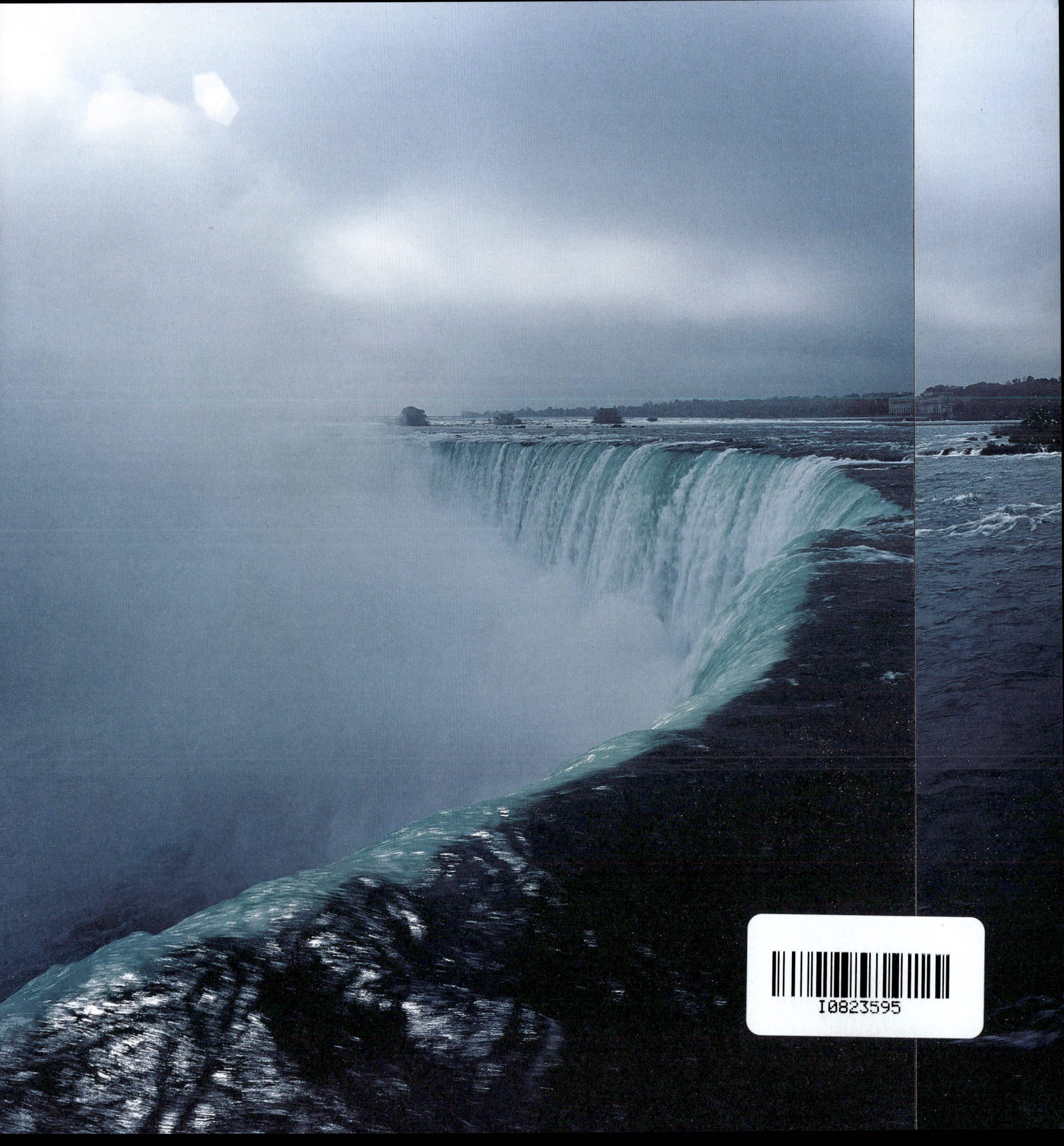
I0823595

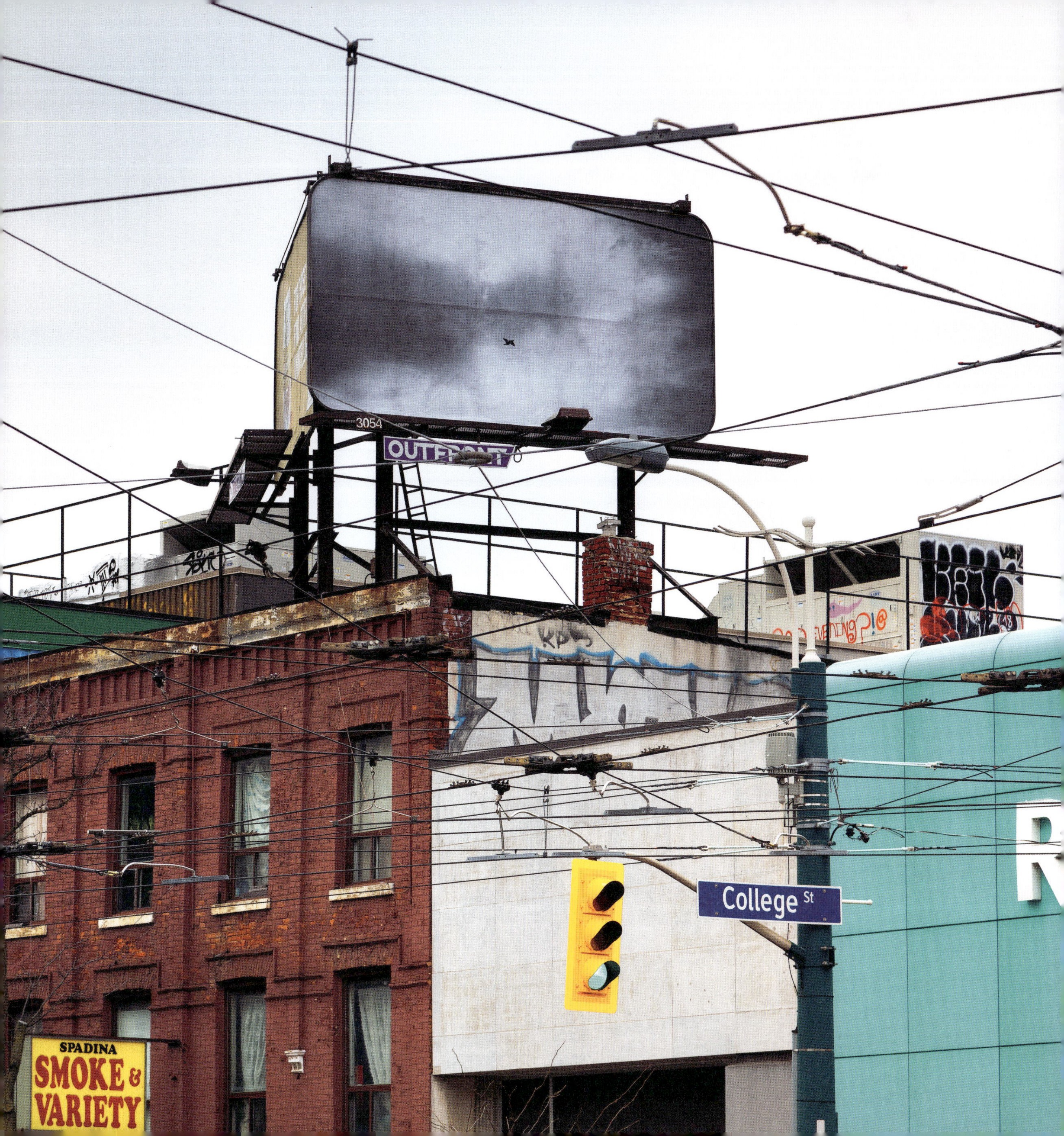
3054
College St
SPADINA
SMOKE &
VARIETY

COLLECTIVE STATES

WORLDS OF PHOTOGRAPHY AT THE AGO

Edited by Sophie Hackett

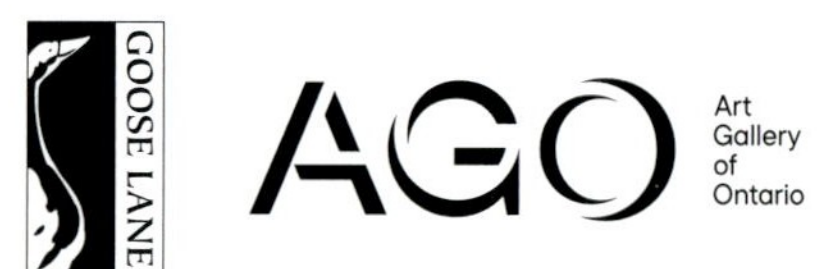

Table of Contents

Felix Gonzalez-Torres
Untitled (Strange Bird)
1993
Billboard, Spadina Avenue and College Street, Toronto, 2022
Gift of Thomas H. Bjarnason, 1998
98/478
(opposite p. 1)

Annie MacDonell
Untitled (detail)
2012
From the series ***The Picture Collection*** (2012)
Inkjet print
76.2 × 55.9 cm
Purchased with the financial assistance of the Art Toronto 2014 Opening Night Preview and the Dr. Michael Braudo Canadian Contemporary Art Fund, 2014
2014/394.1

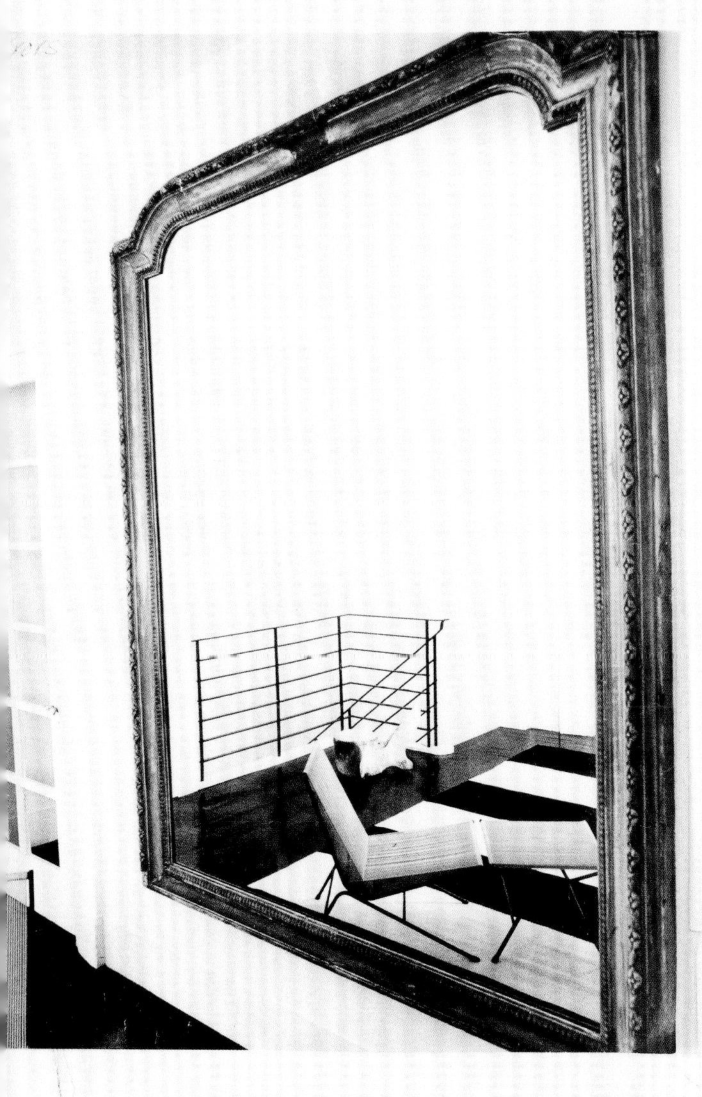
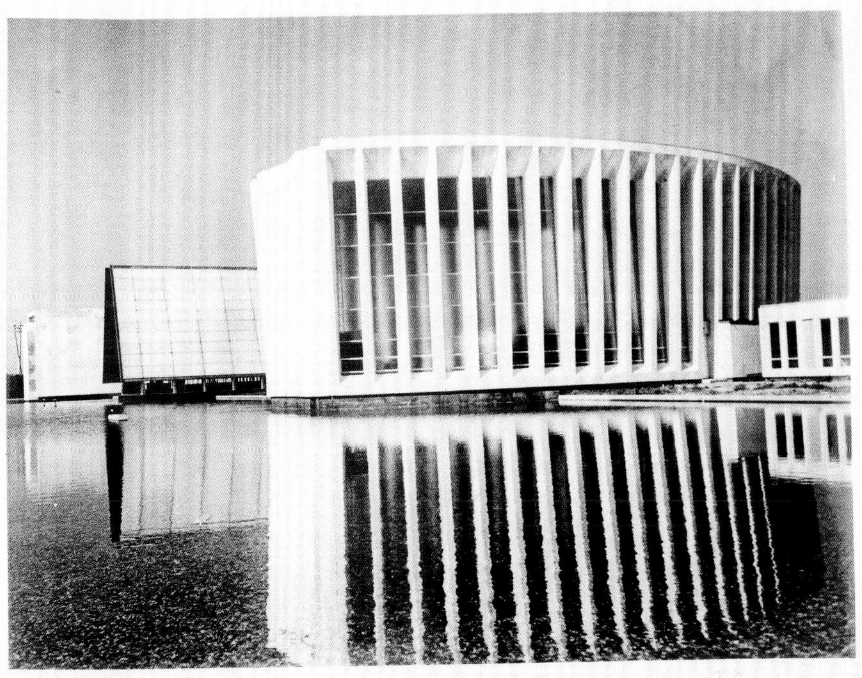
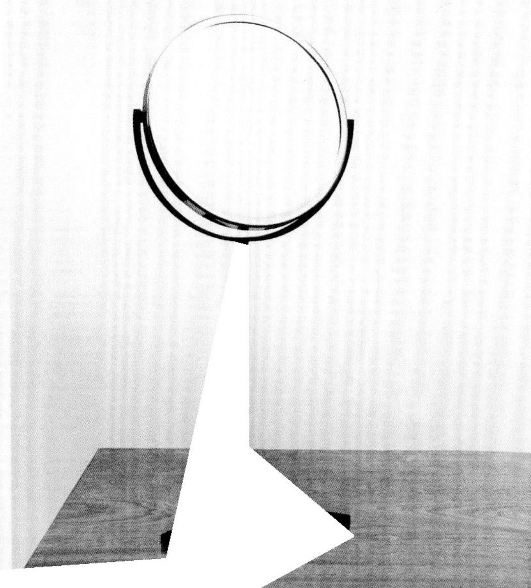
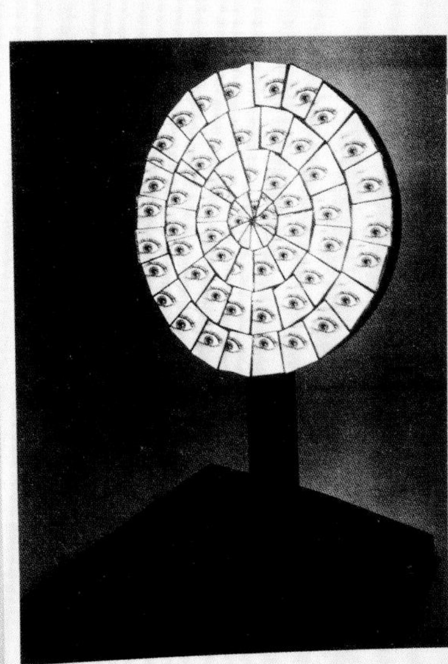

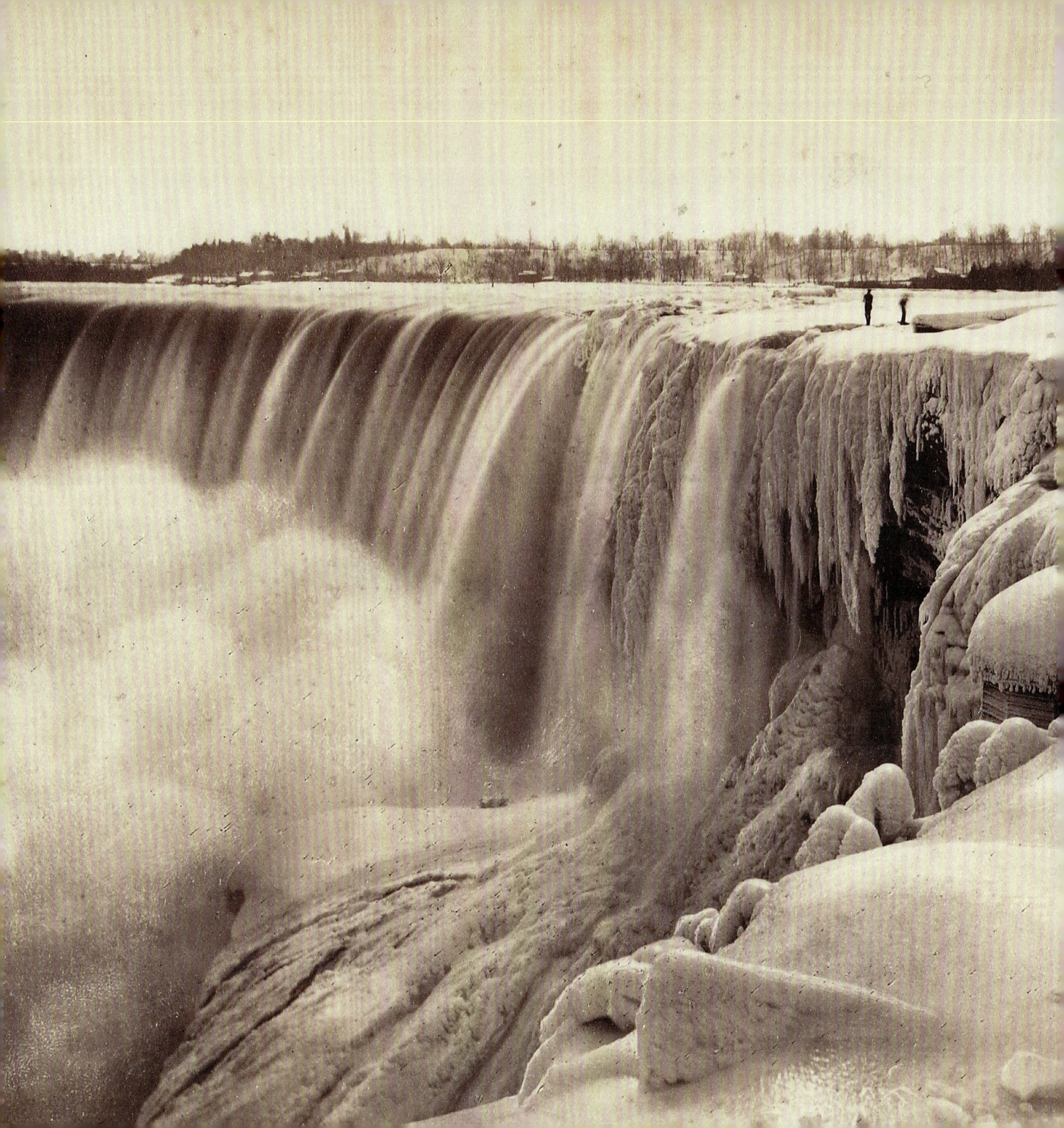

Ki nsadwaamdaming Land Acknowledgement

Maanda Gchi-mzinbiige-gamig Ontario, gii-nokiimgad akiing e-aawang Anishinaabe e- zhimaamoosiwaad debendaagozijig miiniwaa gii-aawan Wendat miiniwaa Haudenosaunee gewi-ina gaazhi-maamooziwaad gii-aawan. Maanda bezhig naagan geye emkwaan Wampum Gchi-pizowin nendimoowin aawan maamowi giizhendamowwaadjin Haudenosanunee e-zhi-maamowiziwaad miiniwaa dash Anishinaabe Nswi Ishkoden, bzandamowaad ji maamowi nakazwaad miiniwaa ji-maamowi gnowenjigaadeg kina gegoo eteg gaataaying Gchi-gimiing. Gewii maanda gchi-oodeno (Toronto ezhinikaadeg) pane gii-zhi-gimaakidaajigaade gchi- kwiinwin nji-sa gchi-gimaanaang mompii Canada miiniwaa giiw Mississaugas odi New Credit Ntam Anishinaabeg. Toronto pane gii-ni-aawan gii-mesh-toonmaaged-enji maawnijiding nji sa giw Ntam Anishinaabeg.

The Art Gallery of Ontario operates on land that is the territory of the Anishinaabe (Mississauga) nation and is also the territory of the Wendat and Haudenosaunee. The Dish with One Spoon Wampum Belt Covenant is an agreement between the Haudenosaunee Confederacy and the Anishinaabe Three Fires Confederacy to peaceably share and care for the resources around the Great Lakes. Toronto is also governed by a treaty between the federal government of Canada and the Mississaugas of the New Credit (Anishinaabe nation). Toronto has always been a trading centre for First Nations.

Alexander Henderson
Horseshoe Falls [Niagara Falls] (detail)
c. 1870
Albumen print
15.7 × 20.7 cm
Anonymous Gift, 2001
2001/185

Rafael Goldchain
Barbershop 2, San Cristobal de las Casa, Chiapas, Mexico
1986
Chromogenic print
50.8 × 61 cm
Gift of Rafael Goldchain in honour of Emilio and Esther Goldchain, 2024
2024/126
(p. 7)

Director's Foreword

Photography's life in most museums has been relatively brief. Queen Victoria and Prince Albert were early fans, and the medium became foundational to London's South Kensington Museum, now the Victoria & Albert Museum, in 1852. In North America, it found limited but significant favour in a handful of Eastern US museums in the early 1900s. Here in Toronto, the most vocal and passionate advocates for photography's place among the other arts, between the 1870s and 1970s—when institutional recognition took root—were the photographers themselves, who organized exhibitions, wrote criticism, and established galleries.

Although our Photography Department is only a few decades old, the AGO's history with photography dates back over 100 years to its early days as the Art Museum of Toronto, when annual exhibitions of the Toronto Camera Club began and a first photograph was donated to seed the collection. Since the 1970s, the museum has built a robust collection of more than 70,000 photographs, stemming from a philosophy that puts equal value on all of the medium's aesthetic forms, across time and place: 1840s daguerreotype portraits; architectural and industrial views from the late 1800s; press photographs from the 1930s; scientific explorations; family photographs gathered in albums; and, of course, the visions of artists who continue to mould the world and the medium to their expressive ends. Reflecting this vital variety, *Collective States* samples the museum's deep and diverse holdings, reproducing many works for the very first time.

The AGO is proud to celebrate these achievements and this landmark twenty-fifth anniversary alongside the Photography Department. Given that my own academic background is in the history of photography, the department has a special place in my heart. *Collective States* is the work of Sophie Hackett, who has served as Curator, Photography, since 2016; Tal-Or Ben-Choreen, Curatorial Coordinator, Photography; and Marina Dumont-Gauthier, Curatorial Assistant, Photography. Maia-Mari Sutnik, Curator Emeritus, Photography, and the department's founding curator, was central to the project as a contributor and as the keeper of vast institutional knowledge. Sophie, Maia, and the team have our deep gratitude and hearty congratulations.

The museum extends our thanks to all the donors, supporters, scholars, interns, members of Toronto's broader photography community, and not least, all the artists who have believed in the AGO as a place for the preservation, research, exhibition, and publication of our photographic heritage, where we lead global conversations from Toronto. The project of a Photography Department and a photography collection have been and continue to be collective endeavours.

We are also grateful to David W. Binet, Gale M. Kelly, Penny Rubinoff, the Schulich Foundation, the Jack Weinbaum Family Foundation, George Yabu & Glenn Pushelberg, and an anonymous donor for their generous support, and to Martha LA McCain for additional assistance.

I commend the AGO colleagues who brought *Collective States* to life on the page. Along with Julian Cox, Deputy Director & Chief Curator, and Jill Offenbeck, Manager, Curatorial Affairs, this book would not have been possible without the dedication of Jim Shedden, Publications Director; Robyn Lew, Publications Coordinator; and Kieran Grant, Content and Production Editor. And we thank Brian Johnson and the team at Polymode for their stunning book design and creative guidance.

Collective States tells a story far beyond photography at the AGO; it is a lens on the nineteenth, twentieth, and twenty-first centuries themselves. Through images that confront, question, and celebrate, this book reveals photography's power to engage with culture, identity, and history. I hope these pages inspire thought, invite reflection, and linger in your mind.

Stephan Jost
Michael and Sonja Koerner Director, and CEO
Art Gallery of Ontario

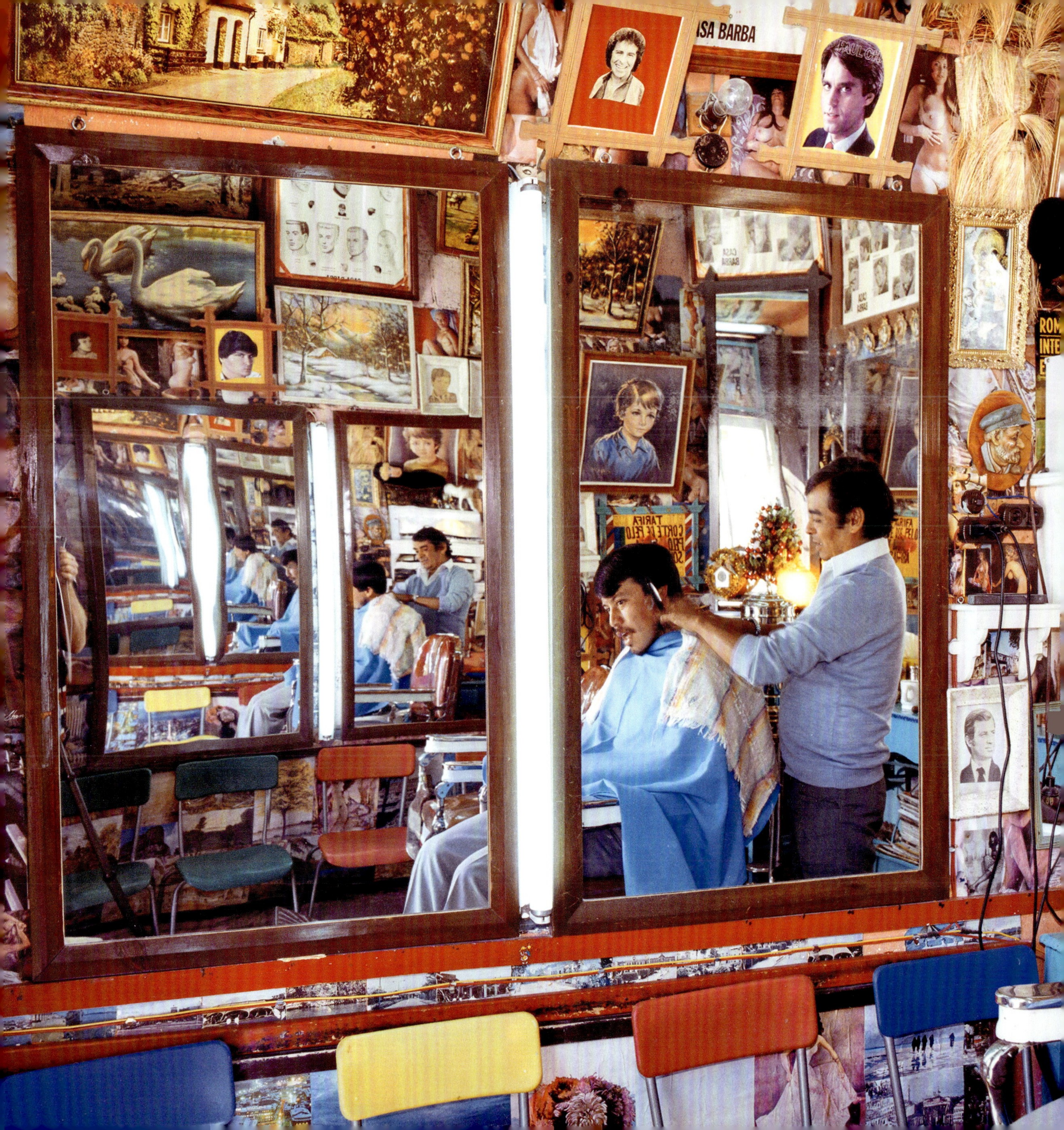

SA BARBA
TARIFA
CORTE DE PELO

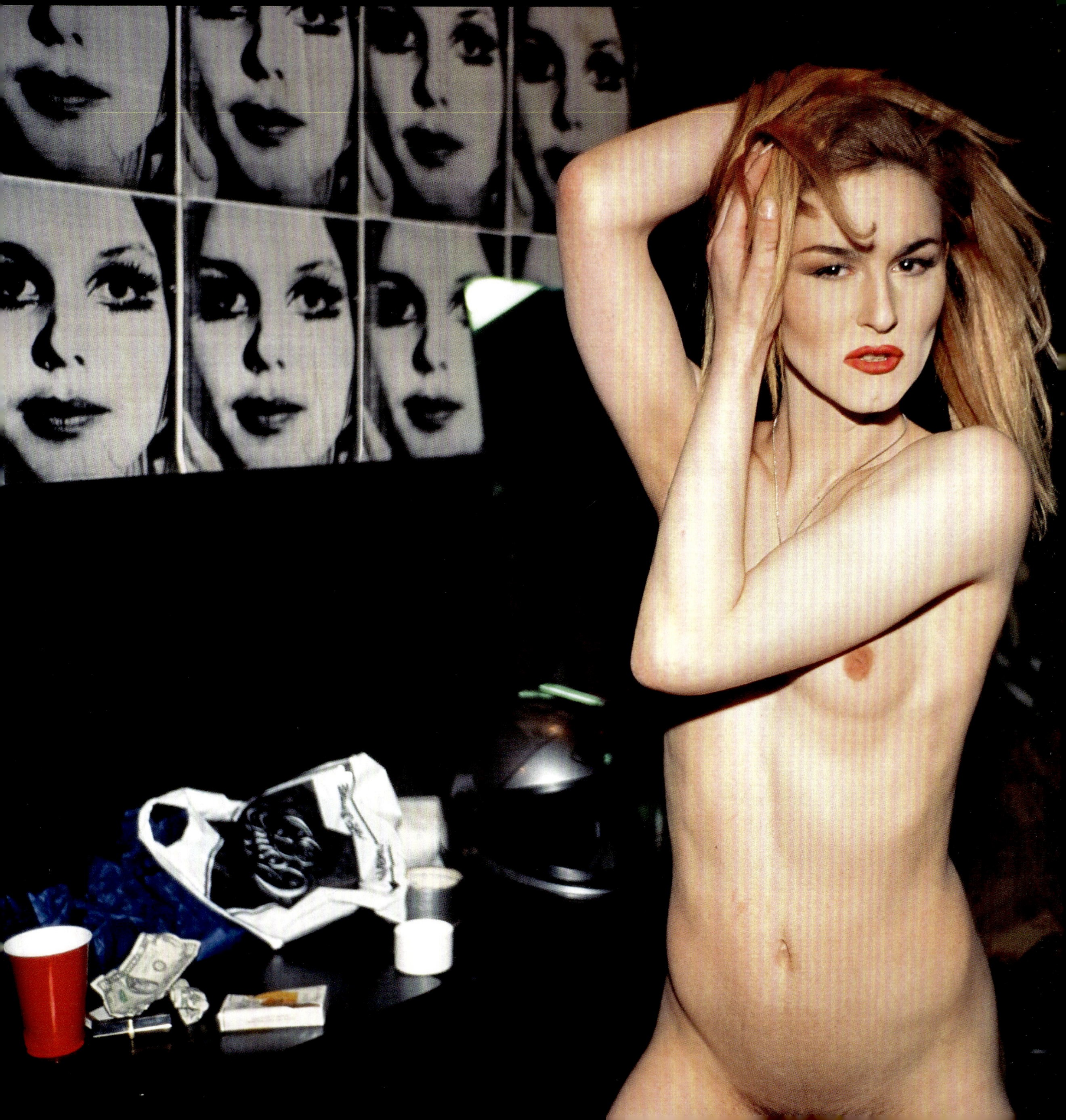

WORLDS OF PHOTOGRAPHY

Sophie Hackett

Twenty-five years ago, the Art Gallery of Ontario (AGO) committed to photography as an official area of focus by establishing a department exclusively dedicated to the medium. This book marks that significant milestone and aims to do two things. First, it seeks to bring a range of works from the AGO's photography collection into view for the first time, underscoring the richness and variety of the gallery's holdings, which are not widely known. Second, it aims to document two decades of advocacy that led to the department's formation in 2000 and its work since then, setting all these activities within the wider context of Toronto's photography scene.

The book's title, *Collective States*, references the department's foundational goals as the gallery's first photography curator, Maia-Mari Sutnik, articulated them: a commitment to "building a collection of primary photographic materials of artistic, historical, and social significance, with emphasis on exploring the collective states of photographic expression and the means by which photographers have achieved their objectives."[1] Sutnik's statement of guiding principles continued:

> The department is committed to exploring not only the wider canon of photography and its renowned historical figures, and the acknowledged "front line" modernists, but also the larger universal scope of photography that has played a seminal role in our visual culture. It takes initiatives to explore the thrusts of creativity in the development of the vernacular and the visual forms of anonymous photography of the past, referenced in the larger body of picture-making that embraces the documentary, photojournalism, reportage, popular photographic objects of everyday life, and the widespread attention to "other pictures" assembled in personal albums. This approach will contribute to the fabric of new ideas and revised studies of how invention, discovery, science, and art have combined to form an account of photography that was unimaginable at the time the medium re-affirmed its practice as a collecting activity.[2]

This guiding vision acknowledged the medium's multiple uses and argued for their importance as part of a broad and interconnected history of photography, highlighting the key roles photographs have played in our visual culture to relay events, act as keepsakes, and create visual narratives.[3] The idea of "collective states" remains a potent and capacious way to describe the medium's multiplicities, its varied uses, and our ongoing engagement as viewers.

The department, with its interest in photography's diverse uses and materials, has aimed to keep its field of inquiry broad and open, like the medium itself. This aim has proactively evolved in recent years to encompass a greater diversity of makers, both known and unknown. It may be no surprise

Nan Goldin
Cody in the Dressing Room at the Boy Bar, NYC
(detail)
1991
Silver dye bleach print
69.4 × 91.6 cm
Gift of Jane Corkin in honour of David Mirvish receiving the Order of Canada, 1996
96/1084

that the core of the AGO's collection reflects photography's origins in France and England in the mid-1800s and follows its numerous paths from there—migratory, colonial, journalistic, familial, mercantile, and expressive. The collection also reflects the North American context, and key practitioners and artistic movements, especially as they connect to Toronto, one of the continent's largest and most diverse cities. A focus on the medium's roles prompts an awareness of the conditions under which any given photograph was created, in the past or in the present: Who held the camera, for whom did they intend the image, for what purpose and in what context, and what materials did they use to produce its finished form.

Acquisitions, exhibitions, and programming have all expanded in recent years to address important gaps. For example, until as recently as 2017, the only photographic work by an artist of Black or African descent was by Lorna Simpson; today our collection includes more than 3,000 such works, including photographs by major artists, snapshots of Black family life, and the Montgomery Collection of Caribbean Photographs.

Colleagues from several curatorial departments, past and present—many from before the advent of the Photography Department—have brought photographic works into the collection, including Alan Wilkinson, Alvin Balkind, Dennis Young, Roald Nasgaard, David Burnett, Philip Monk, Barbara Fischer, Matthew Teitelbaum, Jessica Bradley, Christina Ritchie, Michèle Thériault, Michelle Jacques, Ben Portis, David Moos, Kitty Scott, Adelina Vlas, Xiaoyu Weng, Gerald McMaster, Georgiana Uhlyarik, Wanda Nanibush, Taqralik Partridge, Renée van der Avoird, and Julie Crooks. Each has made their mark, enriching the gallery's holdings, and thus enriching the histories of the field, according to their curatorial expertise and interests.

Today, the AGO photography collection numbers more than 70,000 objects. For staff and interns in the department, the research and curatorial work focused on this collection yields discoveries on a near-daily basis as we explore the objects' subject matter, uses, makers, materials, and connections across time and place. *Collective States* aims to bring this spirit of discovery to life for readers—whether they're familiar with the AGO collection or encountering it for the first time.

The five thematic sections here each point to important ways artists have put photography to use. Although applications of the medium number far more than five, and often overlap, these sections allow us to showcase the idiosyncrasies of the AGO's collection while also calling forth common uses and genres. **Stories We Tell** focuses on the ways we've used photographs to create and share narratives visually, from family albums to press photographs. **People We've Met** centres on the photographic encounter—between photographer and subject, and image and viewer. One of the first threads for collection-building at the AGO was portraits of artists, and these abound in this section; early acquisitions are mainly of painters and sculptors, while later ones see artists harnessing their own image to build new tableaux. The spaces of the photography studio and city streets recur as productive platforms for self-expression and spontaneous exchange. **Things We Make** considers at once the medium's materials—products of European industrialization—and the ongoing inventiveness of makers in adapting and re-presenting these materials to suit a range of wants and needs. Nineteenth-century photocollage, cyanotypes of industrial forms, records of the built environment accompanying mercantile and colonial enterprises, and contemporary photograms all connect here. **Places We've Been** gathers myriad images of the world around us, mapping, evoking, and recording our relationships to and experiences of home, the natural world, cities, migration, places familiar and unfamiliar. Lastly, **What We Imagine** recognizes how we have sought to use photography to express inner states—which have no tangible form—and what we hope for the future. Photographs have long helped create that which does not yet exist and can often only be seen and understood in retrospect.

The "we" that each section title invokes is not static or monolithic. It aims to acknowledge the medium's increasing pervasiveness as much as a diversity of makers, subjects, and viewers. This "we" knows photographs look different to different people, and mean different things. It is a "we" that sees the difficult histories photographs have served to perpetuate and seeks to reckon with these legacies. It is a "we" that, amid these difficult histories, sees the potential for productive exchange—and common ground—in the simple fact that so many of us continue to make, share, and engage with photographs, whether as part of a consciously creative practice or in the course of daily life.

The AGO's photography collection and this book make the case for the social and artistic force of the medium, its open-ended nature and meanings, and ultimately the mysteries of its collective states, which continue to unite and to divide us, to delight and to bedevil us, fuelling our ongoing discoveries and dialogues.

1. Maia-Mari Sutnik, unpublished Departmental Guidelines, April 2007.
2. Ibid.
3. Sophie Hackett, "Encounters in the Museum: The Experience of Photographic Objects" in *The "Public" Life of Photographs*, ed. Thierry Gervais (Cambridge, MA: MIT Press, 2016).

Acknowledgements

Before there could be even the idea of a book on the AGO's photography collection, there were decades of advocacy and dedicated collection-building. I'd like to thank Matthew Teitelbaum, the AGO director who said yes to a photography department twenty-five years ago. To Stephan Jost and Julian Cox, thank you for continuing to support our collection growth and exhibition ambitions. I am grateful to past Photography Curatorial Committee chairs I have worked with—Carol Rapp, Rupert Duchesne, Jay Smith, Judy Schulich, and the current chair, David W. Binet, for their commitment and stewardship—and to all the committee members, past and present, who have brought their curiosity, knowledge, generosity, and openness to our discussions about the photographs we acquire.

To my community of colleagues here in Toronto and further afield, I am deeply grateful for our fellowship and ongoing conversations about the medium, its objects, and its possibilities: To Jim Shedden, Kieran Grant, and Robyn Lew of the ever-resourceful AGO Publishing team, for partnership, patience, perseverance, and always finding a way to make things work. To Craig Boyko in the AGO's Photography Studio, and Tracey Mallon-Jensen and Alexandra Cousins in Rights & Reproductions; to Sara Knelman for crucial editorial support. To Gary Hall, Suzy Lake, and Maia-Mari Sutnik for lending their deep experience to the timeline. To Brian Johnson and the team at Polymode for answering the call and creating such a beautiful way to make this eclectic collection sing.

To Maia-Mari Sutnik for starting it all; to Julie Crooks and Georgiana Uhlyarik for friendship and solidarity; to Amy Langstaff for always making me laugh. To my Photography Department colleagues Jessie Snow, Jill Offenbeck, and Emily Miller, who, though not directly involved in this publication, kept the acquisition, administration, and collections management wheels turning over the years, and with indispensable good humour. Above all, my profound gratitude goes to Tal-Or Ben-Choreen and Marina Dumont-Gauthier: thank you for all the hard work, dedication, sassitude, creativity, intelligence, and unwavering love of photography you brought to this process. This is our book.

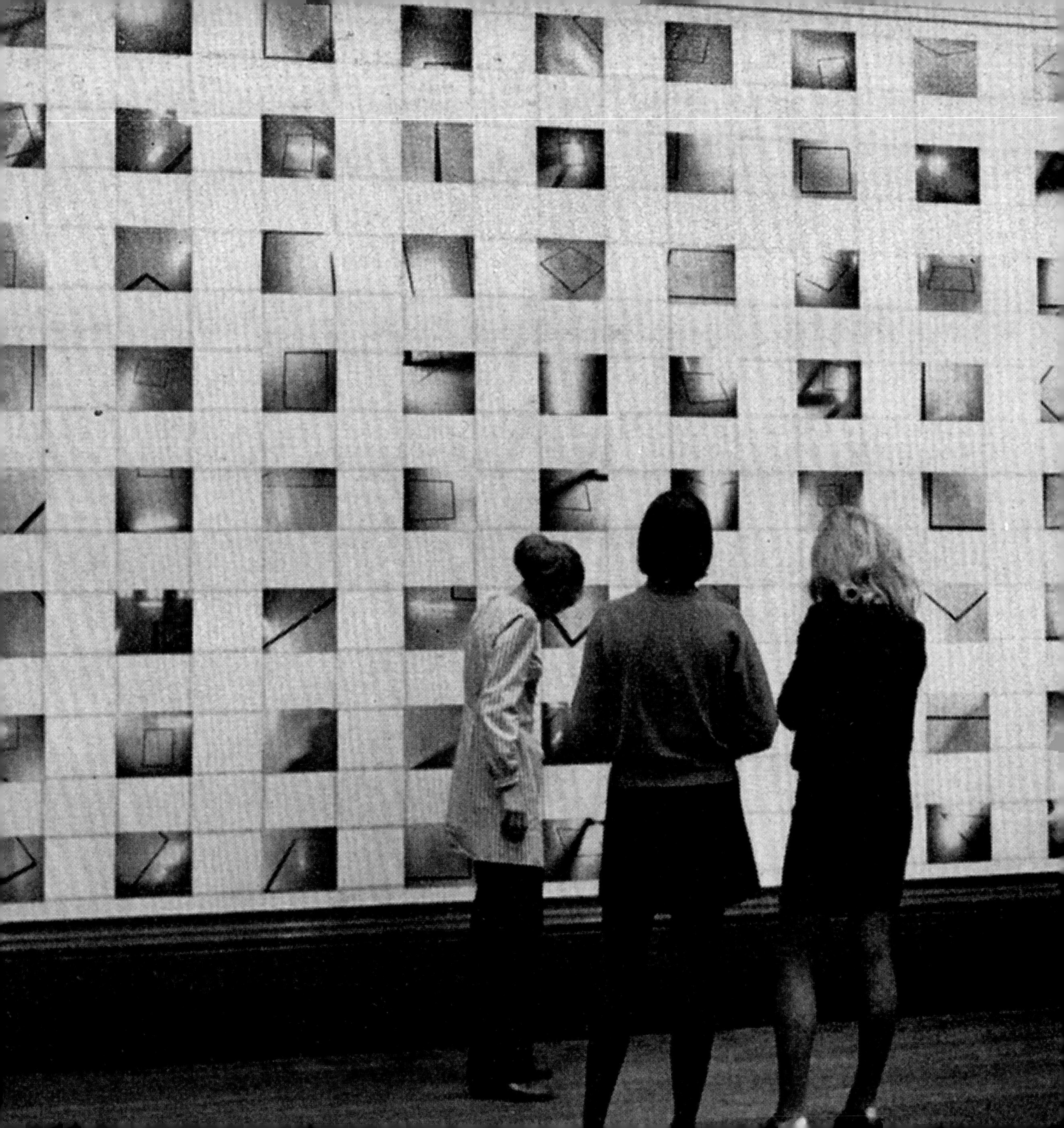

COLLECTIVE STATES

Maia-Mari Sutnik

What is most interesting about photography's career in the museum is that no particular style is rewarded; photography is presented as a collection of simultaneous but widely differing intentions and styles, which are not perceived as in any way contradictory.[1]

Celebrating twenty-five years since the founding of the Photography Department at the Art Gallery of Ontario certainly establishes a notable milestone but, truth be told, it's more like forty-eight years—or fifty, depending how archival the records are.

Recollections

The conviction that photography held the status of art and was worthy of entering museum collections was hardly considered until about 1900. Photography's popularity since the 1840s had evolved through industry and commerce; professional portrait studios, travel photographers, and adventurous painters who turned their sights to the potentials of the new medium as an artistic enterprise. Many photographers sought to embrace new expressions and values—notably in movements that imbued photographic prints with the sheen of art, and as valued objects for contemplation. Often, such photographs did not look like... photographs! Shifting conventions and new points of view aroused ongoing debates about the validation of photography in museum settings.

Installation view of Michael Snow's *8 × 10* (1969) in *Michael Snow / A Survey* at the Art Gallery of Ontario, 1970.

There is a memorable moment that demonstrates such a debate over one photographic work accepted by an arts institution and other works considered as not worthy of inclusion. This issue stirred the growing frustrations of photographers visiting the AGO in February 1970. *Michael Snow / A Survey*, a phenomenal exhibition conceived and installed by Michael Snow and organized by Dennis Young, then the AGO's Curator of Contemporary Art, incorporated many photographic works. The exhibition was unprecedented in representing the concept and scope of Snow's oeuvre—so much so, it was noted in the accompanying catalogue that his were "difficult" works.[2]

One specific work, titled *8×10*, irked various photographers. An 8-by-10-foot grid contained eighty photographs, each an 8-by-10-inch print with elusive surface marks. Detractors thought it bland and meaningless. On the other hand, I expressed admiration. Visually compelling, enriching the parameters of the medium, it was like no other work of photography seen in Toronto. The photographers were not strangers to me. As the AGO's Audio-Visual Librarian—at the time the closest associate in the museum with anything to do with film and photography—they presumed I had answers.[3] Their contention was one of criteria: When is a photograph also art? What distinctions were made? How to account for the AGO's reluctance to exhibit and collect photographs? The photographers were baffled by the anomaly of seeing photography by Snow on view after the medium had been rejected in the past.

8×10 was in every way a photograph—in fact, eighty individual photographs, each taped directly to the wall, equally spaced in a grid. Each showed an outline of a section of a black rectangle at varied angles—the only trace of a subject. This perplexed the photographers, whose own work drew inspiration from historical standards of the medium's achievements, resolving the complexities of camera technique, process, form, style, subject. George Hunter, a photographer noted for his visual narrative and impressive aerial views, declared he was "abandoned!" by the arts establishment.[4] He and his fellow photographers were

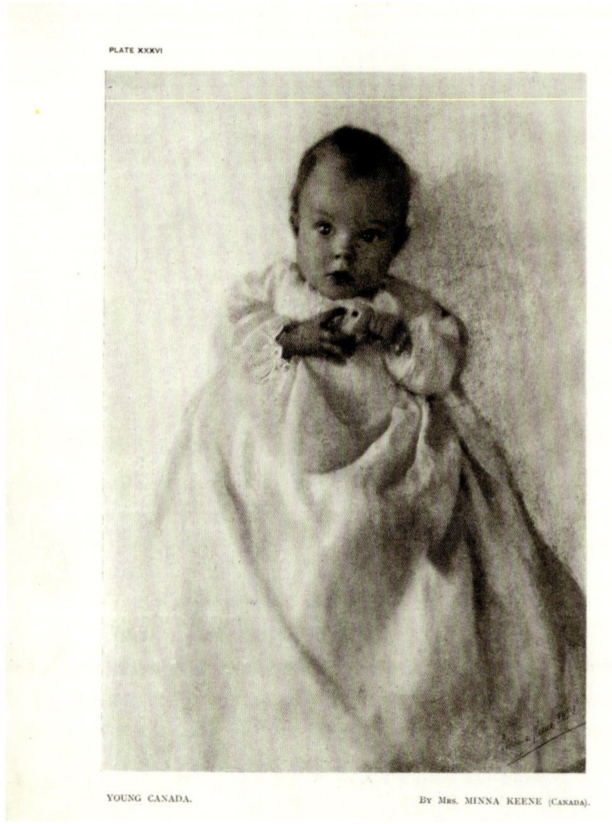

dedicated to perfecting elements of their craft. From their perspective, *8×10* was not aesthetically realized, it was merely radical. Why then was it art?

Snow's contribution was an anthology of photography in parts: the act of photography, vision, seriality, surface, structure, and, significantly, presence of scale. He conjured a witty material reference to photographs, using the 8-by-10-inch paper size dominant at the time, his large grid citing the most prevalent material in photographic culture. This conceptual pun had little effect on his critics—why would eighty prints with minimal content be art?—when photographers working within a tradition of integrated pictorial qualities couldn't even get past the door with one well-realized print.

The question of collecting and what kind of photography passed the test remained an issue. While many museums in the United States and Europe evolved with the medium's new directions, the AGO was still struggling, regardless of *8×10* and other works attracting acclaim and sophisticated readings.[5]

Thirty-nine years later, in 2009, I reflected back on *8×10*'s early critical reception while selecting it for inclusion in the exhibition *Beautiful Fictions*, co-curated with David Moos, then the AGO's Curator of Contemporary Art. I called on Snow to assist with its precise installation. As we measured carefully, he casually mentioned that the size of each photograph is actually less than 8 by 10 inches. Deciding to make the prints borderless, he had trimmed the paper to register a perceptual effect rather than a literal truth—but the originating concept of the popular paper size and its integral role in photography remained. He followed with a wry comment that *this* was indeed the perfect work befitting the "fiction" of the exhibition's title. Snow did not miss a beat.

While *8×10* was a controversial landmark at the AGO in 1970, it was, regardless of the opinions expressed by local photographers, not the real issue. There had been a prolonged void of awareness, as well as suspicions about which lineage of photography was viably artistic. Although the AGO had featured photography in the early 1900s, back when it was still known as the Art Museum of Toronto, by the 1920s radical changes were already in force, emerging in hubs of new artistic, social, and political consciousness—Berlin, Paris, London, New York. Both the conventions of art-making and the new photographic applications and experimentations were being challenged in broad strokes by modernism. Toronto was not on par with this scene.

Photography's links to pluralistic uses contradicted the tenets of fine art as understood in painting, as well as the notion of artistic genius. As the photographic industry entered the public market more freely—most successfully with the roll-film Kodak, introduced in 1888—proliferation of camera clubs with salon exhibitions campaigned for recognition. The Toronto Salon and many cross-country camera clubs showcased photography competitions for artistic evaluations, with titles on par with art displayed in museums. The influential review *Photograms of the Year: 1917–1918* featured only two Canadians, Harold Mortimer Lamb's *Meditation* and Minna Keene's *Young Canada*, a print depicting an infant in a flowing white gown holding a rattle. It was a possible metaphor from Keene, a photographer of considerable recognition outside Canada, that Canadian photography was still in its infancy.[6]

The museum's secretary and curator, Edward R. Greig, had an established affiliation with the Royal Photographic Society of

Minna Keene, *Young Canada* in *Photograms of the Year: 1917–1918* (opposite).

Great Britain (RPS), and this led to the May 1917 opening of the RPS's 26th Annual Exhibition and 14th Salon of the Toronto Camera Club, in The Grange House. Two years later, the future AGO became the Art Gallery of Toronto. Photography was frequently programmed with salon exhibitions and didactic displays from the Ontario Association of Architects, but only two exhibitions by Canadian photographers were significant to the museum's future photography collection. From *Memorial Exhibition of Camera Studies* (1935), by the late M.O. Hammond, a large group of prints was gifted by Skip Gillham in 1985: a summation of Hammond's Canadian scenic views and, more so, a series of fine portraits representing eminent figures active in the arts in Canada. *Plant Patterns in Hawaii and Japan. Photographs by E. Haanel Cassidy* (1938) featured an exceptional body of work created by a self-disciplined practitioner of transcendental theory as the foundation for his photography. In 2007, Cassidy's daughter Sylvia Platt—who had previously contributed archives for the AGO's 1981 exhibition and book on his photography—donated his surviving prints and writings. Between May 1945 and March 1947, Toronto Salon exhibitions took the form of projecting the popular 35mm slide format onto screens.

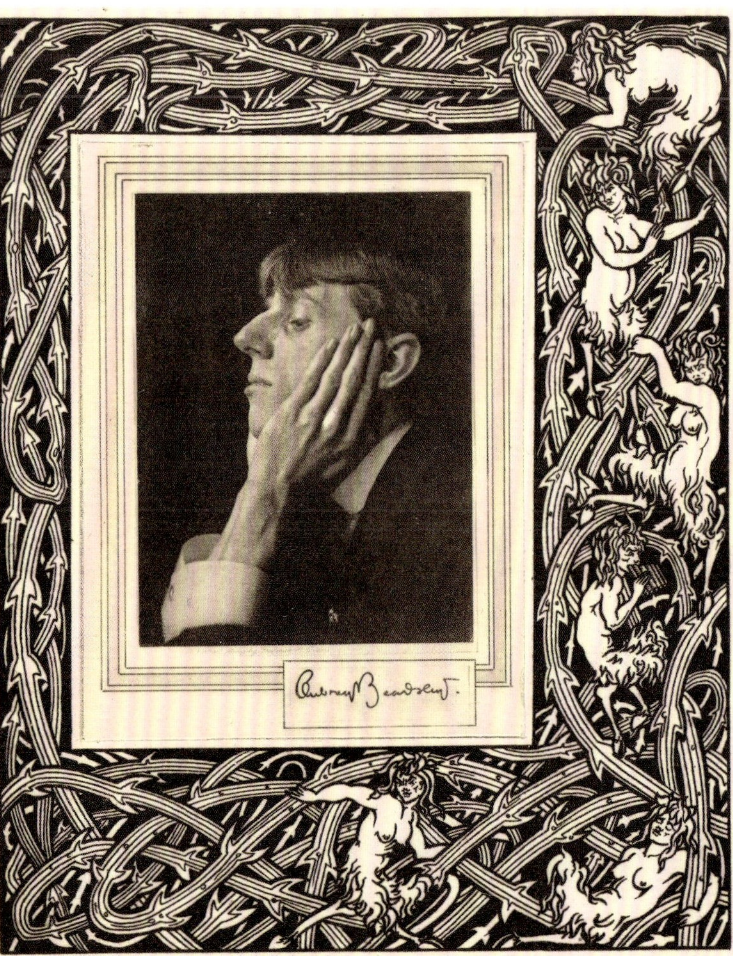

Frederick H. Evans, *A Souvenir of Aubrey Beardsley*, 1893. Platinum print, 20.2 × 14 cm. Gift of Mrs. Gordon Conn, 1979 (79/129).

In 1948, the gallery's first fine arts-educated curator, Sydney Key, who had expertise in British painting, was hired. Few exhibitions featured photography during Key's tenure until 1954. Oddly, postwar commitment to photography at the gallery declined at a time when new, often experimental sensibilities gave new legitimacy to the medium elsewhere. For those photographers engaged in camera clubs and international salons, their aesthetics remained true to their earlier, formative movement, and photography remained a world of competitions and award ribbons. A reliance on such programming left a problematic mark: the ease of ready-made exhibitions failed to motivate exploration, and the authority of camera clubs persisted as the standard. With no discerning or well-defined understanding of the medium's historical lineage or the currency photography exemplified broadly, it was simpler to ignore it.

The interest in photography was so subdued that, in 1950, an offer of sixty platinum prints by renowned British photographer Frederick H. Evans (1853–1943)—famous views of cathedral exteriors and interiors—was rejected. The proposed gift to honour Evans came from Gordon and Rheta Conn, close friends of the photographer from their London days in the 1920s. The assessment by Key and the Executive Committee was that these were merely documents of the history of photography. At a chance meeting in the late 1970s, Rheta Conn, who had been reluctant to part with several favourite Evans prints, was pleased to know of my interest. Evans entered the gallery collection in 1979—including *A Souvenir of Aubrey Beardsley* (1893)—a modest landmark for the collection of photographs.

William Withrow, an acknowledged art educator, became the new director in 1961; his ambition was to increase the gallery's role in art education. With no demonstrated interest in photography, Withrow accepted the National Gallery of Canada's offer of the exhibition *Pleasures of Photography: The World*

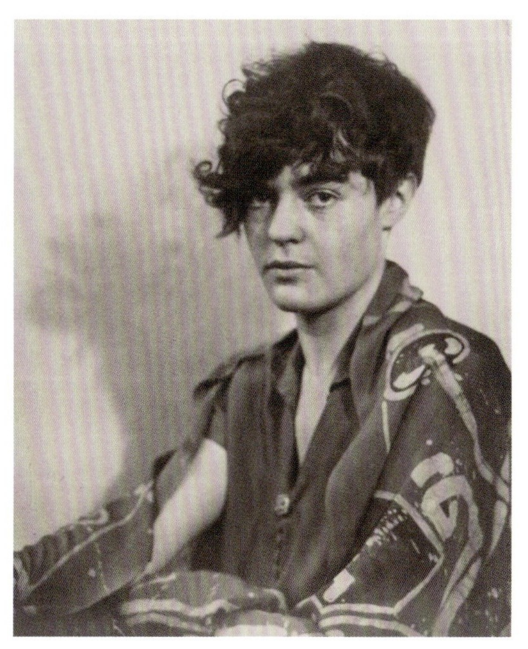

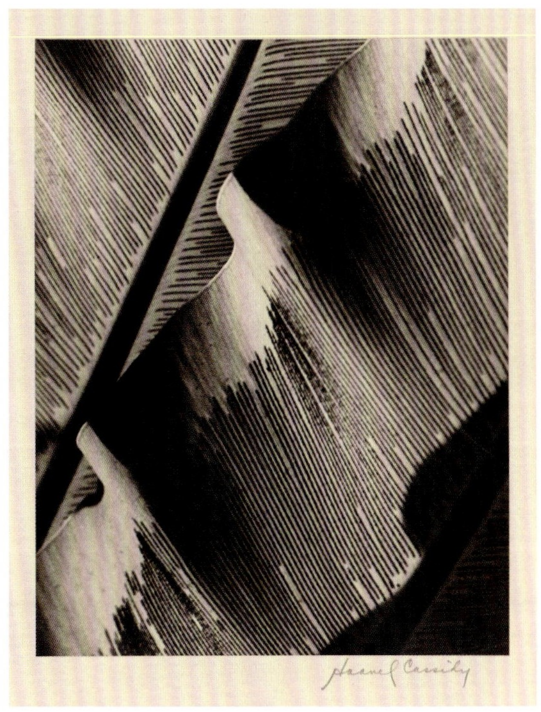

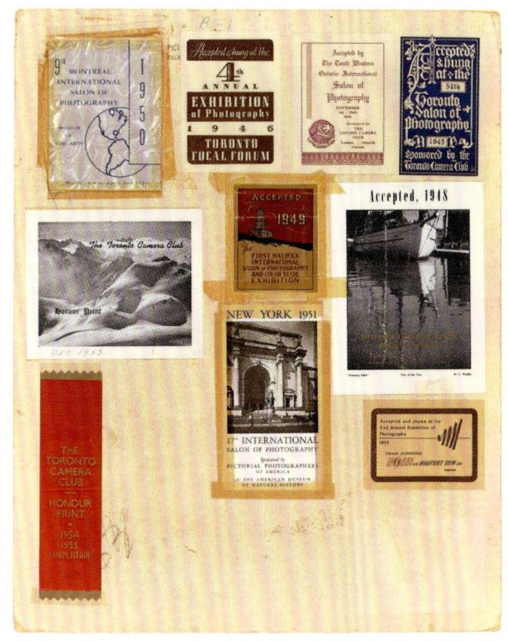
9th MONTREAL INTERNATIONAL SALON OF PHOTOGRAPHY
1950
Accepted & hung at the 4th ANNUAL EXHIBITION of Photography 1946
TORONTO FOCAL FORUM
Accepted by The Tenth Western Ontario International Salon of Photography
Accepted & hung at the 54th Toronto Salon of Photography
1945
Sponsored by the Toronto Camera Club
ACCEPTED 1949
The FIRST HALIFAX INTERNATIONAL SALON of PHOTOGRAPHY AND COLOR SLIDE EXHIBITION
Accepted, 1948
The Toronto Camera Club
Honour Print
DEC 1953
NEW YORK 1951
17th INTERNATIONAL SALON OF PHOTOGRAPHY
Sponsored by PICTORIAL PHOTOGRAPHERS OF AMERICA
At THE AMERICAN MUSEUM OF NATURAL HISTORY
Accepted and shown at the 2nd Annual Exhibition of Photography
1954
THE TORONTO CAMERA CLUB
HONOUR PRINT
1954
1955
COMPETITION

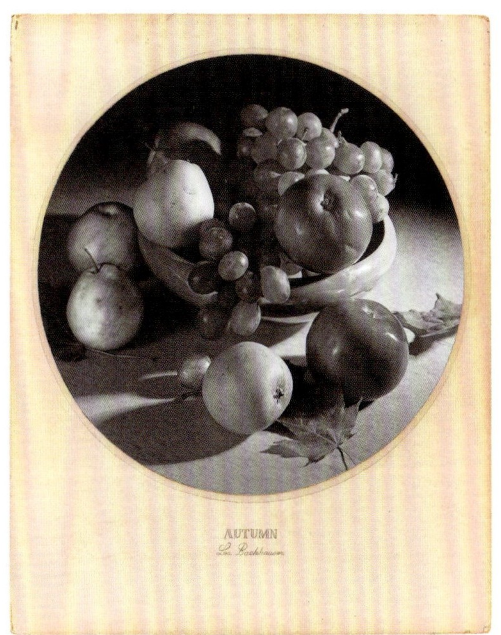
AUTUMN

of Roloff Beny (1966). Canadian-born Beny, then living in Rome, was newsworthy. Beny was once a student of art historian Herbert Read and a friend of renowned art collector Peggy Guggenheim, and these social connections gave his name and work a pedigree. Formerly a painter, he turned to photography, with considerable success in publishing. Large black-and-white photographs of well-measured sheen were displayed on panels, a pleasurable journey through grand art and architecture. The exhibition generated buzz, but not enough to persuade Withrow to commit to a future for photography. A couple of loan exhibitions were given space, but not until Michael Snow's *Survey* did the pressure mount.

The frequent question "What about photography?" was answered most notably by programs generated by the AGO's Extension Branch to circulate art to communities throughout Ontario. From the Canadian government's side, the National Film Board of Canada (NFB) extended photography as a tool to increase awareness of "Canada for Canadians," and many photographers found support in this collective environment. Extension's programs relied on the NFB exhibitions as part of its circulating efforts. On the other hand, a need for more original initiatives was apparent, and Extension programs also gave exposure and recognition to artists of all media, including photographers.

Collecting Reports

In November 1977, the AGO received its first formal request to initiate a photography program. This came from Jim Chambers and twenty-one fellow photographers, including Phil Bergerson, Barbara Astman, Lynne Cohen, George Hunter, and Ken Bell. The proposition was in consideration of the AGO's failure to establish a permanent space for exhibiting (and, presumably, acquiring photographs); it also asked that the gallery support a permanent offsite space for like-minded photographers. The report was assessed by Bill Forsey, the director of the Education and Extension Branch, and he rejected Chambers's proposal as a financially unsustainable "membership club."[7] In January 1978, as the Co-ordinator of Photographic Services / Photographic Resources, I was asked by director Withrow to prepare a proposal for the formation of a Photographic Arts Department. Withrow was all too mindful of the pressures the arts community was placing at his door. The nineteen-page report considered museological requirements as practised in Canada and the United States, and assessed formative objectives: a permanent collection of photographs, exhibitions, research, scholarship, and publications. It included a practical summation of on-site photography exhibitions since 1917, and of the Extension Branch between 1970 and 1977. While the report was viewed as "persuasive" and an "eye-opener," Richard Wattenmaker, Chief Curator and a professed admirer of photography, concluded with Withrow that the curatorial department was underfunded. A new department would compromise ongoing needs. Essentially, they were pleased to know the requirements and remained pleased with my unofficial "caretaking" role in photography.[8]

In addition to their considerations for collecting photography, Extension was expected to generate original exhibitions for circulation. Photography seemed to offer some solutions, including the jury-selected *Exposure: Canadian Contemporary Photographers*, a 1975 survey of the latest trends, demonstrating the AGO's attention to photographers across Canada. However, widely criticized for a jury perceived as biased and the unfortunate choice of letterhead featuring a young nude woman, the project failed to elevate the medium. A scathing review by writer and curator Penny Cousineau did not help, nor did the uproar land well with Withrow, who remained uneasy about the merits of photography even while he paid willing attention to it.[9]

Michael Mitchell's *Nightlife*, which opened in 1978 to acclaim and positive coverage, was a much better experience. Mitchell's luminous use of colour—still controversial in the black-and-white world of photography—and his environmental approach to installation befitted the subjects. The large prints, haloed in darkness with pinpoint lighting, cast a mesmerizing aura and experience. On a tour of the exhibition, Withrow commented, "Photographs can look good on the wall"—a rather rewarding remark!

Wattenmaker, who had studied American and French Impressionism at the Barnes Foundation, had few apprehensions about photographs. His main concern was con-

Melvin Ormond Hammond, *1928*, 1928. Gelatin silver print, 29.8 × 24.5 cm. Gift of Mr. Skip Gillham, Vineland, Ontario, 1985 (85/139). (top left)

E. Haanel Cassidy, *Plant Form - Fugue*, 1938. Gelatin silver print, 35.1 × 27.6 cm. Gift of Sylvia Platt, 2002 (2003/1640). (top right)

Leslie Charles Backhauser, *Autumn* (verso and recto), 1945. Gelatin silver print, mount: 50.7 × 40.5 cm; image: 36 cm (diameter). Gift of E. Dolores Backhauser, 2008 (2009/10). (bottom left and right)

strained resources. He suggested soliciting gifts, and he also drew attention to the collection of photographs, accessioned with the landmark donation of Henry Moore plasters in 1974, eight-five prints by Yousuf Karsh, Roloff Beny, Errol Jackson, and others. One Moore portrait on display was deteriorating and required a replacement. With Alan Wilkinson, the Moore collection curator, the decision was made to purchase something new in 1977: Arnold Newman's *Henry Moore, Much Haddam, England* (1966–1972) was chosen. The possibility of original portraits of artists taken by esteemed photographers motivated Wilkinson to use his department funds for acquisitions. This formally positioned photography as a medium on our collecting agenda. Portraits and photographs related to sculptors and sculpture followed.

In 1988, the anonymous members of a group called Friends of Photography proposed a purchase program offering a large sum of money under a complex system of fundraising and interest on funds. It was speculative, with no clear vision or accounting for the essentials of collections care. Without a model for a holistic and thus successful outcome, the proposal was turned down by management, with criticism from outside interests; I had chased away a generous opportunity.

The AGO appointed a new director, Glenn Lowry, in 1990. A review of all accessioned photographs was scheduled for February 1992. After the presentation, Lowry suggested programming regularly from the more than seven hundred prints and to find a small space for exhibiting. The collection had grown with gifts of work by twentieth-century American and European photographers; and purchases of Canadian historical photographers Richard Maynard and Alexander Henderson strengthened the collecting foundation. Lowry suggested an increased alliance with the Prints and Drawings Department, to pursue programming under its umbrella, a model not unlike that used in several museums in the US, where photography was classified as works on paper. This encouragement to curate collection-based exhibitions and consider suitable gifts seemed like a move toward a program, but a standalone photography department would place budgetary stress on the institution. Once again, not a step closer, but rather a positive "Carry on!"

A curatorial department restructuring in January 1993 left photography floating in no-man's land. The medium did not figure in the plan, even though an exhibition space, the

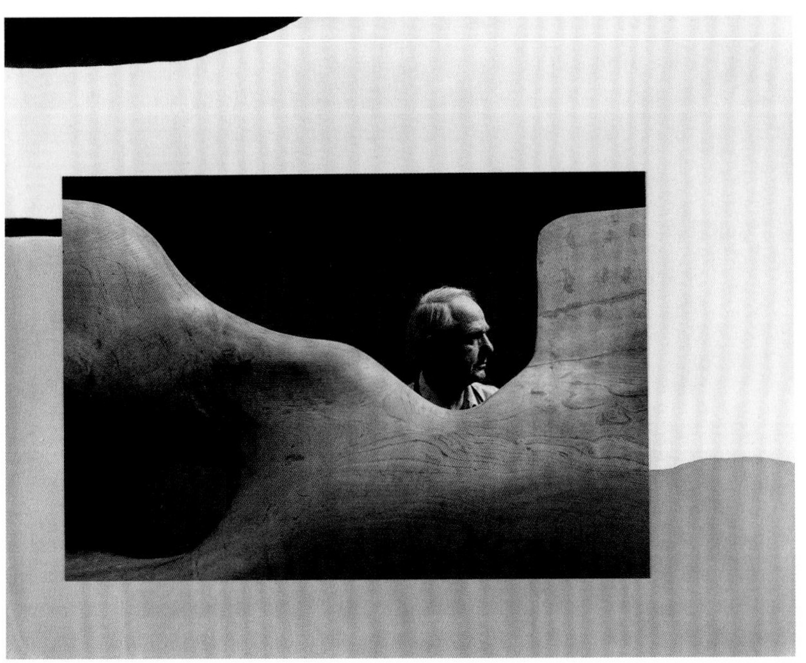

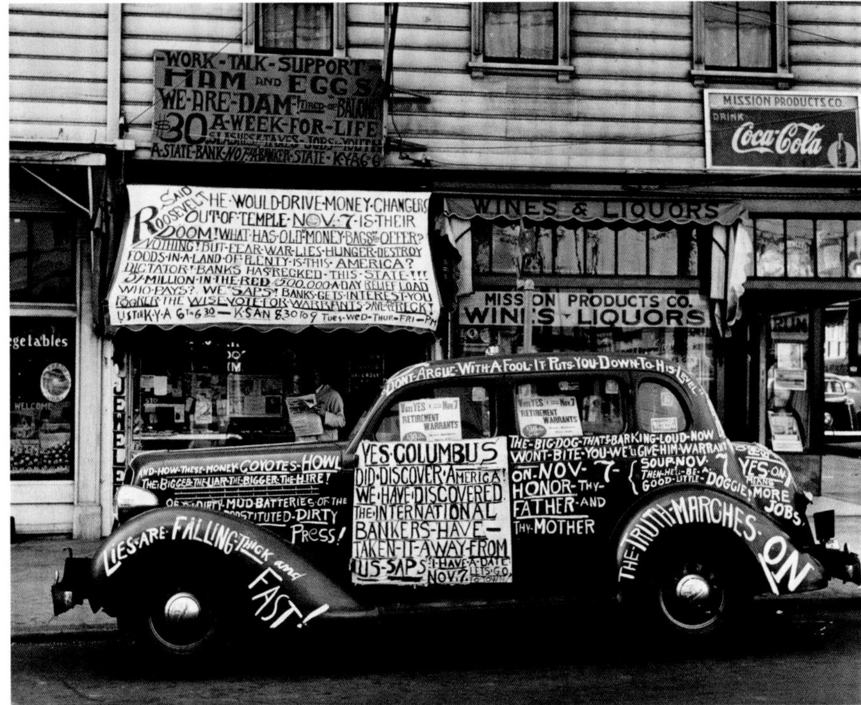

Lozinski Gallery, had been designated to feature photographs. Instead, it was viewed as a kind of tenant entity within Prints and Drawings. This was soon amended by Roald Nasgaard, Chief Curator, with a budget line for installations.

As a follow-up procedure, photographs would be presented to the appropriate acquisition committees for approval: nineteenth-century photographs through the Prints and Drawings Committee with two photographers, Michael Mitchell and Jeff Nolte, as photography voices; work by contemporary artists would be channelled to the Contemporary curatorial department; and historical Canadian photography would be presented through the Canadian Department and/or Prints and Drawings. Although awkward, the new structure provided a working relationship, an opportunity to feature installations complementary to main exhibitions, and demonstrated the collection's active role.

Exhibitions

This new arrangement was highlighted by the fact that major photography exhibitions had been initiated since 1980. These included Robert Frank's *The Americans*, borrowed from the NFB's Still Division. There was also the important addition of Frank's new work. Through direct contact with Frank, who was now living in Cape Breton, Nova Scotia, and his Montreal dealer Michiko Yajima, we were able to give exposure to a group of more recent photographs vested with deeply felt personal messages. The prospect of featuring an artist of Frank's stature would, I thought, certainly affirm photography's importance at the AGO. The exhibition connected well with his devotees but less so with the general public, who saw his social criticism as a dark and tragic journey. This was followed by *E. Haanel Cassidy: 1933–1945* (1981), with its aesthetic lean toward modernism, and Tess Boudreau's *Portraits of Artists* (1984) representing familiar contemporary painters in studio environments in Toronto and Montreal. The *John Gutmann* exhibition (1985) featured the photographer's documentary observations of the United States after he escaped Hitler's regime in Germany in 1933. And *Linnaeus Tripe: Photographer of British India, 1854–1870* (1987) presented early prints from paper negatives, offering an understanding of the origins of photography in a colonial period. *Charles Macnamara and M.O. Hammond: Pictorial Expressions in Landscape and Portrait* (1990) reached back to the AGO's early years in photography, revisiting the alchemy of creating

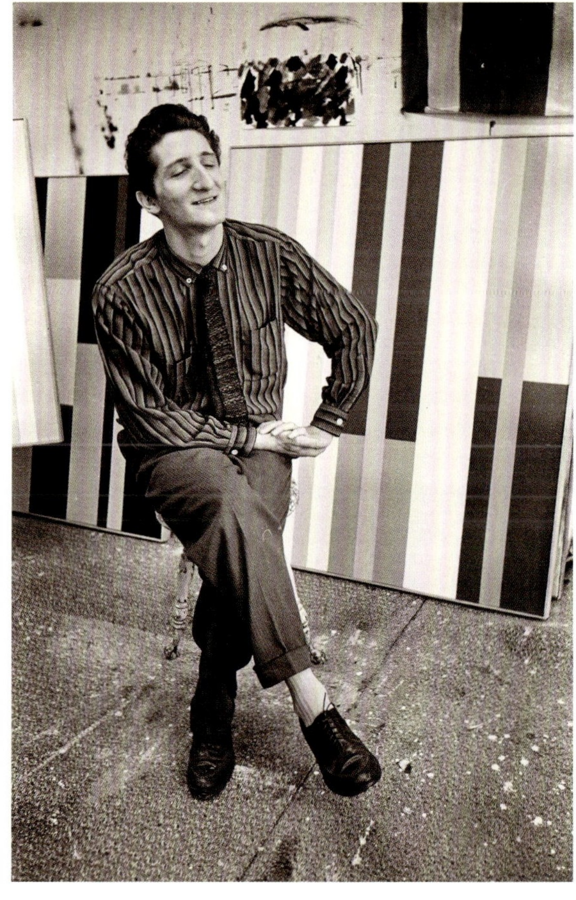

Arnold Newman, *Henry Moore (collage), Much Hadham, England*, 1966–1972. Collage: gelatin silver prints, 26.2 × 33.2 cm. Purchase, 1978 (77/178). (p. 18, top)

John Gutmann, *Yes. Columbus Did Discover America*, 1938. Gelatin silver print, 42.8 × 35.6 cm. Gift of Mark Luca, former student of John Gutmann, 1993 (93/38.9). (p. 18, bottom)

Tess Boudreau Taconis, *Guido Molinari*, early 1960s. Gelatin silver print, 23.5 × 35.4 cm. Gift of the artist, 2007 (2006/453). (above)

artful photographs. These curated exhibitions, and the focus on well-known figures such as Bill Brandt (1982), Harry Callahan (1983), David Octavius Hill and Robert Adamson (1988), and Frederick H. Evans (1990), brought attention to renowned makers. A personal visit by Callahan connected exceptionally well with photographers and audiences.

Supported by Prints and Drawings curator Katharine Lochnan, this clandestine program was an operation without a mandate. It was based on locating opportunities for the AGO to instill a perspective on contributors to the medium's history. These large-scale, open-ended exhibitions would be unthinkable in today's museum environment. It may have been luck that paper-based media were still viewed as minor arts; there was more focus on other forms thought to maximize audiences. In 1981, the photography collection of Sam Wagstaff was featured. He gave two separate talks at which he said he thought of himself as a "garden-variety collector," implicating a wide field of choices in photography as compelling preserves of the medium. Wagstaff's observational approach, freed from chronological movements and standard canonized figures, encouraged digging deeper to discover the creative riches of photography's broad yield.

I had met Wagstaff at a symposium in New York City in 1975, where he presented an overall view of his recent collecting activity. He brought attention to images not only for their unique material qualities but also because they simply stood out from already familiar traditional forms, and to photographers who had been long overlooked and could be defined as singular discoveries. Wagstaff's perception and acumen were well grounded. He believed in photographs as catalysts for the mind, to get one's adrenalin going. Close looking, more looking, to become discerning, would reveal powerful forms of expression, whether the work was created as art or in service of more practical purposes in culture and social history, topics he spoke about with great insight.

From a perspective of mentorship, Wagstaff's approach was truly intriguing. The 1984 exhibition I organized, *Responding to Photography: Selected Works from Private Toronto Collections*, began as a research project to discover the responses of collectors in Toronto. Where did interest reside, and how might this information assist future program choices at the AGO? With the assistance of dealers, doors to Toronto collectors opened. This helped establish a fine array of well-known photographers on one hand, but on the other, there was an absence of hidden gems only rumoured about. I approached collectors, including many artists, who chose specific subjects from a wide spectrum of unattributed images alongside others who encouraged contemporary Canadian photographers. Overall, my research suggested exciting ways to bring variant collecting impulses together—that is, histories rubbing shoulders with one another. In one way, the exhibition amplified some of Wagstaff's discoveries that validated historical relationships by way of both provenance and personal taste. I must now admit that curating this exhibition likely had another, ulterior, motive: that some photographs would find their way to the AGO collection. And, in time, many joined the collection.

A Certain Presence

Since the late 1970s, the AGO collection grew significantly with early gifts that at first appeared as merely promising strays but found value in relationships with other photographs. My ratio-

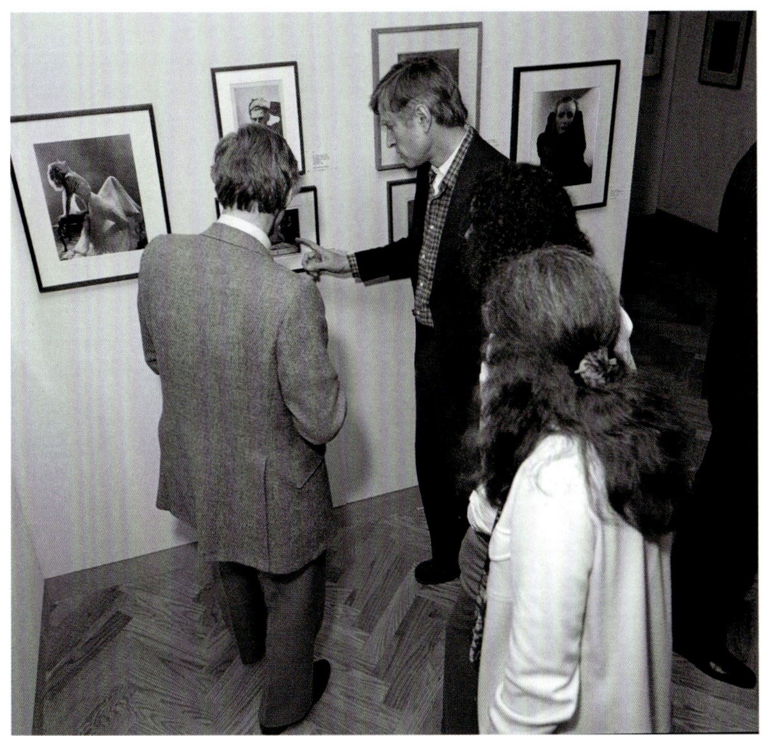

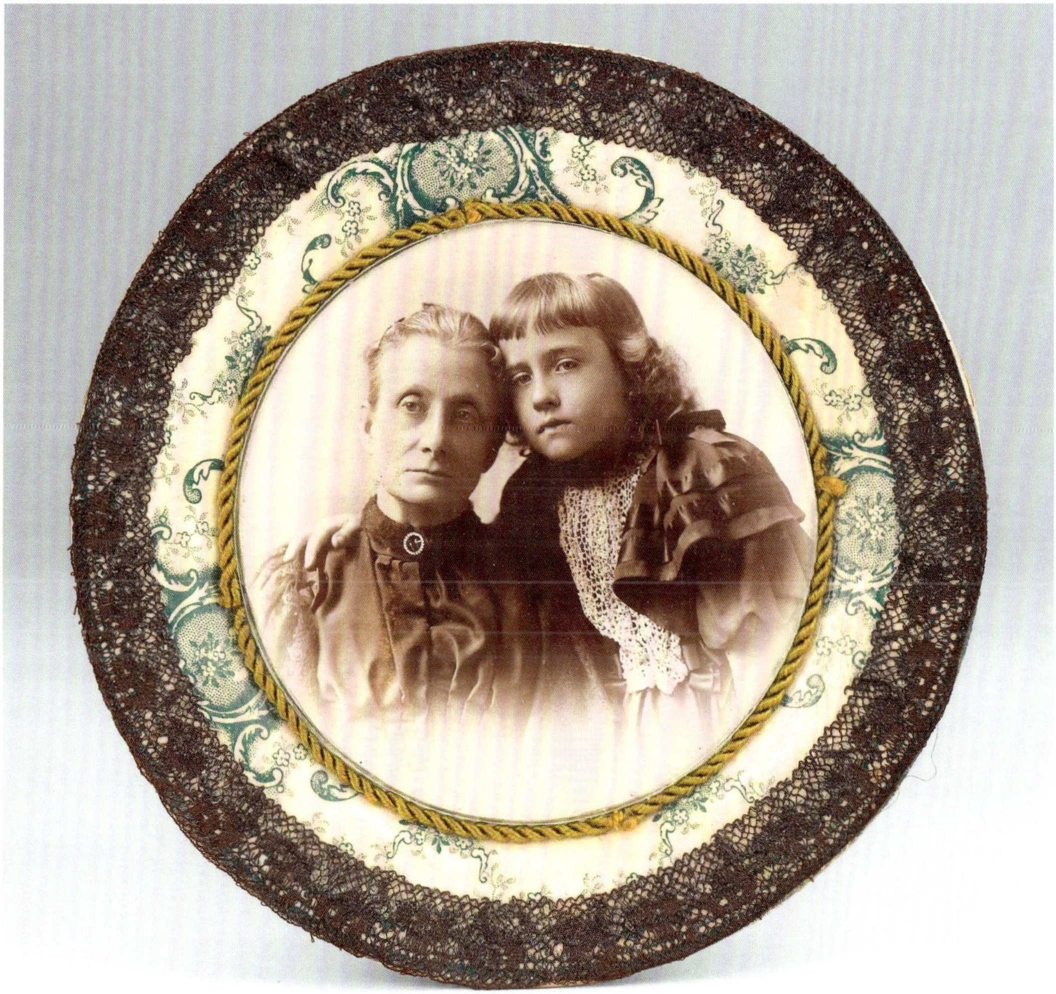

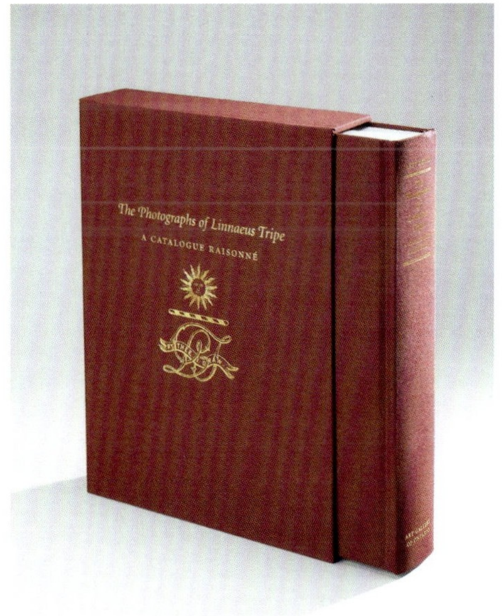

Sam Wagstaff, AGO Director William Withrow, and a visitor view *Photographs from the Collection of Sam Wagstaff*, 1981. (opposite)

Buffalo Pottery, *Decorative plate with portrait of mother and daughter*, plate: 1880s; image: c. 1902. Collodion print on semi-vitreous ceramic with green cord and brown lace, 14 cm. Anonymous Gift, 2004 (2004/144).

The Photographs of Linnaeus Tripe: A Catalogue Raisonné. Art Gallery of Ontario, 2003.

nale and interactions in collection-building called for exploring the collective states of photographic expressions, and how the lineage of those who participated achieved their varied objectives. There were opportunities to trace a historical journey, with examples ranging from the early days of the daguerreotype and cased images to experimental contemporary work—both from photographers with great legacies and those of lesser renown. Photography's uses for more practical purposes and the news media produced memorable images of moments in time. A facet of the collection is sourced from the public domain, from publishers' promotion of "real" photo postcards to personal creations of Pop photographica, memorabilia often referred to as "the vernacular," expressing the idea of unifying forms from the larger public consciousness. These representations, absent from most standard histories, have a meaningful place in our collection, such as a collection of albums from First World War soldiers and their families. Revealing historical moments alongside social narratives and political statements, they signify personal memories and points of view that form a strong basis for the reception of photography.

A solid historical foundation for the collection was established in 1992 when Dr. Shashi B. Dewan and Janet E. Dewan generously donated the work of Linnaeus Tripe, active in British India between 1854 and 1870. Today, the Tripe collection of albumenized prints from paper negatives (calotypes) is a landmark of early photography. The continued support of Janet Dewan reaches many areas that have made a significant difference in our collection development. Since our meeting in 1984, she has contributed to gifting related materials of historical relevance and quietly increased our library holdings. Her curatorial contributions beyond those exclusive to Tripe assisted my archival research in many productive ways. Her dedicated research into Tripe's photographs from more than sixty international collections culminated in an unprecedented work of rigorous scholarship, *The Photographs of Linnaeus Tripe: A Catalogue Raisonné*, published by the Art Gallery of Ontario in 2003 and one of the rare publications of its kind.

In the early struggle to gain a foothold for purchases and not rely solely on gifts, the Nancy and Ken Kembry Endowment Fund made acquisition possibilities real. The Warren Steiner Memorial Fund for Eric Steiner was notable in acquiring photographs that reflected the spirit of Eric's theatrical career and interests. New programming goals were also made possible. Support from Penny Rubinoff funded a successful series of talks by visiting photographers and critics.[10] Her generosity also supported a presentation of works from the AGO collection at the Grand Palais in 2013 at the invitation of Paris Photo. This unconventional installation—*Performance Propositions*, co-curated with Sophie Hackett—could not have been successfully realized without Rubinoff's deep commitment to and engagement with photography.

Final Approach

On August 24, 1997, as Head of Collections, I was invited by Matthew Teitelbaum, Chief Curator and Deputy Director, to review a draft proposal for expanding the AGO's collection mandate. With the curatorial departments now streamlined by Teitelbaum's amalgamations of collection responsibilities, and with vigorous engagement from the Ad Hoc Development Committee, photography was identified as one of three possible new collecting areas. The photography holdings were considered an area that could be enriched with focus on research, promotion of collecting commitments, and new funding targets. The moment seemed hopeful.

Time passed with periodic optimism. In early January 1999,

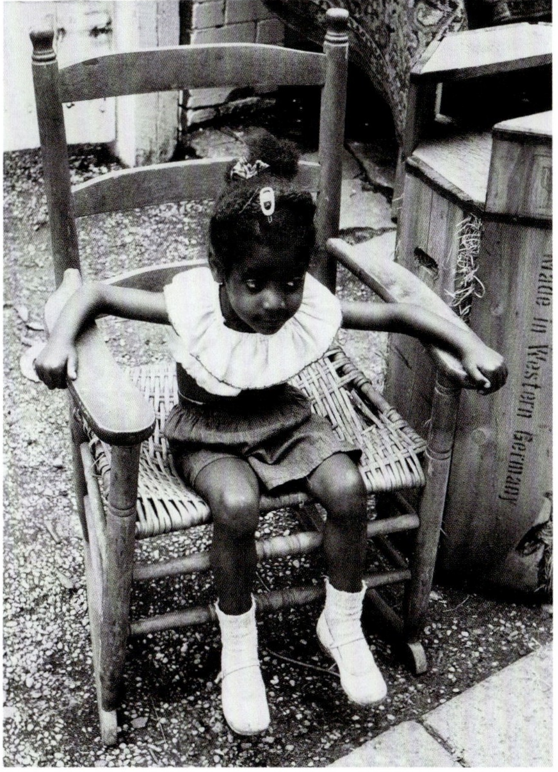

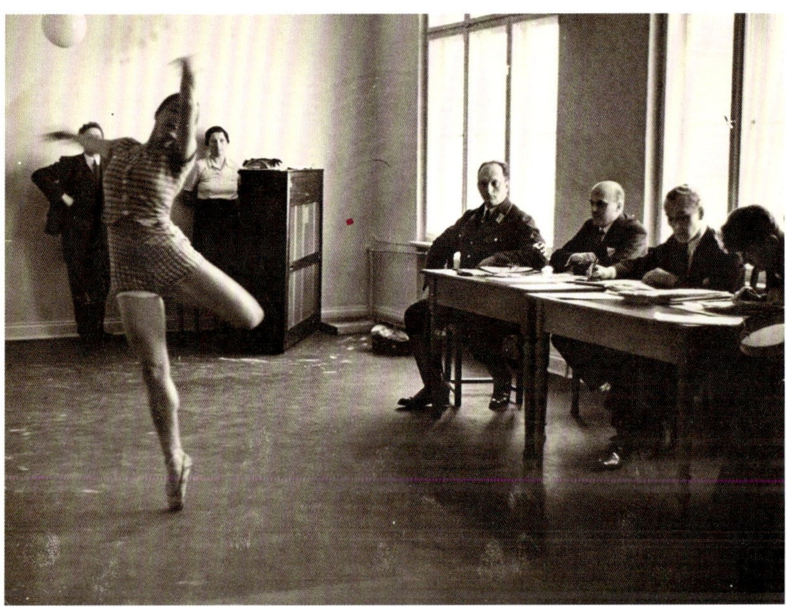

Michel Lambeth: Photographer was about to close. The exhibition showcased Lambeth's empathetic observations and social awareness of Toronto city streets, alongside a group of portraits of artists associated with The Isaacs Gallery, founded by Av Isaacs, Lambeth's dealer, the only one in 1960s Toronto to exhibit photography. This tribute to Michel (1923-1977), comprised in large part of photographs donated by Isaacs, completed one of my more satisfying long-term projects. Even though Lambeth's activist stance against AGO programs made for a contentious relationship with the gallery, he was a central figure in the history of photography in Canada, and his ideological agenda and pursuits for Canadian artists' rights remain only part of the legacy of a vibrant independent photographer. An exhibition on Arthur Goss—Toronto's first official photographer, from 1911 to 1940—expertly guest-curated by photographer Peter MacCallum with prints made from negatives in the City of Toronto Archives, complemented Lambeth. The connection to Goss was Lambeth's rescue of a group of glass-plate negatives from a garbage bin at Toronto City Hall, which Lambeth later published in 1967 as *Made in Canada*.

And then the good news: a January 22, 1999, trip to New York City with Teitelbaum, the AGO's new director as of September 1998. Our task was to look at a large group of photographs by Josef Sudek (1896-1976), from the Czech photography historian Anna Fárová. This remarkable collection spanned all aspects of Sudek's legendary career from the 1920s to the 1960s—photographs richly imbued at once with a sense of place and a sense of timelessness. In my mind, should this valuable gift come our way, it would have to reside in a distinct photography department and not as a subsection of Prints and Drawings. A collection of such extraordinary depth would establish authority for a new photography department. I anticipated that, with Teitelbaum as its well-poised champion, the collection would come to the AGO. Sudek would set the first stage for acquisitions of a critical mass of work by select significant photographers for research and exhibitions.

In December, Teitelbaum proposed that I create a vision statement in preparation for a curatorial committee for photography, essentially to develop objectives and goals, and transition strategically, accounting for potential growth and activities. All topics were crafted as motivational discussion papers, affirming specific departmental goals imbedded in the overarching institutional guidelines, an ongoing process in the management style of Teitelbaum and certainly befitting formation of a new department with its own acquisitions committee.[11]

In 2000, with the Sudek acquisition secured, the annual report announced my appointment as the Associate Curator, Photography. The transition and realignment of responsibilities was gradual. However, by 2002, the Photography Curatorial Committee showed a deep commitment to shaping future advocacy for the medium. Important issues on the agenda included defining terms for photography's collection development relative to other departments and contesting the 1970 end date for the collecting timeframe—not quite an arbitrary date but one proposed because of formative changes that occurred in 1970s visual culture, the prominence of Postmodernism, and its critical practices. (A reminder of the impact of Snow's *8×10*.) The 1970 date constrained the currency of practising photographers whose ideas were responsive to sensibilities that did not embrace the critical art scene as the only relevant activity among contemporary photographers. An equally crucial

Michel Lambeth, *Baldwin Street, Toronto*, c. 1958. Gelatin silver print, 33.2 × 25.9 cm. Gift of Av Isaacs, Toronto, 1994 (94/505).

Alfred Eisenstaedt, *Examination of a German dancer in the Third Reich. A tough examination for the dancer. At the far left of the table sits Karl Schönherr, President of the German Association of Choir Singers and Dancers*, 1934. Gelatin silver print, 18 × 24.4 cm. Anonymous Gift, 2002 (2002/5345).

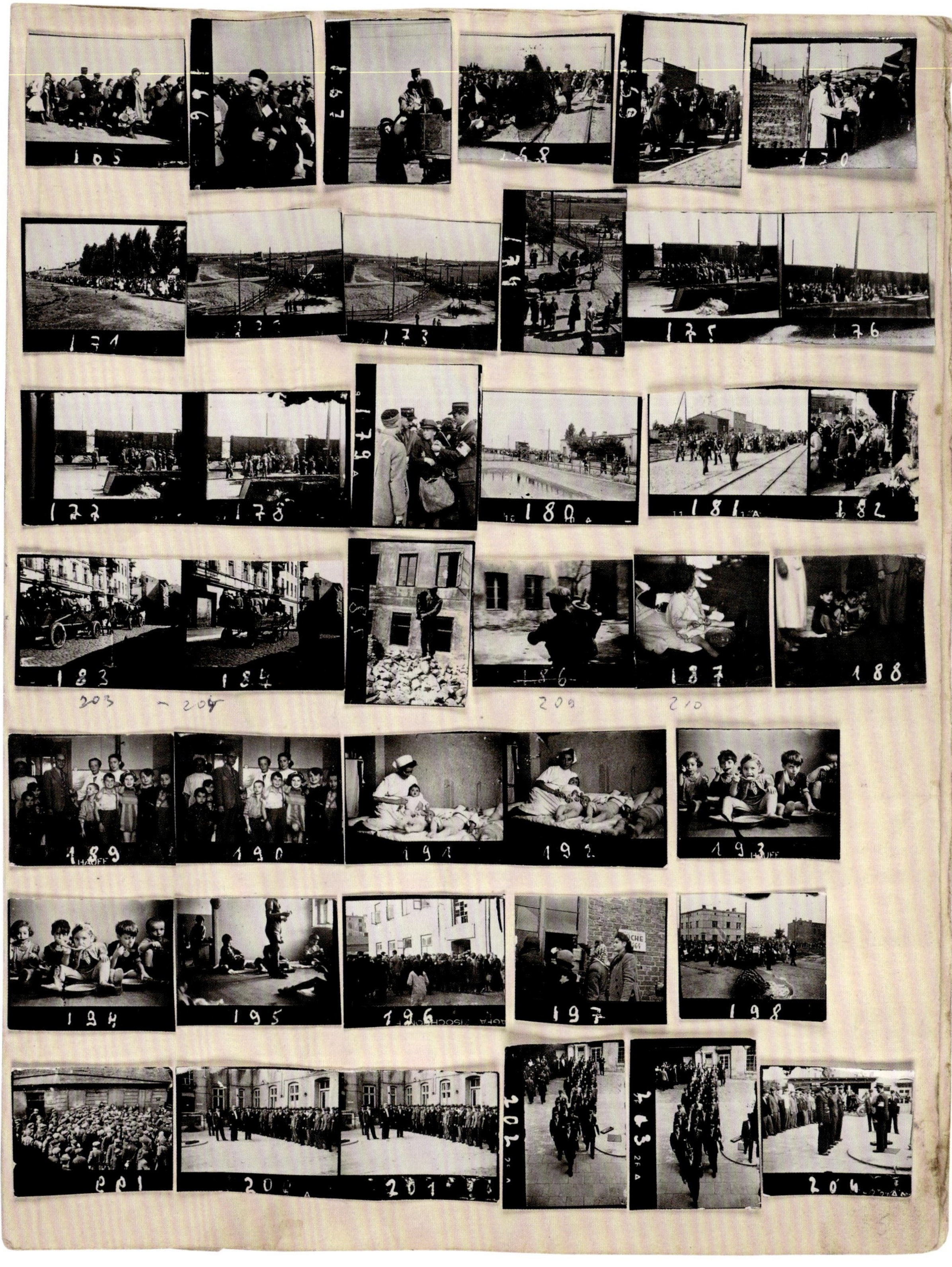

issue was the nature of collecting. My proposition of approximately 450 rare First World War albums that would distinguish the AGO collection, and presented with a rational research report, was not accepted by one member of the committee as art of significance and was followed by a resignation. The proposal passed, but it was a shaky start to overcome!

In 2006, Sophie Hackett joined as Assistant Curator; already familiar with the AGO and the photography collection from her days as collection researcher and intern, she was the perfect choice for the position. Under Teitelbaum's leadership, the AGO enhanced programs and audience engagements by systematically revisiting overarching institutional alertness to vision and future potential. This planted the major task of preparedness for the concept of "Transformation AGO—New art, New building, New ideas, New future," to open in 2008. The focus would be on architect Frank Gehry's building redesign. The buzz was swirling with an abundance of propositions of how to be on the forefront of cultural recognition. Clearly, a new era for the AGO would evolve.

The Photography Department's response to these new ambitions was *Connecting with Photography: Ongoing Dialogues* in the Betty Ann & Fraser Elliott Gallery, newly designated as a permanent space for photography. The thematic structure allowed us to introduce the collection in substantial and multiple, open-ended ways.

The new installation held to the department's founding provocation that the history of photography is still active and transformative. It explored observations and ideas as "touchstones" connecting across times, places, and creative inspirations, evident in photographers' distinct responses to subjects and themes that sparked their moment in time. After a private tour, George Hunter and friends of the Photographic Historical Society of Canada were (finally) pleased.

Not too long after, it was time for Sophie to succeed me as the department's curator. She has mined the photography collections with knowledge and expertise, and made exceptional contributions to its continuing growth with rare and significant additions. Today, she is leading the AGO Photography Department with new agendas and toward new discoveries—and excitement internationally.

After over eighty exhibitions since 1976, I had some collecting goals that needed full concentration. The Sudek gift that planted roots for the new Photography Department in 2000 had only been seen in a small exhibition, *Surrealist Affinities* in 2002. More than 900 prints required research, and my hope was to pursue a major retrospective with Anna Fárová. Sadly, she passed away in 2010, but we had met and shared ideas over the years. The 2012 exhibition *Josef Sudek: The Legacy of a Deeper Vision* conveyed the complex autobiographical journey of an indomitable spirit.[12]

In 2007, we acquired a collection of vast historical importance: photographs by Henryk Ross, who documented all aspects of life in the incarcerated Jewish community of Łódź in occupied Poland, during the Second World War. Ross buried his negatives in the ground before the liquidation of the Łódź Ghetto in August of 1944, fearing their destruction. The following year, after liberation, Ross dug up his box, but many negatives had been destroyed by moisture. The Ross collection, donated by London's Archive of Modern Conflict and

Henryk Ross, *Lodz Ghetto Folio, Page 5*, 1940-1945 (assembled 1962-1987). Gelatin silver prints mounted on paper, 28 × 21.8 cm. Gift from Archive of Modern Conflict, 2007 (2007/2023.5).

Maker once known, *Marksman with Shotgun*, 1901-1922. Charcoal on photographic emulsion, collaged with paper targets, original frame, 49 × 41.5 cm. Anonymous Gift, 2004 (2004/145).

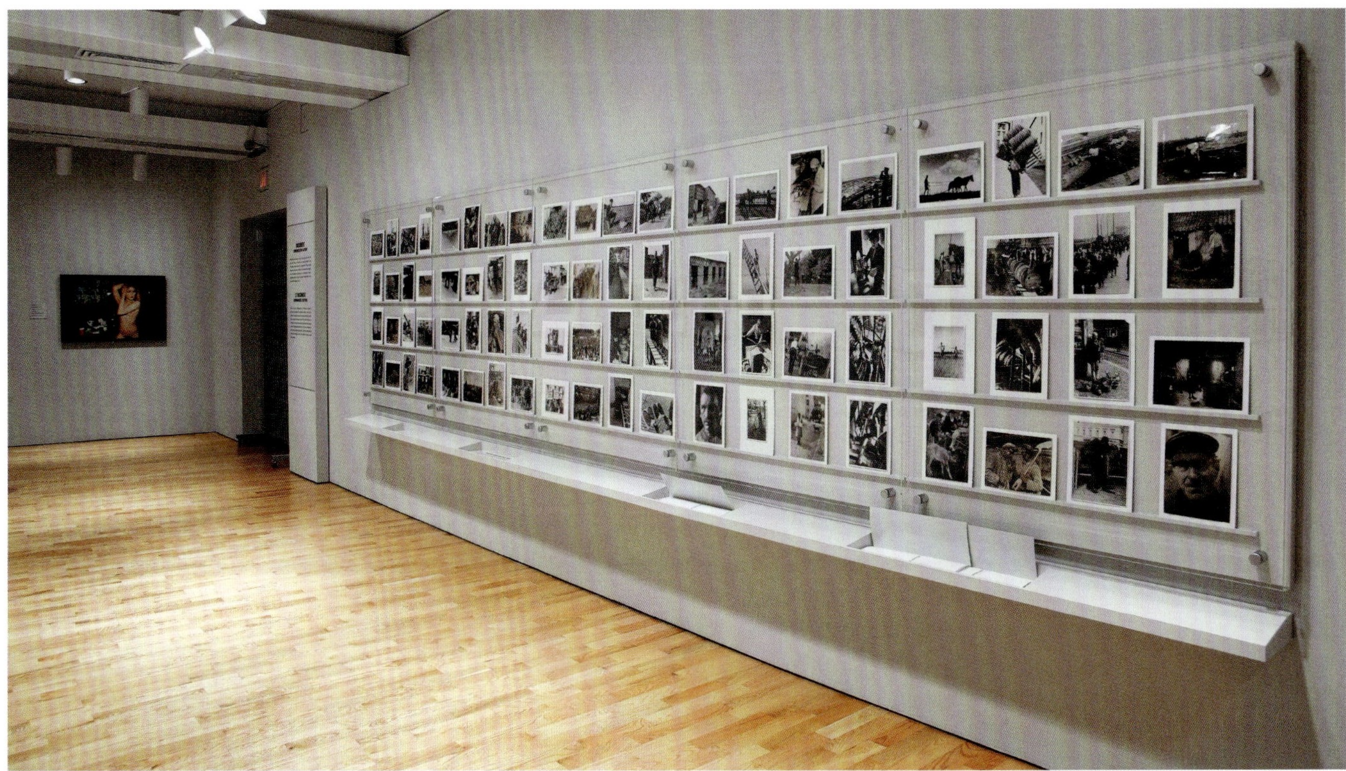

comprising nearly 3,000 surviving negatives, original prints, Ghetto notices, and archival memorabilia, chronicles the tragedy of the Holocaust. The exhibition *Memory Unearthed: The Lodz Ghetto Photographs of Henryk Ross* opened at the AGO in January 2015.[13]

To complete my special assignments, I focused, with support from Matthew Teitelbaum as well as the Photography Committee, on a number of photographers who have joined the collection since Josef Sudek: Harold Edgerton, Arnold Newman, Diane Arbus, Garry Winogrand. These collections join other large holdings of Tripe, Cassidy, Edward Burtynsky, Charles Gagnon, among collections of documentary work that highlight photographic genres and topical subjects—the printed press, political eras, industry, popular culture—all open passages to historic moments captured over the course of photography's evolution. The growing pains of photography collecting is not unique to this institution, but the Museum of Fine Arts, Boston made inroads in the 1920s, New York's Museum of Modern Art in the 1930s, and the National Gallery of Canada established its photography department in 1968 (also late, but thirty-two years ahead of the AGO). Always meaningful were the lively exchanges, debates, and critical opinions. One step forward could feel like two steps backward, but Lowry's "Carry on" was useful: it wasn't "Stop!"

While it's unlikely I could rationalize the insecurities placed on the idea of art in photography, it has perhaps been

Installation view of Klinsky Press Agency Collection and Nan Goldin's ***Cody in the Dressing Room at the Boy Bar, NYC*** (1991) in *Connecting with Photography*, 2008, at the Art Gallery of Ontario.

more contradictory than Susan Sontag observed in "Photography in Search of Itself."[14] When photography was deemed impossible to situate at the AGO, the most logical antidote to calm frustration was turning to Hollis Frampton's proposition that photography arrived in a ballast, possibly from a lost continent. This from the mind of a fascinating fabulist, an apt metaphor for the journey of photography.[15]

The AGO has provided me with an exciting journey. And to top it off, the museum honoured me as its Curator Emeritus, Photography, in December 2015—making my tenure forty-eight years and counting!

1. Susan Sontag, "Photography in Search of Itself," in *The Camera Viewed: Writings on Twentieth Century Photography*, vol. 2, ed. Peninah R. Petruck (New York: E.P. Dutton, 1979), pp. 213-237.
2. William J. Withrow, Introduction to *Michael Snow/A Survey* (Toronto: Art Gallery of Ontario, 1970), p. 4.
3. The Art Gallery of Ontario Audio-Visual Centre was an outreach program supporting art education. To provide supplementary teaching aides, I relied on hiring photographers to make slides and prints of artworks. Frustrations were frequently expressed over the AGO's resistance to program creative photography.
4. The National Gallery of Canada formed a photography department in 1968. The emphasis was on historical and international collecting; George Hunter, among others, felt that Canadian photographers were sidelined. Hunter's achievements in advancing various techniques to realize his documentary assignments were highly praised and existed at the forefront of the medium through his use of the complex dye-transfer printing method to assure greater permanence of colour photographs. Hunter's photographs joined the AGO collection in 2010 with fifty-eight career-spanning photographs.
5. Leah Modigliani's "Michael Snow's Visual Trickery" discusses the range of Snow's works, among them *8×10*, in the context of aesthetics that test human vision and pay homage to boundaries that delineated theories of vision, in *Prefix Photo*, no. 30 (Fall/Winter 2014): pp. 20-31.
6. F.J. Mortimer, ed., *Photograms of the Year: 1917-1918* (London: Hazelll, Watson & Vineyard).
7. At Michael Mitchell's studio, a group of local photographers marked the genesis of the Toronto Photographers Workshop (TPW) in 1977, based on Chambers's proposal for an artist-run centre at the AGO. TPW gained its first exhibition space at Harbourfront Centre in 1980.
8. This "caretaking" refers to the initiation of an in-house photo studio, lab, and staff to consolidate a service for the gallery's photographic needs. This was realized in the John Parkin addition in 1974.
9. Penny Cousineau, "Too Much Exposure—Not Enough Development," *Afterimage*, February 1976, pp. 4-5.
10. The Penny Rubinoff talks series presented Luc Sante, Stephen Shore, Martin Parr, Paul Graham, Antony Penrose, and William Ewing.
11. Committee Chair Carol Rapp, members Marta Braun, Janet Dewan, Av Isaacs, Harry Malcolmson, Aaron Milrad, Michael Mitchell, Jeff Nolte, Bernice Smythe, Michael Stewart, and Howard Tanenbaum.
12. Maia-Mari Sutnik, ed., *Joseph Sudek: The Legacy of a Deeper Vision* (Munich: Hirmer Verlag / Toronto: Art Gallery of Ontario), 2010.
13. Maia-Mari Sutnik, ed., *Memory Unearthed: The Lodz Ghetto Photographs of Henryk Ross* (Toronto: Art Gallery of Ontario), 2015.
14. Sontag, pp. 213-237.
15. Hollis Frampton, "Digressions on the Photographic Agony," *Artforum* 11, no. 3 (November 1972): 43-45. Reprinted in *Circles of Confusion* (Rochester: Visual Studies Workshop Press, 1983), pp. 177-191.

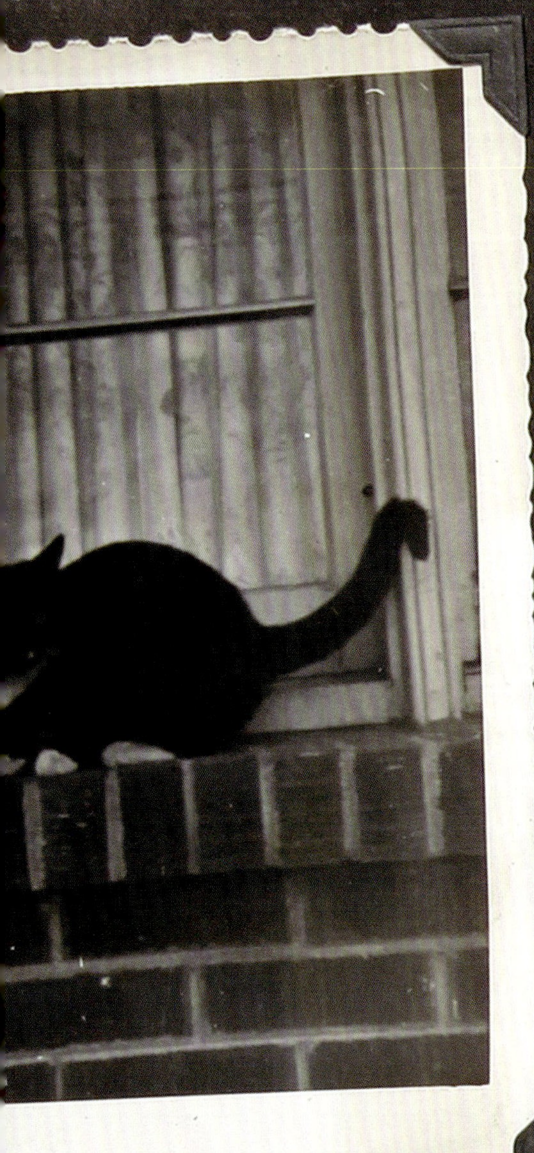

Me in

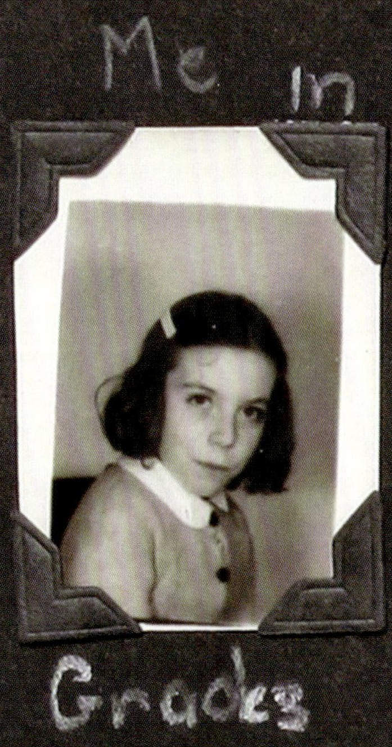

Grades

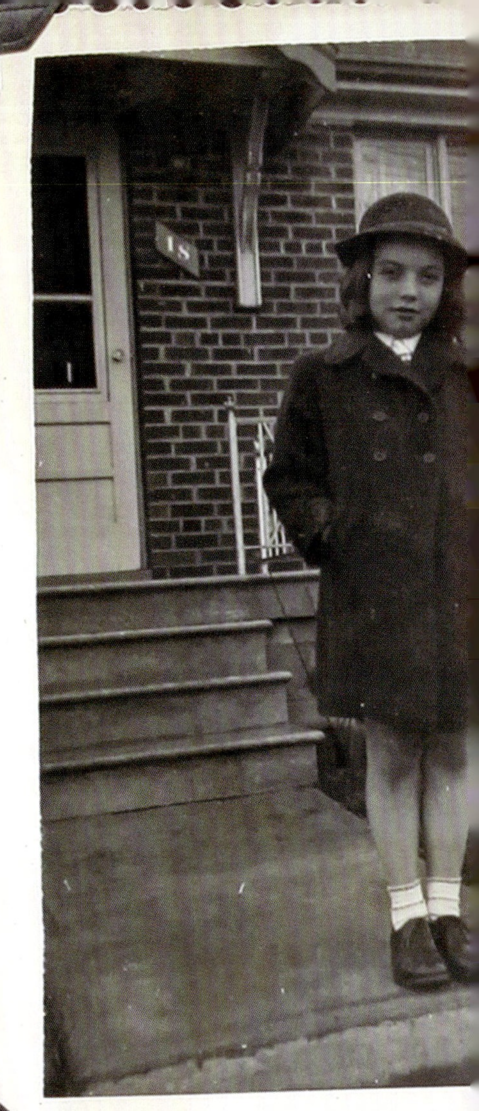

THE Twins

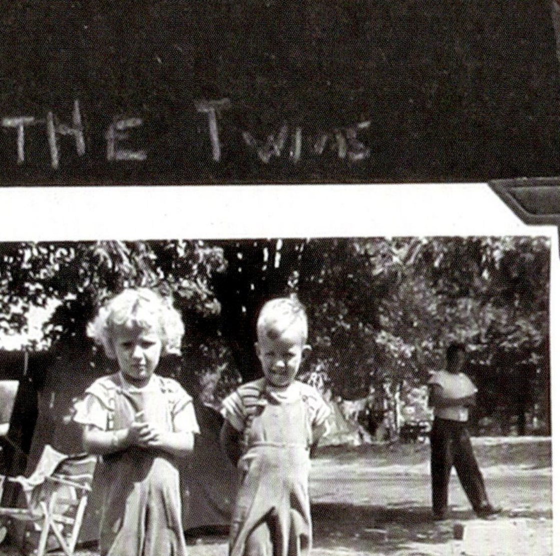

Stories We Tell

Tal-Or Ben-Choreen

Inside a red-covered album from the early 1950s, nine photographs, purposefully askew and secured by black photo corners, form a double-page spread (left and pp. 34-35). A young girl stands upright in a yard; she has inscribed "Me" above several of the photographs. Among the images, a black cat, Vicki, the twins, and Aunt Madge and Don emerge as key characters in her life. A visual narrative of her world unfolds throughout the album in photographs she carefully collected, arranged, and labelled, building her identity and subjectivity. She might keep her story private, or choose to share it with close ones; it may take on a more public life beyond her own. Anonymous and full of life, her effort epitomizes the way photography can build narratives.

Most of us use photographs to tell the stories of our lives, making meaning out of thousands of tiny clusters of silver or pigment on paper, metal, or glass. As our eyes consume these shapes, our minds extrapolate from memory and experience: a loved one, a celebrity, a place, an animal, an object. This evocative visual process encourages—even depends upon—narrative interpretations. Whether physical or digital, organized or haphazard, photography albums reflect something of their makers, and often follow a distinct set of characters over time, seen typically at milestone celebrations, gatherings, and leisure activities. These visual stories affirm memories of moments in our lives, sometimes idealized or even imagined. By sharing them, we weave together, confirm, and fix our collective histories.[1] As artist Max Dean poignantly explained, "Photo albums are the one, and possibly only, story many of us write."[2]

Photographic albums also help mark and study particularly challenging periods of history from different perspectives, as can be seen in the Art Gallery of Ontario's holdings of First World War albums. British Red Cross nurse Emily Maxwell Stuart's album (pp. 38-39) includes photographs of châteaux converted into hospitals, soldiers in trenches, surgeries, and candid images of her colleagues—nurses, doctors, and soldiers—in moments of levity between military duties. Sets of more formally organized stereographs attempt to relay the events of the war retrospectively, if not objectively. Many albums from this time display aerial views and scenes from the frontlines, signalling a shift in the ways conflict could be recorded and shared. Taken together, such photographs underscore how history draws from many perspectives—both exciting and banal, personal and institutional.

Such narratives are expanded upon through the large collection of work by Polish Jewish photographer Henryk Ross (pp. 50-51). One of the official Łódź Ghetto photographers from 1940 to 1944, Ross meticulously documented the grim realities of the ghetto's inhabitants—including his own.[3] While these images record his personal experiences, they act as testimony from the countless people who were unable to doc-

Maker once known, Canadian
Young Girl's Album of Friends, Family and School
(detail)
1949-1954
Gelatin silver prints in a red album with embossed cover
22.4 × 64.4 cm
Gift of Max Dean, 2016
2016/247

Federico Patellani
Vittorio Emanuele Orlando sits in a garden with two other gentlemen (verso detail)
1946
Gelatin silver print
13.4 × 18.5 cm
Anonymous Gift, 2020
2022/6380

ument and share theirs. Such photographs emphasize the way tragic historical events flattened the richness of individual narratives. As such, Ross's photographs stand in for a whole community, blurring the lines between personal and public histories.

In the AGO's collection, documents of private lives sit alongside stories constructed for the public and shared in the press. As the media industry grew in the late 1800s and early 1900s, and newspapers and magazines sought to communicate their coverage more effectively—and to entice more readers to their publications—photography became a primary and seductive tool.[4] The images commissioned and circulated through press photographs—local happenings, international political and social upheavals, sporting events, medical advancements, the glamorous lives of public figures and celebrities—help us understand the interests and values of different communities throughout the twentieth century.

Press photographers were central to this equation, supplying a steady flow of images as printing technologies advanced and distribution networks expanded. They had little control over how their photographs were published and contextualized—few photographers at the time were even credited for their work. In response, seeking greater authorial control over their stories, some came together to create agencies like Magnum, founded in 1947.[5] Half a century later, the shift to digital technologies in the early 2000s led many agencies to dispose of their physical archives. Recognizing the value of these visual repositories, institutions, including the AGO, have collected these press materials, inviting new generations of viewers to encounter and consider them anew, in relation to our evolving understanding of the past.

In the mid-1900s, independent photographers began undertaking prolonged and nuanced visual investigations. Aligned with social documentary practices, artists like Pamela Harris (pp. 59–61) and Michael Mitchell (p. 45) offered expanded views of the world through their photographs, beyond what they saw covered in the popular press.

Later, responding to the perception of photography's innate truth in the popular press, artists in the 1970s began to critique and challenge the possibility of any objective or singular viewpoint. Beyond calling attention to the boundaries of photography's narrative qualities, these makers—such as Carole Condé and Karl Beveridge (p. 55), Martha Rosler (pp. 56–57), and Ken Lum (p. 33)—constructed new stories and addressed a larger set of social concerns.

Spanning the history of the medium, the photographs in this section reflect the stories we tell and share about ourselves and our worlds—through private albums, the popular press, or personal artistic visions. Though the contexts and goals are varied, together these works highlight photography's power to shape and reshape personal and collective histories.

1. For wide discussion of photography's function in the public sphere, see Stephen C. Pinson and Elizabeth Cronin, "Public Eye: 175 Years of Sharing Photography," *Exposure* 48, no. 2 (Fall 2015): pp. 30–35. For discussions of the impact of portraiture and family albums, see Martha Langford, *Suspended Conversations: The Afterlight of Memory in Photographic Albums* (Montreal: McGill-Queen's University Press, 2001); Geoffrey Batchen, *Forget Me Not: Photography & Remembrance* (New York: Princeton Architectural Press, 2004); Thy Phu and Elspeth H. Brown, "The Cultural Politics of Aspiration: Family Photography's Mixed Feelings," *Journal of Visual Culture* 17, no. 2 (2018): pp. 152–165.
2. Quoted in "Max Dean: Album," Art Gallery of Ontario, accessed April 7, 2025, ago.ca/exhibitions/max-dean-album.
3. Maia-Mari Sutnik, ed., *Memory Unearthed: The Lodz Ghetto Photographs of Henryk Ross* (Toronto: Art Gallery of Ontario, 2015).
4. For a longer discussion of the history of photography in the press, see Thierry Gervais with a contribution by Gaëlle Morel, *The Making of Visual News: A History of Photography in the Press* (New York: Routledge, 2017); Mary Panzer with an afterword by Christian Caujolle, *Things as They Are* (New York: Aperture Foundation, 2005); William Hannigan and Ken Johnston, *Picture Machine: The Rise of American Newspictures* (New York: Harry N. Abrams, 2004).
5. Nadya Bair, *The Decisive Network: Magnum Photos and the Postwar Image Market* (Berkeley: University of California Press, 2020).

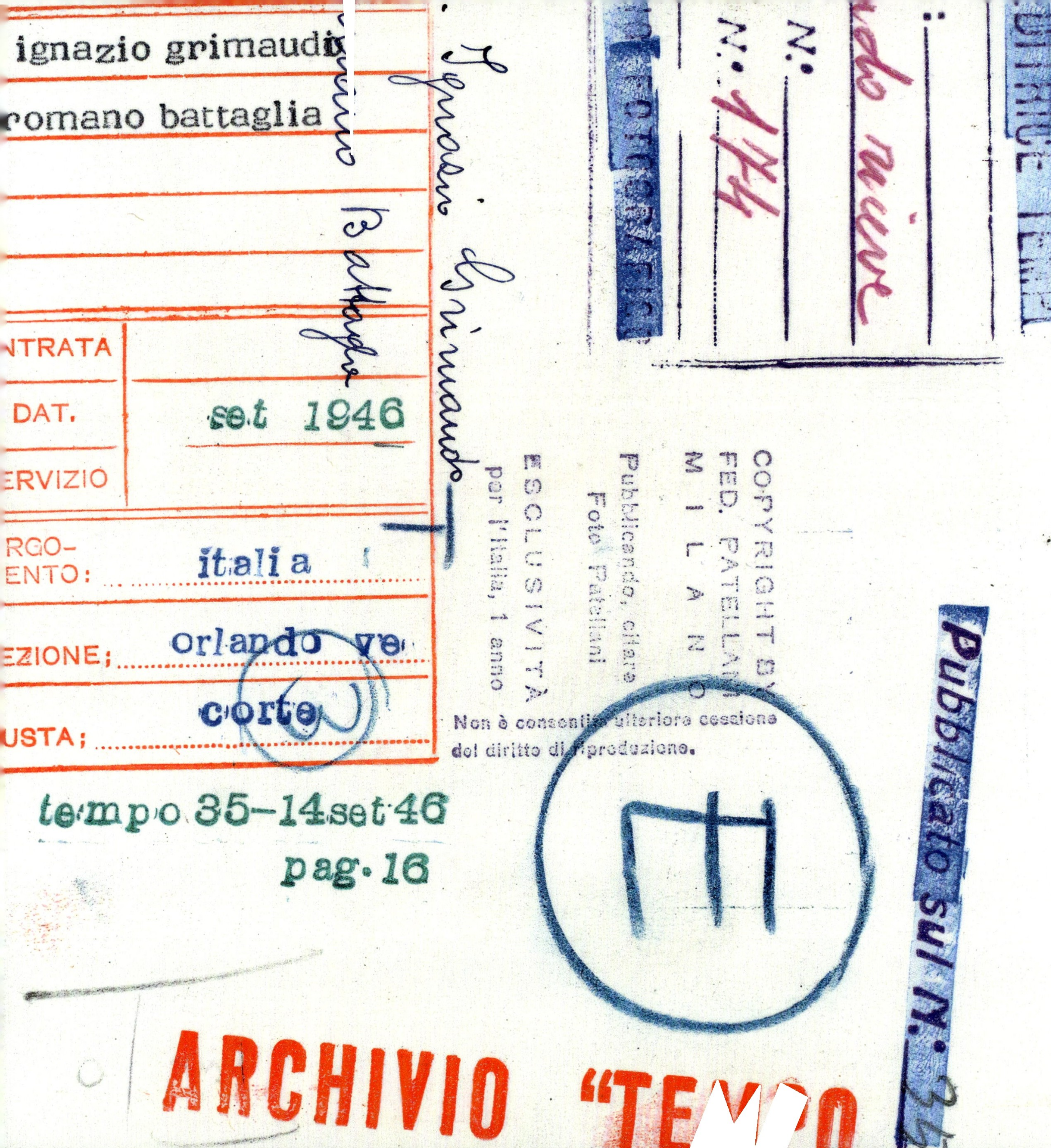
ignazio grimaudo
romano battaglia
set 1946
italia
corte
tempo 35-14set46
pag.16
ARCHIVIO
COPYRIGHT BY
FED. PATELLANI
MILANO
Pubblicando, citare
Foto Patellani
ESCLUSIVITÀ
per l'Italia, 1 anno
Non è consentita ulteriore cessione
del diritto di riproduzione.
Pubblicato sul N.

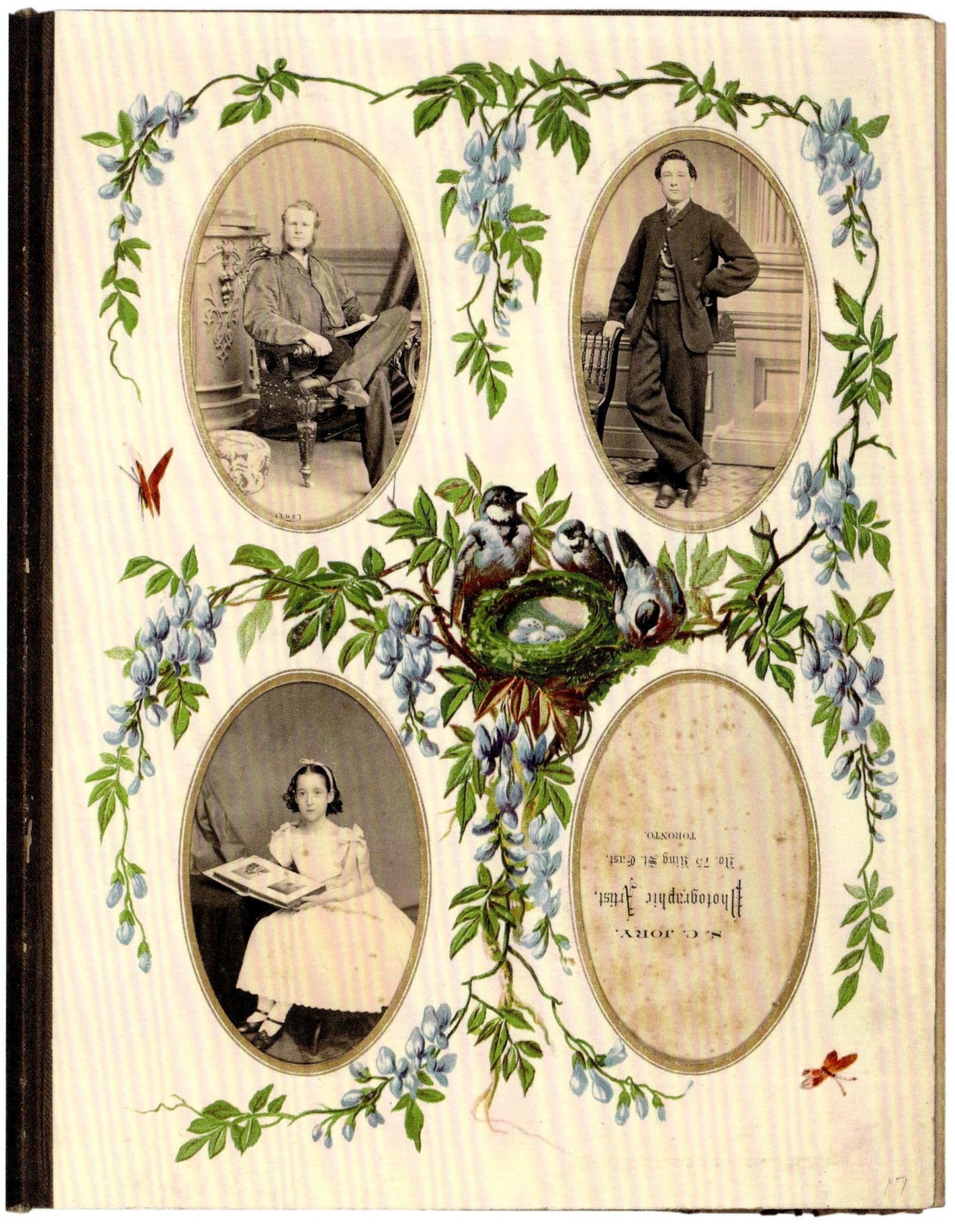
S. C. JORY.
Photographic Artist,
No. 75 King St. East,
TORONTO.

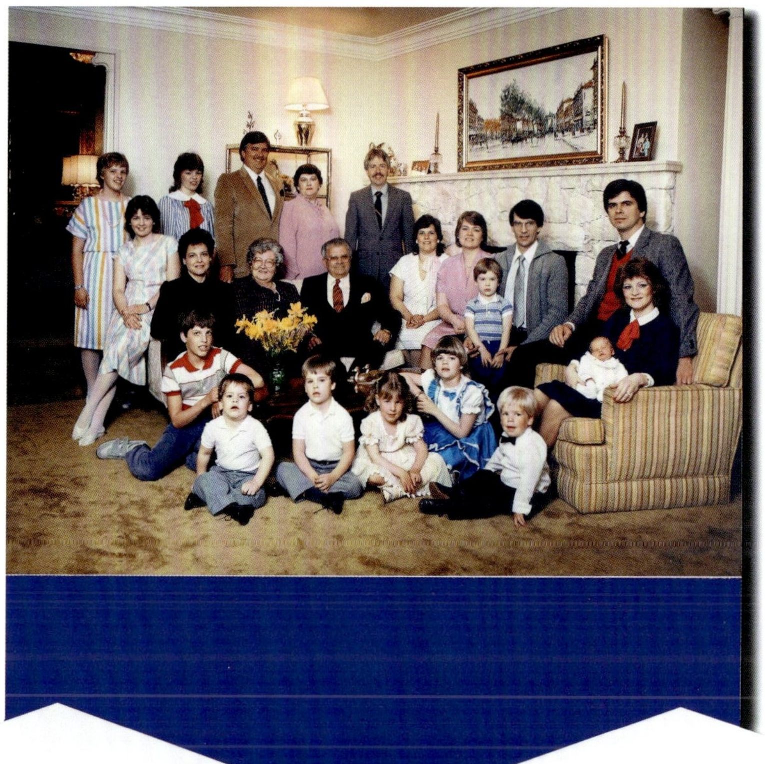

Clockwise from lower left:
J.H. Noverre, James Inglis, Artist once known, and Samuel C. Jory (verso)
Theresa Bywater Peterkin Family Album, Page 17
1867–1973
Cartes-de-visite: albumen prints
27 × 21 cm (page)
Gift of Mary F. Williamson, 2009
2009/180.17

Ken Lum
Jantzen Family
1986
Dye coupler print, acrylic paint on opaque Plexiglas
172.7 × 172.7 cm
Promised Gift of Ydessa Hendeles

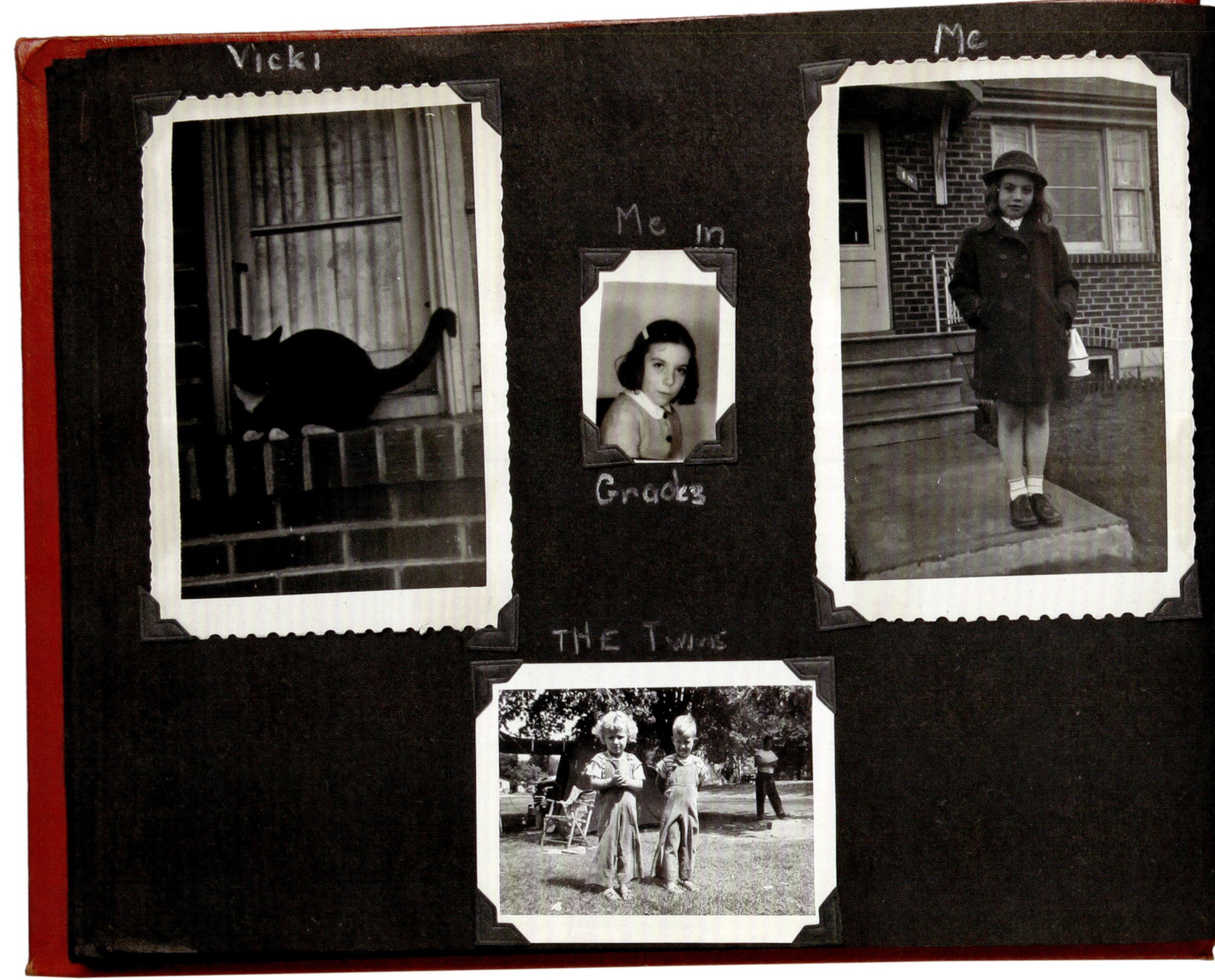

Maker once known, Canadian
Young Girl's Album of Friends, Family and School
1949–1954
Gelatin silver prints in a red album with embossed cover
22.4 × 64.4 cm
Gift of Max Dean, 2016
2016/247

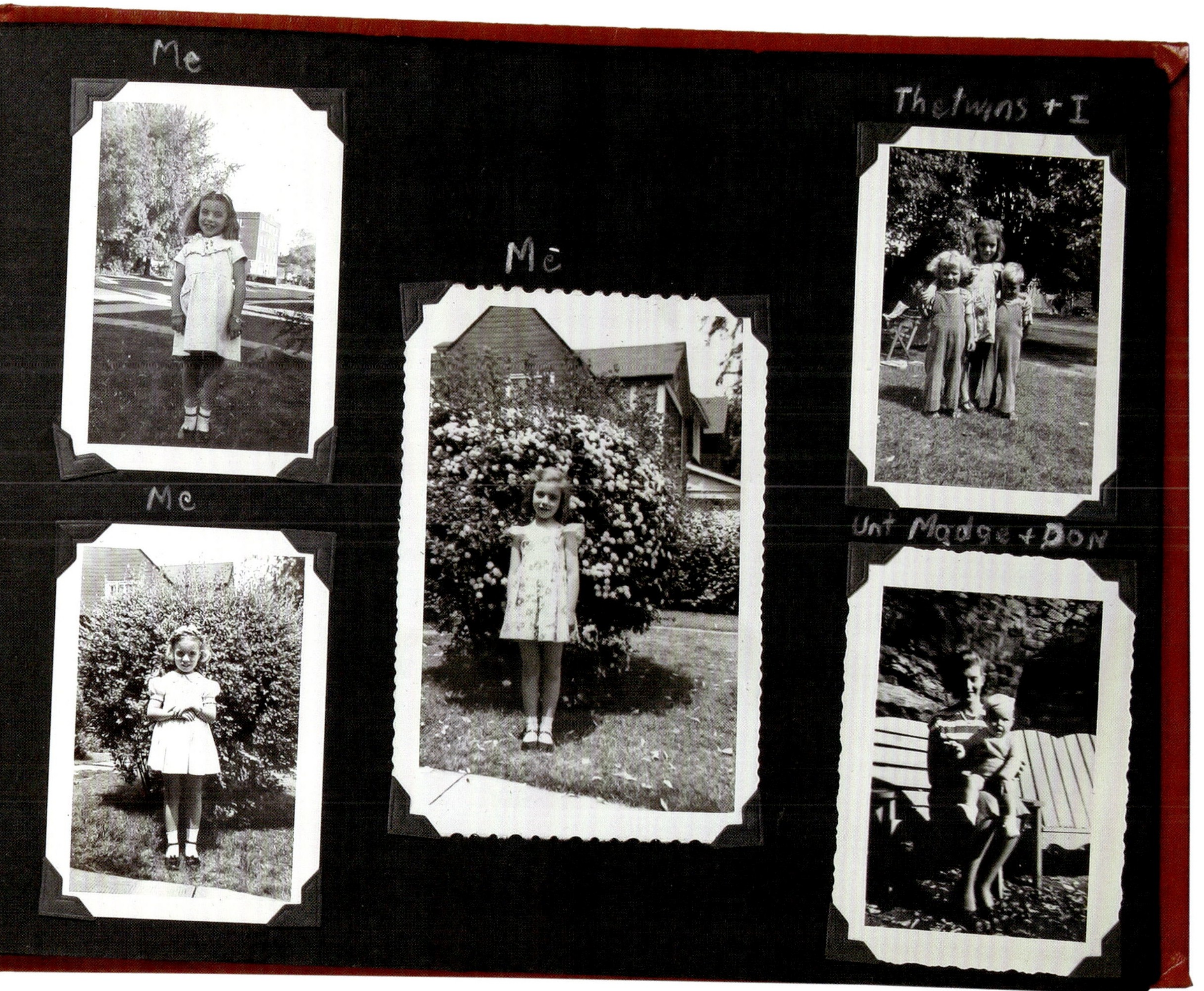
Me
The twins + I
Me
Me
Unt Madge + DON

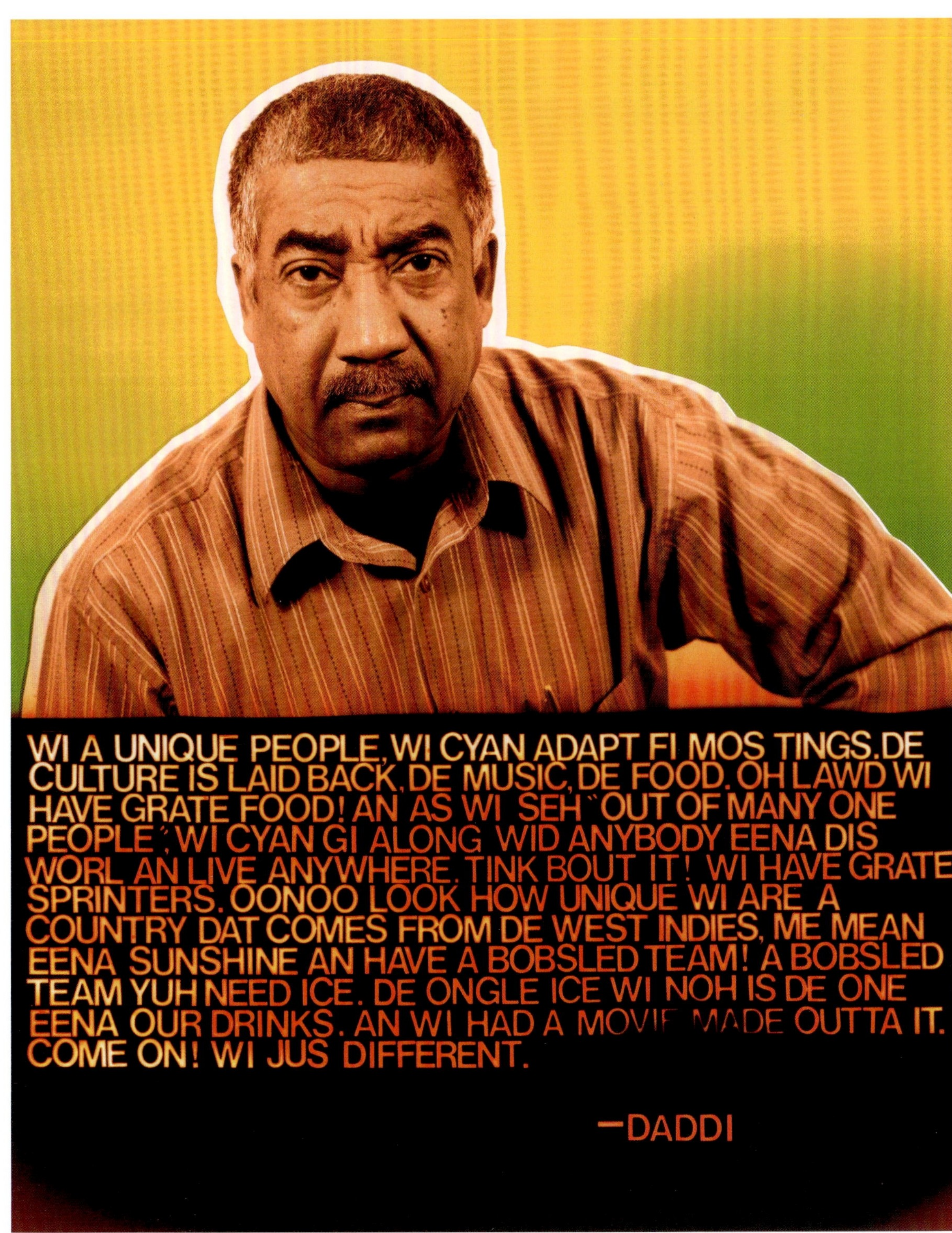
WI A UNIQUE PEOPLE, WI CYAN ADAPT FI MOS TINGS. DE
CULTURE IS LAID BACK, DE MUSIC, DE FOOD. OH LAWD WI
HAVE GRATE FOOD! AN AS WI SEH "OUT OF MANY ONE
PEOPLE", WI CYAN GI ALONG WID ANYBODY EENA DIS
WORL AN LIVE ANYWHERE. TINK BOUT IT! WI HAVE GRATE
SPRINTERS. OONOO LOOK HOW UNIQUE WI ARE A
COUNTRY DAT COMES FROM DE WEST INDIES, ME MEAN
EENA SUNSHINE AN HAVE A BOBSLED TEAM! A BOBSLED
TEAM YUH NEED ICE. DE ONGLE ICE WI NOH IS DE ONE
EENA OUR DRINKS. AN WI HAD A MOVIE MADE OUTTA IT.
COME ON! WI JUS DIFFERENT.
—DADDI

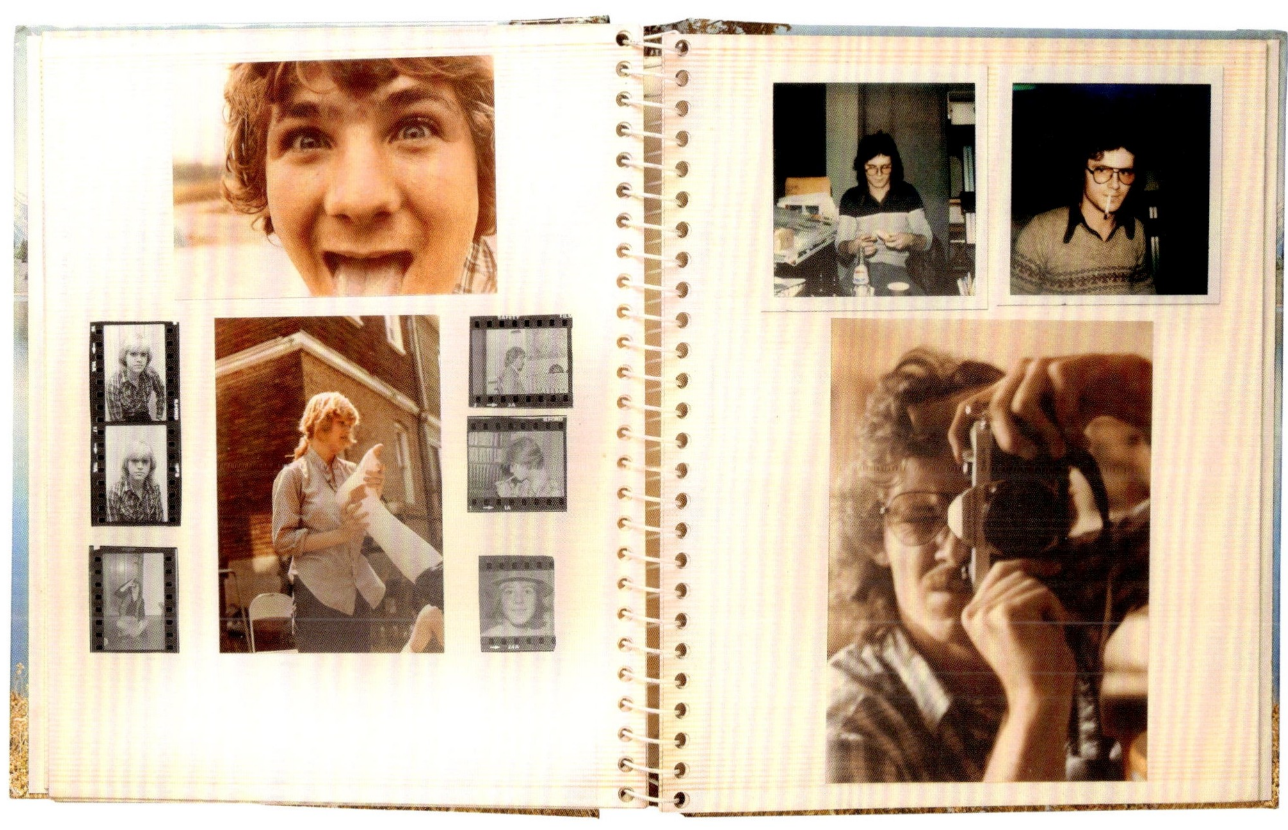

Christina Leslie
Daddi
2006; printed 2023
From the series ***EveryTING Irie*** (2006)
Pigment print
43.2 × 53.3 cm
Purchase, with funds from Friends of Global Africa and the Diaspora, 2023
2023/10

Maker once known, Canadian
Richard Zettler, Cartoonist/Illustrator
c. 1970s
Chromogenic prints
29.8 × 51.6 cm
Gift of Max Dean, 2016
2016/233

FAMILY ALBUMS

Family albums reveal photography's quiet power to shape memory and bind the everyday to history. Tracing more than a century of album-making—its materials, aesthetics, and cultural idiosyncrasies—the hundreds of intimate, often anonymous objects in the collection invite reflection on why they belong in a museum, and how they continue to shape our understanding of ourselves across time and place.

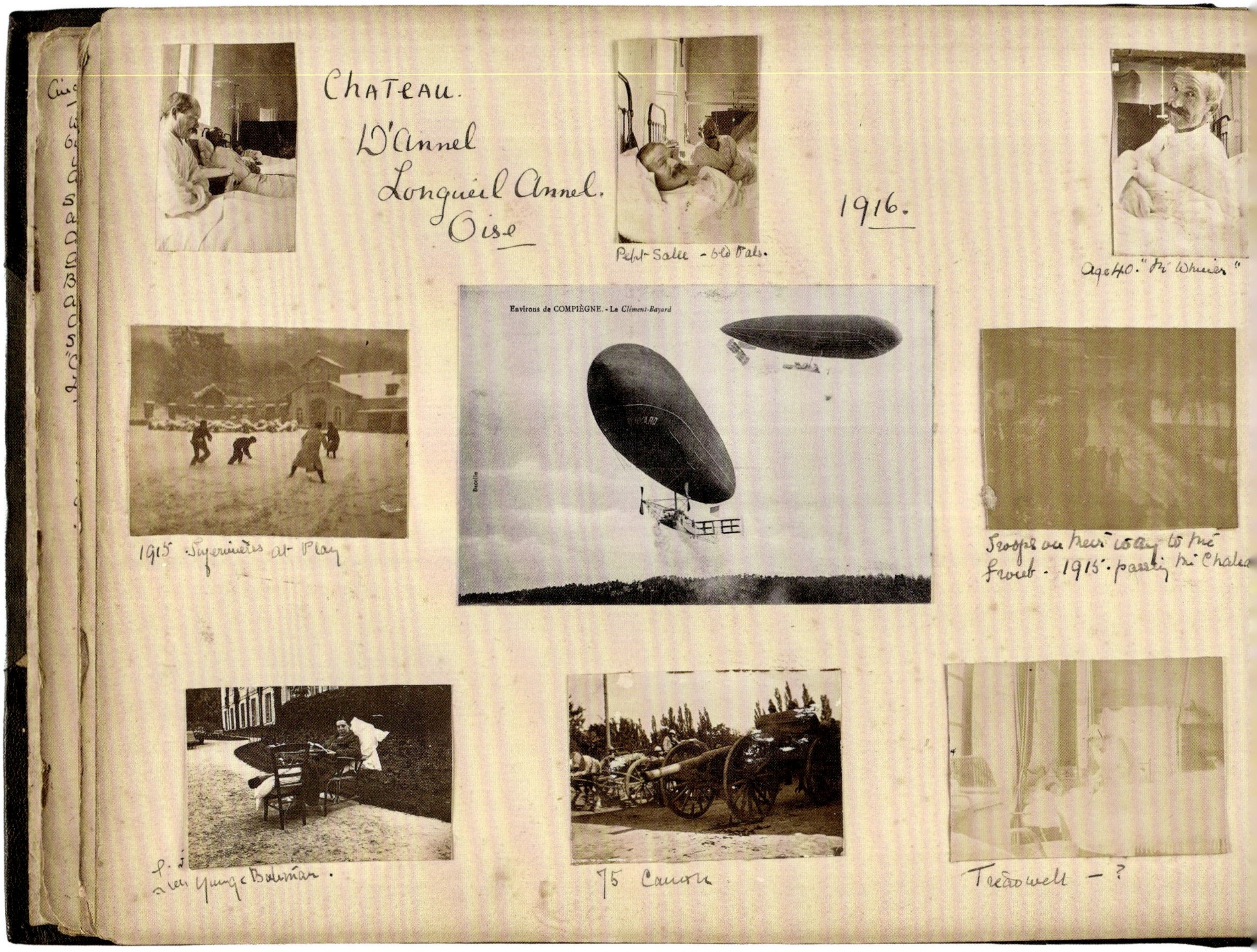

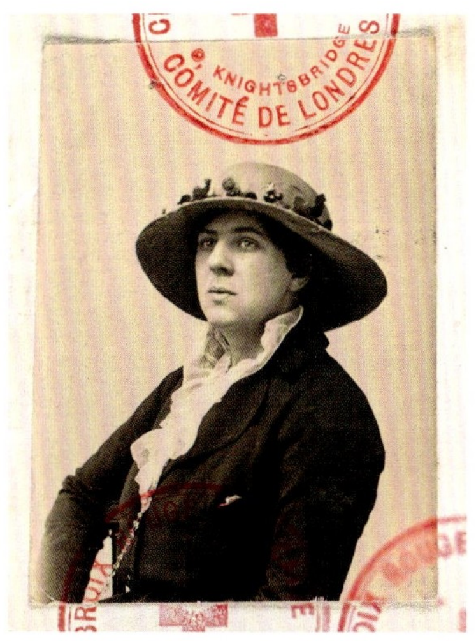

Emily Maxwell Stuart
Emily Maxwell Stuart: Photos taken during the First World War
1914–1918
Album: 354 gelatin silver prints, postcards, ephemera, leather cover
28 × 38.2 × 5.5 cm
Anonymous Gift, 2004
2004/599.2.2, 2004/599.1.27-.28

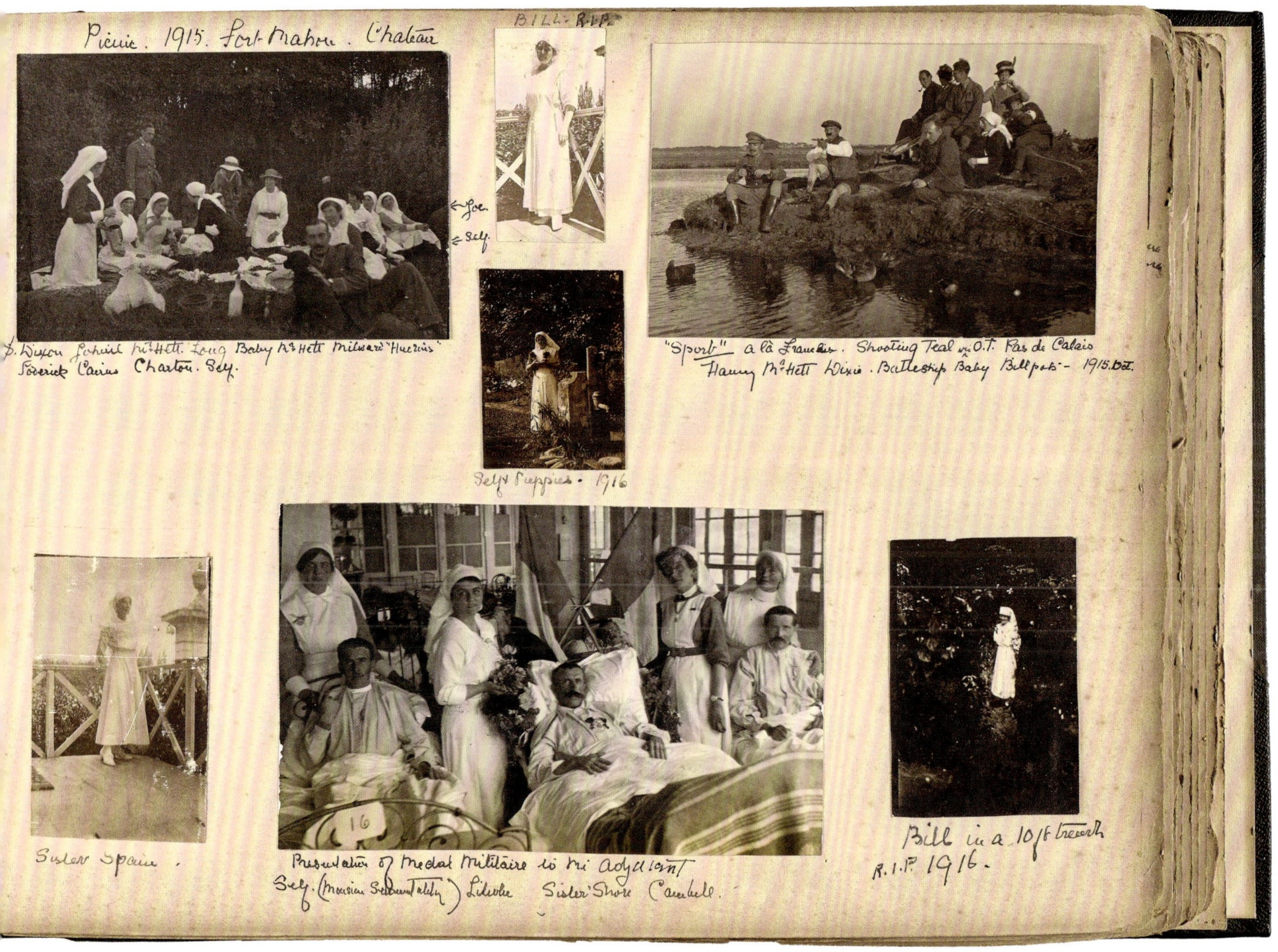

WORLD WAR I ALBUMS

The collection holds nearly 500 photographic albums created by soldiers, nurses, and civilians during the First World War (1914–1918), documenting both private moments and public events. Together, they underscore the war's harsh realities and vast reach, providing an expansive visual record that reveals photography's vital role in recording wide-ranging experiences during a global conflict.

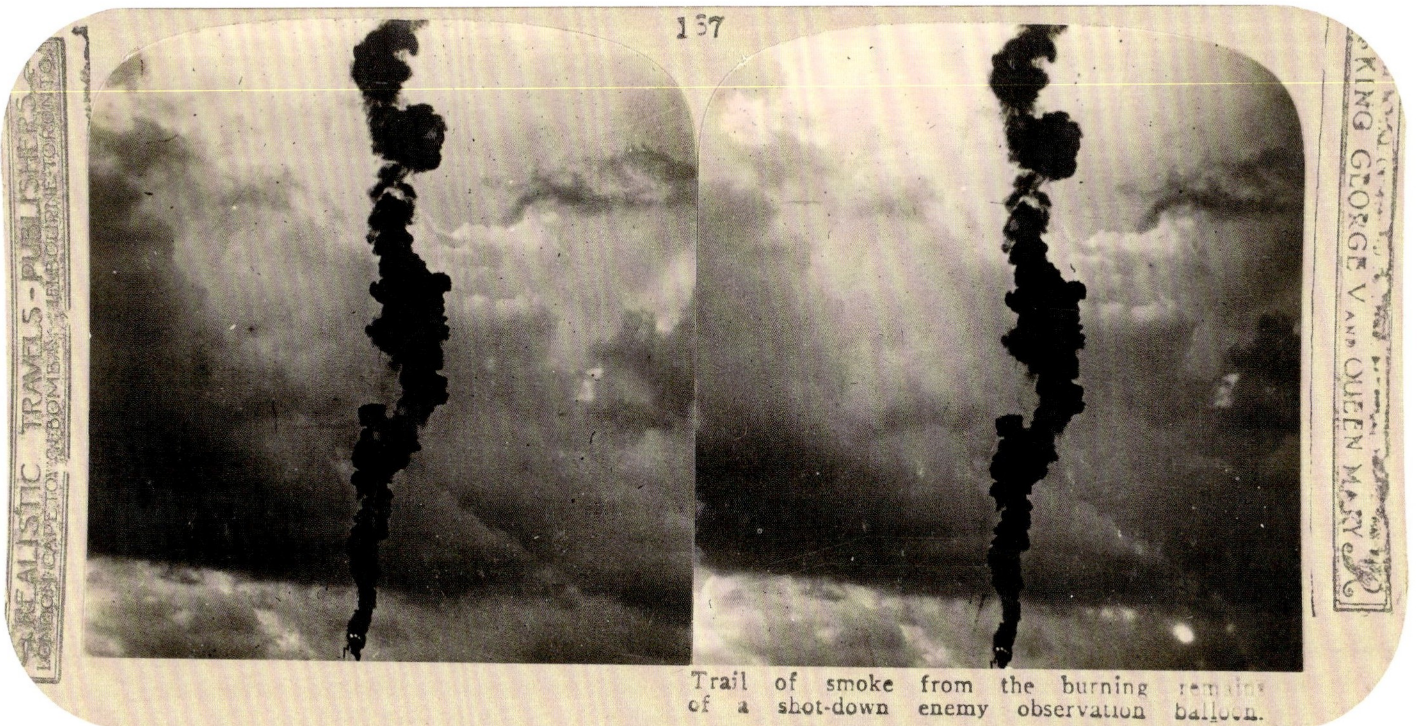

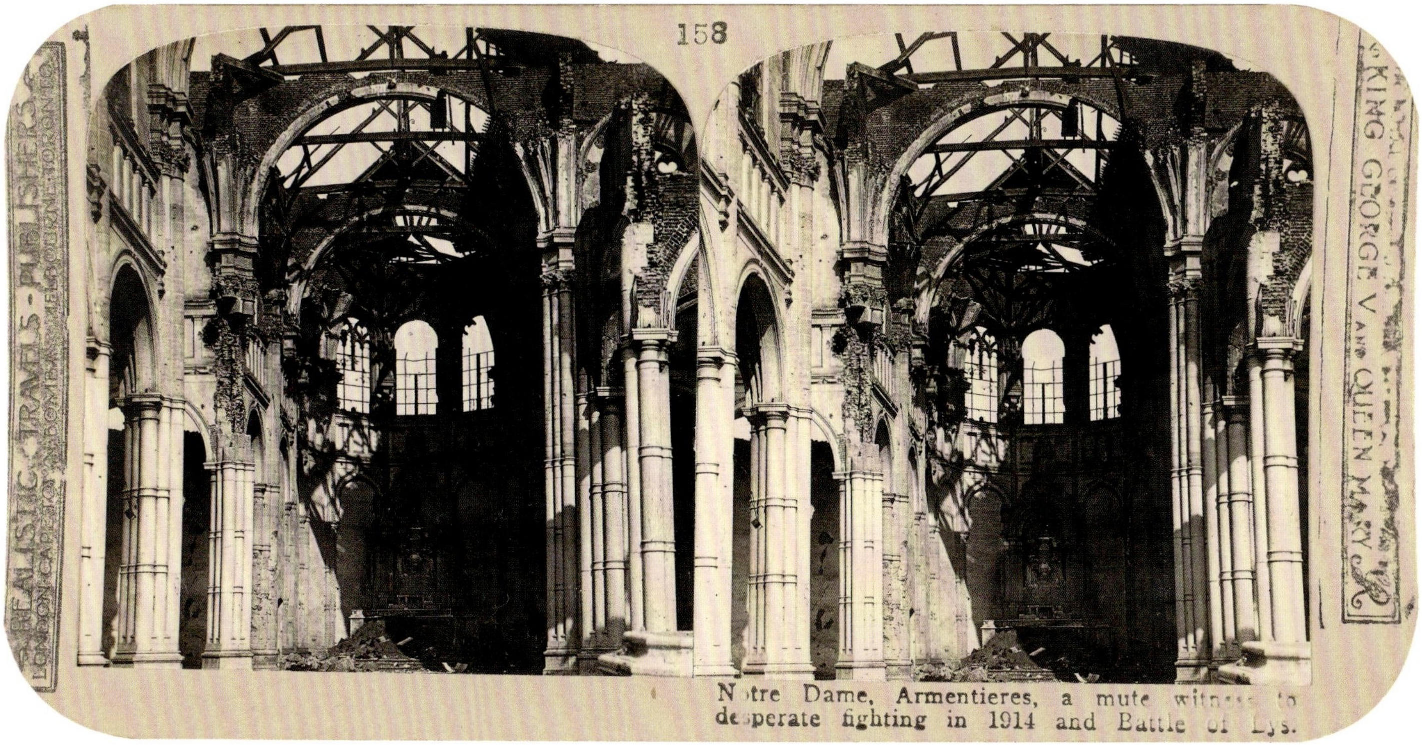

158

REALISTIC TRAVELS - PUBLISHERS

LONDON CAPETOWN BOMBAY MELBOURNE TORONTO

KING GEORGE V AND QUEEN MARY

Notre Dame, Armentieres, a mute witness to
desperate fighting in 1914 and Battle of Lys.

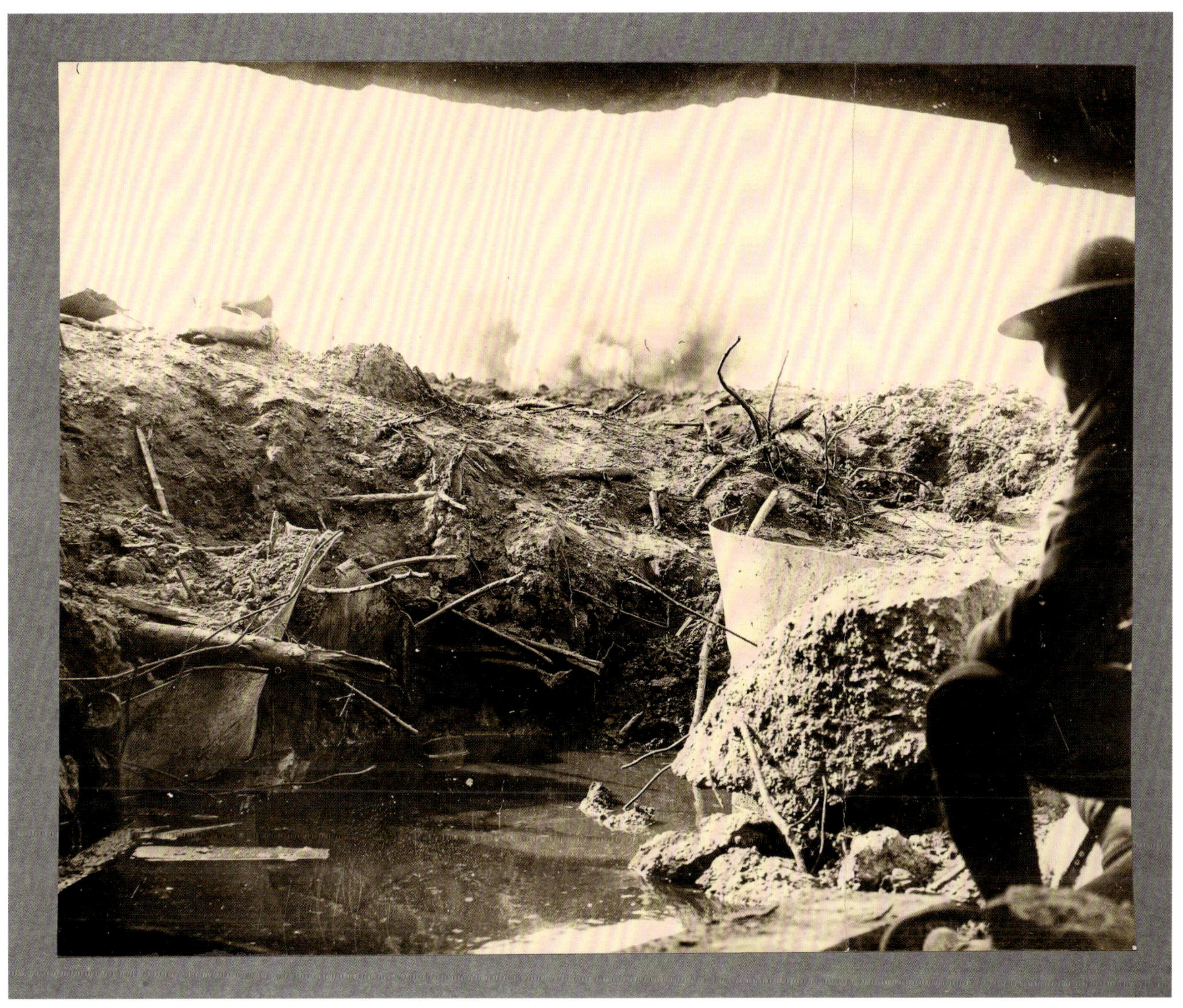

Realistic Travels
British publisher, active London, Cape Town, Bombay, Melbourne, Toronto c. 1908–1921
Other Theatres, Last Battles on the Western Front and War's End*, *#167 and ***#158***
1914–1919
From the set ***Realistic Travels: World War, 1914–1918***
Stereographs: gelatin silver prints
8.9 × 17.7 cm each
Anonymous Gift, 2004
2004/770.24, 2004/770.6

James Francis "Frank" Hurley
From the album ***Western Front, Australians at War***
c. 1917
Album: 37 gelatin silver prints
29.5 × 36.8 cm
Anonymous Gift, 2004
2004/411.3

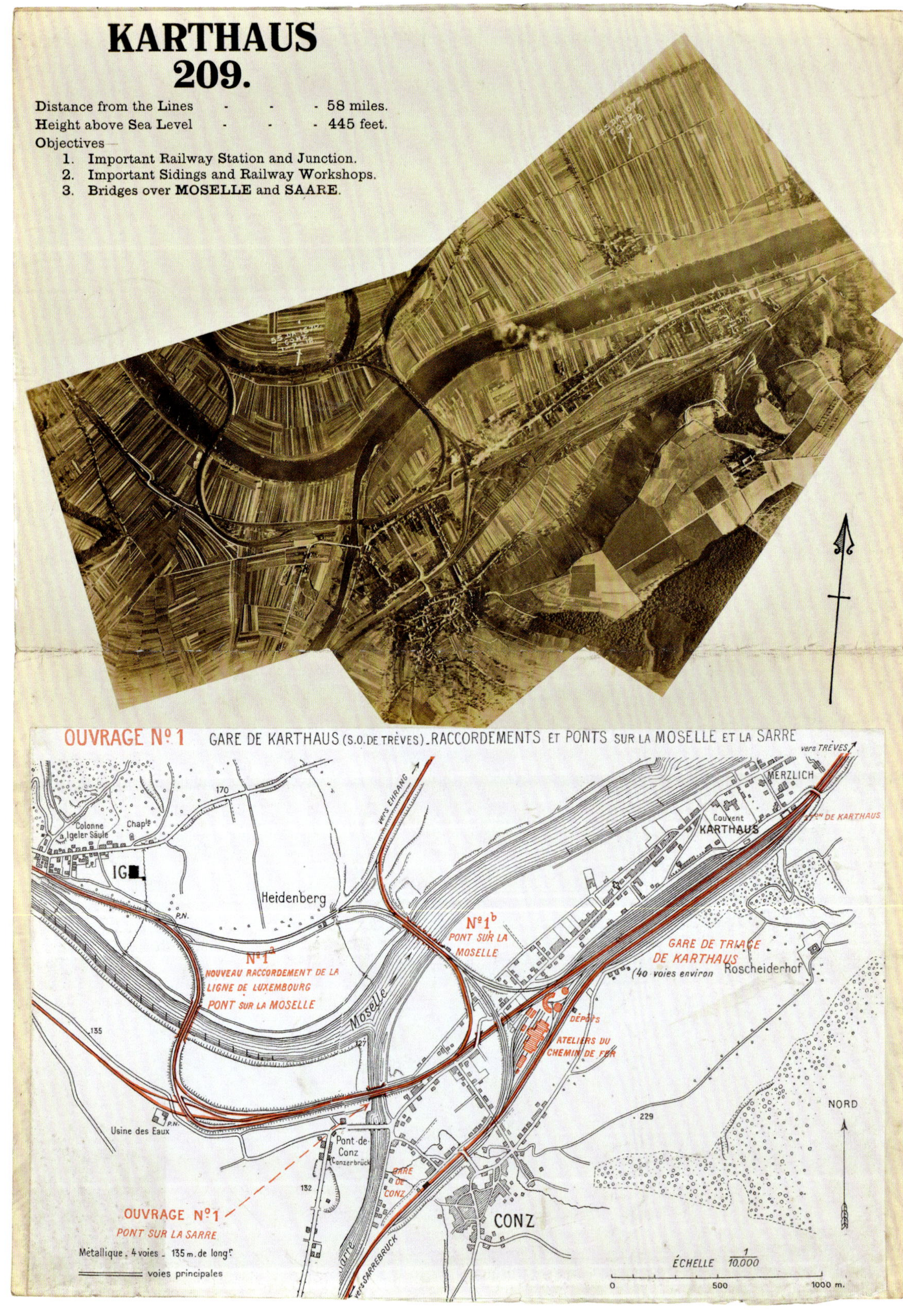
KARTHAUS
209.
Distance from the Lines - - - 58 miles.
Height above Sea Level - - - 445 feet.
Objectives—
1. Important Railway Station and Junction.
2. Important Sidings and Railway Workshops.
3. Bridges over MOSELLE and SAARE.
OUVRAGE N°1 GARE DE KARTHAUS (S.O. DE TRÈVES). RACCORDEMENTS ET PONTS SUR LA MOSELLE ET LA SARRE
vers TRÈVES
MERZLICH
Couvent
KARTHAUS
Colonne Igeler Säule
Chaple
IGEL
170
vers EHRANG
Heidenberg
P.N.
N°1ᵇ
PONT SUR LA MOSELLE
GARE DE TRIAGE DE KARTHAUS
(40 voies environ
Roscheiderhof
N°1ᵃ
NOUVEAU RACCORDEMENT DE LA LIGNE DE LUXEMBOURG
PONT SUR LA MOSELLE
Moselle
135
127
DÉPÔTS
ATELIERS DU CHEMIN DE FER
Usine des Eaux
Pont de Conz
Conzerbrück
229
NORD
132
GARE DE CONZ
CONZ
vers SARREBRUCK
OUVRAGE N°1
PONT SUR LA SARRE
Métallique. 4 voies. 135 m. de longr.
voies principales
ÉCHELLE 1/10.000
0
500
1000 m.

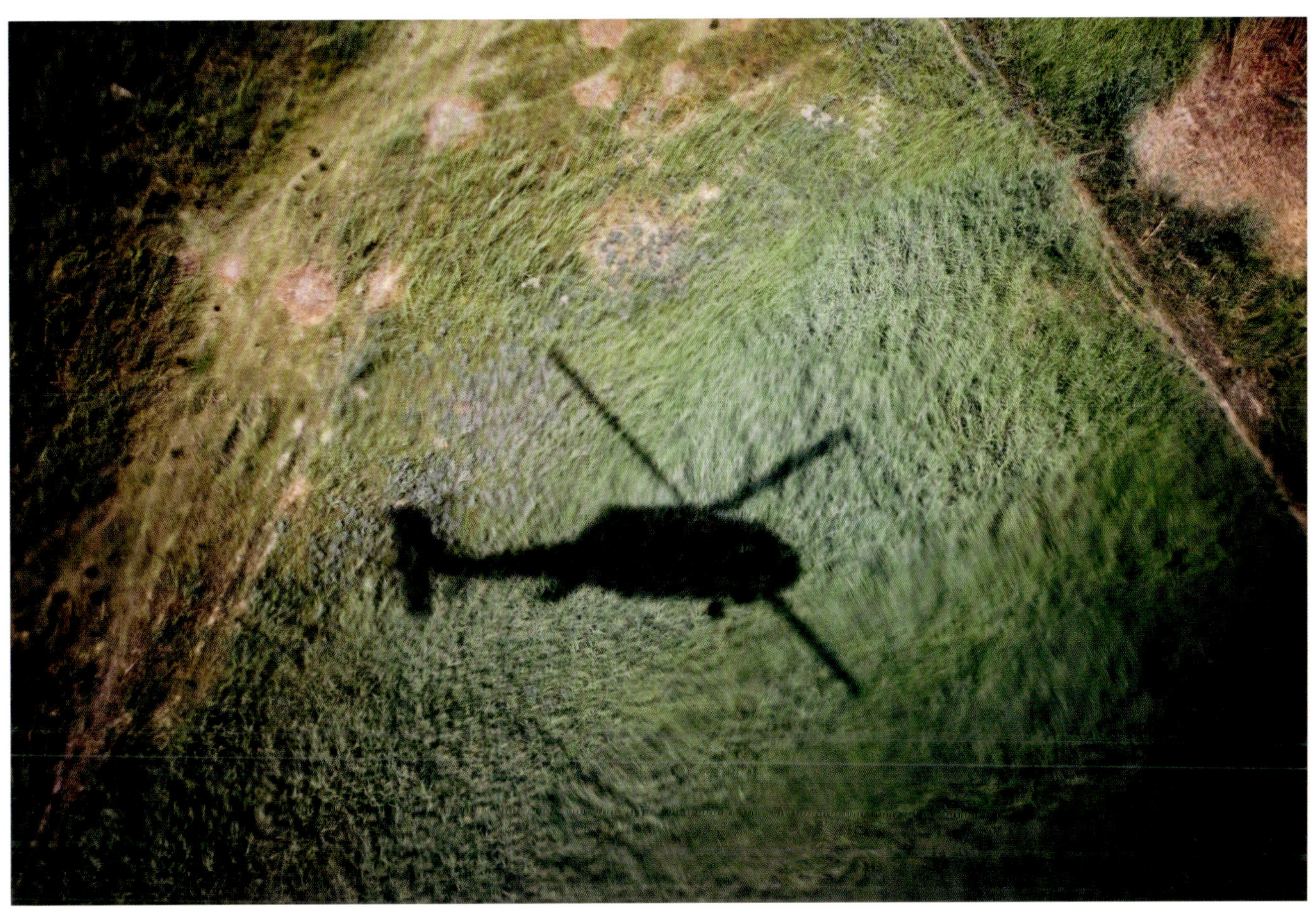

Maker once known
General Staff (Intelligence) Australian Corps
Karthaus 209
July 1918
From the album ***Third Battle of the Somme*** (July 1918)
Ink on paper and gelatin silver prints
34.8 × 42.5 cm
Anonymous Gift, 2004
2004/714.32

Louie Palu
Medevac helicopter on mission over Zhari District, Kandahar, Afghanistan
2010
From the series ***The Fighting Season 1*** (2007–2010)
Pigment print
50.8 × 61 cm
Purchase, Canada Now Photography Acquisition Initiative, with funds from Edward Burtynsky and Nicholas Metivier, 2021
2021/53

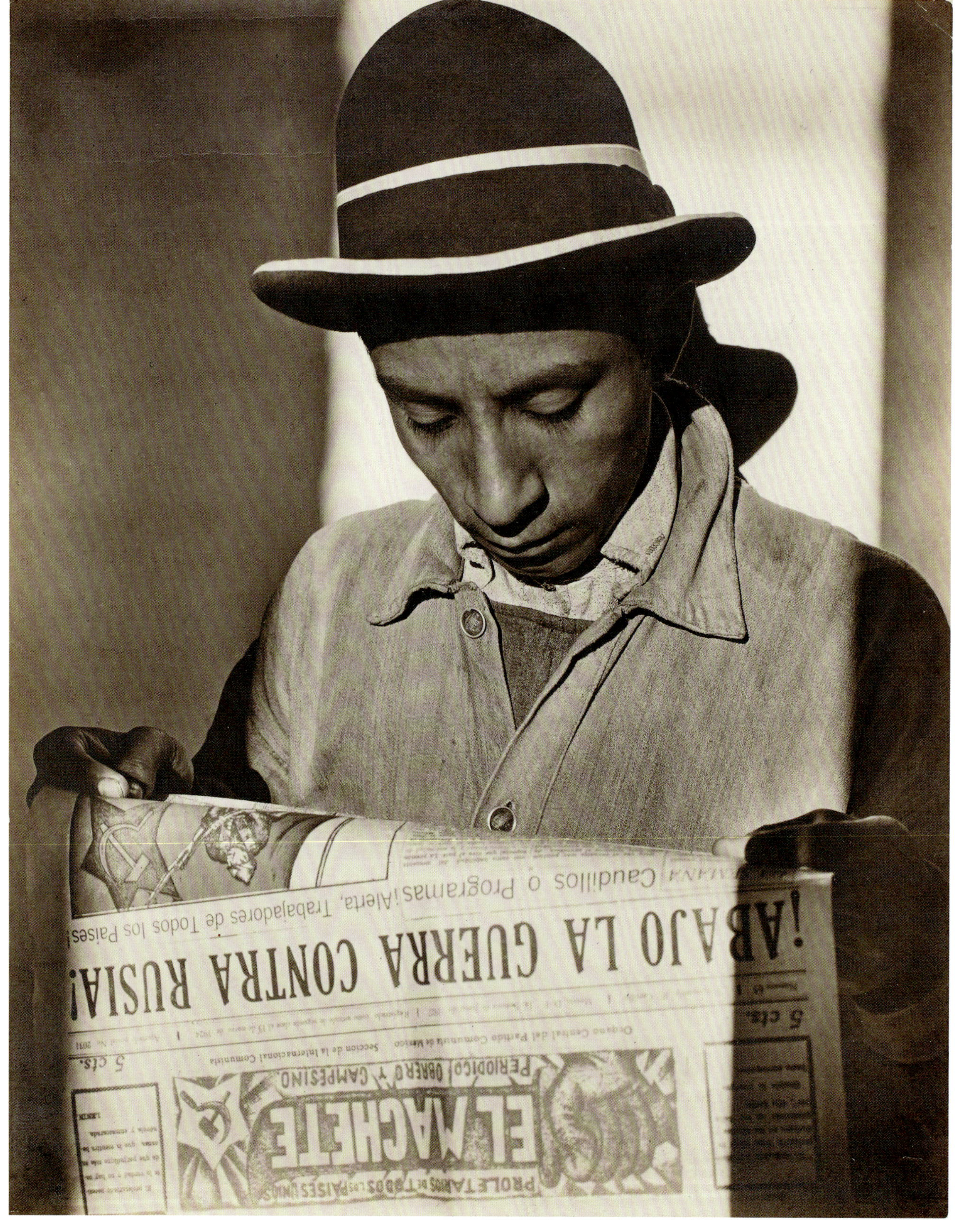
Caudillos o Programas
¡Alerta, Trabajadores de Todos los Paises!
¡ABAJO LA GUERRA CONTRA RUSIA!
5 cts.
Organo Central del Partido Comunista de Mexico
Seccion de la Internacional Comunista
PERIODICO OBRERO Y CAMPESINO
EL MACHETE
PROLETARIOS DE TODOS LOS PAISES UNIOS

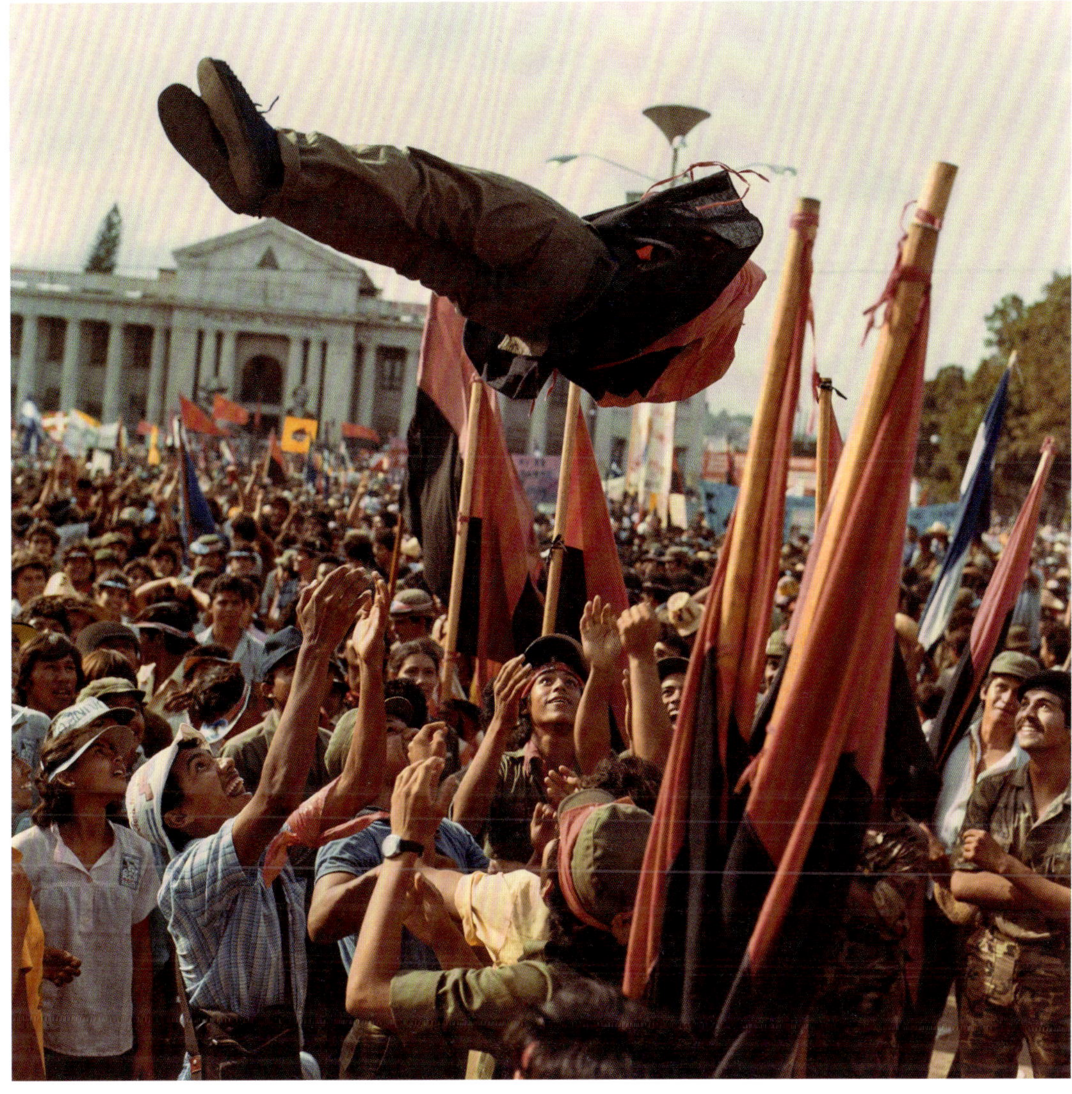

Tina Modotti
El Machete
1926
Gelatin silver print
23.8 × 18.8 cm
Gift of Harry and Ann Malcolmson, 2015
2015/248

Michael Mitchell
Sandinista youths throw each other above the crowd at a mass rally commemorating the 50th anniversary of Augusto Sandino's assassination; Plaza of the Revolution, Managua, February 21, 1984
1984
From the series ***After the Triumph*** (1984)
Chromogenic print
50.8 × 40.6 cm
Purchase, with funds donated by Rupert Duchesne and Holly Coll-Black, 2012
2012/25.3

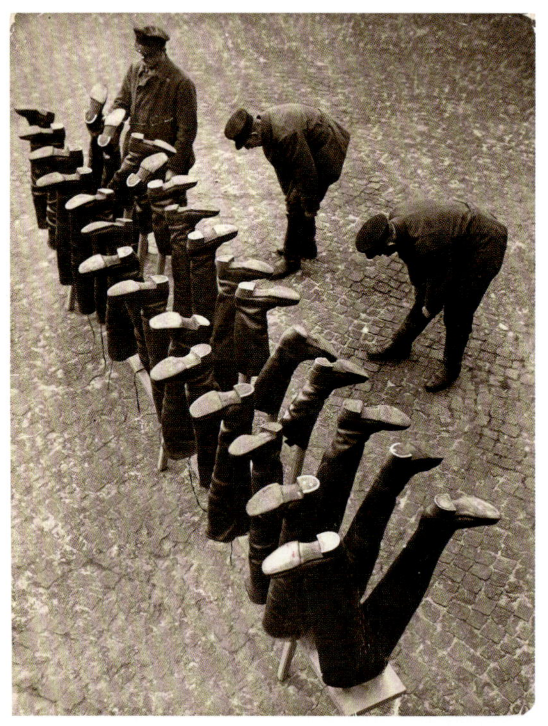

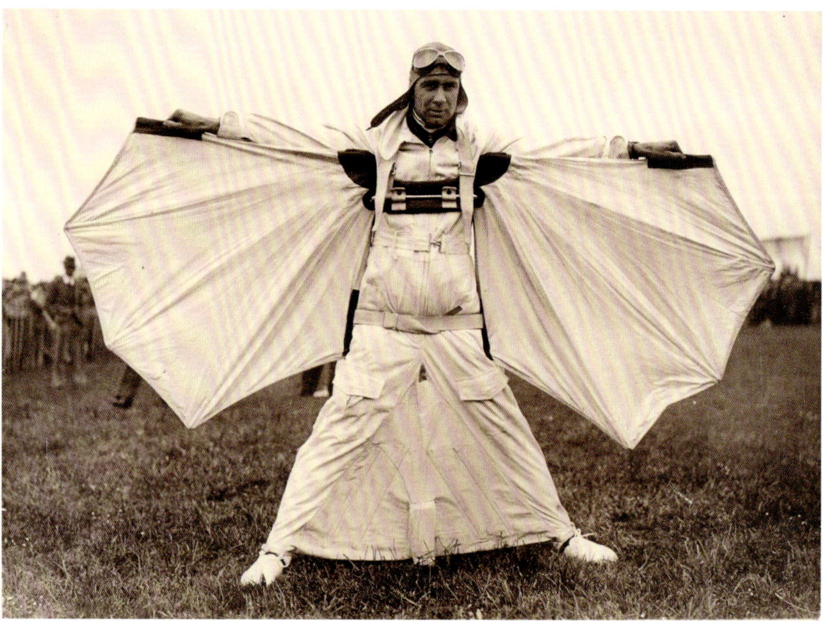

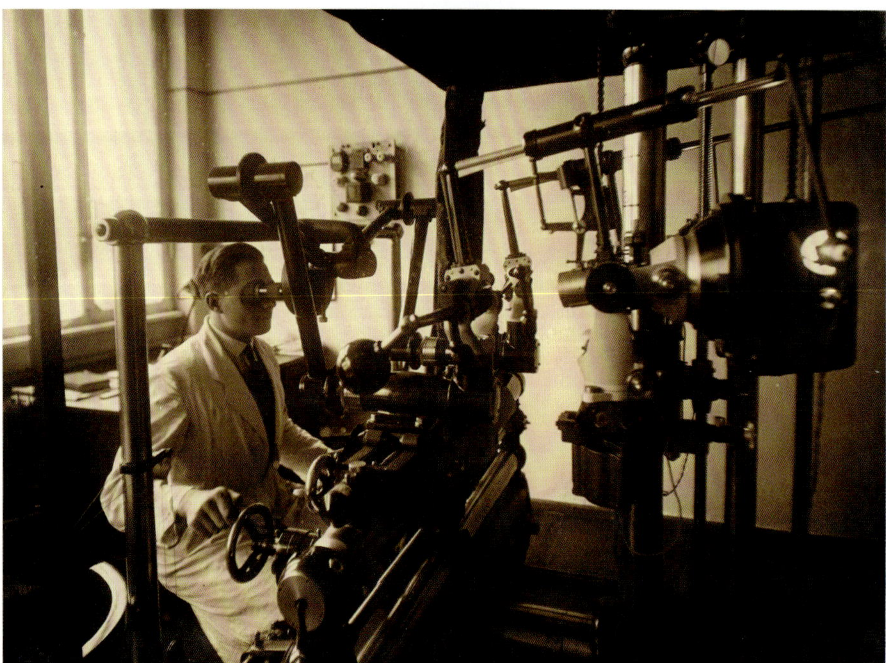

Eric Borchert
The sewer workers, who have to wade through deep water, put on watertight waders
1932
Gelatin silver print
24.2 × 18 cm
Anonymous Gift, 2002
2002/5311

Associated Press (German)
"Birdman" with Artificial Wings, London
1936
Gelatin silver print
14.2 × 18.9 cm
Anonymous Gift, 2005
2005/17375

Willi Ruge
Special Measuring Device
c. 1930s
Gelatin silver print
17 × 23.2 cm
Anonymous Gift, 2002
2002/8660

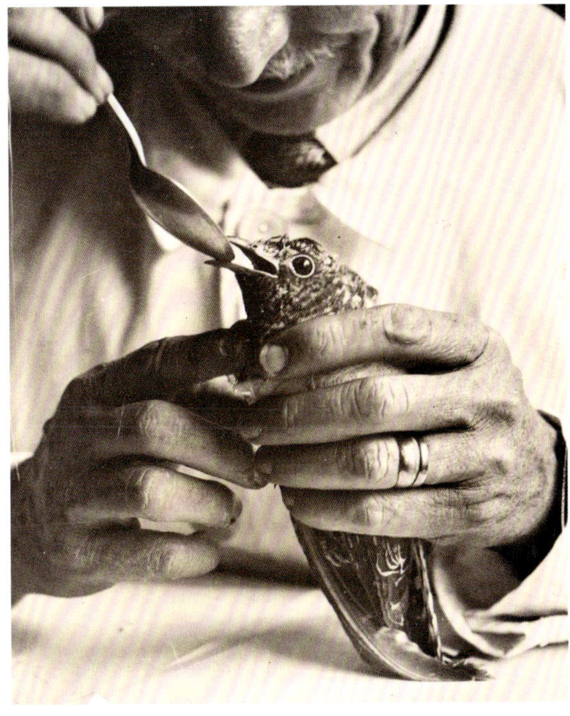

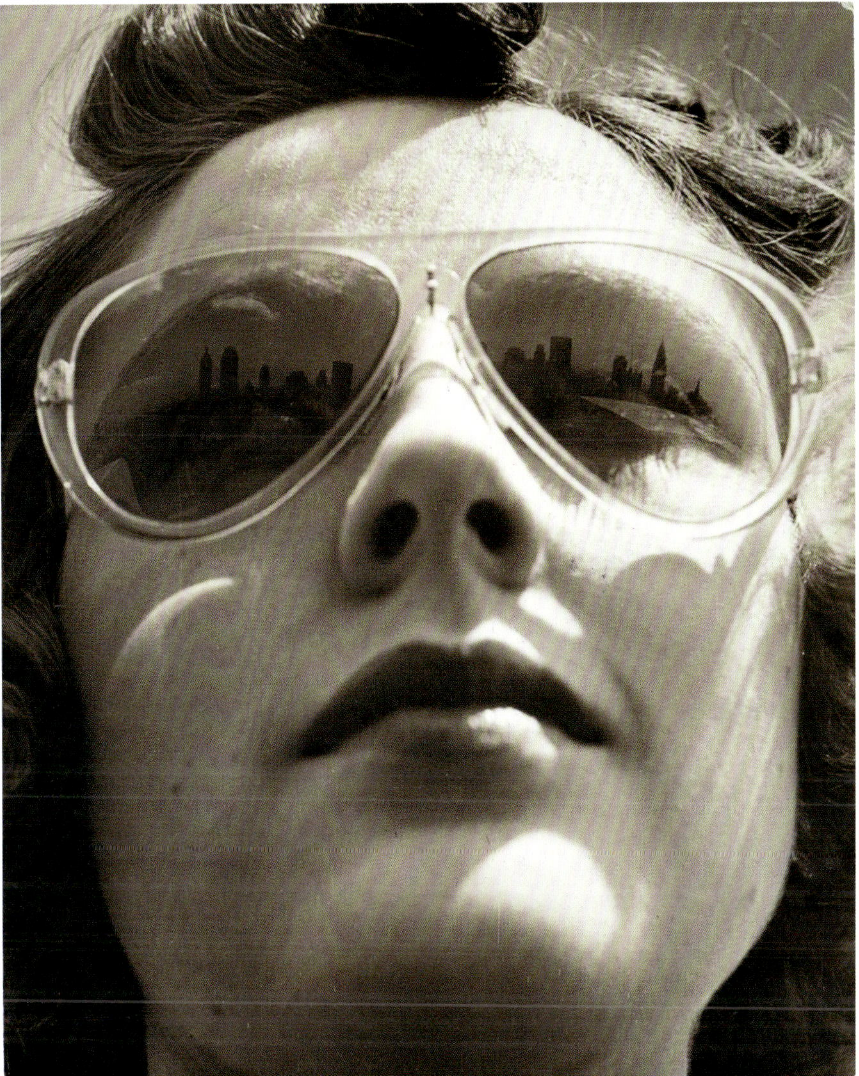

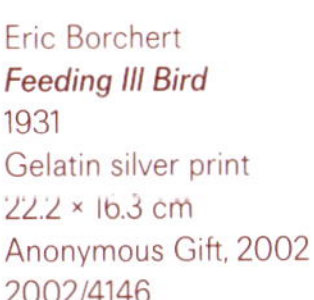

Eric Borchert
Feeding Ill Bird
1931
Gelatin silver print
22.2 × 16.3 cm
Anonymous Gift, 2002
2002/4146

Alfred Eisenstaedt
The Latest Vogue. Here the camera shows the skyline of Manhattan reflected in a pair of sunglasses
c. 1936
Gelatin silver print
22.2 × 16.3 cm
Anonymous Gift, 2002
2002/5005

KLINSKY PRESS AGENCY

The Klinsky Press Agency Collection offers a vivid record of Europe's press photography boom and its international scope. The Amsterdam-based agency, founded by Emil Klinsky, commissioned work by Alfred Eisenstaedt, Eric Borchert, Willi Ruge, and many others. Comprising nearly 19,000 photographs, the collection traces the evolution of illustrated magazines as sources of vivid reportage and, ultimately, their massive social and political influence.

Alfred Eisenstaedt
Emperor Haile Selassie dressed in the uniform of Field Marshall General – a trip to Holeta Military School
1935
Gelatin silver print
18.2 × 24 cm
Anonymous Gift, 2002
2002/4914

Orbis Press Agency
Iraqi people demonstrate unanimously against the British
1939
Gelatin silver print
18.2 × 24.2 cm
Anonymous Gift, 2002
2002/652

Ihee Kimura
Japanese mother walking with her much taller daughters
1935
Gelatin silver print
24.3 × 17 cm
Anonymous Gift, 2002
2002/5816

Thomas Ruff
press++60.01
2015
Chromogenic print
185 × 237 cm
Purchase, funds donated by Donna G. Billes and Diana Billes, 2016
2016/5

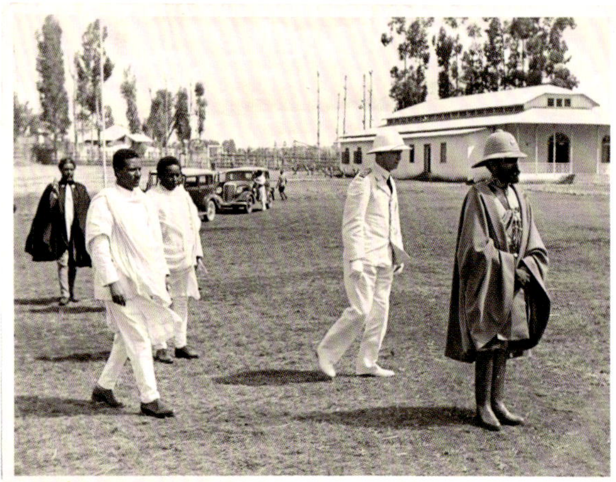

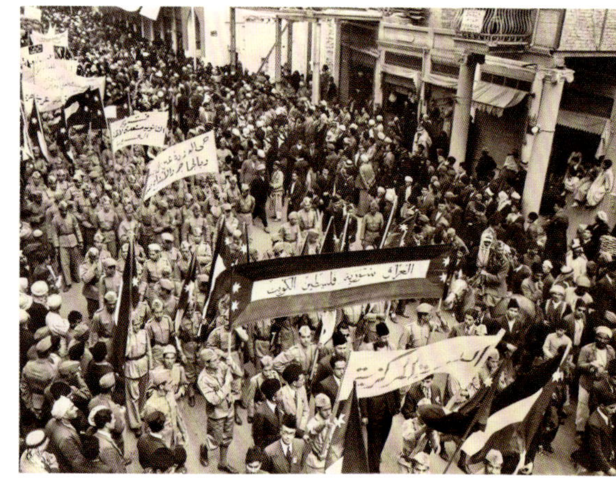

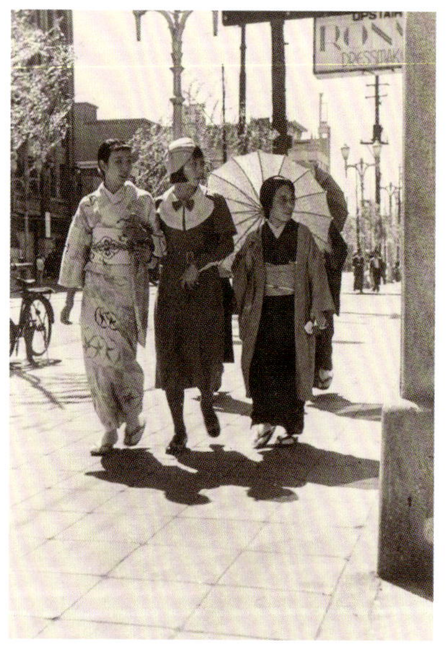

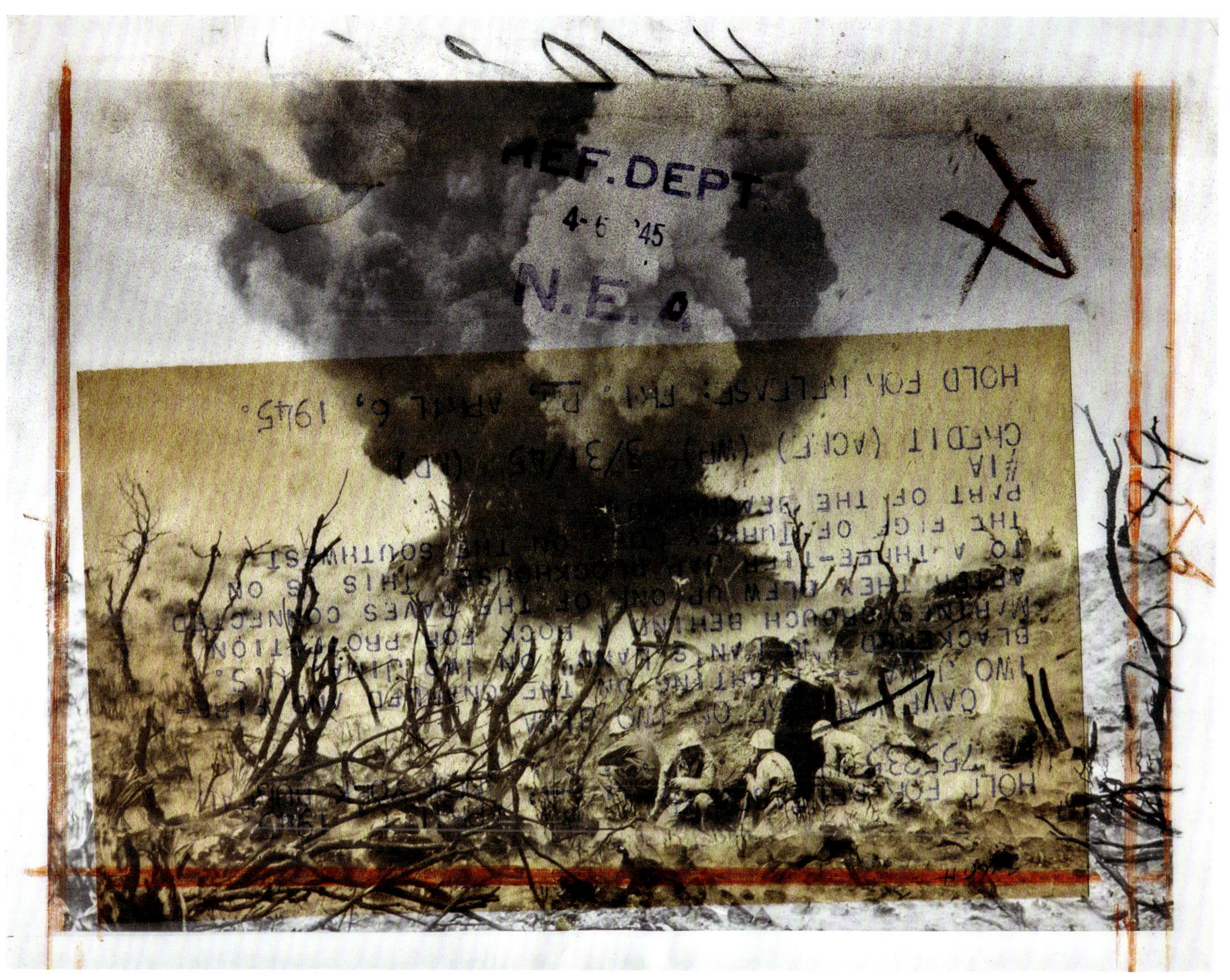
HEF.DEPT
N.E.A

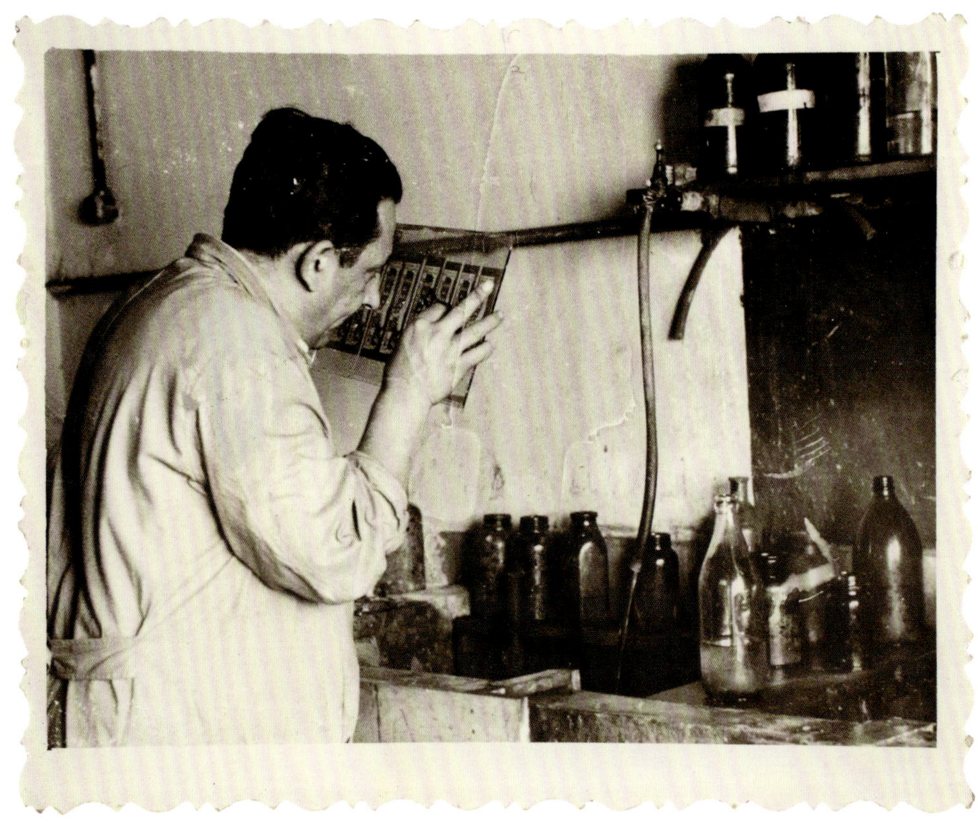

Henryk Ross
Henryk Ross inspecting glass plate negatives
1940–1944
Gelatin silver print
7 × 8.6 cm
Gift from Archive of Modern Conflict, 2007
2007/2372

Clockwise from upper left:
Family portrait
Ghetto residents happily strolling
Family looking out of the window
Family portrait
1940–1944
35mm cellulose nitrate negatives
3.4 × 3.7 cm each
Gift from Archive of Modern Conflict, 2007
2007/1992.4; 2007/1982.3; 2007/1984.28; 2007/2015.24

HENRYK ROSS

Henryk Ross's photographs offer a rare and powerful window into life in Nazi-occupied Poland's Łódź Ghetto during the Second World War. Officially assigned by the local Jewish Council as the ghetto's photographer, he secretly documented its harsh realities, risking his life. Nearly 3,000 negatives survived after Ross buried them before liberation, creating a poignant visual history of Nazi propaganda and the resilience of those imprisoned.

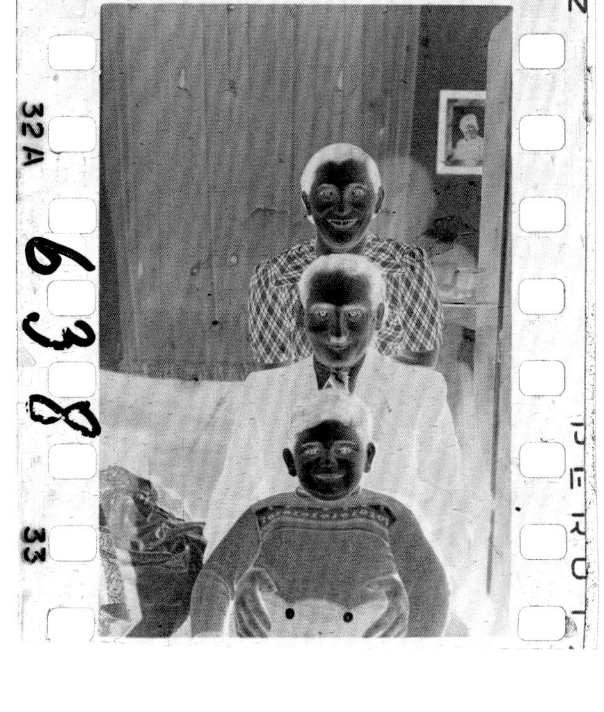
32A
638
33

AGFA ISOPAN F
935
18
17 A

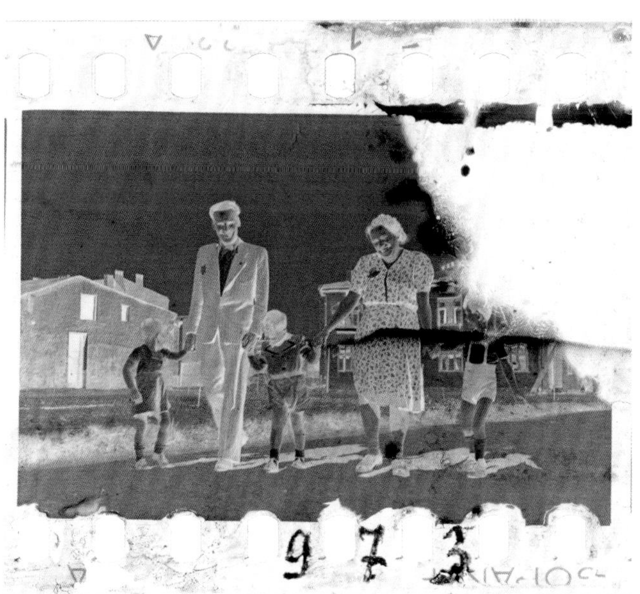

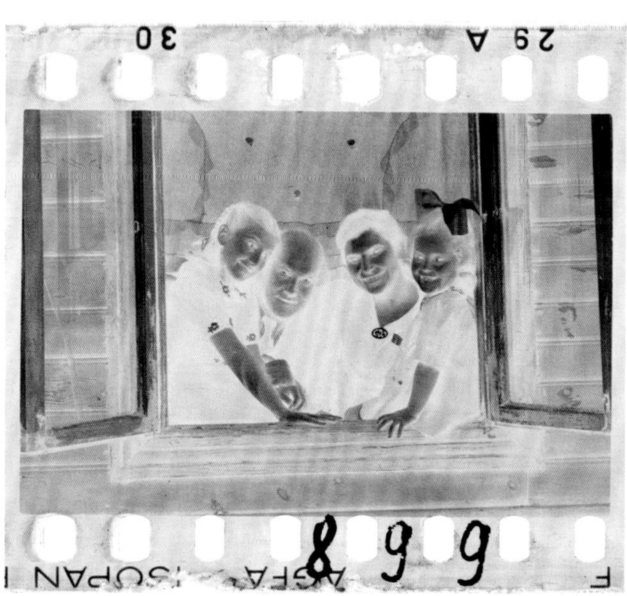

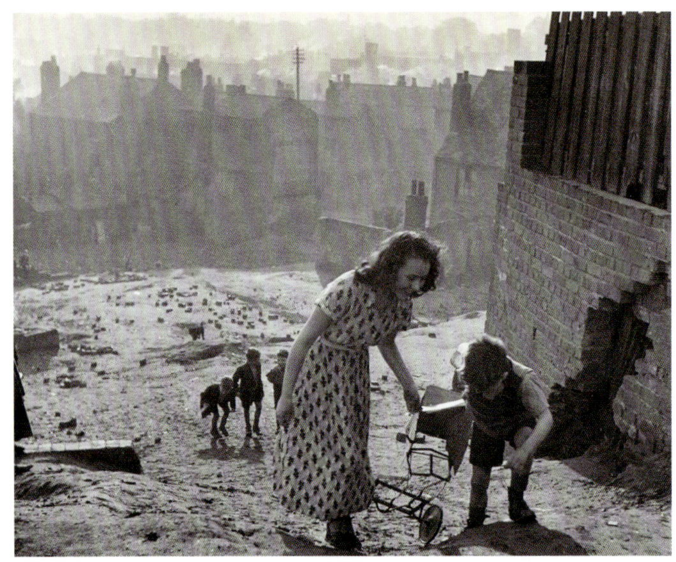

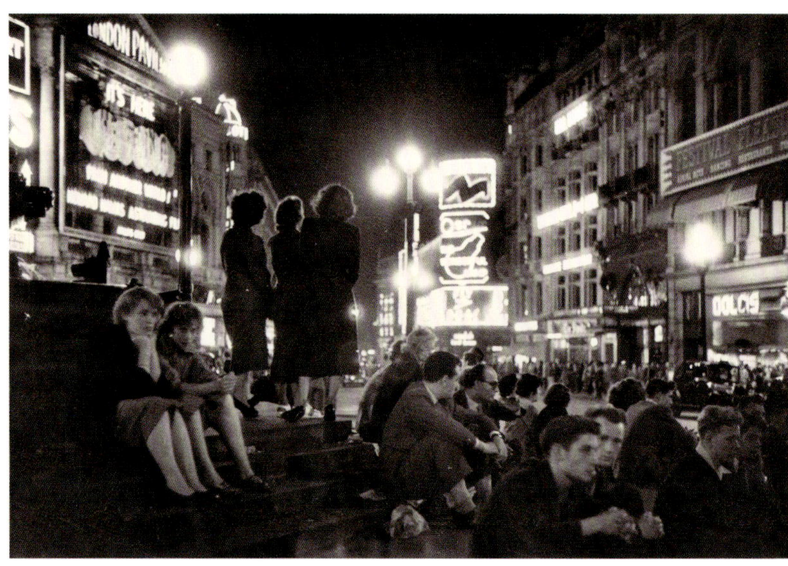

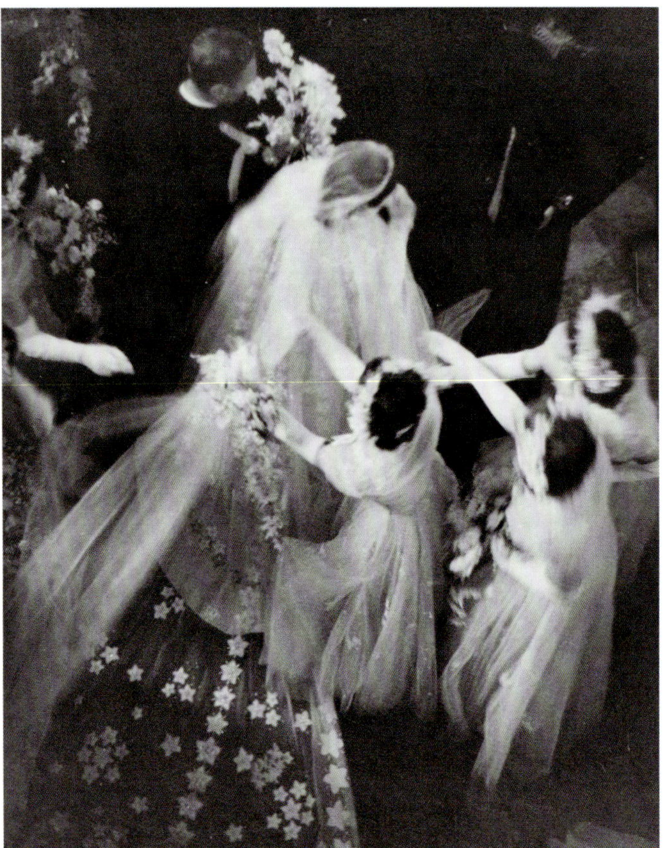

Bert Hardy
Betty Burden with young brother climbs hill, Birmingham
1951
Gelatin silver print
24.5 × 29.5 cm
Anonymous Gift, 2007
2007/1086

Princess Elizabeth and King George V walk down aisle of Westminster Abbey
1947
Gelatin silver print
34.5 × 27 cm
Anonymous Gift, 2007
2007/961

People around Eros steps against nighttime lights of Piccadilly Circus
1953
Gelatin silver print
25.4 × 37.2 cm
Anonymous Gift, 2007
2007/1203

Teenage couple in action jiving on the dance floor
1957
Gelatin silver print
22.9 × 19 cm
Anonymous Gift, 2007
2007/1352

Close up of Bambi dancing
1955
Gelatin silver print
18.5 × 28.7 cm
Anonymous Gift, 2007
2007/1266

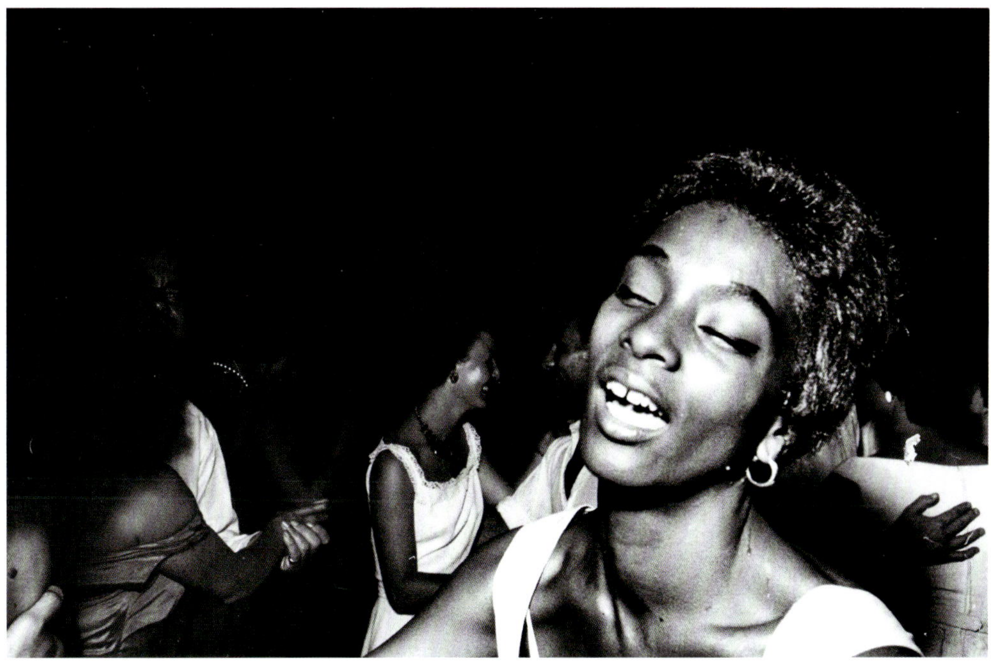

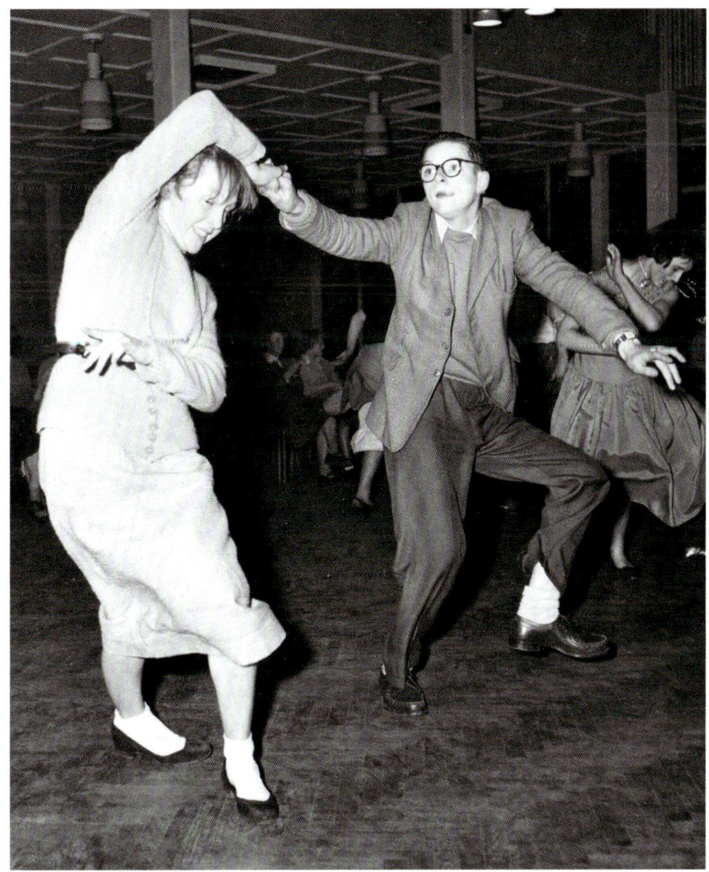

BERT HARDY

Bert Hardy made his mark as *Picture Post*'s staff photographer (1941-1957), pioneering an intimate "slice of life" style that captured everyday working-class Britain. Made without a flash, his images blend warmth and stark realities, revealing resilience and hardship. The collection holds more than 400 photographs spanning essays from London's East End during the Second World War to postwar social transitions across Britain and beyond.

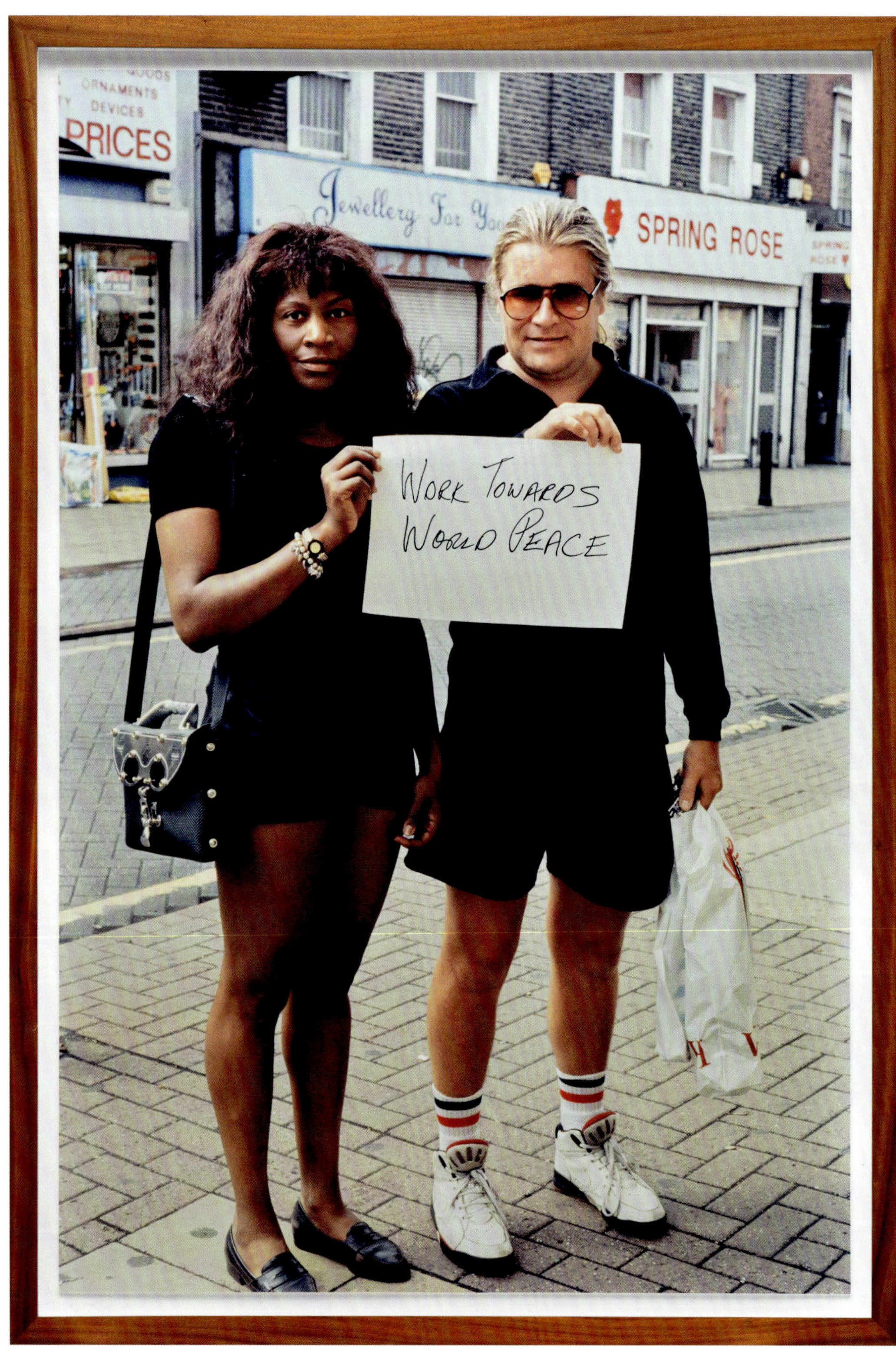

Gillian Wearing
Work towards world peace
1992–1993
From the series ***Signs that say what you want them to say and not Signs that say what someone else wants you to say*** (1992–1993)
Chromogenic print
151.8 × 106.4 cm
Purchase, with funds from Liza Mauer & Andrew Sheiner and Angela & David Feldman, 2022
2022/6

Carole Condé and Karl Beveridge
Standing Up
1980–1981
Silver dye bleach prints
39.8 × 50 cm
Gift from The Peggy Lownsbrough Fund, 1986
86/280.18; 86/280.13

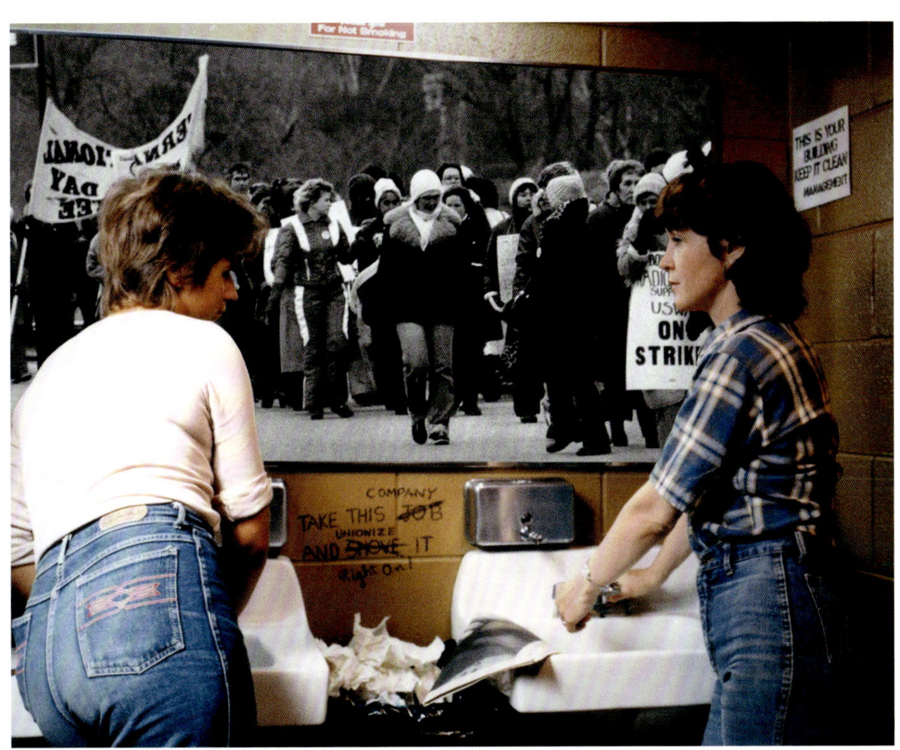
For Not Smoking
THIS IS YOUR BUILDING KEEP IT CLEAN MANAGEMENT
USW
ON
STRIKE
COMPANY
TAKE THIS JOB
UNIONIZE
AND SHOVE IT
right on!

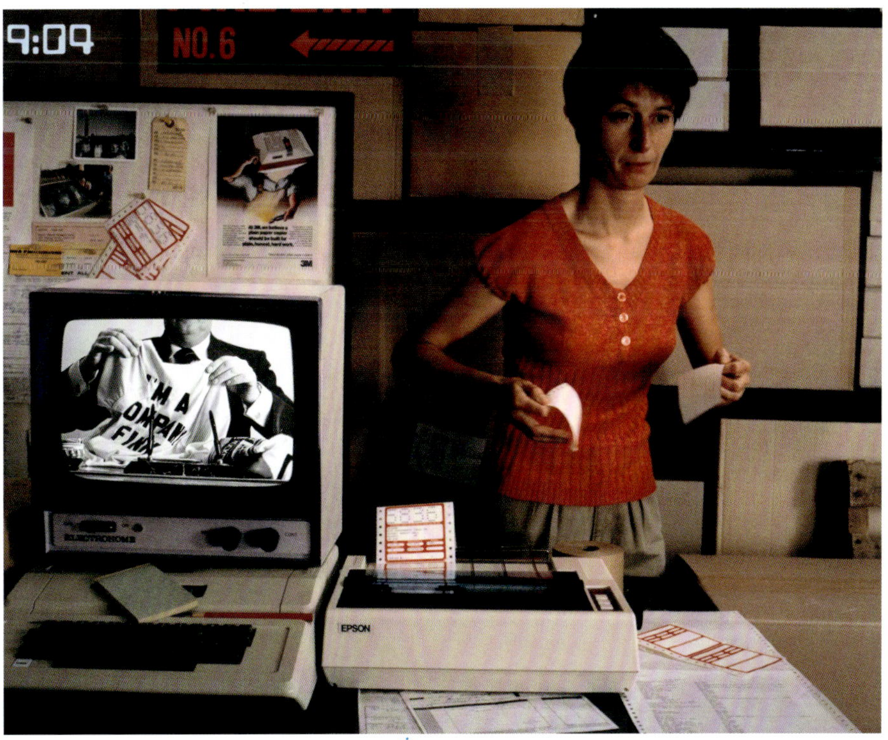
9:04
NO.6
EPSON

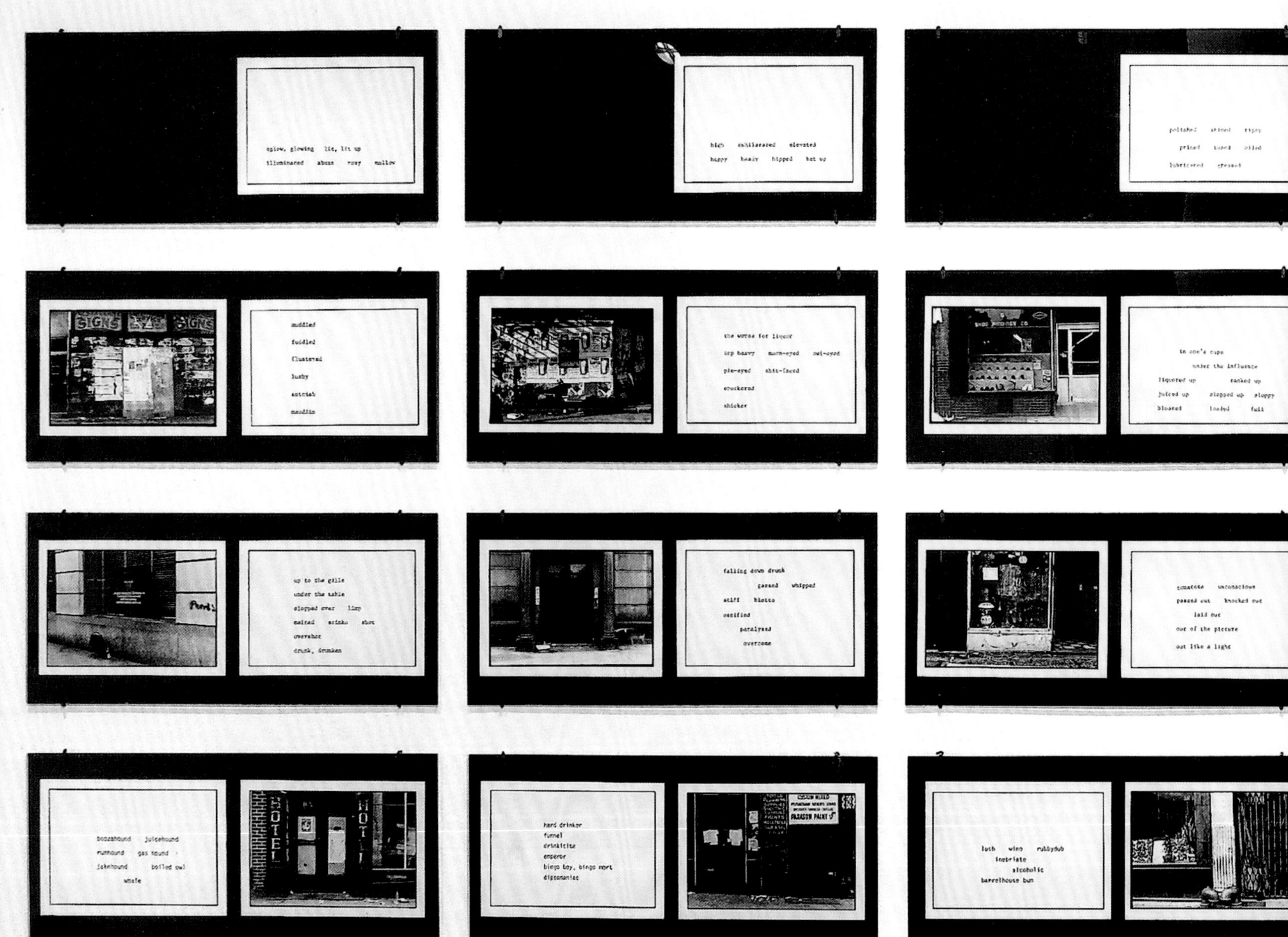
aglow, glowing lit, lit up
illuminated abuzz rosy mellow
high exhilarated elevated
happy heady hipped het up
polished stewed tipsy
primed tuned oiled
lubricated greased
SIGNS
SIGNS
muddled
fuddled
flustered
lushy
sottish
maudlin
the worse for liquor
top heavy moon-eyed owl-eyed
pie-eyed shit-faced
snockered
shicker
in one's cups
under the influence
liquored up tanked up
juiced up slopped up sloppy
bloated loaded full
up to the gills
under the table
slopped over limp
salted drinko shot
overshot
drunk, drunken
falling down drunk
gassed whipped
stiff blotto
ossified
paralyzed
overcome
comatose unconscious
passed out knocked out
laid out
out of the picture
out like a light
boozehound juicehound
rumhound gas hound
jakehound boiled owl
whale
HOTEL
HOTEL
hard drinker
funnel
drinkitite
emperor
bingo boy, bingo mort
dipsomaniac
PARAGON PAINT
lush wino rubbydub
inebriate
alcoholic
barrelhouse bum

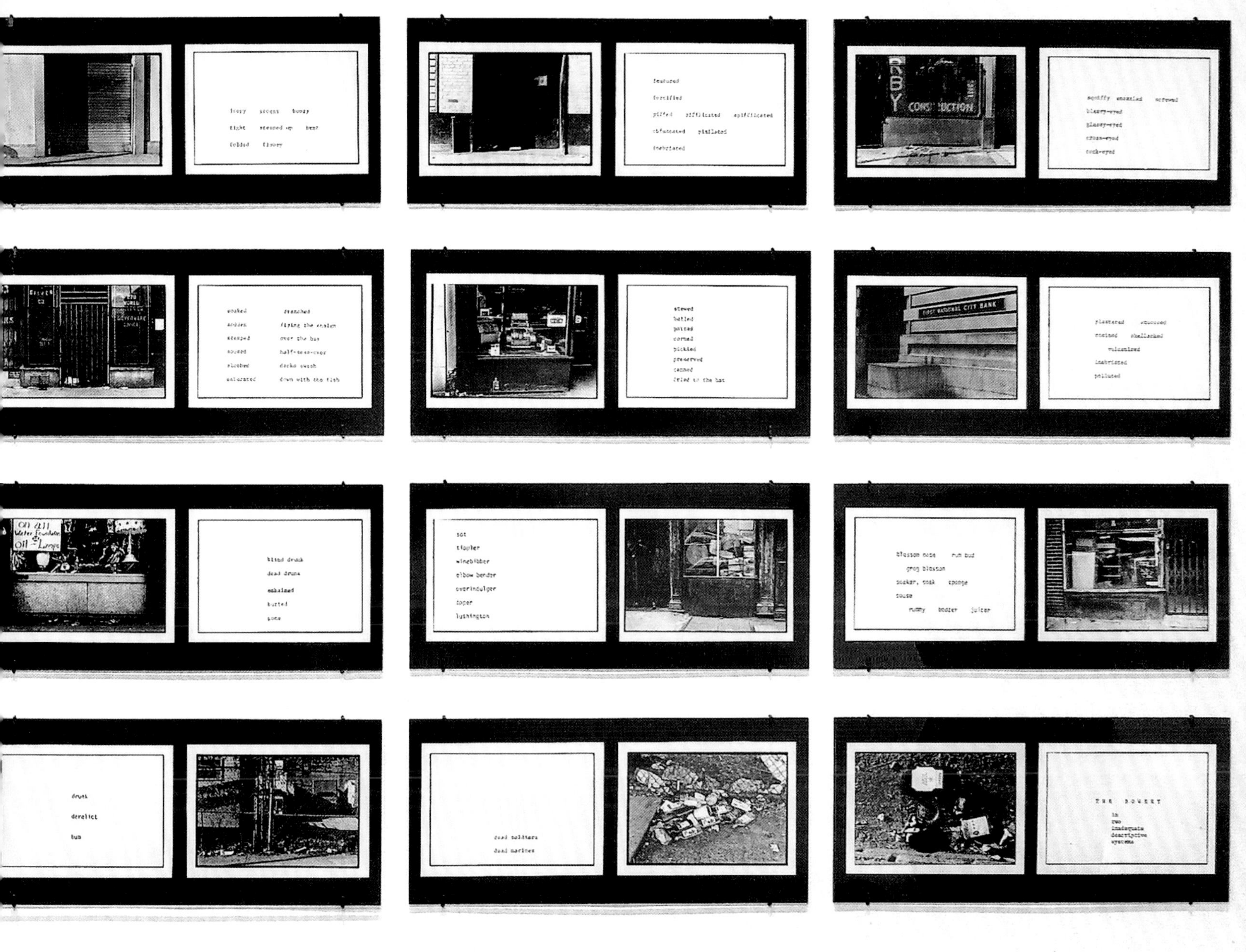

Martha Rosler
The Bowery in two inadequate descriptive systems
1974–1975
Gelatin silver prints
25.4 × 55.9 cm each
Gift from the Junior Committee Fund, 1988
88/140

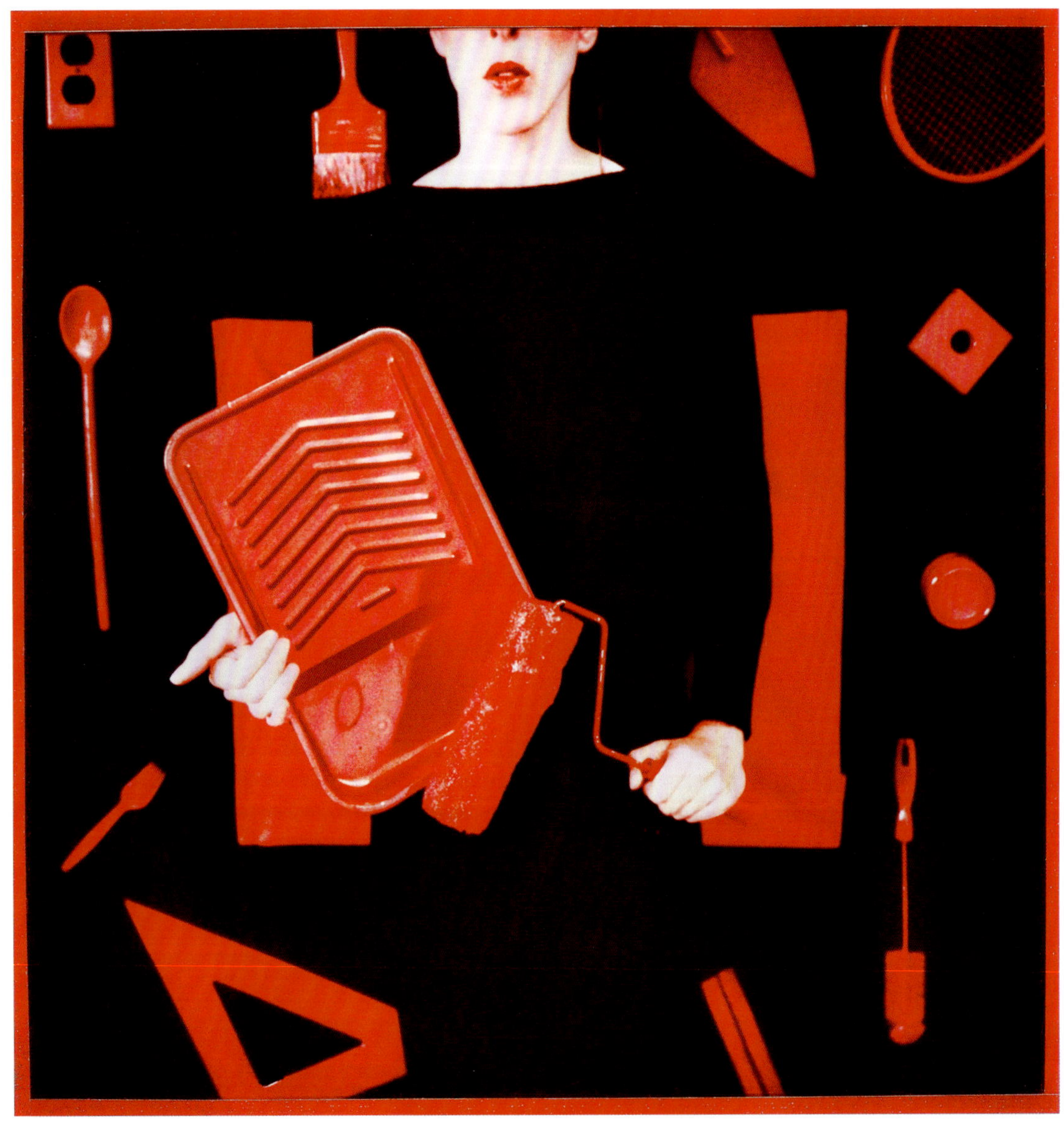

Barbara Astman
Untitled
1981
From the series ***Red*** (1981)
Chromogenic print
121.9 × 119.4 cm
Gift of Margaret and Jim Fleck, 2017
2017/130

Pamela Harris
Arnaoyok Alookee and daughter Haunuaq, Taloyoak, NU
1973
Gelatin silver print
20.3 × 25.4 cm
Gift of Pamela Harris, 2012
2013/227

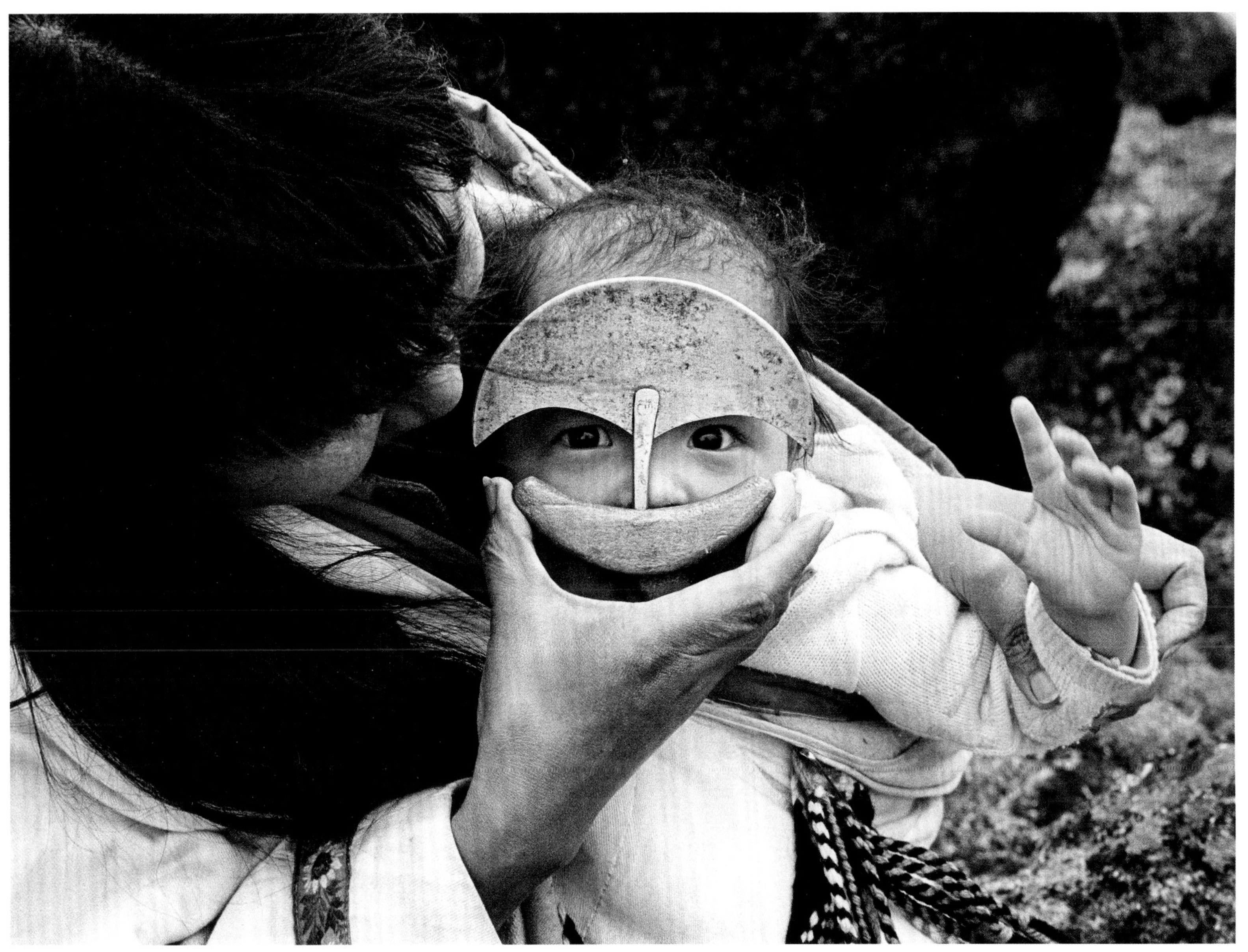

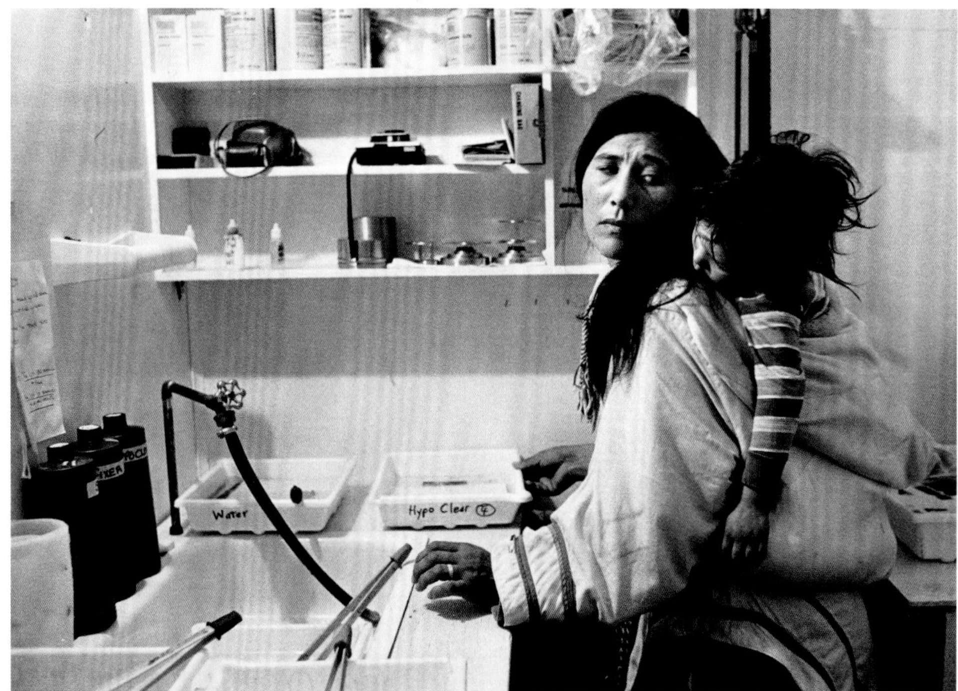

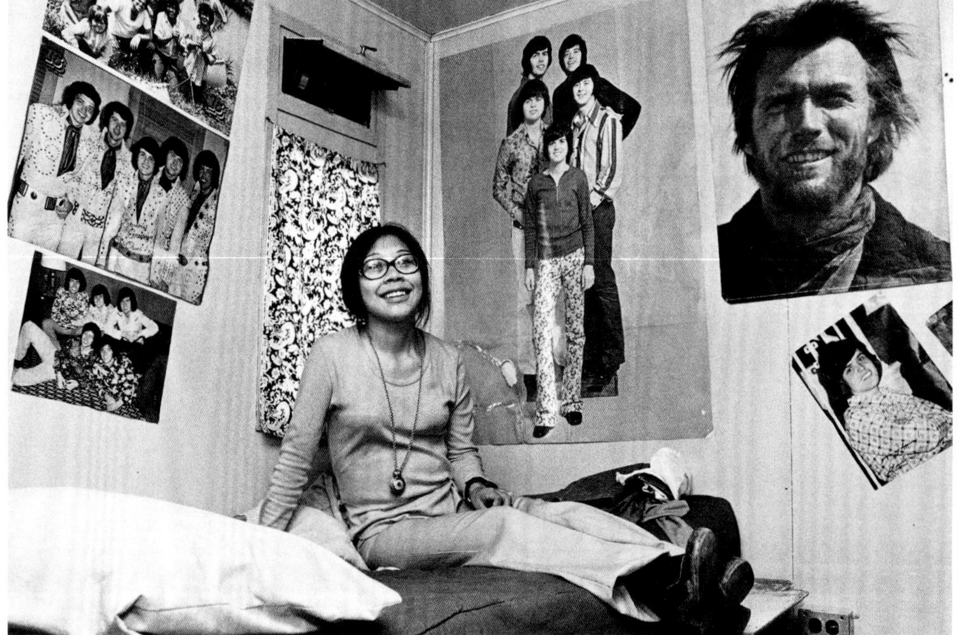

Pamela Harris
Nilaulaq Aglukuk and Willy in women's craft shop darkroom, Taloyoak, NU
1973
Gelatin silver print
20.2 × 25.4 cm
Gift of Randall McLeod, 2012
LA.SC126.S6.F1.6

Mary Neeveakcheak in her room, Taloyoak, NU
1973
Gelatin silver print
27.9 × 35.6 cm
Gift of Pamela Harris, 2012
2013/151

Opposite, clockwise from upper left:
Theresa Quaqjuaq
Pamela Harris in my packing parka with Roland and Brenda
1973
Gelatin silver print
15.6 × 16.7 cm
Gift of Randall McLeod, 2012
LA.SC126.S6.F2.4

Kublu Tucktoo
Natural Dyes Workshop group (and construction workers' graffiti), Taloyoak, NU
1973
Gelatin silver print
17.3 × 17.6 cm
Gift of Randall McLeod, 2012
LA.SC126.S5.1

Theresa Quaqjuaq
Tundra Teabreak, Natural Dyes Workshop, Taloyoak, NU
1973
Gelatin silver print
15.3 × 15.1 cm
Gift of Randall McLeod, 2012
LA.SC126.S5.10

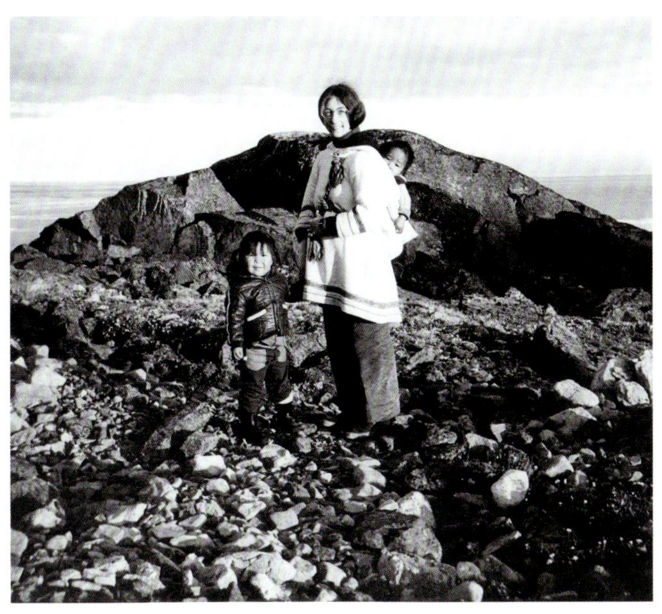

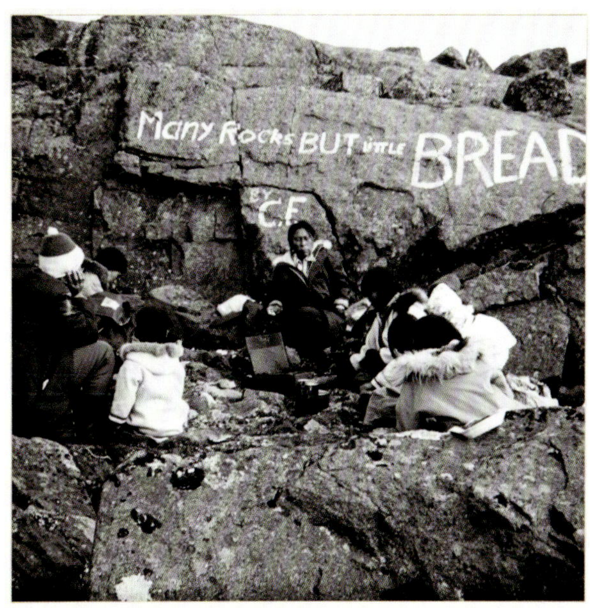

TALOYOAK DARKROOM PROJECT

In 1972, Pamela Harris first visited Spence Bay (now Taloyoak, Nunavut). She photographed daily life, interviewed residents, and established a community darkroom, collaborating with Inuit women—including Kublu Tuktoo and Theresa Quaqjuaq—throughout the photographic process. The collection includes photographs by Harris, Tuktoo, Quaqjuaq, and others, contact sheets, and related materials, offering a significant record of collaborative, self-determined image-making in the North.

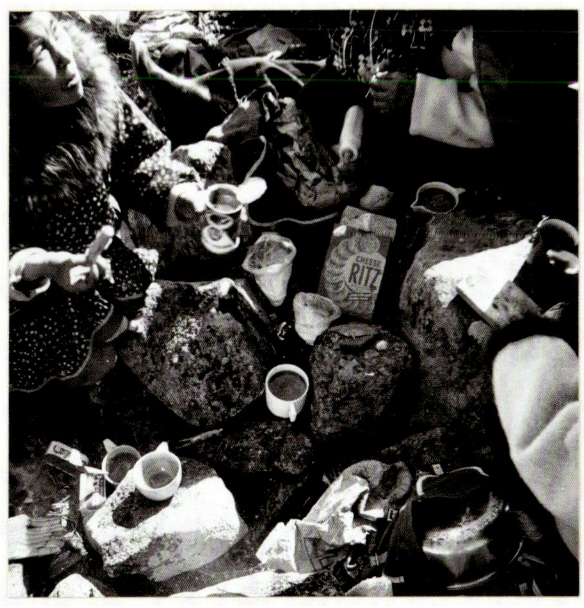

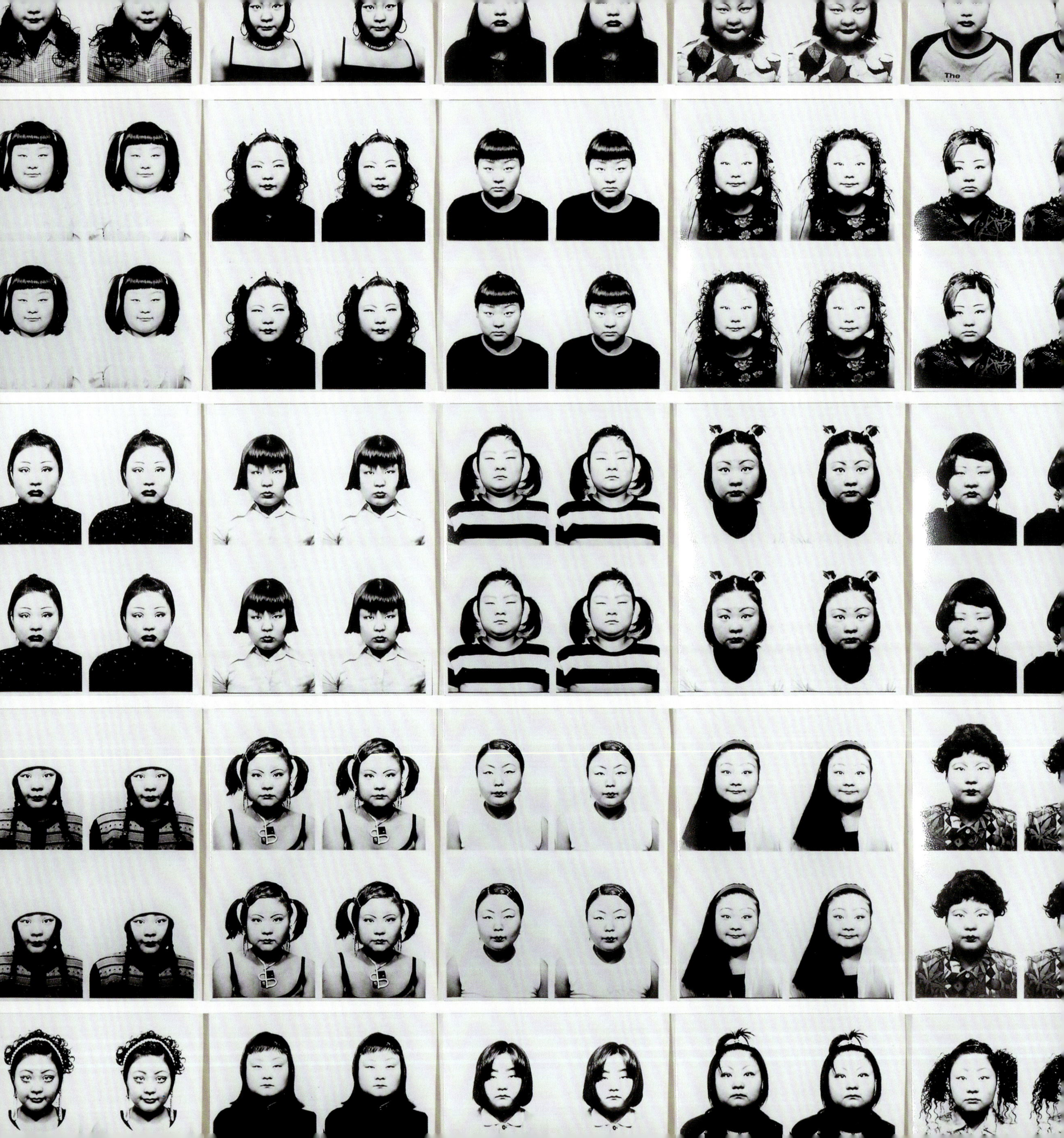
The

People We've Met

Tal-Or Ben-Choreen

Photographic portraits are records of an encounter—be it with the camera or the photographer. Within these exchanges, the subject's body language can offer clues to the ways they relate to the photographer, to their immediate environment, to the historical context, even to their own self-image. Take Tomoko Sawada's *ID 400 (#201-300)* (1998), in which grids of portraits invite viewers to compare and contrast the multiplicity of figures, all of whom, upon close examination, are played by Sawada herself (left, and p. 73). Sawada's riff on the portrait genre betrays its ability to either distill an individual's character, or to project an unexpected persona.

In the early days of photography, portraits required a formal meeting between photographer and sitter, often in a controlled studio environment. This space—specially designed to allow for the brightest daylight to be cast into the room—held the cumbersome equipment needed to produce a photograph, as well as elaborate furniture, backdrops, and props used to reveal the social standing or aspirations of the sitter. In some cases, these portraits follow the conventions of academic painting, but at times new genres emerged, often as solutions to technical problems. For instance, babies and restless children needed someone to hold them in place through long exposure times. The price of portraits was determined by the number of sitters included, so the person holding the child was draped in dark fabric, cropped out, or obscured in other creative ways, yielding a group of portraits that paradoxically highlights these "hidden mothers" (p. 78). The photographic portrait also provided greater access to the kind of ceremonial representation previously reserved for the upper classes, capturing people at communions, graduations, and weddings. Hiring a photographer offered, for some, autonomy and authority over their representations. Many photographers established portrait studios to affirm, preserve, and commemorate their shared identity; James Van Der Zee's (p. 80) powerful portraits of Harlem residents exemplify this effort. Many of us, on the other hand, consciously or unconsciously perform for the camera, influenced by the fame and reputation of politicians and celebrities whose portraits we consume and emulate. In both cases, we are complicit in creating images that reflect the way we *imagine* ourselves and the communities we might represent.[1]

The introduction of amateur photography and handheld cameras in the mid-twentieth century meant that the setting of portraits could now be an open field, a bustling city street, or an intimate room. Encounters with photographers also changed: they could now be a stranger passing by, a loved one, or even oneself. This new-found mobility infiltrated every genre of photography—street, war, documentary, fashion, advertising, and family. The abundance of these images reminds us that we gaze at ourselves and others as a means of confirming our identities and connection to communities.

Tomoko Sawada
ID 400 (#201-300) (detail)
1998
From the series ***ID 400*** (1998-2001)
Gelatin silver prints
127 × 101.6 cm
Gift of Brian J. Henderson, 2023
2023/278

Maker once known
At The Market, Martinique (detail)
1890
Gelatin silver print
22.2 × 18.8 cm
Montgomery Collection of Caribbean Photographs. Purchase, with funds from Dr. Liza & Dr. Frederick Murrell, Bruce Croxon & Debra Thier, Wes Hall & Kingsdale Advisors, Cindy & Shon Barnett, Donette Chin-Loy Chang, Kamala-Jean Gopie, Phil Lind & Ellen Roland, Martin Doc McKinney, Francilla Charles, Ray & Georgina Williams, Thaine & Bianca Carter, Charmaine Crooks, Nathaniel Crooks, Andrew Garrett & Dr. Belinda Longe, Neil L. Le Grand, Michael Lewis, Dr. Kenneth Montague & Sarah Aranha, Lenny & Julia Mortimore, and The Ferrotype Collective, 2019
2019/372

Yet wider power imbalances, both inside and outside the studio, simultaneously led to the use of portraiture to uphold colonial and racist ideologies supported by pseudoscientific and ethnographic studies.[2] In such portraits, the photographer's encounter with his subjects was not established as a partnership or collaboration, but rather as a form of dominance, often in service of national institutions like the police or military. Portraits produced under these conditions often purposefully stripped individuals of their names, contexts, and communities.[3] Some ethnographic images, such as those found in Jacques-Philippe Potteau's *Collection Anthropologique du Muséum de Paris* (1861-1869) (p. 72), complicate this dynamic. Extended captions with each subject's name and other personal details (variously birthplace, age, hair or eye colour), and respectful poses, suggest a more nuanced—though still staunchly colonial—gaze.

Artists have also continuously used portraiture to respond to, challenge, and reject these historical social norms and strategies of control and power. By appropriating or evading such visual tropes, they call attention to their construction and lasting influences. While examples of appropriation, performance, and self-portraiture can be found throughout the history of photography, the 1960s and '70s ushered in a particularly active surge, fuelled by feminist thought and the work of artists such as Suzy Lake (p. 89), Cindy Sherman (p. 90), Rebecca Belmore (p. 96), and Shelley Niro (p. 93), among others. What we understand as portraiture has continuously evolved in work by artists actively incorporating theories that have reshaped identity politics—such as post-structuralism, post-colonialism, and queer theory—and that in turn challenge and expand the boundaries of the genre.[4]

Today, much like the dynamic of early photographic studios, anyone with a smartphone and a social media presence uses posture, dress, sets, and props to construct and communicate identity, and to confirm and actuate desires and ambitions. While many of the visual cues we encounter are drawn from and continue to perpetuate (often harmful) ideas about gender, sexuality, race, and social and economic class, individuals have also harnessed these ideas to explore the fluid construction of identity.

Like many art institutions, the AGO initially overlooked photography as an art form and was slow to collect it. The earliest photographs to enter the collection were portraits of artists represented in the AGO's holdings, like Henry Moore (p. 18) and Rita Letendre (p. 97). This surreptitious way of integrating photography into the collection helped establish it as a creative medium for both gallery staff and the public, paving the way for an expanded mandate, including portraits by a wide range of artists that reflect diverse aesthetic and conceptual approaches. The variety of photographs in the following pages reveals a rich array of encounters between photographers and their subjects, showcasing changing notions of selfhood—from innate to malleable—and our ever-growing desire to see and construct ourselves in pictures.

1. For an overview of the history of photography and portraiture, see John Pultz, *The Body and the Lens: Photography 1839 to the Present* (New York: Harry N. Abrams, 1995), and Max Kozloff, *The Theatre of the Face: Portrait Photography since 1900* (London: Phaidon, 2007).
2. Allan Sekula, "The Body and the Archive," *October* 39 (Winter 1986): pp. 6-7.
3. See Elizabeth Edwards, *Raw Histories: Photographs, Anthropology and Museums* (Oxford: Berg, 2001); *Exposure* 28, no. 3 (Winter 1991-92); Musée du quai Branly, *D'un regard l'autre: photographies XIXe siècle* (Arles: Actes Sud, 2006); Sarah Lewis, *The Unseen Truth: When Race Changed Sight in America* (Cambridge, MA: Harvard University Press, 2024).
4. See, for example, Daniel C. Blight, *The Image of Whiteness: Contemporary Photography and Racialization* (London: SPBH, 2022); Ben Miller, *New Queer Photography: Focus on the Margins* (Dortmund: Verlag Kettler / Richmond, CA: Gingko Press, 2020); Diane Neumaier, ed., *Reframings: New American Feminist Photographies* (Philadelphia: Temple University Press, 1995); Mark Sealy, *Decolonising the Camera: Photography in Racial Time* (London: Lawrence Wishart, 2019).

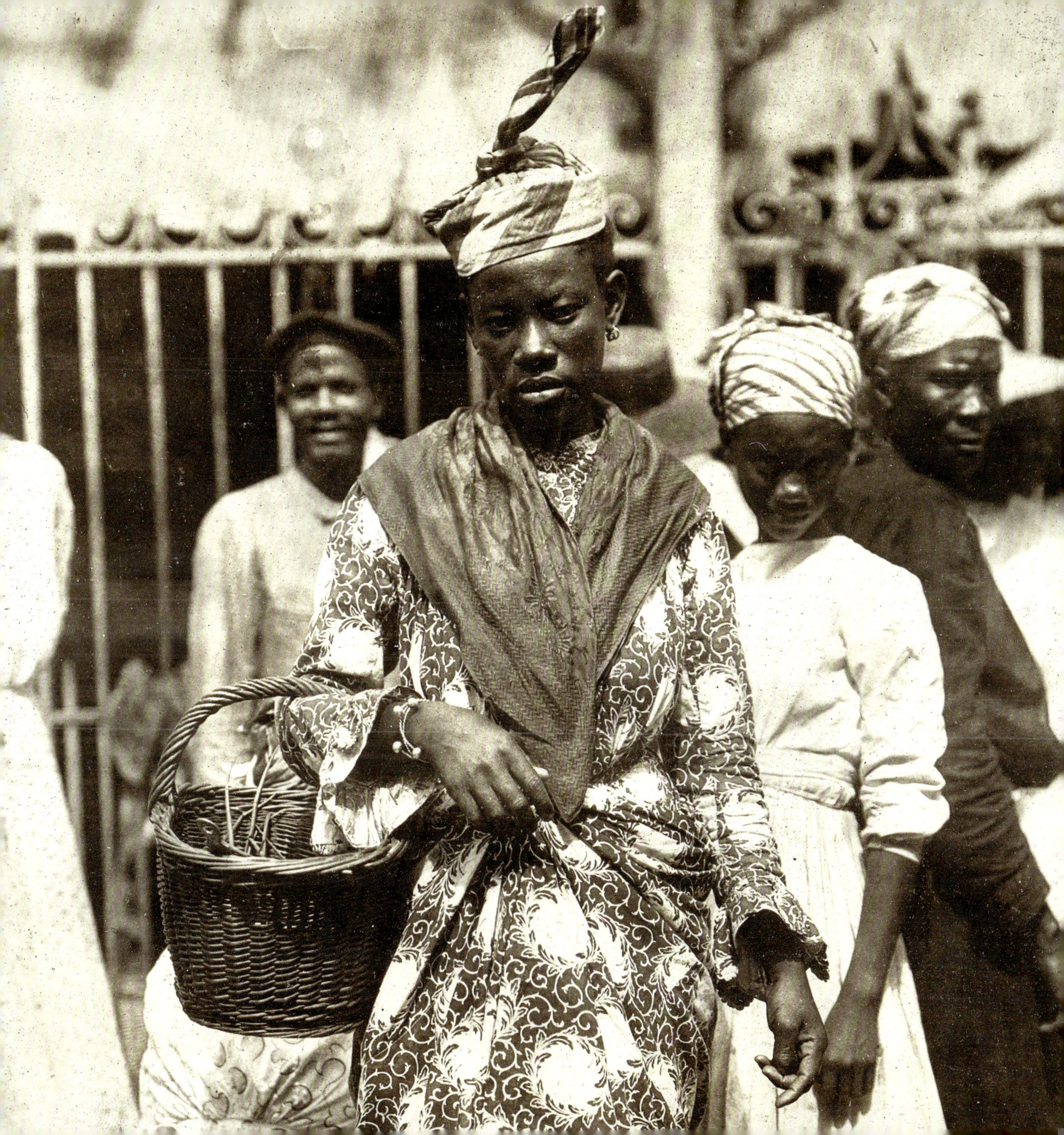

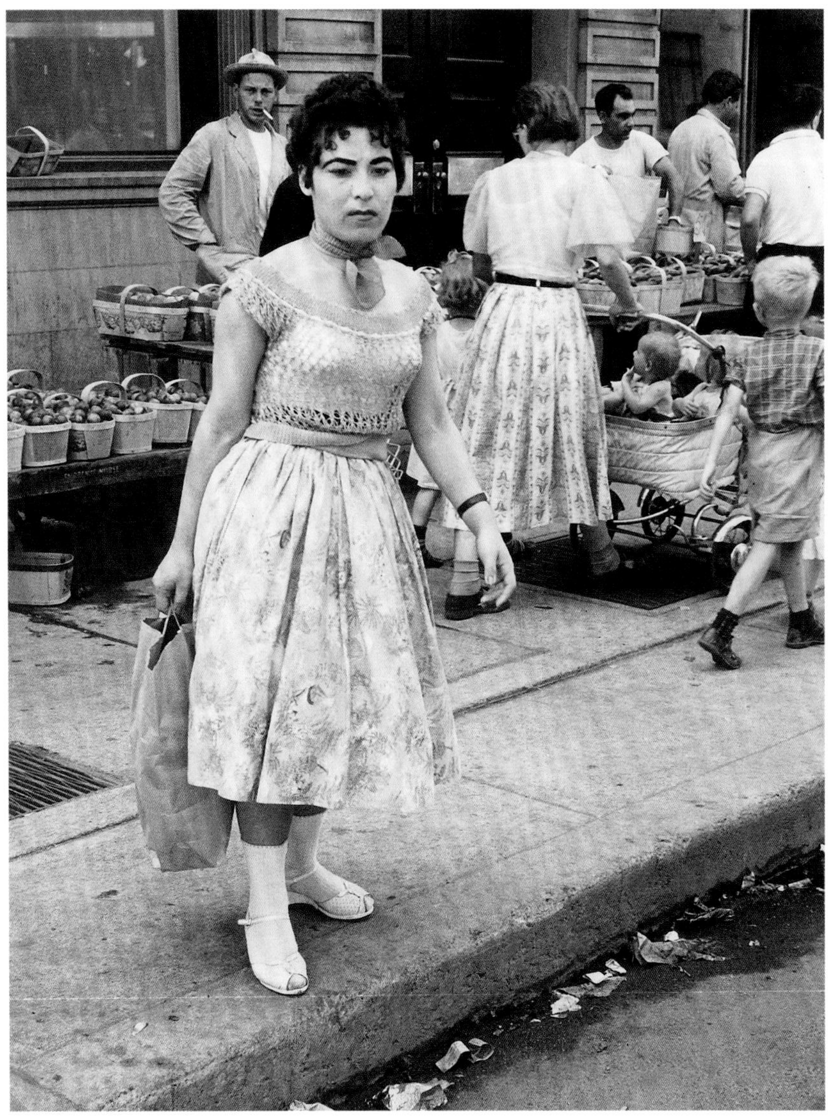

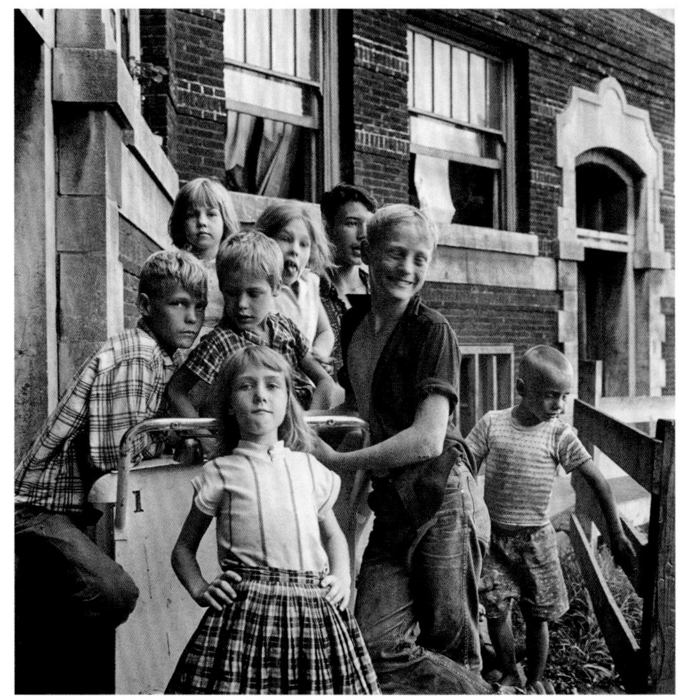

MICHEL LAMBETH

Michel Lambeth is a pivotal figure in Canadian photography, emerging in the 1950s when the medium was still gaining artistic recognition. He photographed Toronto and its people with a deep social conscience and poetic vision. The AGO's holdings of Lambeth's work include such street scenes alongside portraits of the significant artists of his generation, helping to redefine photography as an art form in Canada.

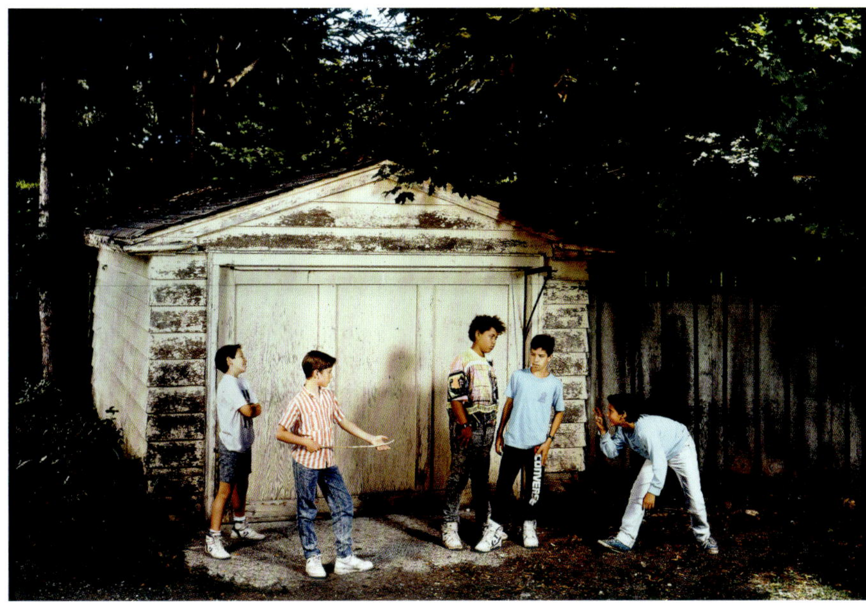

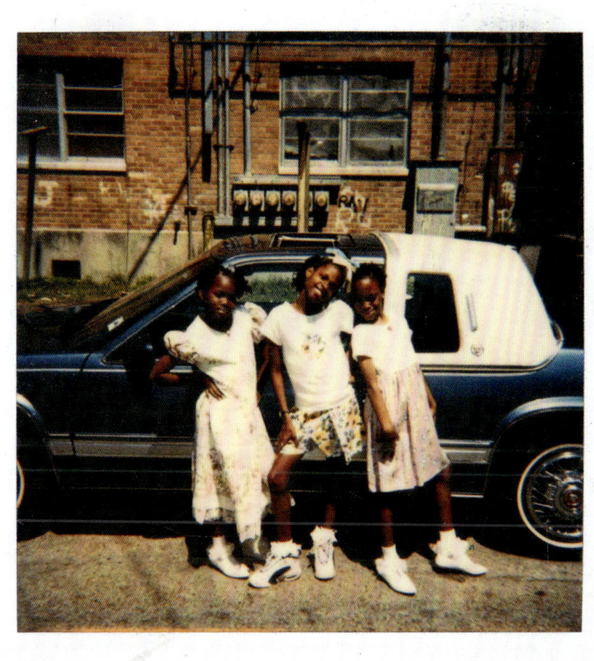

Michel Lambeth
St. Lawrence Market, Toronto
1957
Gelatin silver print
33.8 × 26 cm
Gift of Av Isaacs, Toronto, 1994
94/500

Danny Lyon
Children on Ice Cream Vendor's Box
1965
Gelatin silver print
35.6 × 27.9 cm
Gift of Lewis Richardson, 2015
2016/96

Jeff Wall
The Goat
1989
Transparency lightbox
229 × 308 cm
Purchase, 1989
89/737

Maker once known, American
Three girls posing in floral dresses and skirts standing in front of car
1986–1996
Colour instant print [Polaroid Type 600]
10.8 × 8.8 cm
Fade Resistance Collection. Purchase, with funds donated by Martha LA McCain, 2018
2018/2078

FADE RESISTANCE

The Fade Resistance Collection includes more than 4,000 photographs, chiefly instant prints, ranging from the 1950s to the 2000s, assembled by artist Zun Lee. These poignant representations of daily life, created by and for Black Americans, stand together as a powerful visual record of Black family life, Black self-representation, and Black subjectivity.

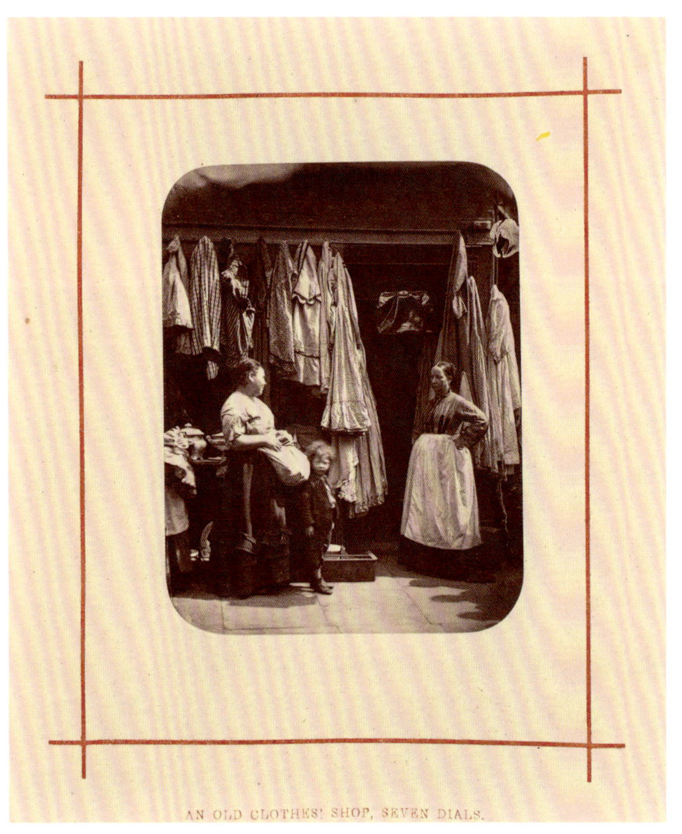
AN OLD CLOTHES' SHOP, SEVEN DIALS.

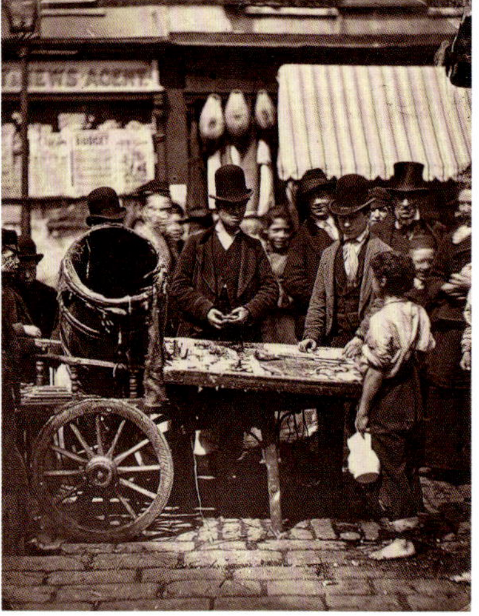

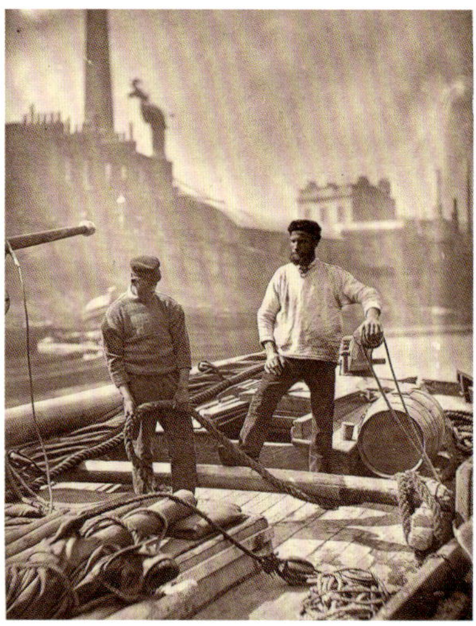

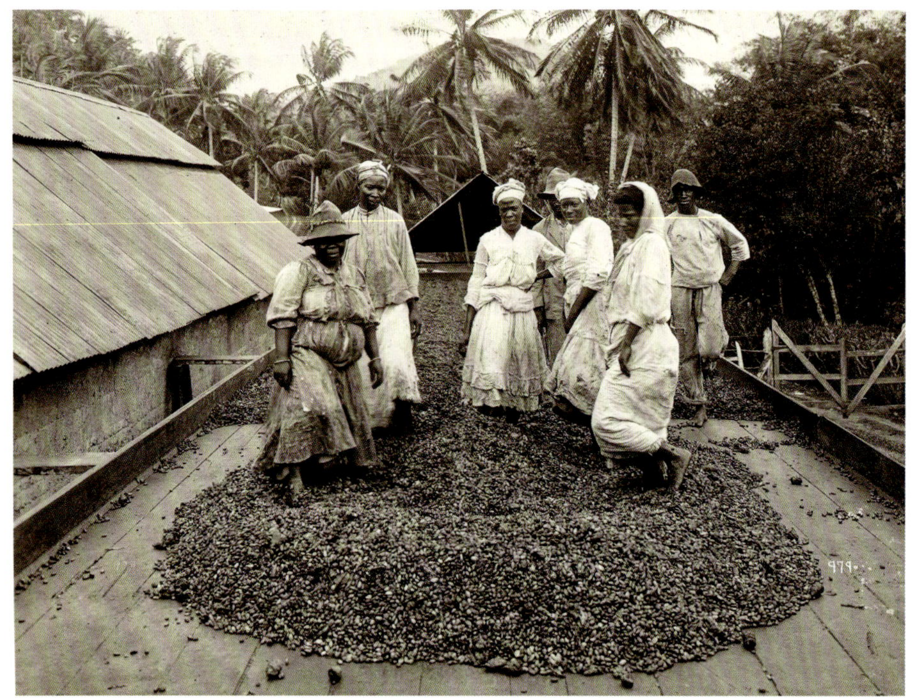

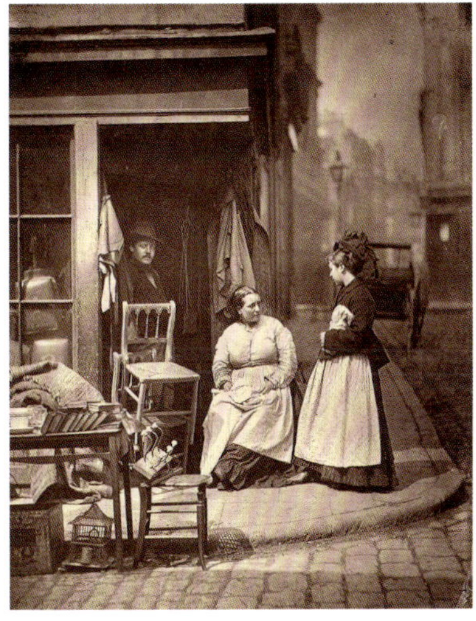

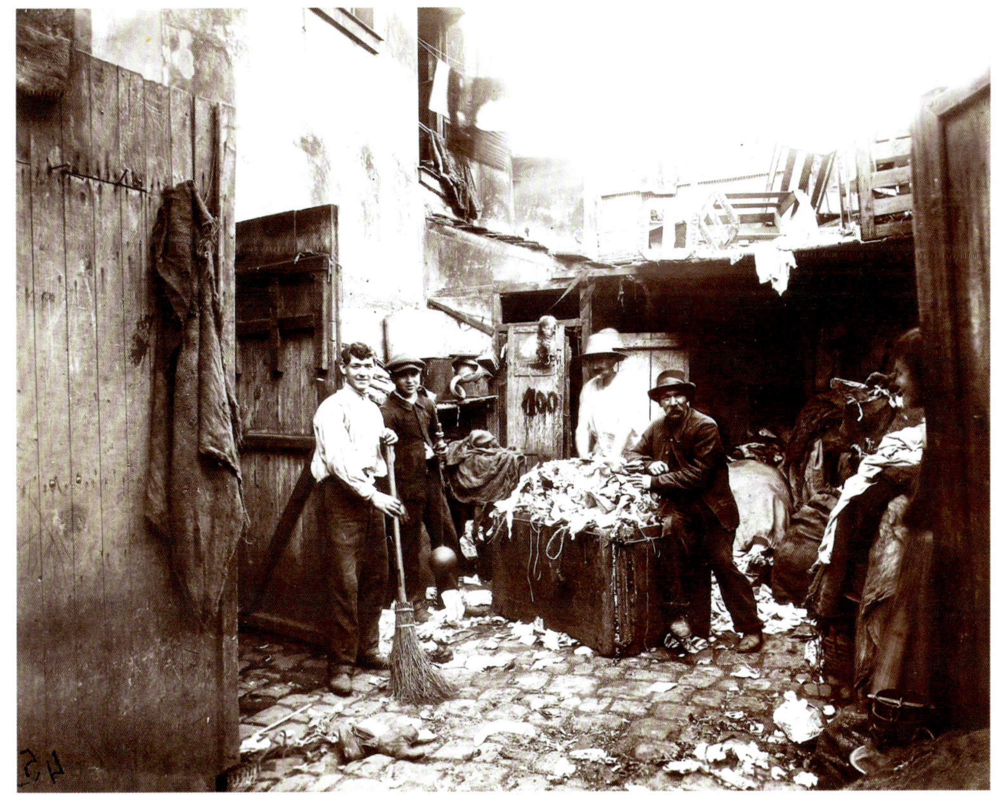

John Thomson
An Old Clothes' Shop, Seven Dials
Cheap Fish of St. Giles
Workers on the "Silent Highway"
Old Furniture
From the series ***Street Life in London*** (1877)
Woodburytype prints
19.9 × 16.8 cm each
Gift of Jane Corkin, 2019
2019/2315.2; 2019/2315.5; 2019/2315.20; 2019/2315.12

Maker once known
Coffee Plantation, Port of Spain, Trinidad
c. 1890
Gelatin silver print
17.4 × 23 cm
Montgomery Collection of Caribbean Photographs. Purchase, with funds from Dr. Liza & Dr. Frederick Murrell, Bruce Croxon & Debra Thier, Wes Hall & Kingsdale Advisors, Cindy & Shon Barnett, Donette Chin-Loy Chang, Kamala-Jean Gopie, Phil Lind & Ellen Roland, Martin Doc McKinney, Francilla Charles, Ray & Georgina Williams, Thaine & Bianca Carter, Charmaine Crooks, Nathaniel Crooks, Andrew Garrett & Dr. Belinda Longe, Neil L. Le Grand, Michael Lewis, Dr. Kenneth Montague & Sarah Aranha, Lenny & Julia Mortimore, and The Ferrotype Collective, 2019
2019/2236

Eugène Atget
Chiffoniers – Cité Valmy
1910
Silver chloride printing-out paper print
17 × 21.6 cm
Gift of Patricia Regan, in memory of Dr. Arthur Rubinoff, 2013
2013/365

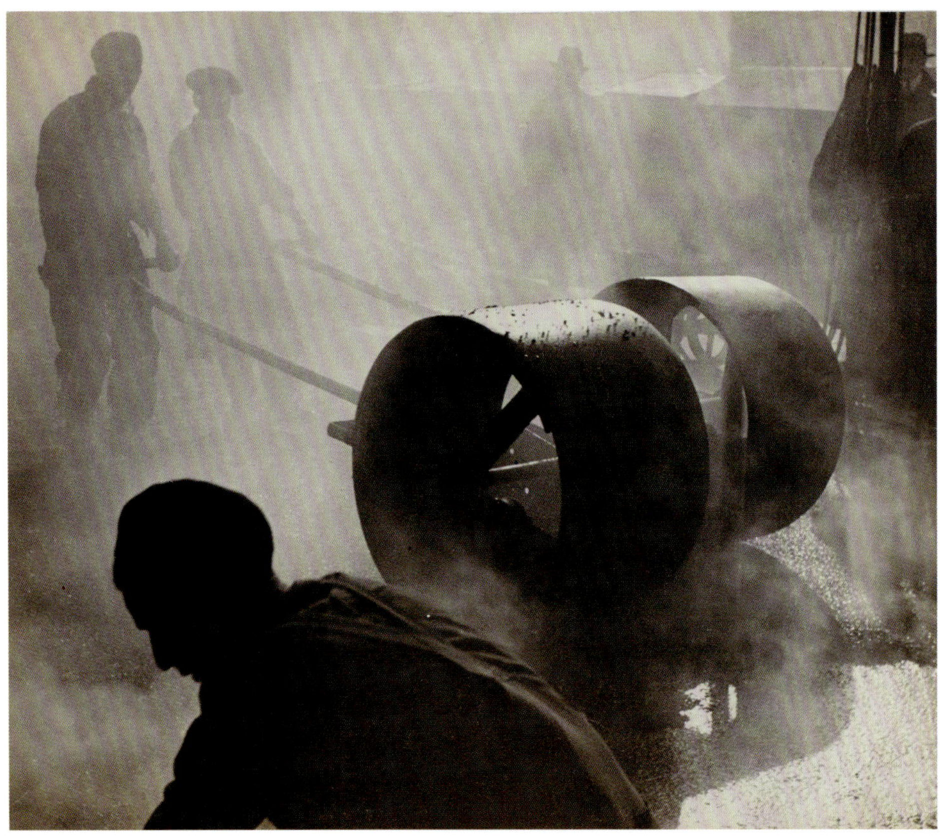

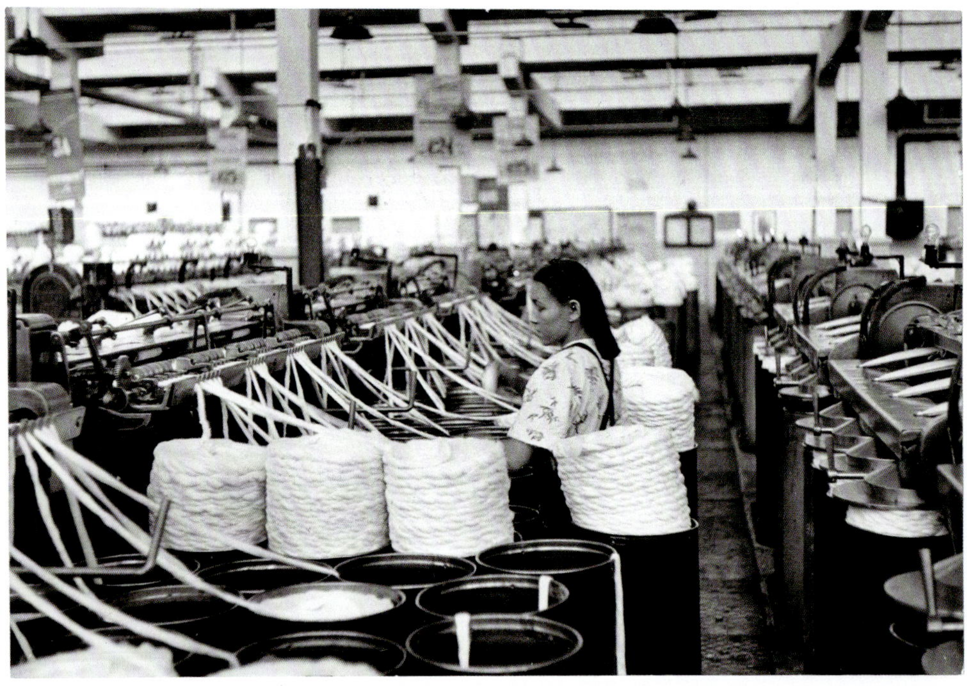

André Kertész
Street Work
1929
Gelatin silver print
24.5 × 29 cm
Malcolmson Collection
Gift of Harry and Ann Malcolmson in partnership with a private donor, 2014
2014/578

Henri Cartier-Bresson
Woman in Soviet Union cotton mill winding rolls of material on machine
1960
Gelatin silver print
25 × 17 cm
Anonymous Gift, 2005
2005/2320

Sarah Anne Johnson
Group Portrait, City Bakery, Calgary
2007
Chromogenic print
76.2 × 101.6 cm
Commissioned and donated by George Weston Limited, 2012
2012/66

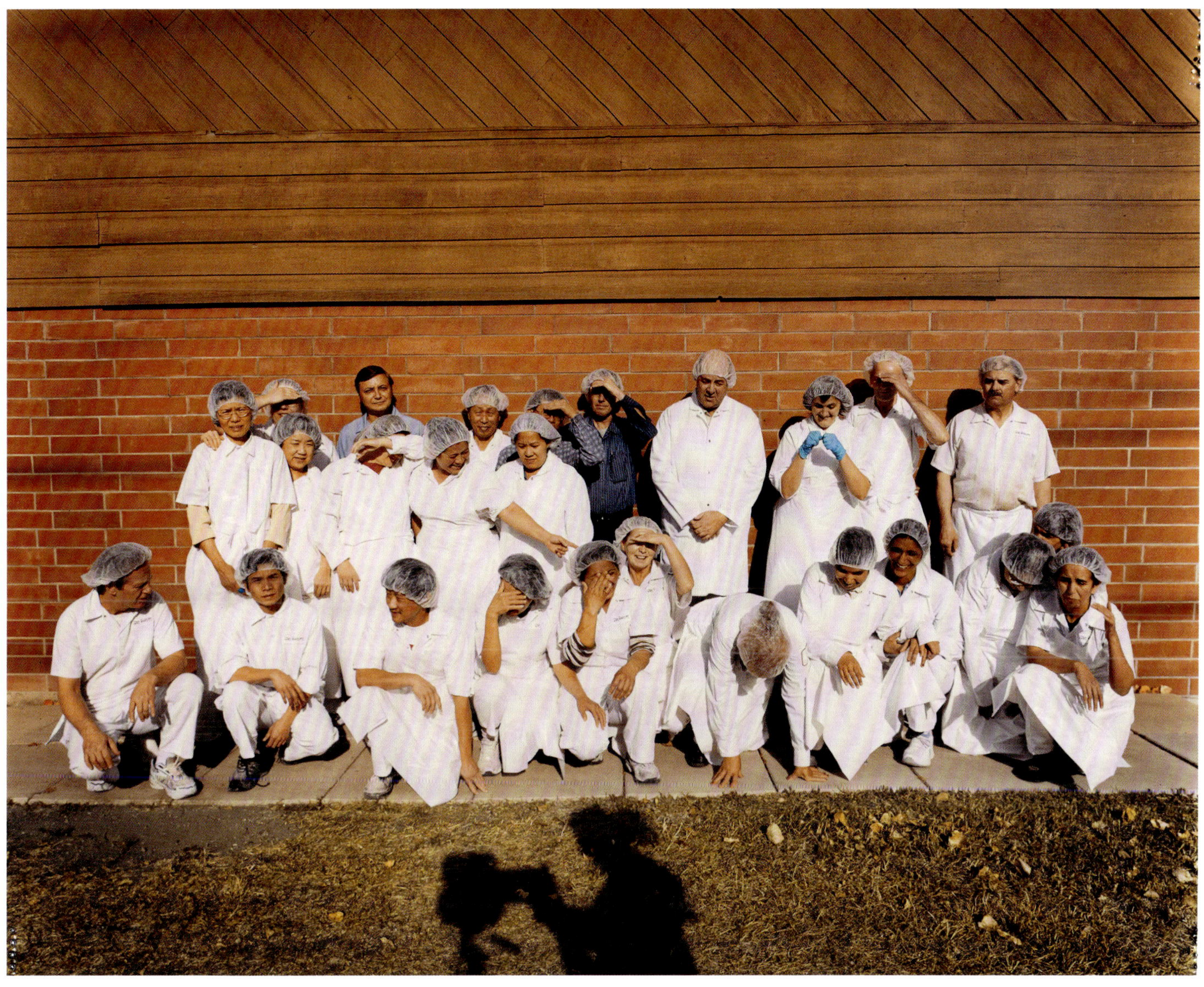

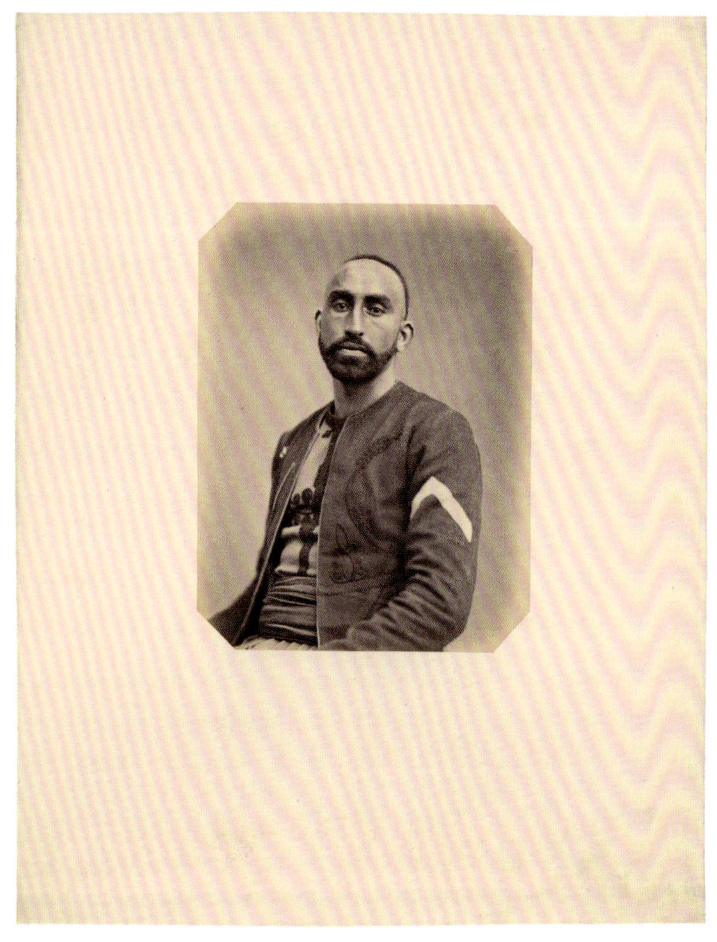

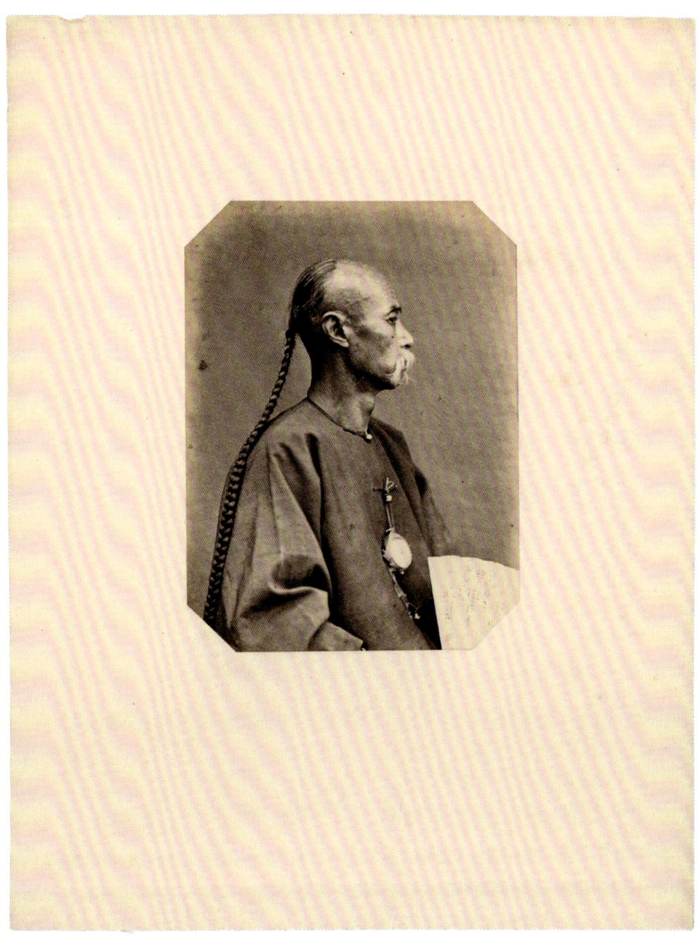

Jacques-Philippe Potteau
126. Brabim-ben Salah (Spahi). Né à Souk Ahras. Province de Constantine (Algérie)
1863
268. Li Yunne Ichiaoh (57 ans) chinois lettré, né à Pékin (Chine). Taille : 1m 74, cheveux noirs, yeux bruns. Père et mère chinois. Suite de la Mission chinoise à Paris
1866
Albumen prints
33.9 × 26.7 cm each
Anonymous gift, 2008
2008/1247; 2008/1413

Tomoko Sawada
ID 400 (#201-300)
1998
From the series ***ID 400*** (1998–2001)
Gelatin silver prints
127 × 101.6 cm
Gift of Brian J. Henderson, 2023
2023/278

JACQUES-PHILIPPE POTTEAU

Jacques-Philippe Potteau's albumen portraits, made between 1855 and 1869, document members of foreign delegations and other visitors to Paris, including people from Siam (now Thailand), Japan, Algeria, Cochinchina (now southern Vietnam), and China. Meticulously labelled with details such as age, birthplace, and parentage, these frontal and profile studies merge misguided scientific inquiry with studio portrait conventions, revealing nineteenth-century ideas about race, colonialism, and a fading pre-industrial world.

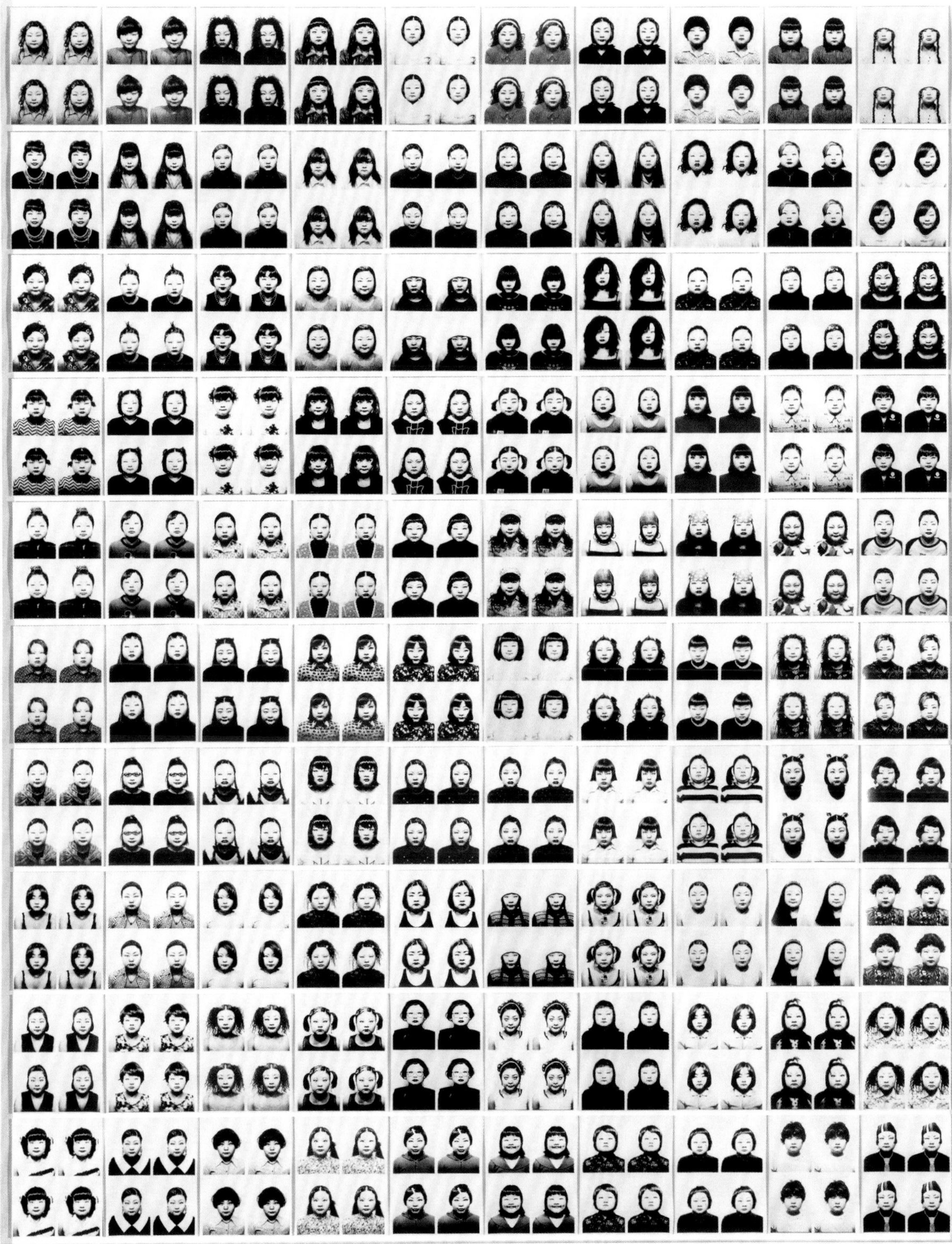

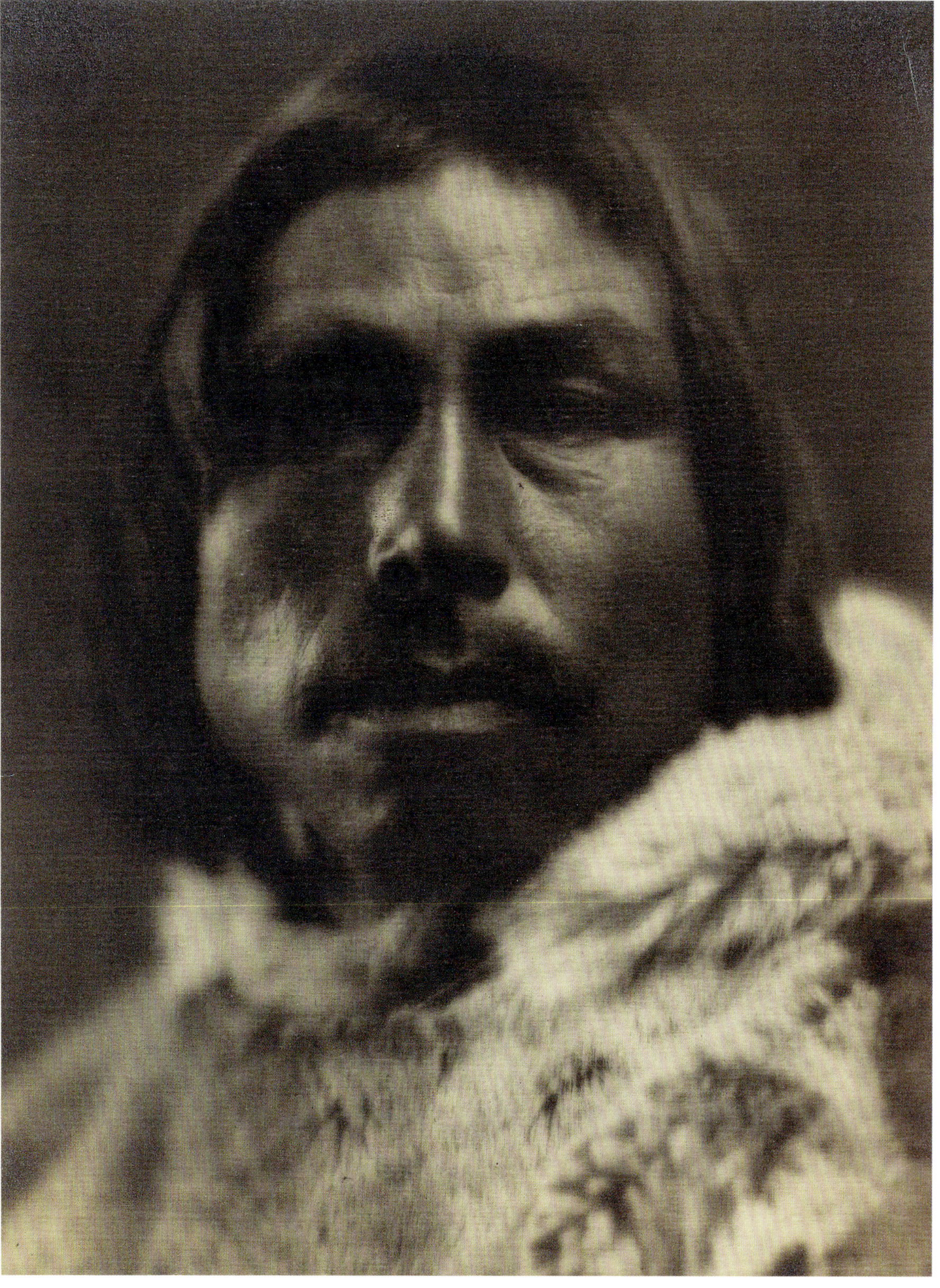

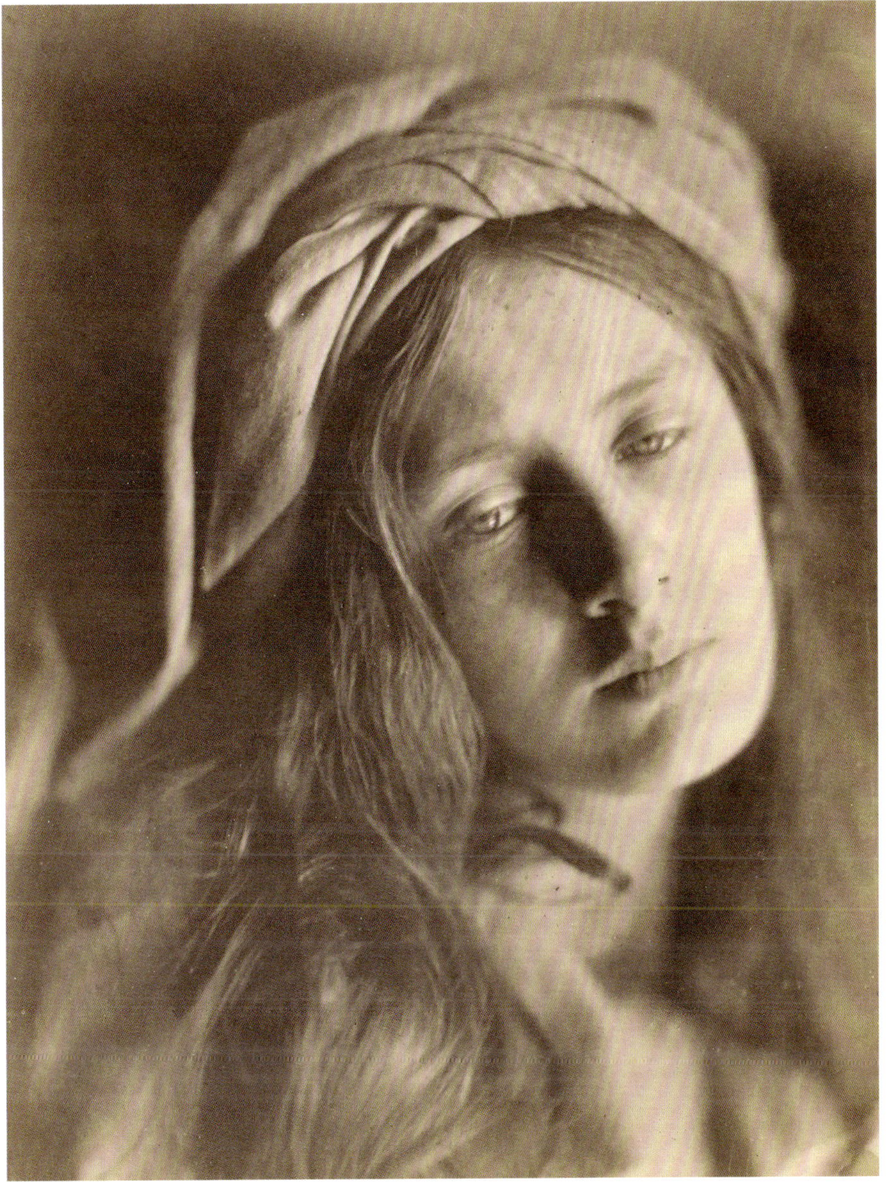

Robert Joseph Flaherty
Tooktoo (The Deer). Chief of Sikoslingmint Eskimos, Southern Baffin Island
1913–1914
Gelatin silver print
24.8 × 18.7 cm
Gift of Gordon M. Robb, 1993
93/280.5

Julia Margaret Cameron
Beatrice
1866
Albumen print
34.5 × 26.1 cm
Gift of Patricia Regan, in memory of Dr. Arthur Rubinoff, 2013
2013/368

ROBERT FLAHERTY

Before his groundbreaking film *Nanook of the North* (1922), Robert Flaherty made gelatin silver prints and photogravures in the 1910s and early 1920s, including *Camera Studies of the Far North* (1922). These works mark a defining moment in early documentary photography and offer a record Flaherty's encounters with various Inuit communities.

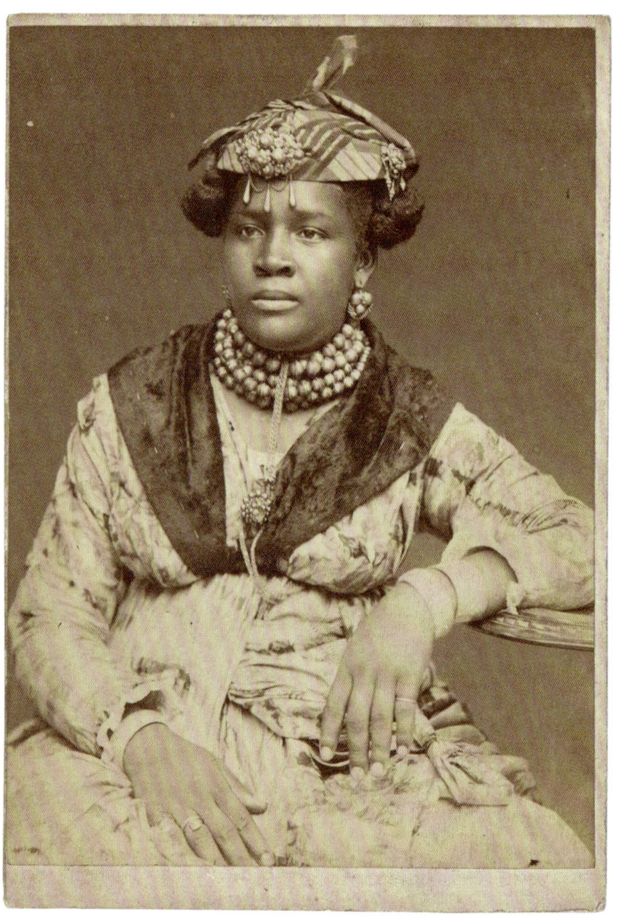

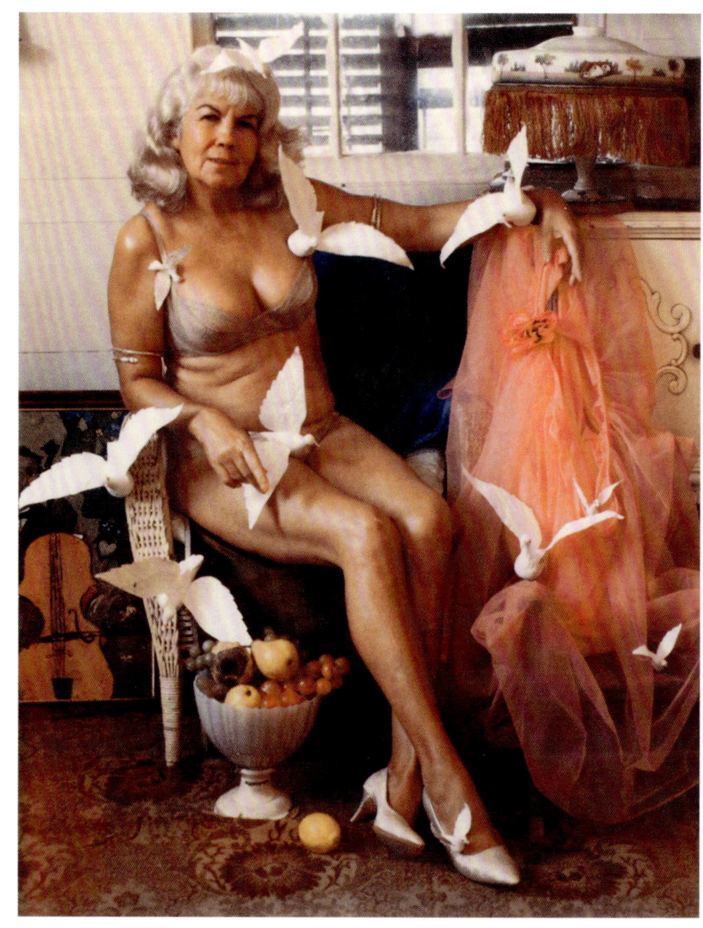

MONTGOMERY COLLECTION OF CARIBBEAN PHOTOGRAPHS

The Montgomery Collection comprises over 3,500 photographs—daguerreotypes, albumen prints, studio portraits, travel views—made in the Caribbean, Bahamas, and Bermuda from the 1840s to 1940s. Created by both local and international photographers, these works depict landscapes, people, and cultures during an era shaped by colonial agriculture and business endeavours, preserving visual histories and documenting profound regional change.

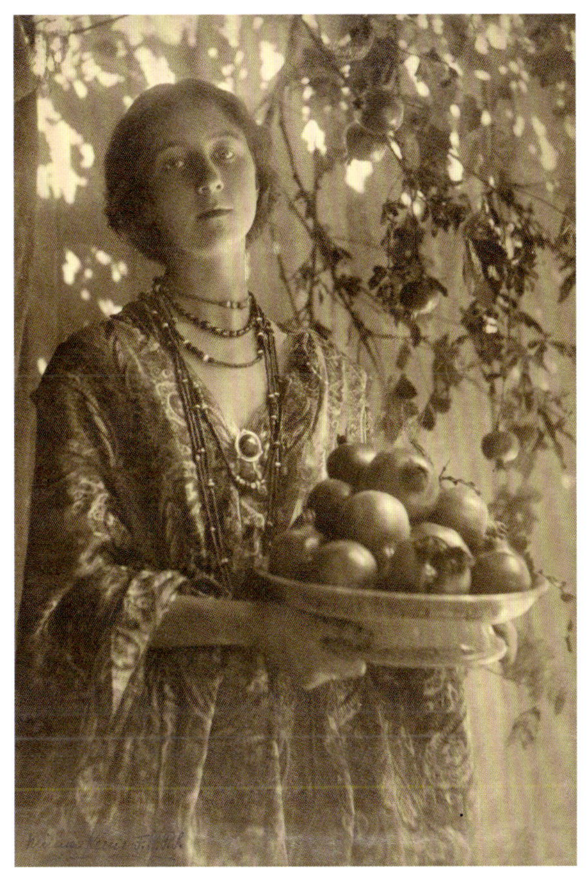

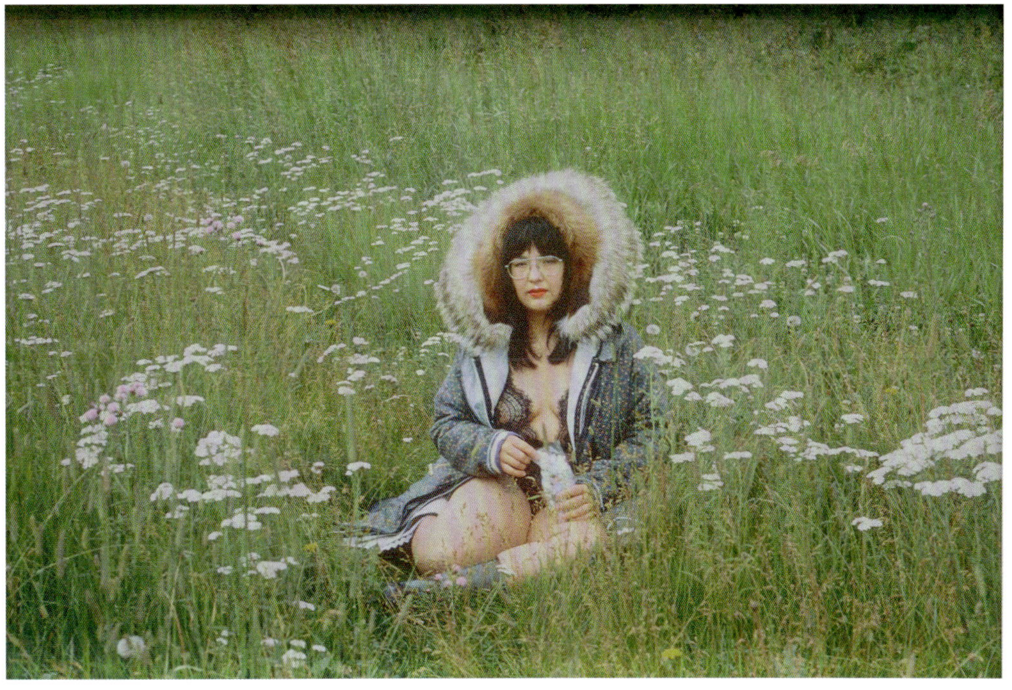

Maker once known
Woman, Martinique
c. 1870
Albumen print mounted to cardstock
14.6 × 10.2 cm
Montgomery Collection of Caribbean Photographs. Purchase, with funds from Dr. Liza & Dr. Frederick Murrell, Bruce Croxon & Debra Thier, Wes Hall & Kingsdale Advisors, Cindy & Shon Barnett, Donette Chin-Loy Chang, Kamala-Jean Gopie, Phil Lind & Ellen Roland, Martin Doc McKinney, Francilla Charles, Ray & Georgina Williams, Thaine & Bianca Carter, Charmaine Crooks, Nathaniel Crooks, Andrew Garrett & Dr. Belinda Longe, Neil L. Le Grand, Michael Lewis, Dr. Kenneth Montague & Sarah Aranha, Lenny & Julia Mortimore, and The Ferrotype Collective, 2019
2019/2208

Marie Cosindas
Princess with Doves
1966; printed c. 1990s
Chromogenic print
36.8 × 29.2 cm
Purchase, funds donated by David G. Broadhurst, 2012
2012/24

Minna Keene
Pomegranates
c. 1910
Carbon print mounted to two-ply period board
33.7 × 22.9 cm
Purchase, 2020
2020/81

Kablusiak
piliutiyara (robin hood)
2021
Inkjet print from faded transparency
61 × 91.4 cm
Purchase, with funds from the Joan Chalmers Inuit Art Fund, 2022
2022/7078

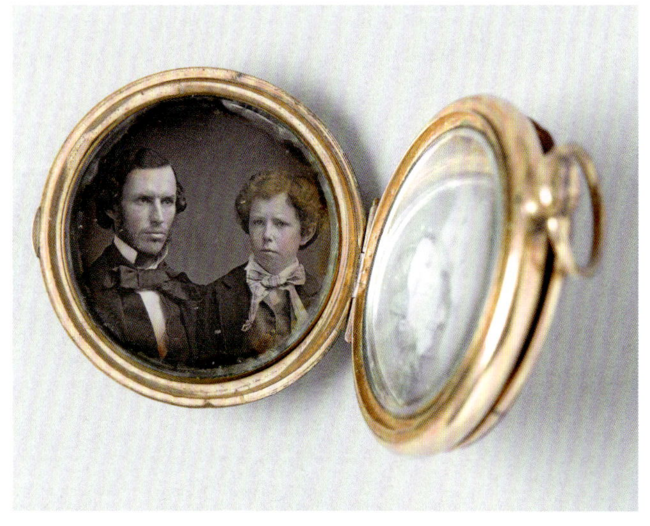

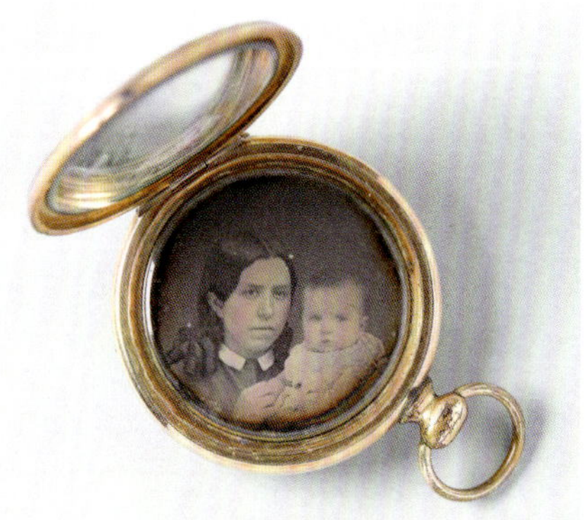

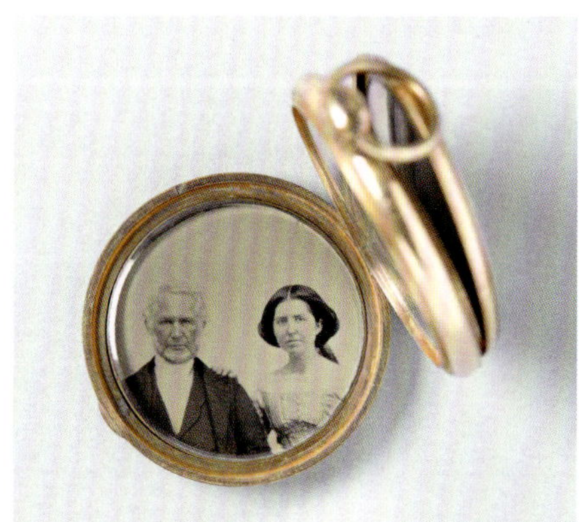

Maker once known, Canadian
Rev. William Henry Williams and family members
1855–1857
Locket: gilded copper alloy with glass cover plates; interior: 3 daguerreotypes and 1 ambrotype
6.3 × 4.3 cm
Gift of Larry Pfaff in honour of Maia-Mari Sutnik, 2021
2021/339

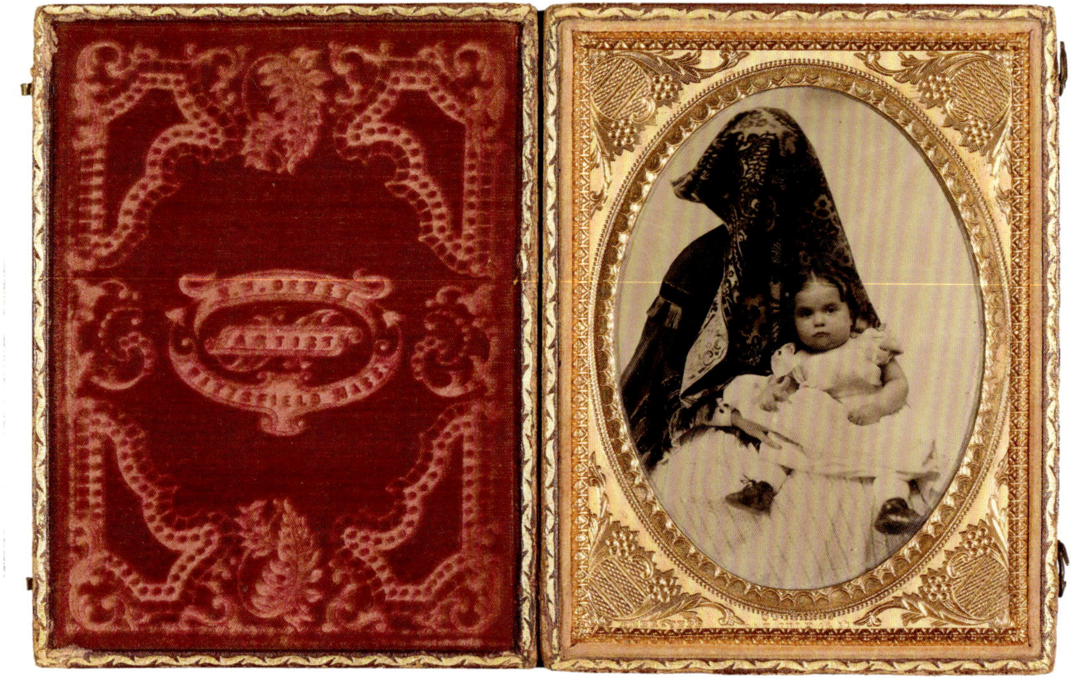

Rodney H. Dewey
Portait of young girl in lap of shrouded figure
c. 1859
Ambrotype, with applied colour in embossed paper-covered wood case with gilt border, brass mat and velvet embossed pad
Anonymous gift, 2009
2009/113

Henry K. Sheldon
Mr. John Shiels, Kingston, Ontario
1856
Daguerreotype, with applied colour
7.1 × 6 cm (image)
Purchase with assistance of the Photography Curatorial Committee, 2008
2008/1

Maker once known, American
Portrait of African American woman
c. 1875
Tintype, in carte-de-visite decorative mat
2 × 1.6 cm (image)
Anonymous Gift, 2000
2000/1320

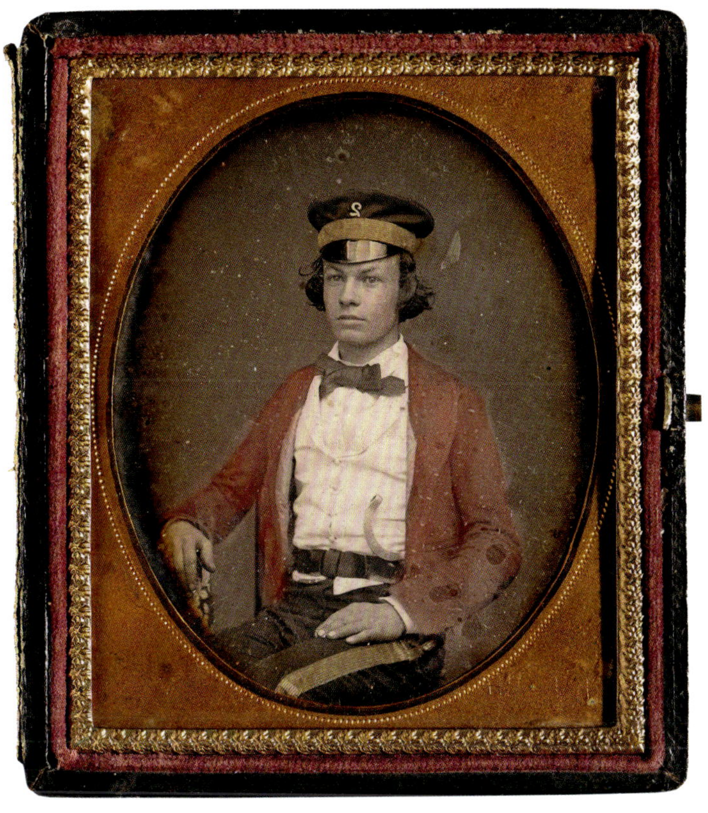

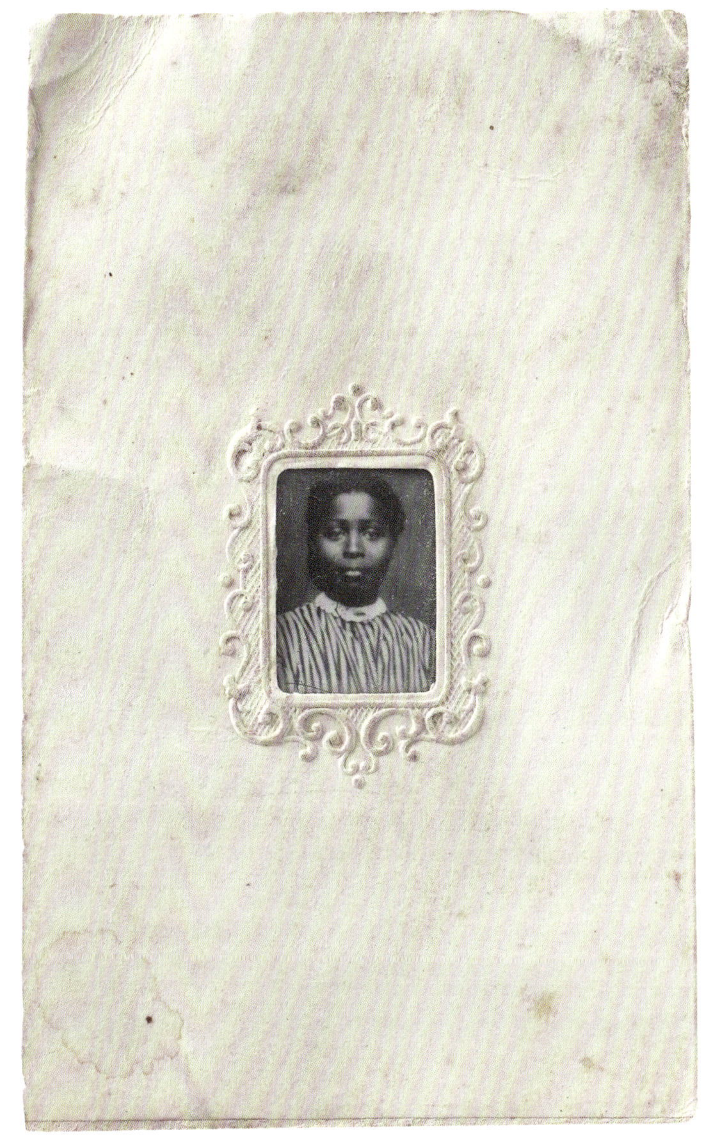

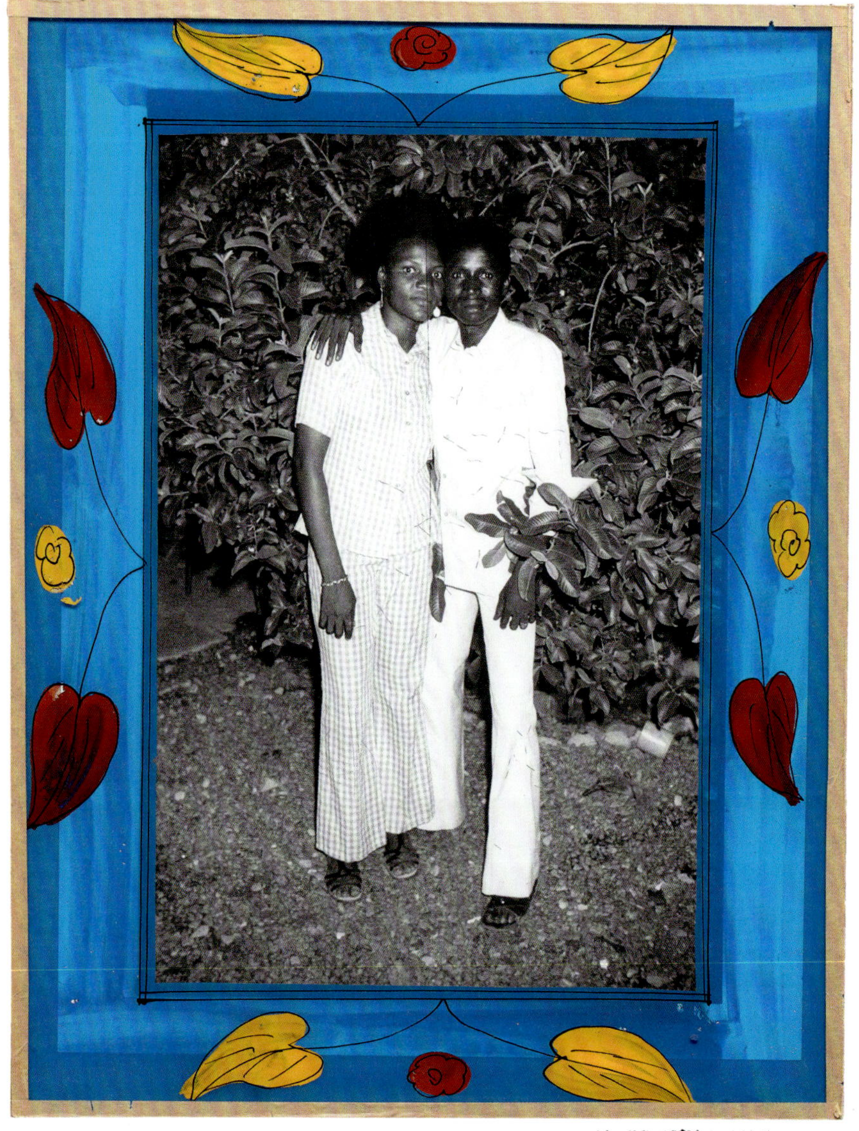

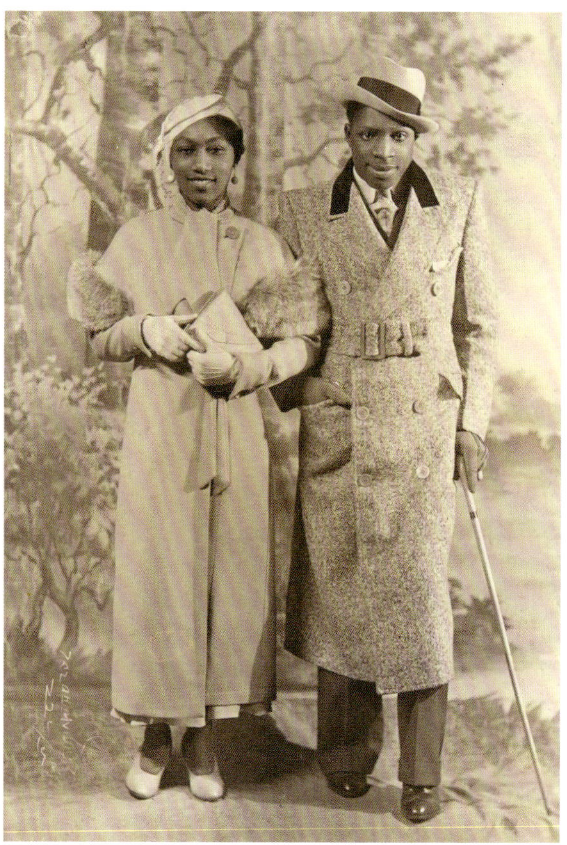

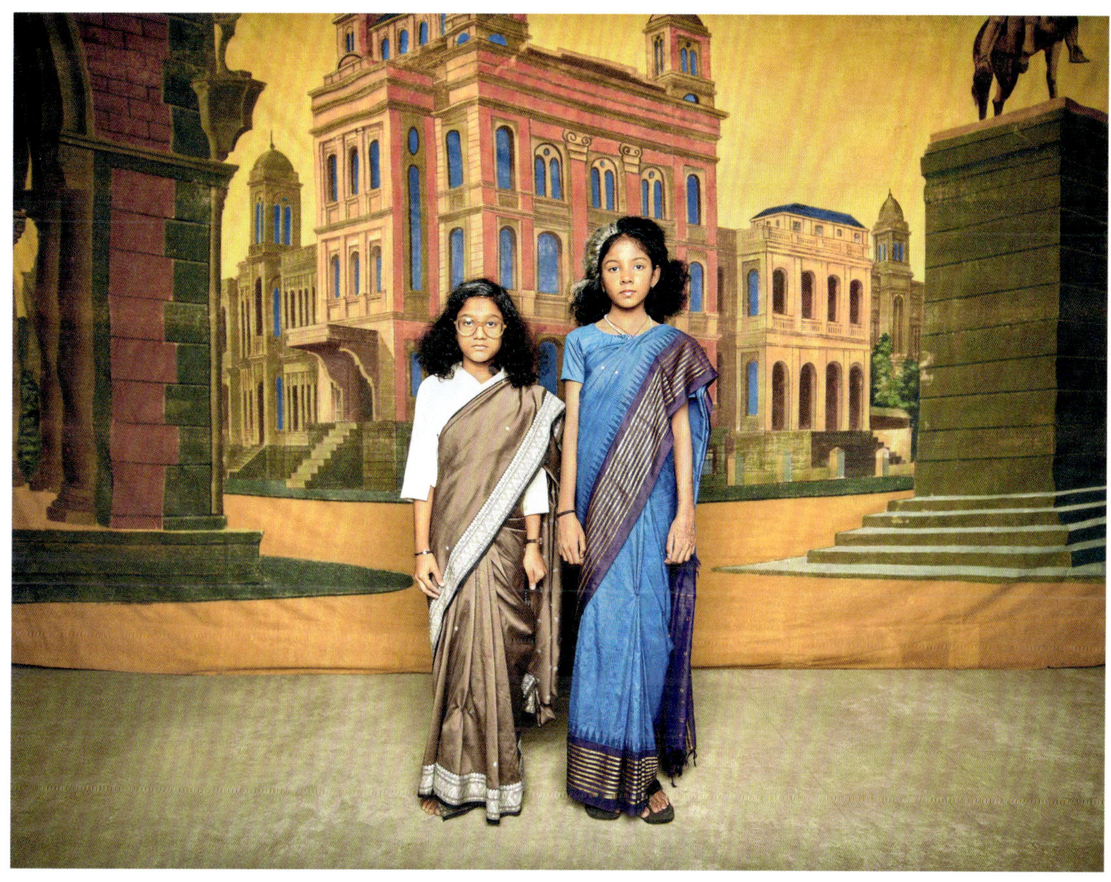

Malick Sidibé
Untitled
2004
Gelatin silver print, glass, paint, cardboard, tape, and string
33 × 22.2 cm (image)
Purchase, with funds from the Photography Curatorial Committee, 2020
2019/23

James Van Der Zee
Strolling
c. 1925
Gelatin silver print
16.8 × 14.9 cm
Purchase, with funds from the Photography Curatorial Committee, 2019
2019/2253

Nandini Valli Muthiah
Two Indira Gandhis
2010
Chromogenic print
48.3 × 61 cm
Gift of Nandini Valli Muthiah, in memory of her father M.C.T. Muthiah (1929-2006), 2014
2014/1578

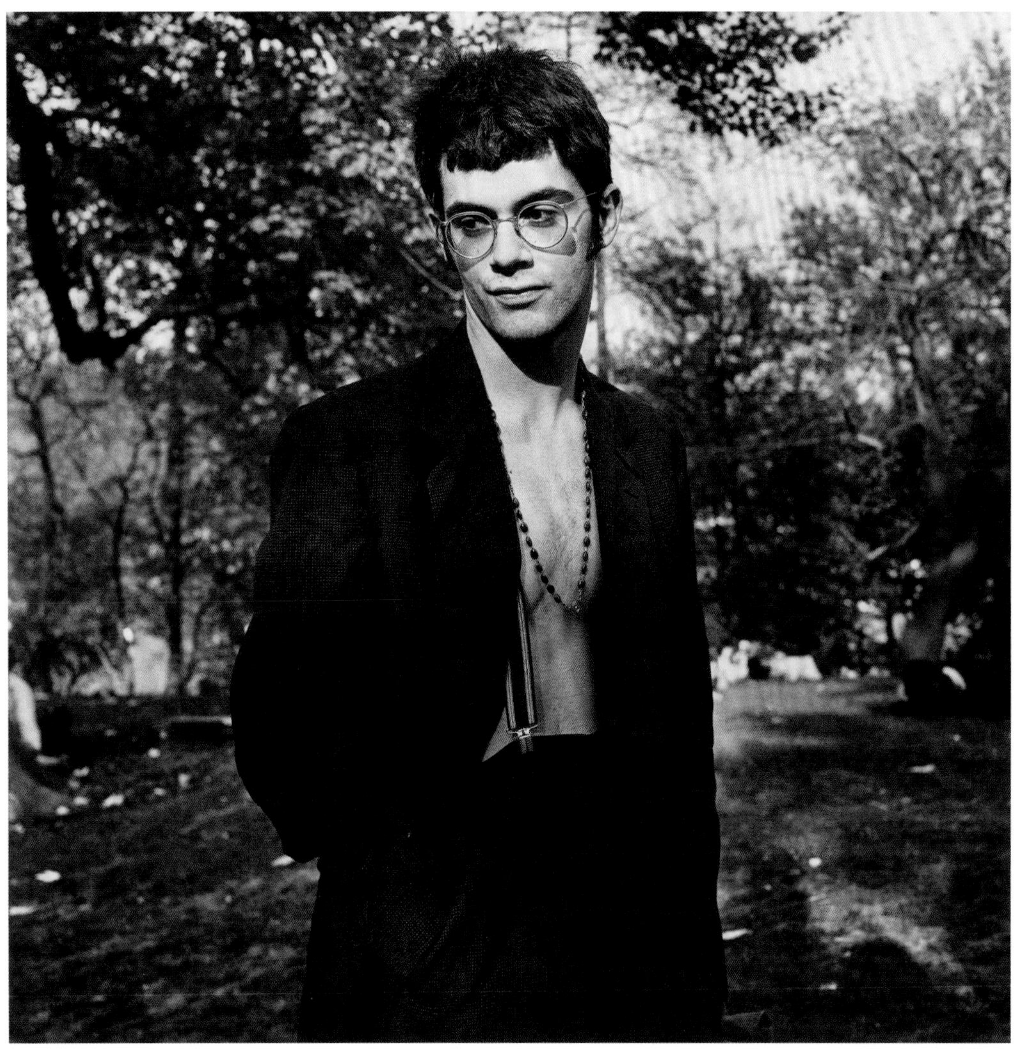

Peter Hujar
Man in Park
c. 1969
Agosto Machado
1980
Gelatin silver prints
50.5 × 40.5 cm each
Purchase with funds from the David Yuile and Mary Hodgson Fund, 2025
2024/413; 2024/525

PETER HUJAR

Peter Hujar's intimate portraits, haunting landscapes, and homoerotic studies reveal a rich emotional and material world shaped by love, loss, and cultural transformation. This collection of over 200 gelatin silver prints spanning the early 1950s to the mid-1980s makes the AGO home to the largest holding of his work outside the United States.

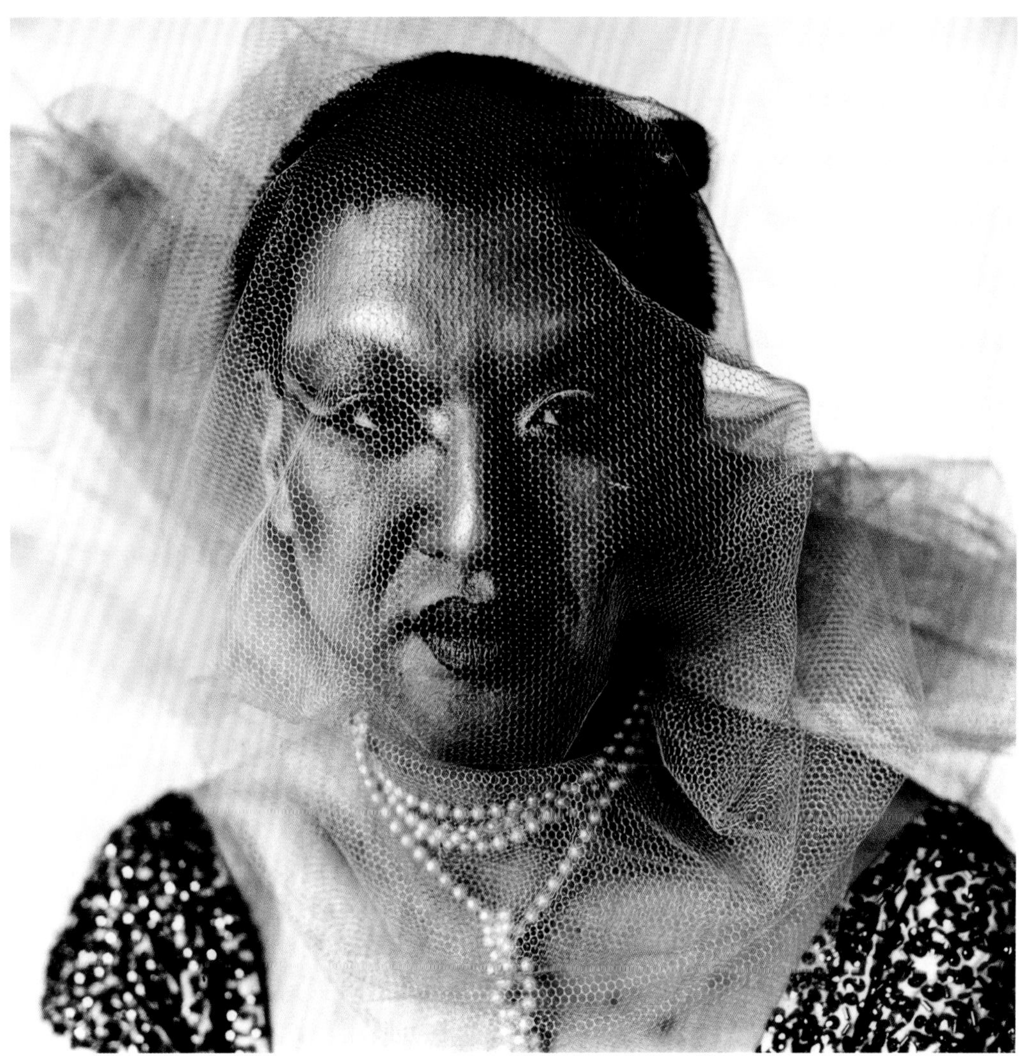

Paul Kodjo
Untitled
c. 1970s
Gelatin silver print
50 × 40 cm
Purchase, with funds from the Photography Curatorial Committee, 2020
2019/2331

Ming Smith
Dexter Gordon, Tenor Saxophonist, Marseille, France
1976
Gelatin silver print
40.6 × 50.8 cm
Purchase, with funds generously donated by Ken Straiton, 2018
2018/34

Opposite, clockwise from upper left:
Nan Goldin
Cody in the Dressing Room at the Boy Bar, NYC
1991
Silver dye bleach print
69.4 × 91.6 cm
Gift of Jane Corkin in honour of David Mirvish receiving the Order of Canada, 1996
96/1084

Paul Graham
Untitled #55
1996–1997
From the series ***End of an Age*** (1996–1998)
Chromogenic print on laminate panel
184 × 143 cm
Gift of Alison and Alan Schwartz, 2000
2000/1348

Don Vincent
Art and Barbara Pratten dancing at Greg Curnoe's studio. New Year's Eve, 1966, London, Ontario
1966
Gelatin silver print
35 × 27.5 cm
Gift of Bernice Vincent, 2000
2000/1306

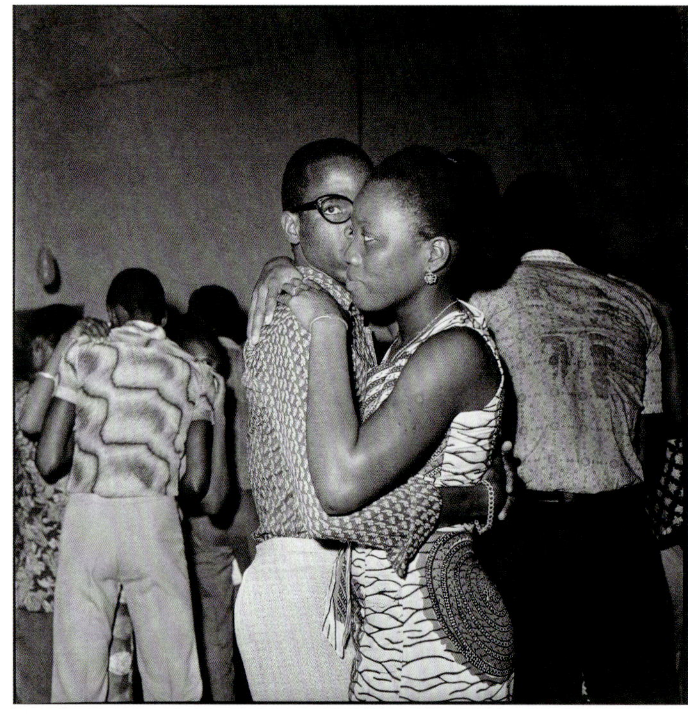

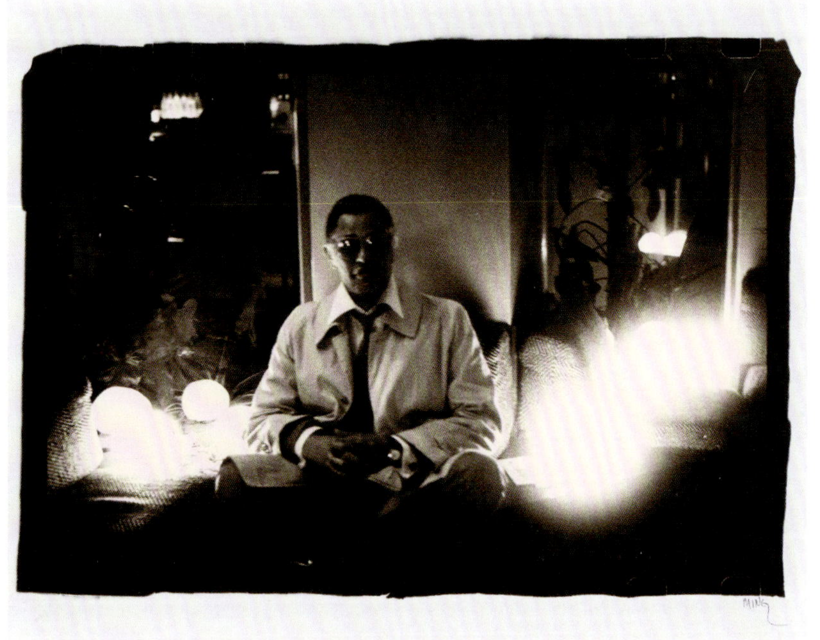

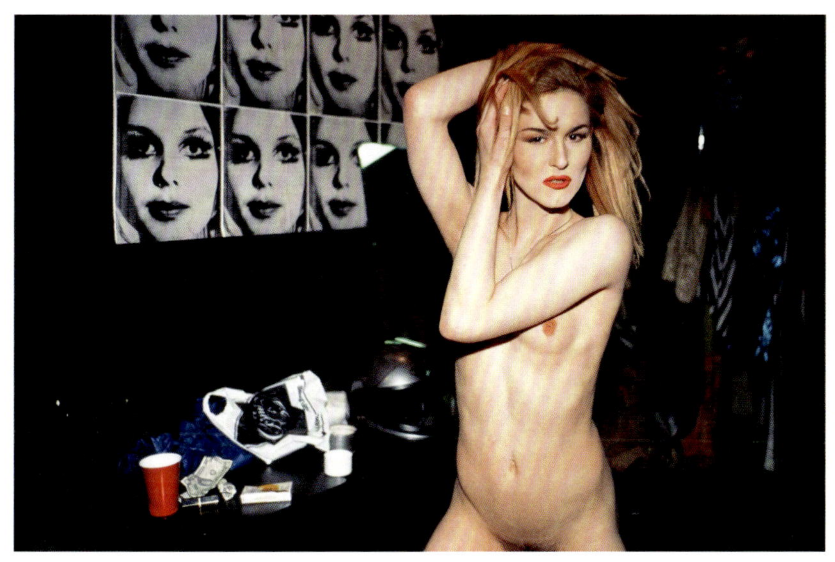

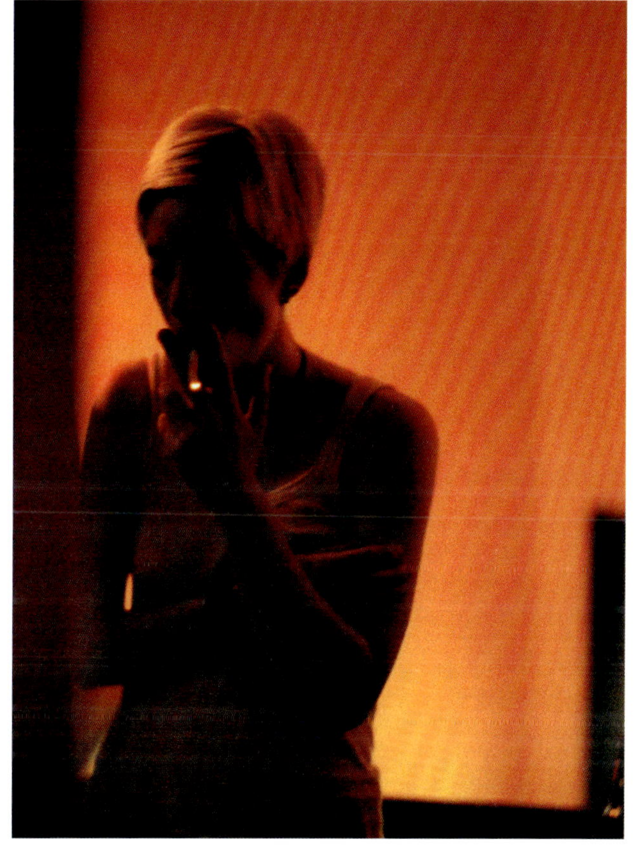

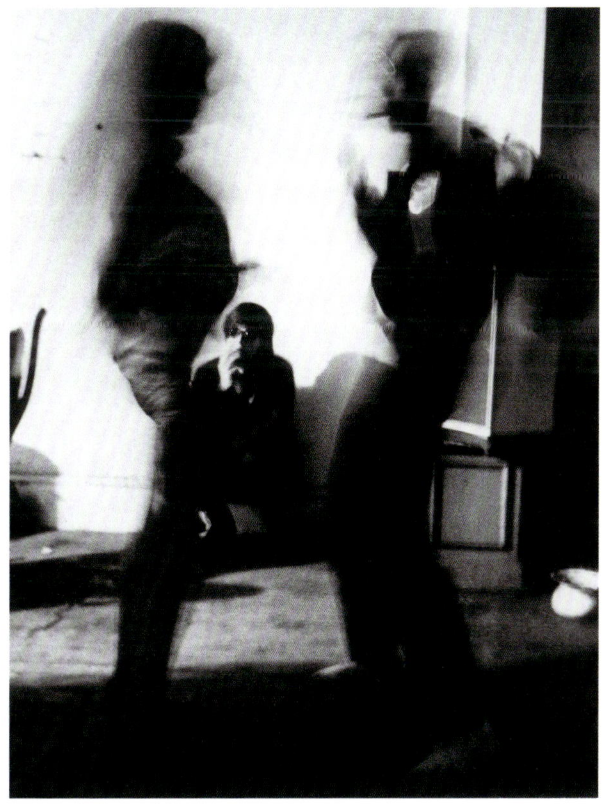

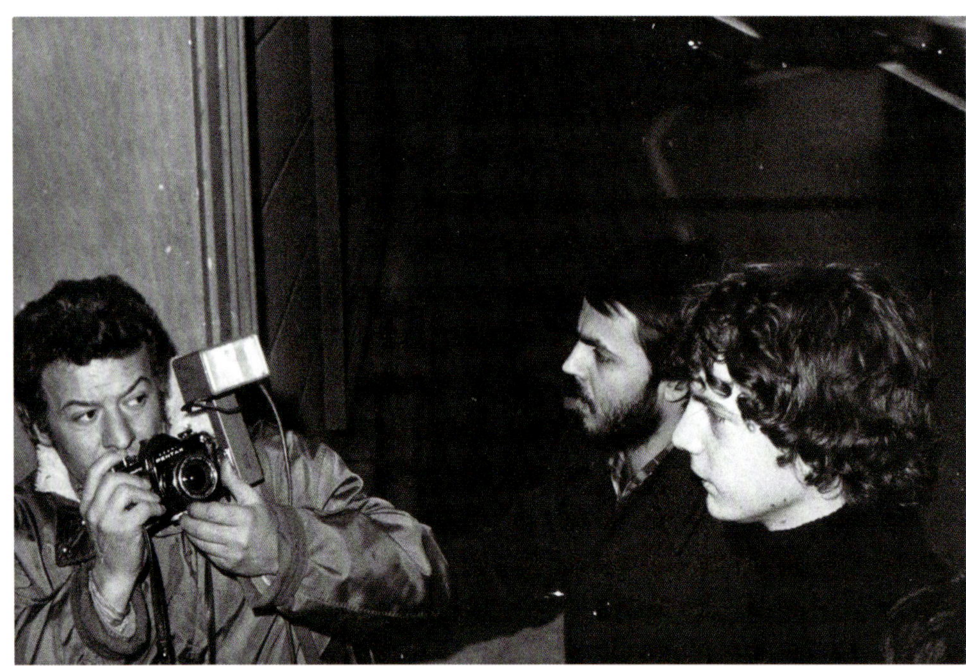

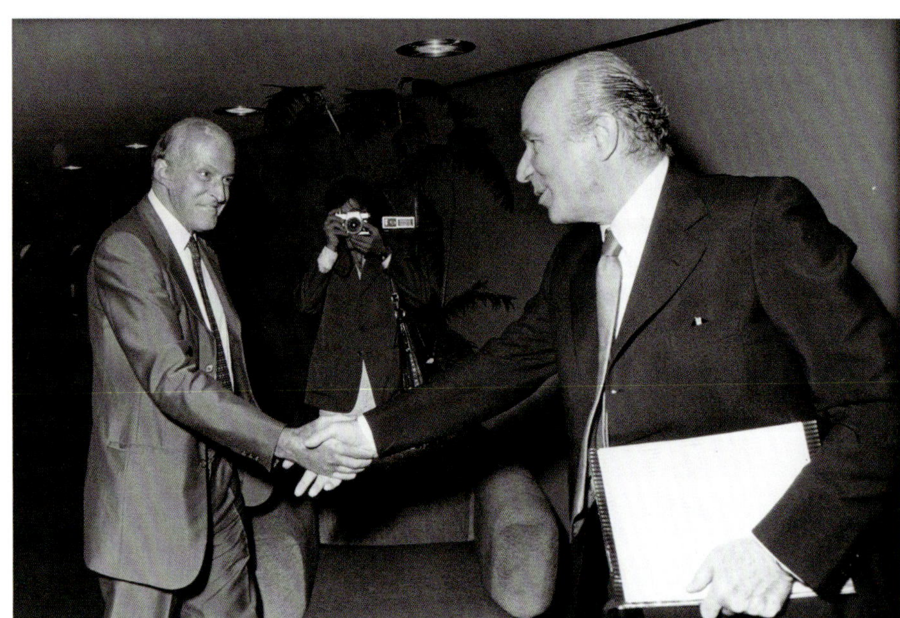

ITALIAN PRESS PHOTOGRAPHY COLLECTION

This collection offers a vivid look at Italy's turbulent postwar decades, drawn from two significant archives: of Rome's Team Editorial Services and of *Tempo*, Italy's leading illustrated weekly. Nearly 7,000 photographs spotlight everything from protests to everyday scenes to media spectacle and the rise of the paparazzo.

Team Editorial Services
John Paul Getty III entering a night club
c. 1969–1973
From the Italian Press Photography Collection
Gelatin silver print
20.5 × 30.6 cm
Anonymous Gift, 2020
2022/3307

Grazia Neri
Leopoldo Pirelli and Guido Carli shake hands for the cameras
c. 1969–1979
From the Italian Press Photography Collection
Gelatin silver print
20.3 × 30.2 cm
Anonymous Gift, 2020
2022/3946

Robert Cohen
Jackie Kennedy and Ron Galella
c. 1960s
From the Amédée Gautier Collection
Gelatin silver print
30.2 × 23.8 cm
Anonymous Gift, 2007
2007/1482

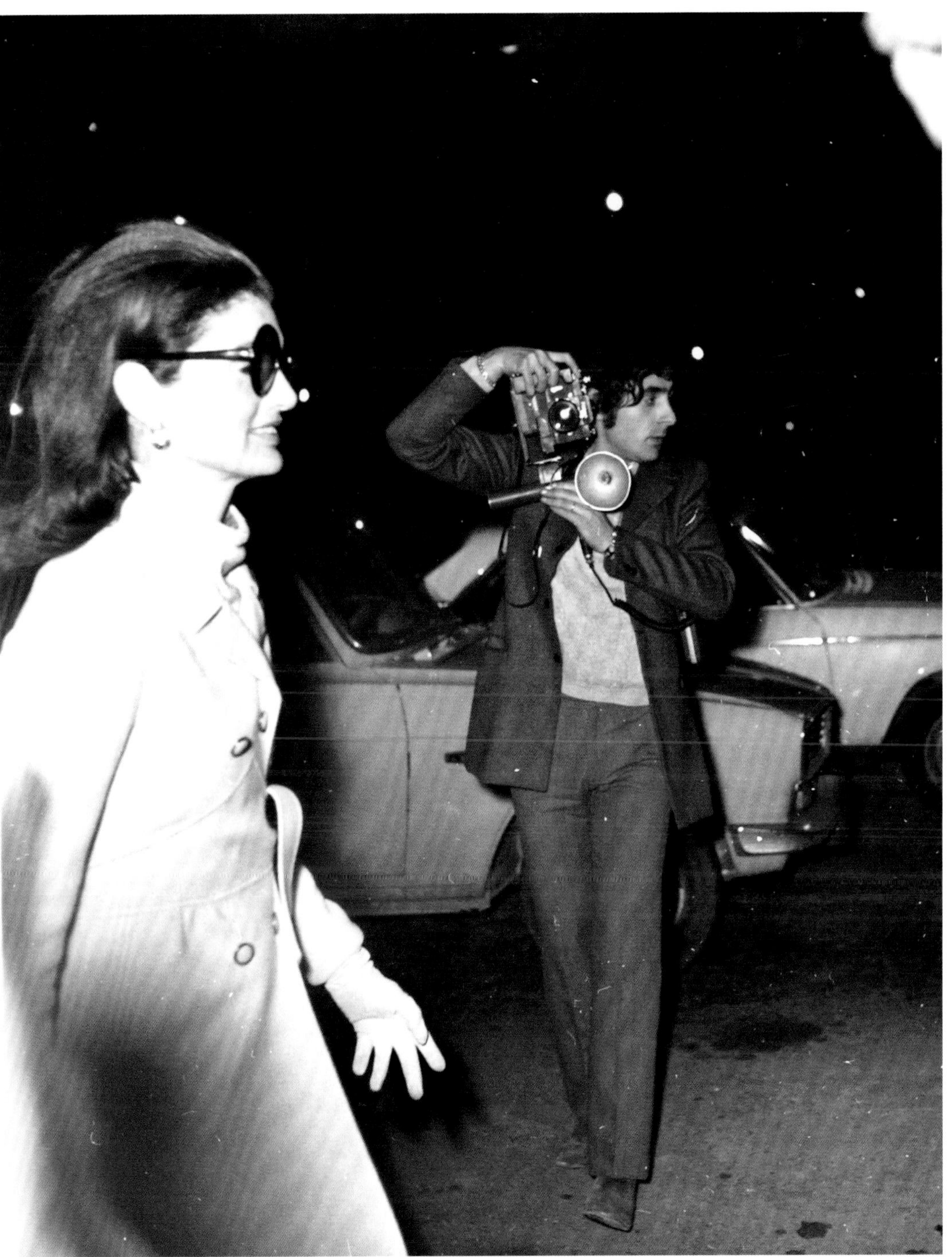

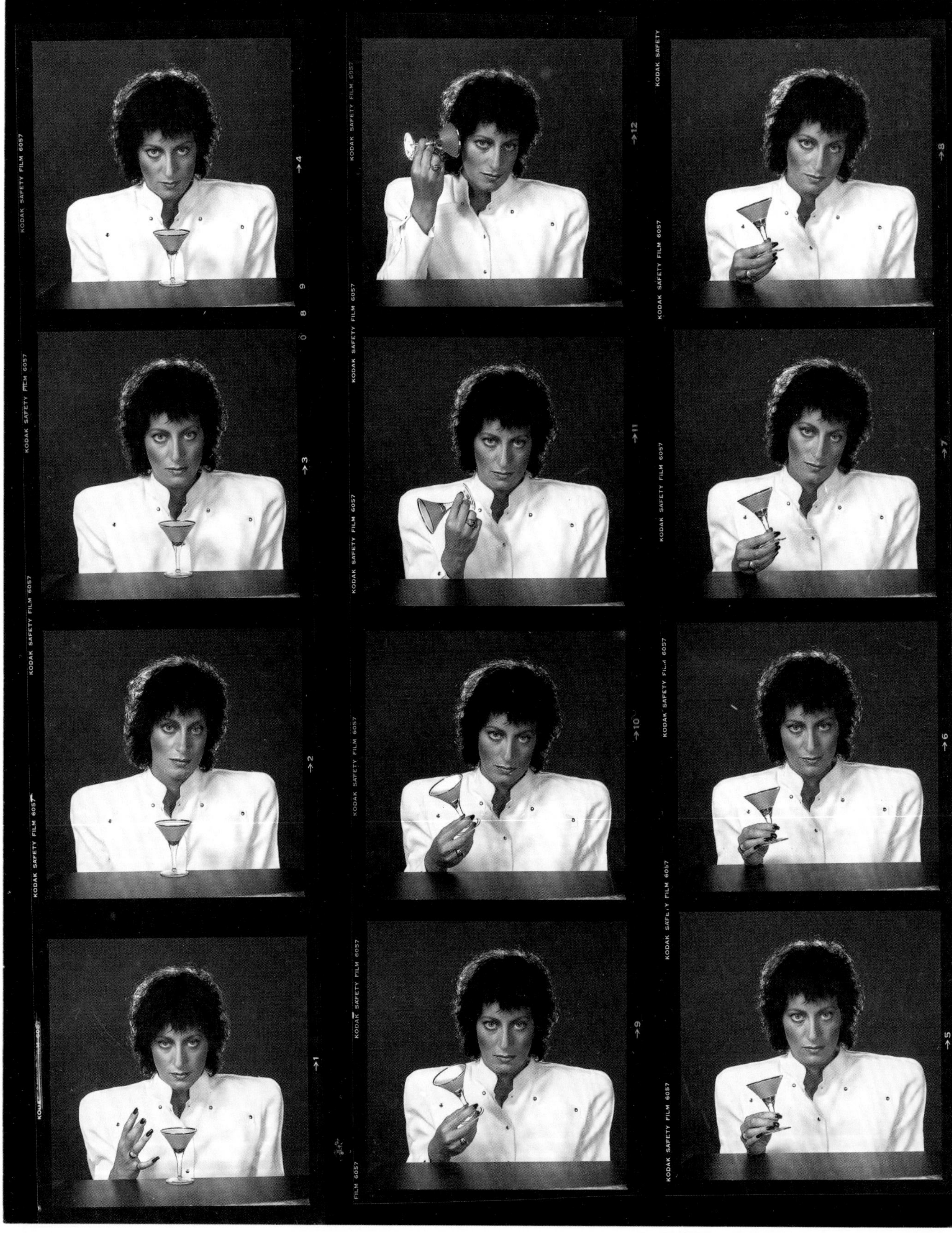

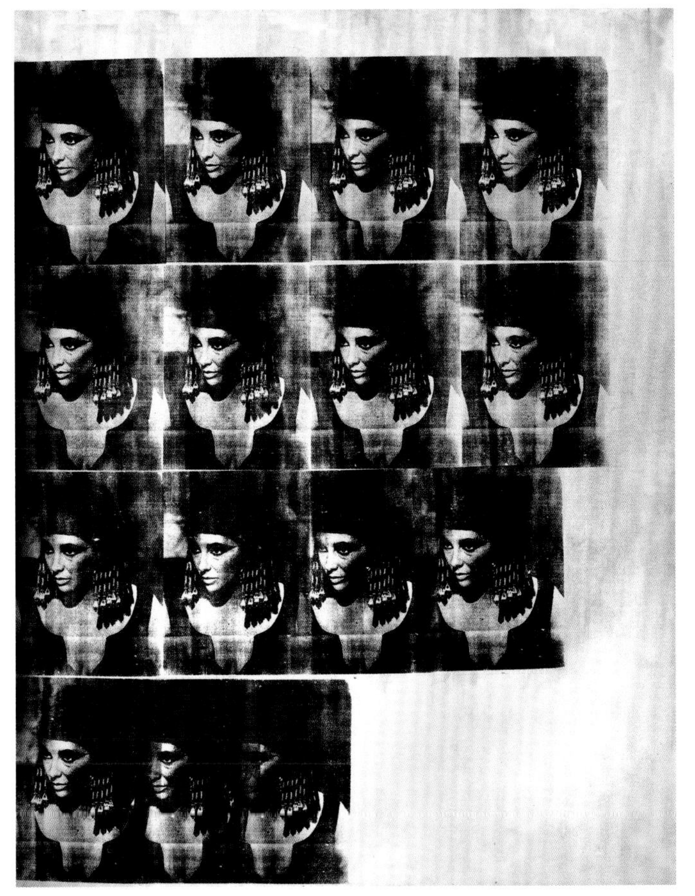

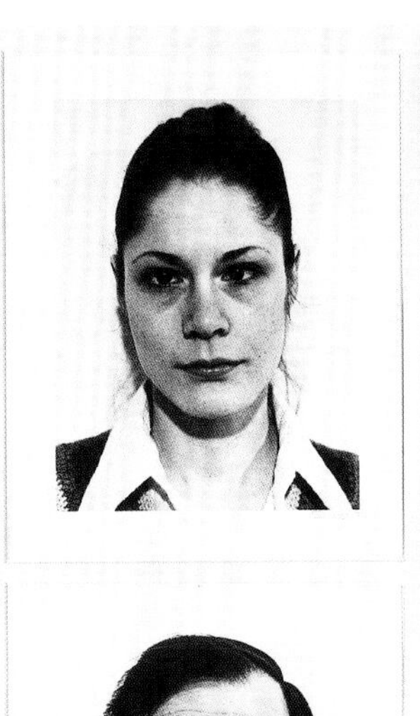

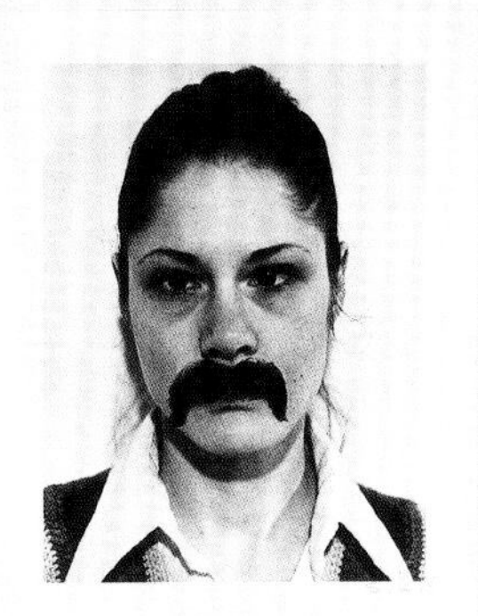

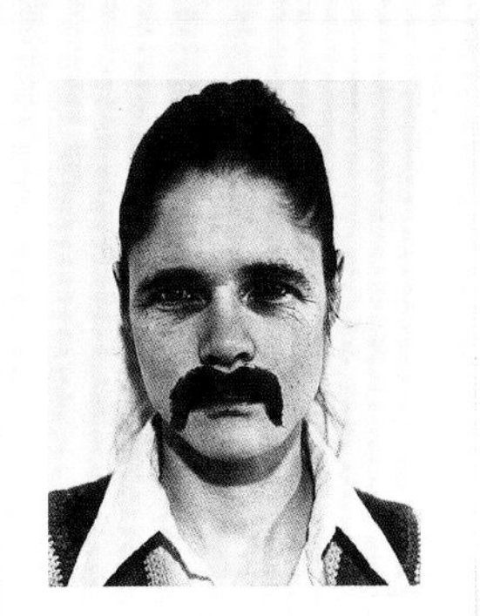

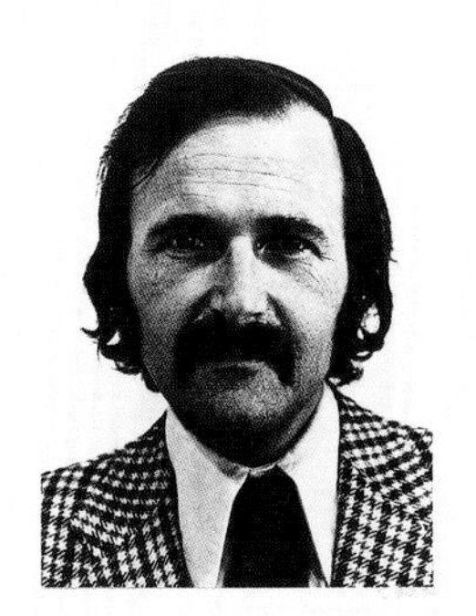

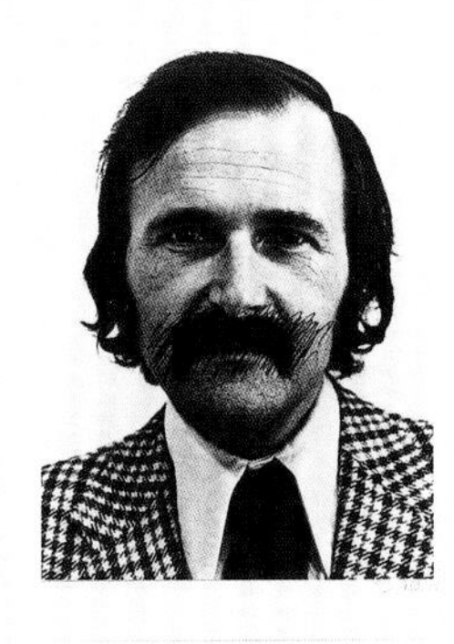

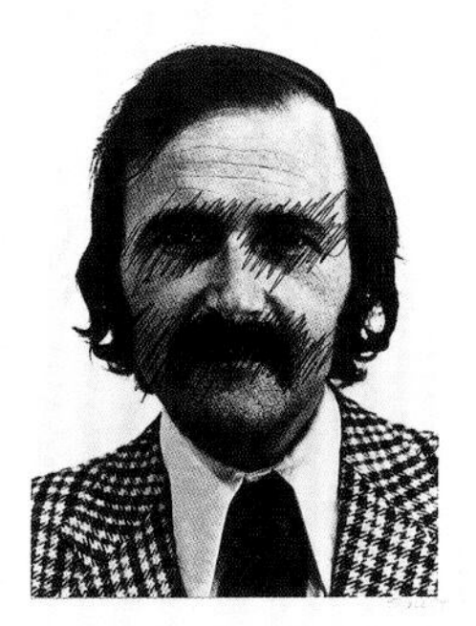

General Idea
Rough Trade, Avoid Freud Album Shoot
1980
Contact sheet: gelatin silver print
17.8 × 12.7 cm
Purchase, with funds from the Photography Curatorial Committee, 2022
2022/7055

Andy Warhol
Silver Liz as Cleopatra
1963
Silver paint, silkscreen ink, and pencil on linen
208.6 × 164.8 cm
Gift of Mrs. Else Landauer, in memory of her husband, Walter Landauer, 1979
79/114

Suzy Lake
Maquette for Suzy Lake as Bill Vazan
1974
Gelatin silver print
34.9 × 27.9 cm each
Purchase with assistance from Wintario, 1978
77/205

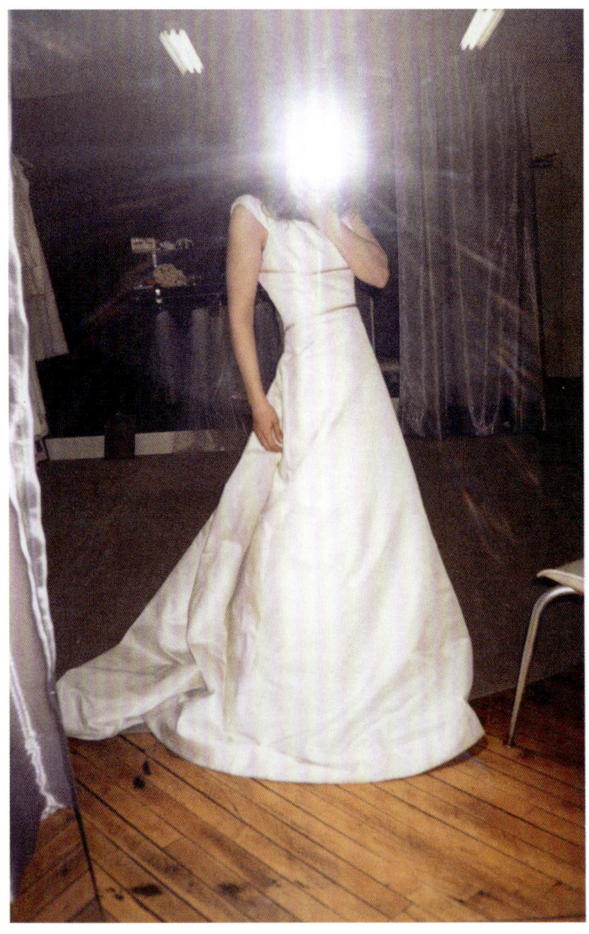

Katharine Mulherin
Untitled
2001
From the series ***Never a Bride*** (2001)
Chromogenic print
15.2 × 10.2 cm
Gift of Pamila Matharu, 2024
2024/239.47

Cindy Sherman
Untitled Film Still #10
1978
From the series ***Untitled Film Stills*** (1977–1980)
Gelatin silver print
20.3 × 25.3 cm
Gift from the Junior Committee Fund, 1988
88/134

Jin-me Yoon
Intersection 2
1998
Diptych: chromogenic prints
143.5 × 109.2 cm each
Gift of Philip B. Lind, 2008
2008/137.1-.2

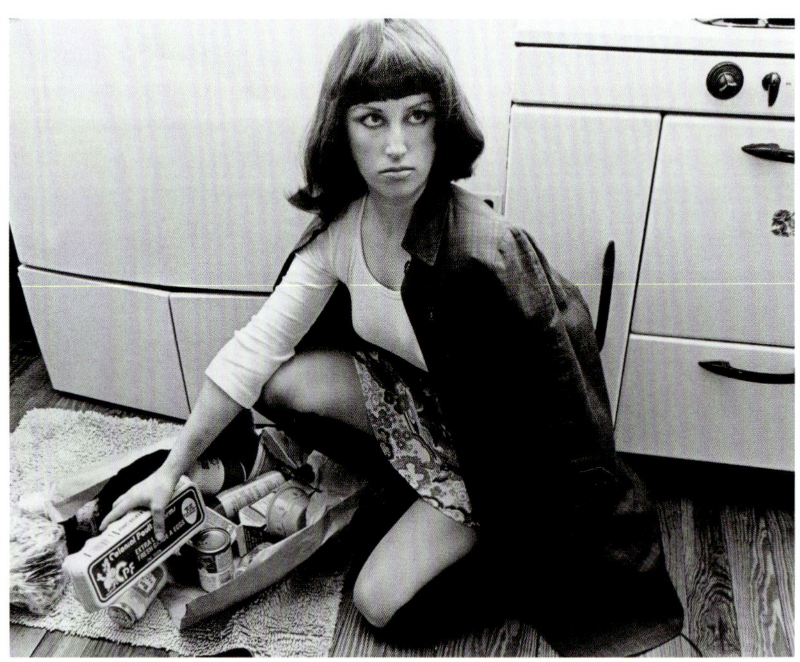

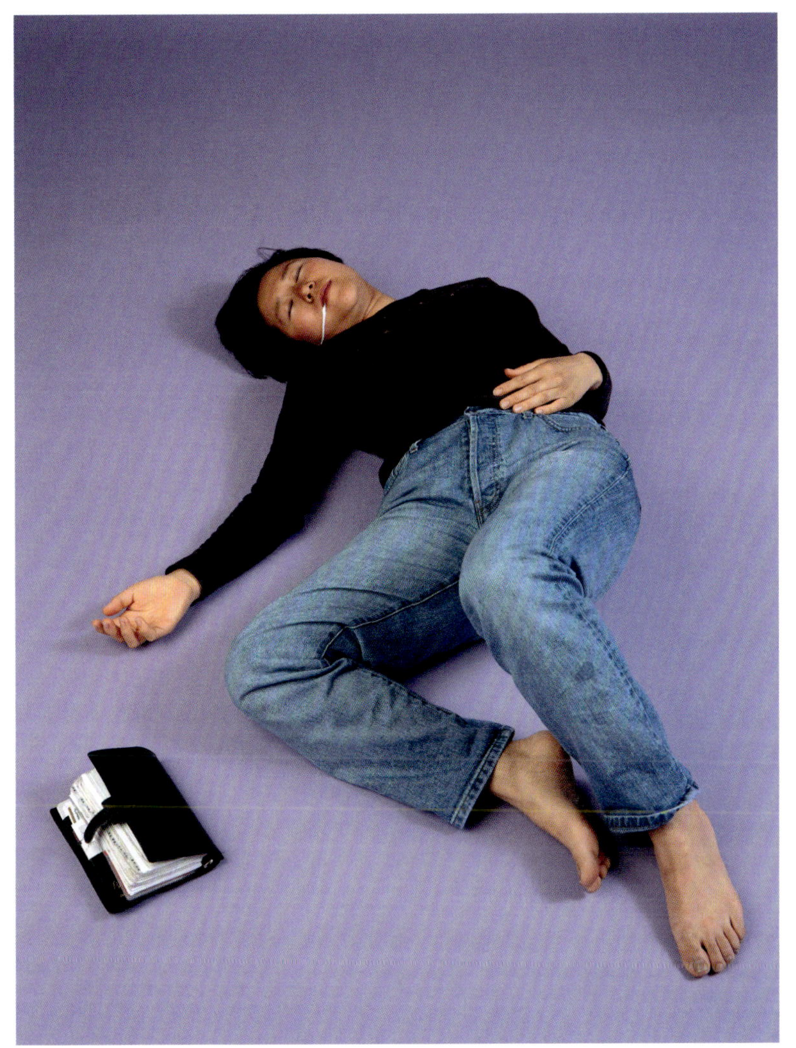

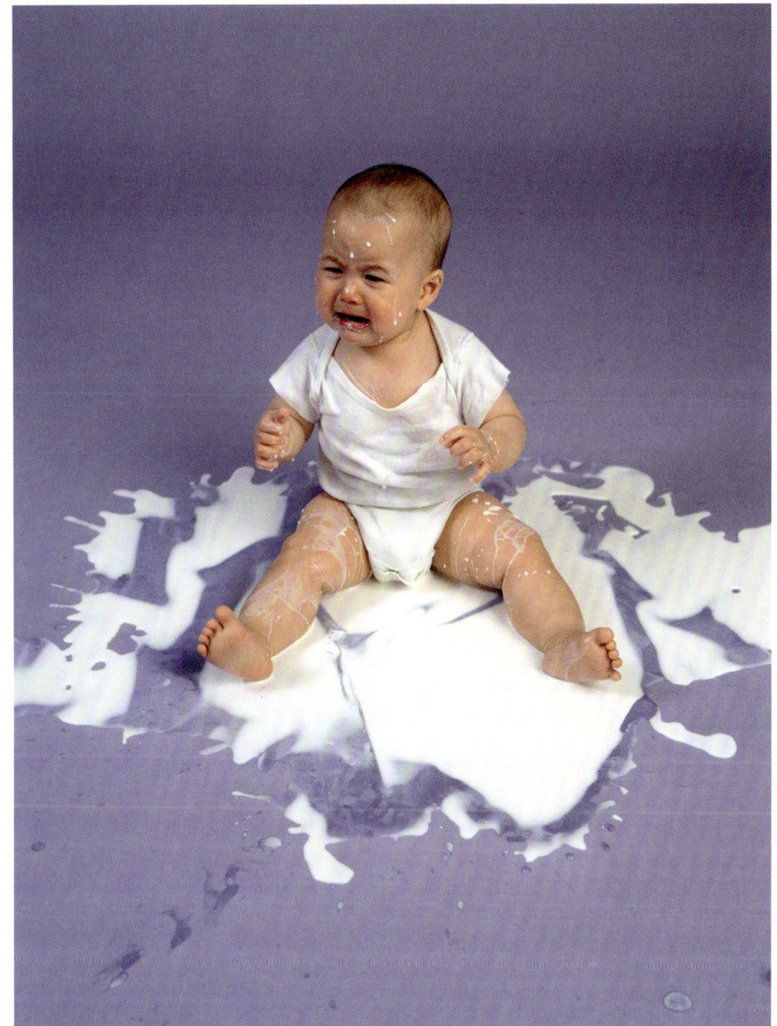

David Goldblatt
At 581 Mapetla, Soweto
1972
Gelatin silver print
25.7 × 20.3 cm
Purchase, with funds from The Schulich Foundation and The W. Garfield Weston Foundation, 2018
2018/3583

George Legrady
Inside Tipi
1973; printed 2017
Gelatin silver print
68.3 × 111.8 cm
Purchase, with funds from the Photography Curatorial Committee, 2021
2021/32

Shelley Niro
Untitled
1991
Collage: gelatin silver prints, some with applied colour, mounted to drilled board
101.6 × 152.4 cm
Purchase, with funds from the Indigenous & Canadian Curatorial Committee and the Photography Curatorial Committee, 2025

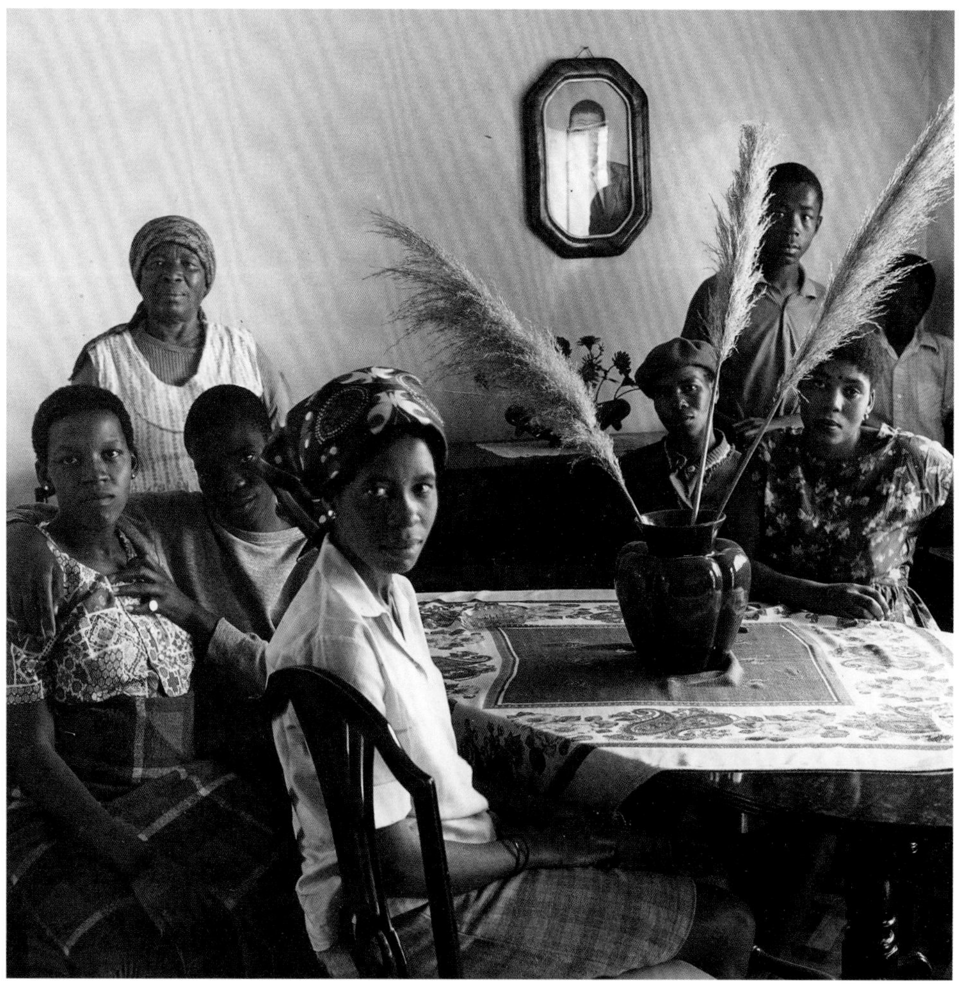

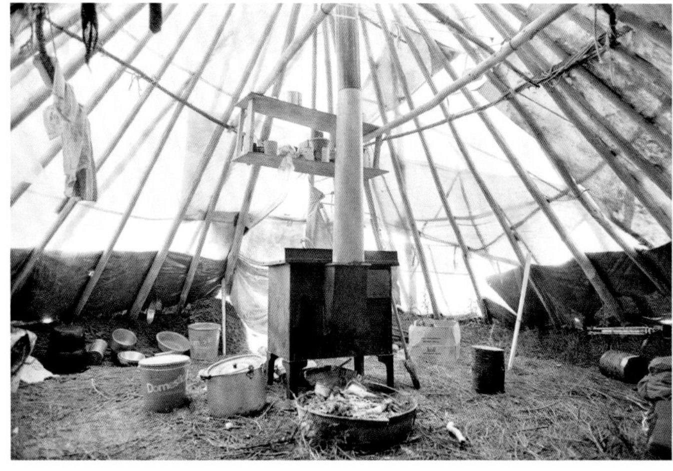

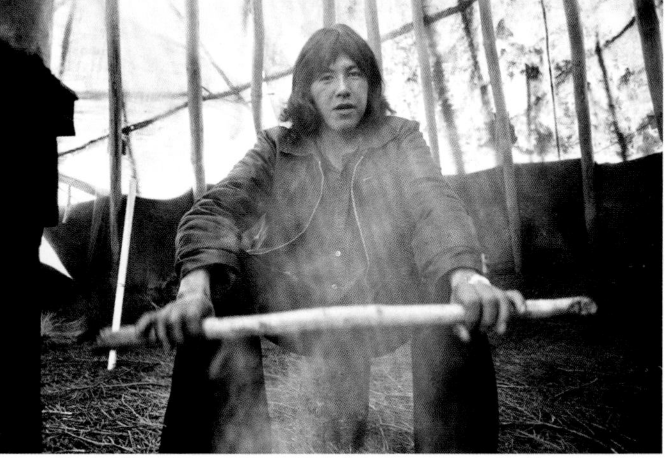

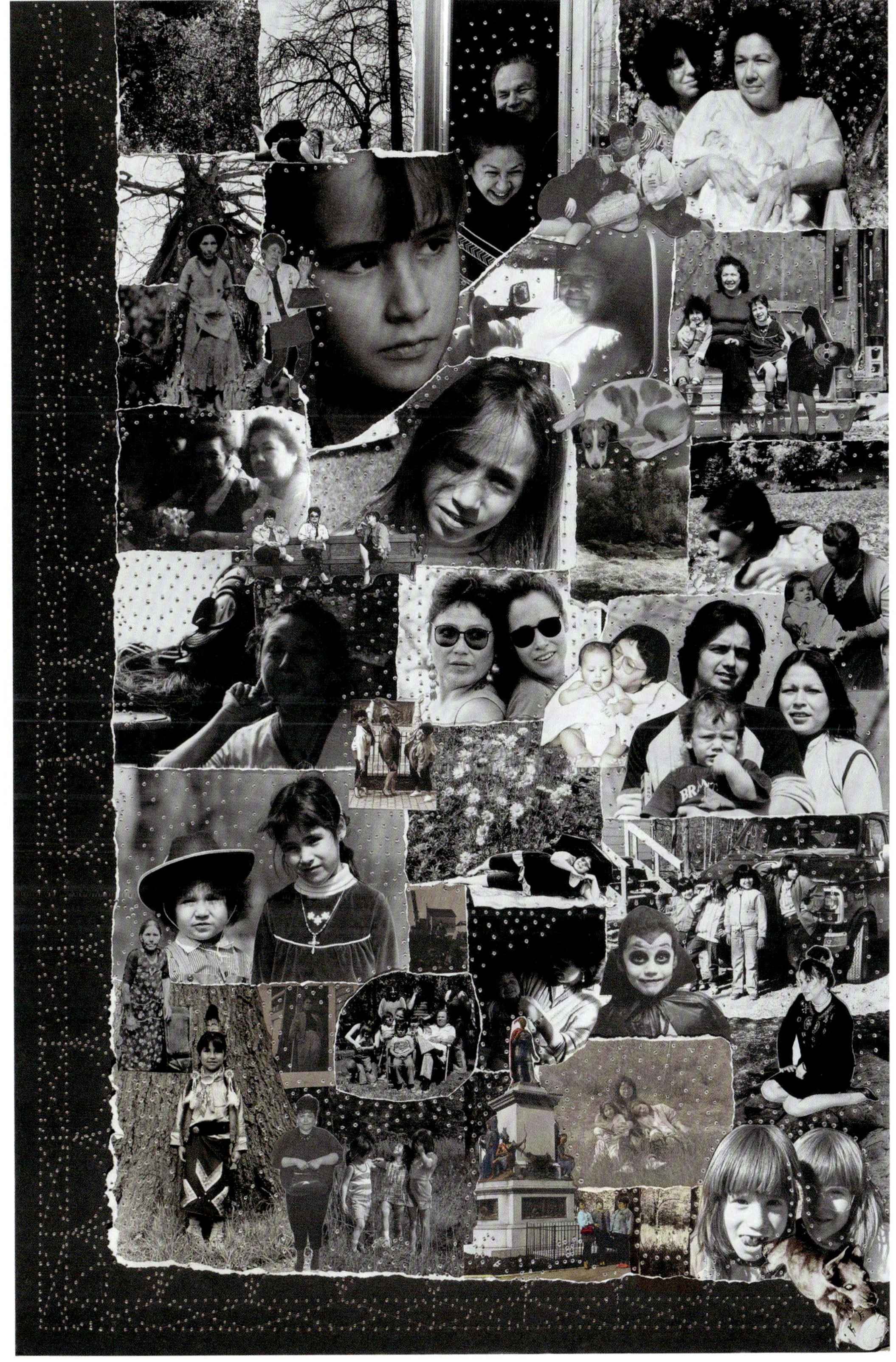

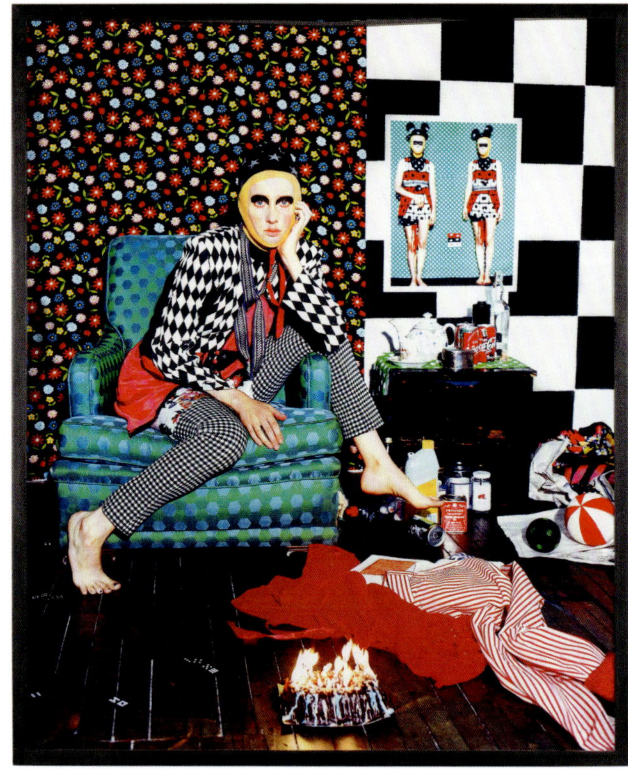

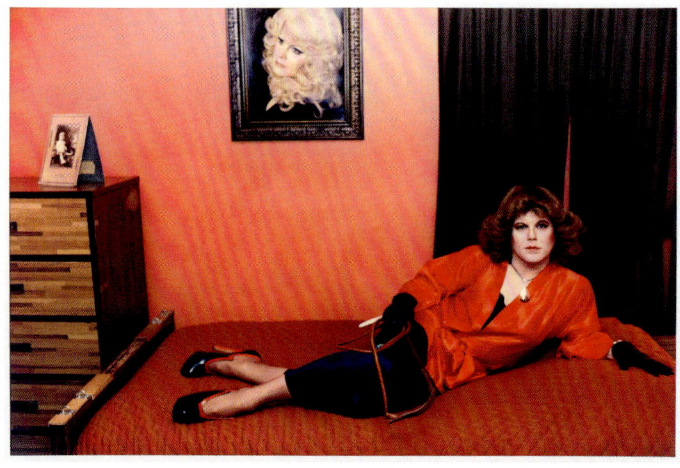

I think at the age of eight I first appeared as Salome;
at that time naked
except for yards and yards and yards of lavatory paper;
my face heavily rouged.
I found that the red ochre of the wall of the dormitory
came off and would apply it to my face
which would always achieve the very desired effect.
I made my first entrance from the one piece of furniture
apart from the bunks in the dormitory
which was a very severe cupboard
which contained hideous blue serge uniforms.
And all the boys from their bunks;
all the toughs from their upper bunks
shone their bicycle lamps on that cupboard
and I believe one or two accompanied me
with "Rustle of Spring" on their mouth organs.
The cupboard doors opened and there I was!
Wonderful dance!
Which needless to say was interrupted
by the headmaster

Janieta Eyre
Burning Cake
1999
From the series ***Lady Lazarus*** (1997–1999)
Chromogenic print
94 × 76.2 cm
Gift of the artist, 2008
2008/254

Mariette Pathy Allen
Kay (Ex-Green Beret)
1978–1989
From the series ***Transformations*** (1978–1989)
Dye transfer print
58.5 × 39.6 cm
Gift of MAVRIK CORP., 2021
2021/347.6

Jake Peters
Matou – Café Debris
1978
From ***The Lindsay Kemp Portfolio***
Silver dye bleach print with typed text
31.1 × 26 cm
Gift of Robert Sirman, 2024
2024/604

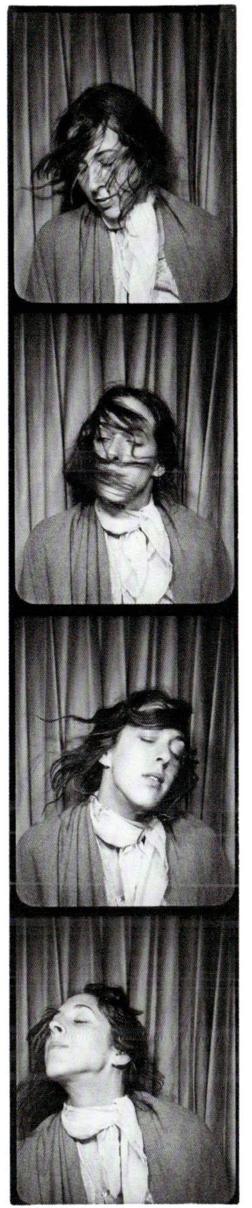
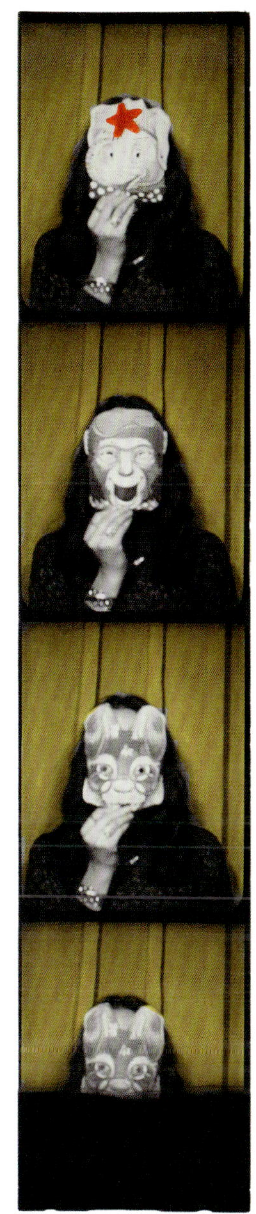
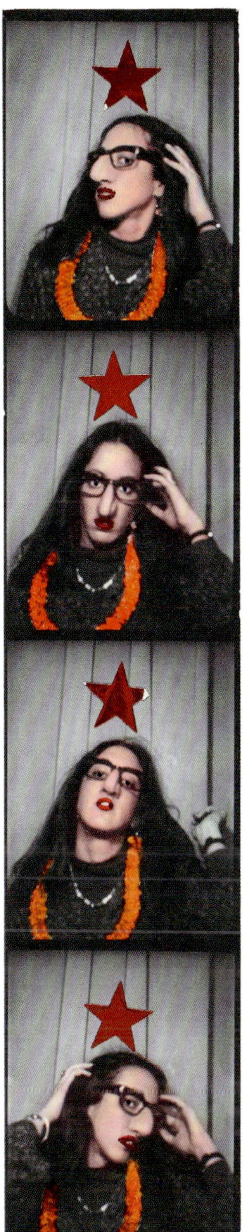
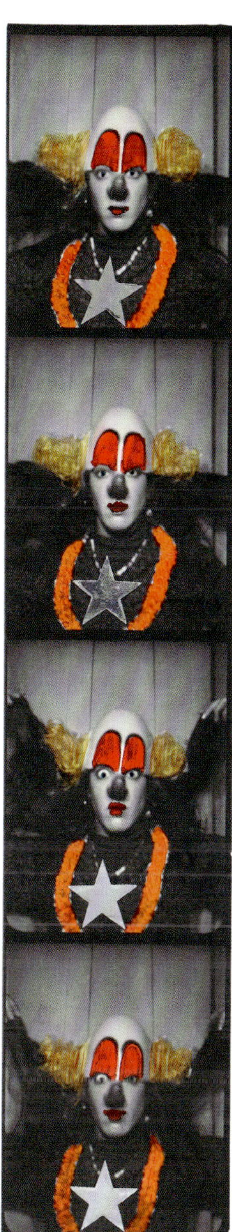
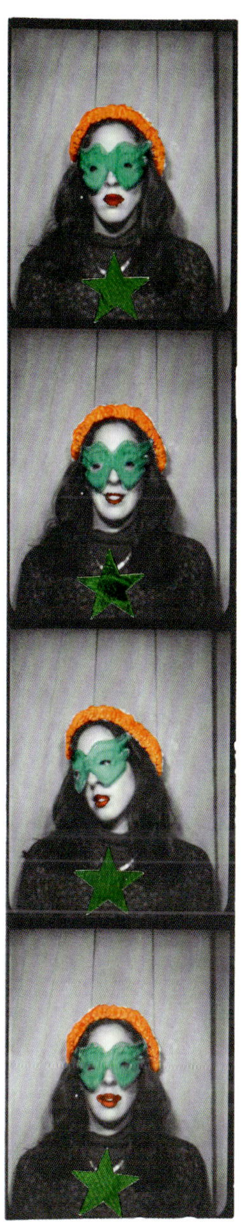

Barbara Astman
Photobooth portraits
c. 1970s
Gelatin silver prints with applied colour, stickers
20.5 × 4 cm each
Promised gift of Barbara Astman

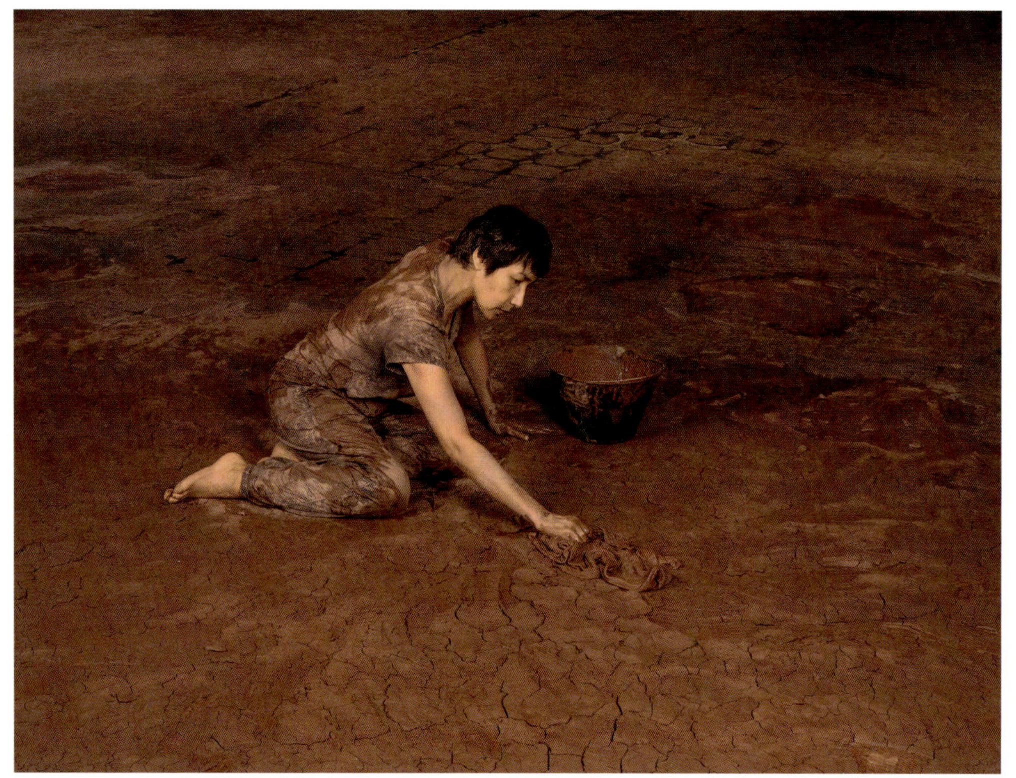

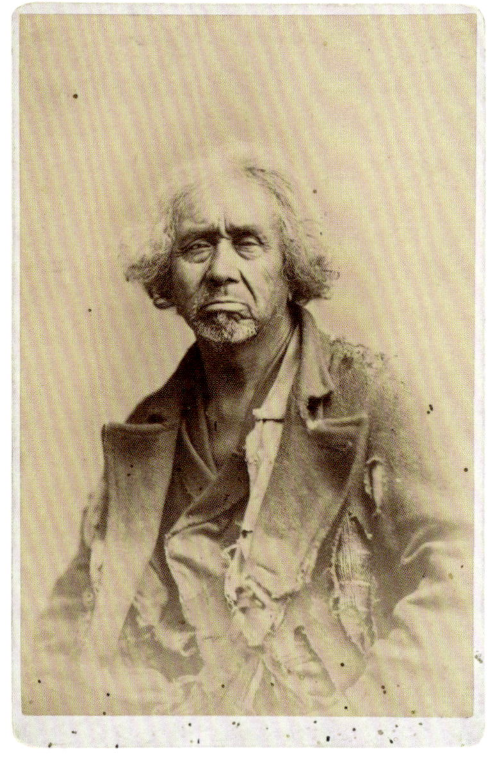

Rebecca Belmore
nindinawemaganidog (all of my relations), keeper
2017
Inkjet print
106.7 × 142.2 cm
Gift of the artist, 2022
2022/7162

Louis-Prudent Vallée
Zacharie Vincent
c. 1870
Albumen print
16.3 × 10.7 cm
Purchase, with funds donated by AGO Members, 2002
2002/48

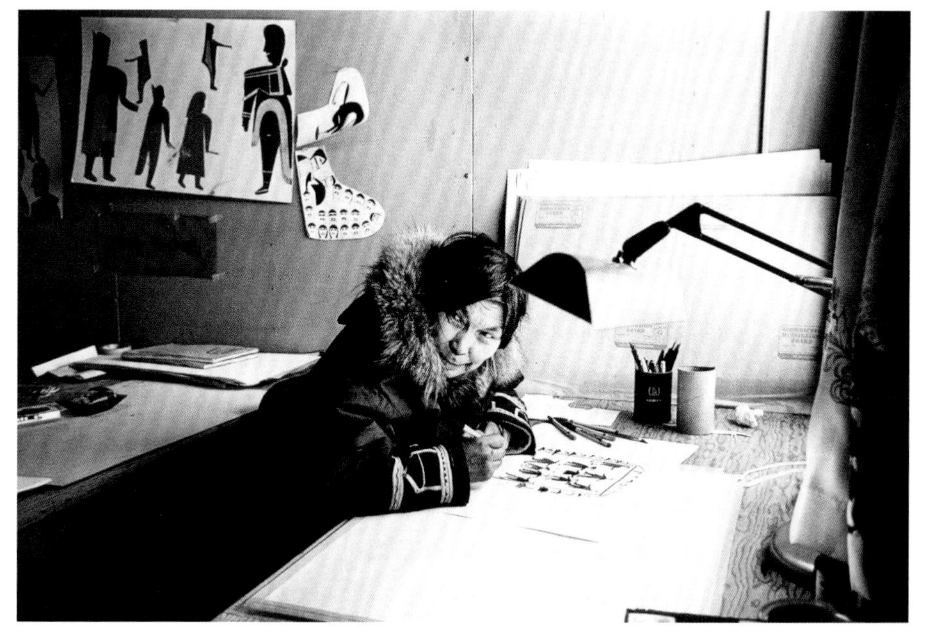

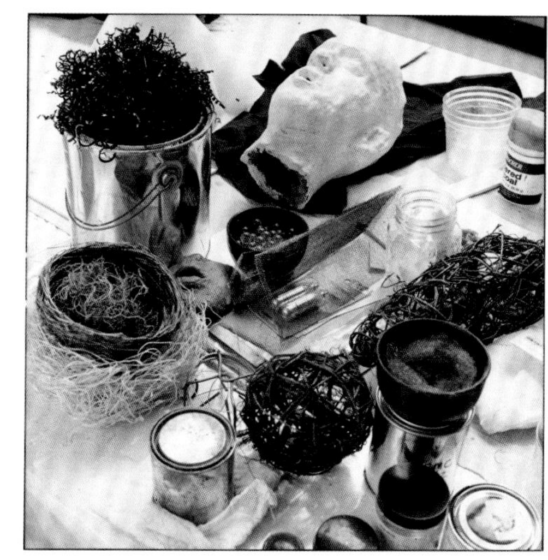

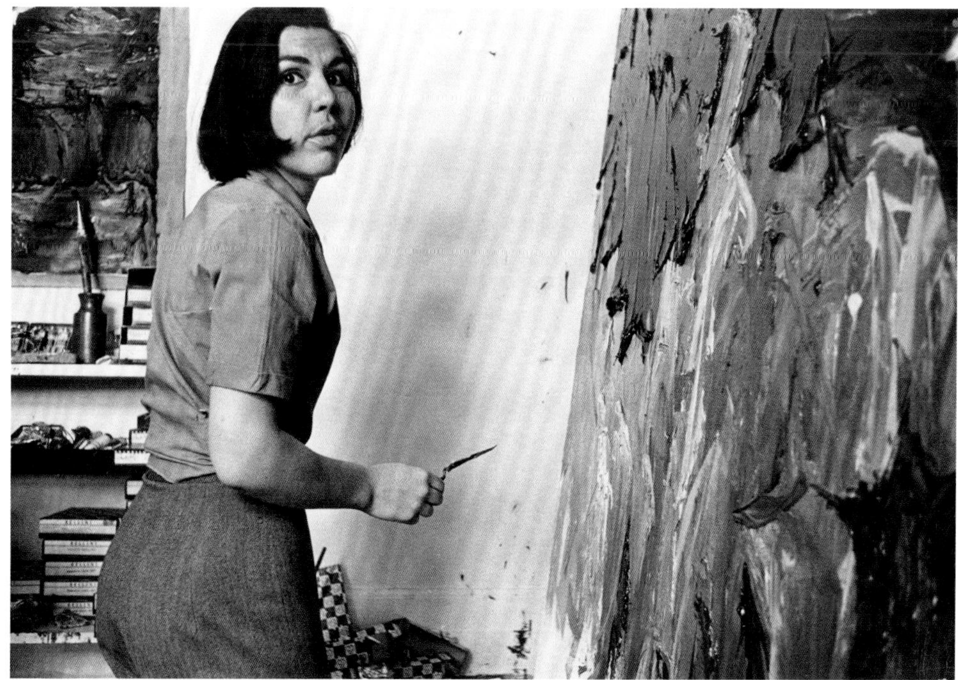

John Reeves
Untitled [Napachie Pootoogook]
1981
Selenium-toned gelatin silver print
27.9 × 35.6 cm
Gift of The Estate of Albert Gilbert CM, 2023
2023/138

Geoffrey James
Betty Goodwin's Studio, Montreal
1994
Gelatin silver print
35.8 × 38 cm
Malcolmson Collection. Gift of Harry and Ann Malcolmson in partnership with a private donor, 2014
2014/568

Tess Boudreau Taconis
Rita Letendre
Early 1960s
Gelatin silver print
23.7 × 34.8 cm
Gift of the artist, 2007
2006/463

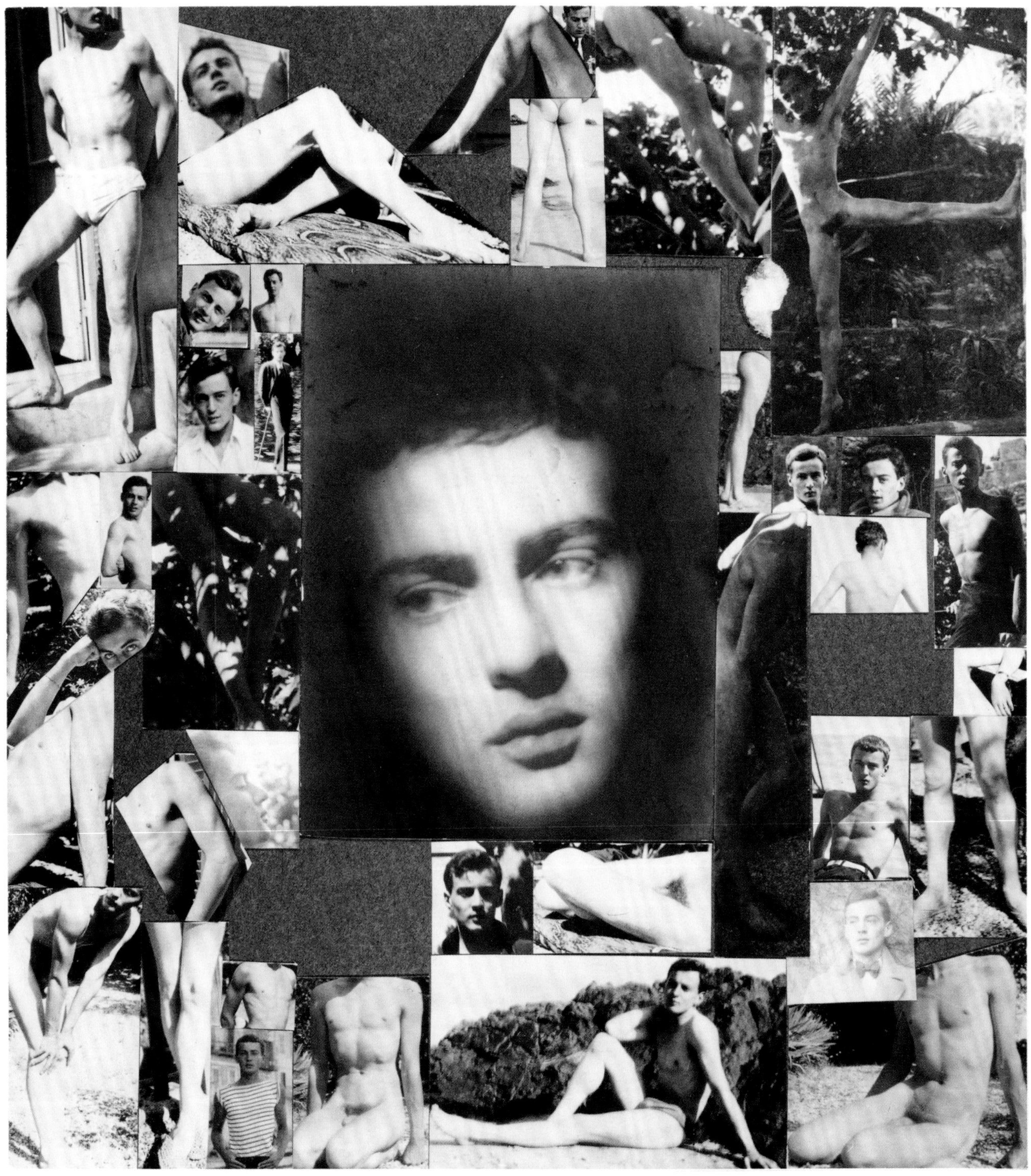

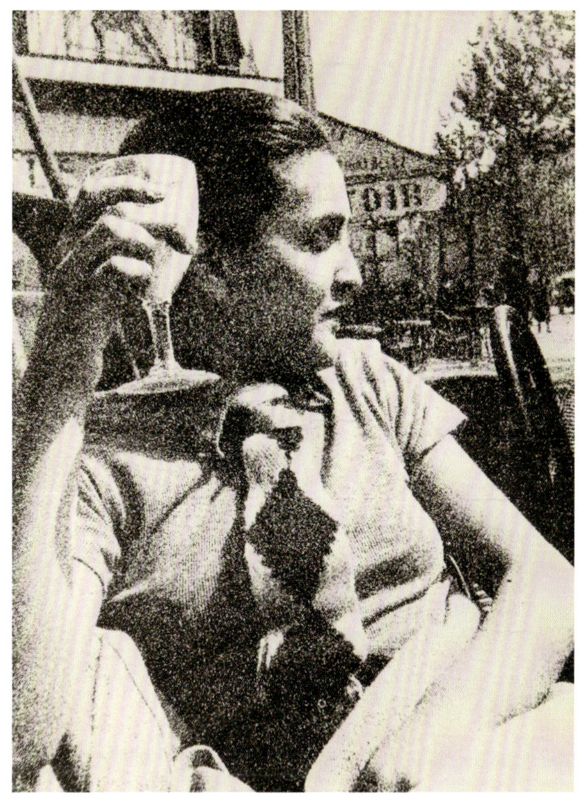

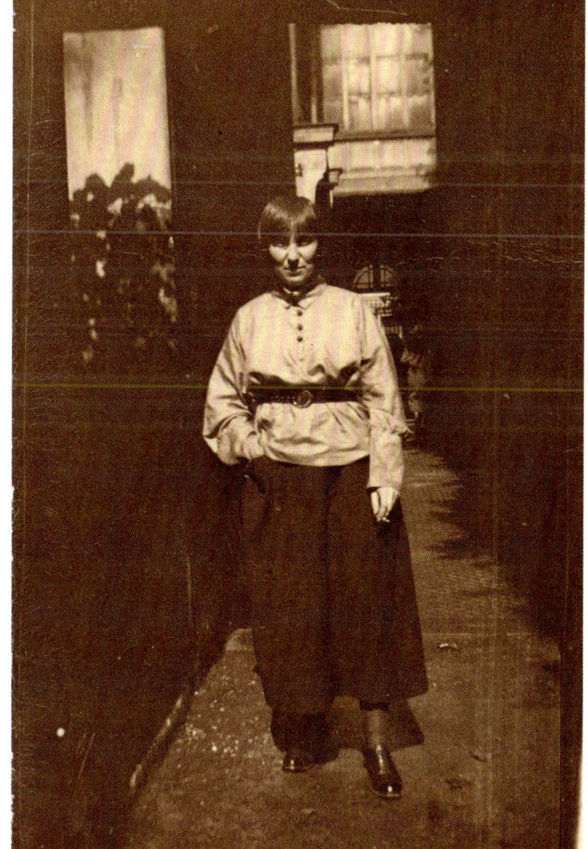

George Platt Lynes
Untitled
c. 1935
Gelatin silver print
21 × 19 cm
Gift of Jane Corkin, 2017
2017/22
(opposite)

Man Ray
Untitled [Meret Oppenheim]
1933
Gelatin silver print
23.4 × 17.4 cm
Malcolmson Collection. Gift of Harry and Ann Malcolmson in partnership with a private donor, 2014
2014/604

Claude Cahun
Portrait of Suzanne Malherbe
1927
Gelatin silver print
8.9 × 6.4 cm
Gift of Jane Corkin, in memory of Frances D. Corkin, 2013
2014/381

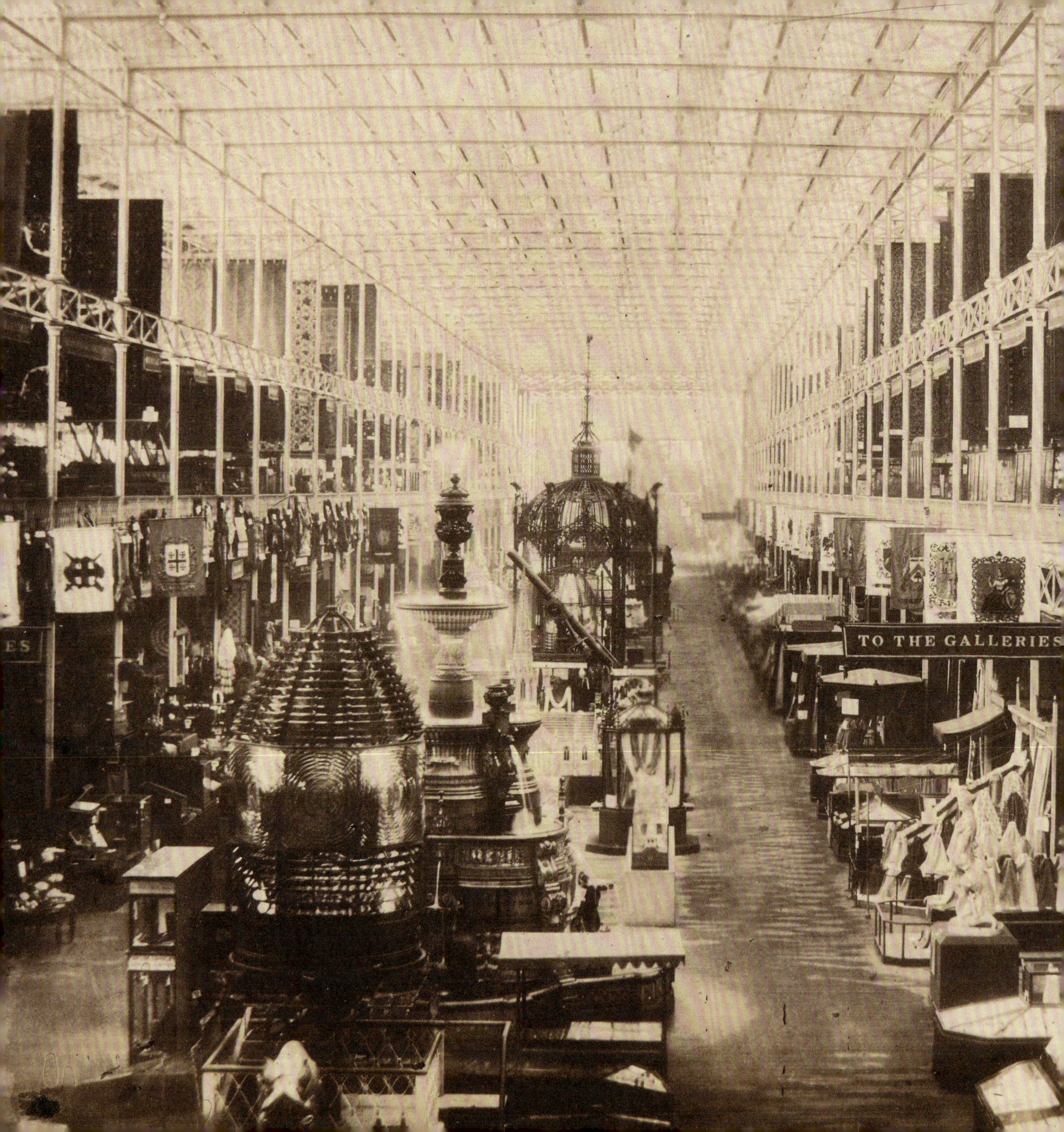
TO THE GALLERIES

Things We Make

Tal-Or Ben-Choreen

Between May and October of 1851, the streets of London were bustling as six million visitors from around the globe descended on Hyde Park to view more than 100,000 displays, coordinated by 14,000 different organizations, highlighting modern industrial feats as part of the *Great Exhibition of the Works of Industry of All Nations*. One image of the grounds showcases the intricate steel-and-glass structure of the Crystal Palace, soaring three stories high and filled with countless objects and booths, stretching far into the distance (left). The then decade-old medium of photography proved a slippery category for the judges of the exhibition, who divided it into two categories: science and art. Credited to "inventors" or "practitioners" rather than to "photographers,"[1] photography was peppered throughout the displays. The following year, a four-volume publication—the *Reports by the Juries*—was released to commemorate the exhibition. Illustrated with 154 salted paper prints, trimmed and pasted into deluxe leather-bound, gilt-stamped volumes, it marked the most ambitious application of the medium in publishing to date (pp. 104–105).[2] Print processes like lithography were widely available and could simultaneously reproduce both illustrations and text; it would have been the pragmatic choice. Opting to use photography instead signalled innovation, an embrace of industry, and a bold aesthetic choice for this modern moment.

In the late 1800s, as many embraced the new mechanical renderings of photography, people also sought ways of personalizing images. Starting with daguerreotypes, held in small cases with velvet-lined pads and brass window mats, photographs have often been housed in unique, purpose-built enclosures. Individuals soon began embellishing photographs more intricately by adding colour, creating elaborate frames, and incorporating them into albums. The appetite for colour in particular led to a surge in demand for hand-colourists, who meticulously tinted both metal and paper photographs.[3] Working with negatives, retouchers could also seamlessly omit or introduce new information to the picture, and skilled printers could combine negatives to create a scene impossible for the camera to capture because of exposure requirements, the scale of the object, or elaborate creative desires. Further interventions include added inscriptions, or cutting up prints to combine them into collages.[4]

These acts of mediation remind us of the people who made these objects. Indeed, our profound personal connections with images led to "pop photographica."[5] Created independently or mass-produced, photographic images were incorporated into functional everyday objects, such as teacups, switchblades, jewellery, and clocks (pp. 114 and 117). These objects make clear that the medium has always been a tool of com-

Claude-Marie Ferrier
View of Western Nave (detail)
1851
Salted paper print
21.5 × 16.4 cm
Anonymous Gift, 2007
2007/1940.4.1

Raymond Boisjoly
From age to age, as its shape slowly unravelled (detail)
2015
Inkjet prints on vinyl, installed: 7
Various dimensions
Purchase, with funds from the Photography Curatorial Committee, 2021
2021/103

memoration connected to consumerism and industry. Today, we continue to embed photographs into a variety of objects, perhaps most notably the smartphone screensaver protecting the thousands of photographs we carry in our pockets.

Photography was likewise adapted for scientific studies,[6] applied in place of drawings and documentation plasters. Amateur and professional scientists soon sought to extend the capabilities of human vision, creating experiments staged specifically for the camera and leading to technological advancements such as faster shutters, more sensitive emulsions, telescopic lenses, and artificial lights. Works by Étienne-Jules Marey (pp. 123–124) and Harold Edgerton (p. 125) showcase these innovations in arresting and original ways.

Enthusiasm for scientific photographs was matched by a desire to document industrial progress and expansion in depictions of architecture, railroads, bridges, mining scenes, machinery, and consumer goods,[7] typically presented to celebrate the innovations and technological advancement. Today, such images reflect two centuries of design—revealing shifting styles and engineering feats across countless disciplines—and trace global trade and markets through the circulation of materials.

Artists also adopted strategies to disrupt or call attention to the medium's mechanization. Dadaists such as Hannah Höch (p. 120) collected and collaged images to create new compositions.[8] Photographers such as Kelani Abass (p. 115) adopted forgotten chemistries or rejected the paper substrate and straight photographic approach, making unique objects and sculptures.[9] Further interventions include the application of paint, multiple and camera-less exposures, combination printing, and other darkroom manipulations.

With all of these potential uses, it is unsurprising that photography's categorization baffled the jury of the Great Exhibition. Since its invention in 1839, photography has positioned the advent of new machines and mechanical processes alongside the imagination of new potentials, which has forever changed our vision of the world. Indeed, the medium has always balanced incorporated aspects of technological innovation and creativity. The works in this section explore the things we make, calling attention to photography's materiality in relation to technological progress, human innovation, and the infinite potential they spark.

1. Anthony Hamber explained of the jury process, "They settled on a structure of four divisions, made up of thirty Classes segmented into sub-classes. It is significant that the *Official Descriptive and Illustrated Catalogue of the Great Exhibition of the Works of Industry of All Nations* did not use the term 'Photographers,' classifying a number of photographers as 'Producers' of photographs. One of the Leading London photographers to exhibit, Antoine Claudet (1797–1867), was described as an 'Inventor.'" Anthony Hamber, *Photography and the 1851 Great Exhibition* (London : V&A Publishing, 2018), 2.
2. Ibid. See also Jill Offenbeck, "The 'Reports by the Juries': A Finding Aid for a Publication from the Great Exhibition of 1851, in the Collection of the Art Gallery of Ontario," MA diss. (Toronto: Ryerson University, 2011; now Toronto Metropolitan University).
3. Heinz K. Henisch and Bridget A. Henisch, *The Painted Photograph, 1839–1914: Origins, Techniques, Aspirations* (University Park: Penn State University Press, 1996).
4. Mia Fineman, *Faking It: Manipulated Photography before Photoshop* (New York: Metropolitan Museum of Art, 2012).
5. Daile Kaplan, *Pop Photographica: Photography's Objects in Everyday Life, 1842–1969*, with an introduction by Maia-Mari Sutnik (Toronto: Art Gallery of Ontario, 2003).
6. Jennifer Tucker, *Nature Exposed: Photography as Eyewitness in Victorian Science* (Baltimore: John Hopkins University Press, 2013); Ann Thomas, *Beauty of Another Order: Photography in Science*, with essays by Marta Braun et al. (New Haven, CT: Yale University Press, 1997).
7. Peter H. Christensen, *Precious Metal: German Steel, Modernity, and Ecology* (University Park: Penn State University Press, 2022).
8. Leah Dickerman, *Dada: Zurich, Berlin, Hannover, Cologne, New York, Paris*, illus. ed., with essays by Brigid Doherty et al. (Washington, DC: National Gallery of Art / DAP, 2008).
9. William Green, "Looking Backward & Looking Forward: Process Photography in the United States, ca. 1970," PhD diss. (New Brunswick, NJ: Rutgers University, 2024); Mary Statzer, *The Photographic Object, 1970* (Berkeley: University of California Press, 2016).

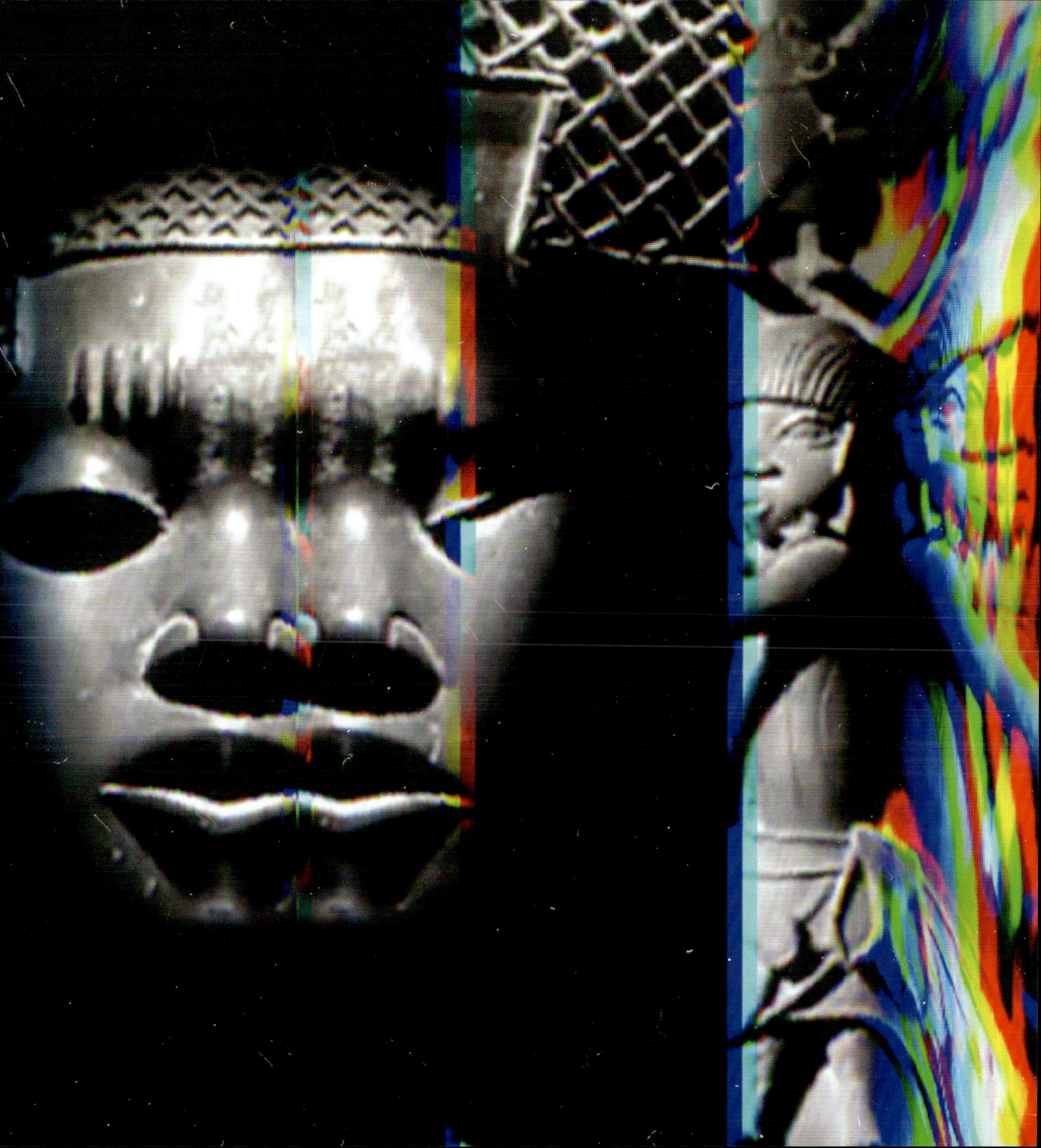

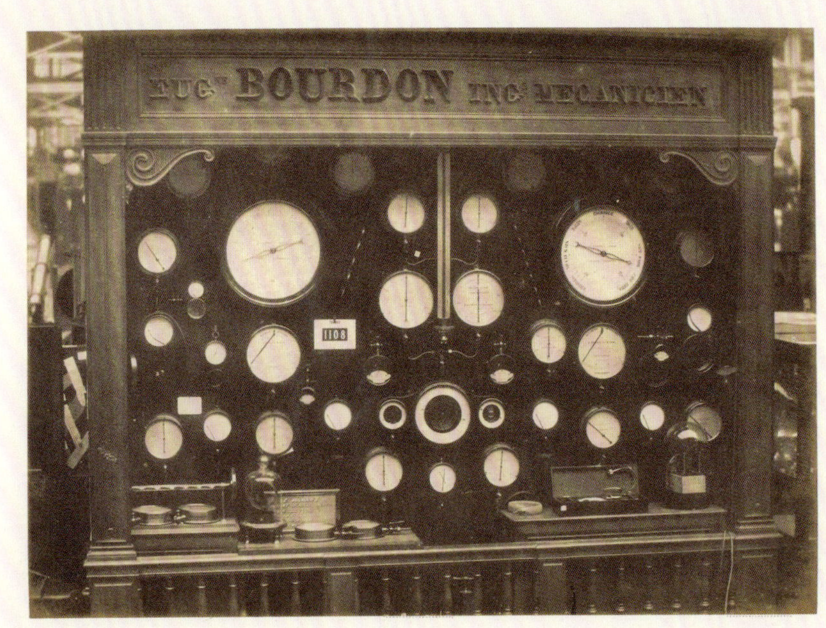

METALLIC BAROMETERS. BOURDON.

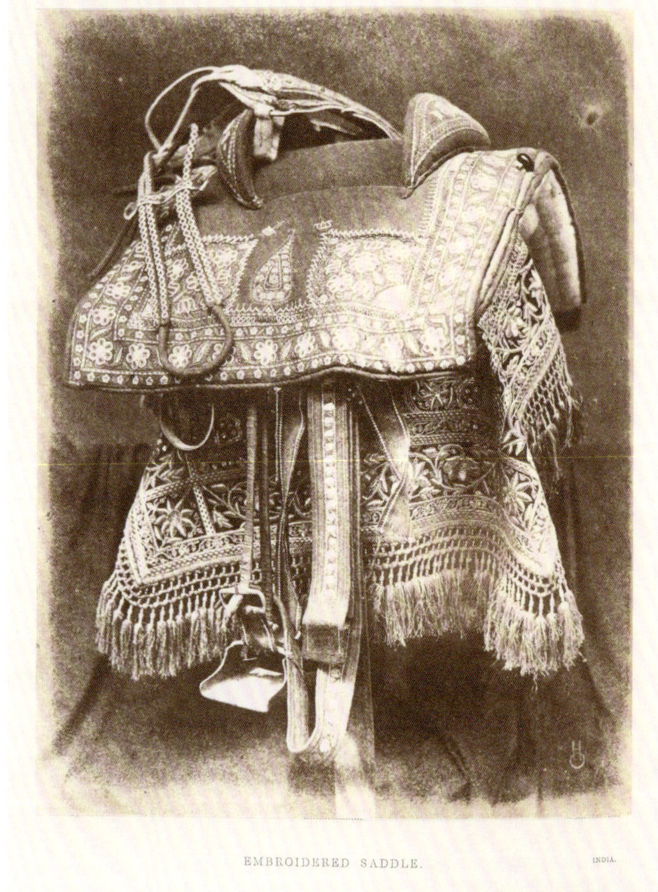

EMBROIDERED SADDLE. INDIA.

Claude-Marie Ferrier
Metallic Barometers, Bourdon
c. 1851
Salted paper print
14.4 × 19.9 cm
Anonymous Gift, 2007
2007/1940.2.37

Hugh Owen
Embroidered Saddle (2)
c. 1851
Salted paper print
22.3 × 17 cm
Anonymous Gift, 2007
2007/1940.3.5

Claude-Marie Ferrier
Double Jacquard Loom, Barlow
c. 1851
Salted paper print
20.9 × 16.2 cm
Anonymous Gift, 2007
2007/1940.2.12

Claude-Marie Ferrier
Disc of Flint Glass, Chance Brothers and Co.
c. 1851
Salted paper print
17.2 × 14.6 cm
Anonymous Gift, 2007
2007/1940.2.33

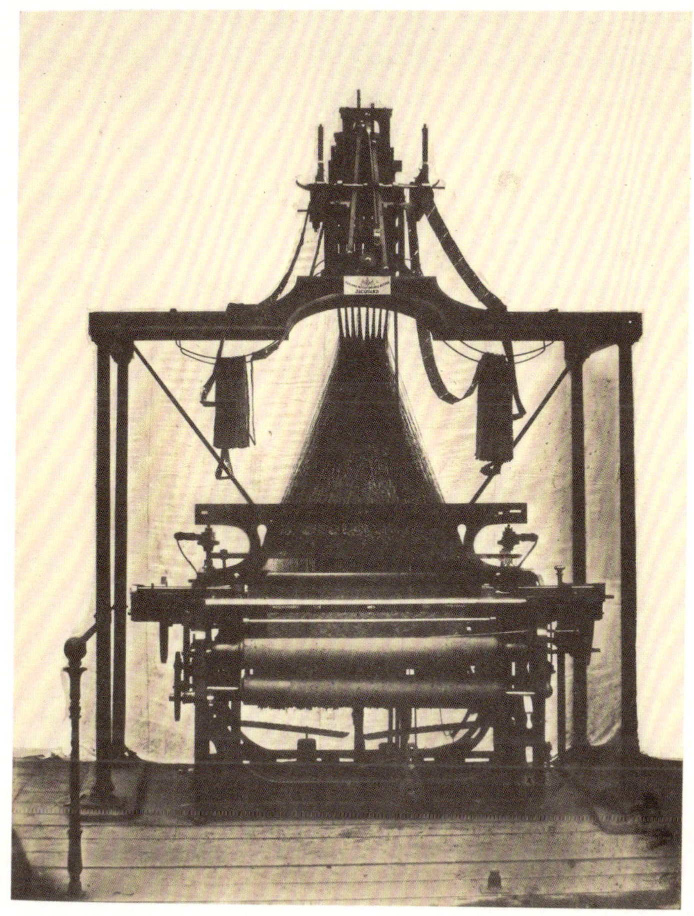

DOUBLE JACQUARD LOOM. BARLOW.

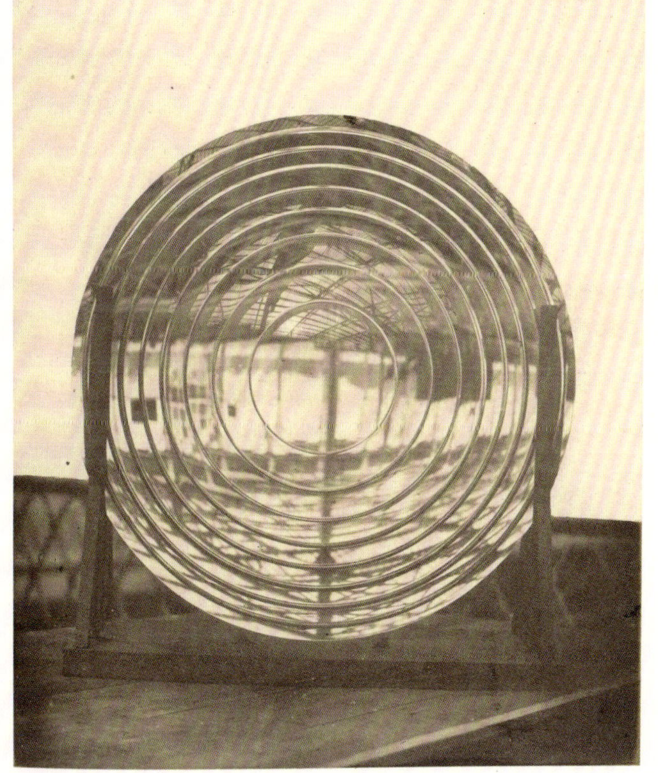

DISC OF FLINT GLASS. CHANCE BROTHERS AND CO.

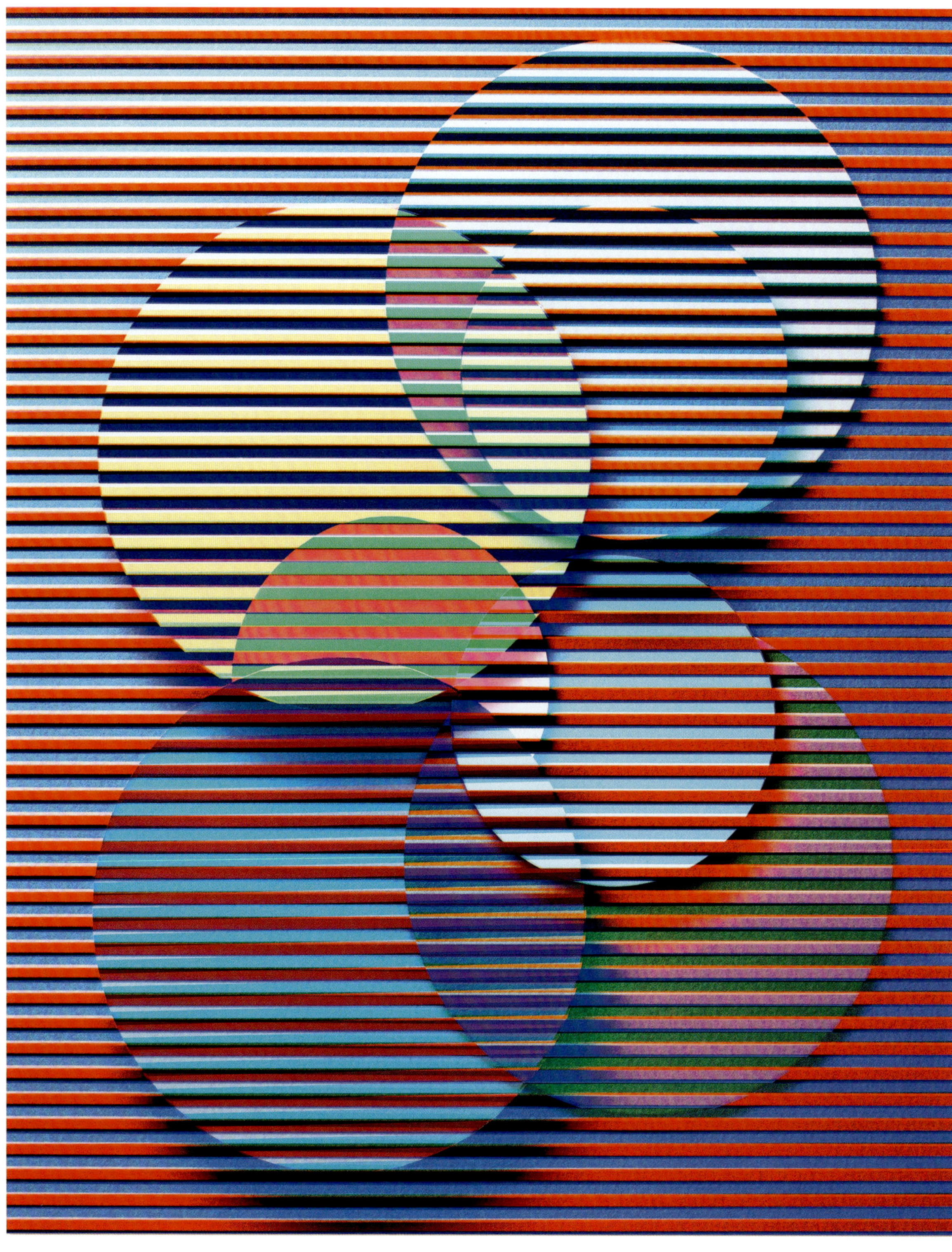

Jessica Eaton
Transition H45
2016
Pigment print
127 × 101.5 cm
Purchased with the financial assistance of the Dr. Michael Braudo Canadian Contemporary Art Fund and the Art Toronto 2016 Opening Night Preview, 2016
2016/159

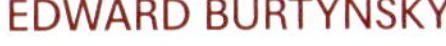

EDWARD BURTYNSKY

Since the 1980s, Toronto's Edward Burtynsky has photographed landscapes reshaped by industrialization—mining sites, manufacturing zones, and expanding cities. His images reveal the profound impact of human activity and how technology and large-scale development are intertwined. The collection holds works documenting these transformations in both rural and urban settings.

Edward Burtynsky
Manufacturing #17, Deda Chicken Processing Plant, Dehui City, Jilin Province, China
2005
From the series ***China*** (2004-2006)
Chromogenic print
121.9 × 182.9 cm
Gift of Edward Burtynsky, 2007
2007/334

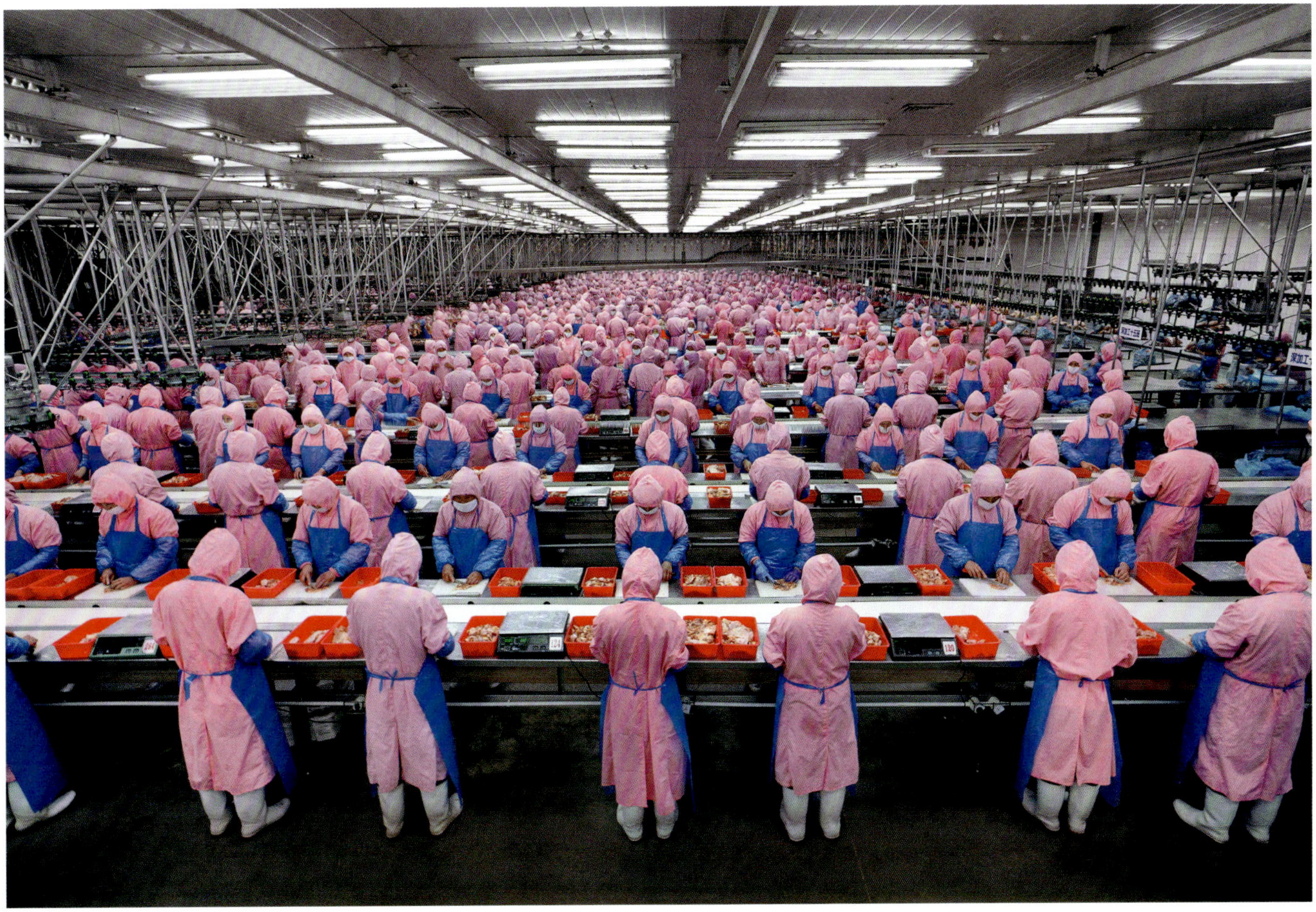

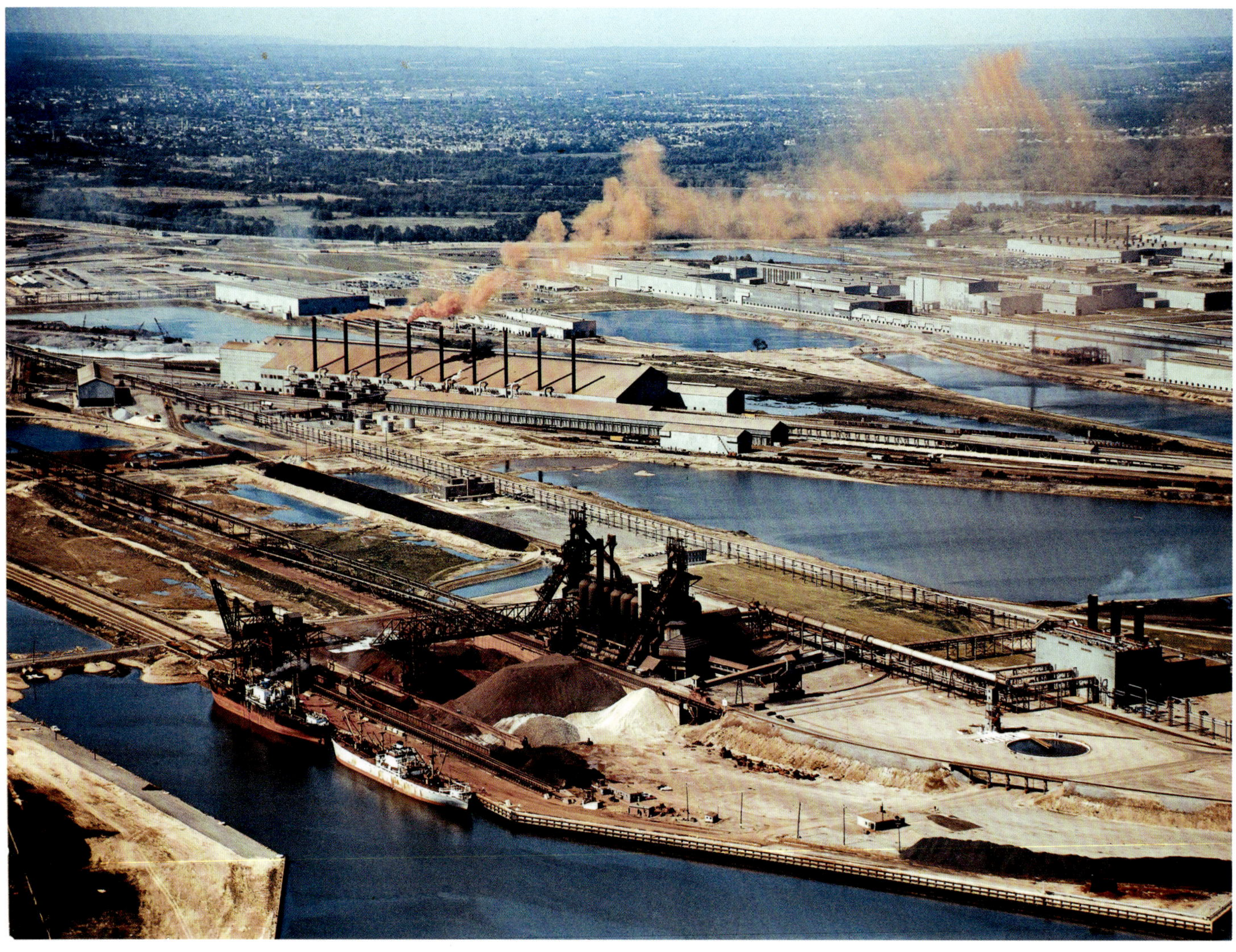

George Hunter
Dofasco and Stelco steel mills, Hamilton, Ontario
1954
Dye transfer print
31.2 × 42.1 cm
Gift of George Hunter, R.C.A., 2010
2010/260

Ralph Greenhill
Prince of Wales Bridge, Ottawa, Ontario
1977
From the series ***Aspects of Industrial Archeology: Machines and Structures*** (1977–1984)
Gelatin silver print
22.6 × 17.4 cm
Gift of Av Isaacs, 2008
2008/165

Photographer once known
"Big Mack"
c. 1940
Cyanotype
30.3 × 25.1 cm
Gift of David Moore and Ross Winter / Camera Lucida, 2007
2007/310

Robert Bourdeau
Lorraine, France
1999
From the series ***Industrial Sites*** (1990–1999)
Gold-toned gelatin silver print
28 × 35.4 cm
Gift of Sean and Jenna Bourdeau, 2018
2019/2485

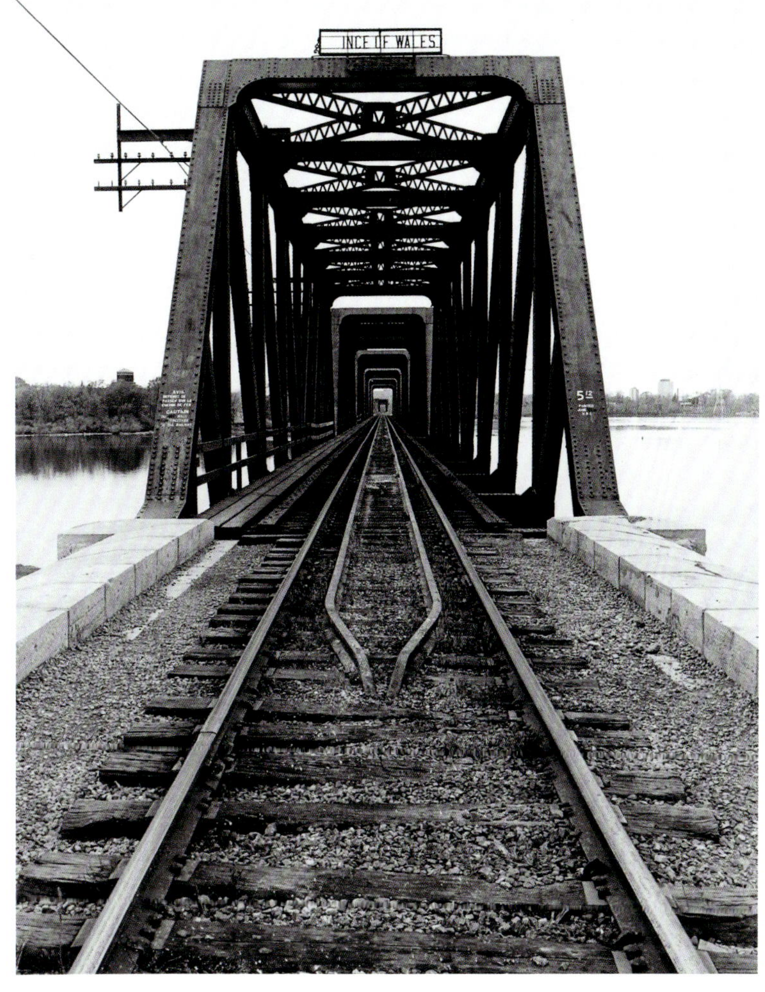
INCE OF WALES

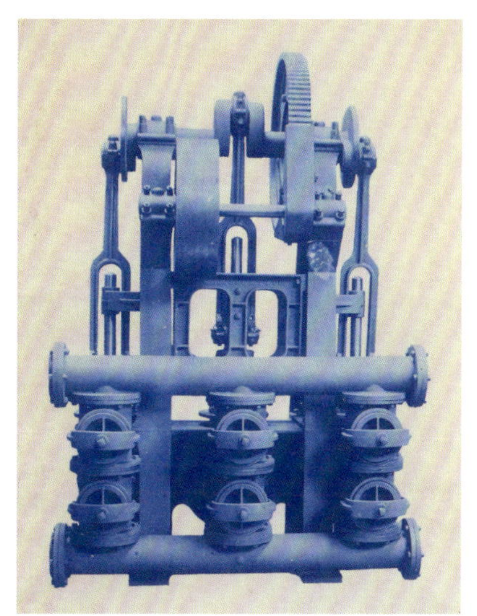

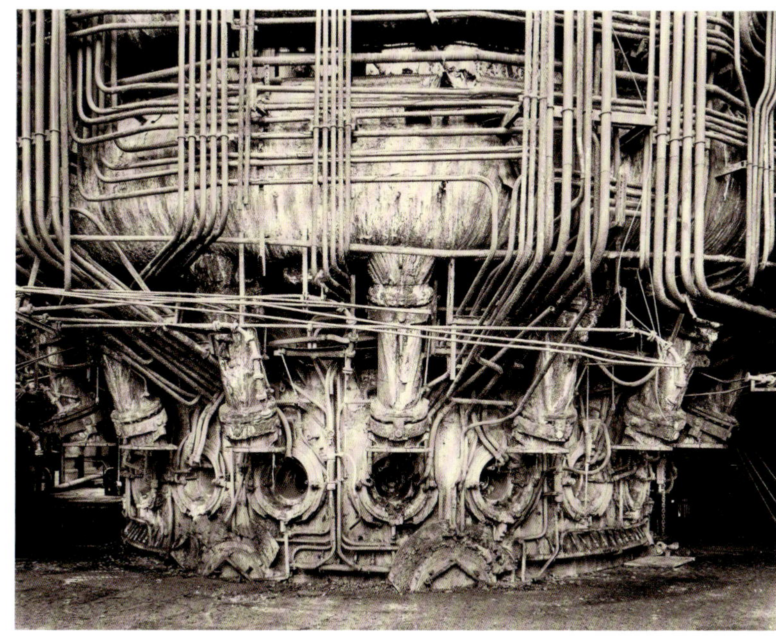

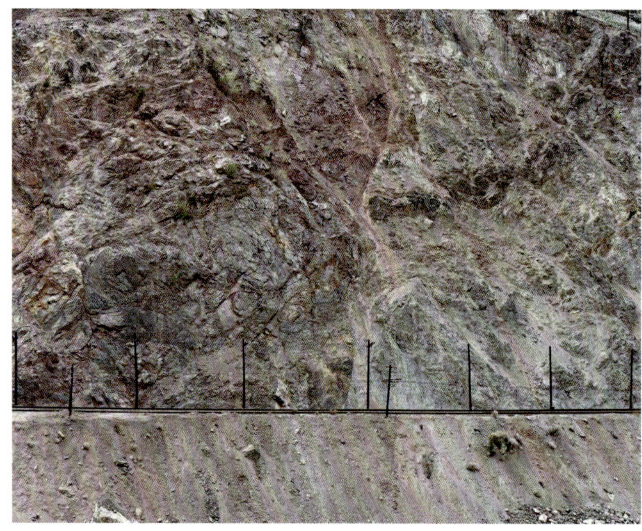

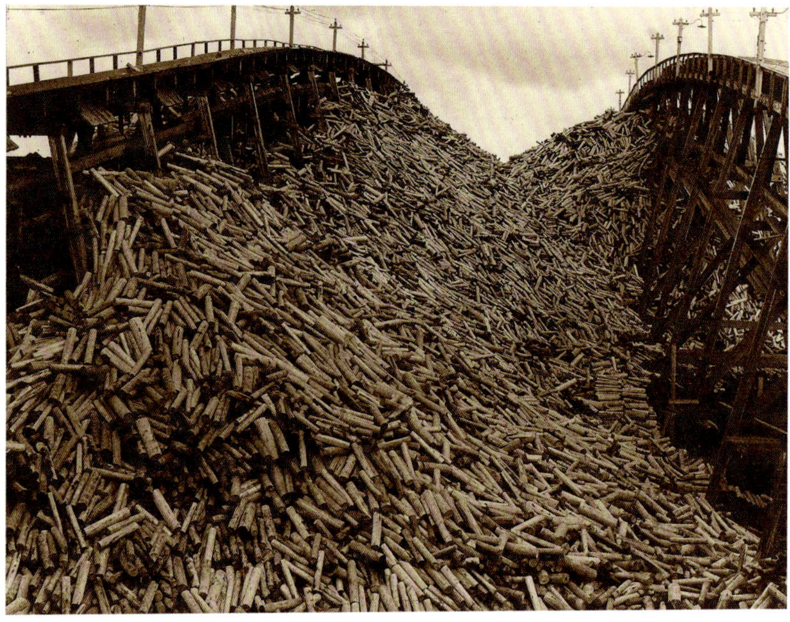

Edward Burtynsky
Railcuts #2, C.N. Track, Thompson River, British Columbia, Canada
1985
From the series ***Railcuts*** (1983-1985)
Chromogenic print
76.2 × 101 cm
Gift of Edward Burtynsky, 1994
94/881

J.C.M. Hayward
Wood Pile
1912
Pulp Pile at Botwood
1912
From the album ***Operations of the Anglo Newfoundland Development Company***
Album: 48 gelatin silver prints
41 × 54 × 5.5 cm
Anonymous Gift, 2008
2008/1144.1-48

Berenice Abbott
Manhattan Bridge, Pier 21, Pennsylvania Railroad
1937
Gelatin silver print
19 × 24.2 cm
Gift of Maia-Mari Sutnik, 2021
2021/349

THE ANGLO NEWFOUNDLAND DEVELOPMENT COMPANY COLLECTION

The Anglo Newfoundland Development Company Collection offers a rare glimpse into industrial expansion in Newfoundland. Established in 1905 to supply raw paper to British newspapers amid political instability in Europe, the company played a critical role in securing newsprint. Assembled by the Beeton family, the photographs—many by Newfoundland-born J.C.M. Hayward—reflect both the scale of the enterprise and their personal engagement with photography.

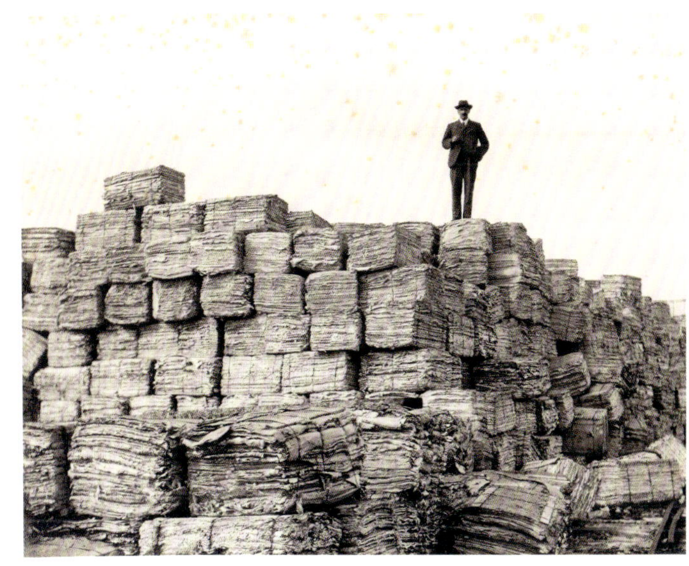

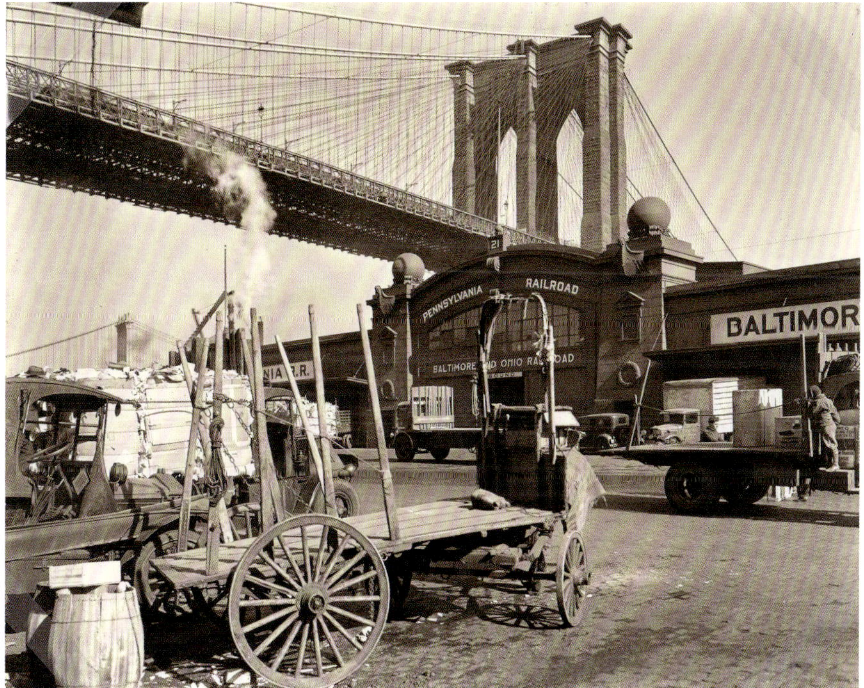
PENNSYLVANIA RAILROAD
BALTIMORE AND OHIO RAILROAD
BALTIMOR

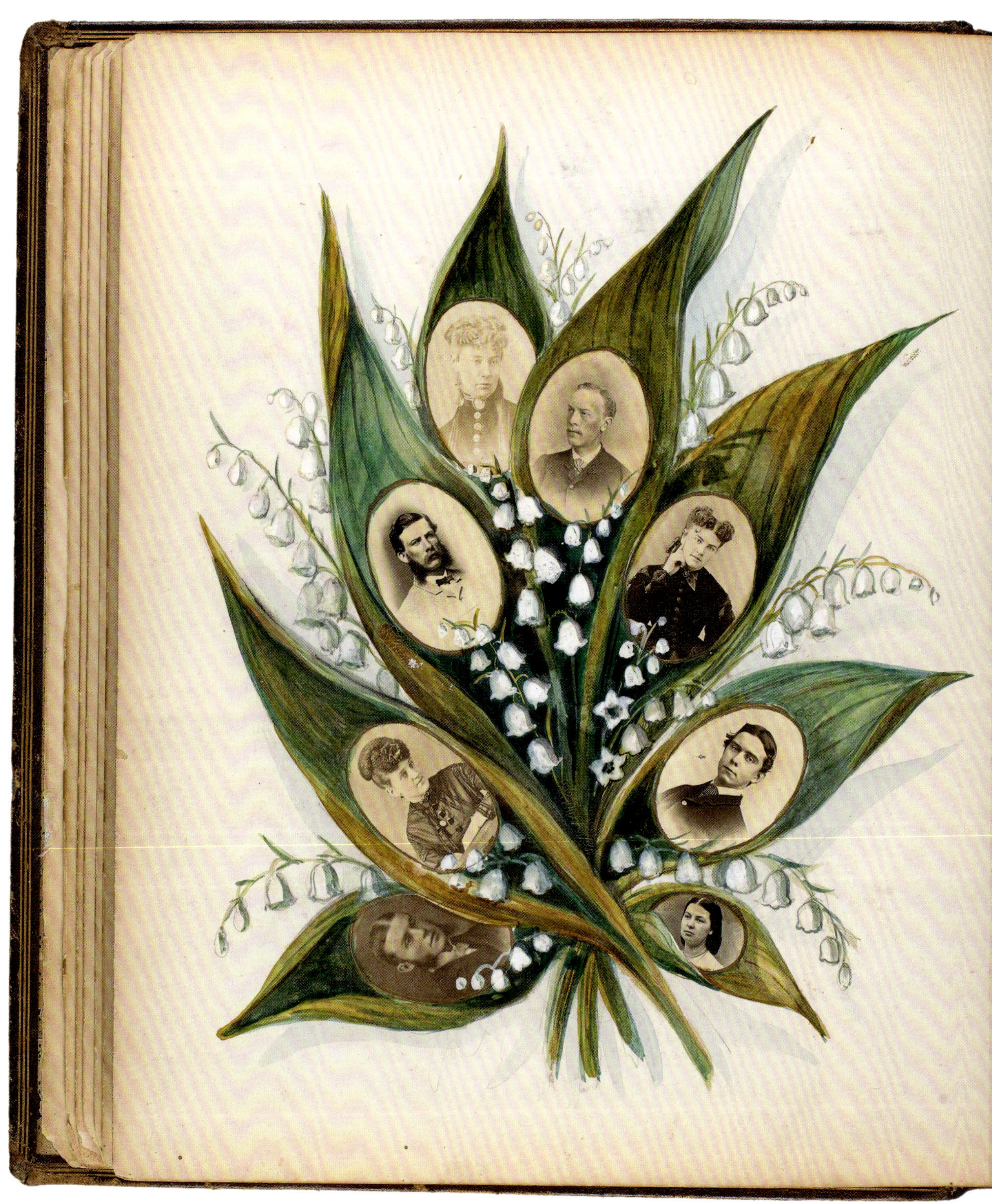

Caroline Walker
C.W. Bell Album
1875
Album: leather bound, gold embossed detailing; 31 albumen prints, watercolour, black ink
33 × 28 × 3.3 cm
Purchase, donated funds in memory of Eric Steiner, 2003
2003/1.12–2003/1.13

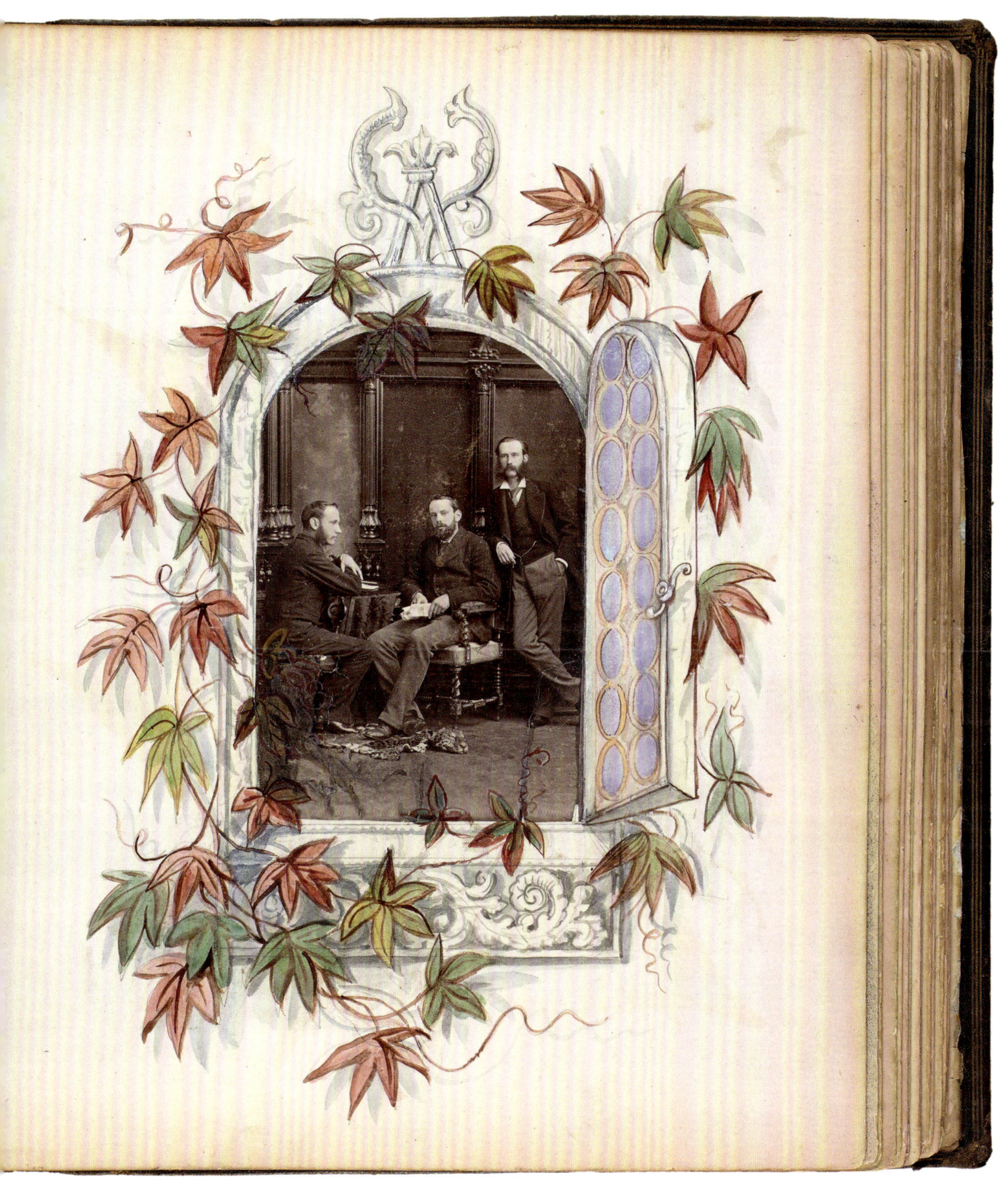

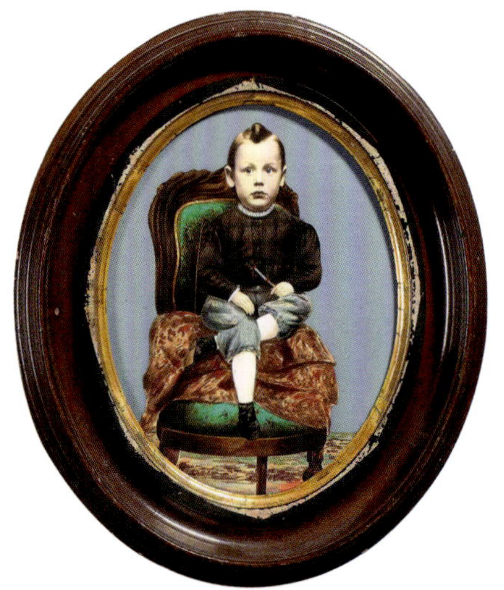

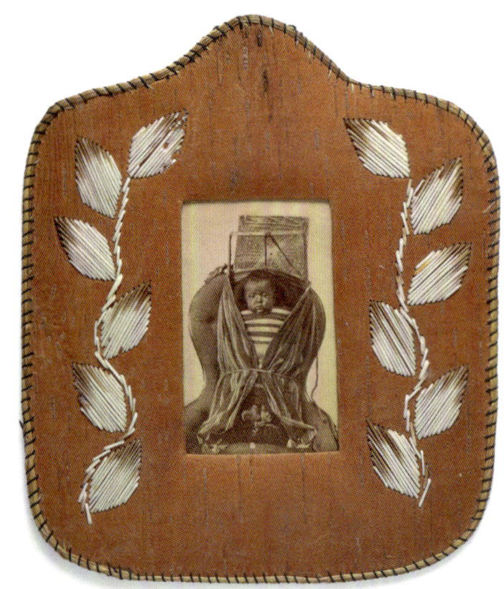

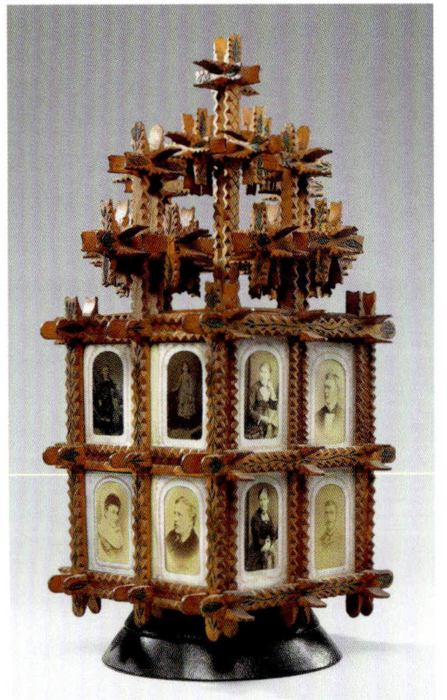

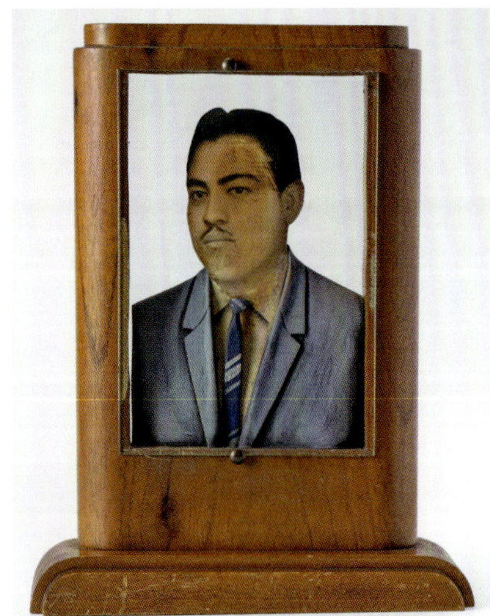

Clockwise from upper left:
Maker once known
Portrait of a boy
c. 1870
Bromide print, watercolour, gouache, on paperboard
23.5 × 18.3 cm
Anonymous Gift, 2006
2006/205

Edric L. Eaton
Sioux Child on Cradleboard
c. 1871
Carte de visite: albumen print in birch bark and quill decorated frame
18.5 × 15.8 cm
Purchase, 2012
2012/22

Maker once known
Fotoescultura
c. 1940–1950
Gelatin silver print with applied colour adhered to carved, polychrome wood (mahogany or mahogany imitation) mount with glass
30 × 24 × 8 cm
Purchase, 2023
2023/173

Maker once known
Tramp Art Photo Display
c. 1885
Cartes de visite: albumen prints, tintypes with applied colour, wood, glass, and paper crown of thorn design with paint applied to rotating base and carved leaf and vine details
63 × 36.5 × 36.5 cm
Purchase, 2011
2011/34

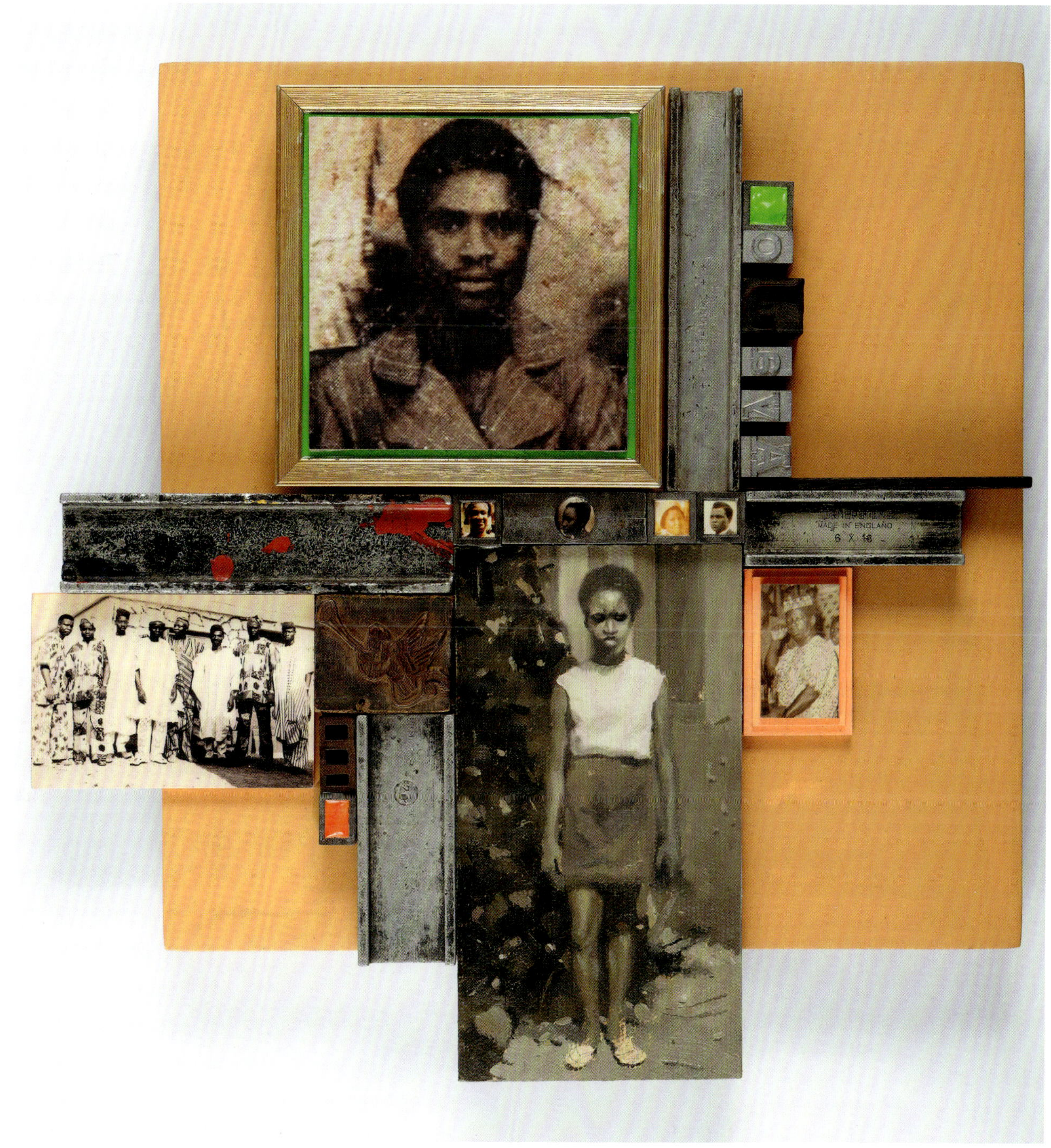

Kelani Abass
Scrap of Evidence, Ayajo
2021
Inkjet prints, oil on canvas, cornerstone, rubber block, antique frame
30 × 35 cm
Purchase, with funds from Friends of Global Africa and the Diaspora, 2022
2022/7085

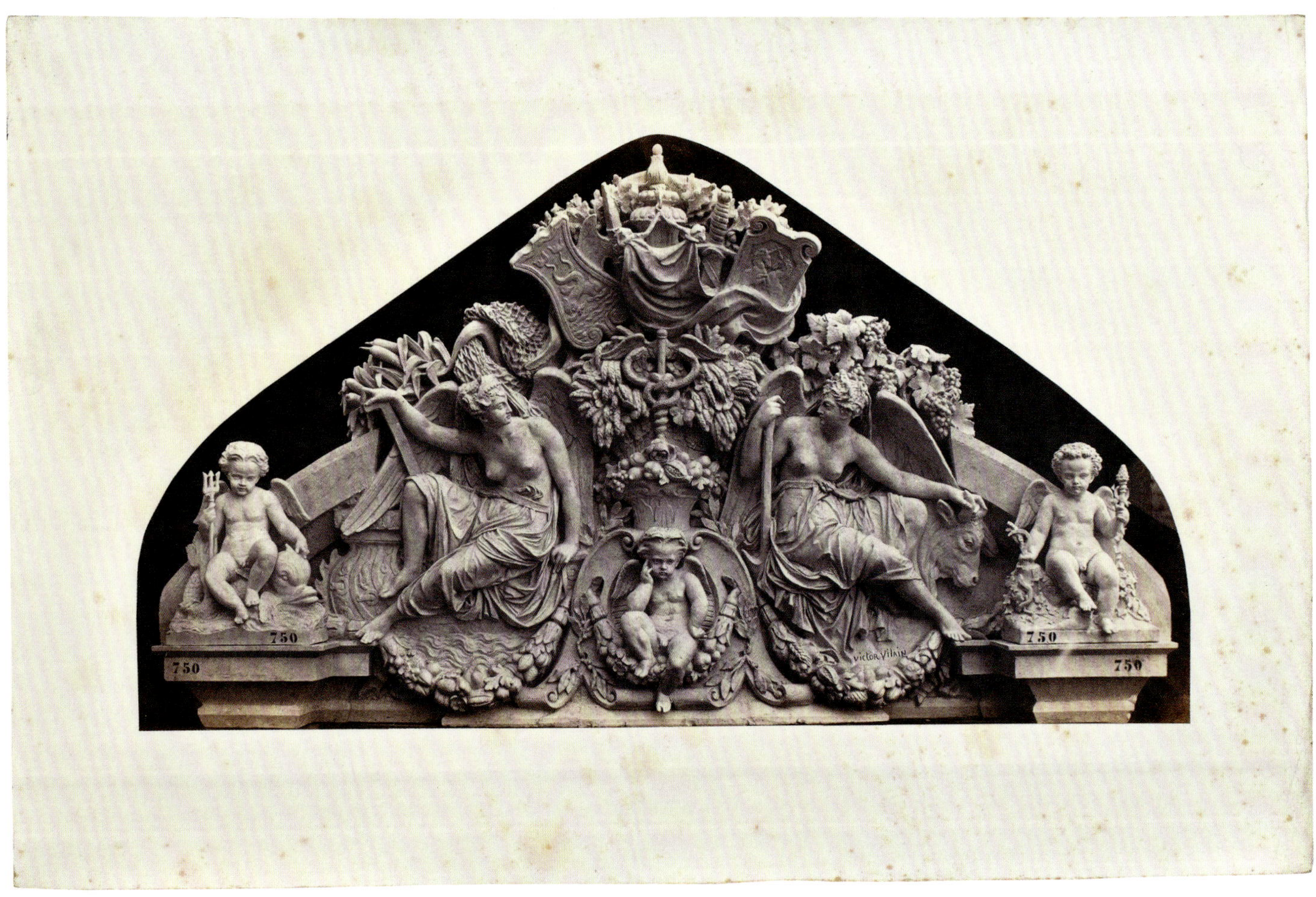

ÉDOUARD BALDUS LOUVRE FOLIOS

In 1855, Édouard Baldus was commissioned to photograph the sculptural elements of the Nouveau Louvre, a vast construction project led by Napoléon III to complete the Louvre as originally envisioned by Henri IV. The salted paper prints served new roles in the building process, as aids to the architect, builders, and sculptors. Their delicate beauty reveals the scale, skill, and ambition of the project.

POP PHOTOGRAPHICA

Since the daguerreotype's invention in 1839, photographs have been integrated into everyday objects—watches, brooches, and teacups. These personal keepsakes highlight the intimate, material culture of photography, revealing how photos have long been woven into daily life, beyond traditional prints. These items remain a vital and distinctive part of the AGO's photography collection.

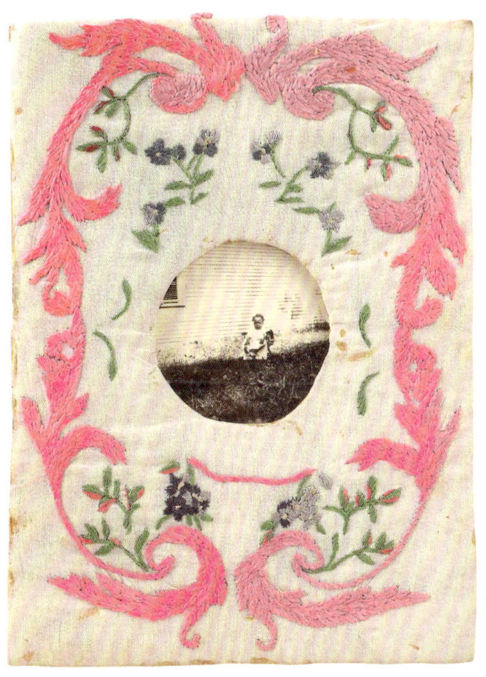

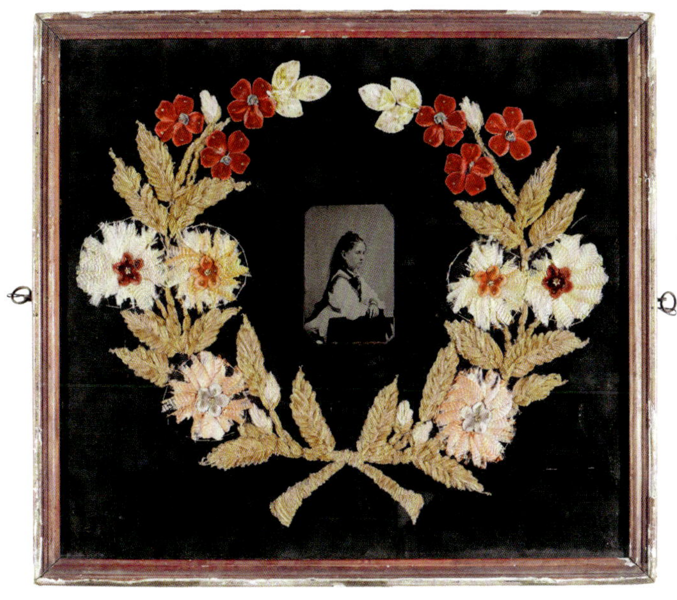

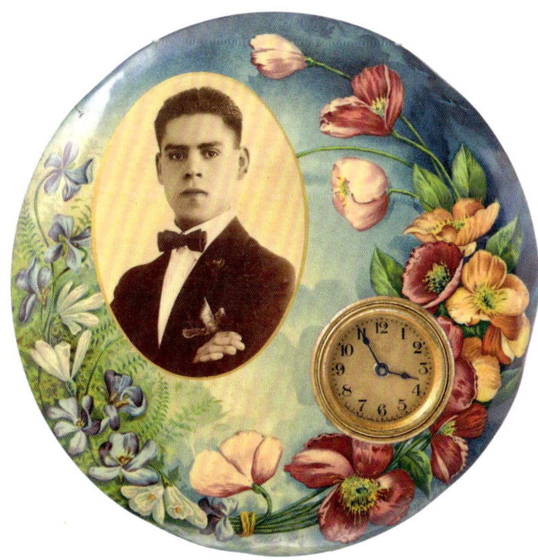

Édouard Baldus
Element No. 750
1857–1858
Salted paper print
31 × 47 cm
Purchase, with funds generously donated by Sandra L. Simpson and David W. Binet
2018/21.74

Maker once known
Young African American Child Seated
c. 1915
Gelatin silver print, multi-colour crewel needlework frame
21 × 15.6 cm
Anonymous Gift, 2000
2000/1325

Maker once known
Portrait of young girl
1860–1900
Tintype, with applied colour, black velvet mount, and hand-sewn fabric flowers; original frame
38.5 × 43.2 cm
Anonymous Gift, 2011
2011/109

Clock: Lux Clock Manufacturing Co.,
Border design: G.F. Eschwei
Portrait of a man
c. 1915
Celluloid print on metal
22.5 × 22.5 cm
Anonymous Gift, 2006
2006/198

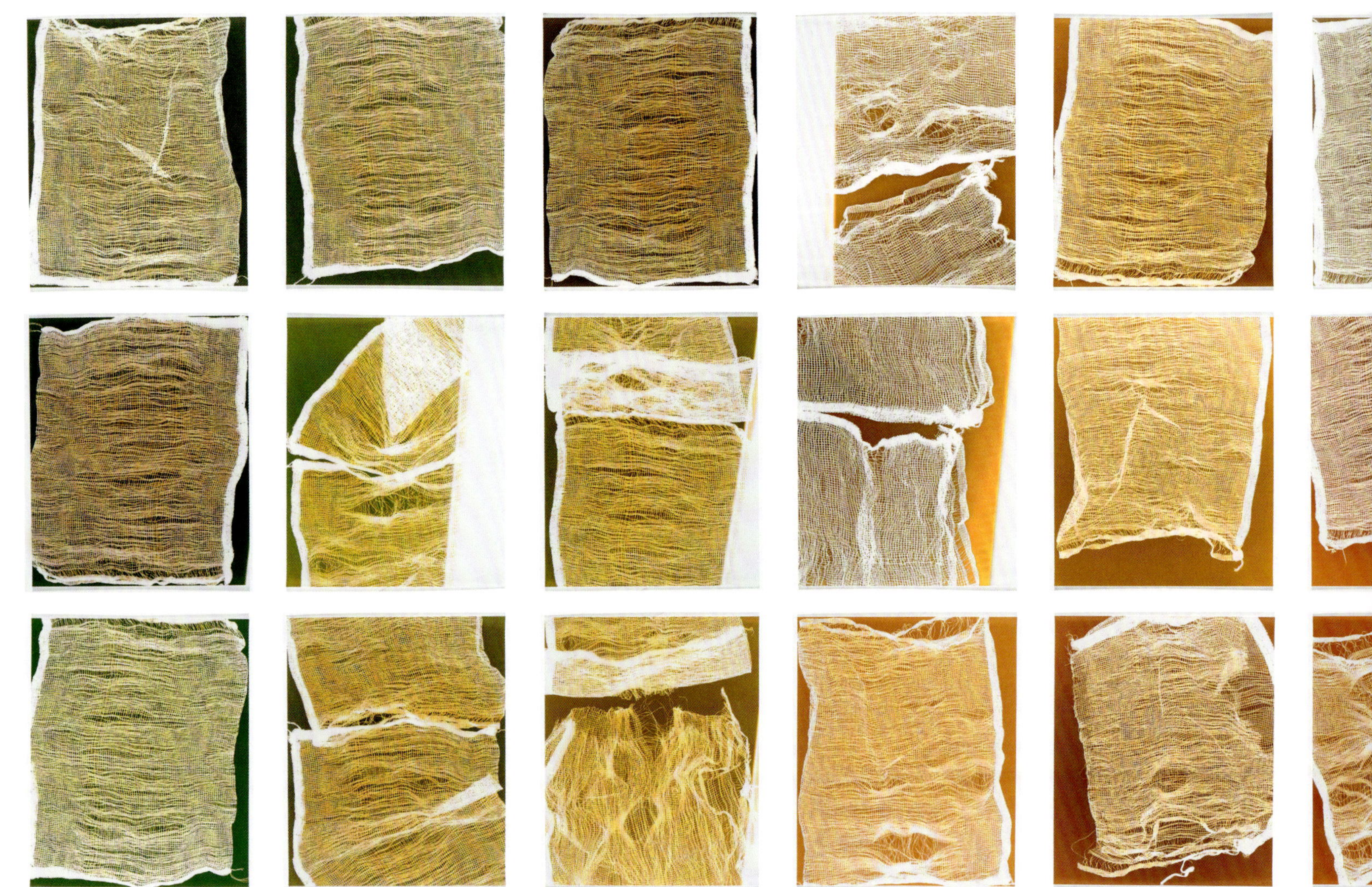

Lotus L. Kang
Her Own Devices
2020
35 photograms
61 × 50.8 cm each
Purchase, Canada Now Photography Acquisition Initiative, with funds from Edward Burtynsky and Nicholas Metivier, 2021
2021/38

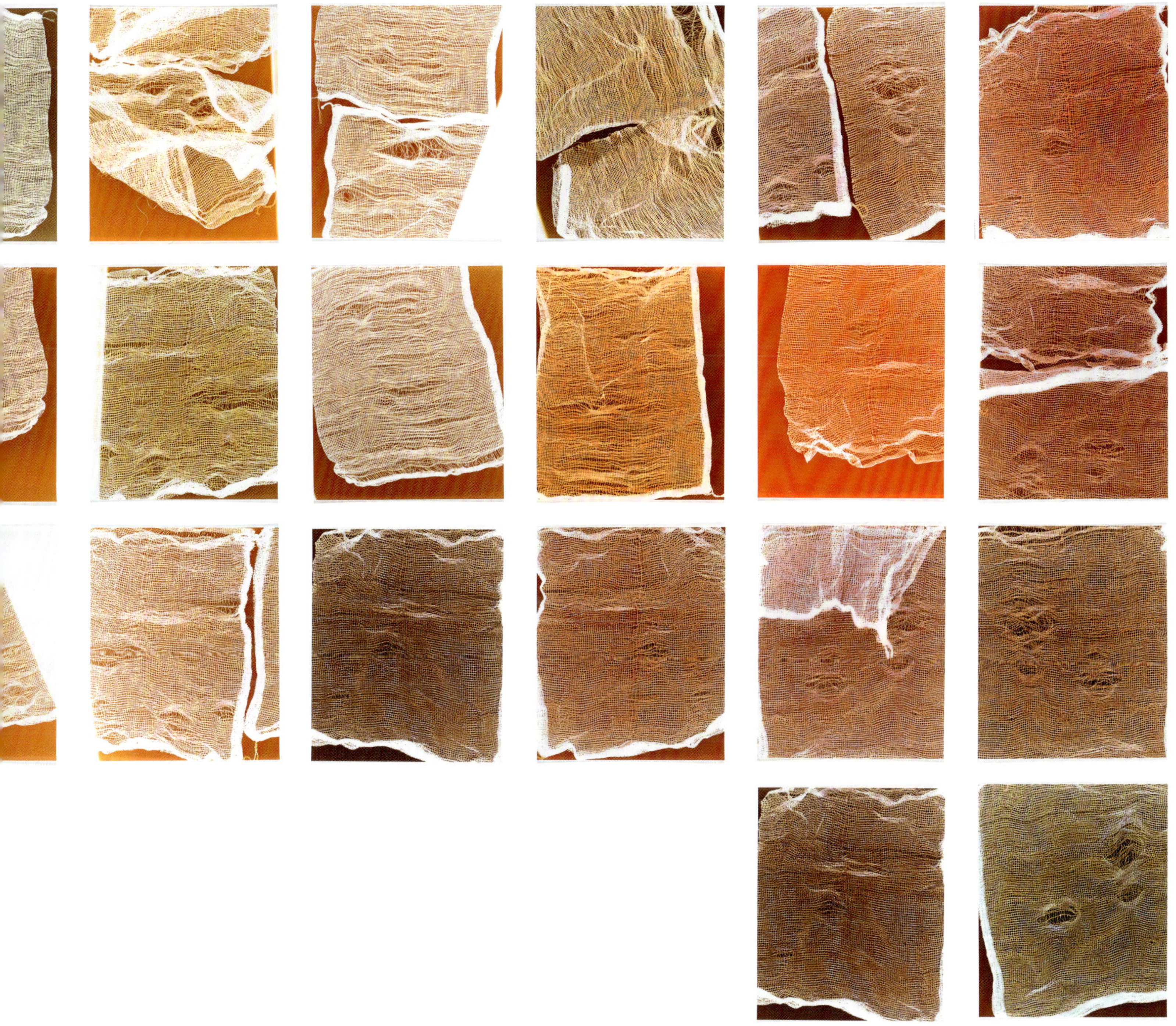

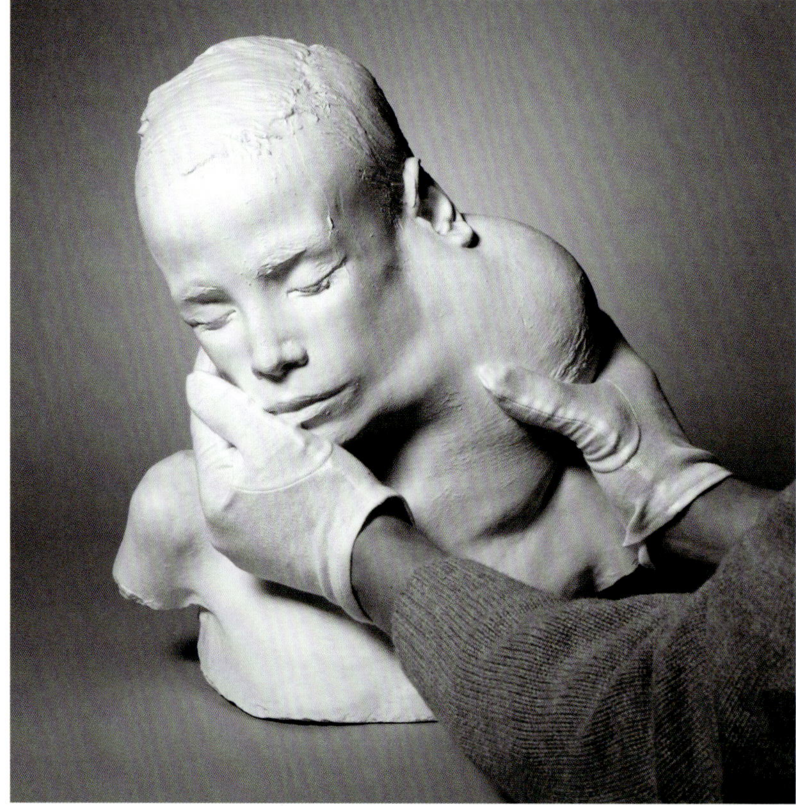

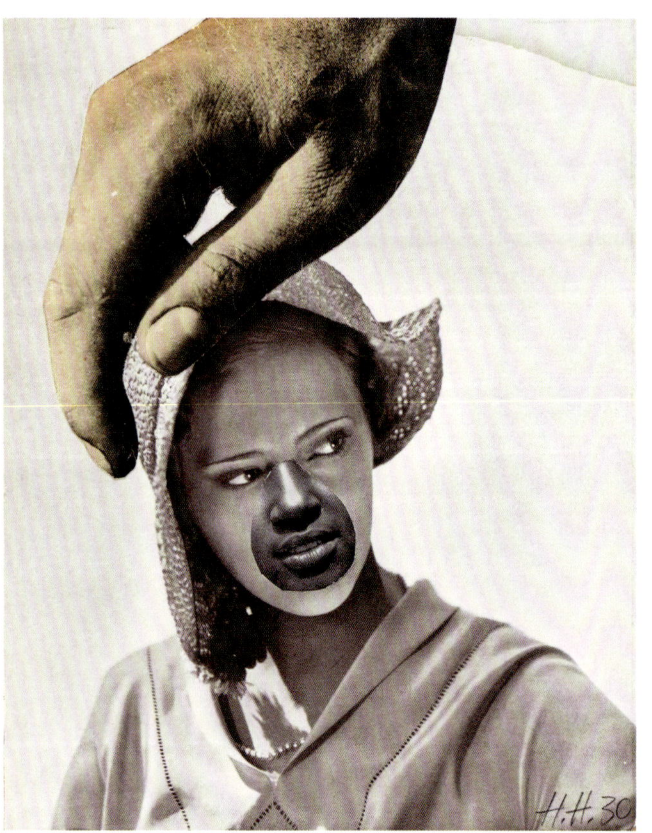

Hannah Höch
Untitled
1930
Photomontage
28 × 22.6 cm
Purchase, 2012
2012/5

Chris Curreri
Lifecast
2017
Gelatin silver print
35.6 × 38.1 cm
Gift of Sara and Michael Angel in memory of Peter Herrndorf, 2024
2024/121

Roy Kiyooka
FRM: StoneDGloves
1969–1976
Collage: gelatin silver prints
68 × 87.5 cm
Purchase with the assistance of the Estate of Christian Claude, 1999
99/417

Max Dean
As Yet Untitled
1992–1995
Metal, rubber, electronic, and mechanical components, photographs, Plexiglas, archival paper board box
157 × 267 × 256 cm
Gift of Jay Smith, David Fleck, Gilles Ouellette, and Terry Burgoyne, 2007
2007/670

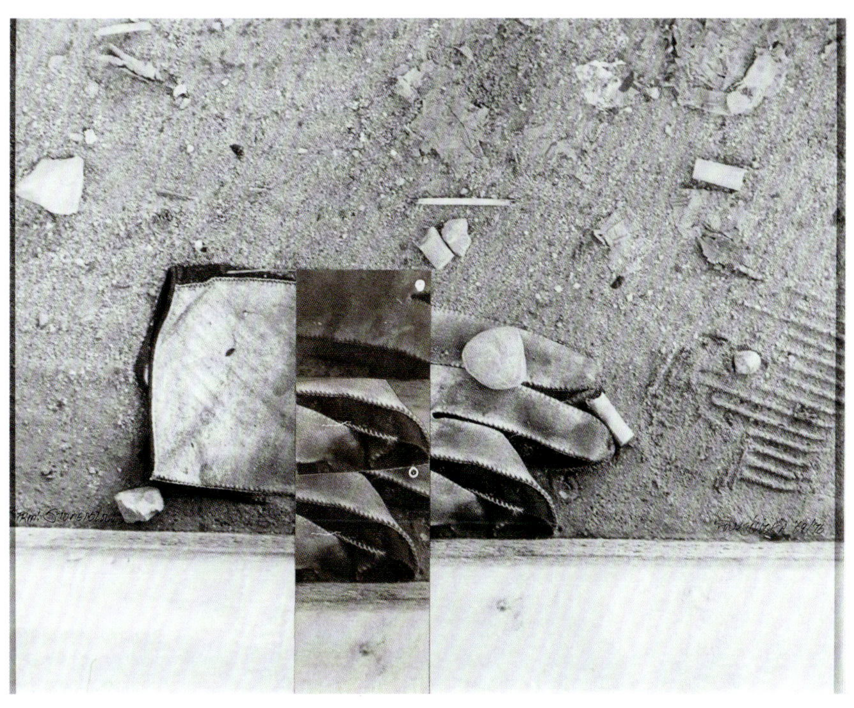

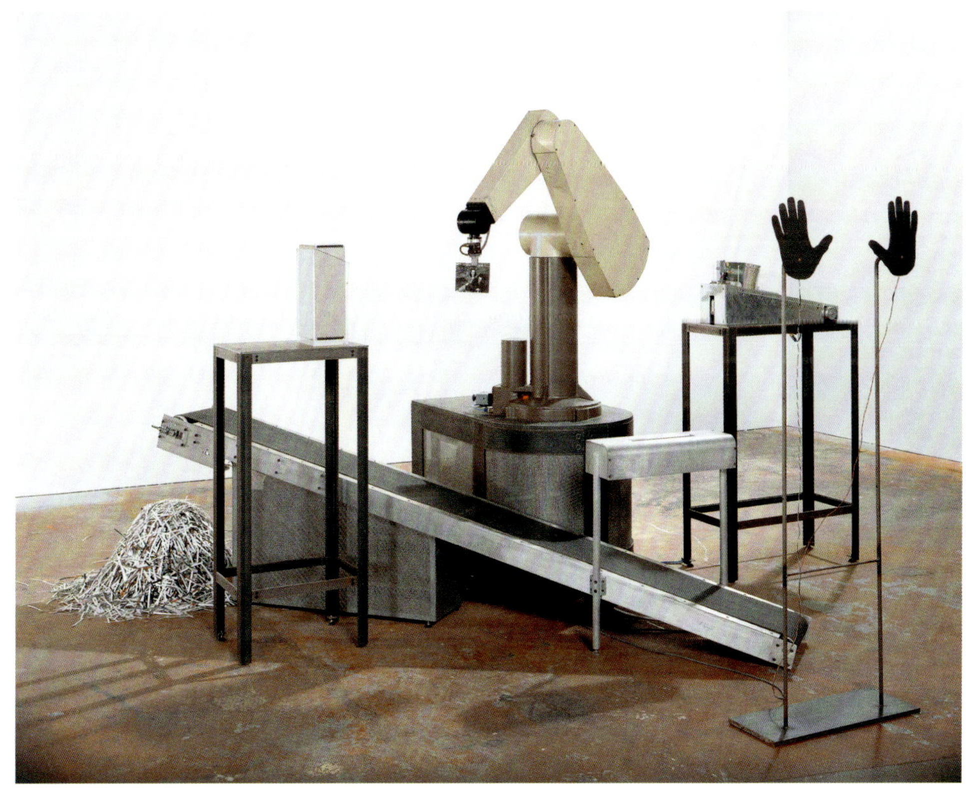

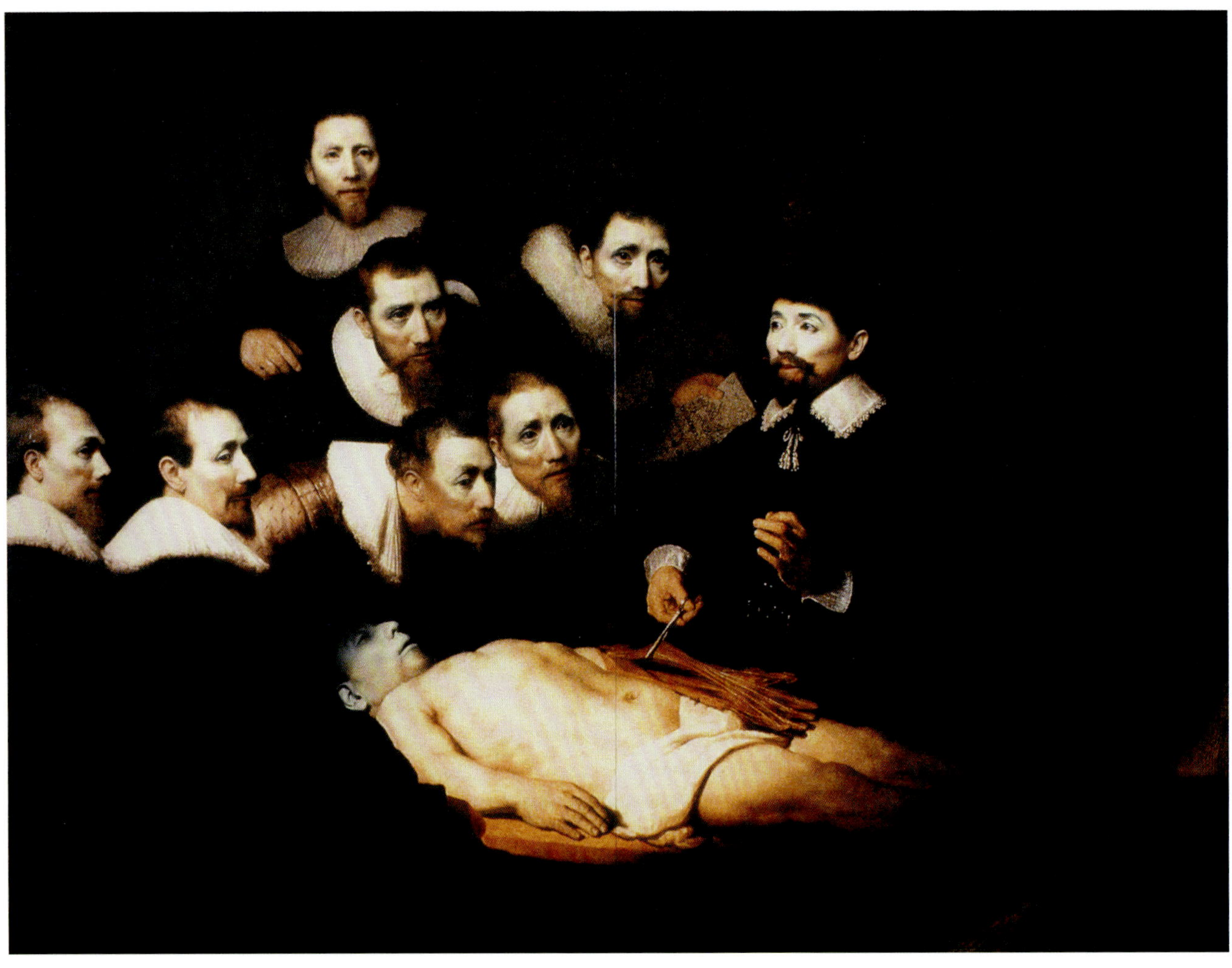

Yasumasa Morimura
Portrait (Nine Faces)
1989
Chromogenic print
196.7 × 250.9 cm
Gift of Vivian and David Campbell, 1998
98/482

Étienne-Jules Marey
Chronophotographic study of the movements of the jaw
1893
Gelatin silver print
23.7 × 17.9 cm
Gift of Marta Braun, 2022
2022/54

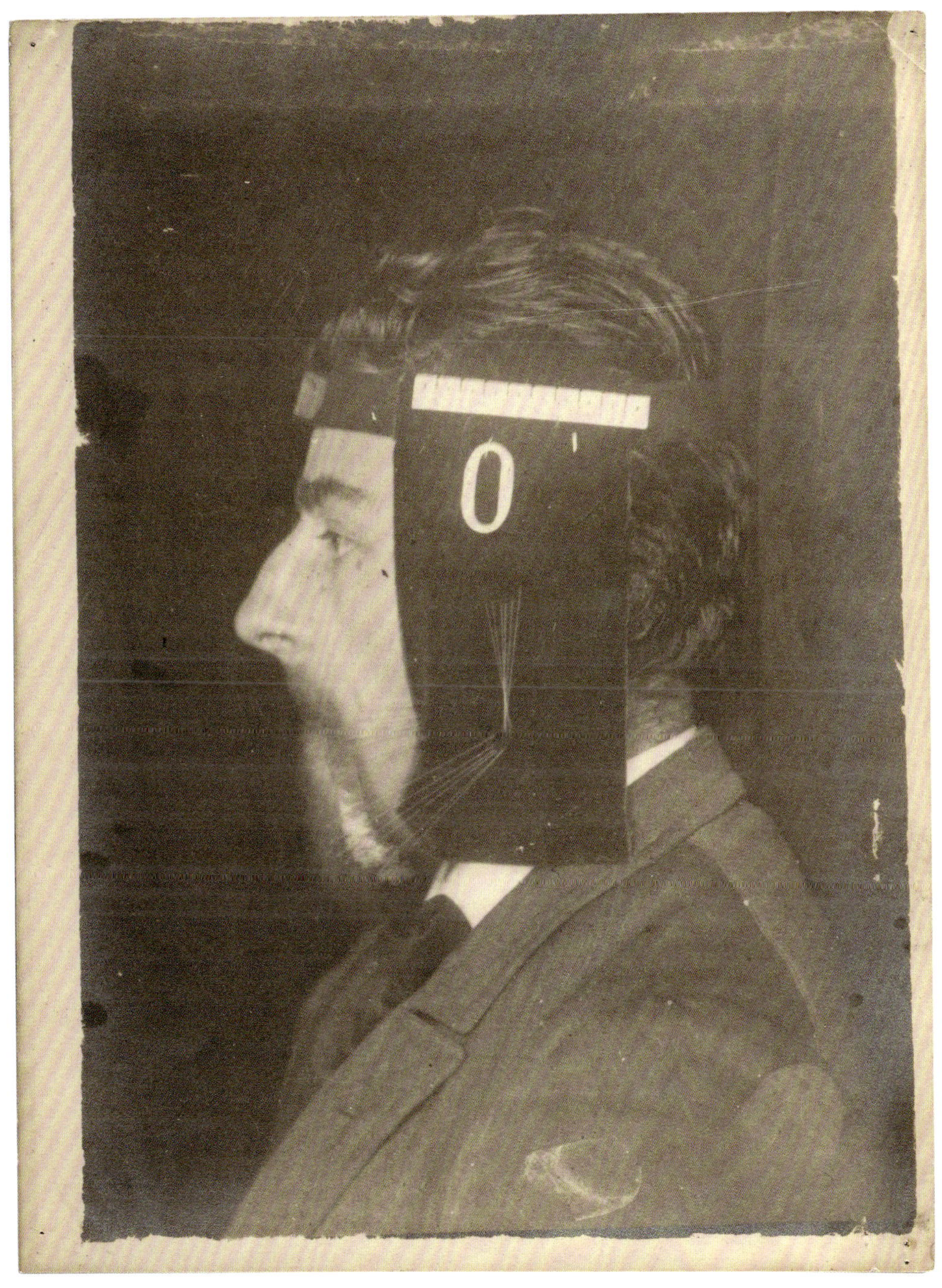
0

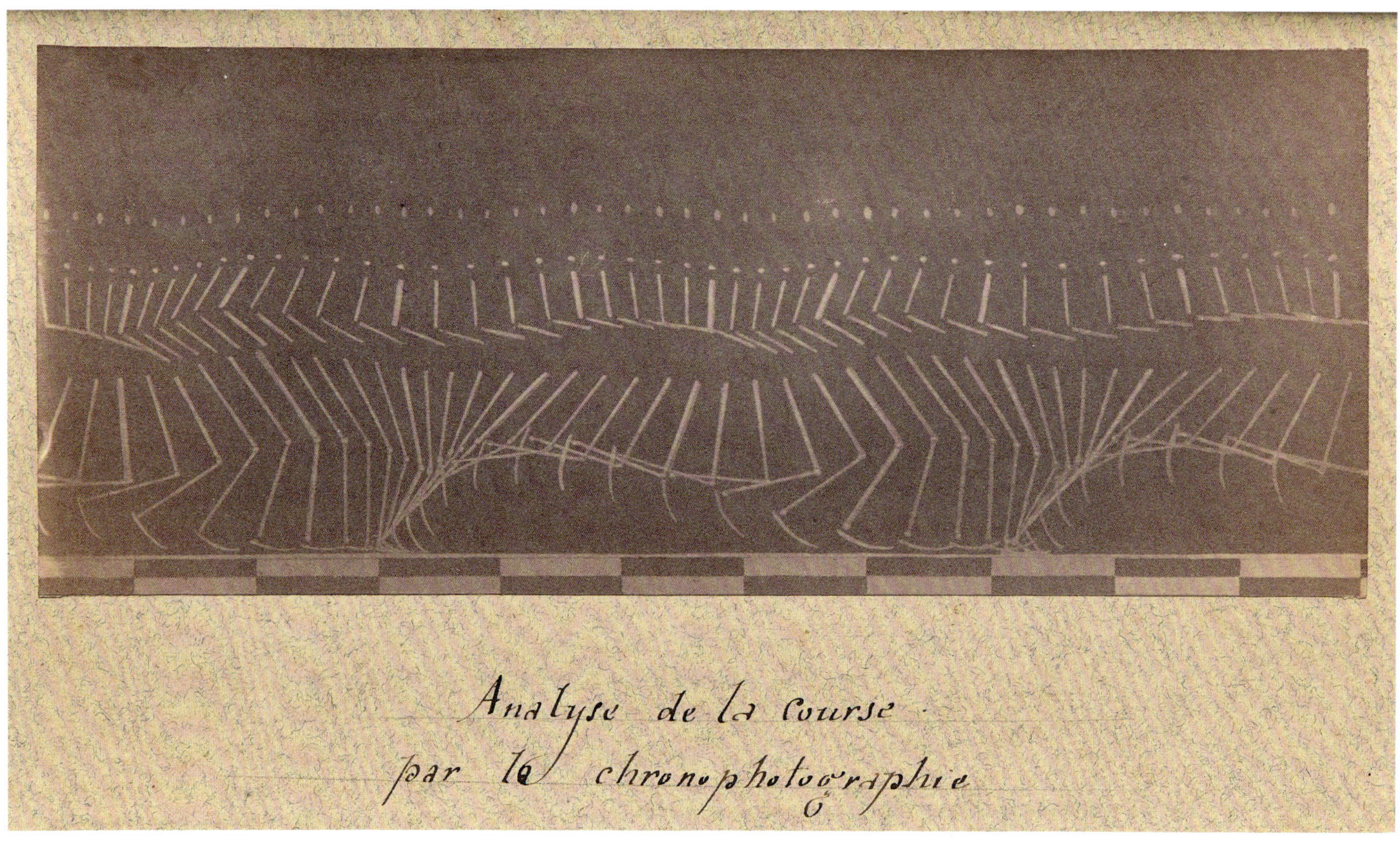

ÉTIENNE-JULES MAREY

Étienne-Jules Marey, a physiologist, focused on visually representing movement using photography as a scientific tool. He advanced photographic technology beyond descriptive uses to capture phenomena imperceptible to the human eye—such as a jaw opening, or a figure running—pioneering visual expressions that influenced both science and the arts, and inspiring movements like Italian Futurism.

Étienne-Jules Marey
Chronophotographic analysis of a run
1883
Gelatin silver print
19.2 × 26.5 cm
Gift of Marta Braun, 2022
2022/41

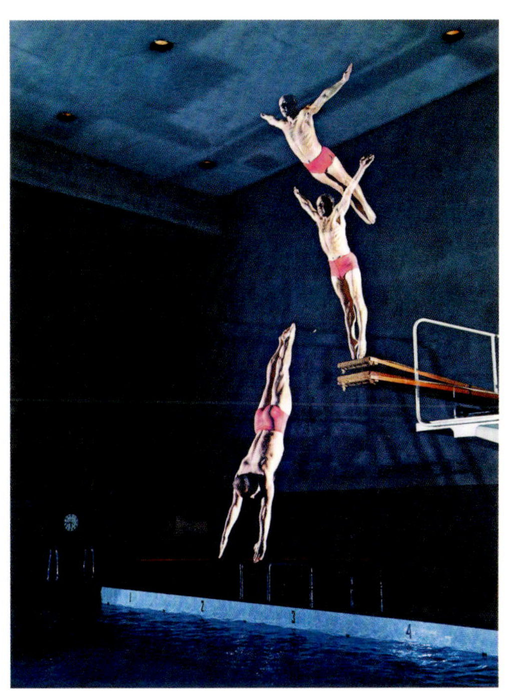

HAROLD EDGERTON

At MIT from the 1930s to the 1980s, Harold Edgerton revolutionized photography's ability to record movement by pioneering stroboscopic flashes, high-speed "rapatronic" cameras, and imaging systems, creating works featuring subjects such as milk drops, birds in flight, and athletes in motion. Comprising over 900 works, the collection offers a rich overview of his scientific breakthroughs and artistic influence.

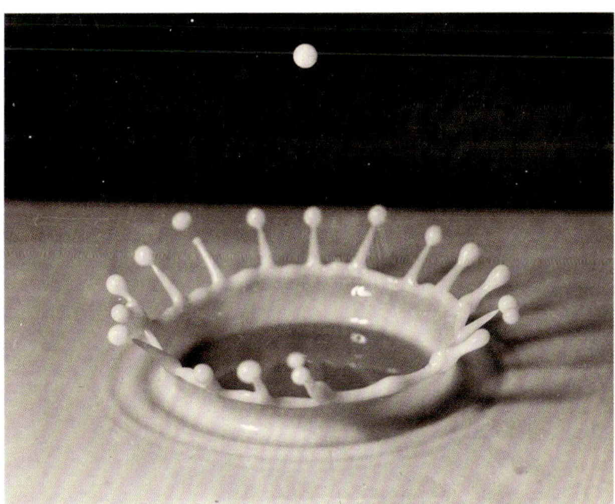

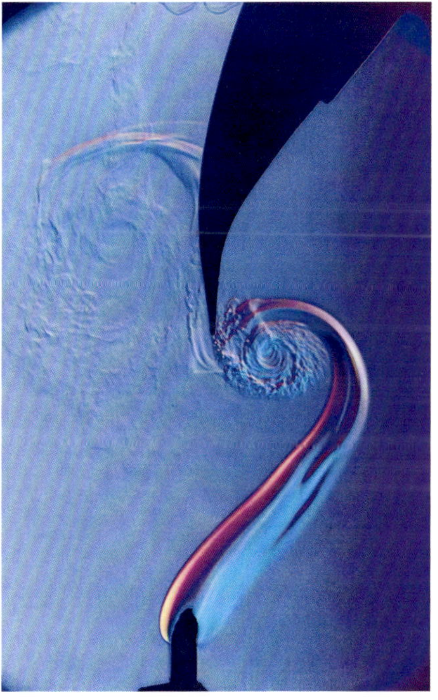

Clockwise from lower left:
Harold Edgerton
Milk Drop Coronet
c. 1935
Gelatin silver print
5.1 × 7.6 cm
2021/1280

Diver
1955
Dye transfer print
50.8 × 38.9 cm
2021/1312

Fan & Flame (blue)
1973
Dye transfer print
61 × 41.9 cm
Gift of Rose Baum and Family,
David Feldman, The Menkes Family, Shabin and Nadir Mohamed, Marc and Alex Muzzo, David Ross, Felicia Ross, Gretchen Ross and Victoria Ross, 2021
2021/1312; 2021/721

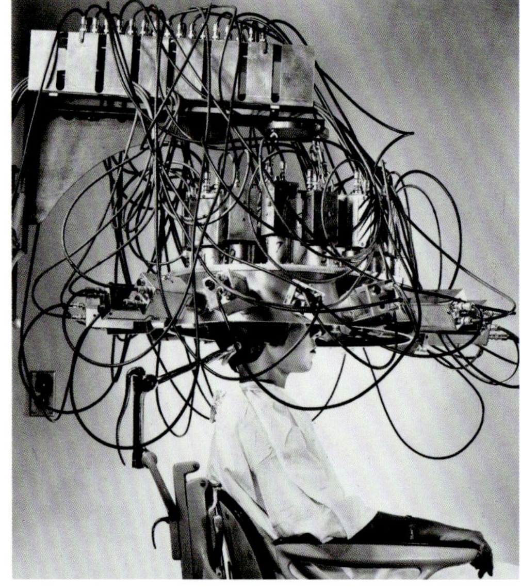

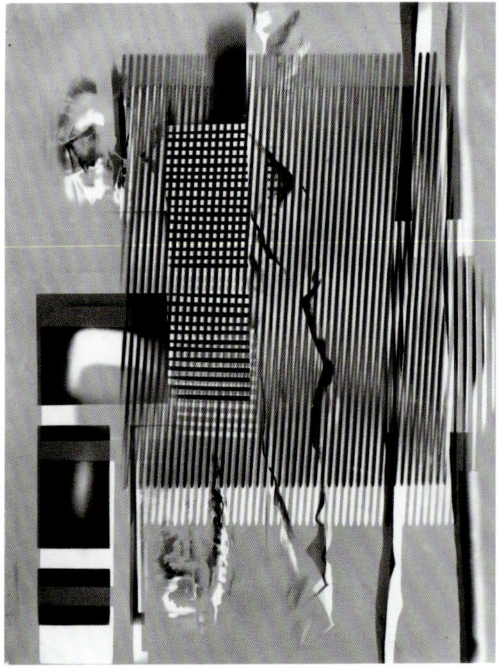

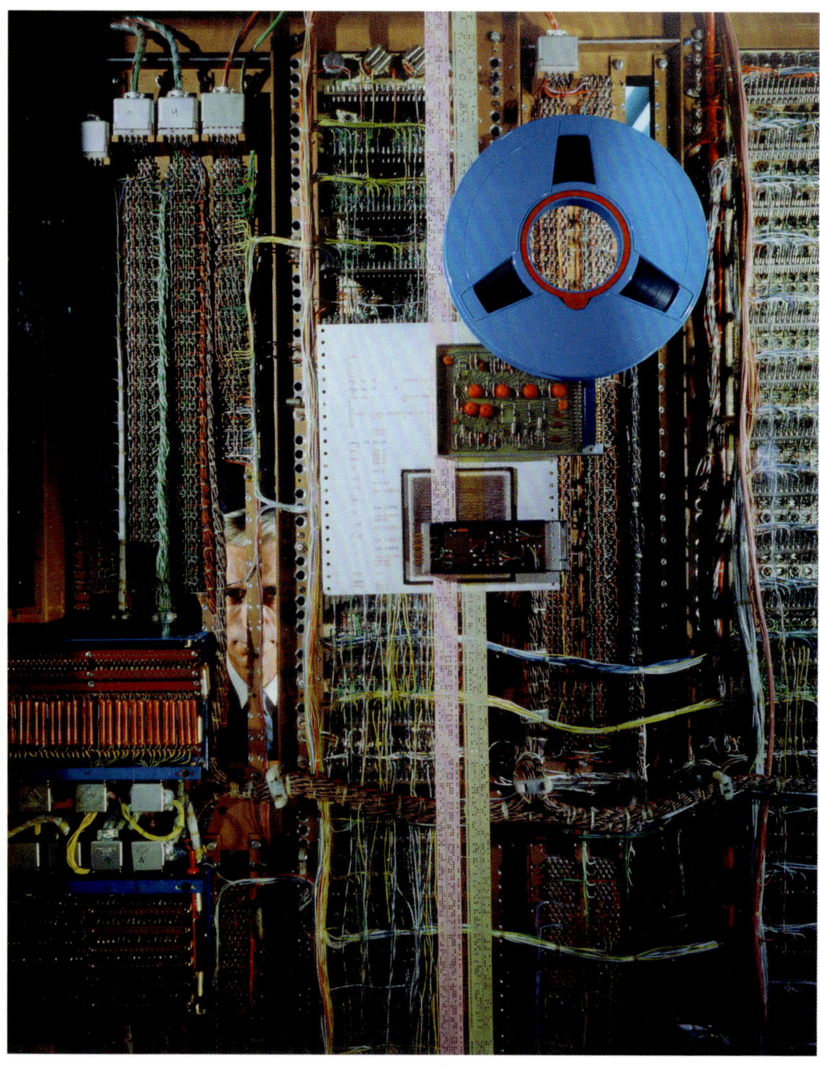

ARNOLD NEWMAN

In a robust career spanning eight decades, American photographer Arnold Newman was renowned for his integrative style of portraits of artists and other notable figures of the post-WWII era in the West, many created as magazine commissions. The AGO holds over 4,830 works by Newman—unique collages, Polaroids, book maquettes, prints autographed by the sitters, and sculptural photographs.

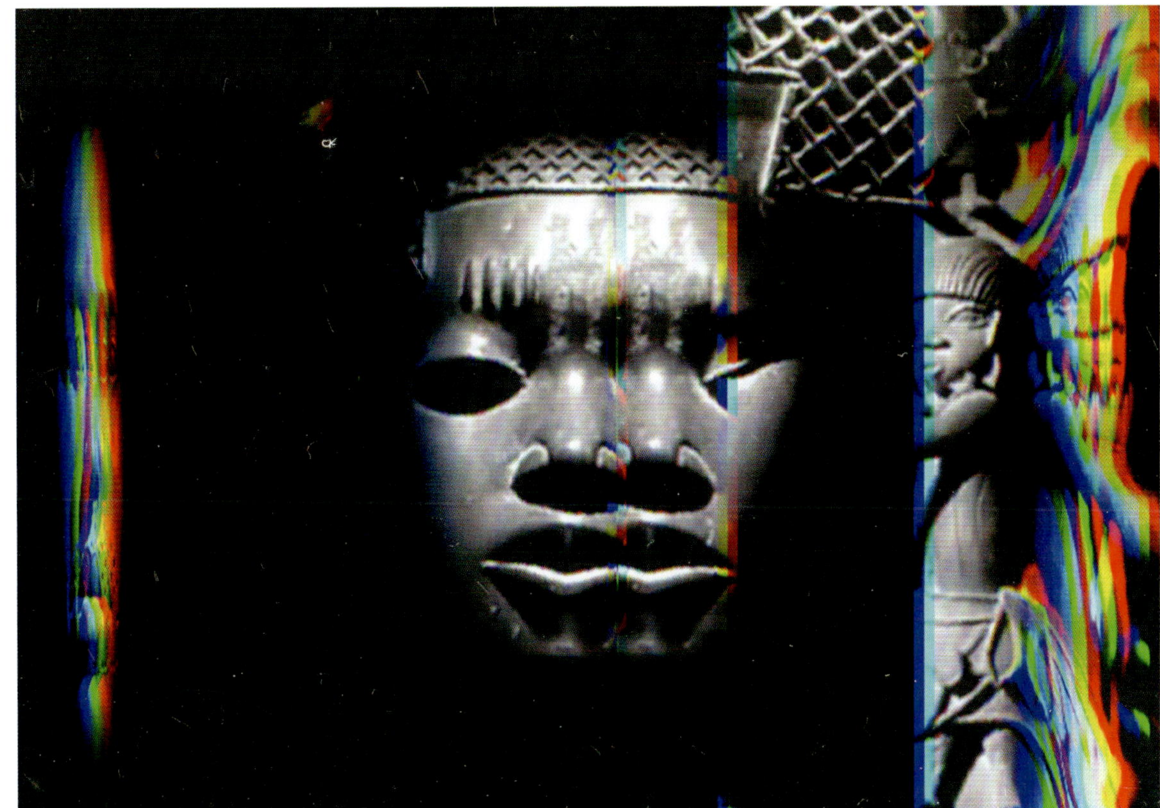

Opposite, clockwise from lower left:
Jaroslav Rössler
Untitled (Abstract Composition with Parallel Lines)
c. 1960
Gelatin silver print
54.6 × 40.6 cm
Anonymous Gift, 2018
AGO.136408

United States Information Services
Picture Story No. 1016: Detecting disease with atoms. The complicated contrivance with dangling wires, called a multi-detector, pinpoints brain tumors
1950s
Gelatin silver print
26 × 20.5 cm
Anonymous Gift, 2005
2005/5218

Arnold Newman
Dr. Claude E. Shannon, Scientist, Massachusetts Institute of Technology
1962
Commissioned by *Holiday*
Chromogenic print
50.8 × 40.6 cm
Anonymous Gift, 2012
2015/4044

Raymond Boisjoly
From age to age, as its shape slowly unravelled
(detail)
2015
Inkjet prints on vinyl: 7
Various dimensions
Purchase, with funds from the Photography Curatorial Committee, 2021
2021/103

Geoffrey Farmer
Look in my face; my name is Might-have-been; I am also called No-more, Too-late, Farewell
(installation view)
2013
Computer generated algorithmic montage sequence projection
Purchased with funds from David & Yvonne Fleck, the Dr. Michael Braudo Canadian Contemporary Fund, the Ivey Foundation Contemporary Art Endowment Fund, the Janet & Michael Scott Fund, and the Contemporary Circle Fund, 2015
2015/14

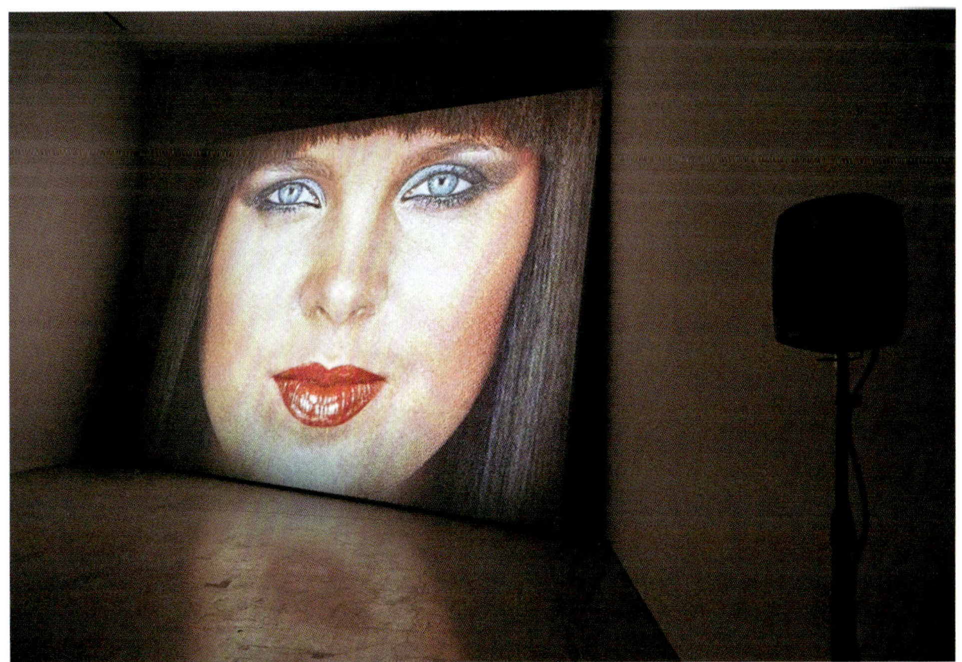

Places We've Been

Tal-Or Ben-Choreen

The velvety darkness of Dawoud Bey's photograph *Untitled #19 (Creek and Trees)* (left and p. 132), appears like a minimalist painting. As our eyes adjust, details of a landscape begin to emerge: a creek runs through the bottom centre of the frame and bare tree branches from a dense forest tangle reach out. The image evokes the feeling of moving by moonlight, the stillness of the forest interrupted by the sounds of leaves and twigs crunching underfoot. Bey made this work as part of his series *Night Coming Tenderly, Black* (2016–2017), where he envisioned the movement of enslaved individuals who travelled on the Underground Railroad roughly 160 years earlier. Although the depicted scenes show real places, Bey imposes on them an imagined history, a communal experience of "the perilous flights of self-emancipating people."[1]

The idea of place is ephemeral, changing in relation to industrialization, population and economic shifts, conflicts, ecological disasters, and climate change. Photographers have been central to mapping our perceptions and experiences of specific environments and locations, and their work provides us with a sense of grounding and an understanding of ourselves. We continue to use photography to document our homes, cities, monuments, and natural wonders. Just as the scenes of each place vary, so do their meanings, shaped by the agendas of institutions and agencies, the image-makers, and ultimately the viewers of the pictures.

Since the nineteenth century in the West, photographs have transported us to locations far from our homes and introduced us to different ways of living. Photographers in this era also studied the wilderness and human feats exerted to traverse it, often including people only to emphasize the vast scale of the landscape. While this ability to see the world without leaving home is profound, many of these depictions purposefully affirmed Western power, and reinforced narratives to justify colonial and imperialist claims while also bolstering commercial and mercantile interests,[2] for instance, in the photographs of Linnaeus Tripe (p. 145) and Alexander Henderson (p. 4). The variety of approaches photographers undertook reveals their specific interests and agendas, and the deep complexities of recording place.[3]

Twentieth-century photographers, motivated by both curiosity and ideology, also used the medium to build and project national identity. Image-makers documented local workers and the yields of their industries, ritual activities, and changing landscapes, dress, and architecture, creating cultural records of places around the world. Edith S. Watson (pp. 134–135), for example, travelled throughout Canada making pictures from the 1890s to the 1920s. In addition to publishing individual pho-

Dawoud Bey
Untitled #19 (Creek and Trees) (detail)
2017
From the series ***Night Coming Tenderly, Black***
(2016–2017)
Gelatin silver print
121.9 × 149.9 cm
Purchase, with funds generously donated by Susan & Larry Dime, Hugh Hall, Gale M. Kelly, Jack & Harriet Lazare, Edward Redelmeier, and Kenneth Straiton, 2020
2020/20

Sunil Gupta
The Wedding (detail)
1987
From the series ***Exiles*** (1986–1987)
Chromogenic print
40.7 × 58.5 cm
Purchase, funds from Robyn McCallum and Stephan Delaney, 2024
2024/93

tographs in the popular press, she collaborated with her work and life partner, journalist Victoria Hayward, to publish *Romantic Canada* (1922), an idealistic portrayal of pre-industrialized rural communities with an emphasis on women and their work. The first published instance describing Canadian culture as a mosaic, the book and Watson's photographs contribute to a complex and evolving idea of a vast and diverse country.

Street photography emerged as industrialization in the late 1800s and early 1900s encouraged urban migration and the growth of densely populated centres. Photographs of this phenomenon document poverty, and the rapid expansion of both infrastructure and consumerism. Many images offer distinct views of neighbourhoods through the gestures and fashion of strangers, details from posters and signage, shop displays, the technology and aesthetics of transportation, weather, and the bright lights that illuminate the lively events of the street. Photographers working in the mid- and late twentieth century and into the twenty-first century continued to explore city streets, tracing changes in demographics and ecology, including locally, here in Toronto (pp. 158–165).

Photography has also cemented the appeal of places with collective significance; as images of monuments or sites of historical import circulate, they fuel the desire to visit, often prompting us to make near identical images to further affirm our experiences or to record our presence there. The introduction of the automobile and the construction of highways in the early 1900s made such visits more accessible, encouraging a new trend many were keen to record photographically: the road trip.[4] Soon, road signs were erected to suggest spots for picturesque sightseeing.[5] As a result, our sense of many locations is tied to a single point of view.

More recently, artists have leveraged the clichés of travel photographs to both contemplate and criticize the activity of tourism. Some have explored the social construction of identity and otherness in relation to place, as in Tseng Kwong Chi's series *East Meets West* (1979–1989) (pp. 140 and 142). Others have contemplated the history of places, creating visual archives to fill in perceived gaps in our pictorial records and to imagine spaces anew, such as in Sunil Gupta's series *Exiles* (1986–1987) (right, and p. 144), which visualizes the experience of gay men in India. Of this work, Gupta said: "It seemed wherever we lived, we were cut off from India and there was an overwhelming, deeply frustrated desire to claim some part of it for ourselves."[6]

Over nearly two centuries, we have delighted in the capacity to make photographs of the spaces we inhabit and move through, creating portraits of our countries, neighbourhoods, and homes, and exploring our complicated and shifting relationships to them. From vast landscapes to bustling cityscapes, the destruction of war to the creation of new architectural forms, we understand ourselves and construct our identities in response to these depictions. The works in the following pages illustrate different understandings of places and a shared desire to map them as a way of defining, and commemorating, our experiences.

1. Shawn Michelle Smith, "Photography, Darkness, and the Underground Railroad: Dawoud Bey's *Night Coming Tenderly, Black*," *American Quarterly* 73, no. 3 (March 2021), p. 28.
2. Jarrod Hore, *Visions of Nature: How Landscape Photography Shaped Settler Colonialism* (Oakland: University of California Press, 2022); Eleanor M. Hight and Gary D. Sampson, *Colonialist Photography: Imag(in)ing Race and Place* (New York: Routledge, 2002).
3. M. Christine Boyer, "*La Mission Héliographique:* Architectural Photography, Collective Memory and the Patrimony of France, 1851," in *Picturing Place: Photography and Geographical Imagination*, ed. Joan Schwartz and James Ryan, (London: I.B. Tauris, 2003), pp. 21–54.
4. David Campany, *The Open Road: Photography & the American Road Trip* (New York: Aperture Foundation, 2014).
5. Leslie K. Brown, "The Kodak Picture Spot Sign: American Photographic Viewing and Twentieth-Century Corporate Visual Culture," PhD diss. (Boston: Boston University, 2019).
6. Sunil Gupta, "Exiles," in *From Here to Eternity*, ed. Mark Sealy (London: Autograph, 2020), p. 43.

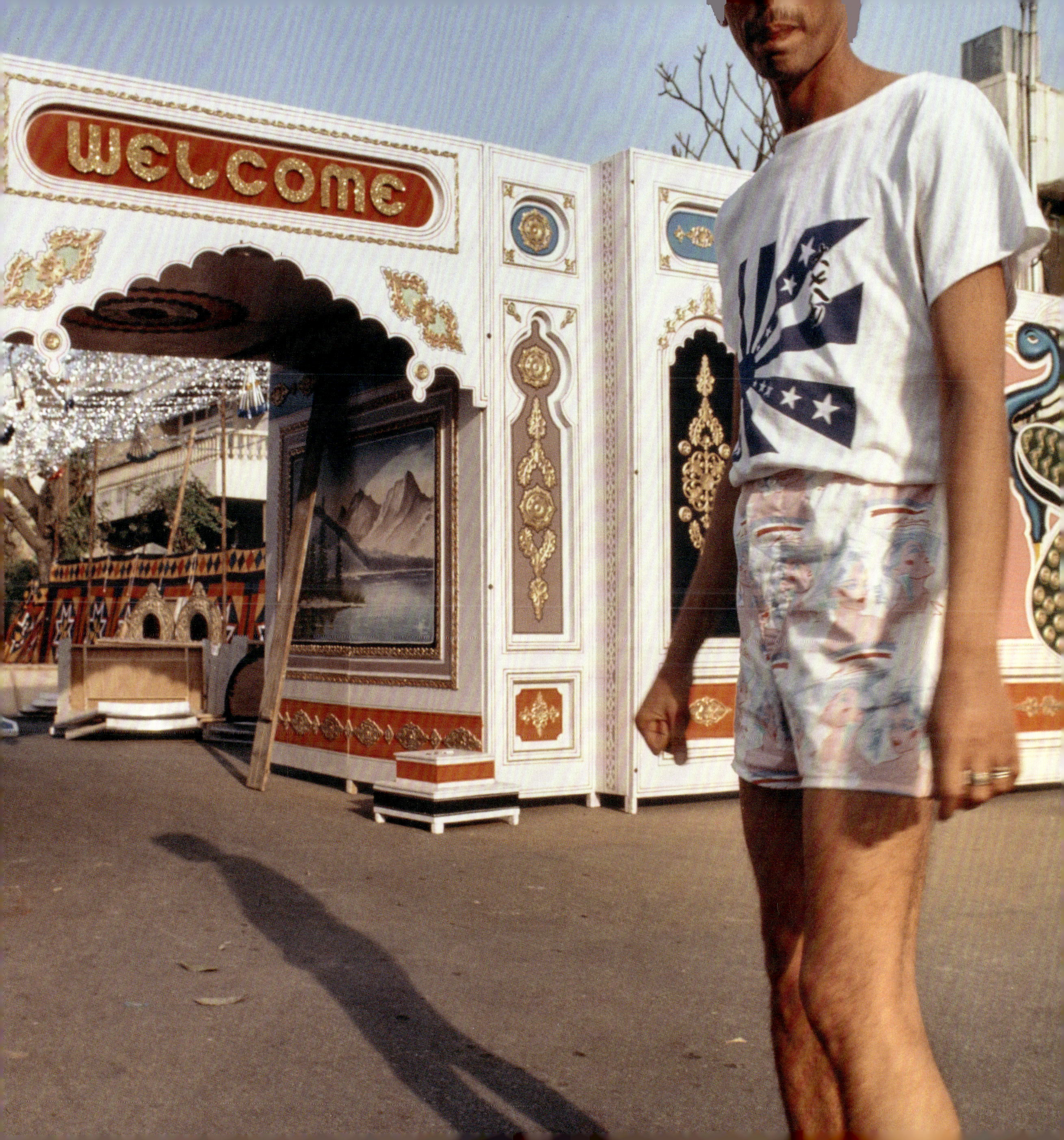
WELCOME

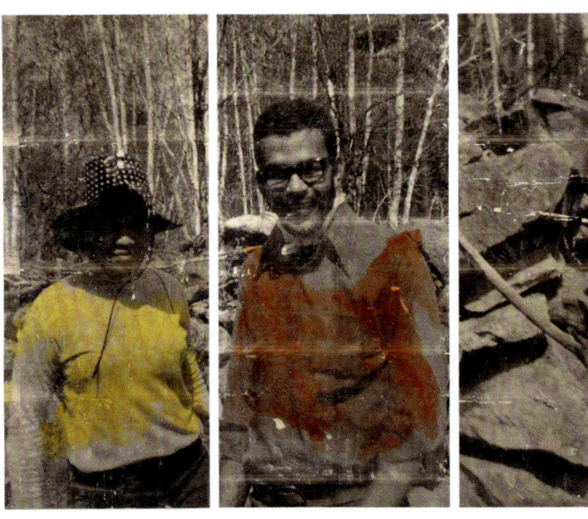

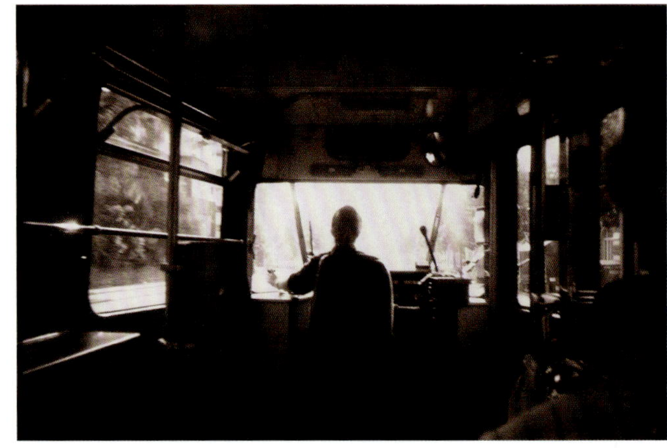

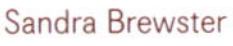

Sandra Brewster
Hiking Black Creek
2018
Gel medium transfer, charcoal, acrylic on wood
335.3 × 406.4 cm
Purchase, with funds by exchange from a gift in memory of J.G. Althouse from Isobel Althouse Wilkinson and John Provost Wilkinson, 2020
2020/17

Angela Grauerholz
La Conductrice
1992
Silver dye bleach print
122 × 185.4 cm
Gift of Alison and Alan Schwartz, 1997
97/1587

Dawoud Bey
Untitled #19 (Creek and Trees)
2017
From the series ***Night Coming Tenderly, Black***
(2016–2017)
Gelatin silver print
121.9 × 149.9 cm
Purchase, with funds generously donated by Susan & Larry Dime, Hugh Hall, Gale M. Kelly, Jack & Harriet Lazare, Edward Redelmeier, and Kenneth Straiton, 2020
2020/20

Reva Brooks
La Perequinación, San Miguel
1950s
Gelatin silver print
50.7 × 40.4 cm
Gift of the Estate of David Silverman in memory of Reva Brooks, 2004
2004/79

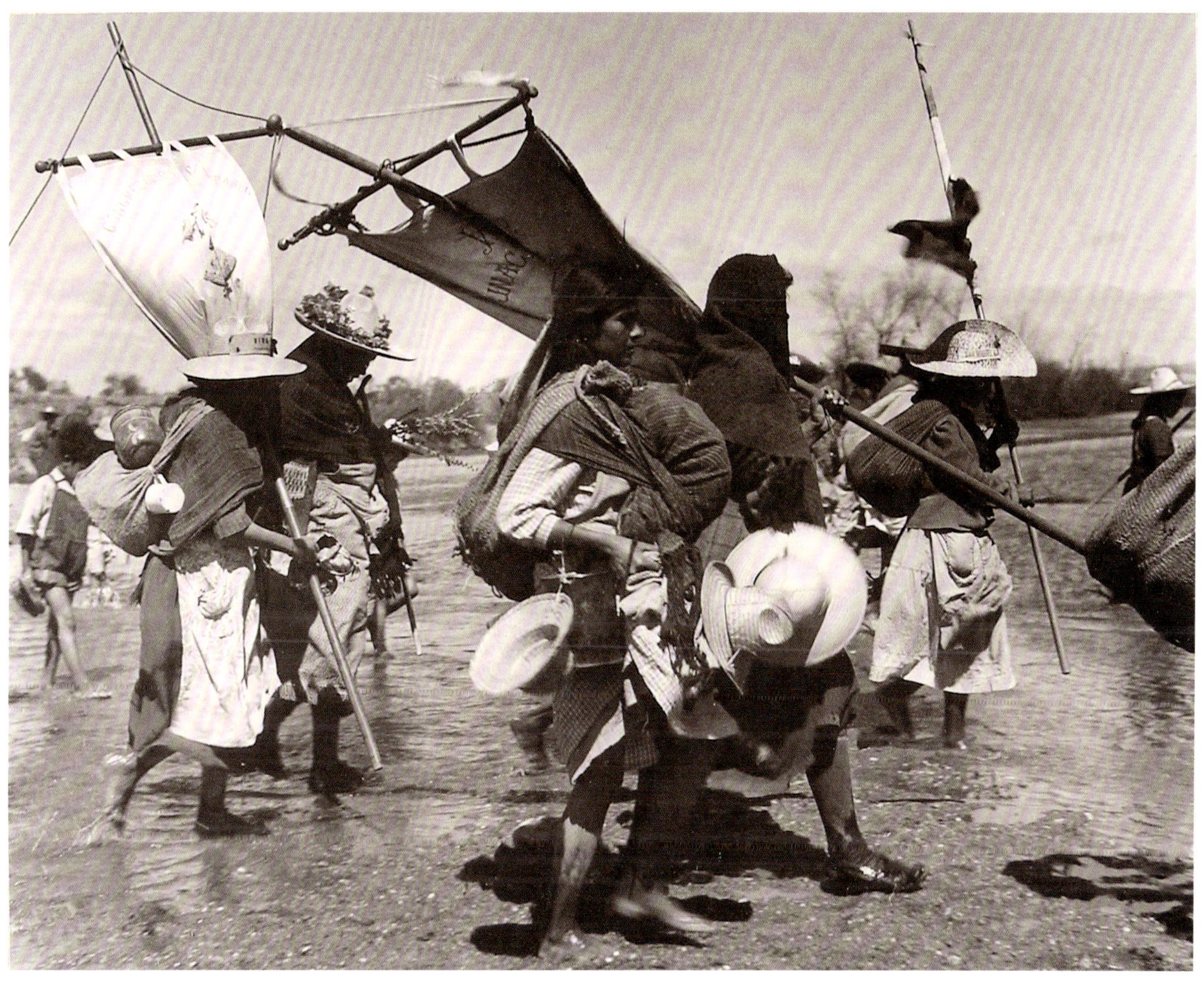

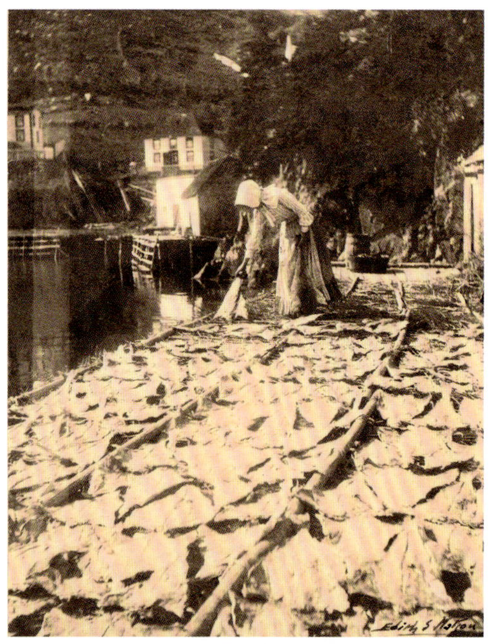

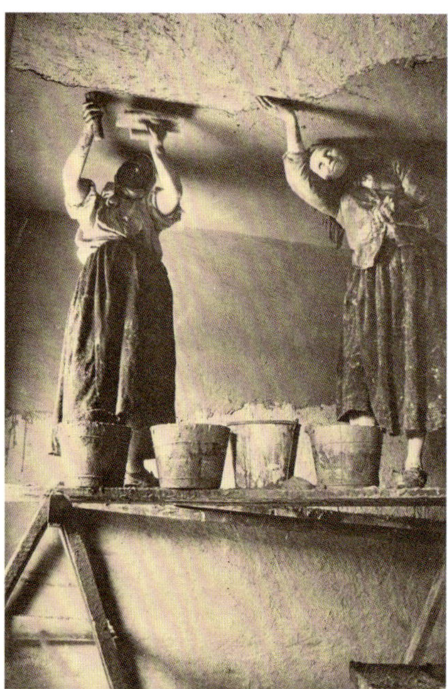

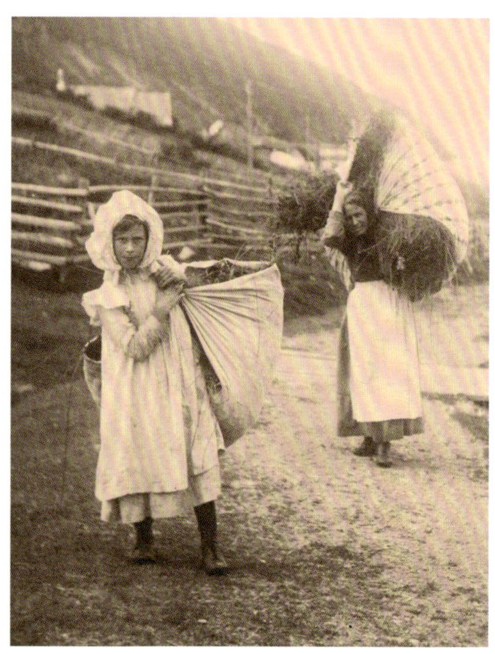

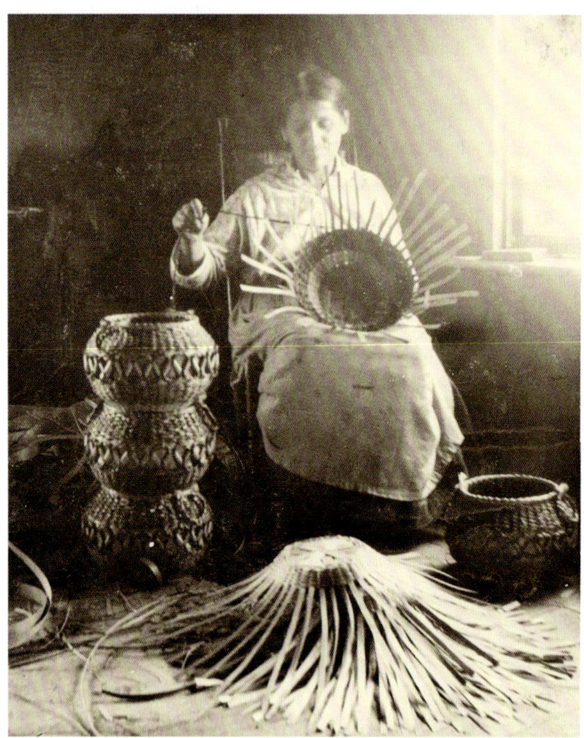

EDITH WATSON

The sixteen albums in this collection, holding over 1,000 photographs, form the core of Edith Watson's Canadian work. Assembled geographically or thematically and often captioned by hand, they document women and families—both Indigenous and immigrant—across communities from Newfoundland to Haida Gwaii, from Abenaki lands and Doukhobor settlements, offering an unprecedented record of rural life from 1896 to 1921.

Edith Watson
Heads and Tails, Path End, Newfoundland
1896
From the album ***Happy Souvenirs of trips made alone to Newfoundland, and to Labrador in company with Miss Victoria Hayward, the writer*** (1896–1921)
Gelatin silver print
12.4 × 10 cm

Two women stand on a work table to plaster a ceiling with bare hands
1919–1920
From the album ***The Doukhobours II*** (1918–1920)
Gelatin silver print
25.4 × 17.2 cm

Hermitage (Carrying Hay)
1919–1921
From the album ***Children from here and there! A picture book of children we have happened upon in Canada, Newfoundland, St. Pierre et Miquelon and The Bahamas*** (1890s–1930s)
Gelatin silver print
22 × 16.8 cm

An expert basket maker, in the Abenaki Reservation, Odanak, Quebec
1919–1921
From the album ***A souvenir of our days among the makers of sweetgrass baskets, in the reservation of the Abenaki, near Pierreville, Quebec*** (1911–1921)
Gelatin silver print
19.1 × 17.3 cm

On the pier head, Quebec (Victoria Hayward)
1919–1931
From the album ***Happy Voyages with Queenie*** (1911–1931)
Gelatin silver print
22.3 × 17 cm

Frances Rooney Collection. Purchase, with funds generously donated by Martha LA McCain, 2018
2018/3588.76a; 2018/3598.38a; 2018/3594.76a; 2018/3590.11; 2018/3603.1a

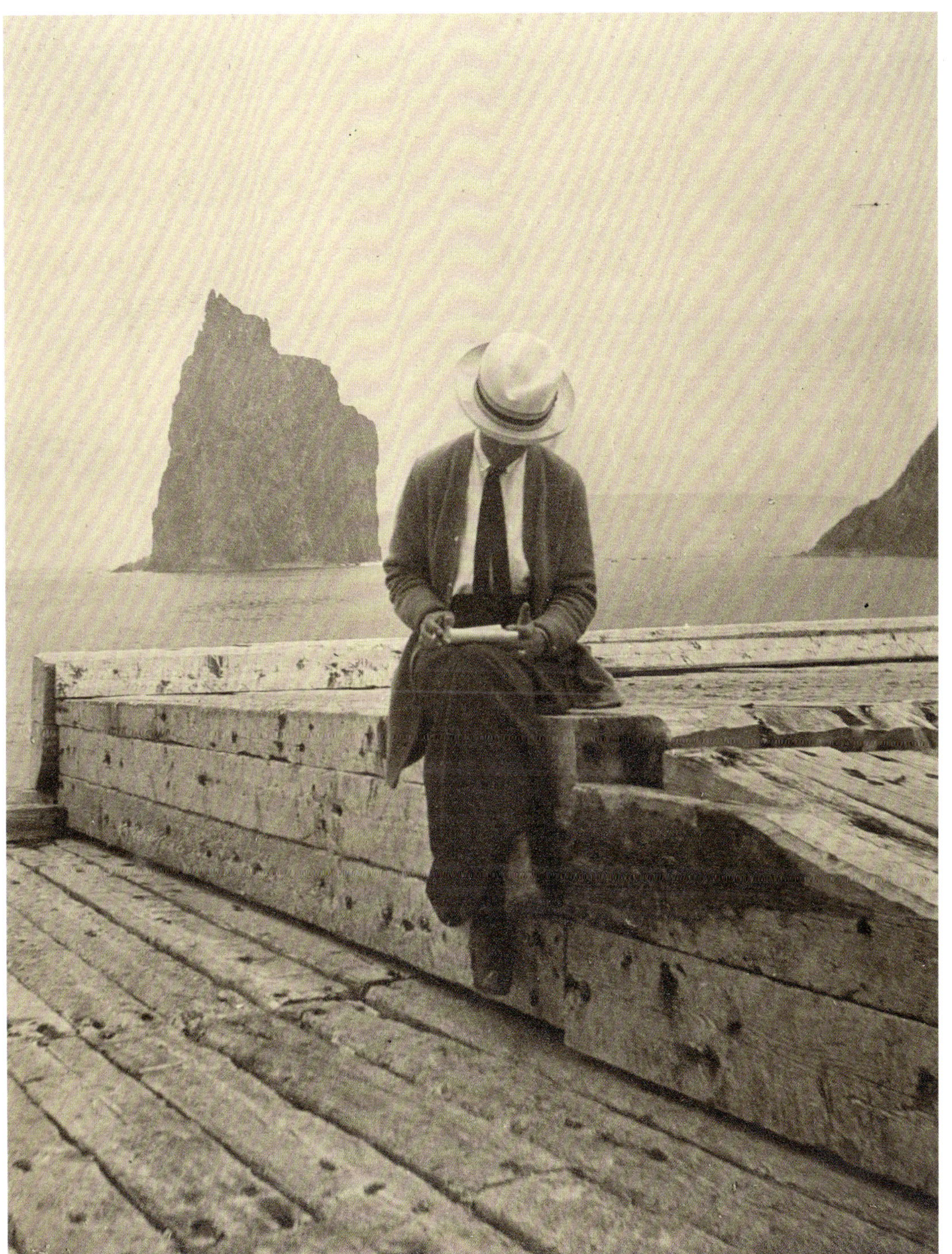

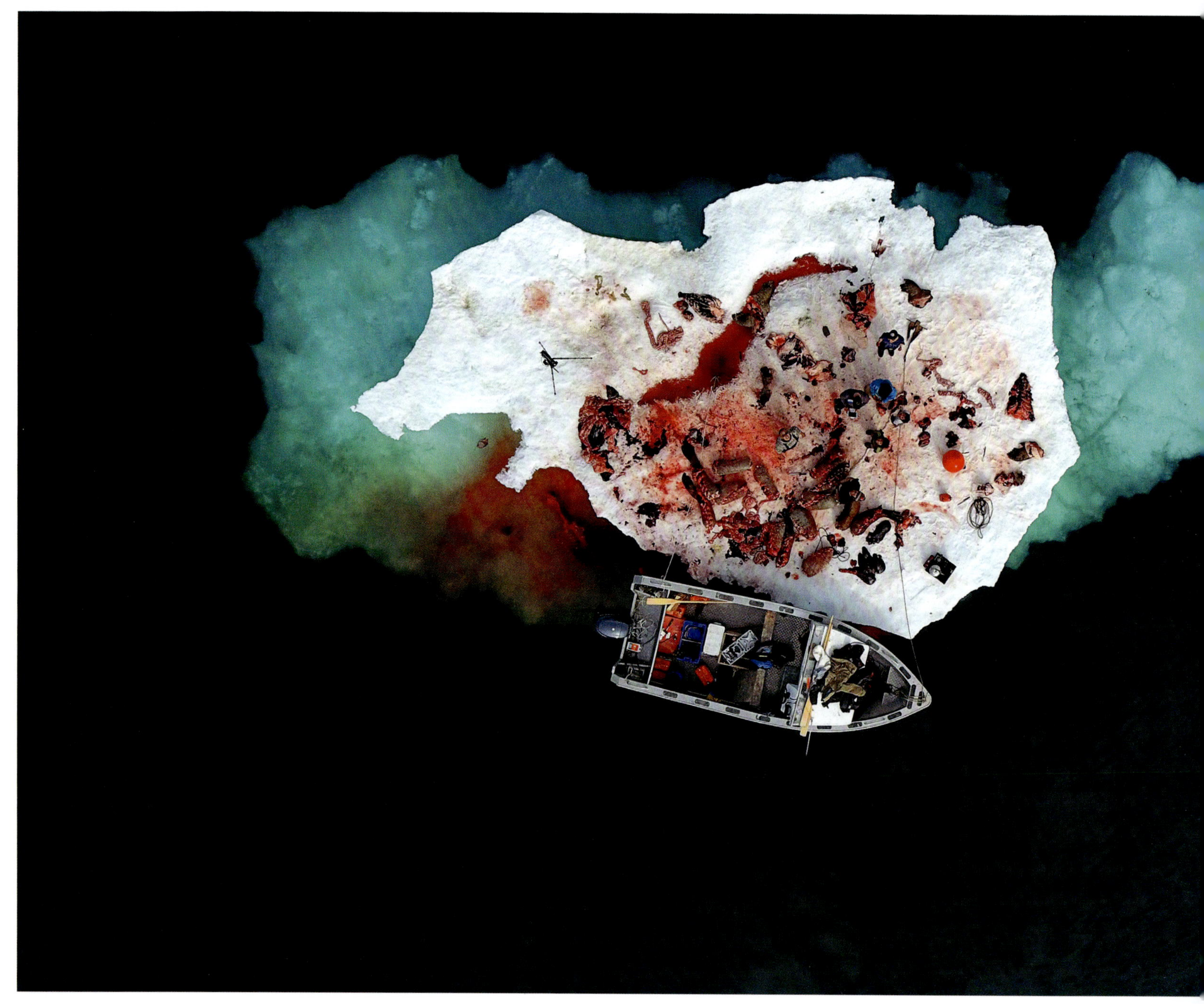

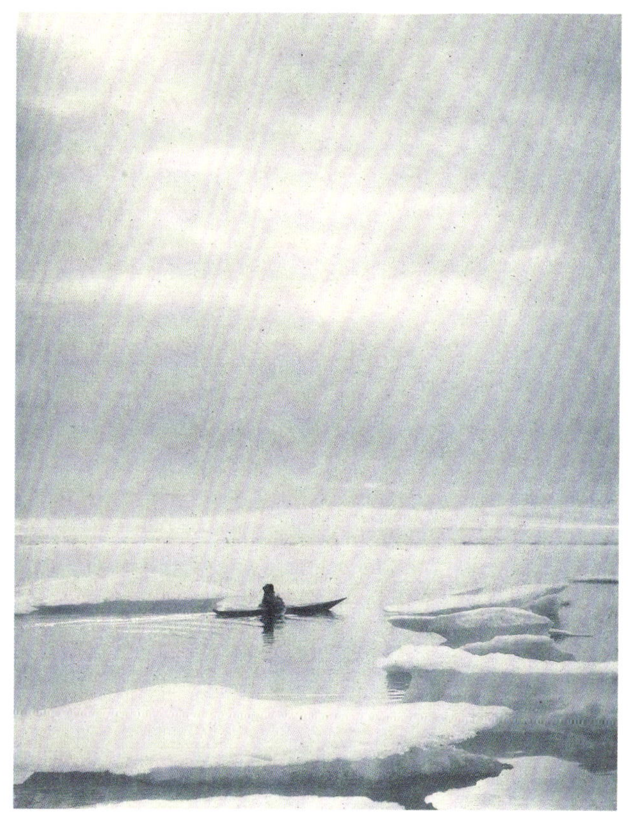

Robert Kautuk
Walrus Hunt
2016
Inkjet print
53.3 × 90.8 cm
Purchase, Canada Now Acquisition Initiative, with funds from Edward Burtynsky and Nicholas Metivier, 2022
2022/7046

Robert Flaherty
Summer (August), Kayak in Northeastern Hudson Bay
c. 1925
Photogravure
51 × 33.8 cm
Gift of Sandra Ball and Marcia Reid, 1987
87/322

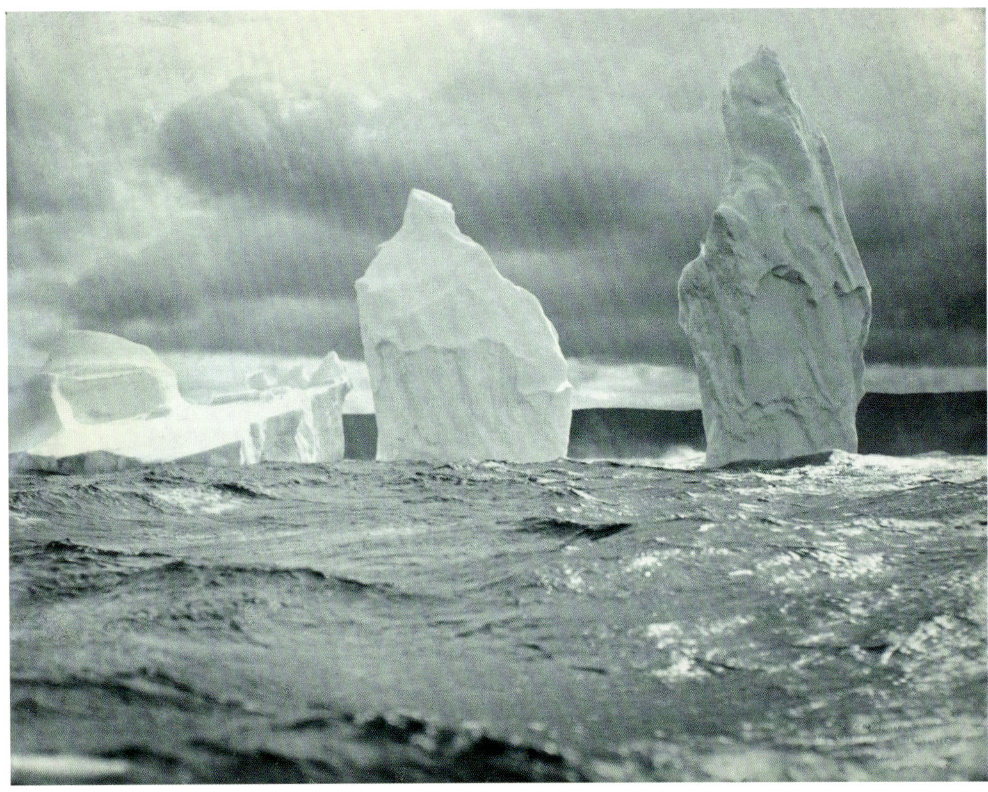

Elizabeth "Elsie" Holloway, The Holloway Studio
Iceberg, Newfoundland
c. 1920
Carbon print
29.8 × 38.1 cm
Purchase, with funds from the Kenneth and Nancy Kembry Fund, 2024
2024/5

Dawit L. Petros
Act of Recovery (Part II)
2016
Pigment print
50.8 × 66 cm
Purchase, Canada Now Photography Acquisition Initiative, with funds from Edward Burtynsky and Nicholas Metivier, 2021
2021/50

Robert Frank
Another World (Mabou Harbour, Nova Scotia)
1976-1977
Photo off-set line screen print
47 × 69.2 cm
Purchase, Penny Rubinoff Fund for Photography, 2010
2010/85

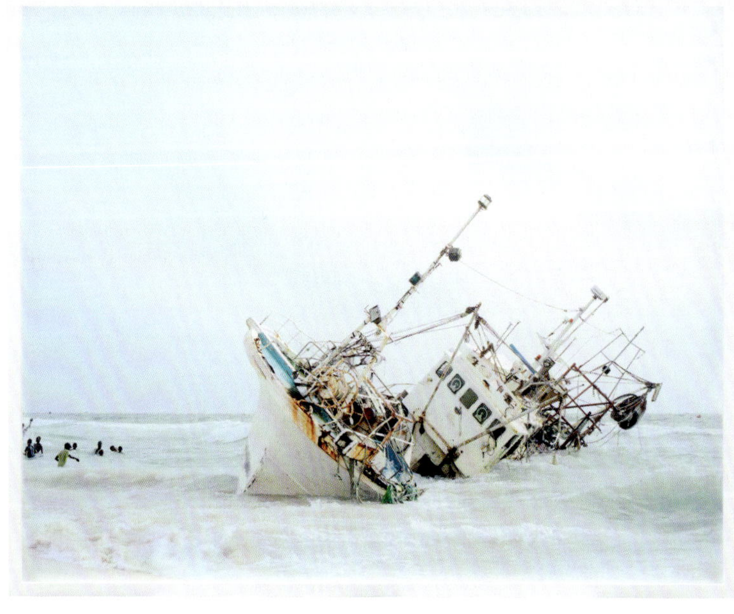

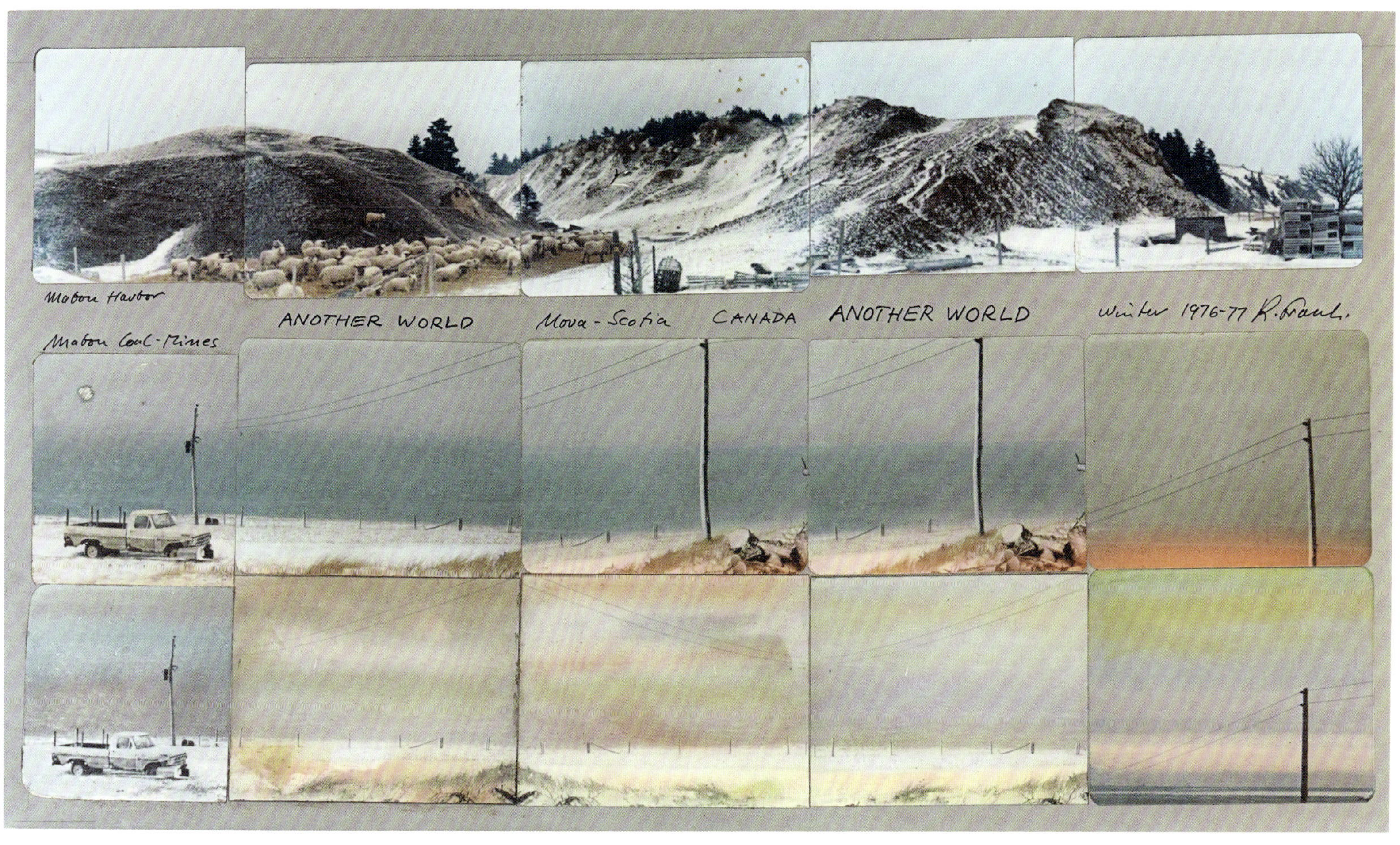
Mabou Harbor
ANOTHER WORLD
Nova - Scotia
CANADA
ANOTHER WORLD
Winter 1976-77 R. Frank.
Mabou Coal-Mines

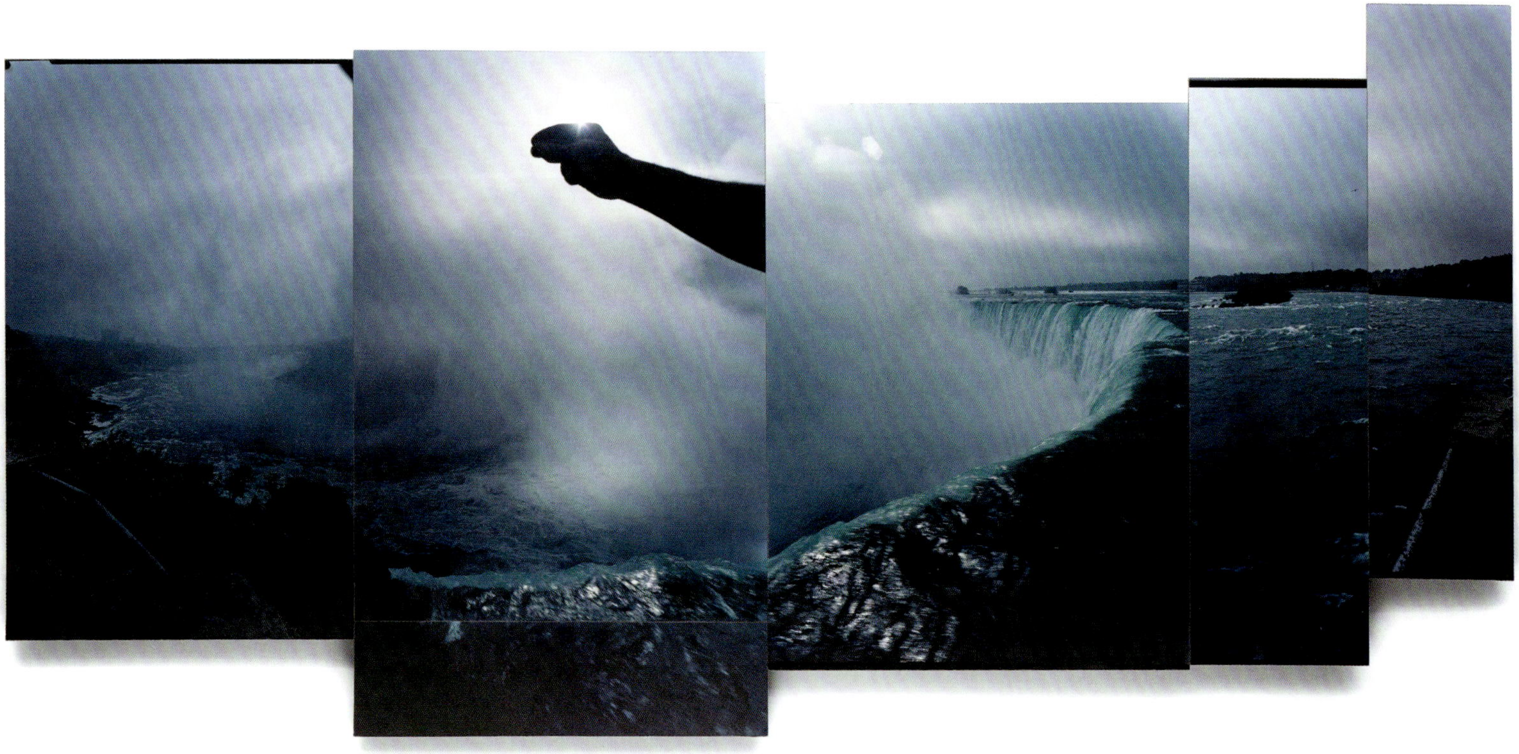

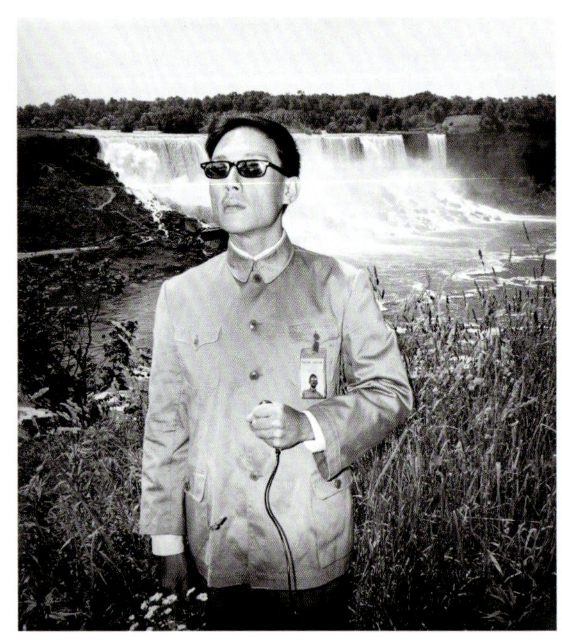

TSENG KWONG CHI

Born in Hong Kong and raised in Vancouver, Tseng Kwong Chi was a photographer and performance artist active in 1980s Manhattan. The definitive working set of his best-known series *East Meets West* (1979–1989) is now held in the collection. In a thrifted Mao suit and sunglasses, Tseng assumed the persona of an "ambiguous ambassador," cleverly subverting stereotypes to interrogate cultural narratives.

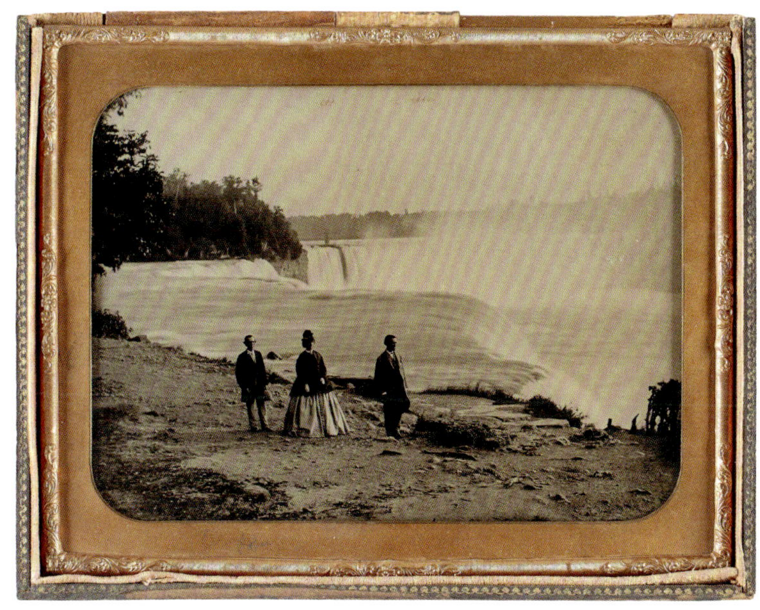

Max Dean
Snap (after Robert Frank)
2004
Chromogenic prints, mounted
76.5 × 160 cm
Malcolmson Collection
Gift of Harry and Ann Malcolmson in partnership with a private donor, 2014
2014/524

Tseng Kwong Chi
Niagara Falls, Canada
1984
From the series ***East Meets West*** (1979–1989)
Gelatin silver print
25.3 × 20.2 cm
Purchase, with funds from the Marie-Louise Stock Fund in memory of Valentine Stock, George Yabu & Glenn Pushelberg, Judy Schulich in honour of Julie Saul, Eleanor & Francis Shen in memory of Laura Rapp, Woodrow A. Wells, Kate Subak, Andrew Grimes and Jamie Stagnitta, 2024
2024/176

Platt Babbitt
A Party of Three Tourists Visiting Niagara Falls
c. 1855
Ambrotype
17.9 × 23 × 1.3 cm
Purchase, funds donated by Penny Rubinoff, 2015
2015/13

Maker once known, American
Studio Portrait: Arthur I. Rothwell of Burlington Ontario, taken at Niagara Falls, N.Y.
1894
Tintype in original paper folder
12.8 × 8.5 cm
Anonymous Gift, 2004
2004/152

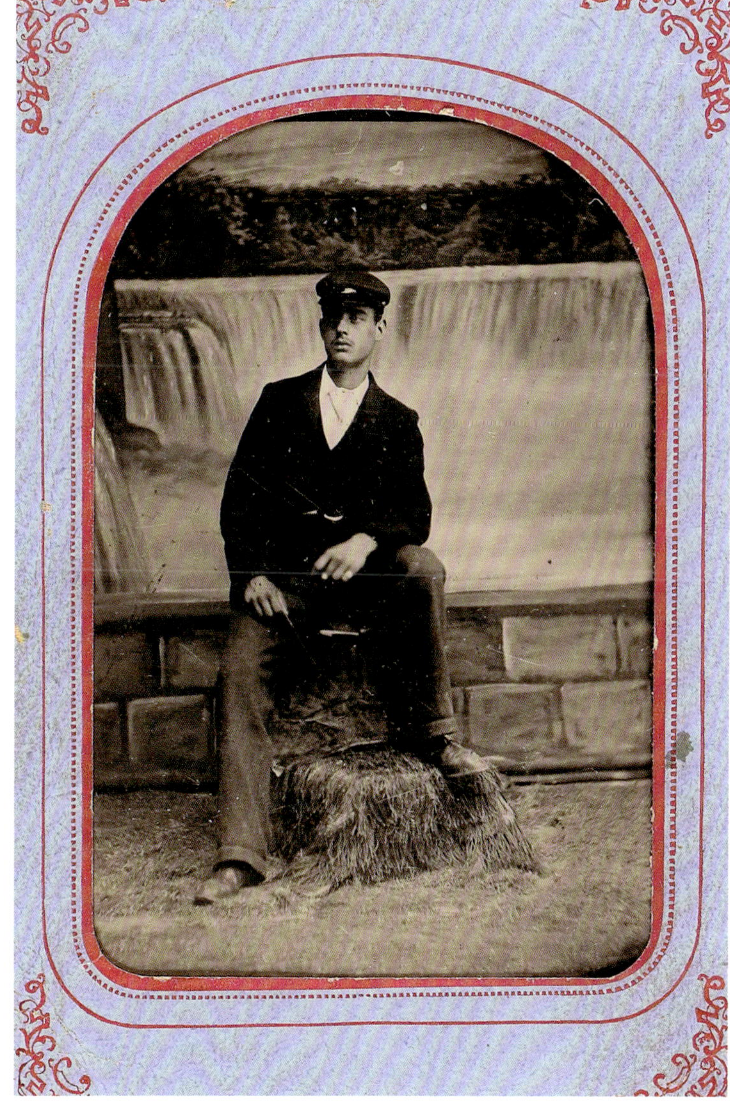

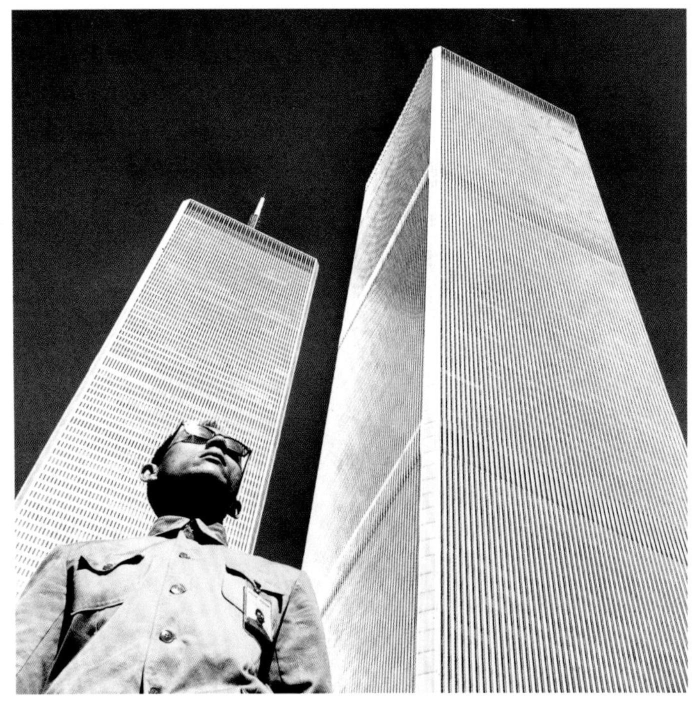

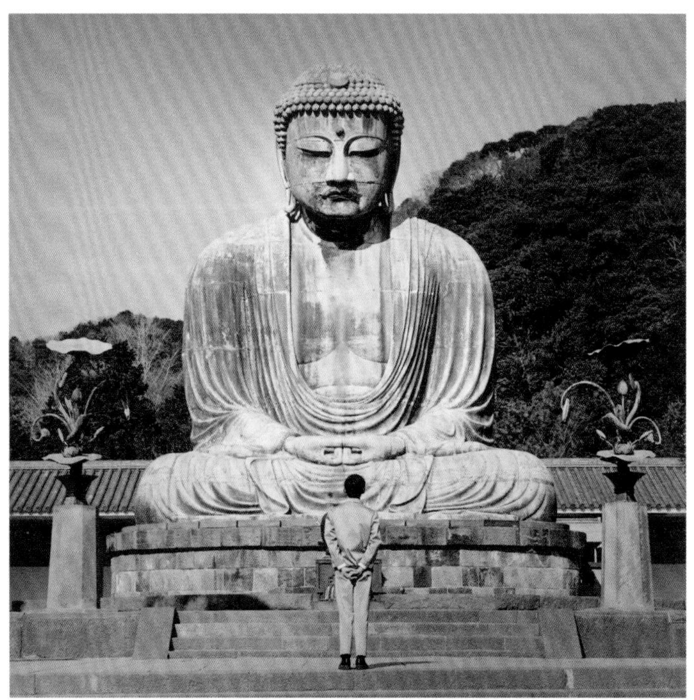

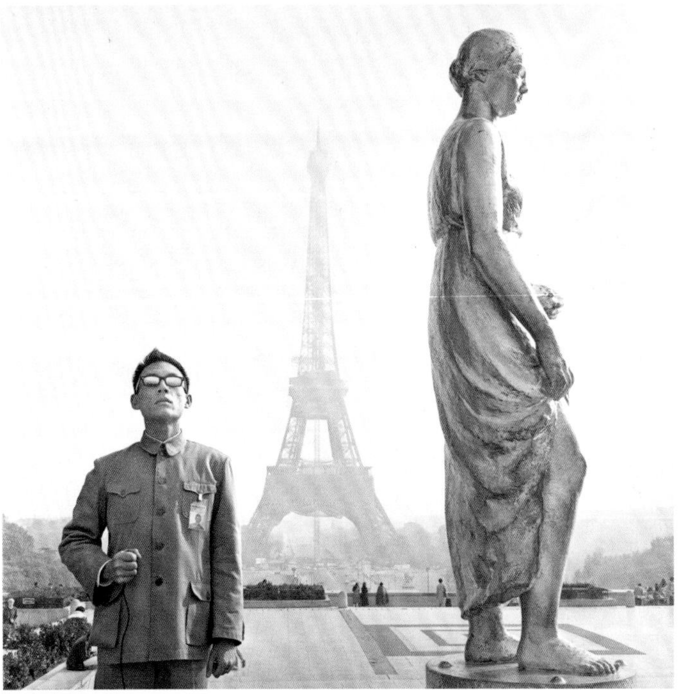

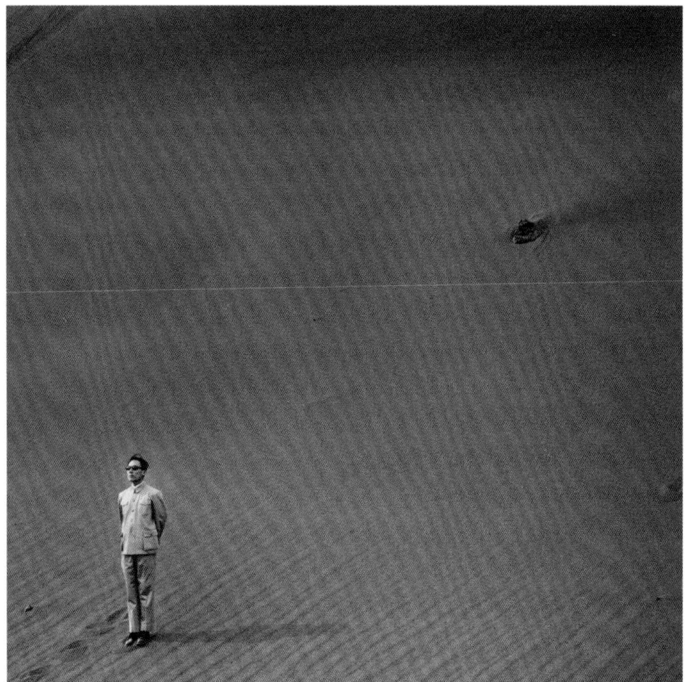

Tseng Kwong Chi
From the series ***East Meets West*** (1979–1989)

World Trade Center, New York
1979

Kamakura, Japan
1988

Paris, France
1983

Oshima, Japan
1988

Gelatin silver prints
25.3 × 20.2 cm each
Purchase, with funds from the the Marie-Louise Stock Fund in memory of Valentine Stock, George Yabu & Glenn Pushelberg, Judy Schulich in honour of Julie Saul, Eleanor & Francis Shen in memory of Laura Rapp, Woodrow A. Wells, Kate Subak, Andrew Grimes and Jamie Stagnitta, 2024
2024/148; 2024/202; 2024/169; 2024/203

Greg Girard
House on Zixua Lu, #14 Lu
2005
Chromogenic print
183 × 213 cm
Purchased with the assistance of the Toronto International Art Fair 2007 Opening Night Preview, and with the Financial Support of the Canada Council for the Arts Acquisition Assistance Program, 2008
2007/249

Maker once known, China
Nanking Road, Shanghai
1870s
From the album ***Views of Japan, China and Hong Kong*** (1870s–1890s)
Albumen print
21.4 × 26.5 cm
Gift of Neil B. Cole, 2007
2007/275.1-.75

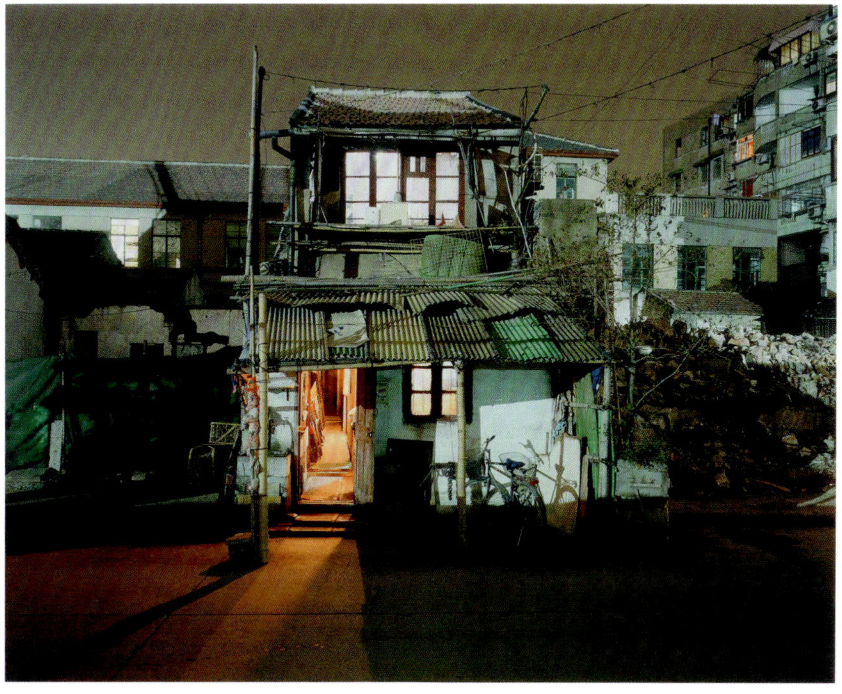

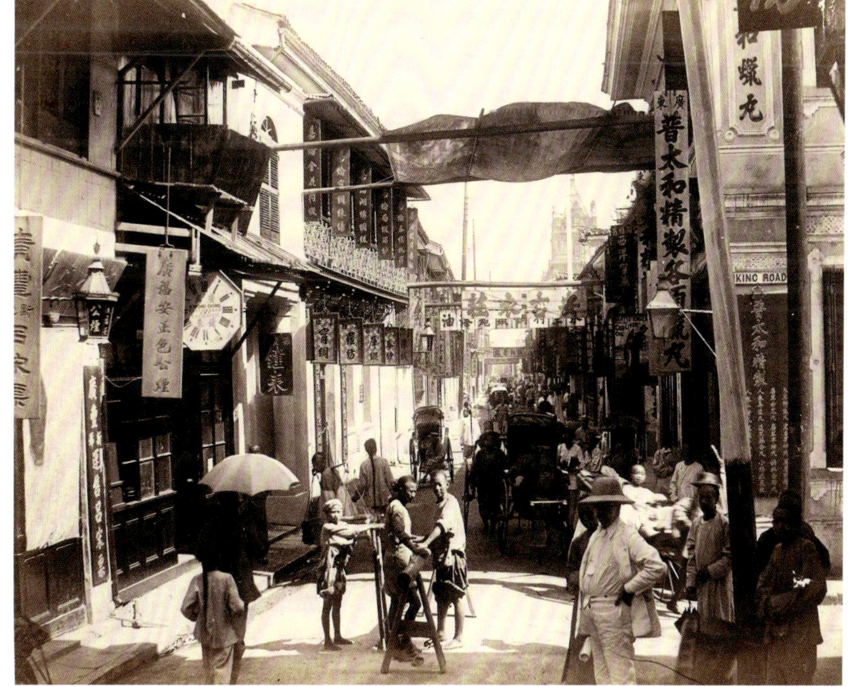

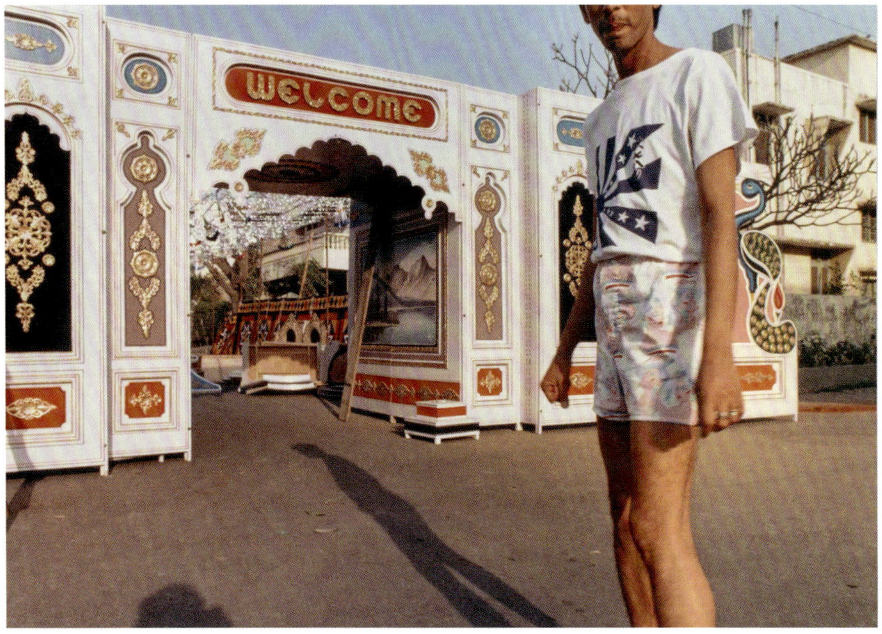

The Wedding
Everyone is married. Mother wants me to get married. I probably will, there is the family name, and respect to consider.

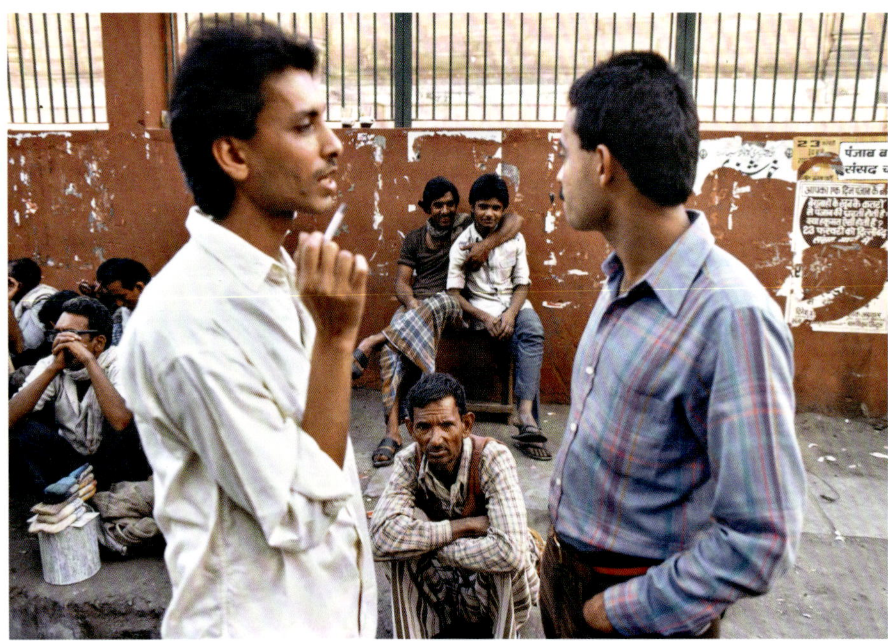

Jama Masjid
I love this part of town. It's got such character and you can have sex just walking in the crowd.

LINNEAUS TRIPE

Linnaeus Tripe created photographs of architecture and artifacts in South India and Burma (now Myanmar) in the 1850s—made from calotype negatives—that rank among the medium's boldest and most inventive early works. The comprehensive collection exemplifies the artistic and documentary ambitions of this British government-appointed photographer, highlighted by the 2003 publication of *Linnaeus Tripe: Catalogue Raisonné*, one of the first to be devoted to a photographer.

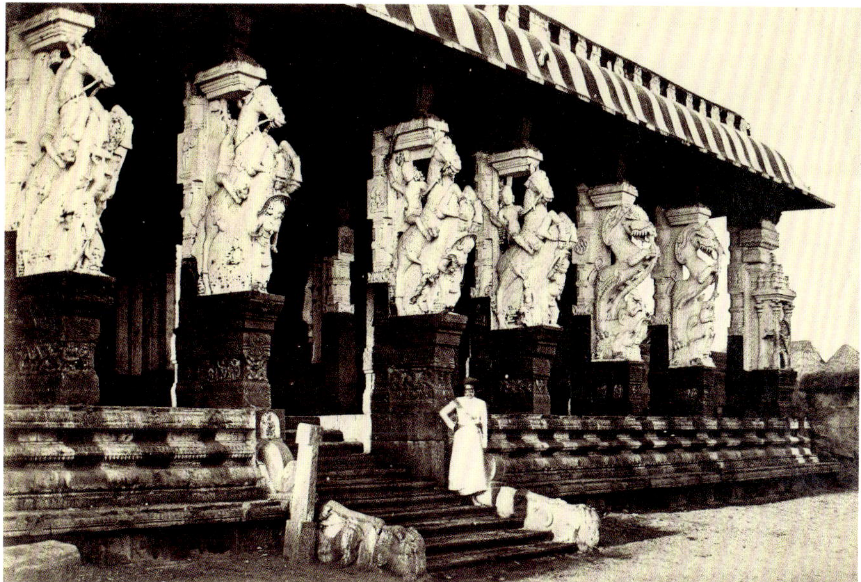

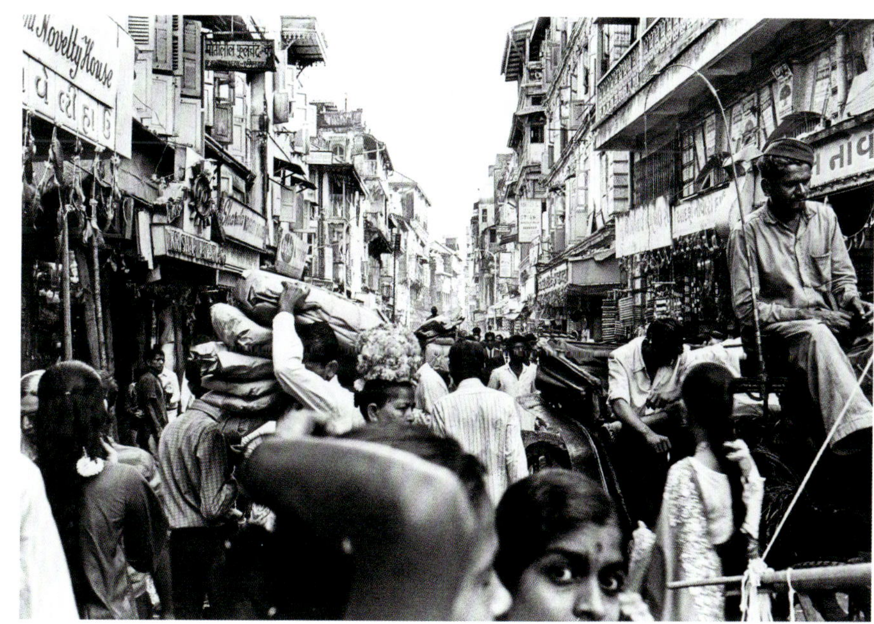

Sunil Gupta
From the series ***Exiles*** (1986-1987)

Jama Masjid
1989
Chromogenic print
40.5 × 58.4 cm
Gift of Stephen Bulger and Catherine Lash, 2024
2024/376

The Wedding
1987
Chromogenic print
40.7 × 58.5 cm
Purchase, funds from Robyn McCallum and Stephan Delaney, 2024
2024/03

Linnaeus Tripe
Secunder Malay. Munduppum, in Front of the Therooparungoonrum Pagoda
1858
Albumen print from a waxed paper negative
24.5 × 37.5 cm
Gift of Dr. Shashi B. Dewan and Janet E. Dewan, 1996
96/1267

Bhupendra Karia
Population Crisis, B96.70 Bombay
1968-1971
From the series ***Population Crisis*** (1968-1971)
Gelatin silver print
28 × 35.5 cm
Purchase, 2016
2016/166

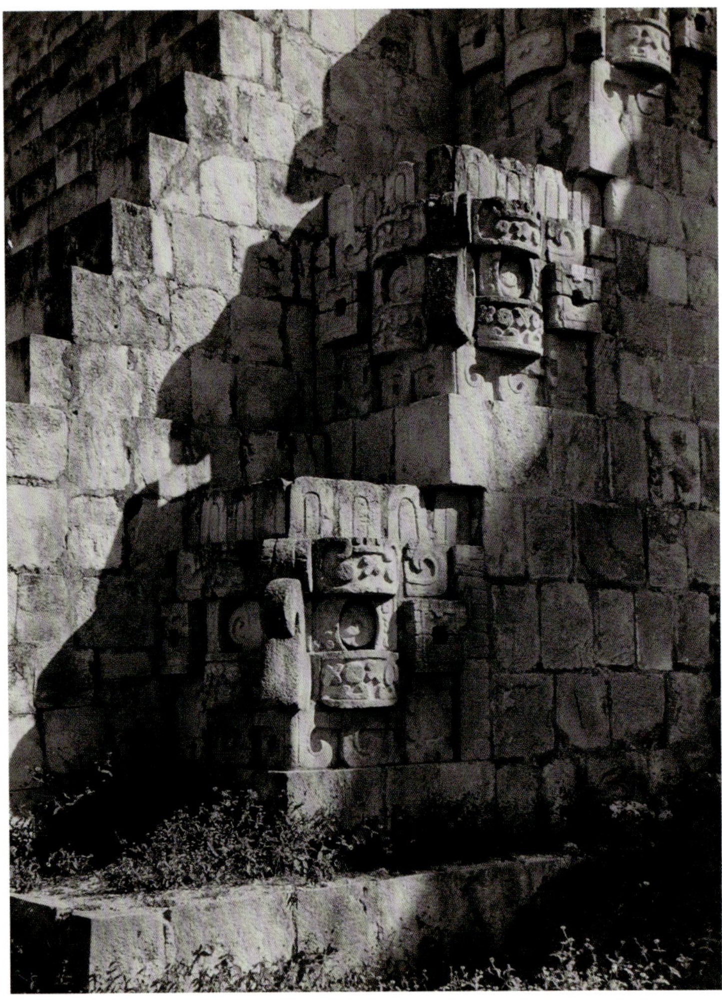

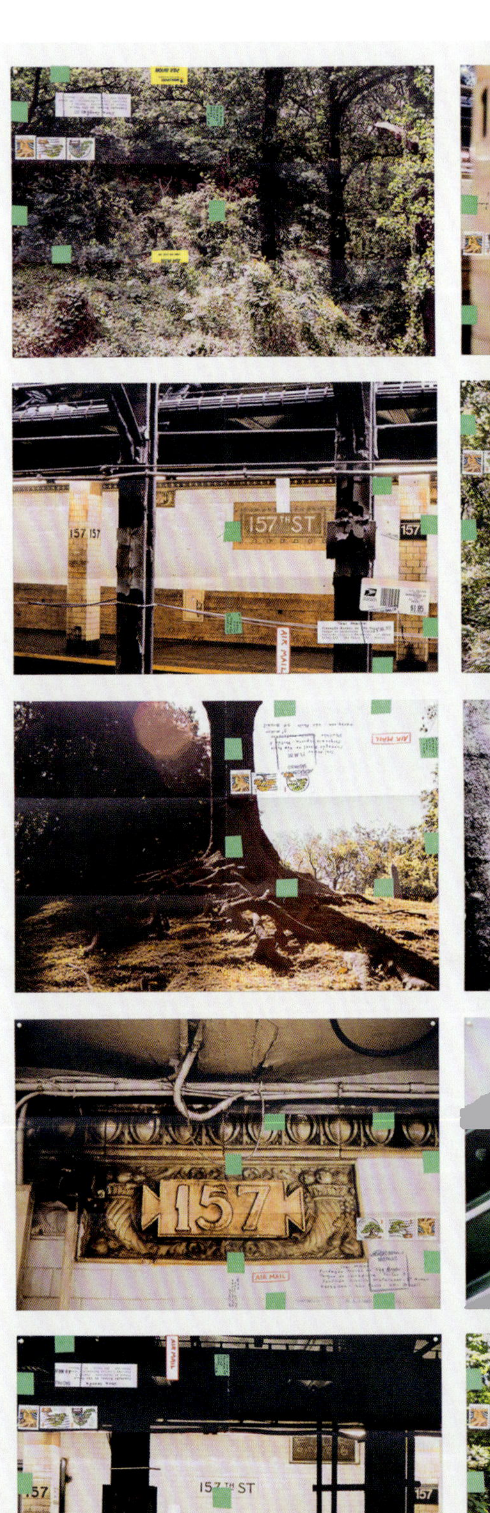

LOLA ÁLVAREZ BRAVO

Lola Álvarez Bravo is one of Mexico's most influential photographers. Over a fifty-year career, she captured the spirit of her country through striking images of its people, landscapes, and architecture. The collection's significant holdings of her photographs of Mexico's pre-Hispanic sites reveal a quiet, powerful facet of her work, honouring the past while shaping a distinctly modern visual language.

Lola Álvarez Bravo
Uxmal: Pyramid of the Magician, stair carvings
1950s
Gelatin silver print
24.3 × 17.2 cm
Anonymous Gift, 2007
2007/898

Moyra Davey
157 Women
2012
Chromogenic prints (25), tape, postage, ink
30 × 45 cm each
Gift of Robin and Malcolm Anthony, Alexandra Babcock and Todd Cowan, Kim Bozak and Phil Deck, Susan Caskey and John Francis, Angela and David Feldman, Liza Mauer and Andrew Sheiner, Elisa Nuyten and David Dime, Donna and Robert Poile, and Anne and Lawrence Ullman, 2020
2020/52.1-.25

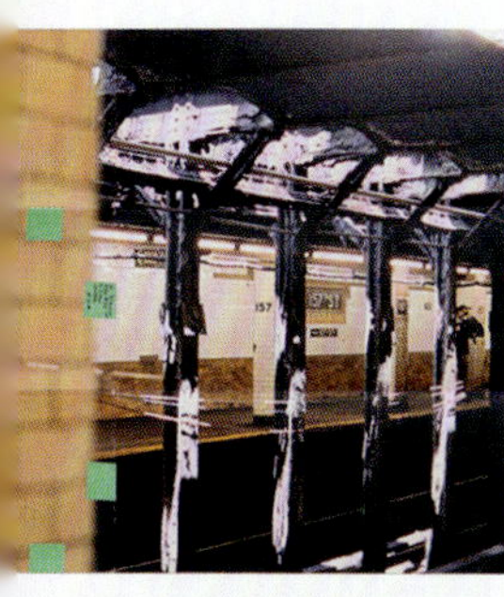
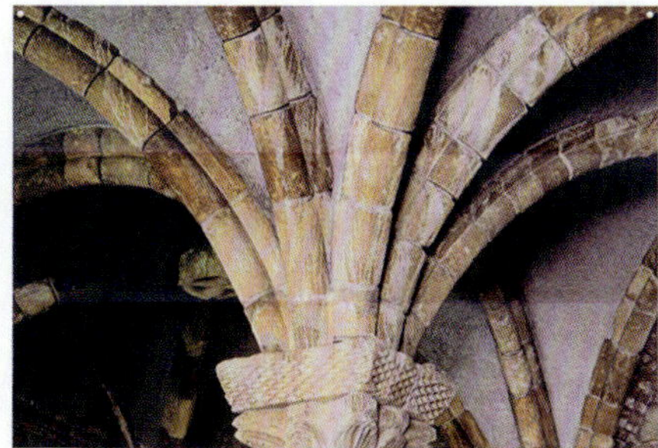
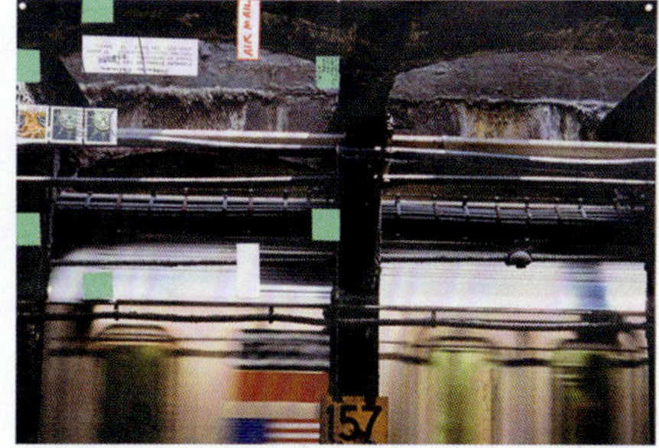
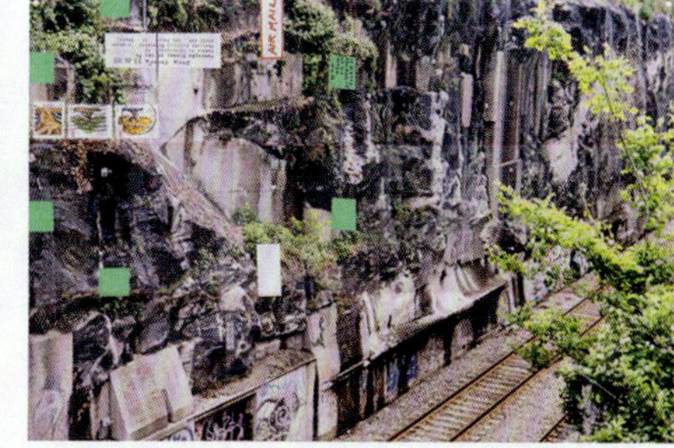
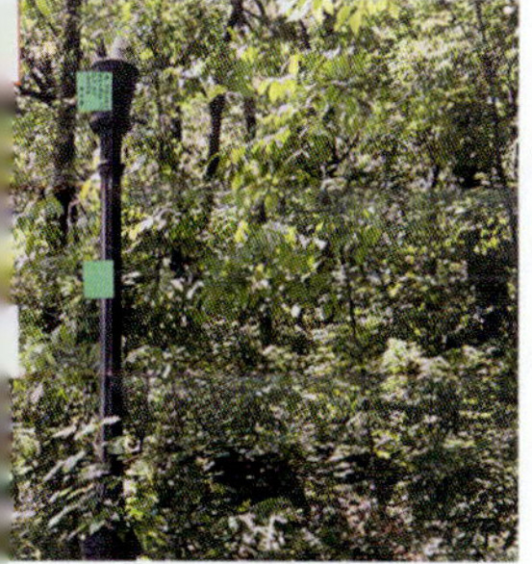
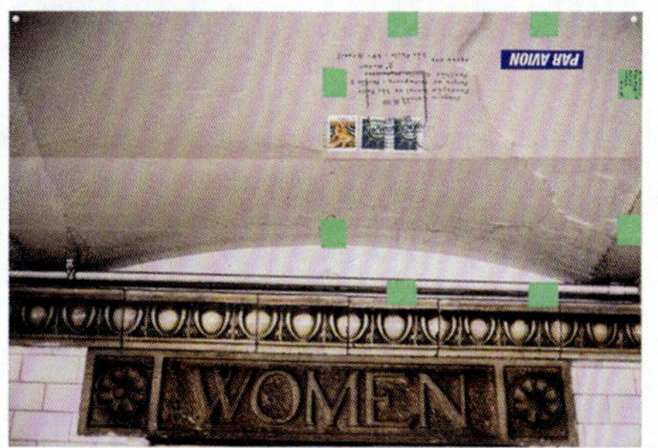
PAR AVION
WOMEN
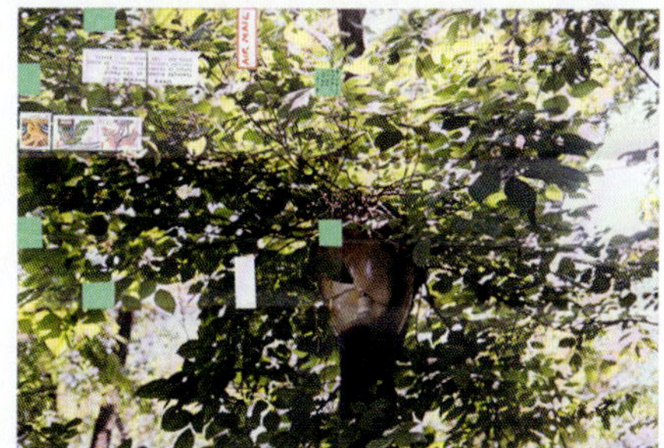
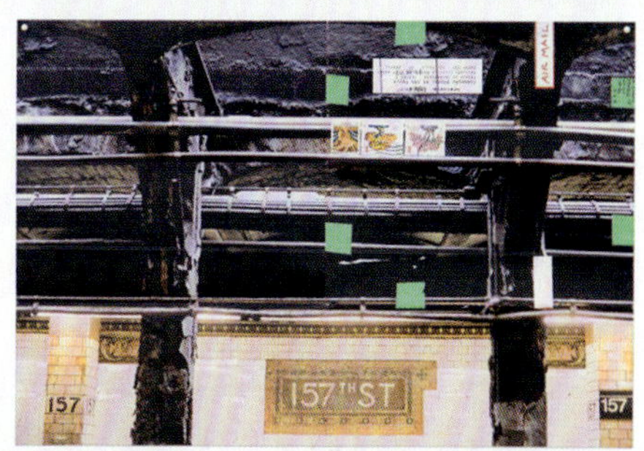
157TH ST
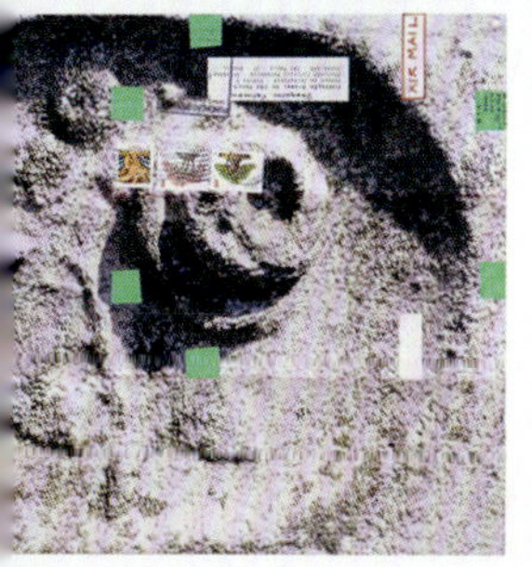
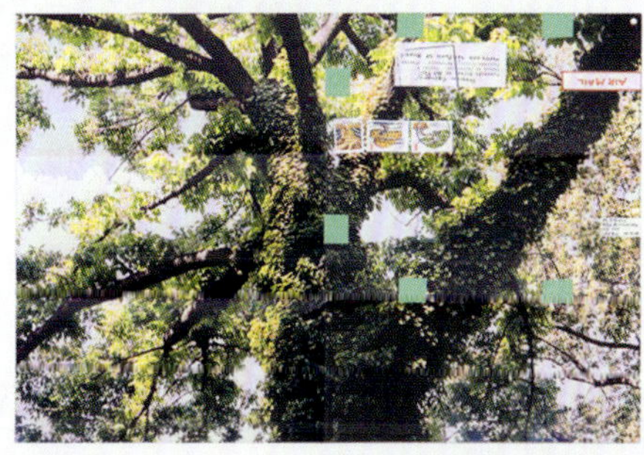
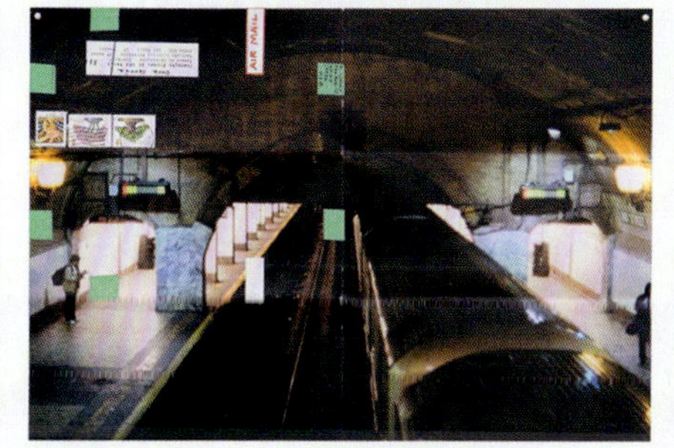
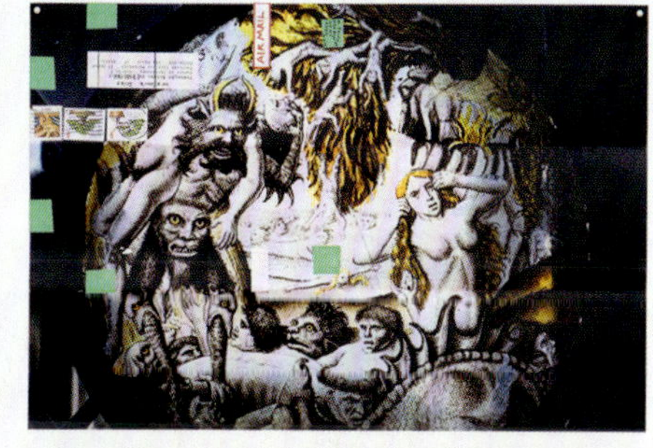
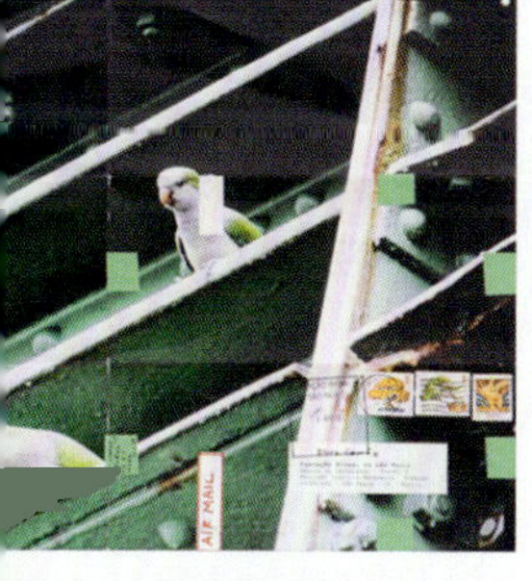
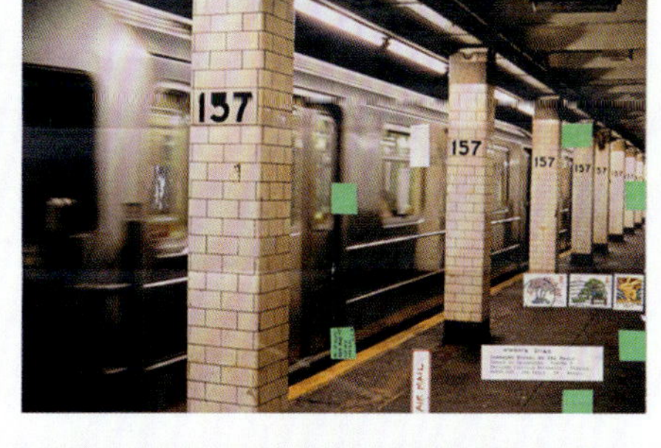
157
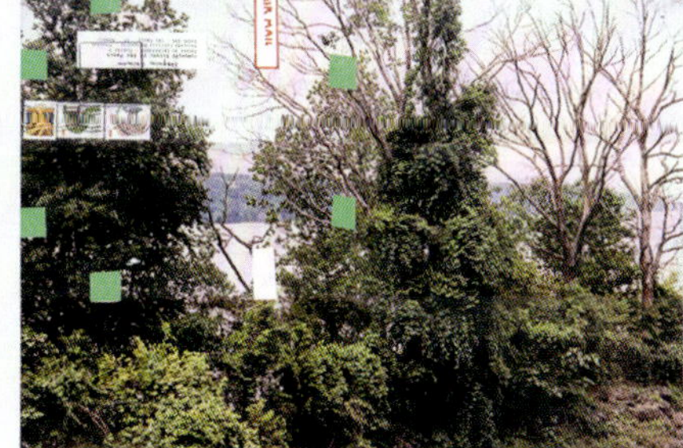
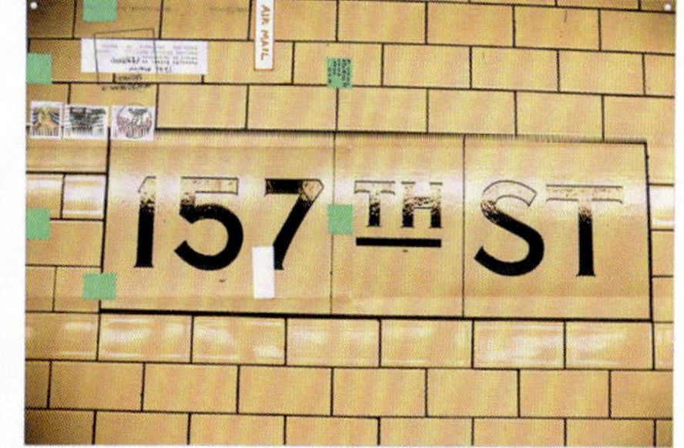
157 TH ST
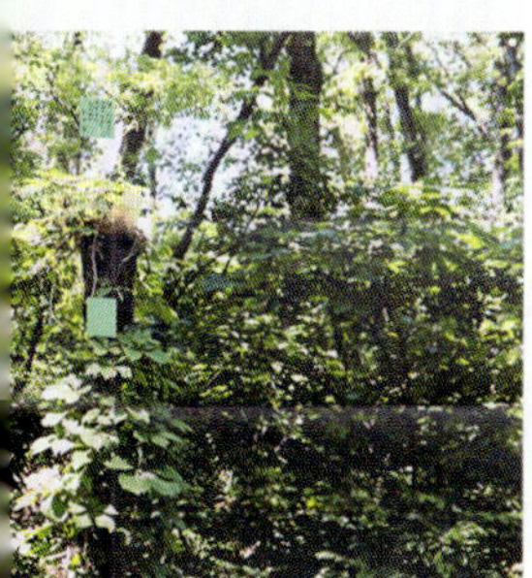
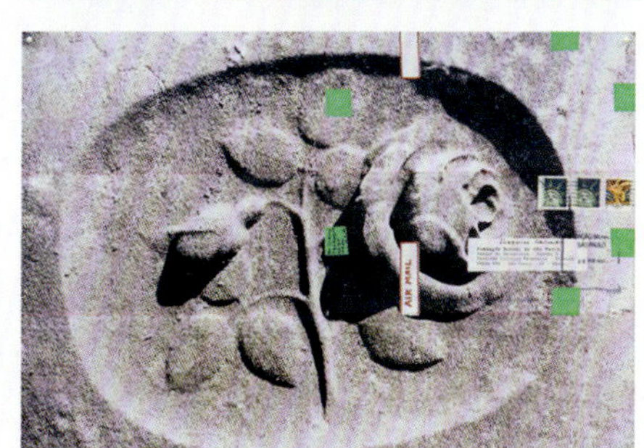
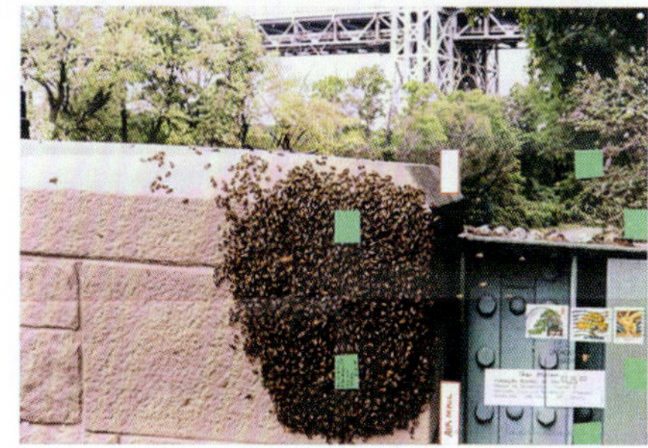
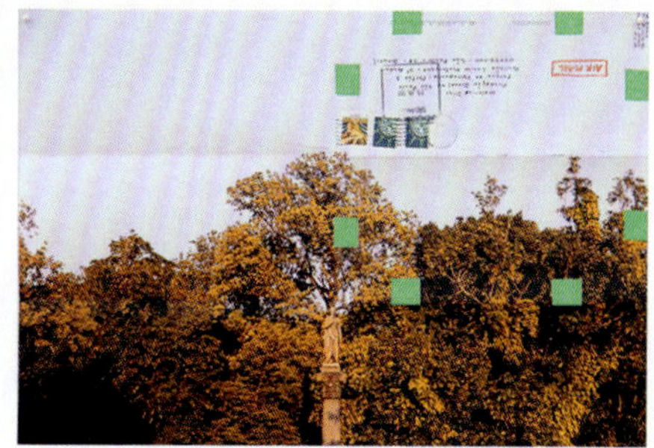

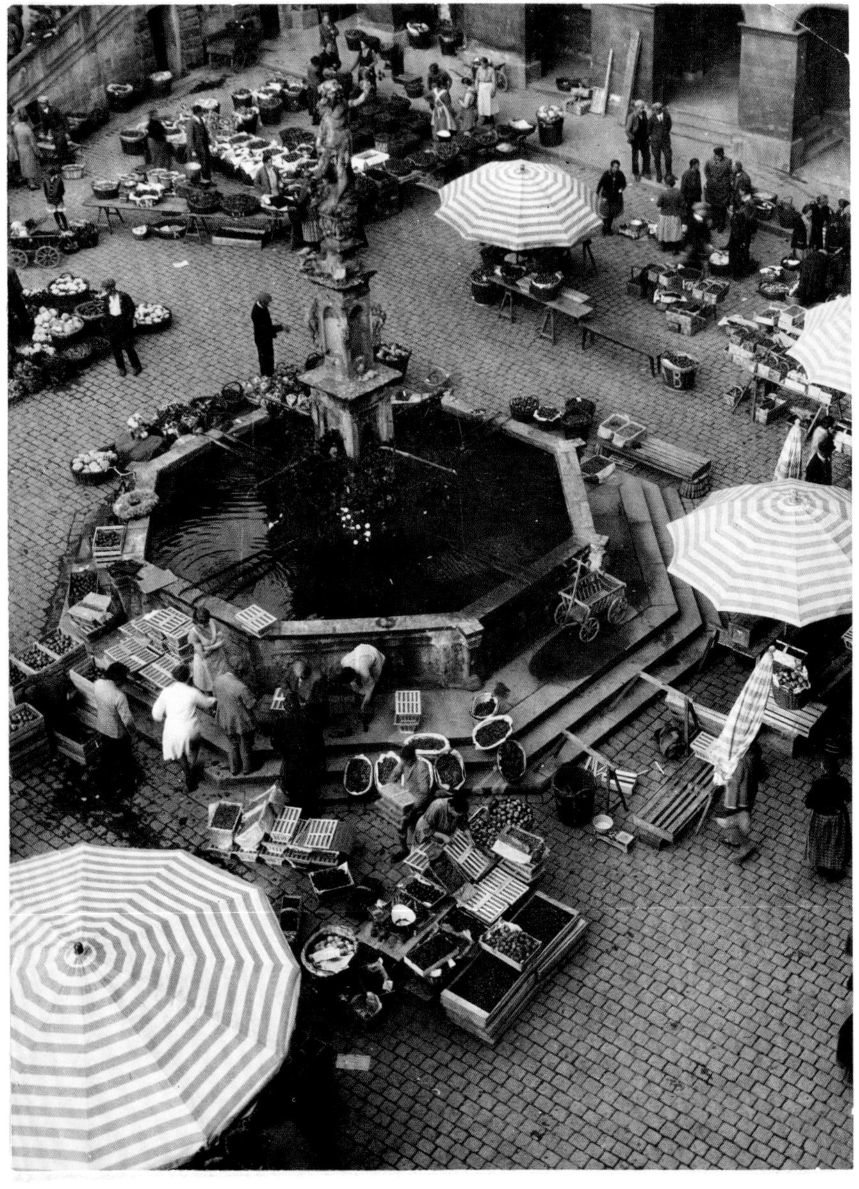

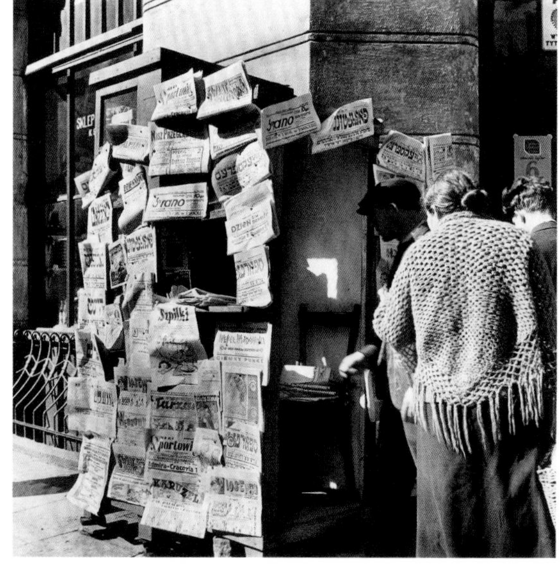

László Moholy-Nagy
Marketplace and Fountain, Berlin
c. 1928
Gelatin silver print
23 × 17.1 cm
Gift of Jane Corkin in honour of Alkis Klonaridis, 1996
96/1085

Roman Vishniac
There Were 402 Jewish Publications...Warsaw
1937; printed later
Gelatin silver print
25.4 × 20.4 cm
Gift of Sandra Ball and Marcia Reid, 1987
87/221

Ian Wallace
Untitled (Main Street, Lodz)
1990
Acrylic and photograph on canvas
152.5 × 152.5 × 3.4 cm
Gift of Alison and Alan Schwartz, 1999
99/649

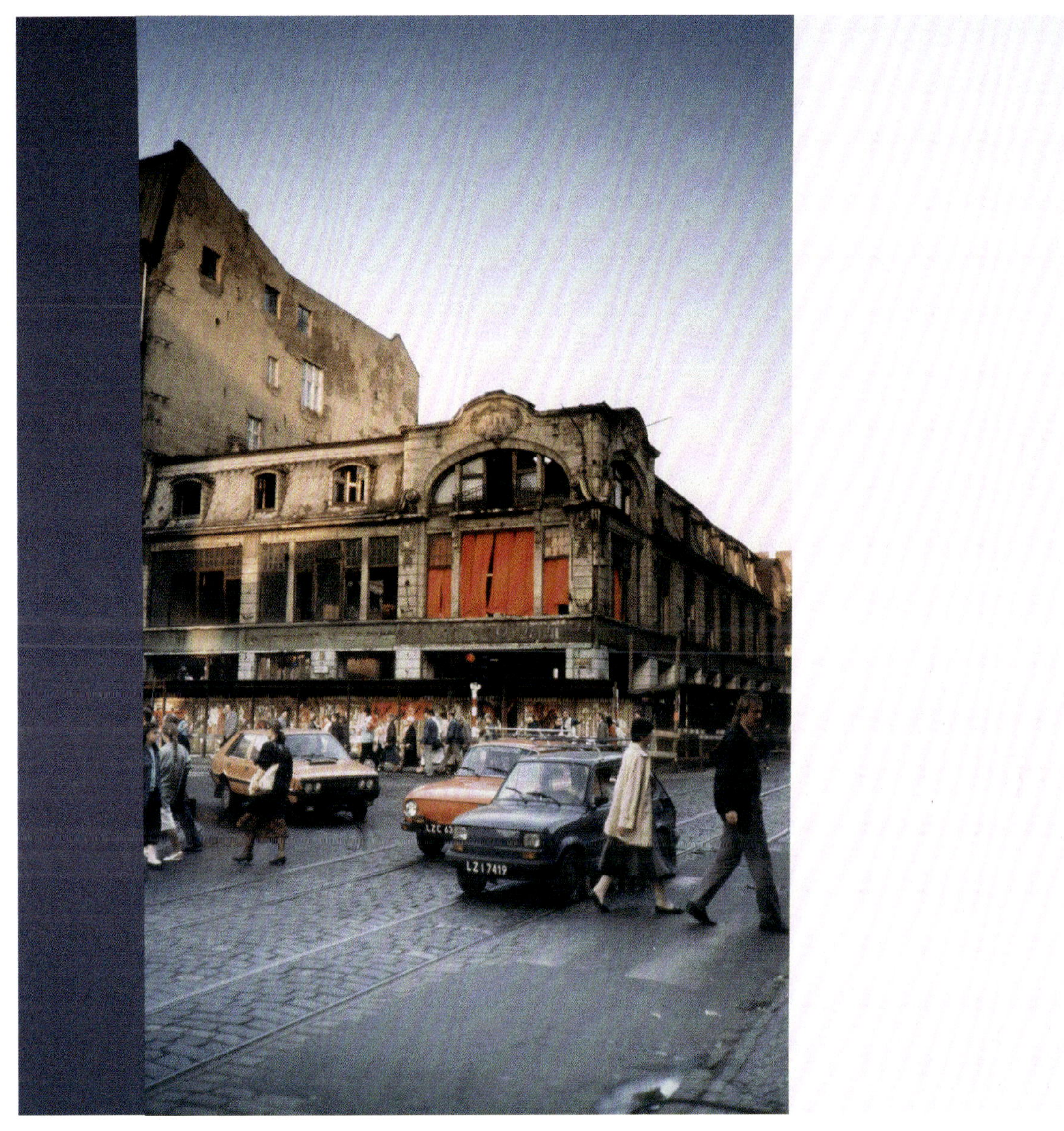

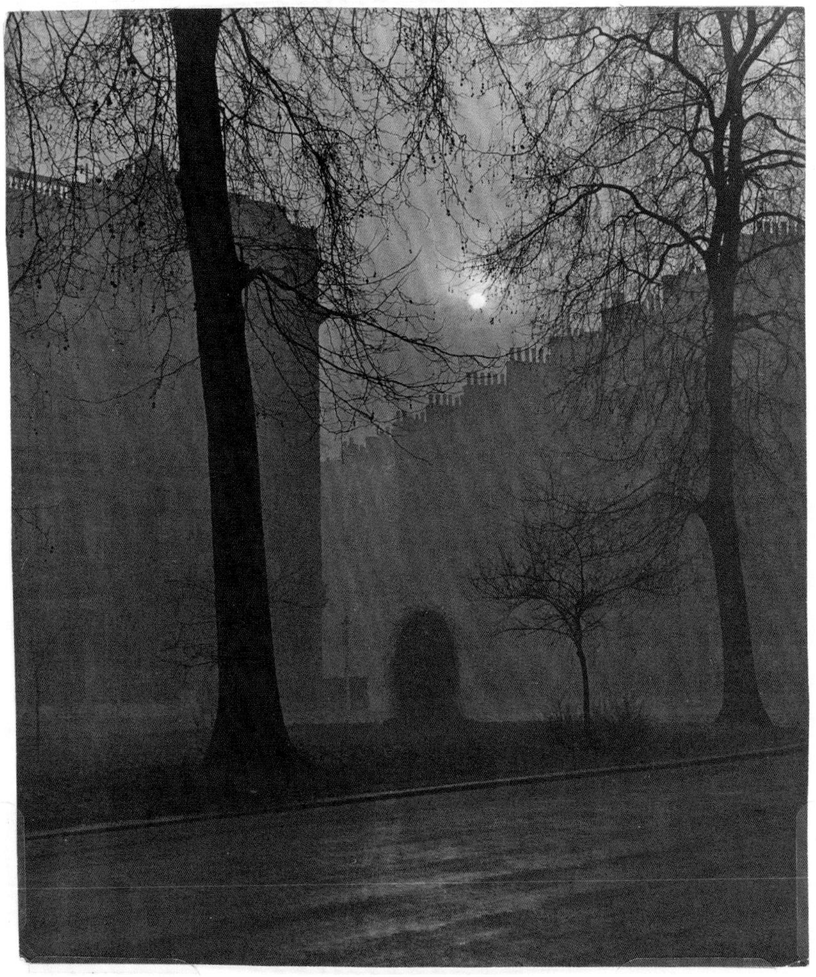

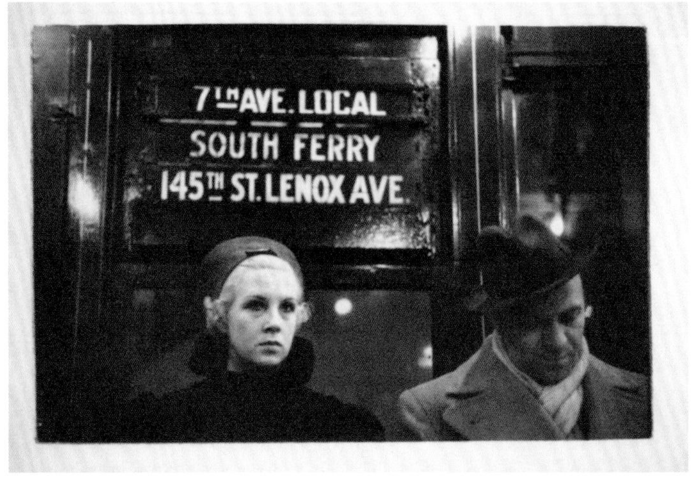

Bill Brandt
Square in Bayswater, Blackout, London
c. 1942
Gelatin silver print
19.6 × 22.9 cm
Gift of the Applebanks Collection, Toronto, 2024
2025/49

Walker Evans
Untitled
1938–1941
Gelatin silver print
20.3 × 19.1 cm
Anonymous Gift, 2006
2006/225

André Kertész
On the Boulevards
1934; printed c. 1960
Gelatin silver print
25.5 × 19.2 cm
Malcolmson Collection. Gift of Harry and Ann Malcolmson in partnership with a private donor, 2014
2014/576

John Vanderpant
Window Patterns
1920s–1930s
Gelatin silver print
34.6 × 26.7 cm
Malcolmson Collection. Gift of Harry and Ann Malcolmson in partnership with a private donor, 2014
2014/699

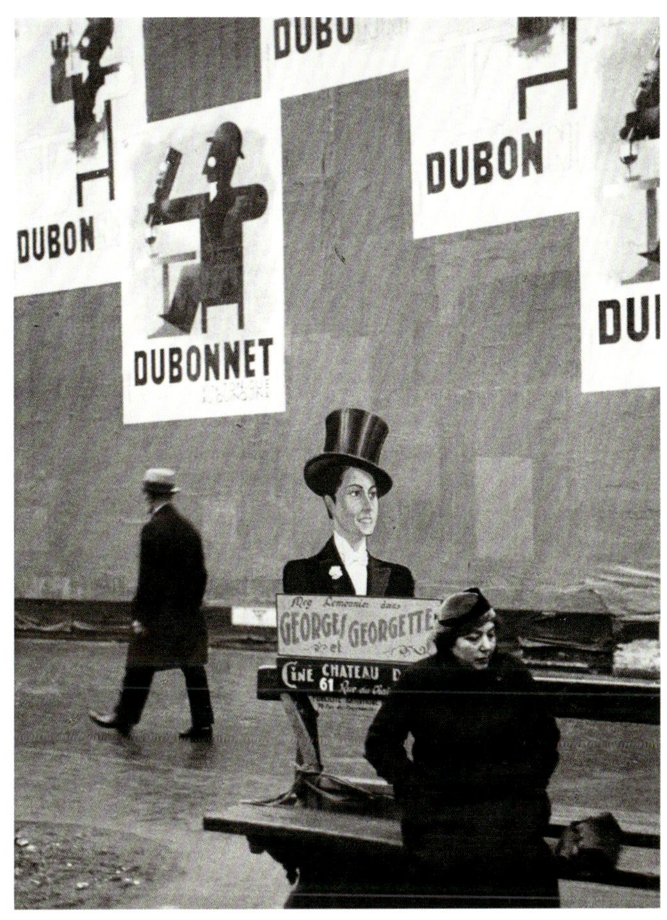
DUBO
DUBON
DUBONNET
DUBON
GEORGES
et
GEORGETTE
CINE CHATEAU
61

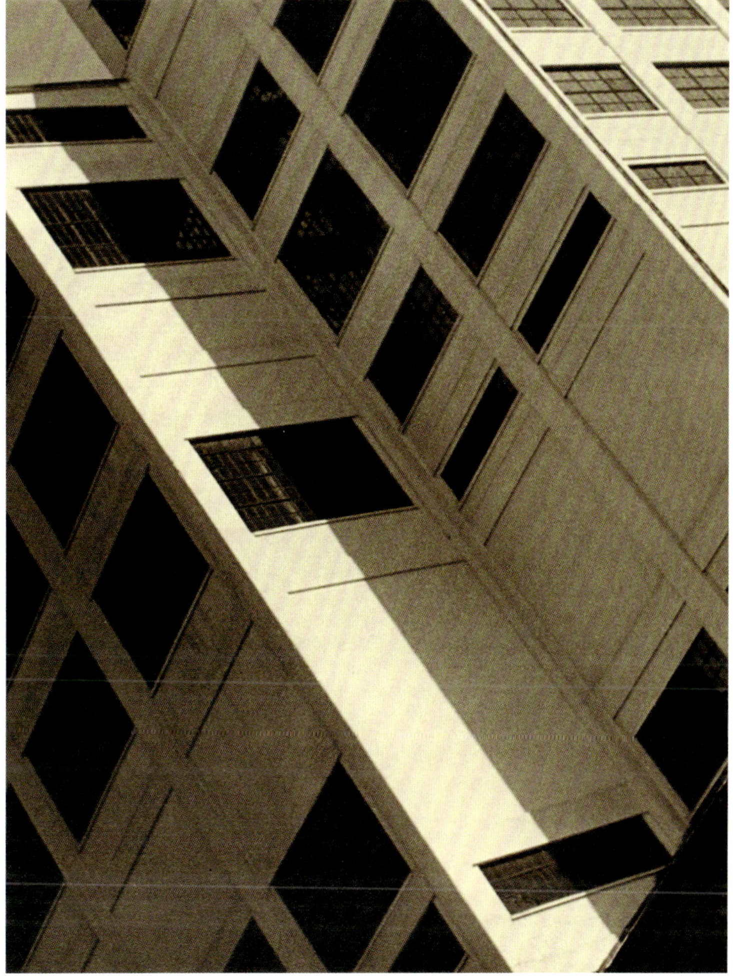

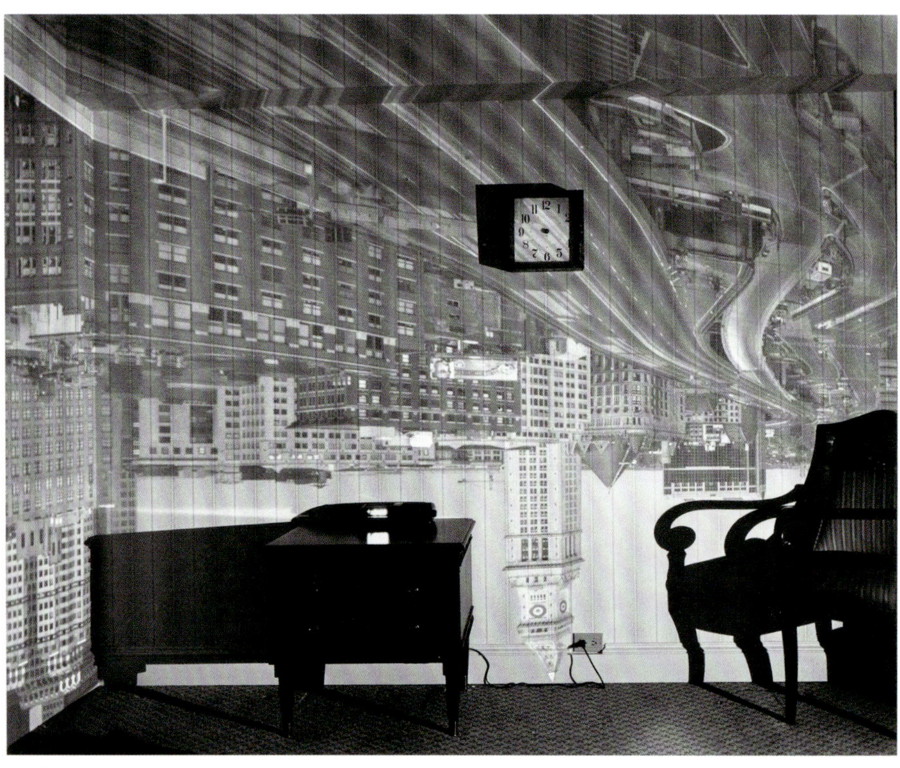

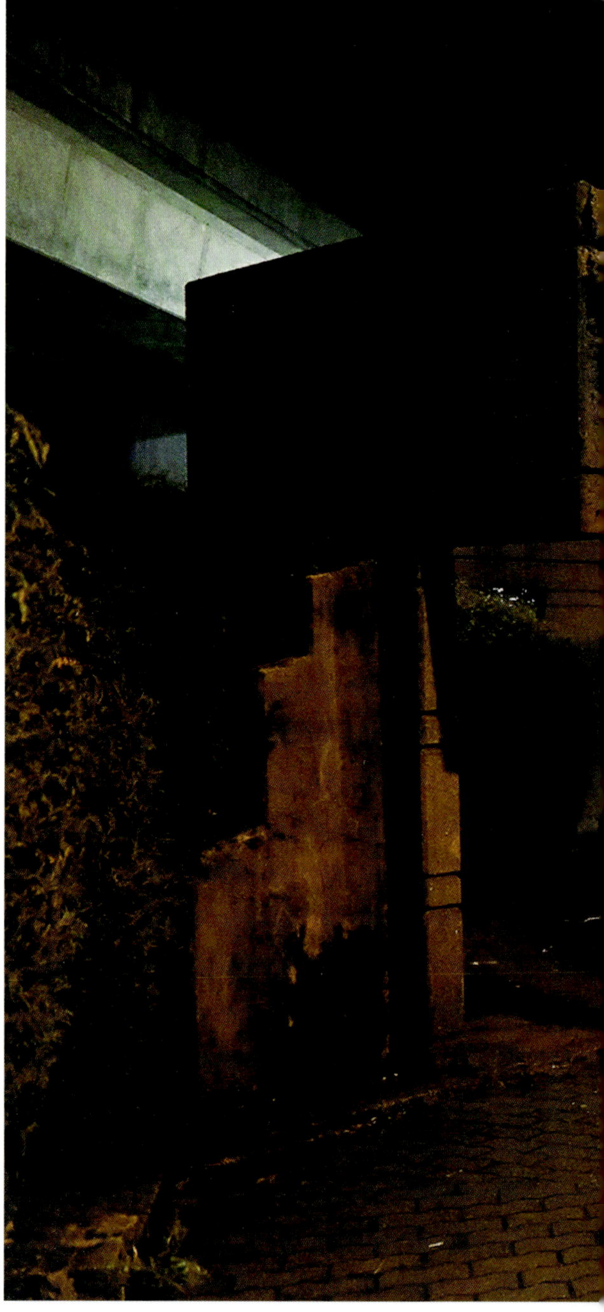

Abelardo Morell
Camera Obscura Image of Boston's Old Custom House in Hotel Room
1999
Gelatin silver print
45.9 × 57 cm
Gift of Ross Winter and David Moore, Camera Lucida, in honour of Maia-Mari Sutnik, 2023
2023/263

Gabrielle L'Hirondelle Hill
Monument to Piazza Italia
2014
Inkjet print
61 × 110 cm
Purchase, with funds from Robyn McCallum and Stephen Delaney, 2021
2021/73

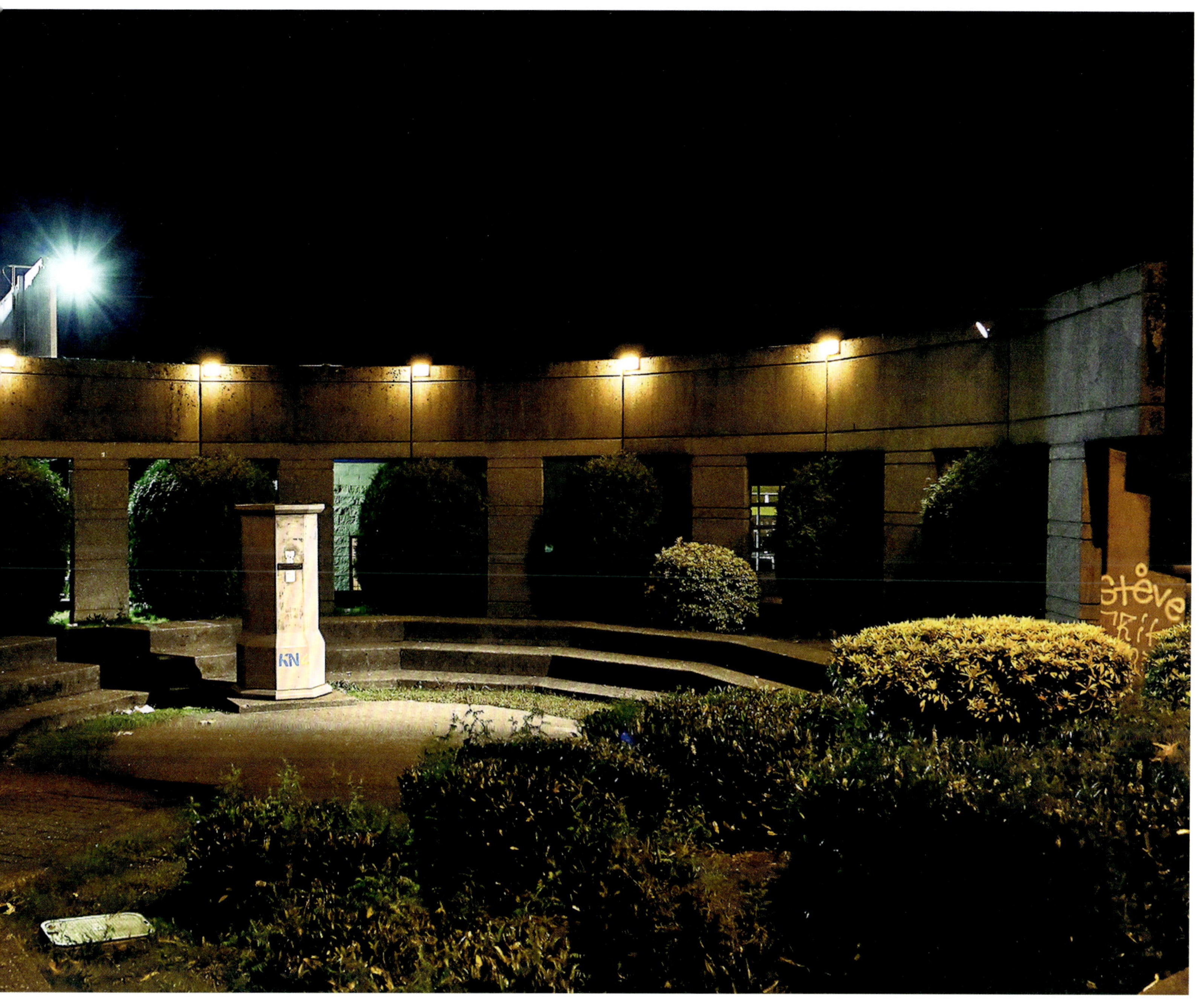

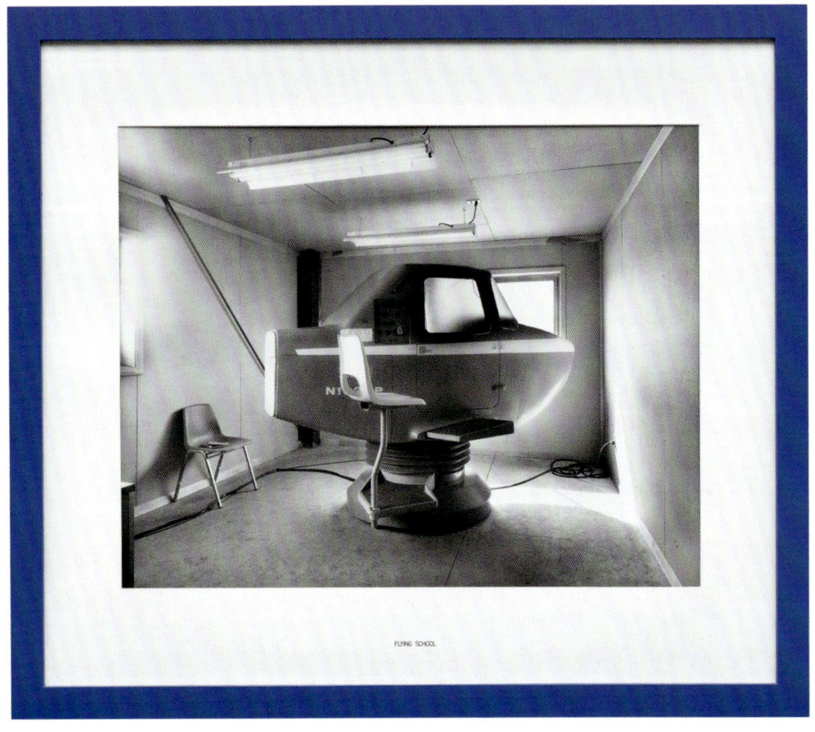

LEE FRIEDLANDER

Lee Friedlander's photographs—wry, rigorous, and deeply rooted in American vernacular culture—have expanded the possibilities of the medium, revealing the layered strangeness of familiar places. The collection offers an unparalleled view of his career, spanning from the 1950s to the mid-2010s, and includes self-portraits, street scenes, portraits, nudes, and family photographs. Notable is the complete set of prints from Friedlander's 1989 retrospective *Like a One-Eyed Cat*.

Lynne Cohen
Flying School
1989
Gelatin silver print
101.6 × 119.4 cm
Gift from The Peggy Lownsbrough Fund, 1990
90/69

Lee Friedlander
Philadelphia
1961; printed c. 2010
From the series ***Little Screens*** (1960–1969)
Gelatin silver print
40.6 × 50.8 cm
Gift of Mazyar Mortazavi and Bita Doagoo, 2024

Cheryl Sourkes
Game
2006
From the series ***Homecammers*** (2006)
Chromogenic print face-mounted to Plexiglas
101 × 132 cm
Anonymous Gift, 2023
2023/285

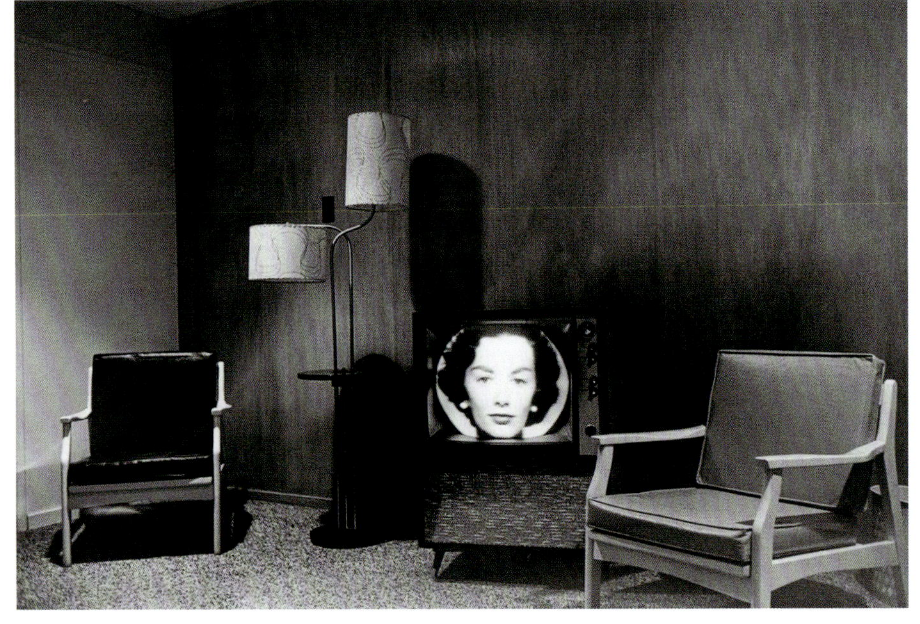

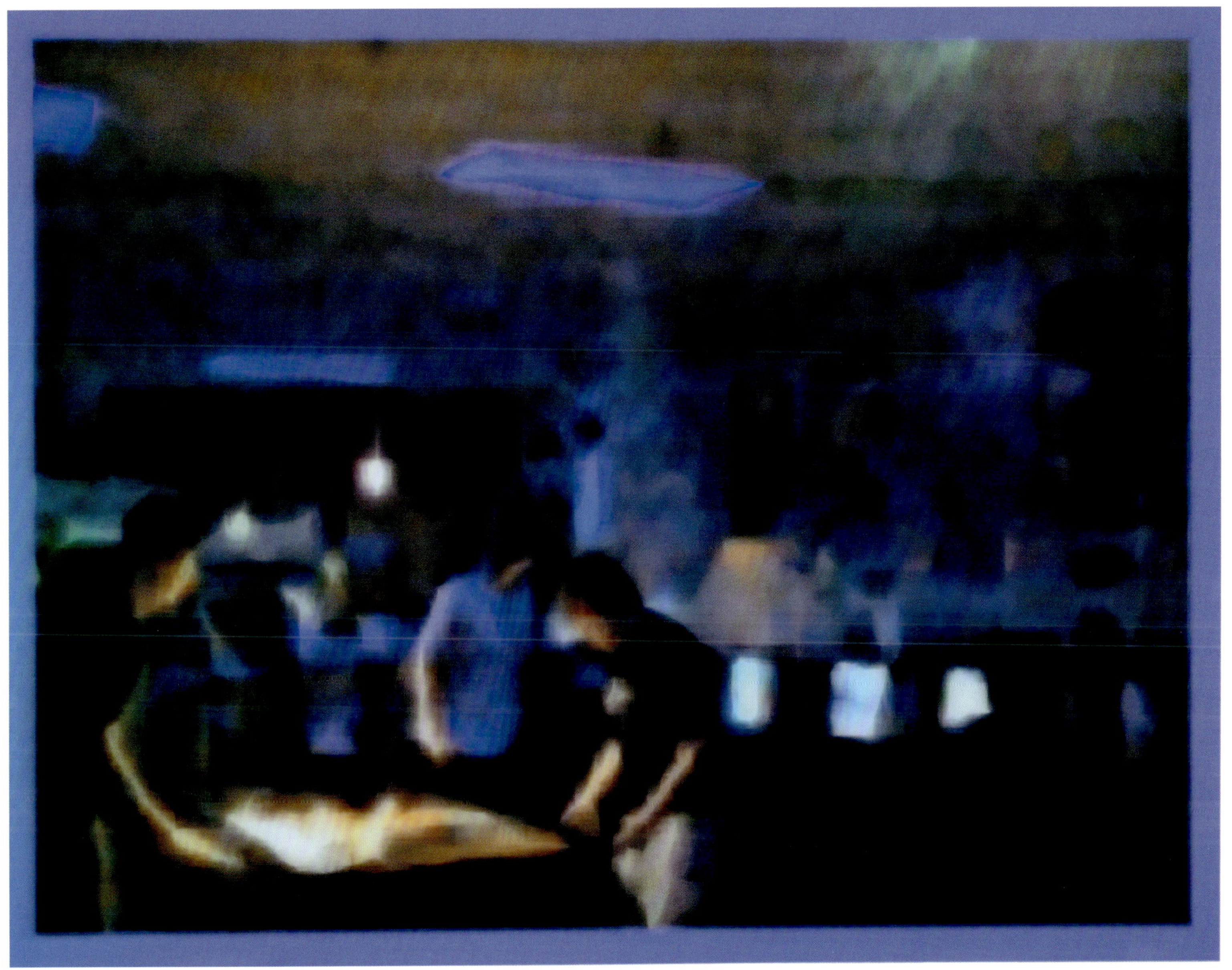

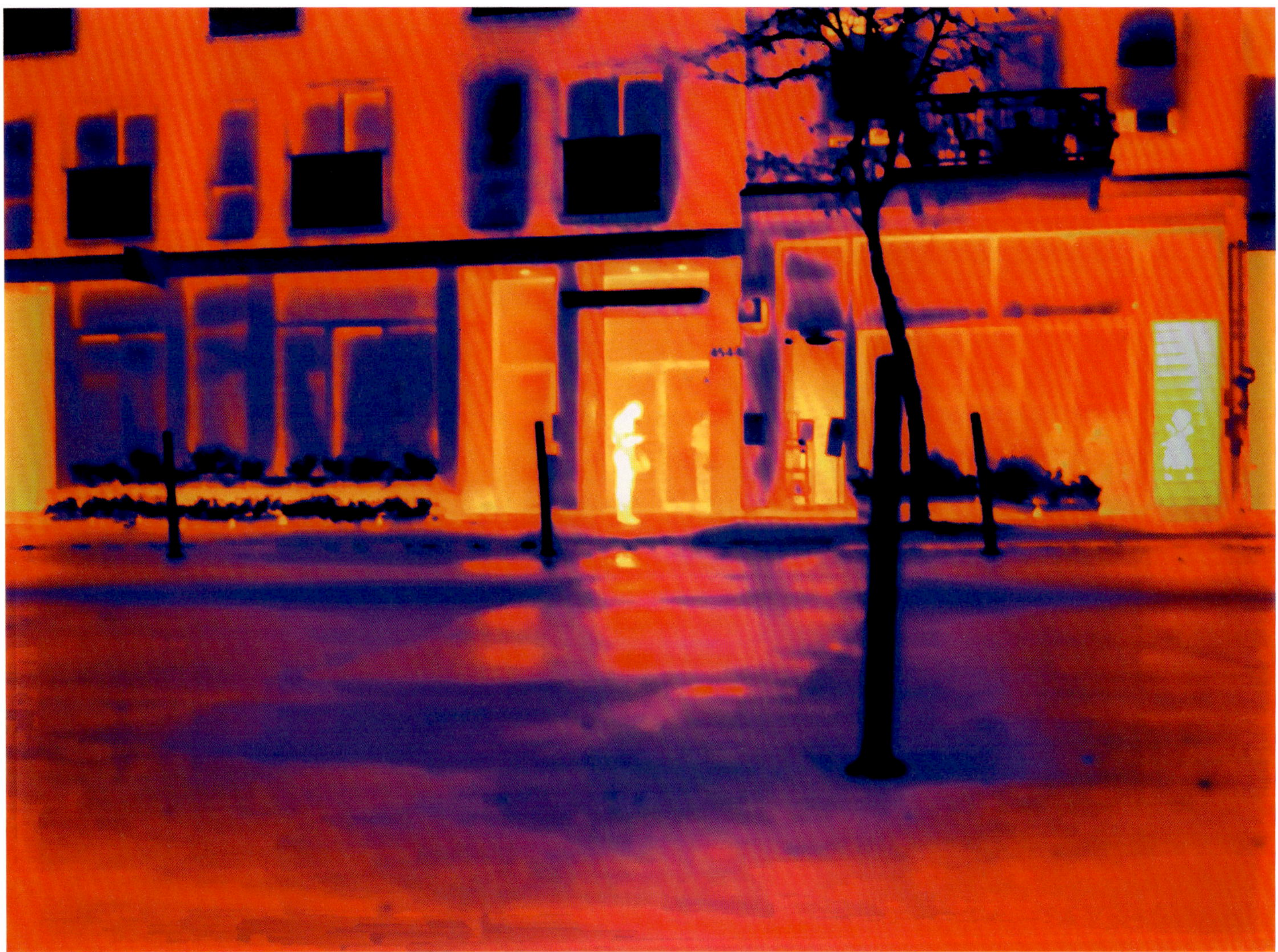

Emmanuelle Léonard
Le livreur et sa cliente, 22:53 (Delivery person and Client, 10:53pm)
2022
Heat-sensitive image, inkjet print
110 × 152 cm
Purchase, with funds from the Photography Curatorial Committee, 2022
2022/7054

Jalani Morgan
Protesters perform a "die-in" by laying on the ground at Yonge and Dundas Square in Toronto
2014
From the series ***The Sum of All Parts*** (2017)
Inkjet print on vinyl
273 × 206.5 cm
Purchase, Canada Now Acquisition Initiative, with funds from Edward Burtynsky and Nicholas Metivier, 2022
2022/7056

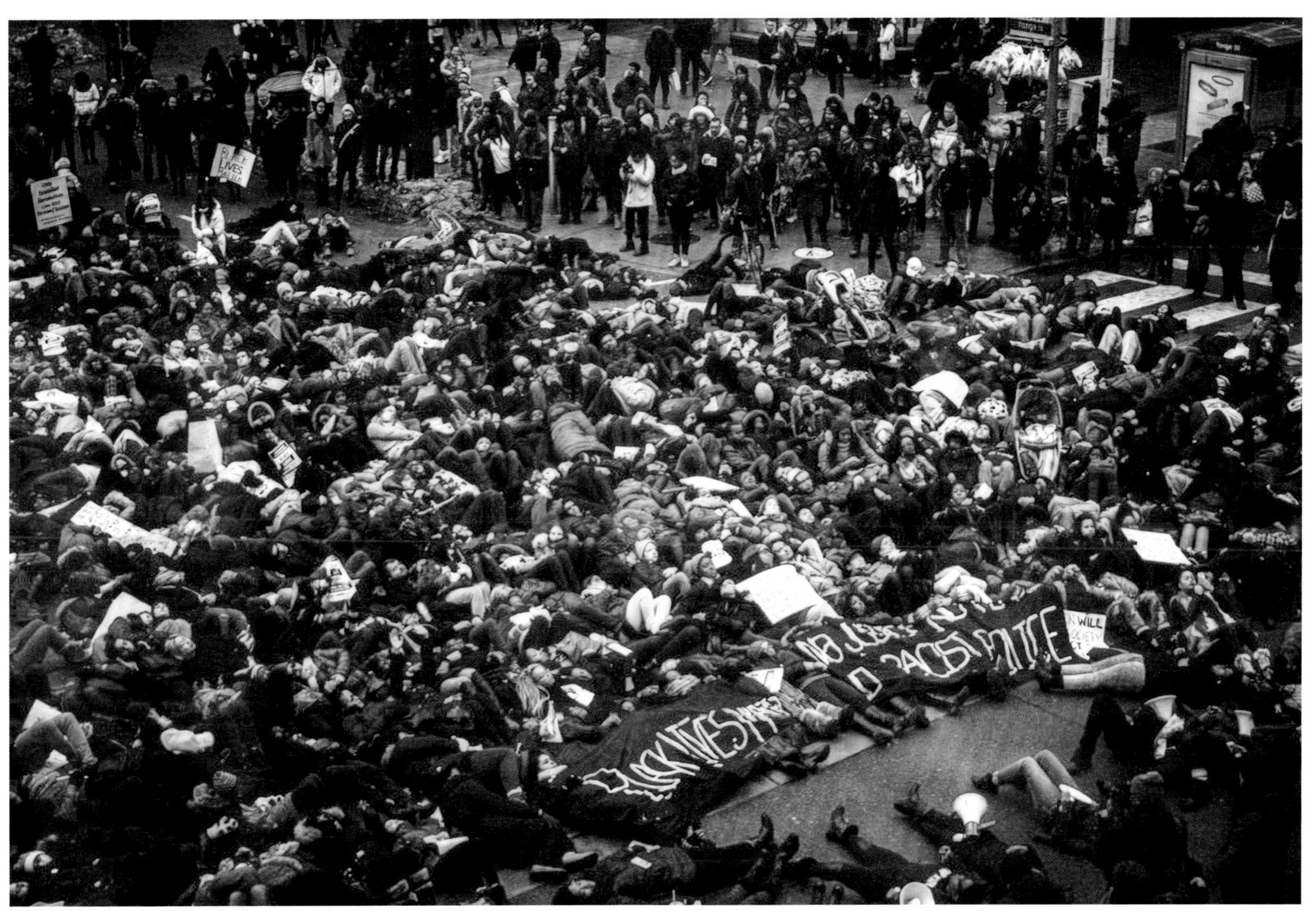

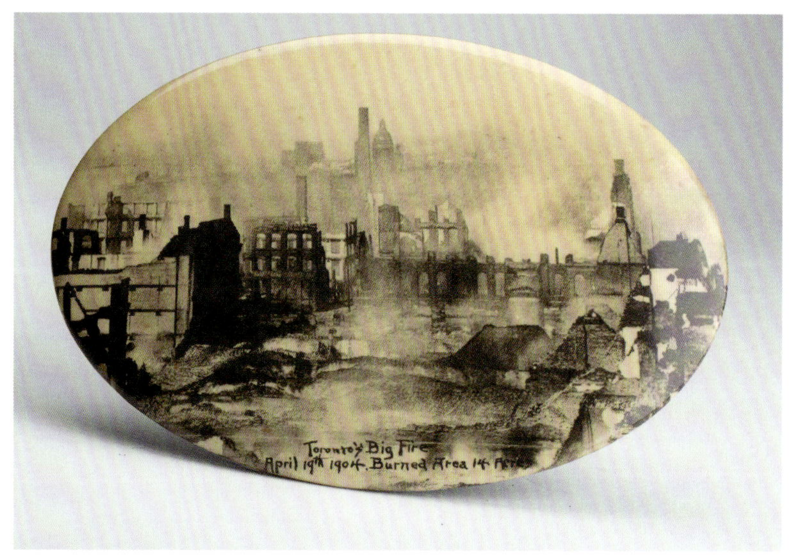

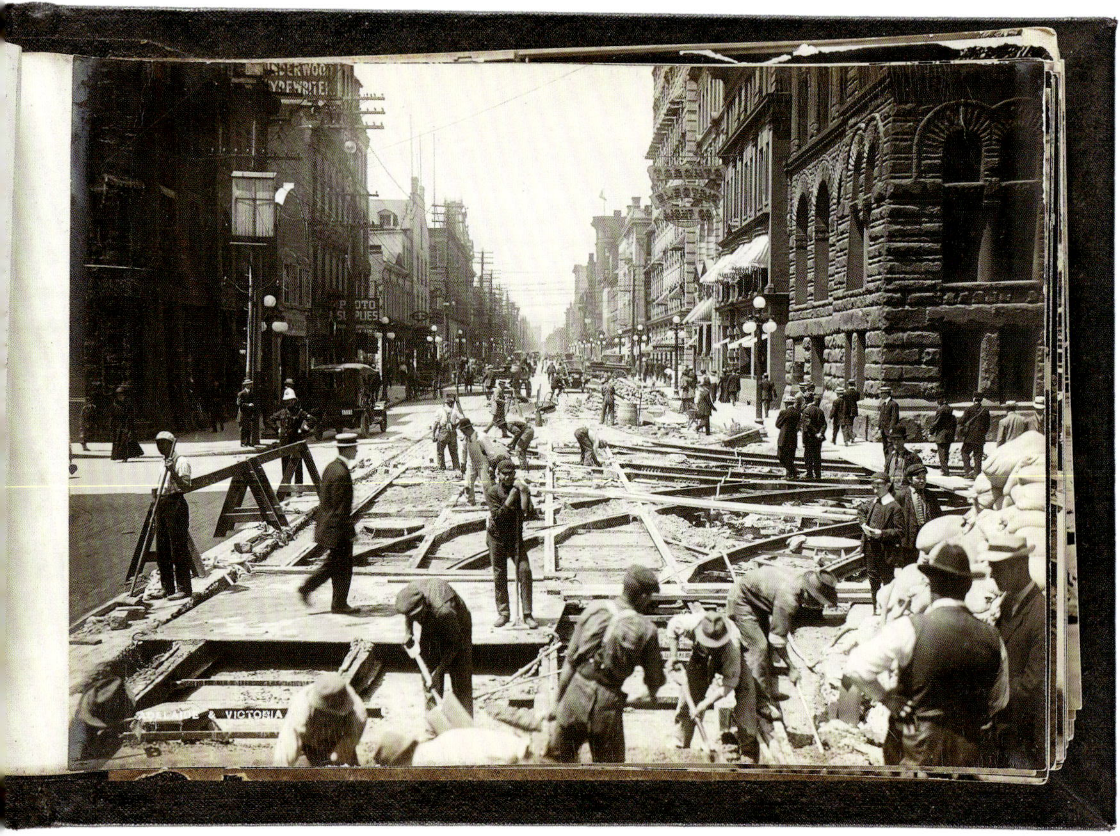

Maker once known, Canadian
Toronto's Big Fire
1904
Celluloid over paper, board, metal
11.5 × 16.5 cm
Anonymous Gift, 2011
2011/132

Arthur Goss
Adelaide & Victoria Streets
1911
From the album ***Toronto Street Construction: Street-car tracks and paving*** (1910–1912)
Gelatin silver print
16.5 × 11.5 cm
Anonymous Gift, 2014
2014/1155.35

Jeff Thomas
Toronto Series: Queen St West
1984, printed 2016
Pigment print
88.7 × 67 cm
Gift of Jeff Thomas, 2016
2016/439

Garry Winogrand
Toronto
1969
Gelatin silver print
27.9 × 35.6 cm
Purchase, 2009
2009/49

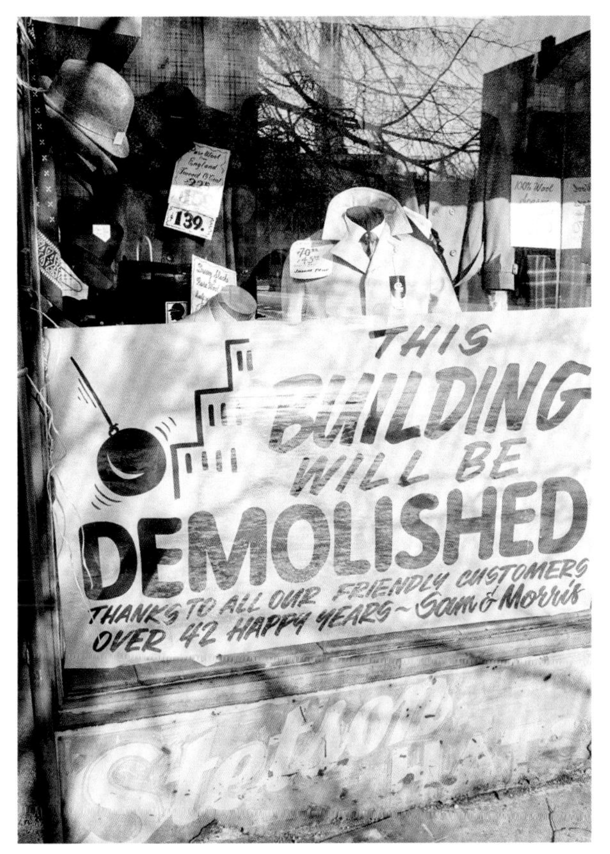
THIS
BUILDING
WILL BE
DEMOLISHED
THANKS TO ALL OUR FRIENDLY CUSTOMERS
OVER 42 HAPPY YEARS ~ Sam & Morris
139.

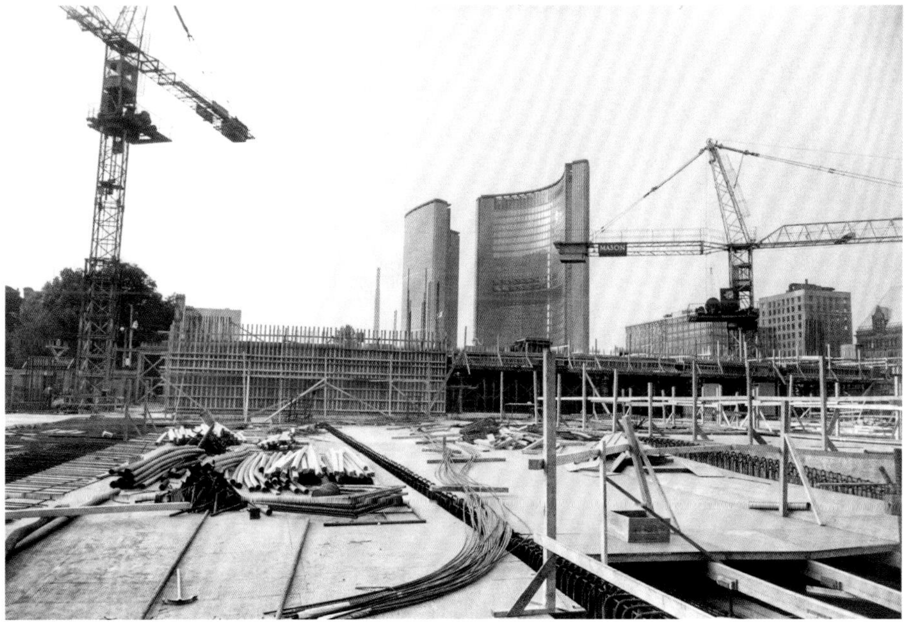

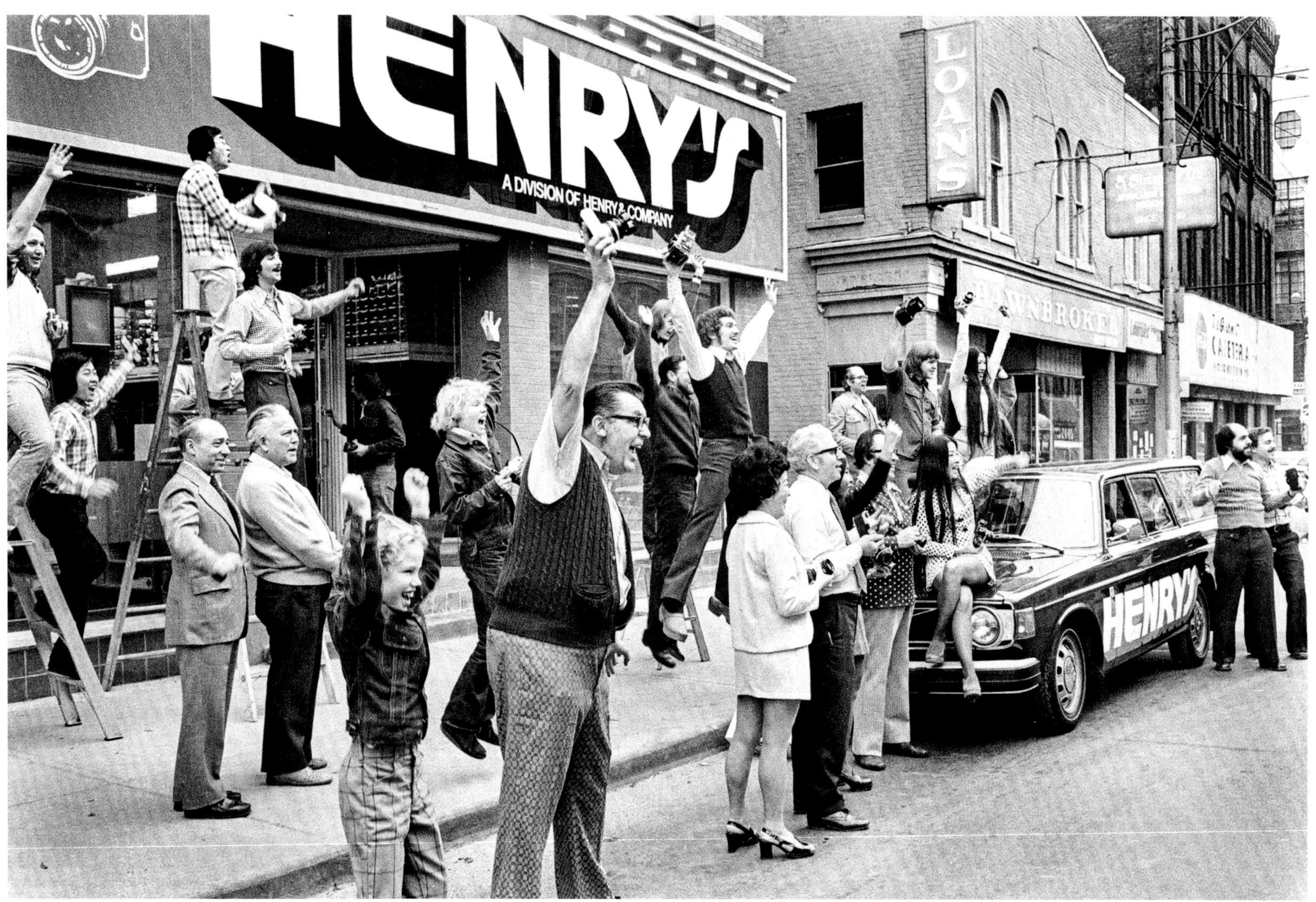
HENRY'S
A DIVISION OF HENRY & COMPANY
LOANS
HENRY'S

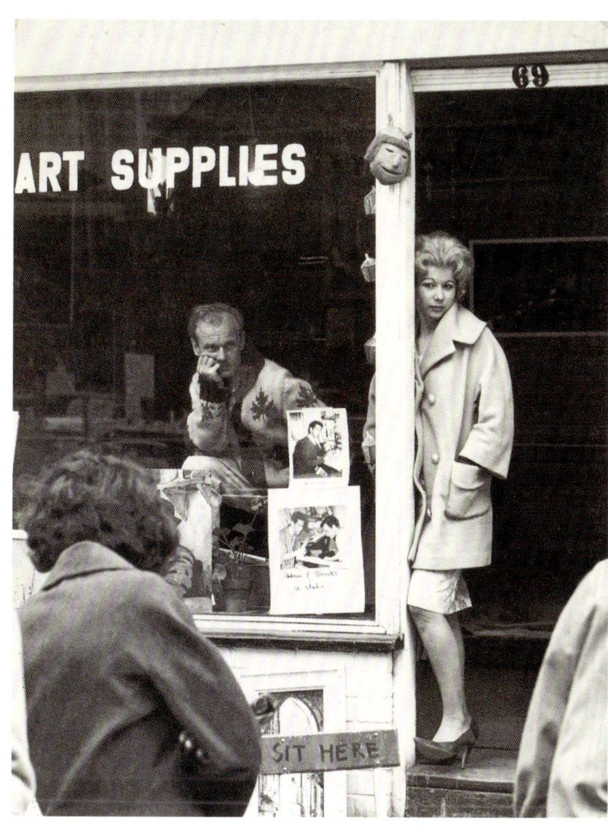

June Clark
Henry's on Church Street
1974; printed 2023
Gelatin silver print
21 × 30.5 cm
Purchase, 2023
2023/103

Michel Lambeth
Hayter Street, Toronto
1962
Gelatin silver print
33.8 × 26 cm
Gift of Av Isaacs, Toronto, 1994
94/497

Thaddeus Holownia
Cameron House, Toronto
1996
From the series ***Our City Our Walls*** (1988–1996)
Chromogenic contact print
17.8 × 43.2 cm
Gift of Stephen C. Brown, 2009
2009/45

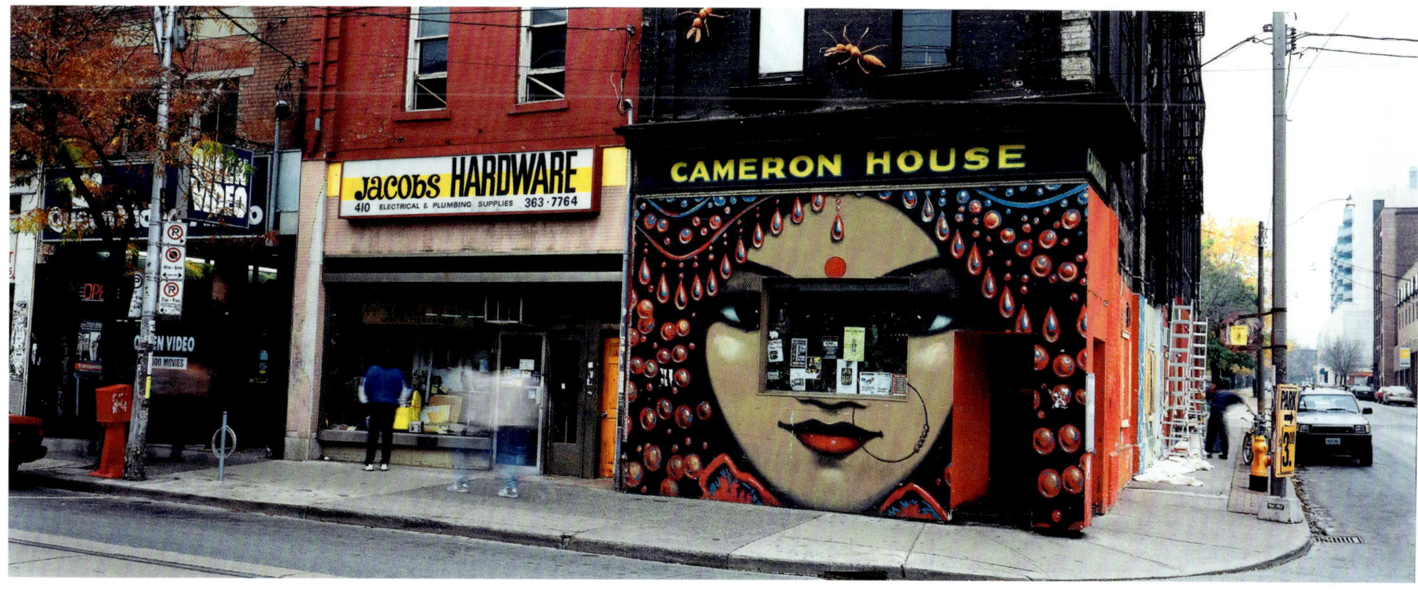

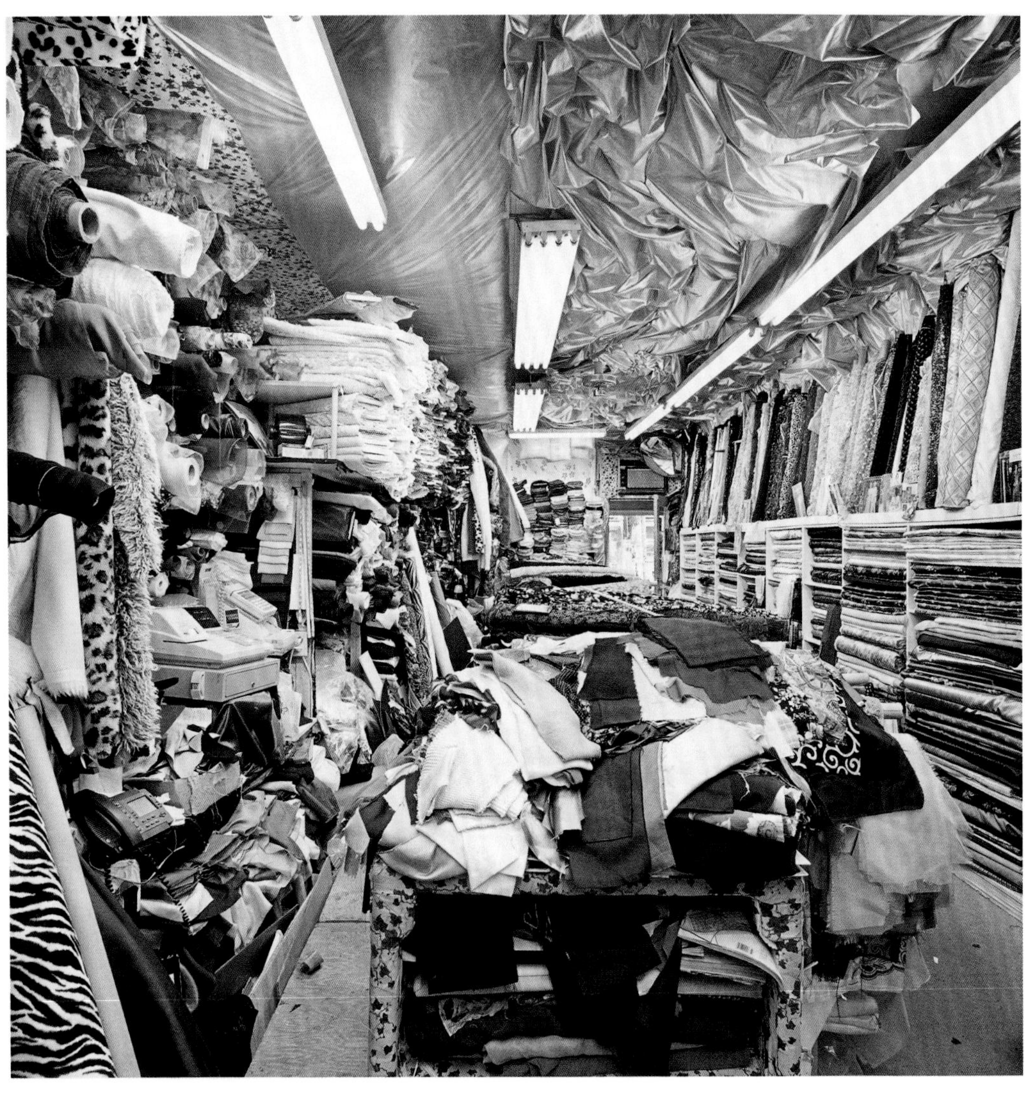

Peter MacCallum
Leo's Textiles, 473 Queen Street West
1997
Gelatin silver print
50.7 × 40.5 cm
Malcolmson Collection. Gift of Harry and Ann Malcolmson in partnership with a private donor, 2014
2014/596

Steven Evans
Tank Bases, Stone Distillery
1997
Gelatin silver print
27.7 × 34.5 cm
Gift of the Volunteer Committee in memory of Carol Sprachman, 2001
2000/140

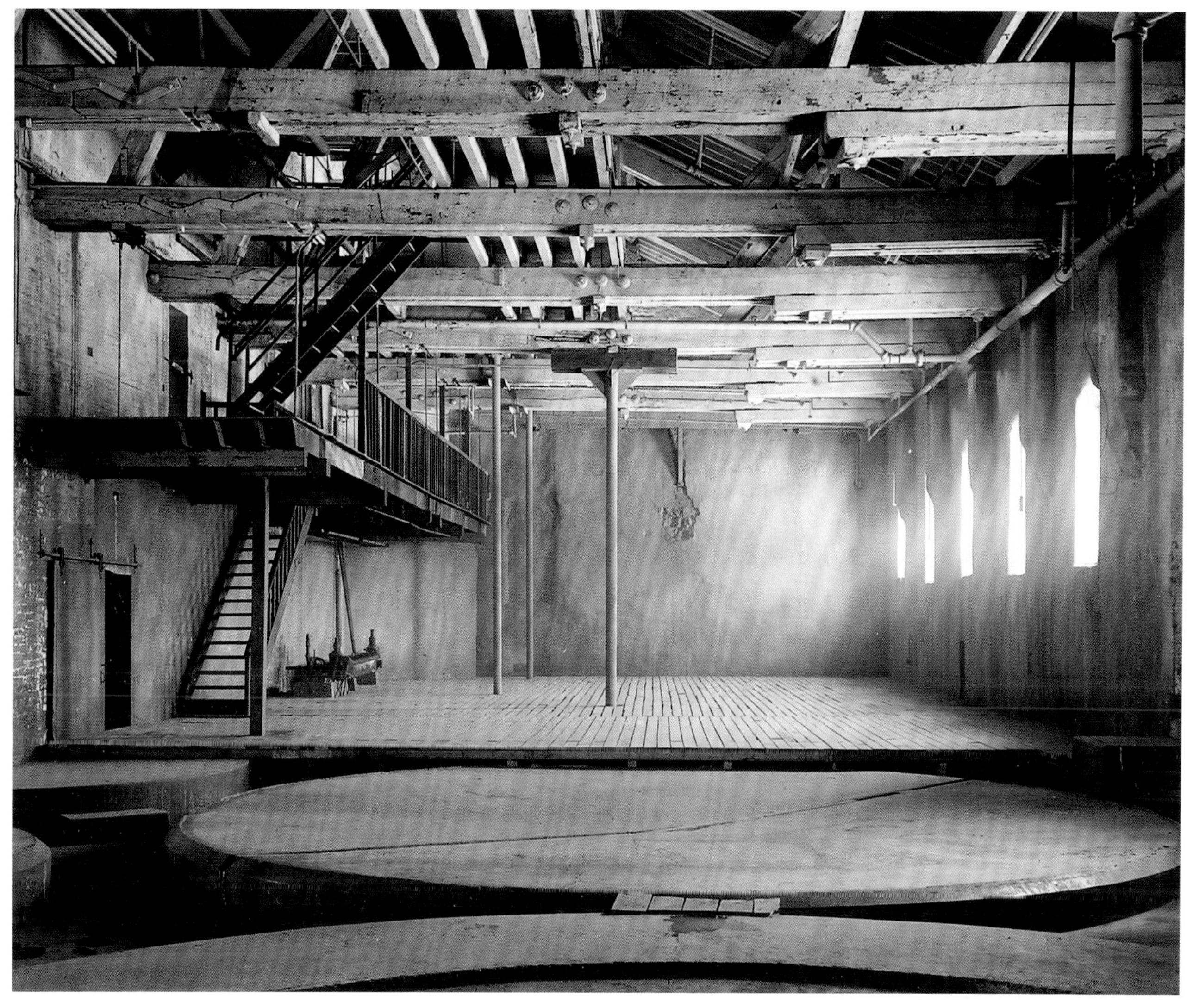

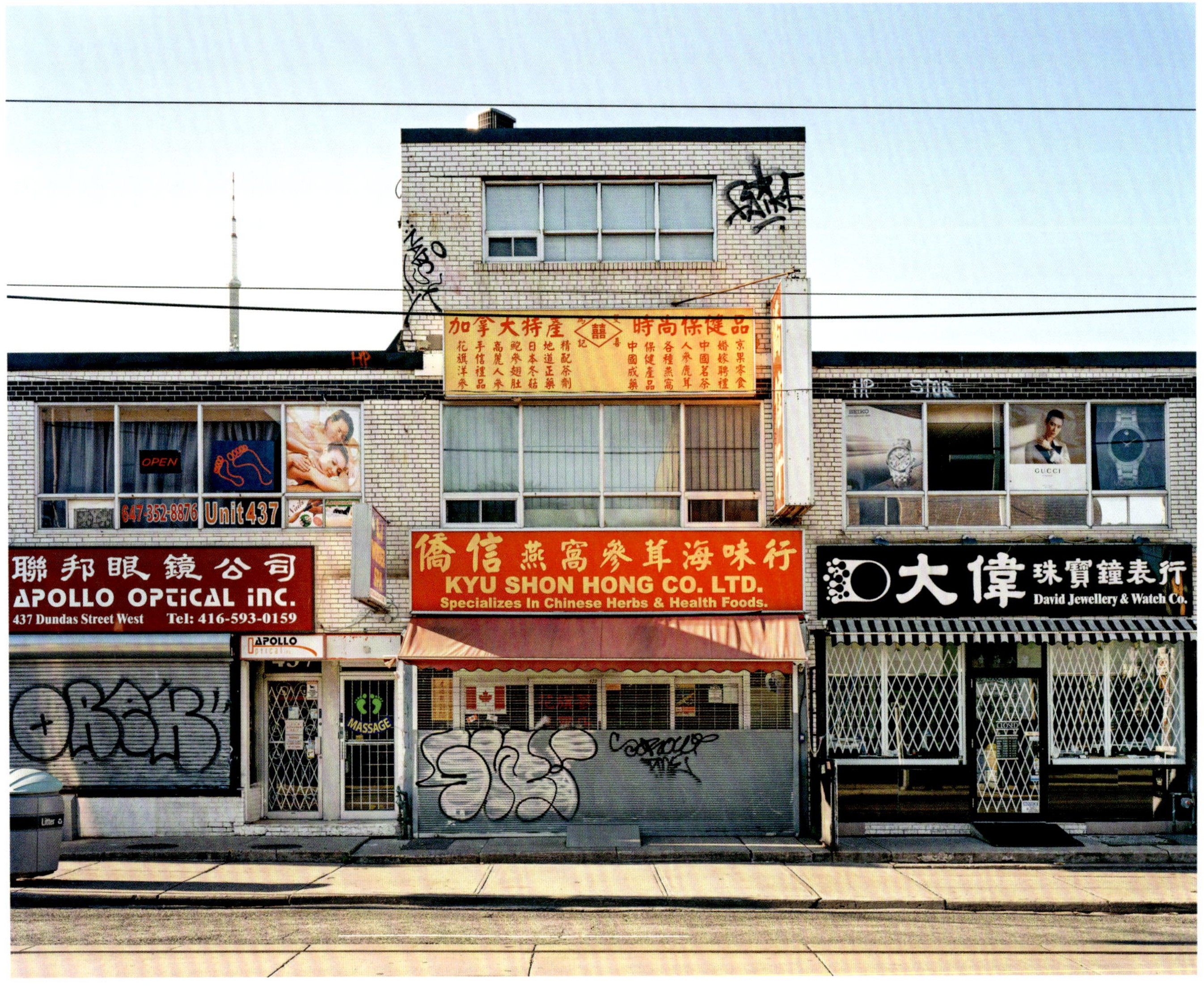

Morris Lum
Kyu Shon Hong Co. Ltd.
2016
From the series ***Tong Yan Gaai (Chinatown)*** (2012–ongoing)
Pigment print
50.8 × 60.96 cm
Purchase, 2025
Purchase, with funds from Photography Curatorial Committee, 2025

Jeff Thomas
Dundas Street Car, Toronto, Ontario, N43 39.211 W79 23.718
1990; printed 2016
Pigment print
71.1 × 91.4 cm
Purchase with assistance from an anonymous donor and James Lahey, 2016
2016/44.4

Jorian Charlton
Georgia & Kukua
2020
Inkjet print
139.7 × 111.8 cm
Purchase, with funds from the Garrett-Longe Family, 2022
2022/7087

Bidemi Oloyede
Untitled, Toronto
2018
Inkjet print
71.1 × 71.1 cm
Purchase, with funds from the Friends of Global Africa and the Diaspora, 2021
2021/83

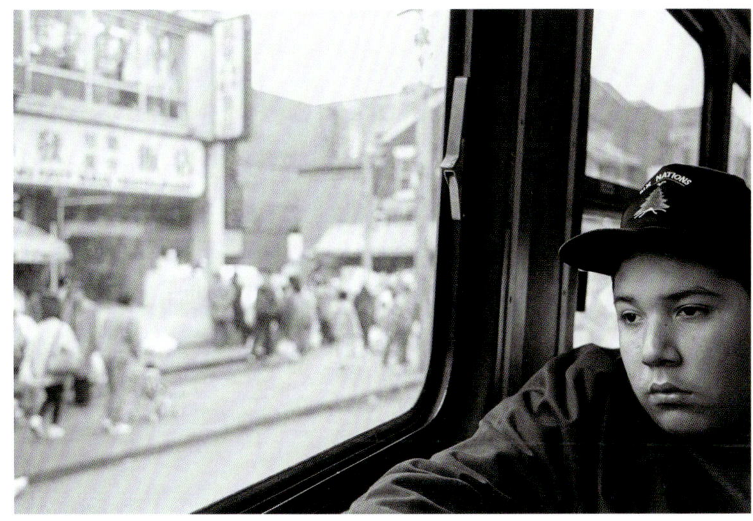
NATIONS

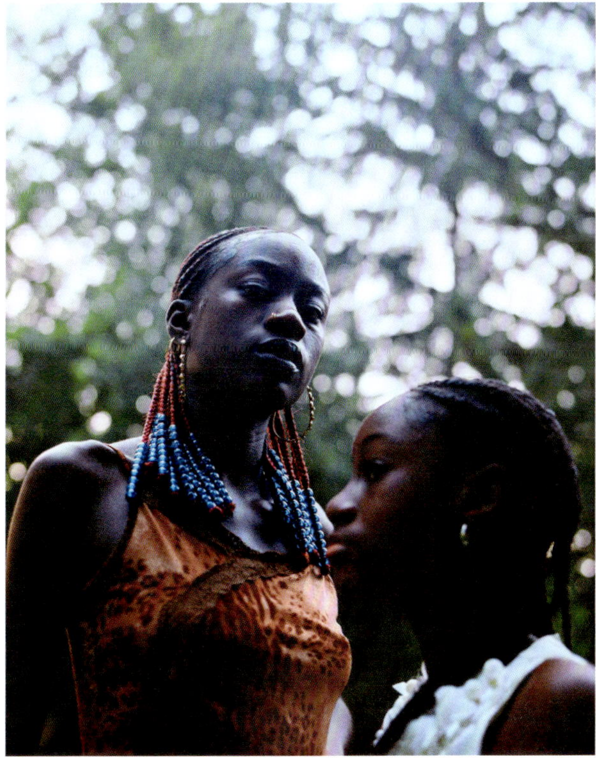

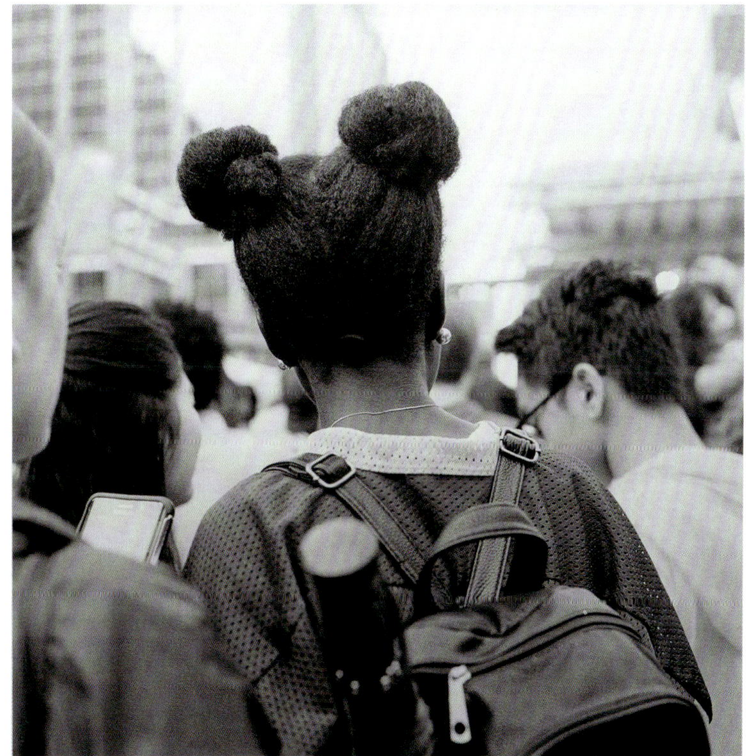

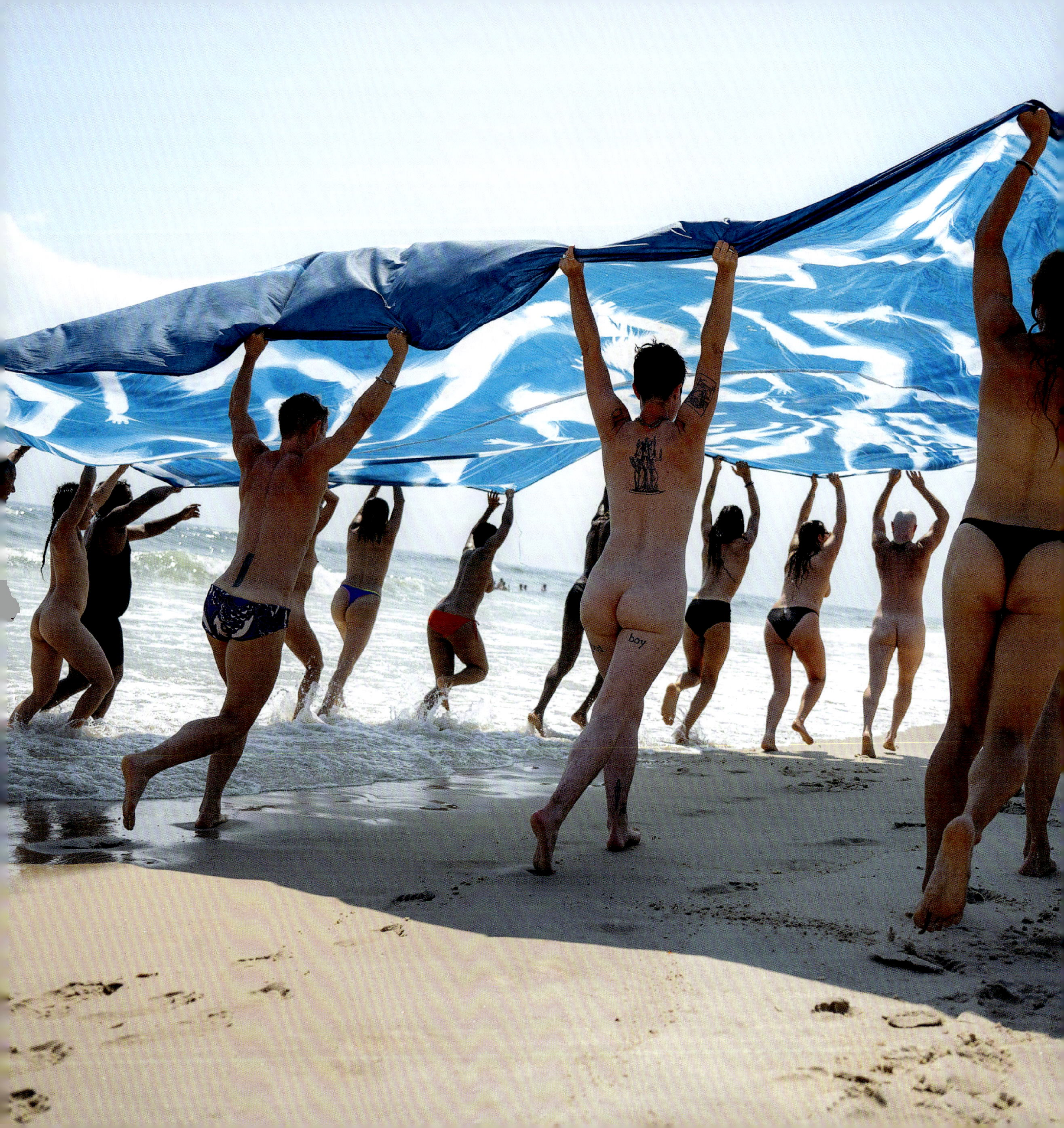
boy

What We Imagine

Tal-Or Ben-Choreen

On August 12, 2023, a group of twenty trans and non-binary people rushed into the waters of the Atlantic Ocean, along Fire Island, trailing a large sheet of muslin. When they emerged from the water, they revealed a tapestry of rich cyan blue outlining silhouettes of figures mirroring the clouds above them. The massive cyanotype, *Etched in Light* (left, and p. 189), was conceptualized by artist Cassils, who invited participants to position their bodies on the light-sensitive fabric, asking that they make at least a single point of contact with another participant. As they lay on the beach, the sunlight traced their forms, rendering a record of these communal temporal connections—what Cassils called "moments of care and touch and pause and community building."[1]

Performance art, which is rooted in experimental twentieth-century movements, allows artists to express aspects of their interior states. Although it can be experienced only within a specific temporal and physical context, photographic documentation can extend these creative acts, allowing access to a new and broader audience, like in Francoise Sullivan's 1948 work *Danse dans la neige* (p. 169). Photographers have recorded performances on the stage, in the street, or in nature—both public and private—as well as those expressed through acting, dance, or protest. At times, artists have conceptualized performances solely for the camera's audience, as in the work of Luther Konadu (pp. 180–181) and Gauri Gill (p. 187). Such activities push and blur the boundaries of these tangled modes of creative expression.

Photographers have long used the unique qualities of daylight, darkness, and artificial light to craft evocative scenes. Their choices in exposure, tone, and print saturation shape what we see and how we feel. By framing fragments of our lives—our social circles, environments, and objects—photographers highlight their significance. Yet since its invention, photography has also helped us *imagine* a different world, giving form to our as of yet unrealized desires and dreams. The simple yet powerful act of photographing can transform the intangible into something concrete or make the invisible visible. The medium's alchemy creates opportunities not only to show the world as it is but to imagine it as we want it to be.

From photography's earliest days, in the 1840s, individuals created abstract, camera-less photographs by placing plant specimens or everyday objects on light-sensitive paper, giving them a new, magical presence. In the early 1900s, various artistic movements embraced the possibilities of abstraction to generate new visions of a fast-changing world. Recognizing the power of photography for recording encounters, surrealists used the medium to summon the subconscious, rendering depictions of varying stages of dreaming, and exploring a plethora of psy-

Nir Arieli
Cassils's ***Etched in Light, BOFFO Performance Festival, Fire Island, New York***
2023

Françoise Sullivan, in collaboration with Maurice Perron
Danse dans la neige (detail)
1948
Gelatin silver prints (17), mounted on wood
39 × 39 cm each
Gift of Barry Campbell & Debra Grobstein Campbell, Henry M. Campbell, and Jeffrey & Lesley Campbell, 2012
2012/108.1-.17

chological states and desires. They appropriated and decontextualized photographs from the media, creating new, unlikely juxtapositions, conjuring new visual worlds. Such works invent and explore the uncanny, dreams, even forbidden sensualities and sexualities.[2] The darkroom and later digital technologies continued to offer opportunities for creative experimentations such as solarization and photomontage.

Similarly, photographers shook free from the burdens of societal norms by decentering, distilling, and rejecting established narratives about who they should be. Through the camera, they reimagined their experience and challenged power structures to confront class, gender roles, and sexualities. Their images destabilized reality and allowed them to shape their environments according to their own perspectives. These resulting visions acted as a call to action, pushing beyond the status quo and laying the groundwork for new futures.

Photographs can accrue new and different meanings over time and in relation to one another. Artists have gathered images from various sources to reveal through their regathering new patterns, ideas, and stories, as can be seen in the work of Claude Cahun (p. 174) and Shelagh Alexander (p. 179). Simultaneously, the prevalence and influence of photography have prompted individuals to create reflexive works that respond to widely circulated images. These appropriated pieces reclaim and challenge dominant visual narratives while constructing new, often subversive, compositions. Wardell Milan's *Michael Ross* (2018) (p. 170) offers one such compelling example. Engaging with the leagcay of Robert Mapplethorpe's *Black Book* (1986), he cut pages from the volume and reassembled the fragments into a transformative collage. The desire to align the external world with a photographer's imaginative vision has historically driven artists to modify their cameras, emulsions, and photographic substrates—continually pushing the boundaries of the medium itself.

To make a photograph is to conjure a personal vision. Much like our lived experiences, each of the images we create is unique, shaped by an infinite string of responses to events and encounters that trace and test our existence. Through photographs we also build communities that nourish and affirm our creativity. The photographs included in this section underscore the medium's ability to activate and embody our imaginations.

1. Michael Bullock, "Striving Towards Utopia": Inside the BOFFO Performance Festival," *Interview* (August 18, 2023), accessed May 8, 2025, https://www.interviewmagazine.com/art/striving-towards-utopia-inside-the-boffo-performance-festival.
2. Rosalind Krauss and Jane Livingston, *L'Amour fou: Photography & Surrealism,* with an essay by Dawn Ades (Washington, DC: Corcoran Gallery of Art / New York: Abbeville Press, 1985); David Bate, *Photography and Surrealism Sexuality: Colonialism and Social Dissent* (London: I.B. Tauris, 2003).

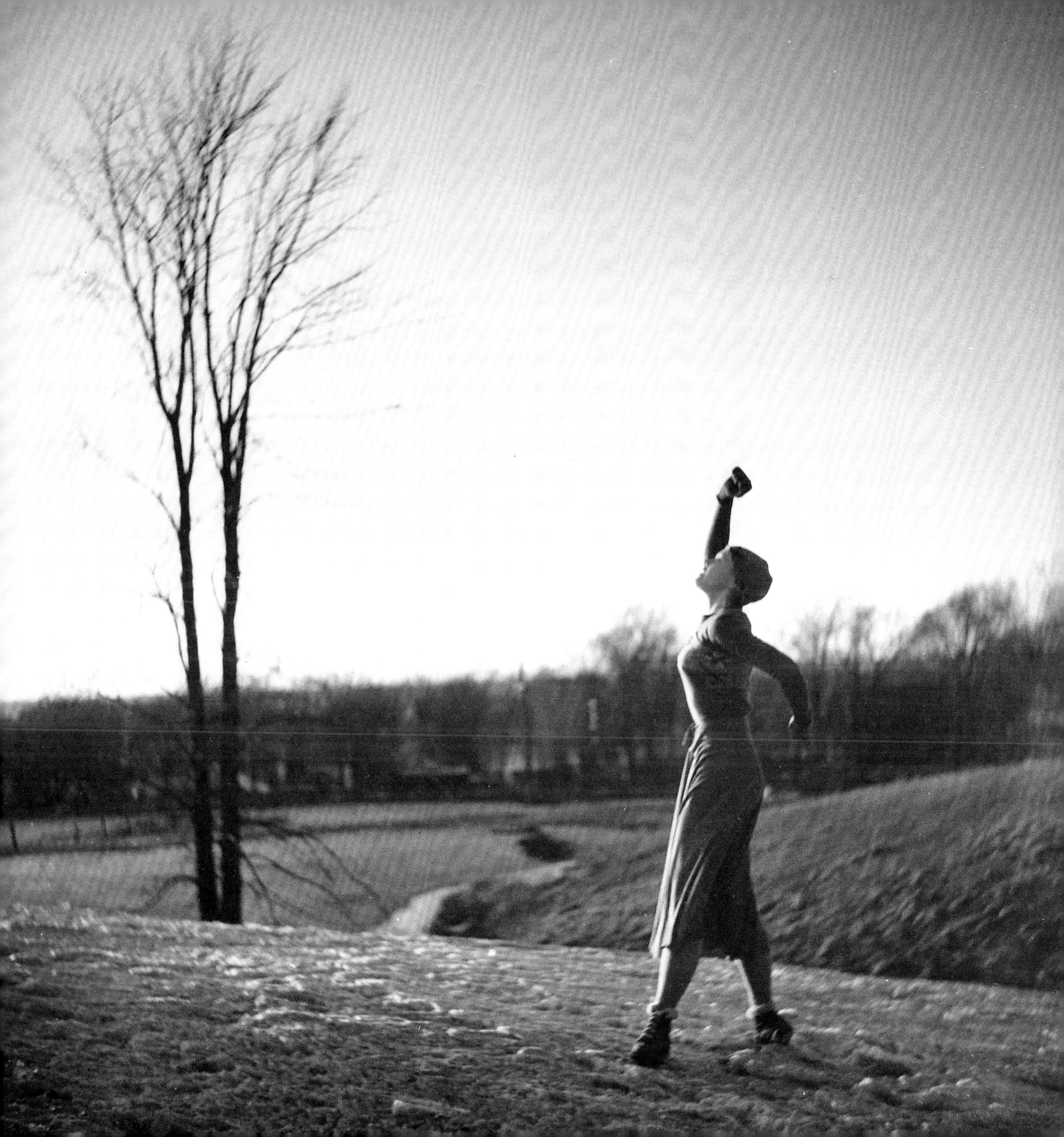

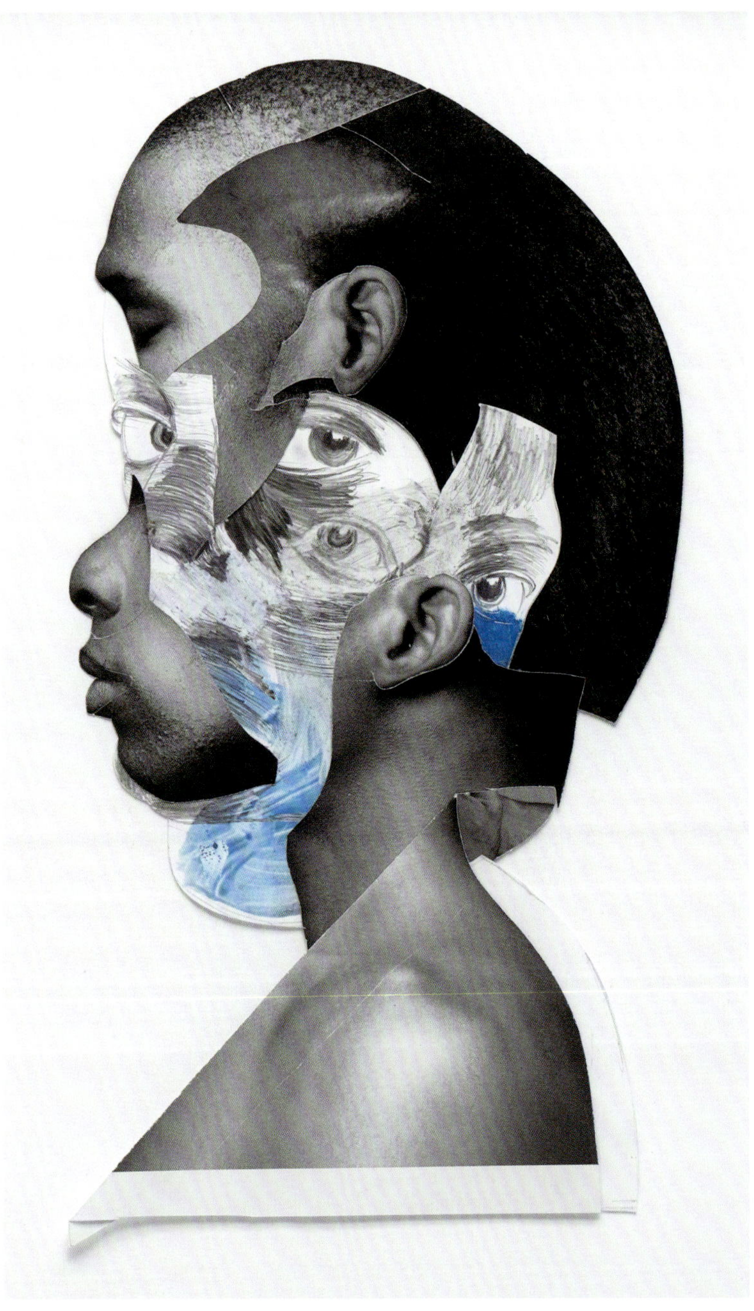

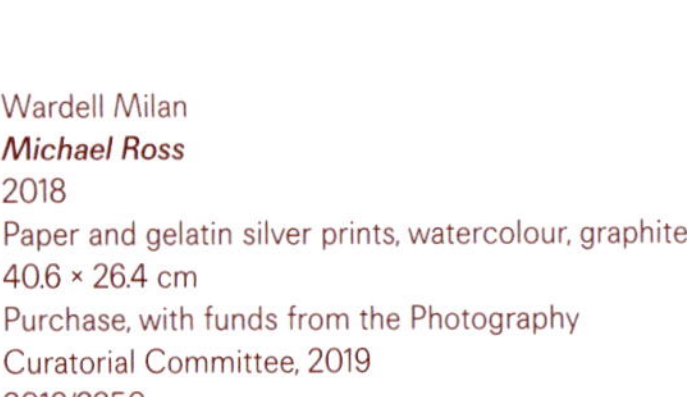

Wardell Milan
Michael Ross
2018
Paper and gelatin silver prints, watercolour, graphite
40.6 × 26.4 cm
Purchase, with funds from the Photography Curatorial Committee, 2019
2019/2250

Ming Smith
Alvin Ailey Revelation, Harlem, NY
c. 1975
Gelatin silver print
27.6 × 35.3 cm
Purchase, with funds generously donated by the Photography Curatorial Committee, 2018
2018/31

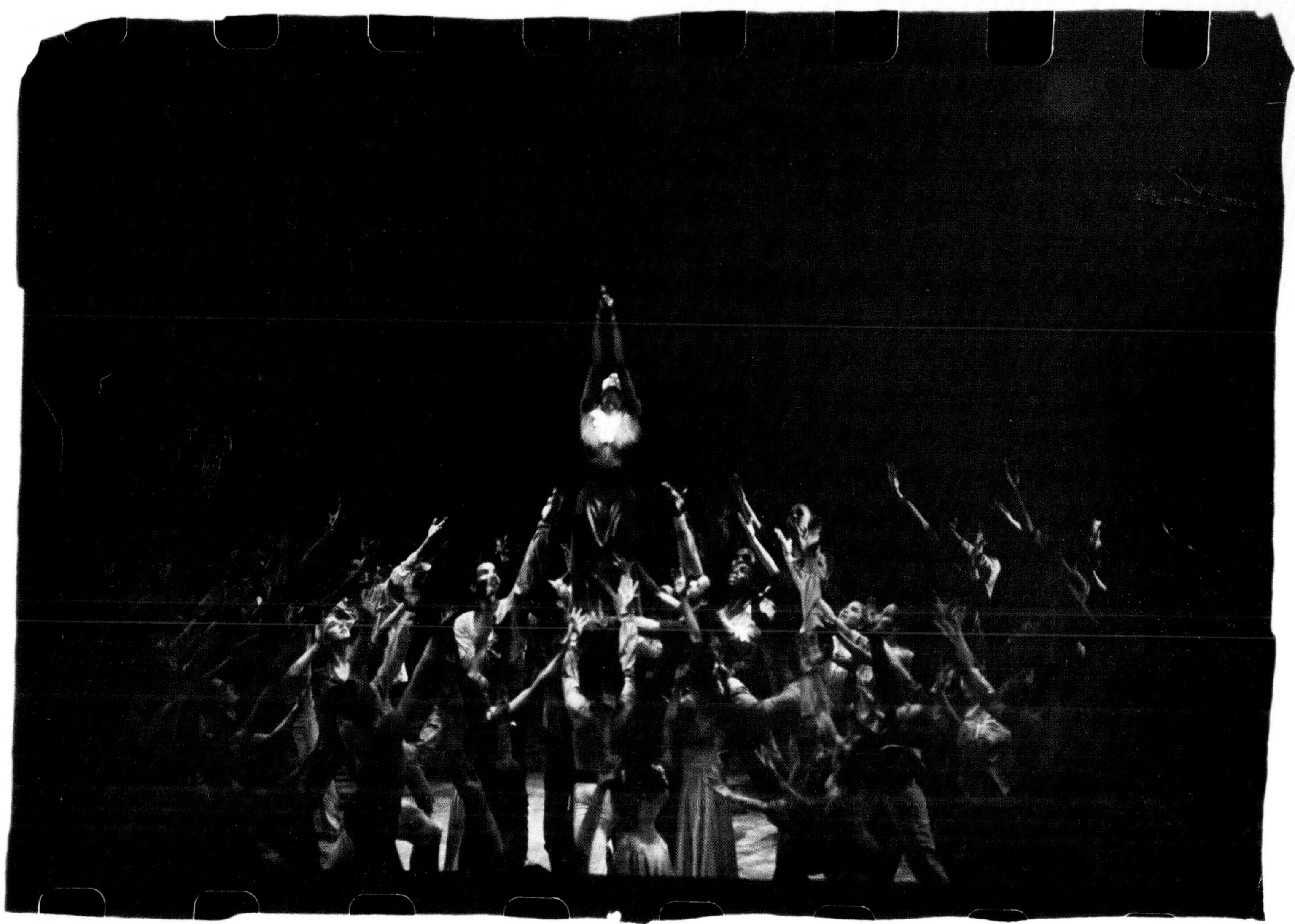

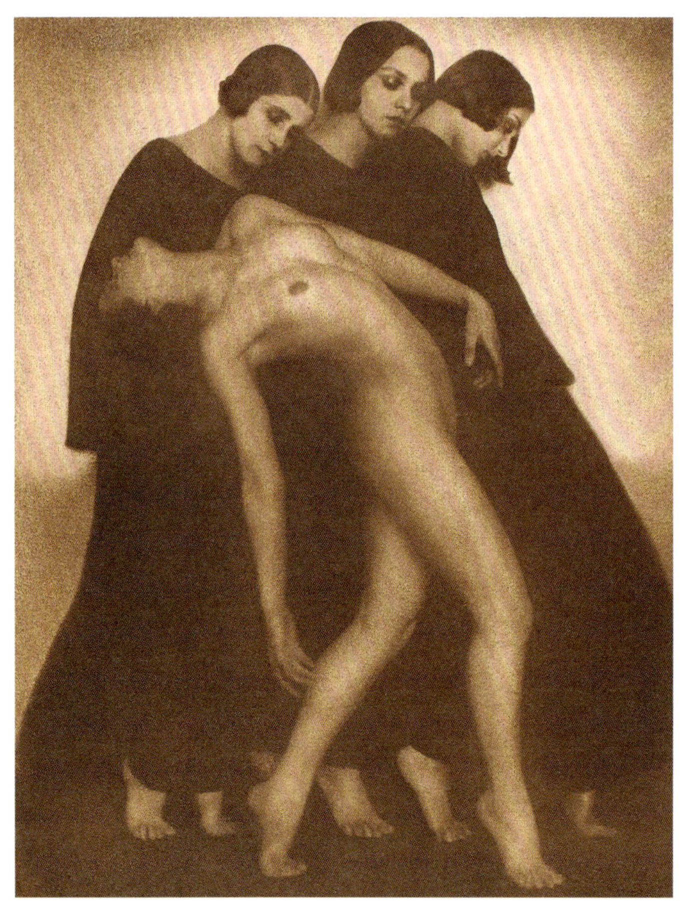

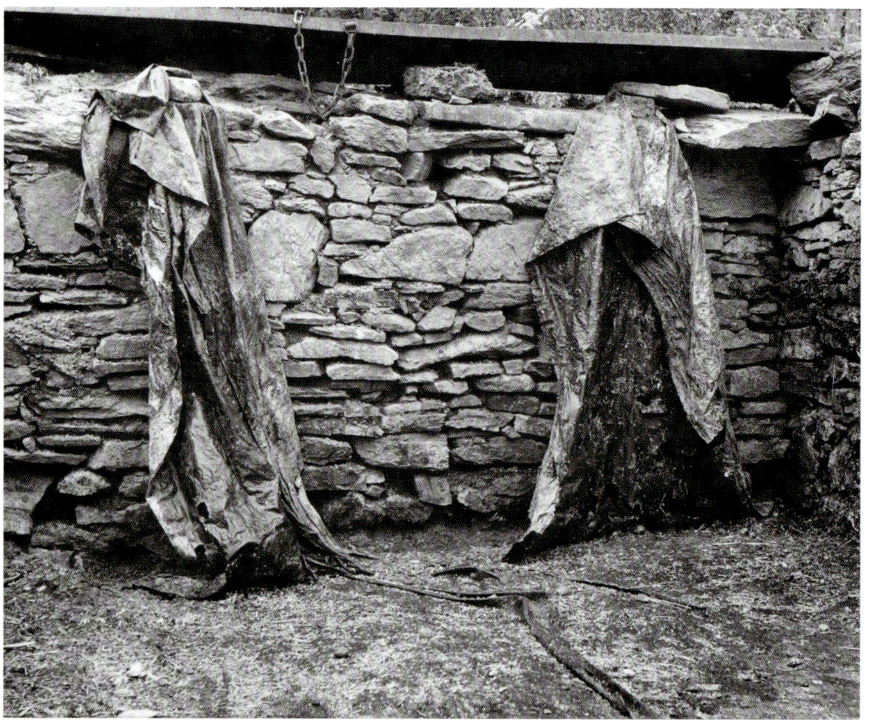

CZECH PHOTOGRAPHY COLLECTION

The Czech Photography Collection provides an exemplary overview of the country's photographic production from the 1950s to the 1990s, with more than 6,000 works by over 350 photographers. Largely unknown until after the 1989 Velvet Revolution, these photographs—ranging from documentary to surreal abstraction—present a distinct lens on daily life shaped by layered histories and creative vision.

Rudolph Koppitz
Bewegungsstudie
1926
Bromoil print
59.8 × 43.8 cm
Gift of Patricia Regan, in memory of Dr. Arthur Rubinoff, 2013
2013/373

Emila Medková
Dvě Vdovy (Two Widows)
c. 1955
Gelatin silver print
40.4 × 50.5 cm
Anonymous Gift, 2018
2019/8048

Josef Sudek
In the Magic Garden
1954–1959
Gelatin silver print
29.7 × 39.6 cm
Anonymous gift, 2000
2000/554

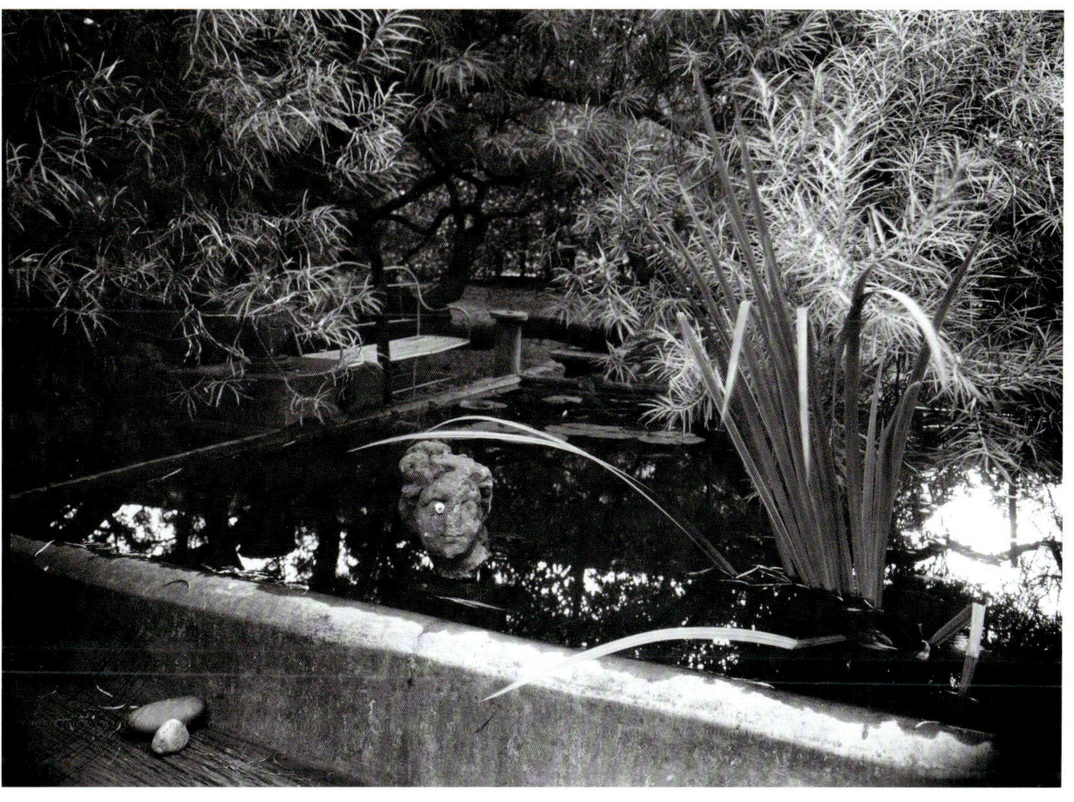

JOSEF SUDEK

Josef Sudek's photographs—from early atmospheric scenes, to his prolonged cycle of poetic studies from his studio windows, to surrealist experimentations, and his lifelong exploration of Prague—have transformed ordinary subjects in the real world into extraordinary objects. In 2000, a landmark acquisition of 973 works spanning his sixty-year career led to the formalization of the Photography Department.

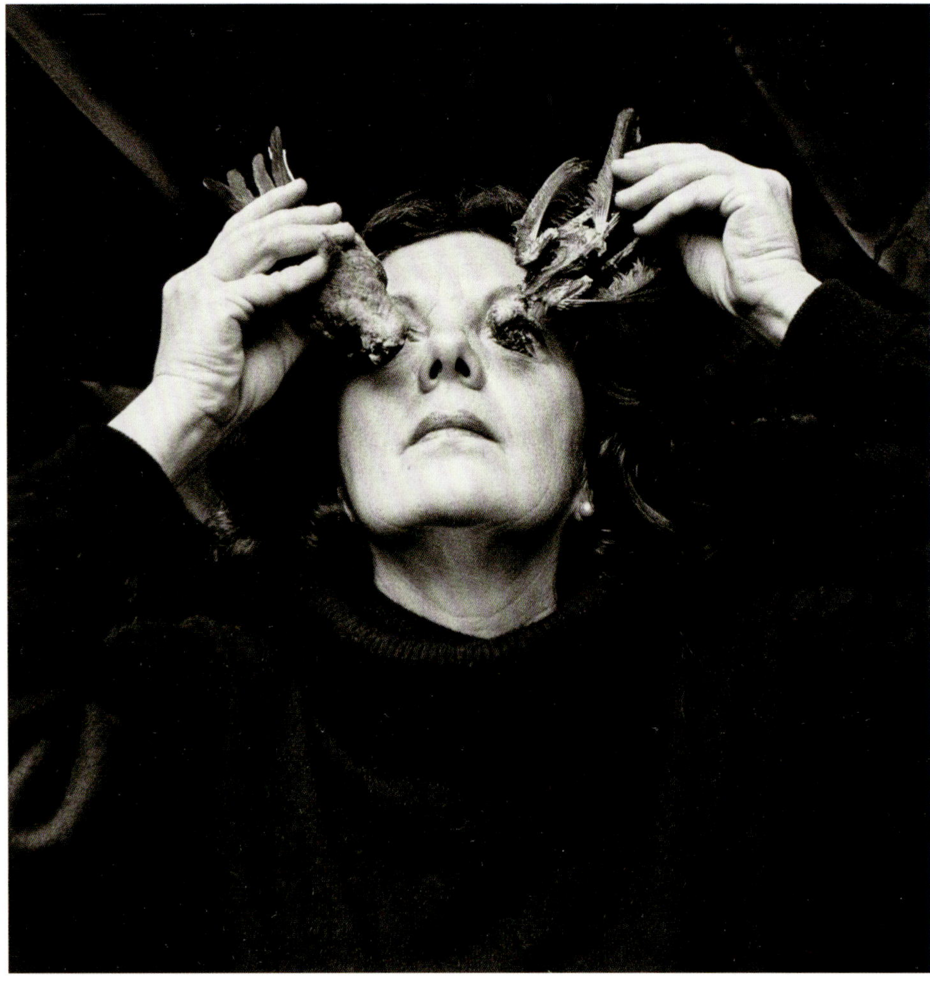

Graciela Iturbide
¿Ojos para volar? Coyoacán, México (Eyes to Fly With? Coyoacan, Mexico)
1991
Gelatin silver print
35.6 × 27.9 cm
Purchase, with funds from the Photography Curatorial Committee, 2023
2023/55

Claude Cahun
Aveux non Avenus
1930
Photogravure (Éditions du Carrefour, Paris)
22 × 17 cm
Special Collections, Edward P. Taylor Library & Archives, Art Gallery of Ontario

Lorna Simpson
Tense
1991
Gelatin silver prints, engraved plastic plaques
165.1 × 312.4 cm
Gift of Alison and Alan Schwartz, 2000
2000/1343

GRACIELA ITURBIDE

Graciela Iturbide is one of Latin America's most impactful photographers, known for her deeply personal and poetic exploration of Mexican society. Since the late 1970s, she has photographed the everyday life, rituals, and traditions of her country and abroad. The collection spans her prolific career, featuring work with the Seris in Sonora, the Zapotecs of Juchitán, self-portraits, and scenes from India.

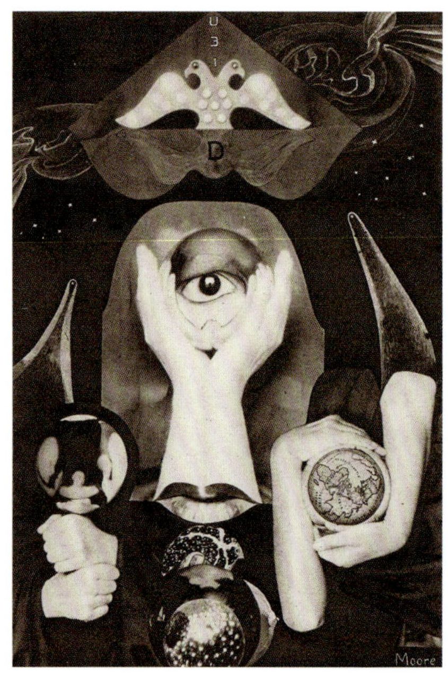

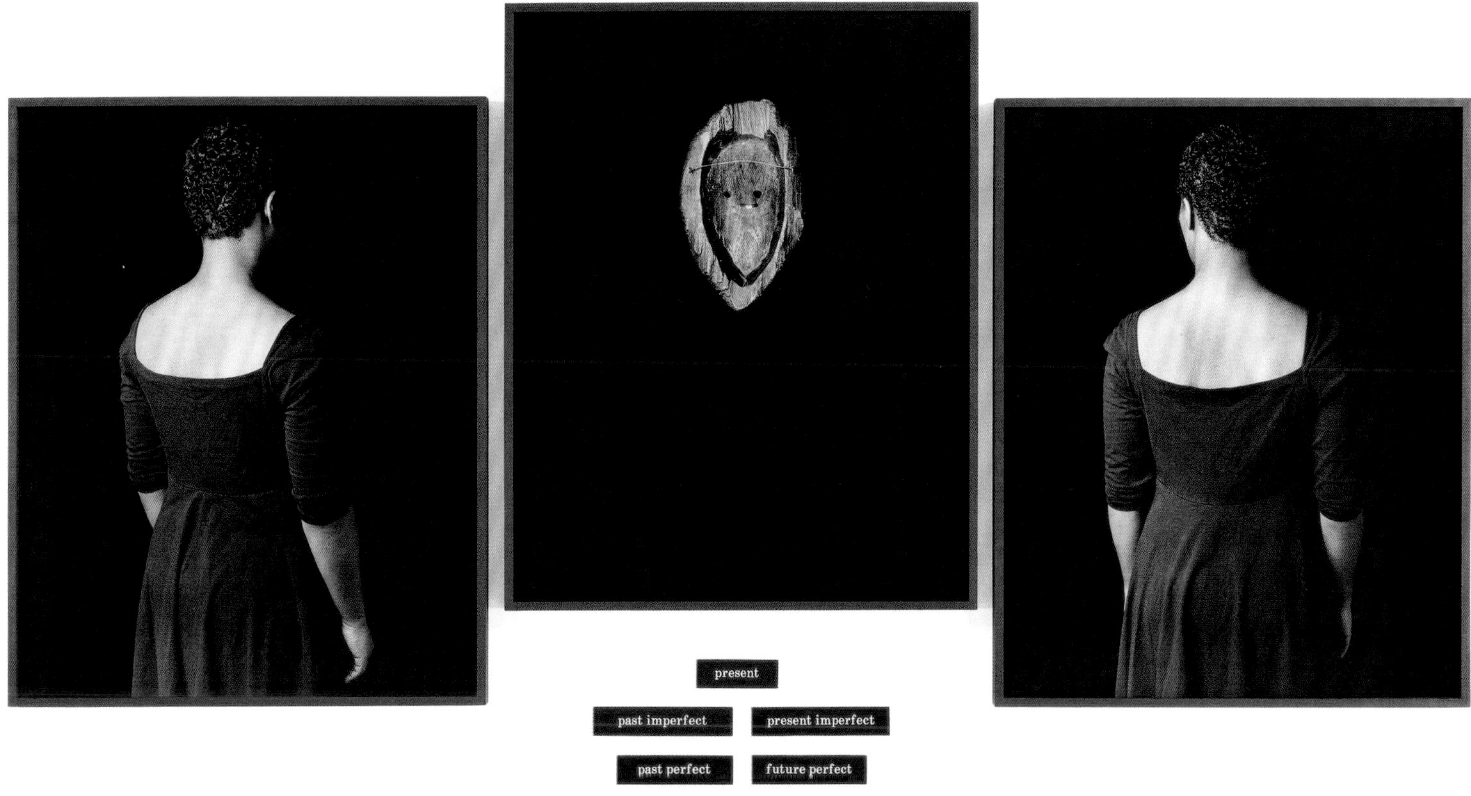
present
past imperfect
present imperfect
past perfect
future perfect

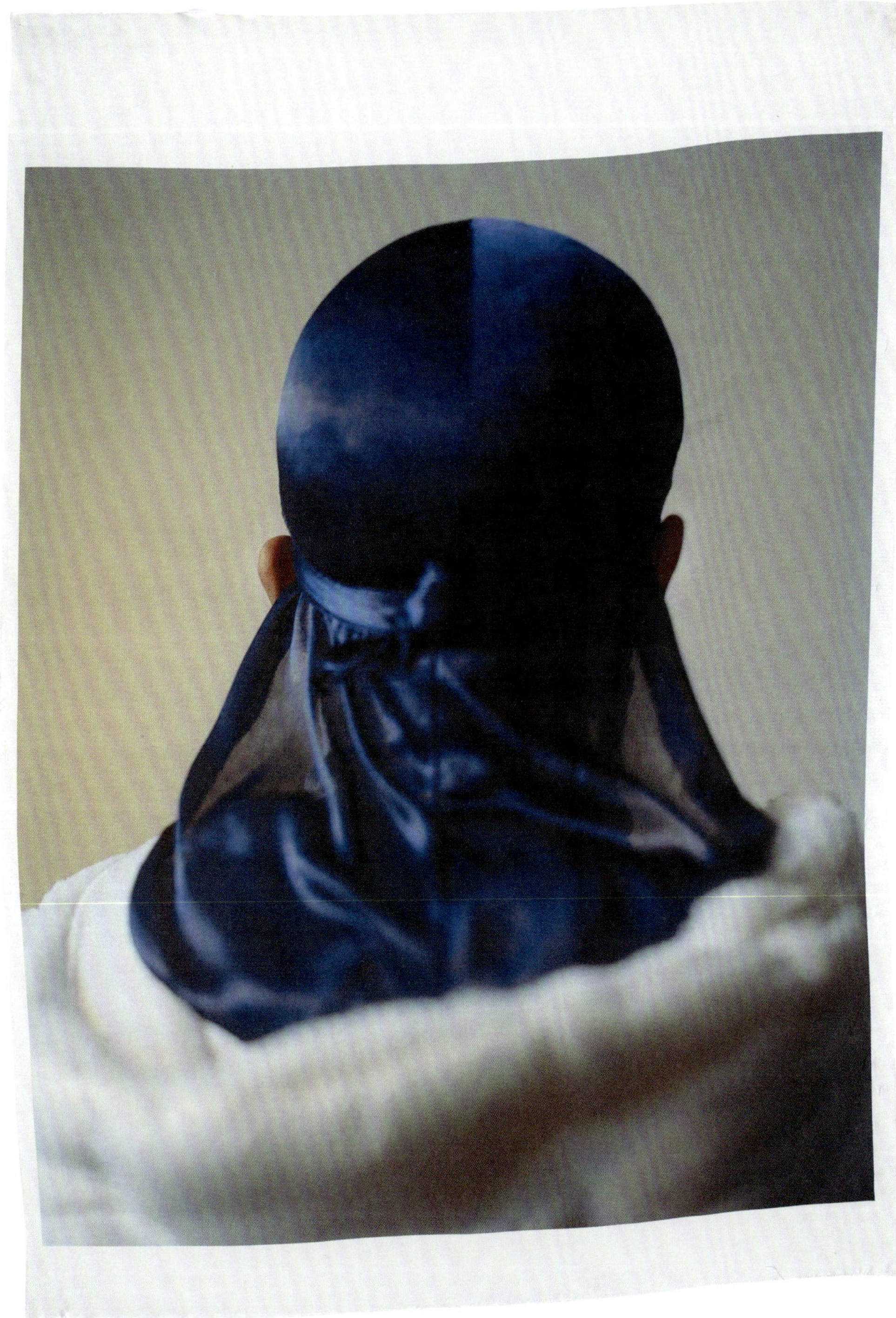

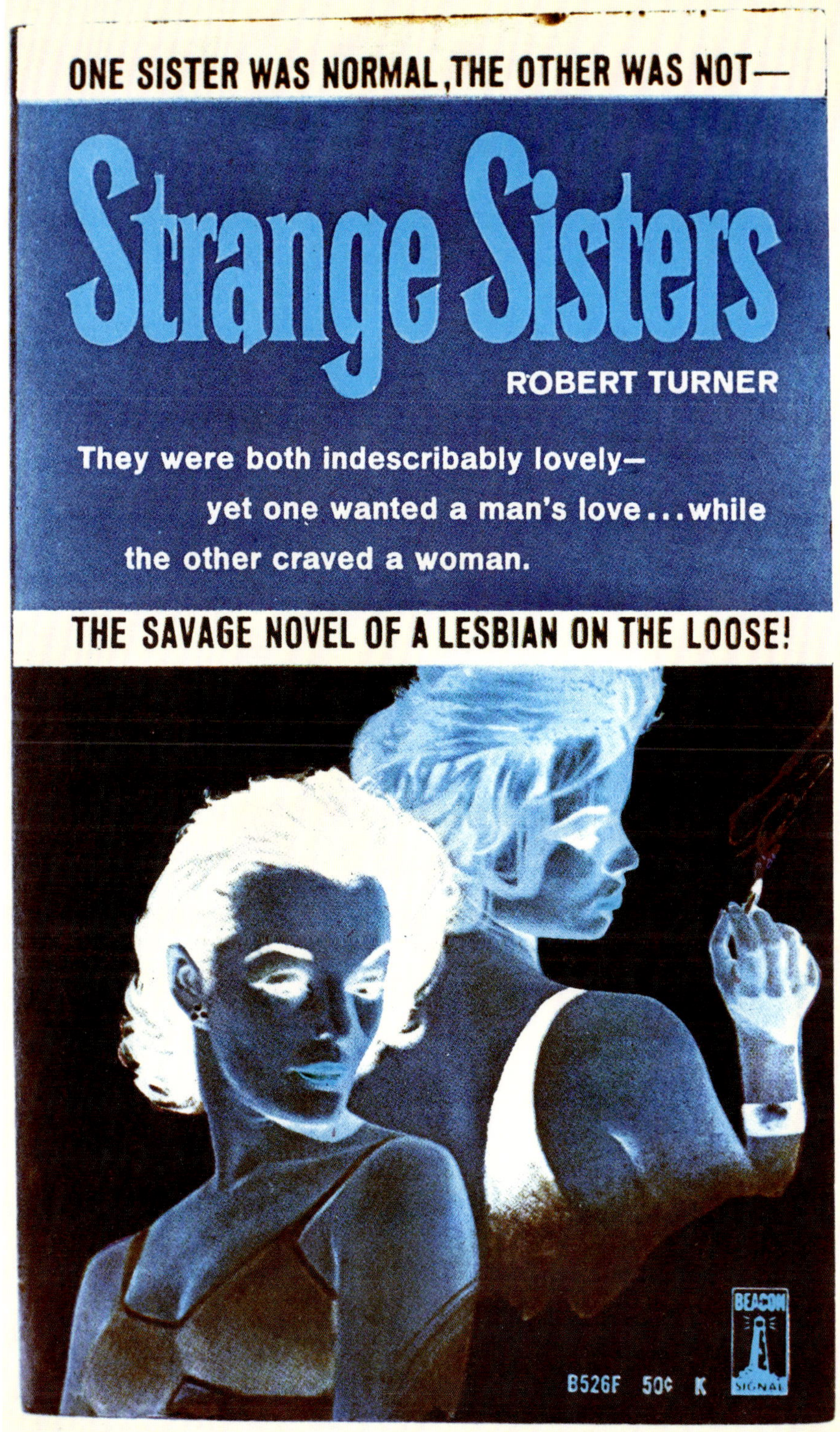

John Edmonds
Untitled (Du-Rag 2)
2017
Pigment print on Japanese silk
150 × 107.5 cm
Purchased with the assistance of Art Toronto 2017 Opening Night Preview, 2017
2017/41

Nina Levitt
Conspiracy of Silence (detail)
1987
Chromogenic prints: 5
76.2 × 101.6 cm
Purchase, with funds from the Photography Curatorial Committee, 2022
2022/7044

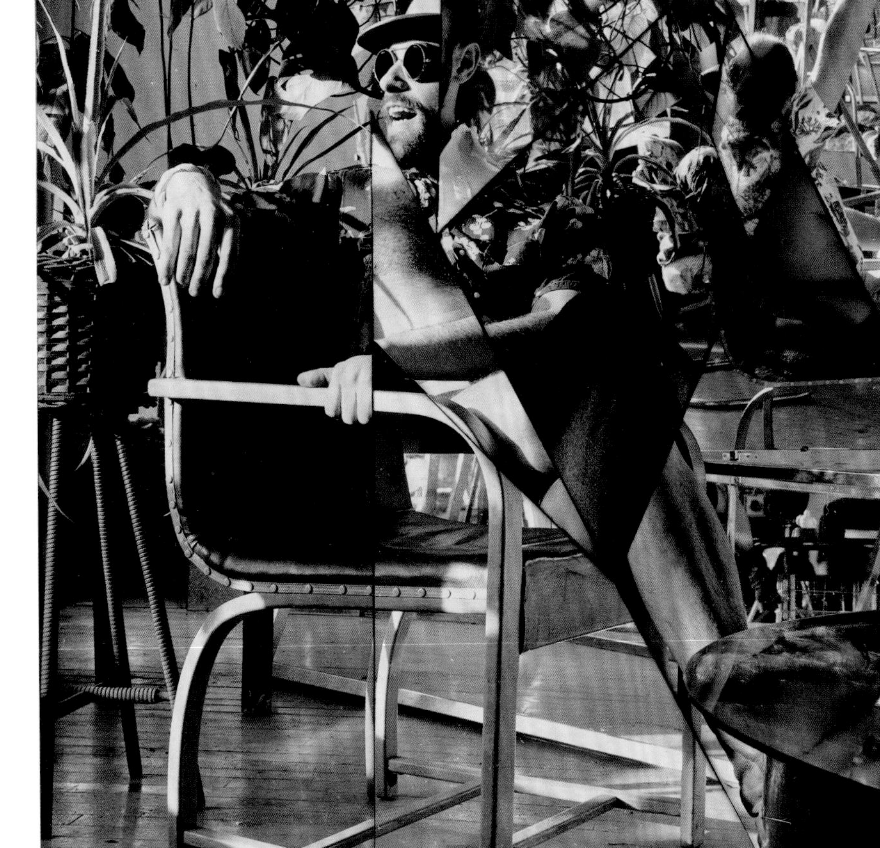

Rodney Werden
Portrait of Jorge Zontal (darkroom collaboration)
Gelatin silver print
50.5 × 40.6 cm
Purchase, with funds from the Photography Curatorial Committee, 2024
2024/87

Susie King
Elizabeth Chitty Performing at the Chromaliving Vernissage Gala
Wooden bikini: Tanya Mars
1983
Gelatin silver print
50 × 60 cm
Gift of Elizabeth Chitty, 2022
2022/7103

Shelagh Alexander
Untitled (Wish)
1988
Photomontage: gelatin silver prints
157.8 × 208.6 cm
Gift of Alison and Alan Schwartz, 1997
97/1548

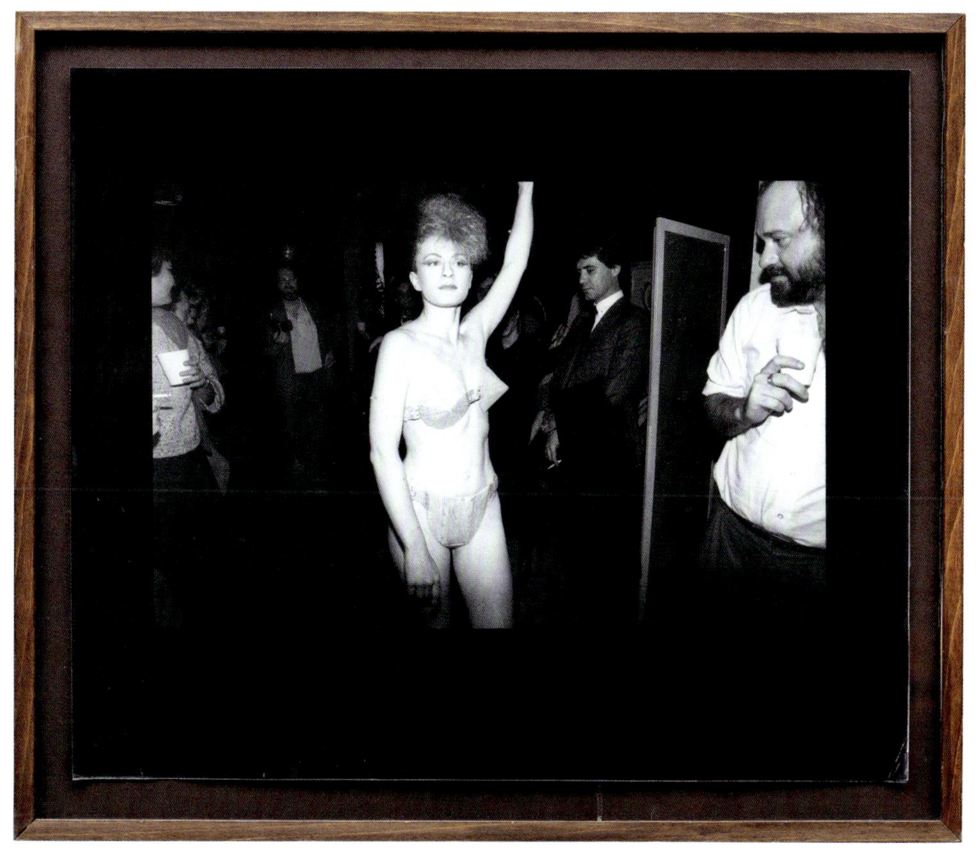

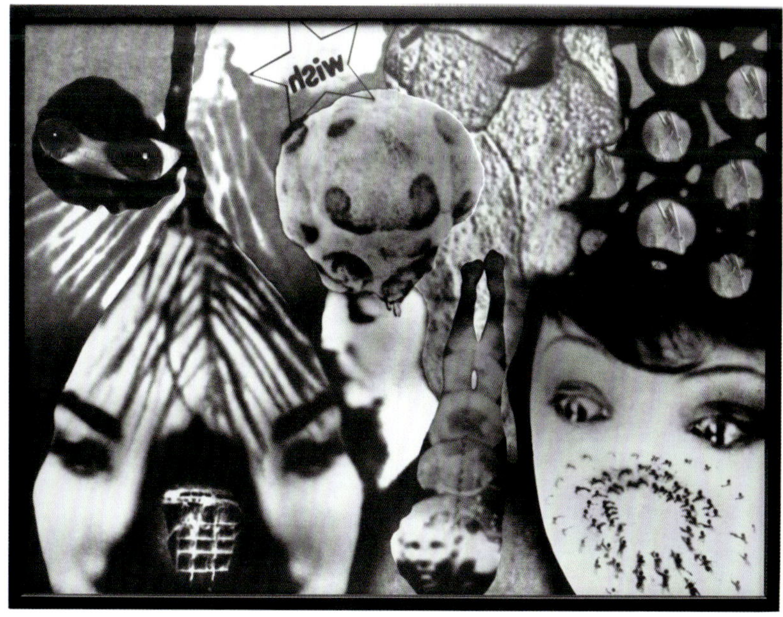
wish

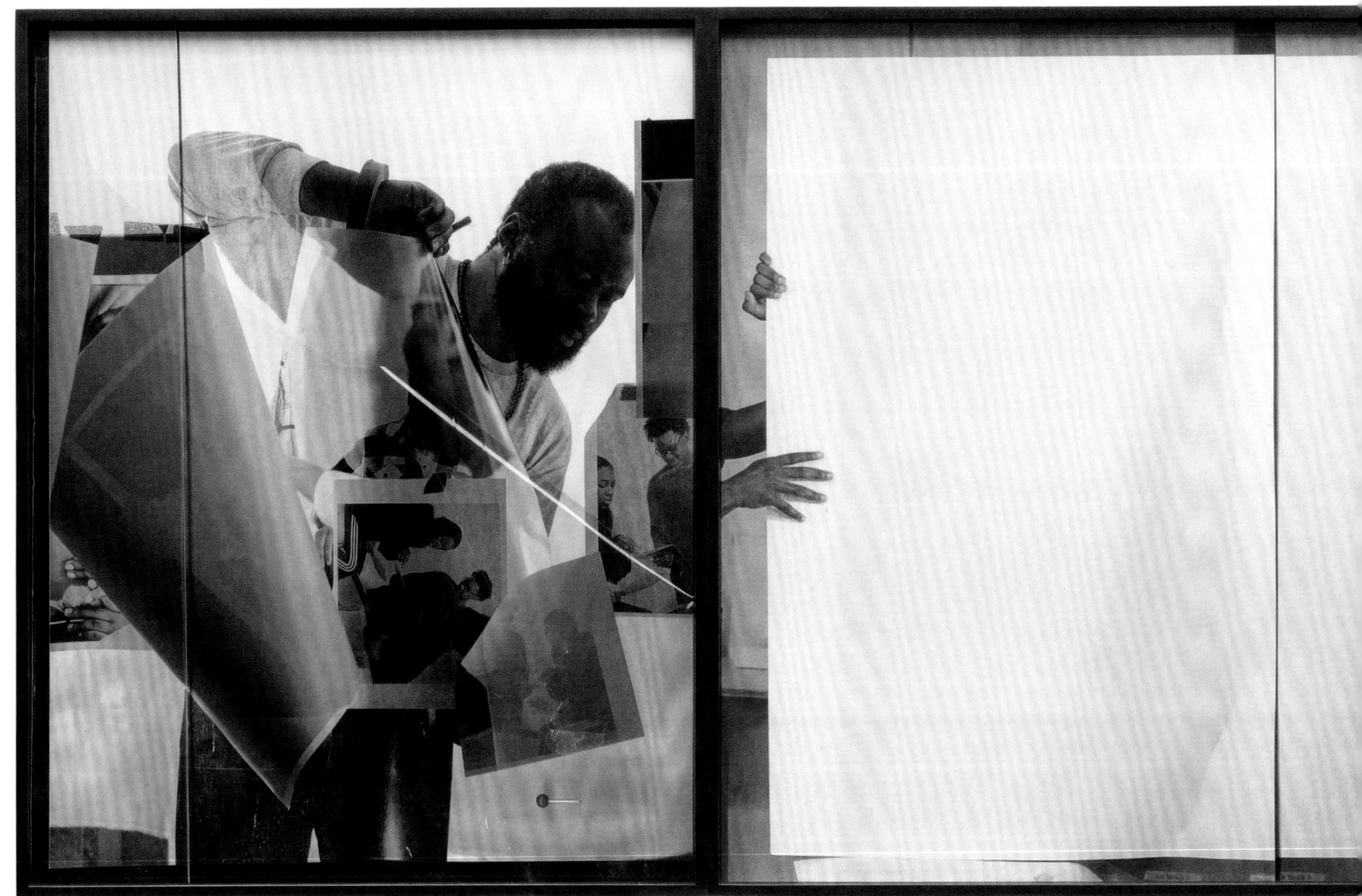

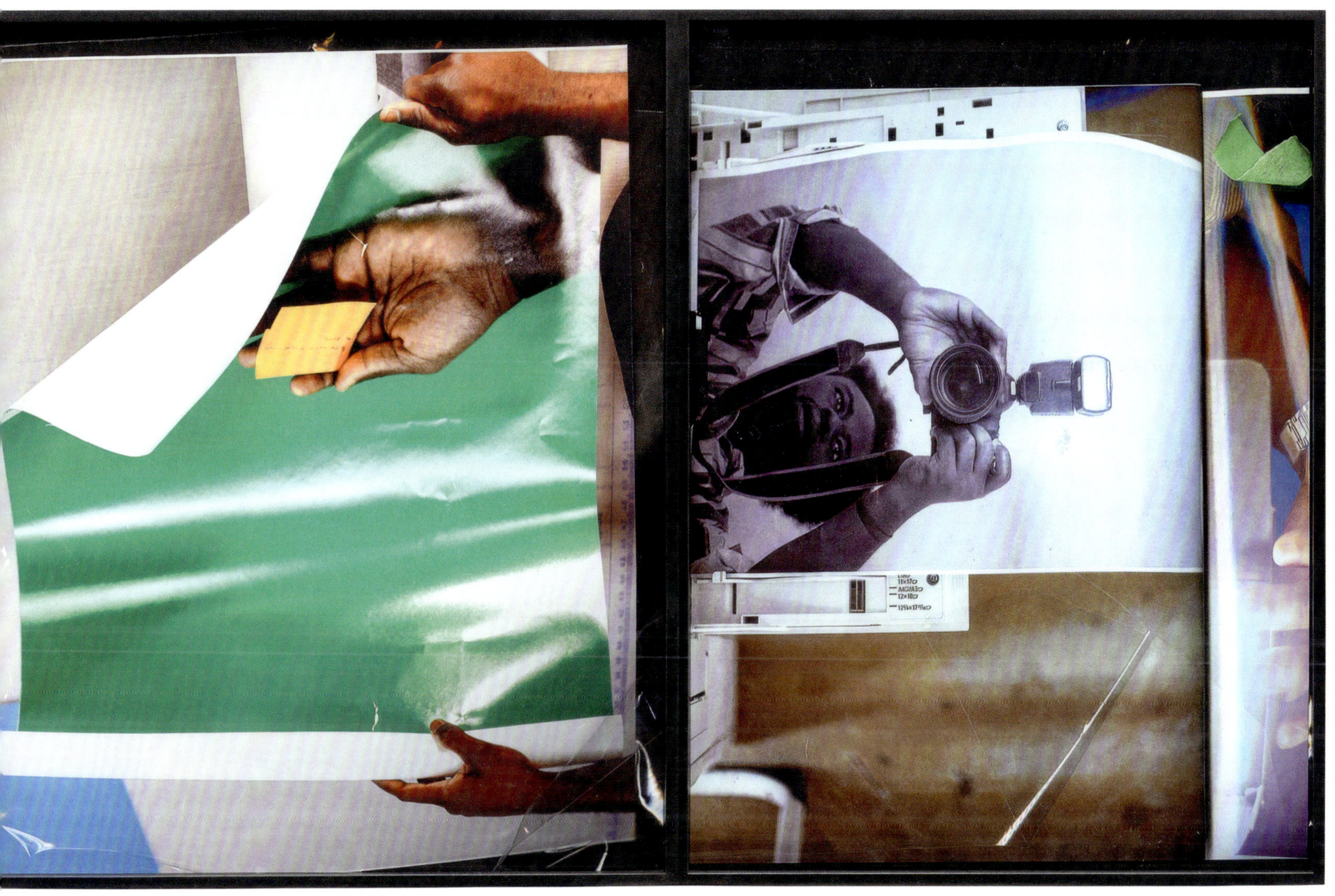

Luther Konadu
Ambient Photo
2025
Pigment prints, mounted
73 × 96.5 cm each
Purchase, with funds from James Lahey & Pym Buitenhuis and Dr. Kenneth Montague & Sarah Aranha, 2025
2025/202

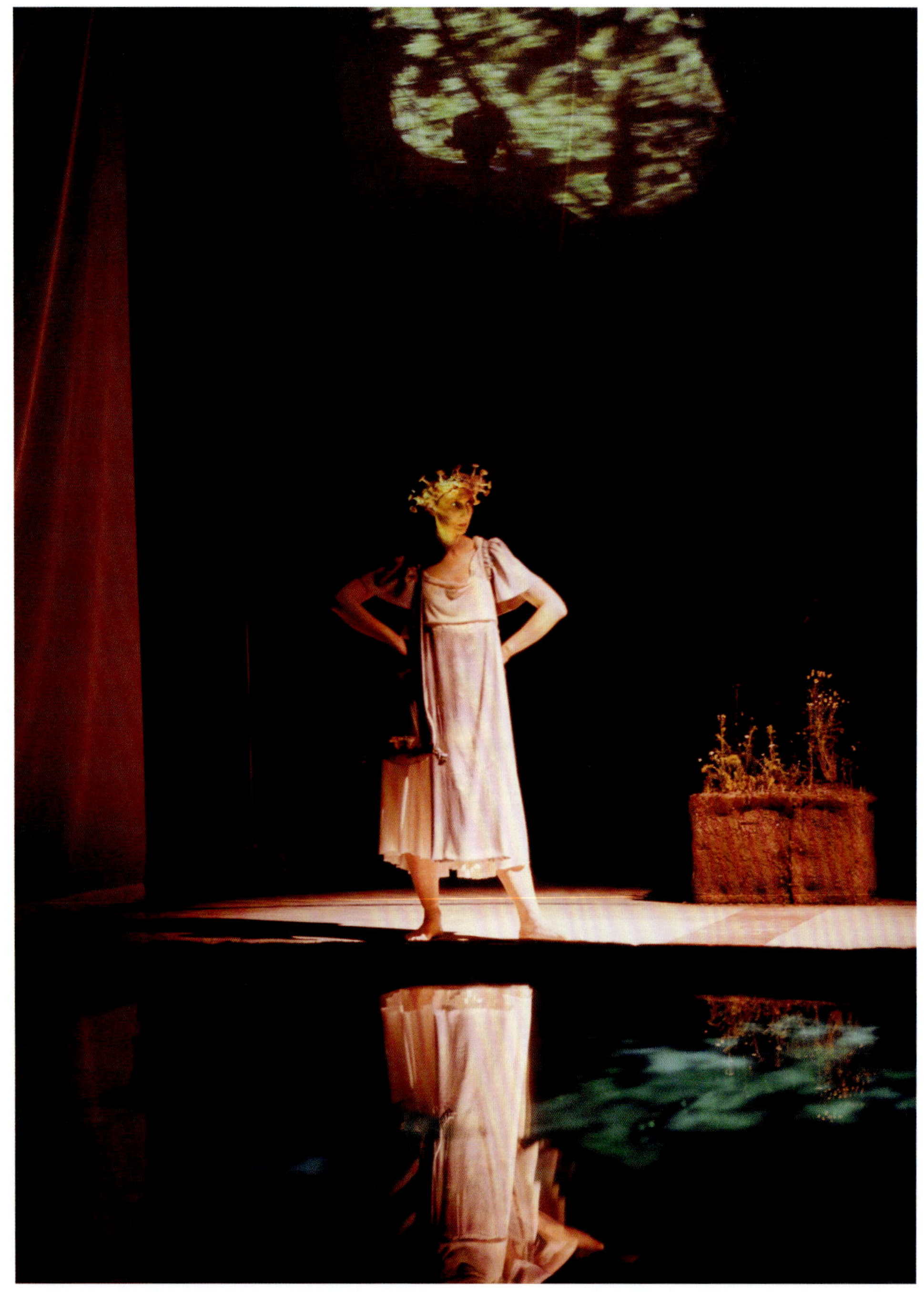

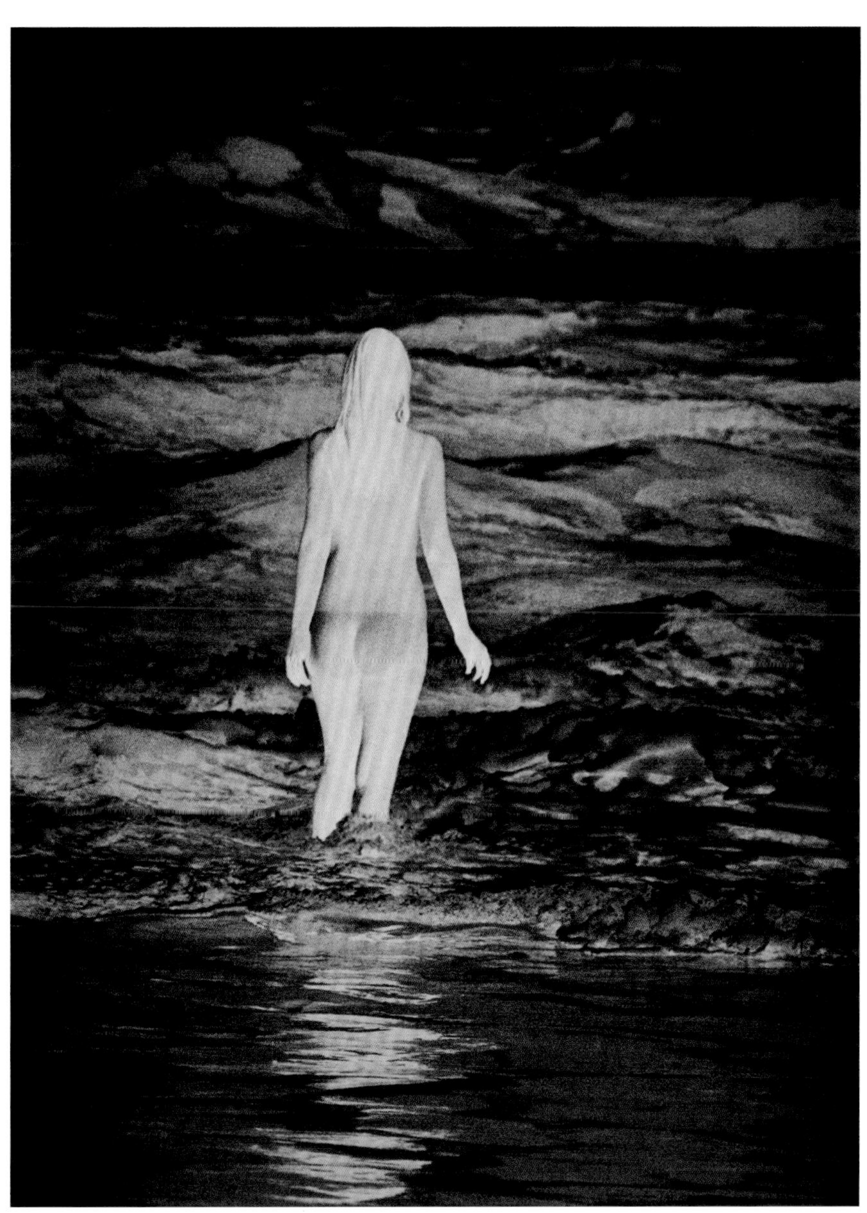

David Hlynsky and Elizabeth Chitty
Costume design: Shelagh Young
Winter: Strength, Lake Suite
1990
Chromogenic print
76.2 × 101.6 cm
Gift of Elizabeth Chitty, 2022
2022/7104.1

Anne Collier
Negative (California)
2013
Chromogenic print
226.4 × 180.3 cm
Promised Gift of Robin & Malcolm Anthony
and Donna & Robert Poile

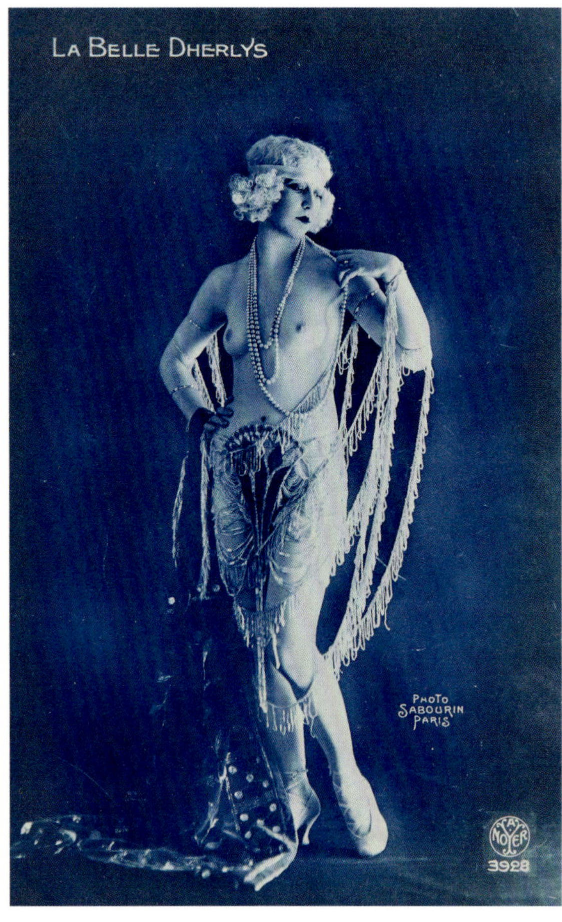

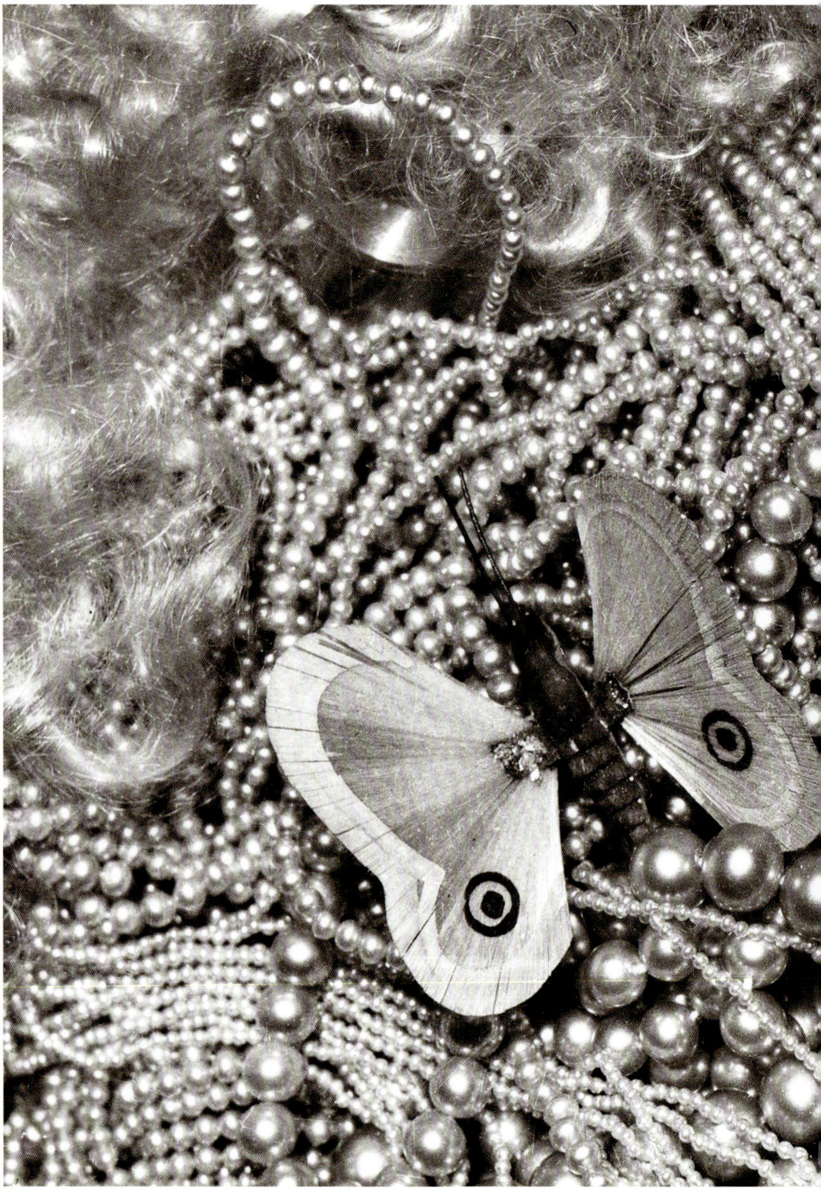

Alfred Noyer
La Belle Dherlys
1900s
Cyanotype
13.5 × 9 cm
Gift of Carol and Morton Rapp, 1997
97/1826

Herbert Bayer
Paris
1930
Gelatin silver print, ferrotyped
27.9 × 21.6 cm
Purchase, with funds from the Photography
Curatorial Committee, 2025
2024/391

Isabel Okoro
Spirit Traveller
2021
Pigment print
65.6 × 55.4 × 5.1 cm
Purchase, with funds from Friends of Global Africa
and the Diaspora, 2022
2022/32

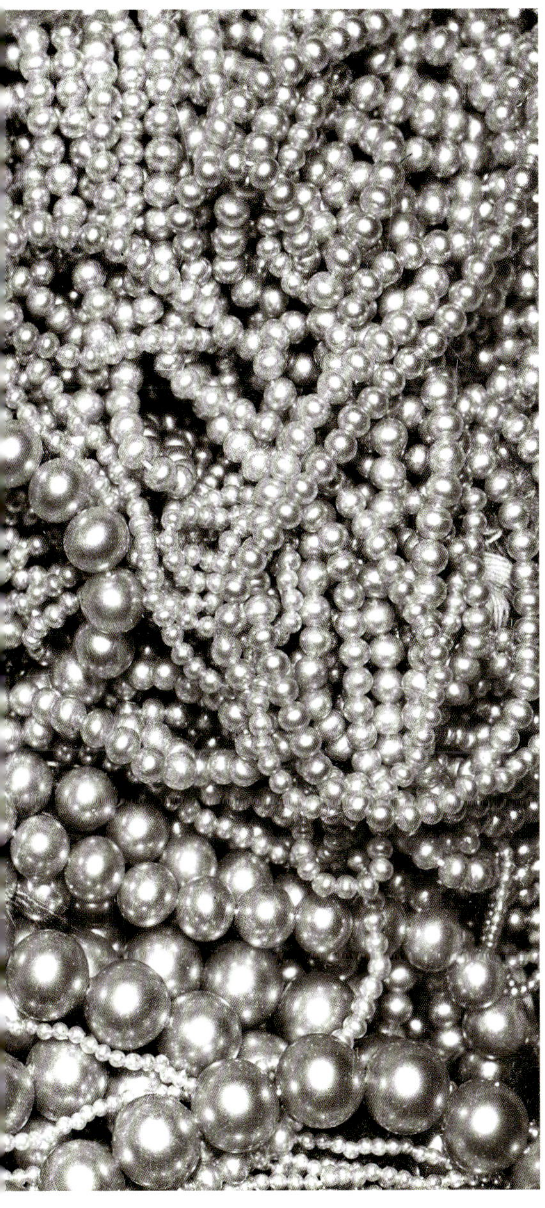

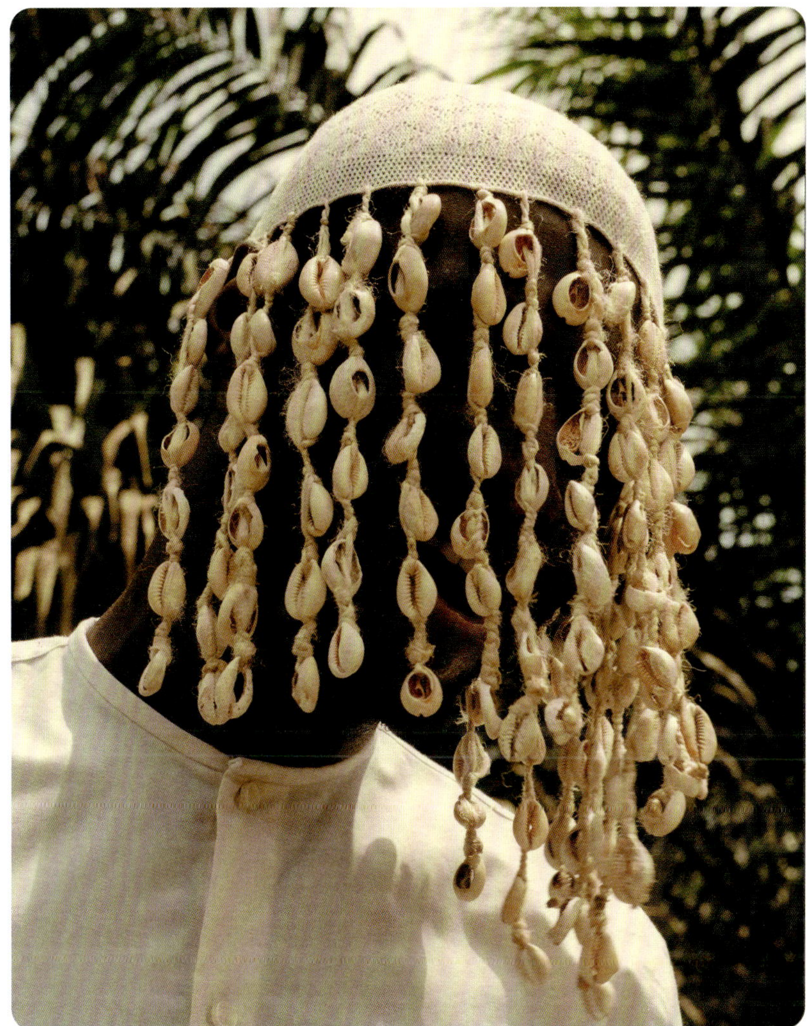

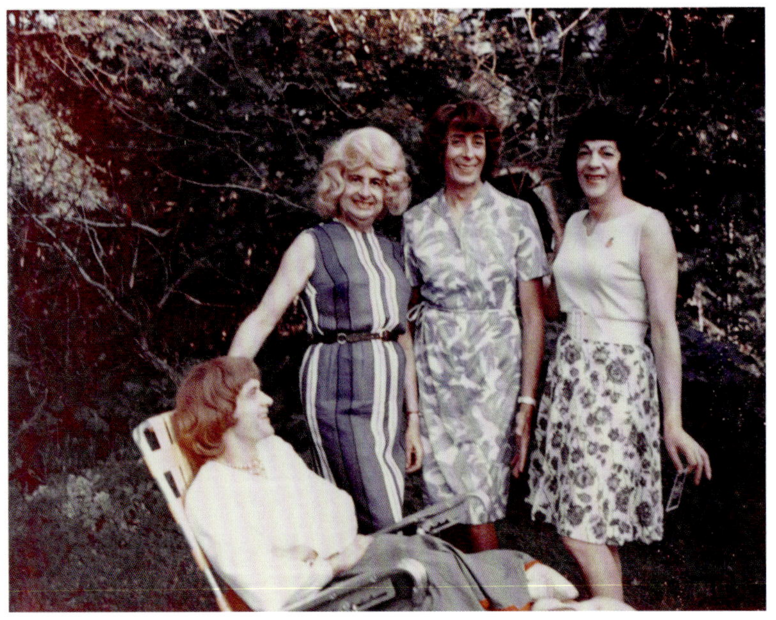

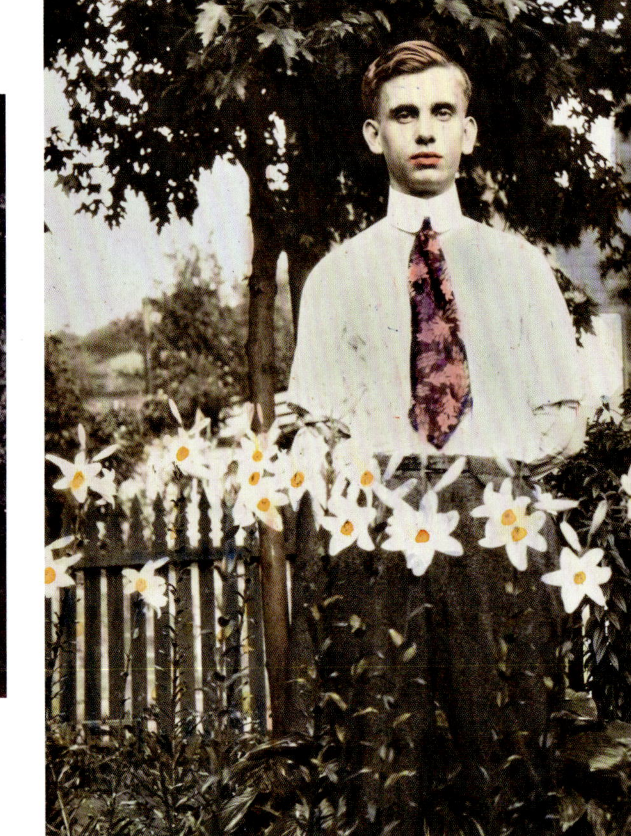

CASA SUSANNA

In the 1960s, Casa Susanna, a quiet resort in the Catskills, offered a rare safe space for cross-dressers to explore and celebrate their femininity. Run by Susanna Valenti and her wife, Marie, it became a central hub for this community in the United States. The photographs, rediscovered at a flea market in 2000, reveal the community's connection, playfulness, and joy.

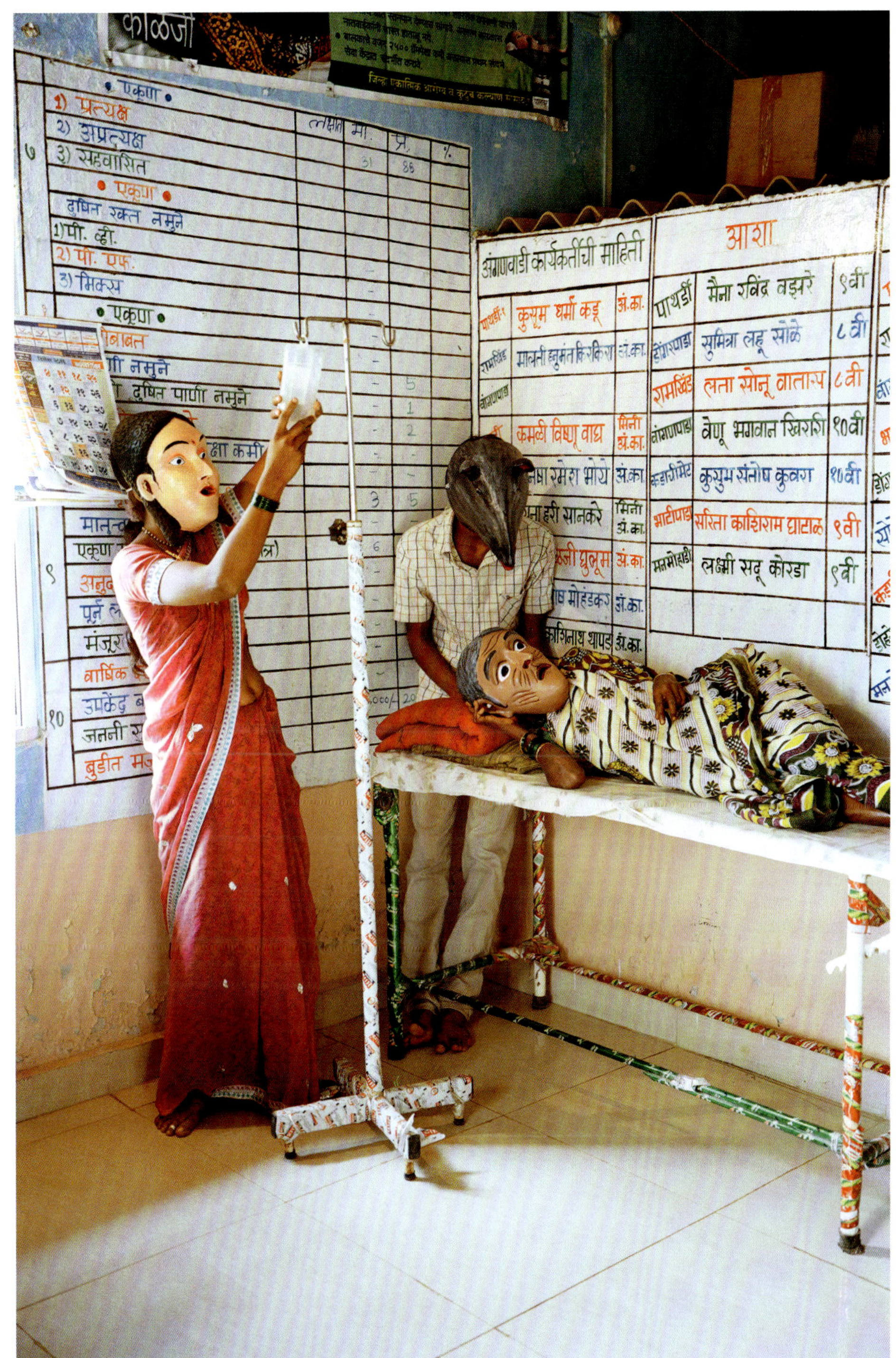

Attributed to Andrea Susan
Daphne sitting on a lawn chair with Ann, Susanna and a friend outside, Casa Susanna, Hunter, NY
1964–1968
Chromogenic print
8.9 × 10.8 cm
Purchase, with funds generously donated by Martha L A McCain, 2015
2014/820

Maker once known
A young man wearing a purple tie
c. 1920
Gelatin silver print, with applied colour
21.3 × 16.6 cm
Purchase, donated funds in memory of Eric Steiner, 1999
99/397

Gauri Gill
Untitled (9)
From the series ***Acts of Appearance*** (2015–ongoing)
Archival pigment print
152.4 × 101.6 cm
Purchase, with funds from the Photography Curatorial Committee, 2022
2021/278

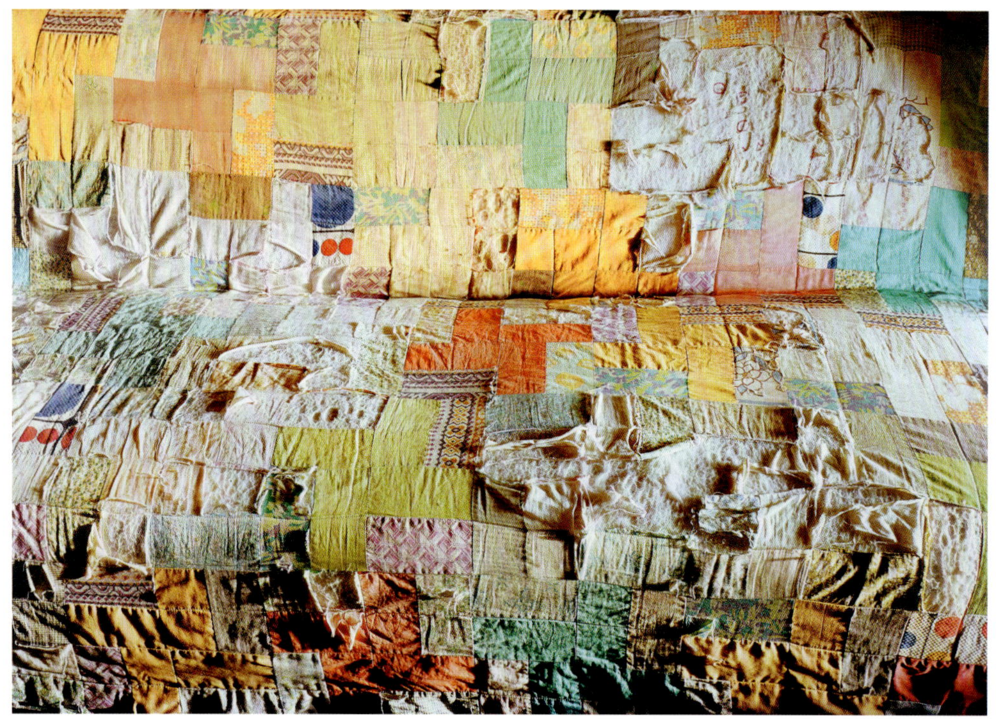

Scott McFarland
Torn Quilt the Effects of Sunlight
2003
From the series ***Cabin*** (2001-2004)
Pigment inkjet print
139.7 × 148.6 cm
Gift of François R. Roy, 2013
2013/388

N.E. Thing Co.
Nude
1969
photographic transparency, metal, illumination
34.6 × 50.2 × 13.7 cm
Gift of Mr. and Mrs. Aaron Milrad, 1975
75/48

Cassils
Etched in Light
2023
Installation view, BOFFO 2023 Benefit Exhibition, kurimanzutto New York
Cyanotype on cotton fabric
609.6 × 579.1 cm
Purchase, with funds from the Christian Claude Fund and Martha LA McCain, 2024
2024/16

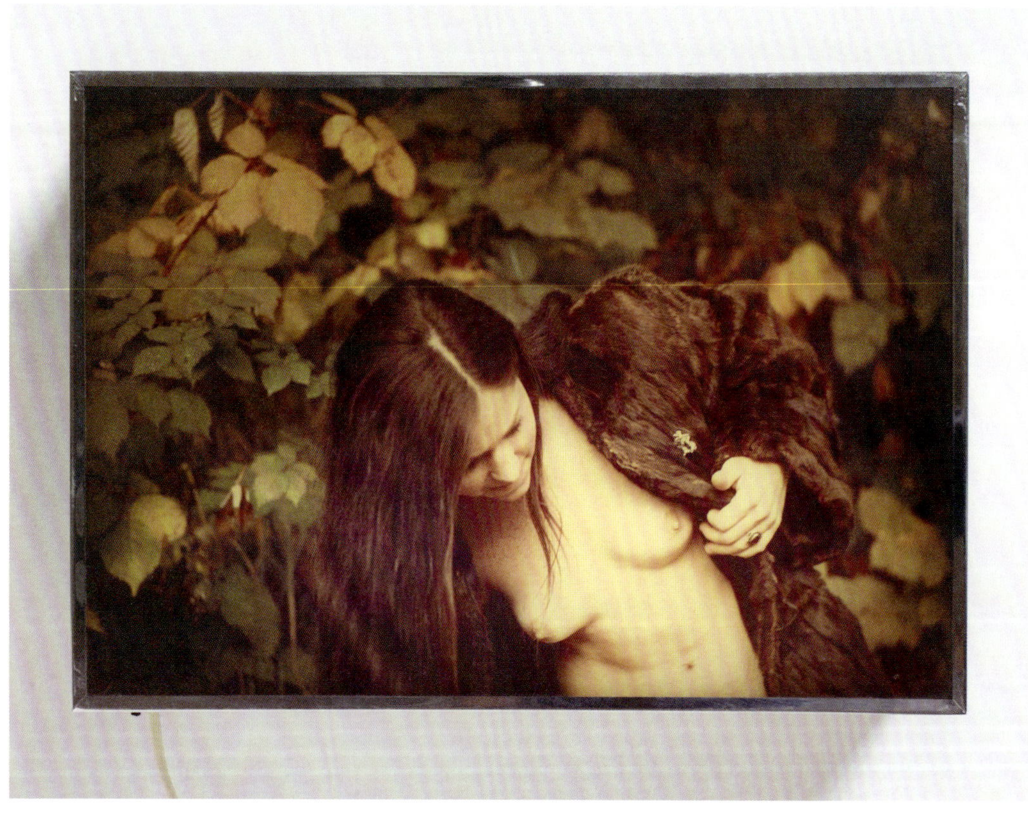

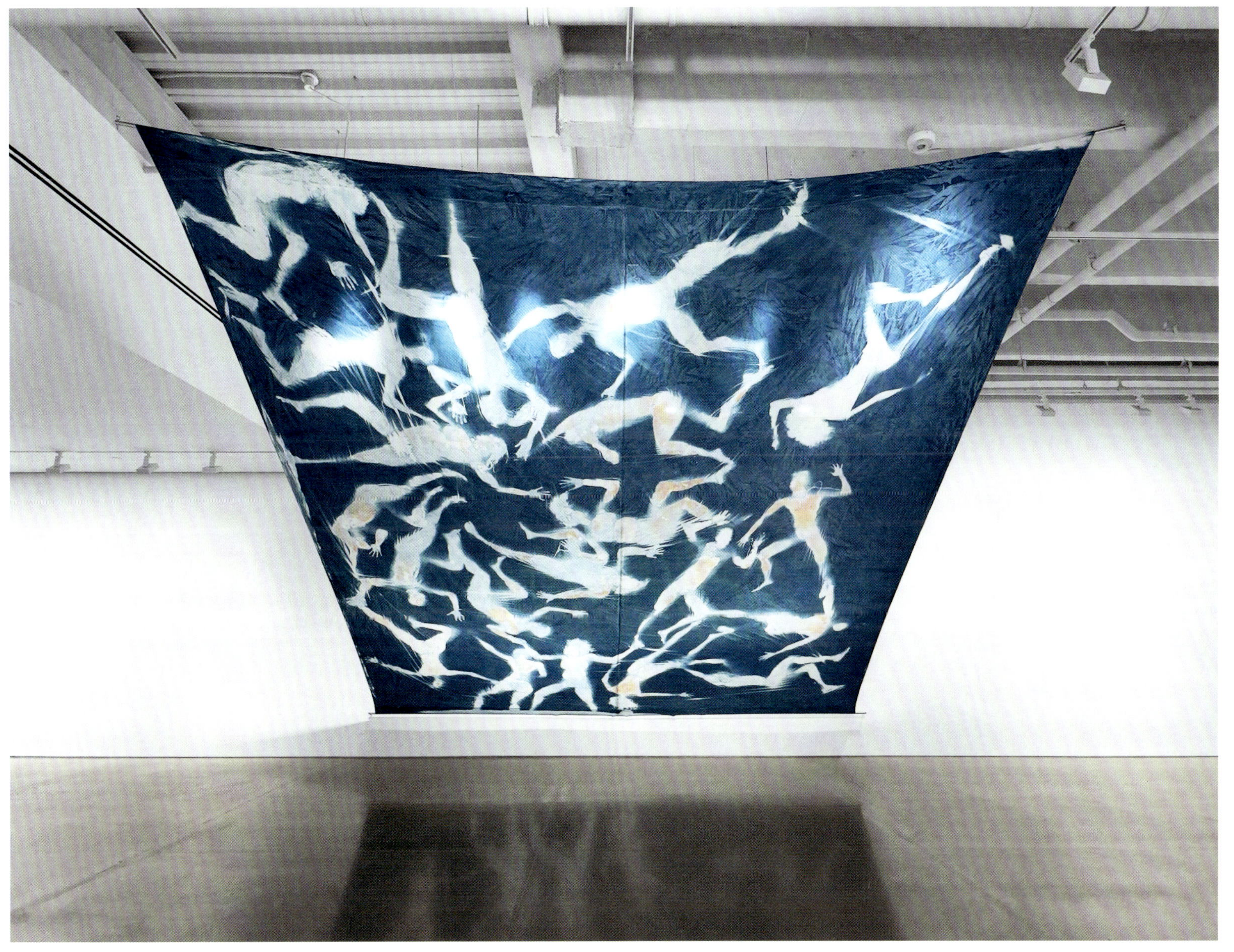

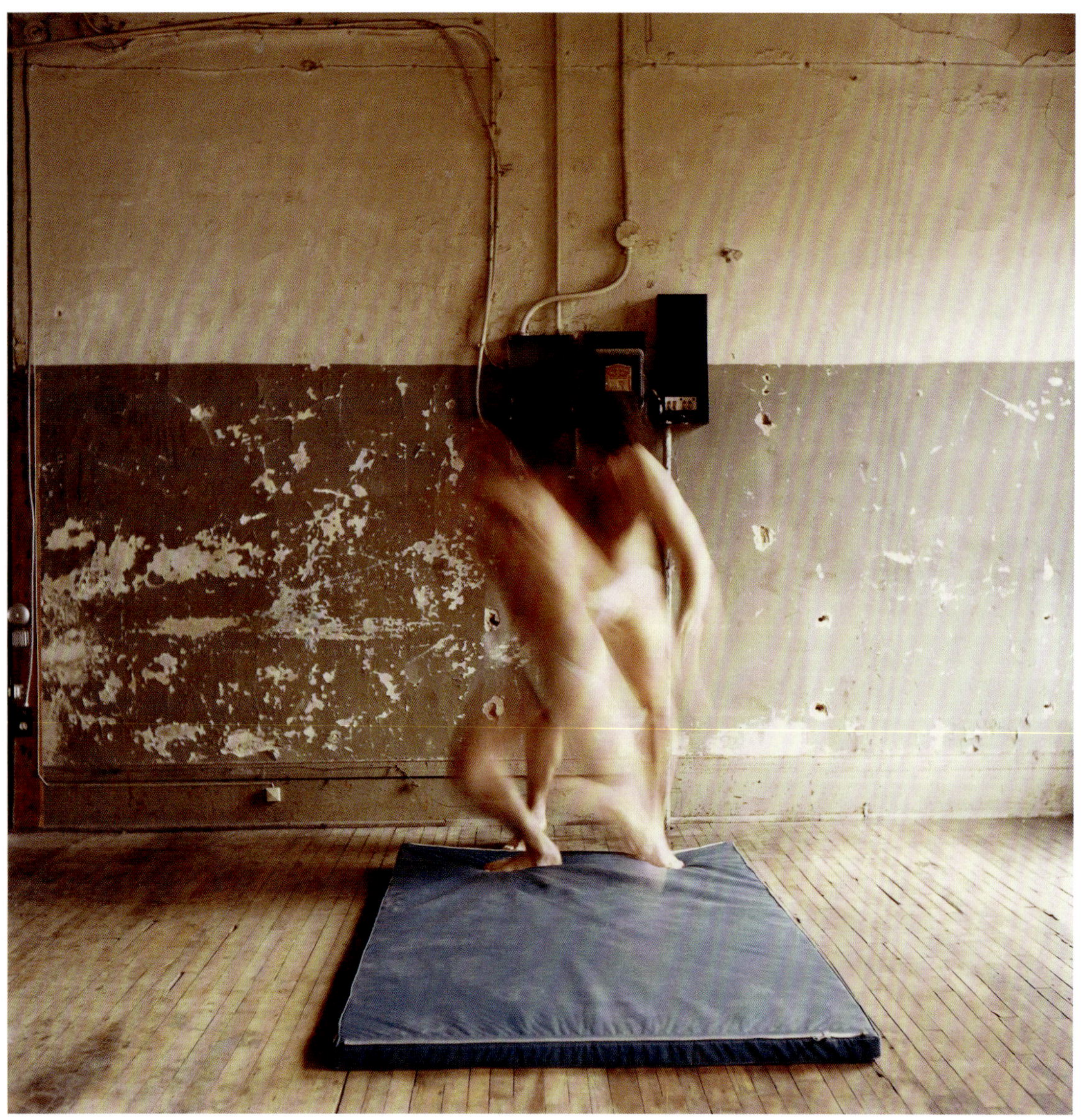

Sorel Cohen
After Bacon/Muybridge, Coupled Figures/Shoulder Toss #1 (detail)
1980
Pigment prints (4)
50 × 50 cm each
Gift of Alison and Alan Schwartz, 1994
94/851.1.4

Alec Soth
Helena, Arkansas
2002
From the series ***Sleeping by the Mississippi***
(1999–2002)
Pigment print
81.3 × 101.6 cm
Gift of Richard J. Balfour, 2025
2025/216

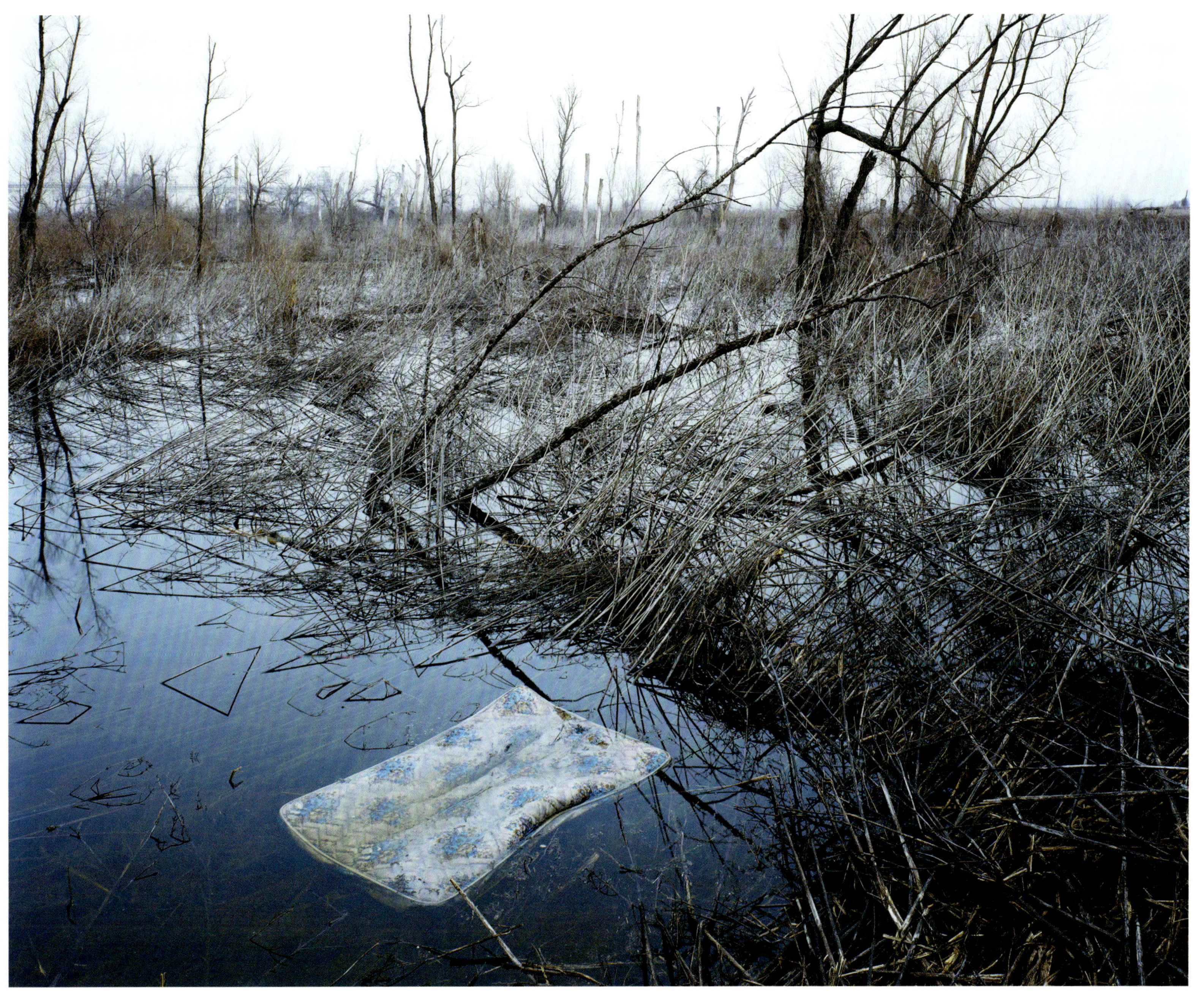

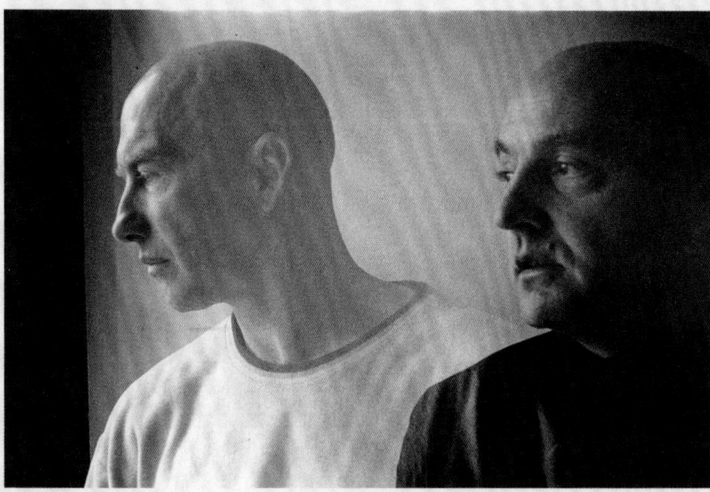

Duane Michals
Self Portrait with my Guardian Angel
1974–1975
Gelatin silver print
36.8 × 40.8 cm
Gift of Lynn and Stephen Smart, 2012
2012/174

Spring Hurlbut
Deuil I: Mary 1
2006
From the series ***Deuil*** (2005–2008)
Pigment print
72.7 × 82.9 cm
Purchased with the assistance of the Toronto International Art Fair 2008 Opening Night Gala and the Hal Jackman Foundation, 2009
2008/111

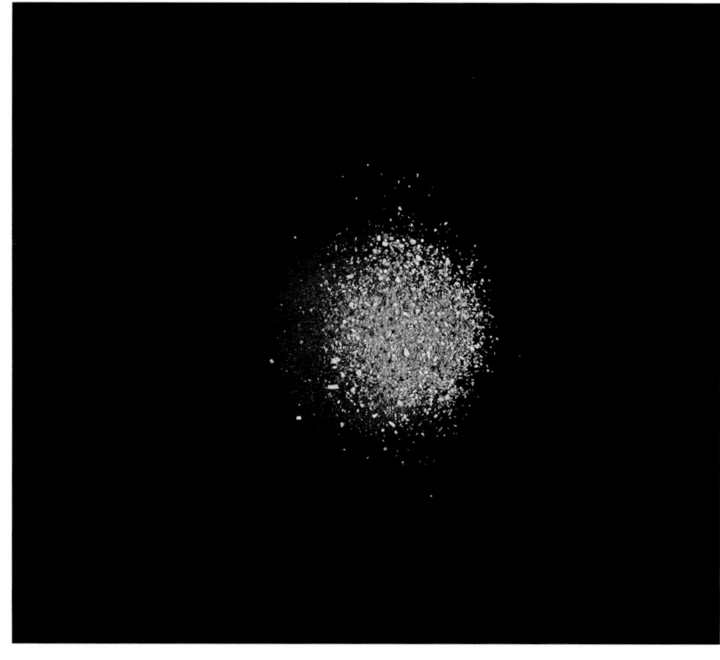

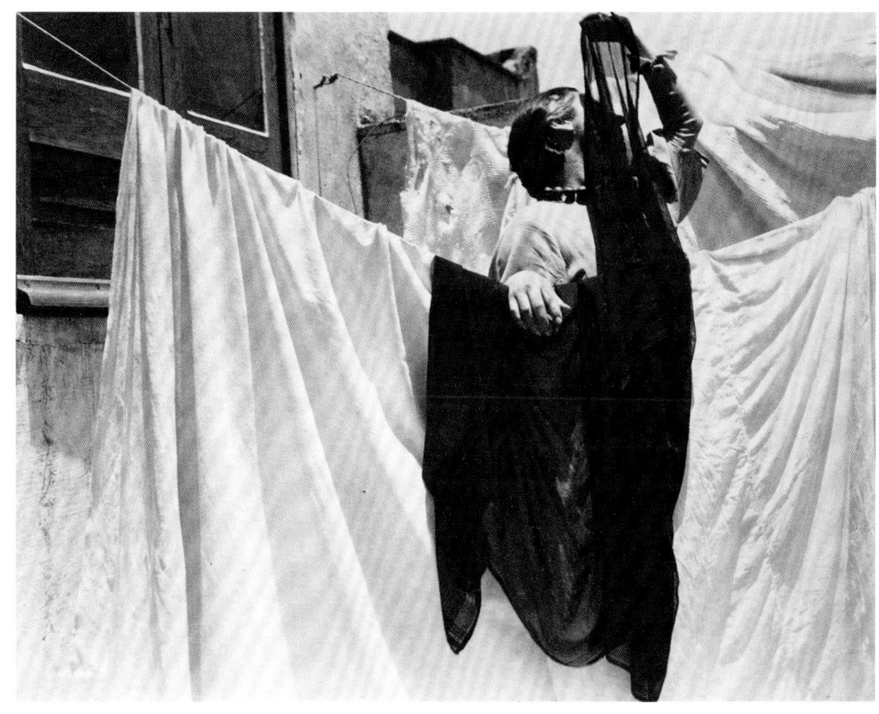

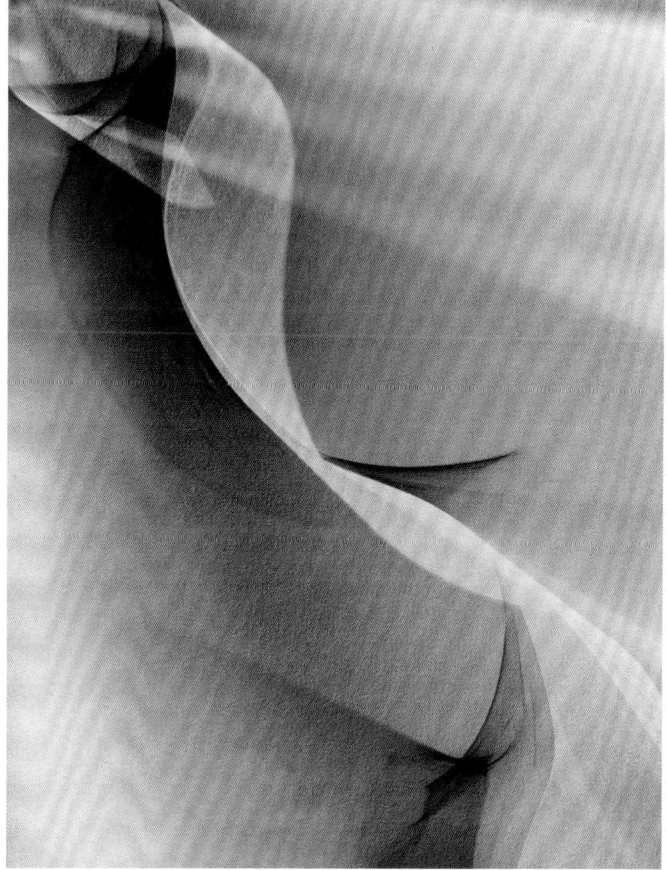

Manuel Álvarez Bravo
Eclipse
1933
Gelatin silver print
19.9 × 25 cm
Malcolmson Collection. Gift of Harry and Ann Malcolmson in partnership with a private donor, 2014
2014/462

Lotte Jacobi
Large Photogenic (#3)
c. 1950–1956
Gelatin silver print
50.1 × 38.7 cm
Gift of Dr. Roxane Connick Carlisle in memory of John J. Connick (1883–1972), PEI, 1995
95/285

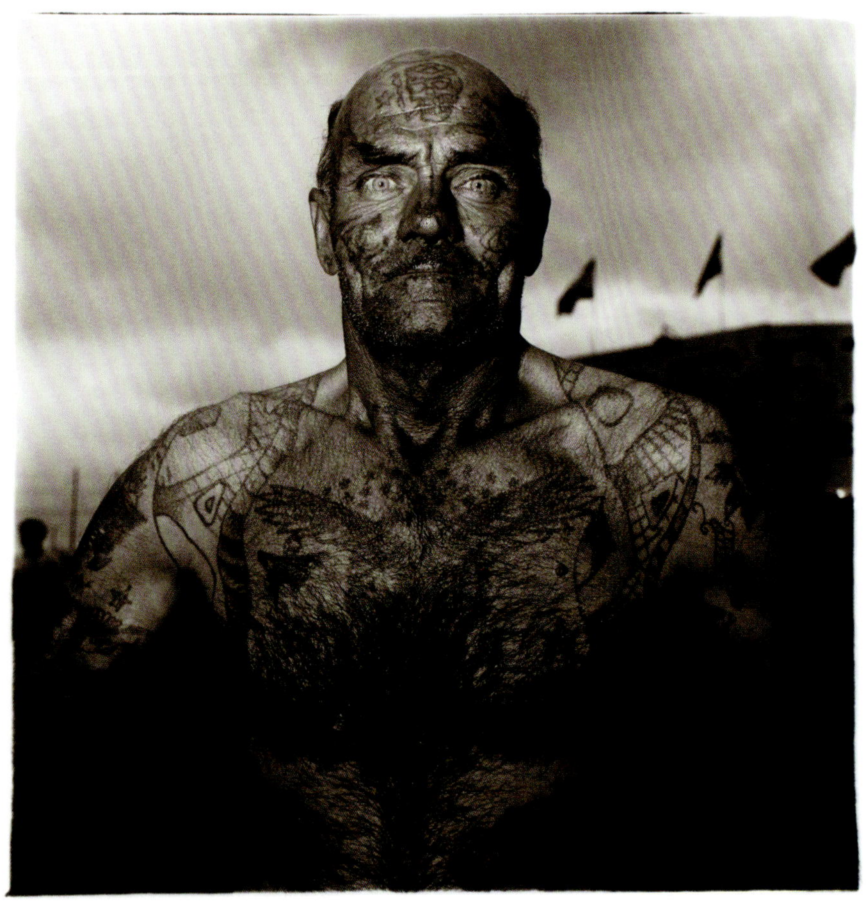

DIANE ARBUS

Diane Arbus revolutionized portraiture with her striking black-and-white photographs. Her work captured a diverse range of subjects—couples, children, nudists, suburban families, circus performers, and celebrities, among others—in a crisp, direct style that became her signature. The AGO's collection of 522 photographs spans her career from 1945 to 1971, making it one of the most significant international holdings of her work.

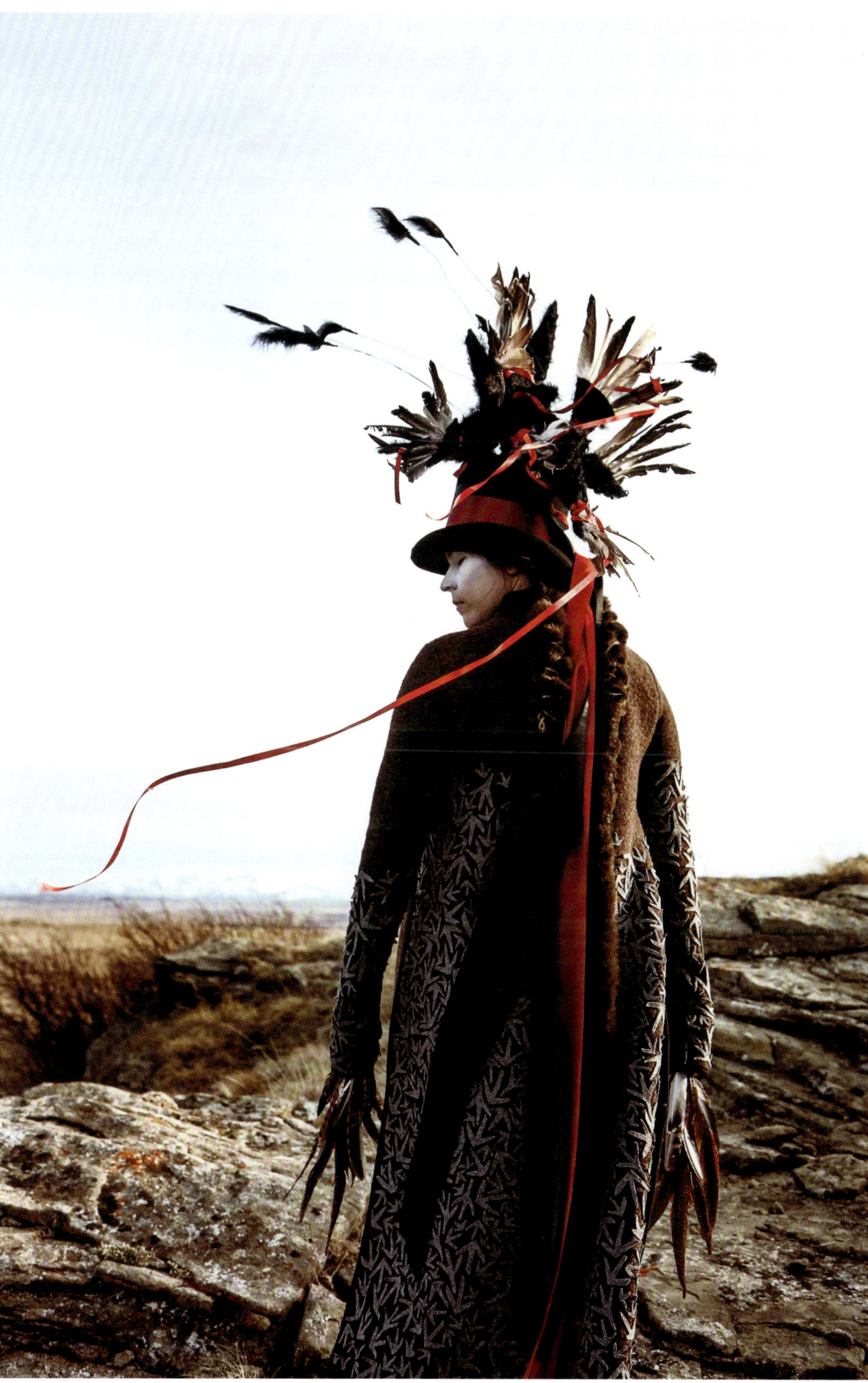

Diane Arbus
Tattooed man at a carnival, Md., 1970
1970
Gelatin silver print
50.8 × 40.6 cm
Gift of Robin and David Young, 2016
2016/932

Meryl McMaster
Bring me to this place
2017
Pigment print
152.4 × 101.6 cm
Purchased with the assistance of the Dr. Michael Braudo Canadian Contemporary Art Fund and the Art Toronto 2017 Opening Night Preview, 2017
2017/43

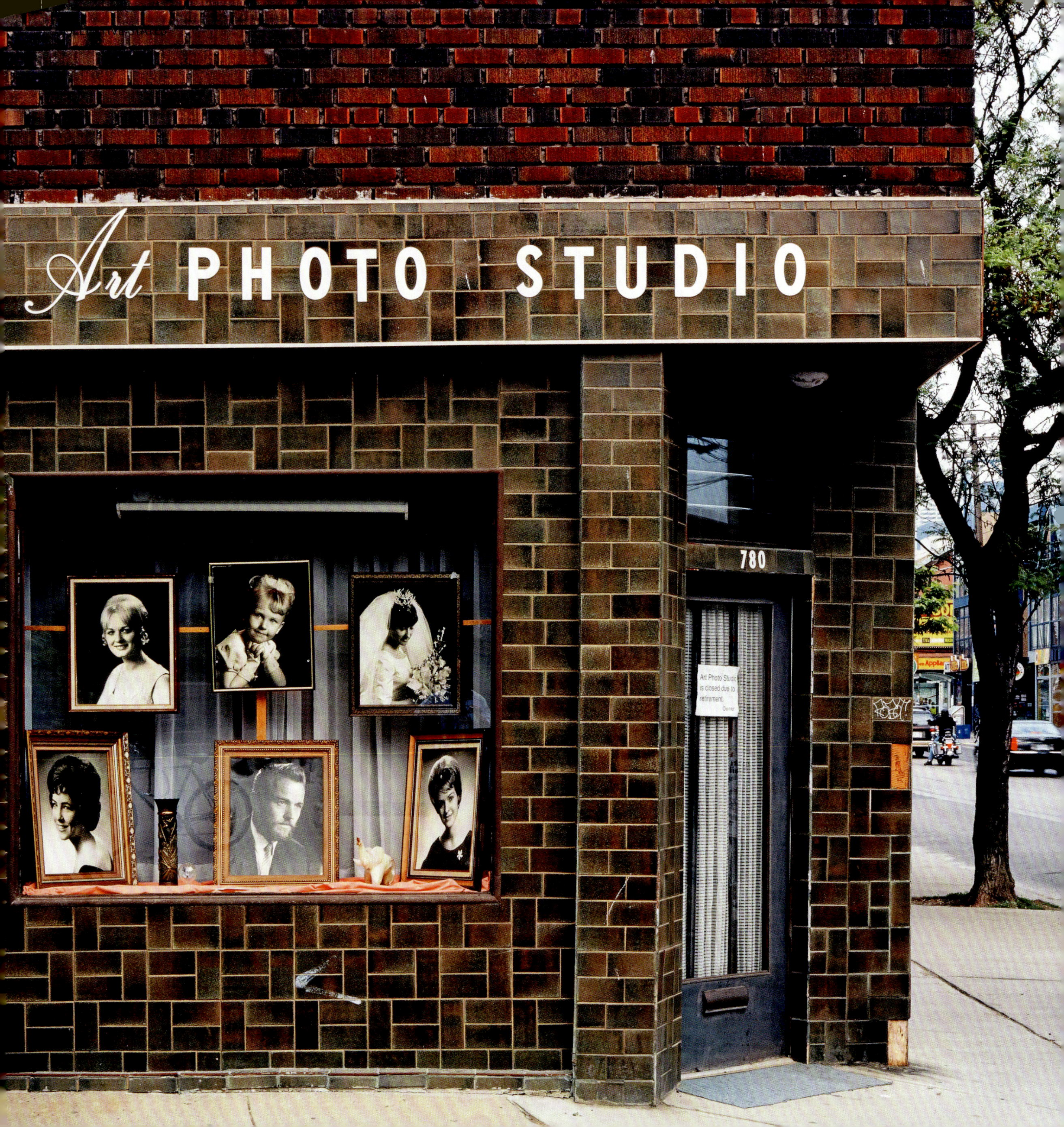
Art PHOTO STUDIO
780
Art Photo Studio
is closed due to
retirement.
Owner

Framing the Scene

A PHOTOGRAPHY TIMELINE IN AND AROUND THE AGO

Marina Dumont-Gauthier

Photography has long held a mirror to Toronto—its shifting architecture, layered histories, contested identities, and imagined futures. Since the inception of the medium in 1839, the city has been a site of photographic experimentation, documentation, and artistic expression. While much of Toronto's photographic scene has grown outside traditional institutions, this timeline foregrounds the AGO's role in collecting, exhibiting, and publishing photography, and that, long before the creation of a Photography Department in 2000.

Nothing grows in a vacuum and this timeline underscores the reciprocal nature of this growth, underlying how artists, curators, collectors, gallerists, historians, and photo enthusiasts have all shaped a photographic culture that is as plural and complex as the city itself. It documents nearly a century of photographic developments, outlining key figures, milestones, and turning points in the medium's expansion in the city and beyond. It frames the trajectory of photography at the AGO as the central thread through which to explore the broader photographic life of Toronto, recognizing the many diverse forces and communities that have shaped it.

A timeline is never neutral; it is a constructed form, a narrative scaffold that privileges certain events, dates, and names. In that way, it is not intended as a comprehensive account but rather as an exercise in recollection that invites reflection rather than closure. Tracing the history of photography in Toronto is to follow a tapestry of interwoven narratives—personal memories and public histories, local practices and global exchanges, artistic innovation and curatorial engagement—shaped by cultural shifts, institutional resistance, and technological change. As the AGO celebrates this milestone for its Photography Department, *Collective States* can be seen as both a commemoration and a window into the future, honouring the past and those who have paved the way for new voices, new forms, and new aspirations.

Robert Burley
Art Photo Studio: Closed Due To Retirement, Toronto, Ontario (detail)
2005
Inkjet print
40 × 48 cm
Purchase, with funds from Ken Straiton, 2019
2019/1

Artists noted in red are part of the AGO permanent collection.

1840

English industrial chemist Hugh Lee Pattinson makes the first known daguerreotypes of Niagara Falls. One of them is later published as a lithograph in Noël-Marie Paymal Lerebours's *Excursions daguérriennes* in 1841.

1847

Eli J. Palmer opens one of Toronto's first photography studios at King and Church Streets, specializing in daguerreotypes and helping popularize photographic portraiture. The neighbourhood becomes a hub for photography studios in the latter half of the 1800s.

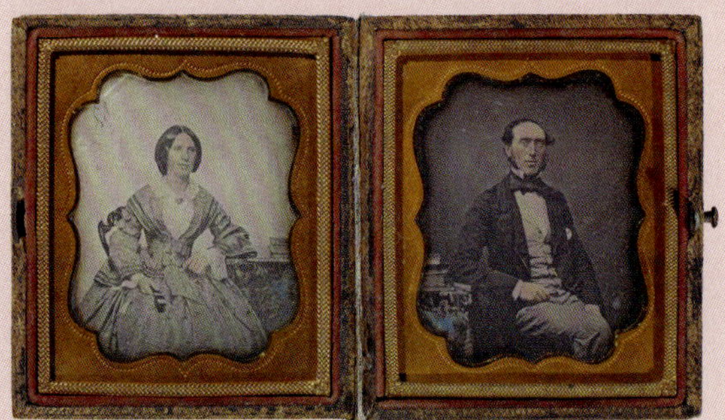

Eli J. Palmer, *Portrait of a man seated at table with books; Portrait of a woman seated at table with books*, c. 1855. Daguerreotypes, tinted, 6.5 × 5.5 cm each. Gift of John Richmond Harris, 2006 (2006/300).

1868

Octavius Thompson publishes *Toronto in the Camera*. Featuring forty-eight albumen prints of key buildings, it is one of the earliest visual records of the city's architecture.

John A. Fraser opens the Notman, Notman & Fraser Photographic Studio in Toronto as a branch of **William Notman**'s business at 39 King Street East. The studio becomes a meeting place for artists. In 1872, Fraser and a group of friends form the Ontario Society of Artists, whose first exhibition opens at Notman & Fraser in 1873.

1888

The Toronto Amateur Photographic Association is founded, evolving into the Toronto Camera Club in 1893. The club fosters a growing community of photographers, with key members like **Arthur Goss** and Sidney Carter playing a leading role in advancing pictorialism in the city and promoting photography as an art form.

1891

The Globe publishes an engraving of Wilfrid Laurier, marking the first use of a photograph-based image in a Canadian newspaper.

1900

The Art Museum of Toronto is established, finding a home in the Grange Manor in 1913. It becomes the Art Gallery of Toronto in 1919, and the Art Gallery of Ontario in 1966. The Grange is now a designated national historic site and remains central to the AGO's identity.

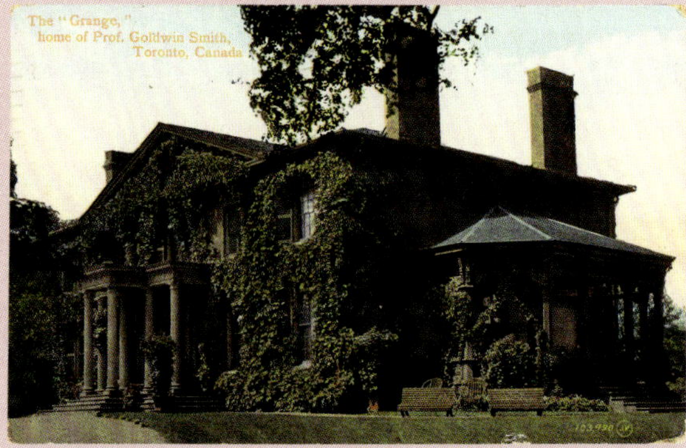

Valentine & Sons Co. Ltd., The Grange home, future site of the Art Museum of Toronto, c. 1912–1916. Edward P. Taylor Library & Archives, Art Gallery of Ontario.

1911

Arthur Goss becomes the first official photographer for the City of Toronto, a position he maintains until 1940.

1917

The Toronto Camera Club holds its first annual salon at the Art Gallery of Toronto. The club's association with the museum continues until the outbreak of the Second World War, in 1939.

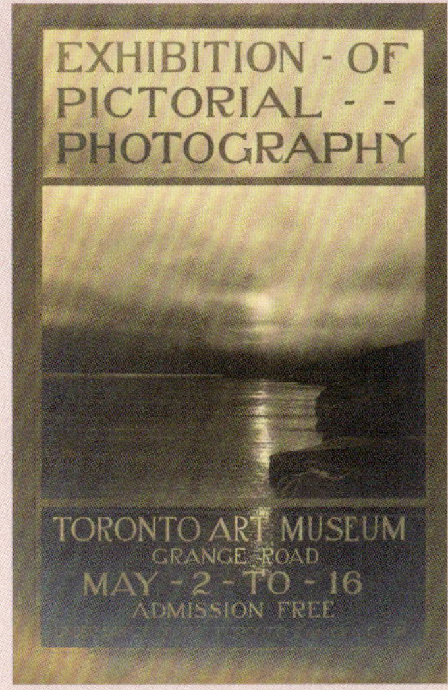

Arthur Goss, poster for Toronto Camera Club's Exhibition of Pictorial Photography at the Toronto Art Museum, 1917. Edward P. Taylor Library & Archives, Art Gallery of Ontario.

1919

Minna Keene, the first woman fellow of England's Royal Photographic Society, moves to Toronto from Montreal and opens a studio with her daughter **Violet Keene Perinchief**.

1920–1949

These decades see a diverse range of photographic exhibitions at the Art Gallery of Toronto. Along with the Toronto Camera Club salons, noteworthy exhibitions include *Photographs by the Royal Photographic Society of Great Britain* (1929), *Plant Patterns in Hawaii and Japan: Photographs by E. Haanel Cassidy* (1938), and the *First Canadian International Colour Slide Salon of Photography* (1945).

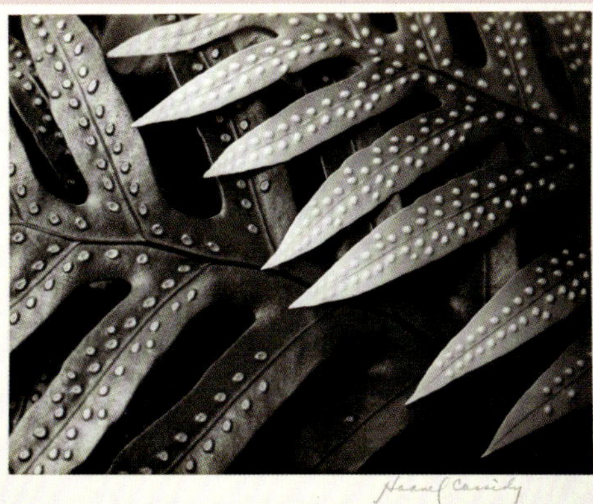

E. Haanel Cassidy, *Plant Form Leaves with Circular Protrusion*, 1938. Chlorobromide print, 39.9 × 50.9 cm. Gift of Sylvia Platt, 2002 (2003/1638).

1925

The first photographic object, a portrait of *Jane Eyre* author Charlotte Brontë, is donated to the AGO. An ambrotype made from an engraving after a drawing by George Richmond, it carries the inscription: "A birthday present to dear Fanny from her loving friend EA, March 28, 1858." This inaugural gift highlights the role personal photographs continue to play in the collection.

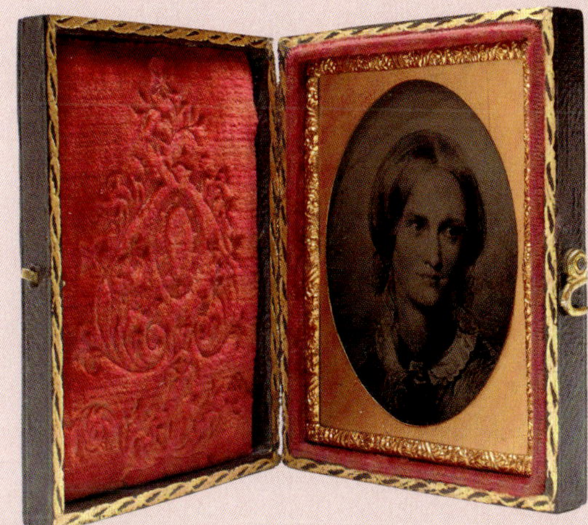

Maker once known, Charlotte Brontë, from engraving after the 1850 drawing by George Richmond, 1858. Ambrotype, brown leather with medallion and scroll design, interior with embossed red velvet pad (case), 6.4 × 5 cm (image). Gift of Ronald Hewat, Kaslo, BC, 1925 (782).

1935

Memorial Exhibition: Photographs by M.O. Hammond opens at the Art Gallery of Toronto. **Hammond** was a pioneering figure in Canadian photography, noted for his pictorialist vision and his advocacy for the medium. The AGO later acquired 101 of his works, in 1985.

1941

The National Film Board of Canada (NFB) forms its Still Photography Division, commissioning photographers to document life across the country as part of a nation-building effort to visually define Canadian identity. Early contributors include Nicholas Morant, **George Hunter**, and Chris Lund.

1948

The School of Photography is established in the founding year of the Ryerson Institute of Technology (now Toronto Metropolitan University). The program evolves to produce notable graduates such as **Robert Burley**, **Edward Burtynsky**, **Cheryl Sourkes**, and **Nina Levitt**.[1]

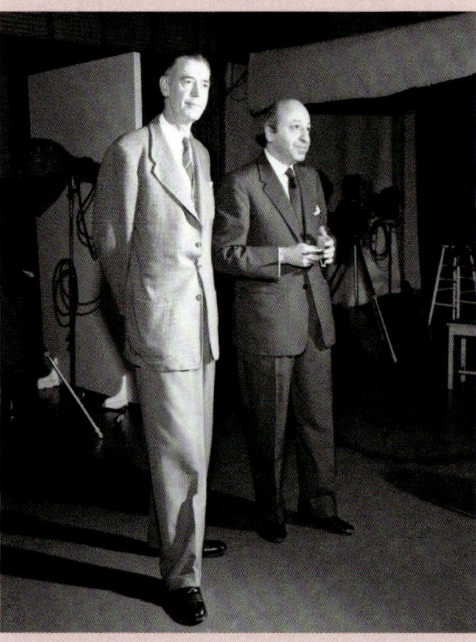

Maker once known, Canadian, Yousuf Karsh visit to the School of Photographic Art, December 4, 1957. Photograph courtesy of Toronto Metropolitan University Libraries, Archives and Special Collections (RG 95.1.72.12.01).

1. Toronto Metropolitan University had four previous official names: Ryerson Institute of Technology (1948–1966); Ryerson Polytechnical Institute (1966–1993); Ryerson Polytechnical University (1993–2001); and Ryerson University (2001–2022). The Ryerson Image Centre was renamed the Image Centre in 2022. This chronology refers to these institutions by the name they held at the time of each event.

1960

Lorraine Monk becomes executive producer of the National Film Board's Still Photography Division. Her leadership ushers in a shift toward more subjective, personal approaches to documentary photography by photographers like **Michel Lambeth**, **Lutz Dille**, and Michael Semak.

1961

Av Isaacs moves his Greenwich Gallery from Hayter Street (near Bay and Gerrard) to 832 Yonge Street. Renamed The Isaacs Gallery, it becomes a vital space for contemporary Toronto artists, including **Joyce Wieland**, **Michael Snow**, and **Michel Lambeth**.

Canadian Art magazine publishes its first-ever feature on the medium, "Photography and the Image of Canada," by photographer Philip Pocock.

1964

Maia-Mari Sutnik begins her career at the Art Gallery of Ontario, initially part-time in the Education Department teaching children's art classes and supporting front-of-house operations. The AGO Women's Committee, which operates the Gallery Shop, asks her to supervise book, reproduction, and product sales. In 1968, she becomes Audio-Visual Librarian, initiating a new program of films on art and media aids.

1965

Ralph Greenhill's newly published *Early Photography in Canada* becomes the first book of its kind to focus on the history of photography in the country. An expanded edition appears in 1979, co-authored by photography historian Andrew Birrell.

1968

The National Gallery of Canada (NGC), under the directorship of Jean Sutherland Boggs—the museum's first woman director—establishes its Photography Department, appointing James Borcoman as its inaugural curator.

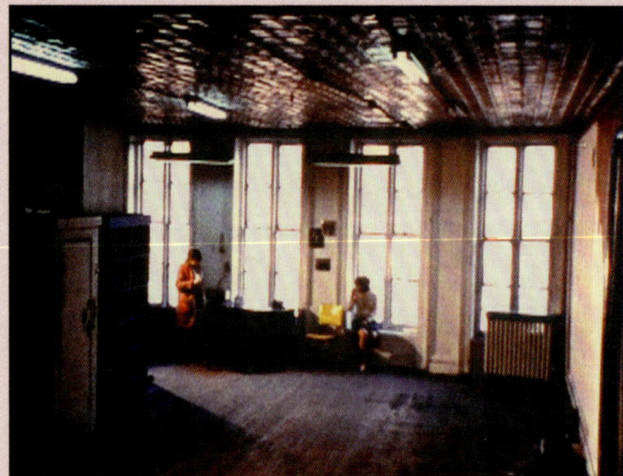

Michael Snow, *Wavelength* (film still), 1967.

The Art Institute of Ontario is absorbed by the AGO's Extension Services Department. Offering programming throughout Ontario, the department promotes art appreciation and education through lectures, workshops, exhibitions, and educational materials. Extension Services played a key role in supporting and raising the visibility of photography at the gallery until 1995.

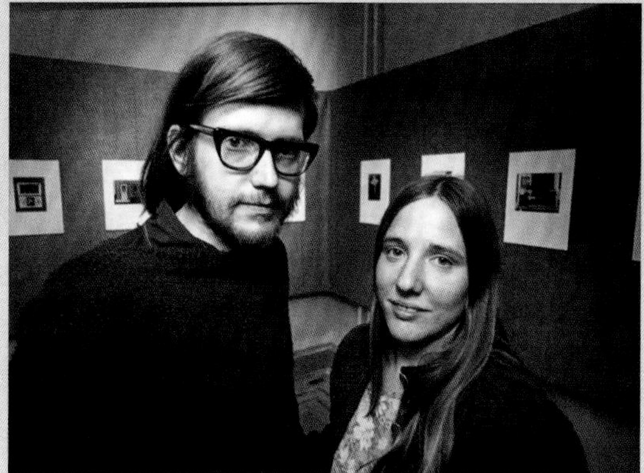

Maker once known, Canadian. John F. Phillips and Laura Jones, Baldwin Street Gallery of Photography, c. 1969. Gelatin silver print. Courtesy of Laura Jones.

1969

Under the guidance of Sutnik, the AGO acquires **Michael Snow**'s landmark experimental film *Wavelength* (1967) for the museum's film program.

The Baldwin Street Gallery of Photography, Canada's first independent photography gallery, is founded by American expats John Phillips and Laura Jones. It becomes a hub for Canadian talent, showing artists like **Barbara Astman, Pamela Harris, George Legrady,** and **Marian Penner Bancroft**, as well as major international figures, both historical and contemporary, like **Julia Margaret Cameron, Barbara Morgan, and Ansel Adams.**

Canadian Art (renamed *artscanada* between 1967 and 1983) devotes an entire issue to photography, featuring essays by scholars, curators, and photographers such as Peter Bunnell, James Borcoman, and **Geoffrey James.** This marks a pivotal moment in the recognition of photography as a legitimate and significant art form in Canada.

1970

The AGO presents *Michael Snow / A Survey*. Curated by Dennis Young, the exhibition included a number of Snow's conceptual photographic works, which sparked controversy among traditional photographers who felt they had been overlooked by the AGO.

1971

The Body Politic, a groundbreaking Canadian LGBTQ+ magazine, is launched. Operated as a collective, members including Gerald Hannon, Jearld Moldenhauer, and Rick Bébout taught themselves photography to document stories important to the community. The publication folded in 1987, but its legacy continues through the Canadian Lesbian and Gay Archives (now The ArQuives), which it helped found in 1973.

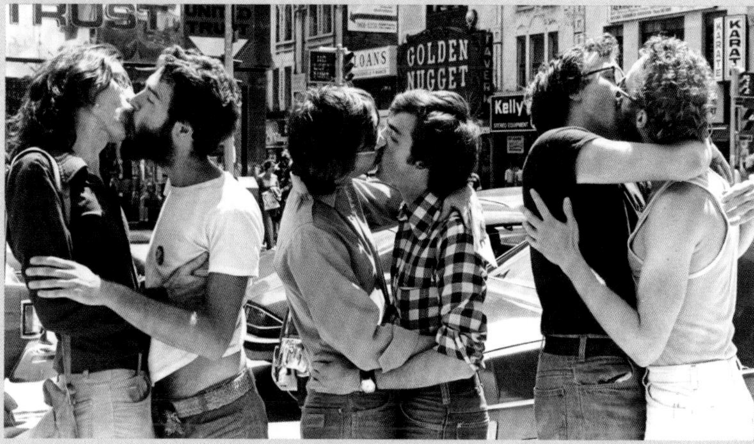

Gerald Hannon, *Kiss-in (Yonge and Bloor, Toronto)*, 1976. Gelatin silver print, 13.5 × 24 cm. File no. 1986-032/155P(01). Photograph Collection Box no. 6. The ArQuives: Canada's LGBTQ2+ Archives, Toronto, Canada.

General Idea's *Miss General Idea Pageant* takes place in Walker Court. Marcel Dot, the alter ego of the Vancouver artist Michael Morris, is crowned. **Rodney Werden** is among the key photographers who help immortalize the event at the AGO.

Sandra Ball and Marcia Reid's Déjà Vu Gallery operates in Yorkville during the 1970s and 1980s. In 1987, Ball and Reid gift the AGO fifty-four works—including ones by **Roman Vishniac, Edward Weston, Lotte Jacobi,** and **André Kertész**—a significant grounding for the museum's modernist photography holdings.

The collective *Mind and Sight* is co-founded by twelve photographers. The gallery, workshop, and resource centre opens the following year on St. Joseph Street with the exhibition *Arthur Goss, Toronto Photographs*, organized by **Michel Lambeth.**

1972

The **Baldwin Street Gallery** becomes co-operatively run by the Women in Photography Co-op—Laura Jones, **June Clark**, Judy Holman, **Lisa Steele**, Linda Rosenberg, Liz Mancell, **Pamela Harris**, and Lynn Murray. In response to the lack of visibility for women photographers, the group organizes *Photographs of Women by Women*, selecting 230 works from over 1,500 submissions.

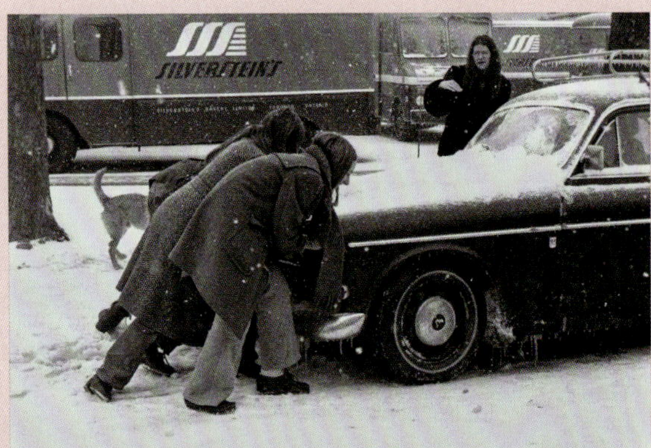

June Clark, *Untitled*, members of the Women in Photography Co-op, c. 1974. Gelatin silver print, 21.6 × 30.5 cm. Gift of June Clark, in memory of her parents Anne and Joseph Clark, 2023 (2023/108).

1973

Two galleries presenting a mix of Canadian and international contemporary artists open their doors in Toronto: Gallery O (later Olga Korper Gallery) on Markham Street, featuring artists like **Lynne Cohen**, Barbara Steinman, and **Robert Mapplethorpe**; and Jared Sable Gallery (later Sable-Castelli) at 401 King Street East, showcasing US artists such as **Andy Warhol**, **James Rosenquist**, and **Frank Stella**, alongside Canadians **Barbara Astman**, **Suzy Lake**, and **Spring Hurlbut**.

1974

Sutnik is appointed head of the AGO's Photographic Resources Department, where she leads the revitalization of a comprehensive slide library for the study and dissemination of artworks, including photographs. She works closely with Eberhard Otto, who consulted on developing a program of slide sales as teaching aids in art and, more significantly, in designing the museum's first in-house photography studio and darkroom facilities. The first studio head and photographer under this newly established department was Jim Chambers.

The Henry Moore Sculpture Centre opens at the AGO. A foundational gift from the artist establishes the world's largest public collection of his work. The donation also includes eighty-five photographs by **Roloff Beny**, **Yousuf Karsh**, and others.

The Extension Services Department launches the *Artists with Their Work* series, a focused program of exhibitions that significantly increases the presence of photography at the AGO and provincially with artists, including **David Hlynsky**, Shin Sugino, April Hickox, **Barbara Astman**, and Andrew Danson.

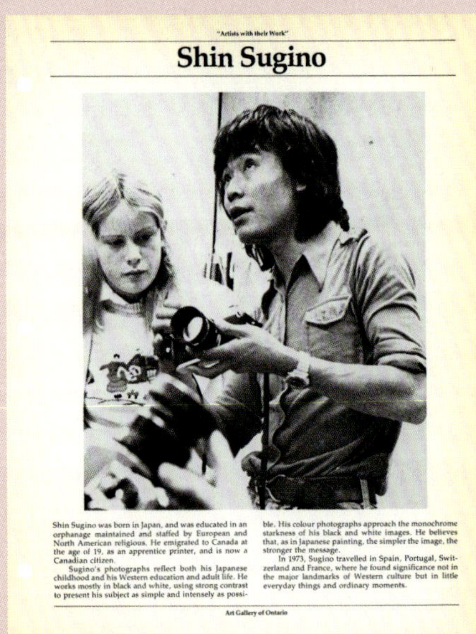

"Artists with their Work"

Shin Sugino

Shin Sugino was born in Japan, and was educated in an orphanage maintained and staffed by European and North American religious. He emigrated to Canada at the age of 19, as an apprentice printer, and is now a Canadian citizen.

Sugino's photographs reflect both his Japanese childhood and his Western education and adult life. He works mostly in black and white, using strong contrast to present his subject as simple and intensely as possible. His colour photographs approach the monochrome starkness of his black and white images. He believes that, as in Japanese painting, the simpler the image, the stronger the message.

In 1973, Sugino travelled in Spain, Portugal, Switzerland and France, where he found significance not in the major landmarks of Western culture but in little everyday things and ordinary moments.

Art Gallery of Ontario

"Shin Sugino" in *Artists with Their Work* catalogue, 1977. Edward P. Taylor Library & Archives, Art Gallery of Ontario.

Art Metropole is founded by the Canadian artist collective **General Idea** at 241 Yonge Street, becoming a key hub for artists and for contemporary art publications.

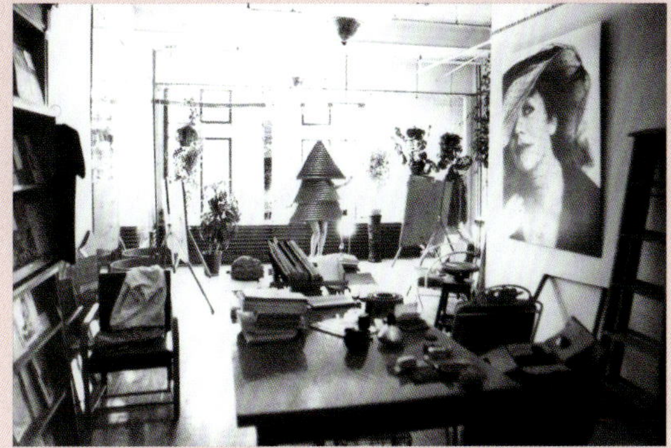
General Idea studio / Art Metropole, 241 Yonge Street, Toronto, 1974. Courtesy of General Idea.

Phil Bergerson establishes the annual International Lecture Series on Photography, which later evolves into the Kodak Lecture Series at Ryerson Polytechnical Institute. A must-attend event in the field, more than 200 influential artists, curators, and scholars come to speak. In the 1990s, several of the lectures, including those by **Robert Frank** and **Michael Snow**, are held in collaboration with the Art Gallery of Ontario. The series concludes in 2007.

1977

In the wake of the **Henry Moore** gift, Alan Wilkinson and Sutnik purchase **Arnold Newman**'s *Henry Moore (collage), Much Hadham, England* (1966–1972), signalling a new focus on photographic portraits of artists.

Jim Chambers, along with a group of photographers including Phil Bergerson, **Barbara Astman**, and **Lynne Cohen**, submit a formal request to the AGO calling for a photography program. The proposal criticizes the lack of a permanent exhibition space for photography and urges institutional commitment to the medium. It is rejected.

In response to the lack of venues for contemporary photography, artists convene in **Michael Mitchell**'s studio at 641 Queen Street East to share and critique each other's work and to mobilize efforts to advance photography's place in the city. This group evolves into the Toronto Photographers Workshop and later Gallery TPW, founded in 1980 with Gary Hall as its first executive director. During the same decade, other artist-run centres open in Toronto, including Mercer Union (1980) and Gallery 44 Centre for Contemporary Photography (1987).

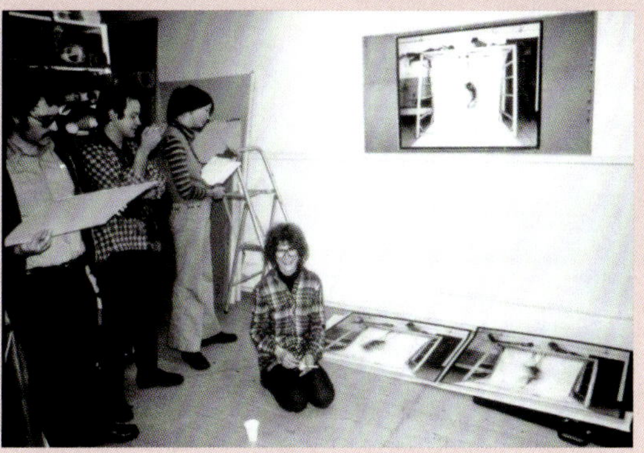
Maker once known, Canadian, *Suzy Lake installing photographs at TPW*, c. 1980. Edward P. Taylor Library & Archives, Art Gallery of Ontario (LA.161642).

1978

Sutnik presents her proposal for a photographic arts department at the request of AGO director William Withrow. The document outlines a vision for developing a permanent collection, regular exhibitions, scholarly publishing, and educational programming, as well as the resources required. The proposal is well received but does not move forward.

Michael Mitchell's daring solo exhibition *Nightlife* opens at the AGO, signalling the arrival of a new era in colour photography. The show draws new audiences and contributes to a growing interest in photography within the gallery's exhibition program. **Suzy Lake**'s first AGO exhibition, *Impositions*, opens the same year.

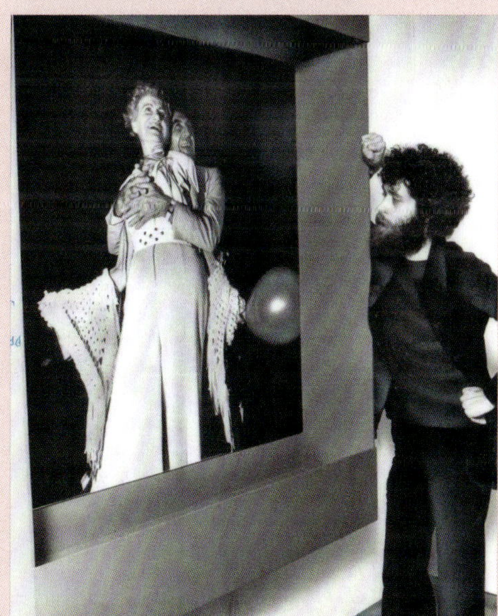
Michael Mitchell in his *Nightlife* exhibition, January 13, 1978 (Ron Bull / *Toronto Star* via Getty Images).

Jane Corkin Gallery (now Corkin Gallery) moves from Markham Street to 144 Front Street, opening the new space with an exhibition by **André Kertész**. Corkin played a central role in establishing photography as a serious art form in the city, and in creating a collector base both locally and internationally. Her gallery introduced international artists such as **Horst**, **Irving Penn**, Sarah Moon, and **Nan Goldin**, while also supporting Canadian voices like **Barbara Astman**, **Robert Bourdeau**, and **Thaddeus Holownia**.

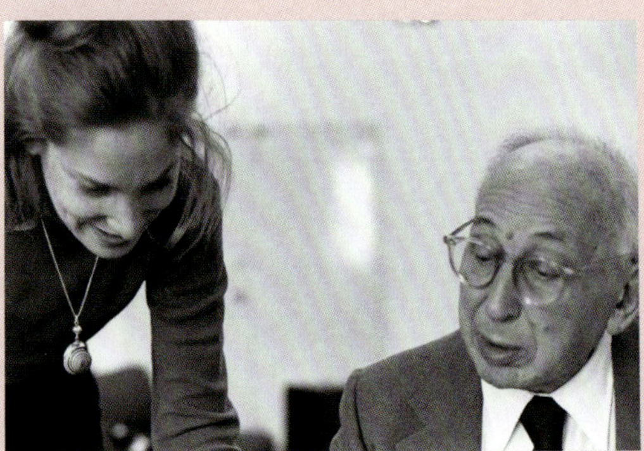

Patricia Fitzpatrick, *André Kertész and Jane Corkin*, 1979. Courtesy of Corkin Gallery.

1979

Martha Rosler presents *The Bowery in Two Inadequate Descriptive Systems* (1974–1975) at A Space Gallery.

The Ryerson Polytechnical Institute hosts Canadian Perspectives: A National Conference on Canadian Photography. Organized by Phil Bergerson, the conference brings together leading photographers, scholars, and curators—among them Ann Thomas, Rudolph Arnheim, Claudia Beck, and Penny Cousineau—to discuss the state of Canadian photography.

Michael Snow's *Flight Stop* is installed at Toronto's Eaton Centre. Made up of sixty fibreglass Canada geese, each surfaced with tinted black-and-white photographs and suspended from the ceiling. This beloved landmark remains today.

1970–1979

A strong program of Canadian photography is presented through AGO-organized and touring exhibitions, including *The Notman Collection of Photographs* (1968–1970s), *Photography in Canada* (1969–1971), *The Many Worlds of Lutz Dille* (1970–1971), *Zoo Sights: A Photographic Perspective of the Metro Toronto Zoo /Michael Mitchell, Shin Sugino, Susan Trow* (1975), *Ian Wallace* (1975), *Exposure: Canadian Contemporary Photographers* (1975), and *Sanctuary: Photographs by Michael Torosian* (1978–1979).

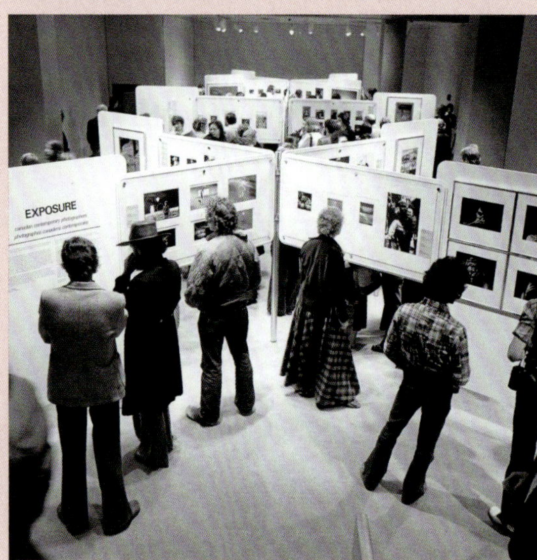

Opening of *Exposure: Canadian Contemporary Photographers*, 1975. Edward P. Taylor Library & Archives, Art Gallery of Ontario.

Magazines dedicated to contemporary art, visual culture, and photography emerge in Toronto, including *Image Nation* (1970–1982), *Impressions* (1970–1983), *Impulse Magazine* (1971–1990), and *Photo Communiqué* (1979–1988). These publications contribute to a broader conversation on photography's role in Canadian visual culture.

1980

Robert Frank – Photographs, on loan from the NFB, opens at the AGO. Sutnik supplements the show with Frank's more recent work, created in Mabou, Nova Scotia.

The Harbourfront Community Gallery presents *The Banff Purchase*—an exhibition drawn from a landmark acquisition by the Walter Phillips Gallery—featuring works by **Robert Bourdeau**, **Lynne Cohen**, **Charles Gagnon**, **Tom Gibson**, **David McMillan**, **Orest Semchishen**, among others.

Ydessa Hendeles launches the Ydessa Gallery on Queen Street West, championing Canadian artists like **Rodney Graham**, **Liz Magor**, **Jana Sterbak**, and **Ken Lum**.

Sandra Simpson establishes S.L. Simpson Gallery at 515 Queen Street West, becoming a key venue for conceptual photographic practices and featuring both Canadian and international artists like **Laurie Simmons**, **Ian Wallace**, **Sarah Charlesworth**, among others.

Loretta Yarlow and Greg Salzman co-found Yarlow-Salzman Gallery on Baldwin Street, focusing on experimental and contemporary art, as well as historical photography.

The Canadian Centre of Photography and Film opens at 596 Markham Street with backing from photographer Al Gilbert. A gallery dedicated to showcasing both national and international photographers, it also offers seminars, workshops, and lectures, and publishes the periodical *596* to promote public awareness of photography as a creative medium. Notable figures **Irving Penn**, **Alfred Eisenstaedt**, **André Kertész**, **Henri Cartier-Bresson**, **Sam Tata**, and **John Reeves** pass through its doors.

1981

Photographs from the Collection of Sam Wagstaff opens at the AGO. Wagstaff, who deeply influenced Sutnik's collecting approach, emphasized building a collection that goes beyond the canonical history of photography.

1983

MUSE magazine dedicates an issue to the 150th anniversary of photography, with contributions by Sutnik and Ann Thomas. This marks a rise in critical discourse around photography.

1984

Sutnik curates *Responding to Photography,* an exhibition of 156 works borrowed from over thirty-five Toronto collectors. The exhibition underscores photography's presence in Toronto collections and significantly advances the case for a dedicated photography department at the AGO.

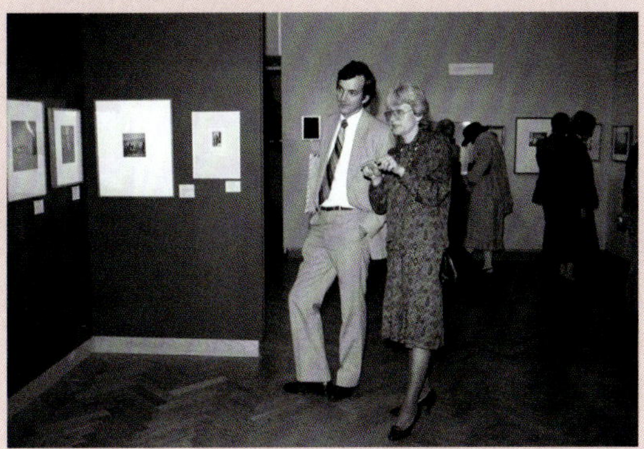

Maia-Mari Sutnik and collector Robert Wilson at the *Responding to Photography* exhibition, 1984. Edward P. Taylor Library & Archives, Art Gallery of Ontario.

Gallery TPW, in collaboration with Photo Communiqué and The Art Gallery at Harbourfront, present the *Toronto Documentary Photography Project*. The project reveals a multitude of contemporary approaches to recording local life, with contributions from artists including Margaret Bélisle, **Robert Burley**, **Karl Beveridge and Carole Condé**, **Pamela Harris**, Judy McClard, Frank Pimentel, and Graham Smith.

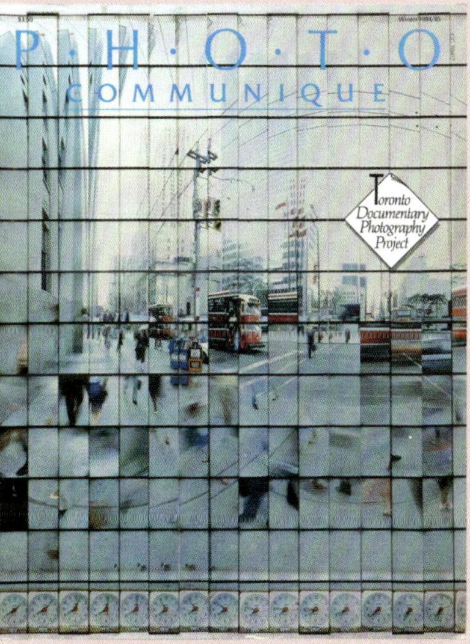

"Toronto Documentary Photography Project" (special issue). *PHOTO Communiqué* 6 no. 4 (Winter 1984/85). Courtesy of the Thomas Fisher Rare Book Library, University of Toronto.

1985

The Canadian Museum of Contemporary Photography (CMCP) is founded in Ottawa, with Martha Langford as director and chief curator.

The Native Indian/Inuit Photographers' Association (NIIPA) is founded in Hamilton by a group of Indigenous image-makers, including Rick Hill, Yvonne Maracle, Brenda Mitten, and **Greg Staats**, to support and promote Indigenous photographers across Canada. As one of the first national Indigenous artist-run organizations, NIIPA plays a pivotal role in reshaping the photographic landscape and advocating for self-representation in visual culture.

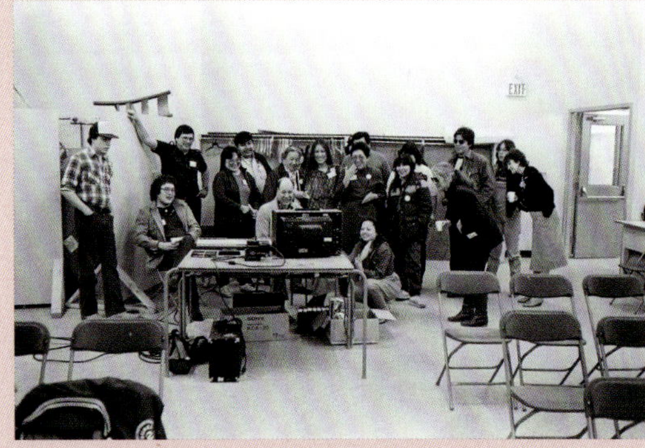

Attendees of the *VISIONS* conference gather around a TV, including future NIIPA founders Murray McKenzie, Yvonne Maracle, and Brenda Mitten. Photograph courtesy of Cees van Gemerden.

1986

Linnaeus Tripe: Photographer of British India, 1854–1870 opens at the AGO. The exhibition marks the beginning of a long association between Sutnik and Janet Dewan—a Toronto-based descendant of Tripe—which ultimately leads to the gift of 159 works by Tripe, donated between 1992 and 2008.

Michael Torosian establishes Lumiere Press, dedicated to producing special-edition letterpress photography books, including of work by **Edward Weston**, Gordon Parks, and Saul Leiter, among others.

1987

Pressure to establish a photography department at the AGO continued to build both internally and from Toronto's photography community, with many advocates playing a key role in pushing the initiative forward, including the group Friends of Photography.

1988

Photographs: Selected Gifts from the Collection opens at the AGO as the institution's first major exhibition showcasing photographs from its collection.

Ydessa Hendeles establishes the Ydessa Hendeles Art Foundation at 778 King Street West and inaugurates the space with a major exhibition of French artist **Christian Boltanski**'s work. A dedicated photography collector, Hendeles also organizes major shows, including a landmark **Diane Arbus** exhibition in 1991 and *The Teddy Bear Project*, presented in the exhibitions *sameDIFFERENCE* (2002) and *Partners* (2003), a collection of more than 3,000 photographs of people posing with teddy bears.

The Canadian Artists Network: Black Artists in Action (CAN: BAIA) is founded to provide information, advocacy, and education for Black Canadian artists across various disciplines, including photographers Karen Tyrrell, Cameron Bailey, and **David Zapparoli**.

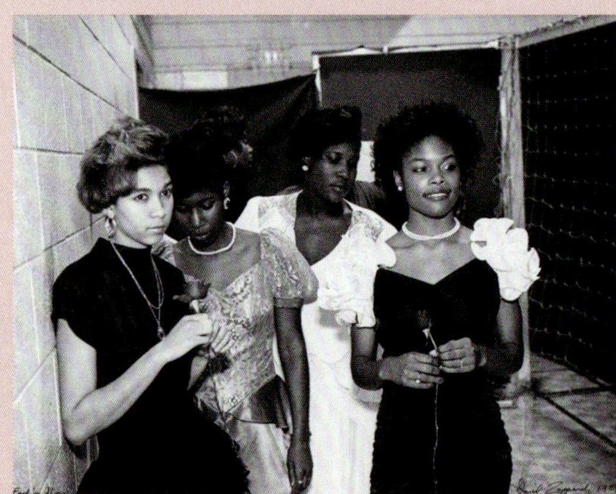

David Zapparoli, *Backstage at Fashion Show*, 1989. Gelatin silver print, 34.3 × 24.1 cm. Purchase, with funds from Ken Straiton, 2019 (2019/2261).

1989

Edward Burtynsky opens Toronto Image Works (TIW) at 80 Spadina Avenue, offering darkrooms and photo-processing services. Still in operation today, TIW remains an indispensable resource for the city's photographers.

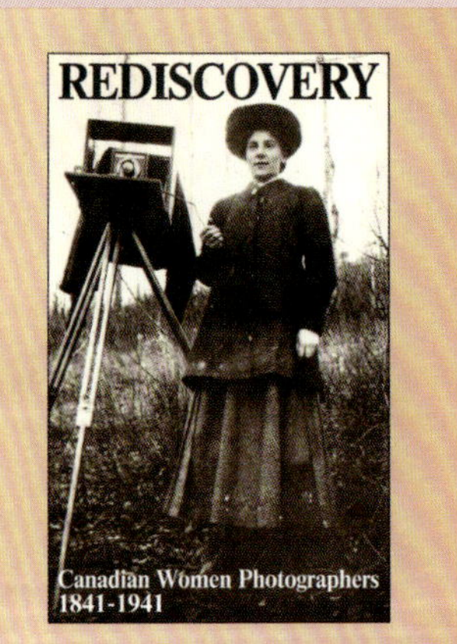

Rediscovery: Canadian Women Photographers, 1841–1941. Published by the London Regional Art Gallery, 1983.

1980–1989

A wide array of exhibitions includes *E. Haanel Cassidy: Photographs, 1933–1945* (1981), *Rediscovery: Canadian Women Photographers* (1984, loaned from the London Regional Art Gallery, London, Ontario), *Tess Boudreau: Portraits of Artists* (1984), *John Gutmann* (1985), *Photographs of László Moholy-Nagy* (1986–1987, loaned from the Goethe Institute), *Carole Condé and Karl Beveridge: Standing Up* (1988–1989), and *Edward Curtis: Photographs of Indians* (1988–1989).

1990s

The AGO acquires works by key nineteenth-century photographers, including **Carlo Naya**, **Édouard Baldus**, **Julia Margaret Cameron**, and **Eadweard Muybridge**, along with over 300 French *cartes postales* of "naughty ladies." These acquisitions signal a growing commitment to collecting works by established artists as well as more popular forms.

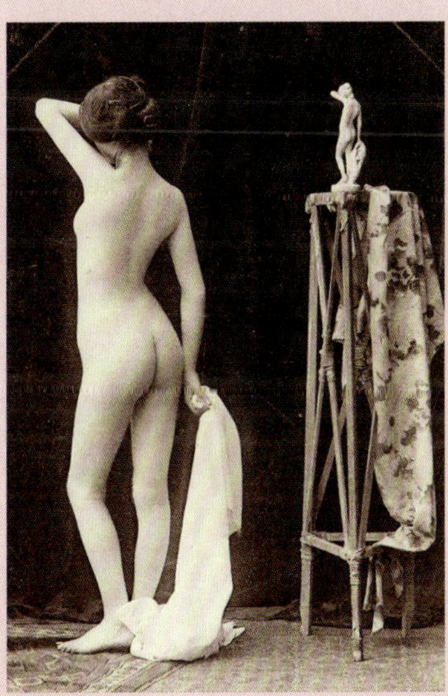

Maker once known, French, c. 1900s. Collotype print, 13.5 × 9 cm. Gift of Carol and Morton Rapp, 1997 (97/1947).

1993

The Marvin Gelber Print and Drawing Study Centre opens for the care and study of works on paper, including the growing collection of photographs. The home of the Prints and Drawings Department, the space now also houses the Photography Department.

1994

Toronto gallerist Av Isaacs donates seventy-seven **Michel Lambeth** photographs, forming the foundation for a major 1998 exhibition and catalogue curated by Sutnik.

1995

Edward Burtynsky / Richard Maynard: Photographs opens at the AGO, pairing **Maynard**'s nineteenth-century views of British Columbia with **Burtynsky**'s industrial landscapes. It is Burtynsky's first institutional exhibition.

Stephen Bulger Gallery opens its doors at 700 Queen Street West with a two-person exhibition featuring Wright Morris and Phil Bergerson. While presenting a wide range of photographic work, the gallery becomes particularly known for supporting artists with strong documentary practices, including Marion Post Wolcott, **Robert Burley**, **Sunil Gupta**, **Sanaz Mazinani**, and **Louie Palu**.

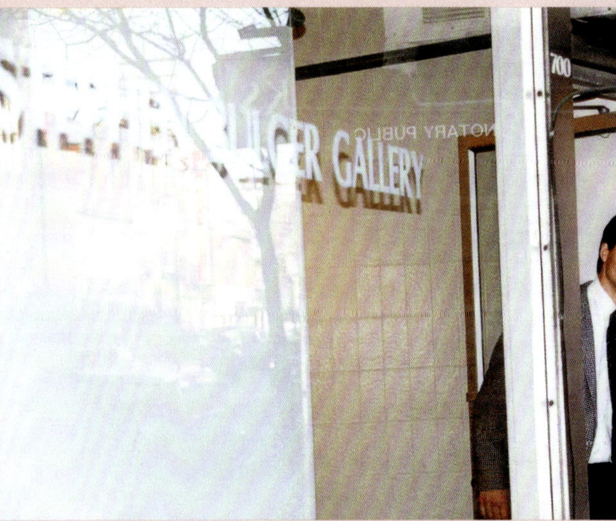

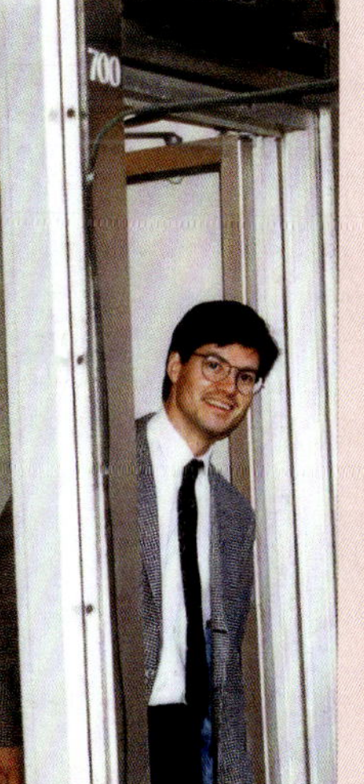

Stephen Bulger on the opening day of his gallery on Queen Street, 1995. Photo credit: Dr. Dermon McCarthy. Courtesy of Stephen Bulger Gallery.

Hiroshi Sugimoto opens at the Art Gallery of York University (now the Joan and Martin Goldfarb Gallery of York University). Under directors like Loretta Yarlow (1987–1997), the gallery regularly presents photography in dialogue with installation and video.

1997

CONTACT Photography Festival launches in Toronto as a city-wide celebration of photography. Founded by Darren Alexander, Linda Book, Stephen Bulger, and Judith Tatar, with Lesley Sparks as its first director, the festival quickly gains momentum.

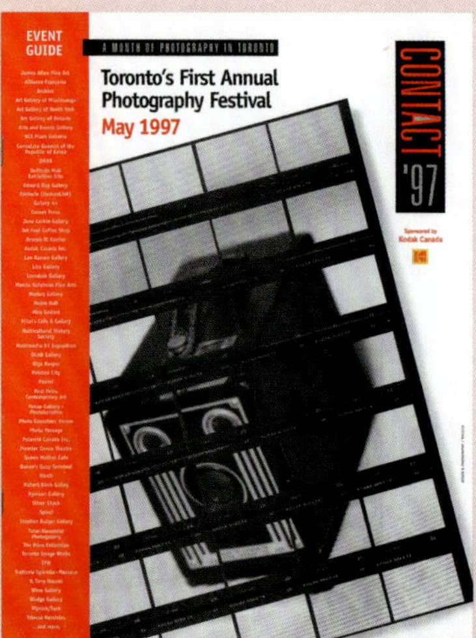

Contact '97: *Toronto's First Annual Photography Festival* [event guide], 1997. Edward P. Taylor Library & Archives, Art Gallery of Ontario.

Dr. Kenneth Montague inaugurates The Wedge Gallery in his Toronto home with the exhibition *Michael Chambers: Transforming Reality*. The endeavour evolves into Wedge Curatorial Projects, alongside what is now one of Canada's largest private collections focused on African diasporic culture.

Arts magazine *Lola* (1997–2003) is launched by artist and writer Sally McKay, curator John Massier, and arts writer and editor Catherine Osborne to reinvigorate Toronto's visual arts scene with this new forum to critique and discuss local exhibitions and events.

The AGO launches a photography lecture series, sponsored by Fujifilm Canada, with a lecture by **Duane Michals**. The program expands to feature leading photographers from Canada and abroad, including Susan Meiselas, **Greg Staats**, and **Vince Pietropaolo**.

1990–1999

The decade features notable solo exhibitions, including of **Jeff Wall** (1990), **John Gutmann** (1995), **Michel Lambeth** (1998), **Claude Cahun** (1999), and **Cindy Sherman** (1999).

2000

The acquisition of 973 works by Czech photographer **Josef Sudek** instigates the founding of the Photography Department at the AGO, affirming photography's place within the museum's curatorial framework. Sutnik is appointed as its inaugural curator, bringing deep expertise and a vision for a collecting strategy that acknowledges the diverse uses of the medium. Three key exhibitions herald the occasion: *A Practical Dreamer: The Photographs of Man Ray* (on loan from the J. Paul Getty Museum), *The Bigger Picture: Contemporary Photography Reconsidered*, and *Paris Itineraries: Photographs by Eugène Atget* (on loan from the Musée Carnavalet).

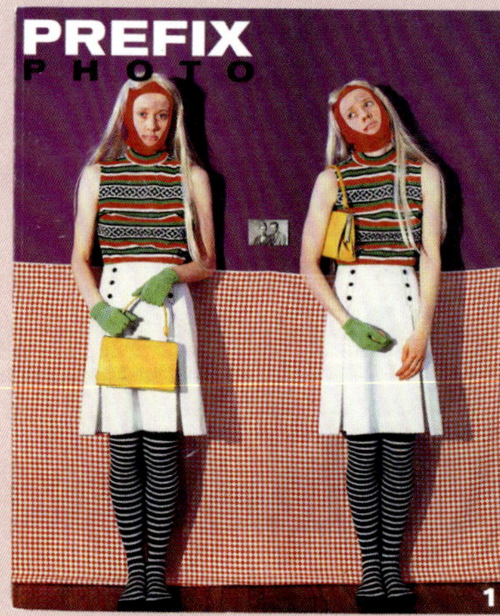

Prefix Photo [cover], vol. 1 (Spring/Summer, 2000).

Prefix Photo is founded in Toronto by curator Scott McLeod as a quarterly magazine dedicated to Canadian and international photography. The first issue features **Janieta Eyre**.

2001

The Power Plant presents *Substitute City*, curated by Philip Monk. Seventeen artists in photography, film, video, and graphic novels explore Toronto's role as a stand-in for other urban environments in film and television, while also navigating and engaging with the city's unsupervised and overlooked spaces.

Vancouver's Monte Clark Gallery opens a Toronto location at Queen and Augusta before moving to the Distillery District in 2003. The gallery showcases a diverse range of work by both emerging and established artists, including artists associated with the Vancouver School, like **Scott McFarland** and **Greg Girard**.

2002

The Klinsky Press Agency Collection is acquired, featuring over 9,000 press photographs from the 1930s, a period when illustrated magazines emerged as a powerful new vehicle. This marks the first of many press collections to join the department's holdings, among them Information et Documents (2005), Schostal Press Agency (2008), Hillelson Agency Collection (2007), the World War I British Press Bureau Collection (2008), and the Italian Press Photography Collection (2022).

Ken Lum, *I Don't Know Whether to Laugh or Cry*, Art Gallery of Ontario. Public installation in partnership with CONTACT Photography Festival, 2003. Courtesy of CONTACT.

Under the directorship of Bonnie Rubenstein, CONTACT launches feature public installations as part of the festival. For this first iteration, Sutnik installs a work by **Ken Lum** above the entrance to the AGO's Jackman Hall, then home to Cinematheque Ontario. "Close Encounters," a program inviting the public to view works from the photography collection during the festival is also inaugurated.

Dr. Deepali Dewan joins the Royal Ontario Museum (ROM) as Associate Curator of South Asian Civilizations, deepening the museum's engagement with photography. Her curatorial projects include *Embellished Reality: Indian Painted Photographs* (2008) and *Between Princely India & the British Raj: The Photography of Raja Deen Dayal* (2013–2014).

2003

Pop Photographica: Photography's Objects in Everyday Life, 1842–1969 opens, guest-curated by Daile Kaplan and organized by Sutnik. The exhibition and accompanying publication make the case for vernacular photographs as objects worthy of art-historical inquiry.

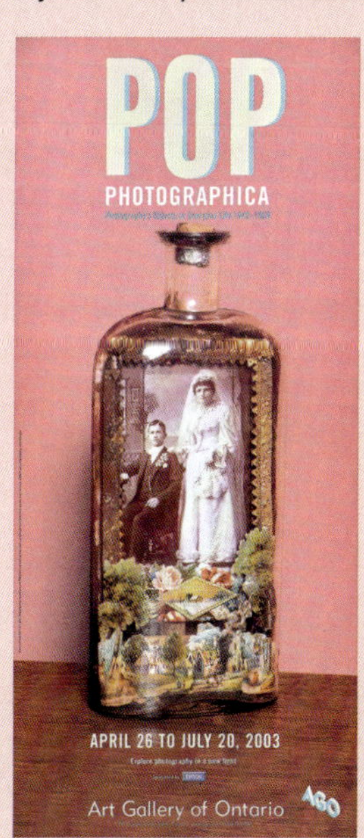

Pop Photographica [exhibition pamphlet], April 26 – July 20, 2003. Edward P. Taylor Library & Archives, Art Gallery of Ontario.

The Photographs of Linnaeus Tripe: A Catalogue Raisonné is published, authored by Janet Dewan. It is one of the first such catalogues dedicated to a photographer.

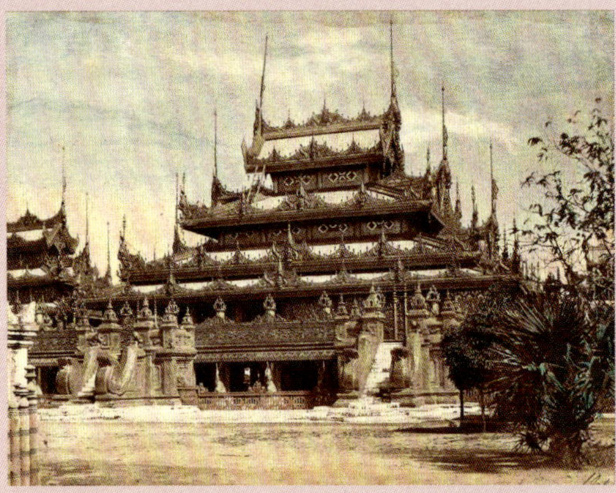

Linnaeus Tripe, *Amerapoora. Maha-Too-Lo-Boughian Kyoung*, 1855. Albumen print from a waxed paper negative tinted in watercolour, 26.6 × 35 cm. Gift of Dr. Shashi B. Dewan and Janet E. Dewan, 1996 (96/1249).

2004

The AGO acquires 495 photographic albums related to World War I. In 2018, the collection is showcased in the two-part exhibition *Photography: First World War, 1914–1918*, highlighting photography's central role in shaping and documenting the conflict.

Nicholas Metivier Gallery opens its doors on King Street West. The inaugural exhibition is dedicated to the work of **Edward Burtynsky**.

2005

Extensive holdings by two French makers are added to the AGO collection: 218 photographs and negatives by **Charles Nègre** and 1,703 works by **Abel Boulineau**.

2006

Sophie Hackett joins the AGO as Assistant Curator, Photography.

The AGO acquires 113 photographs by **Tess Boudreau Taconis** and 107 works by **Larry Fink**, increasing the collection's focus on portraiture and social documentary practices.

2007

The AGO acquires the **Henryk Ross** Collection, a vital record of nearly 3,000 photographs and negatives documenting life in the Łódź Ghetto during the Second World War. In 2015, the AGO presents *Memory Unearthed: The Lodz Ghetto Photographs of Henryk Ross*, which tours internationally and further cements Ross as a crucial witness to the Holocaust.

2008

Suzy Lake creates the site-specific work *Rhythm of a True Space* for the CONTACT Photography Festival, installed on construction hoarding outside the AGO during the gallery's closure for the Frank Gehry expansion.

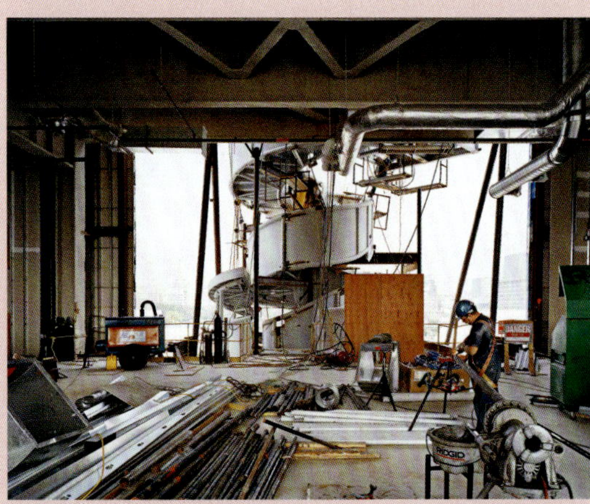

Edward Burtynsky, *Fourth floor - looking North*, July 26, 2007. Chromogenic print, 136.3 × 170.4 cm. Gift of the artist, 2008 (2008/627). © Edward Burtynsky / Art Gallery of Ontario.

When the AGO reopens to the public, so does a new space for the photography collection in the Betty Ann & Fraser Elliott Gallery. The opening installation *Connecting with Photography: Ongoing Dialogues* features a diverse selection of photographs installed thematically.

Canadian artist **Sarah Anne Johnson** wins the inaugural Grange Prize (later the Aimia | AGO Photography Prize), a photography award decided by public vote. In its decade-long run, the prize awards and shortlists artists **Jin-me Yoon**, **Gauri Gill**, LaToya Ruby Frazier, David Hartt, Hank Willis Thomas, **Hito Steyerl**, and Liz Johnson Artur, among many others. It expands in 2014 to include a national scholarship program.

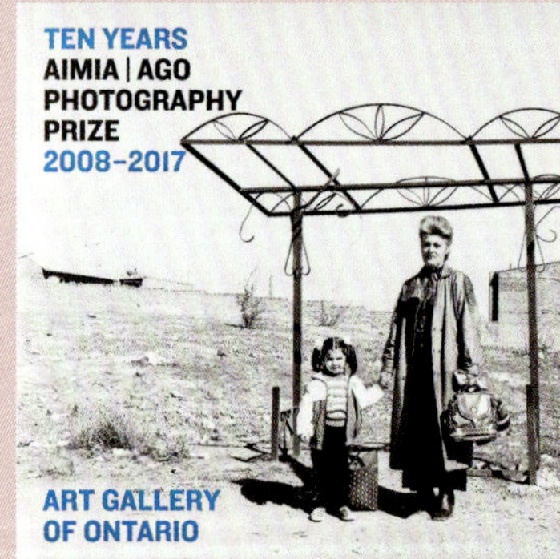

Ten Years: AIMIA | AGO Photography Prize, 2008–2017. Published by the Art Gallery of Ontario and Goose Lane Editions, 2017.

The Film + Photography Preservation and Collections Management (FPPCM) program at Ryerson University and the AGO form a partnership for graduate students to learn and participate in the department's activities.

2009

Beautiful Fictions: Photographic Art at the AGO, featuring the David and Vivian Campbell Collection, opens, co-curated by Sutnik and David Moos. A related symposium features speakers such as **Axel Hütte**, **Lorna Simpson**, and **Michael Snow**.

Sutnik becomes Curator, Special Projects, Photography.

Feeling Photography symposium is held at the University of Toronto. Organized by Elspeth H. Brown and Thy Phu, the event brings together scholars and artists to explore photography's role in shaping and expressing affect and embodiment. It situates Toronto as a key site for critical discourse around the politics and poetics of feeling in photography.

2000–2008

Prior to the museum's temporary closure for the AGO Transformation in 2008, Sutnik presents a dynamic series of photography exhibitions, including *To Look Again: André Kertész* (2000–2001), *Photographs Witnessing War and Conflict* (2001–2002), *Reva Brooks: Photographs of Mexico* (2002), *Josef Sudek: Surrealist Affinities* (2002), *Larry Fink: Social Graces* (2004–2005), and *Isaacs Seen: Two on the Scene* (2005), and *Volker Seding, Extended Environments: Zoo Sites* (2006).

2010

US artist **Barbara Kruger** creates site-specific project *Untitled (It)* for the museum's Dundas Street facade as part of the CONTACT Photography Festival—an ambitious initiative curated by Hackett.

Black Artists' Network in Dialogue (BAND) is founded by Karen Carter, Julie Crooks, Karen Tyrell, and maxine bailey as a platform for showcasing Black artistic expression. Its inaugural exhibition, featuring the work of Gordon Parks, is presented in 2014 in collaboration with Nicolas Metivier Gallery.

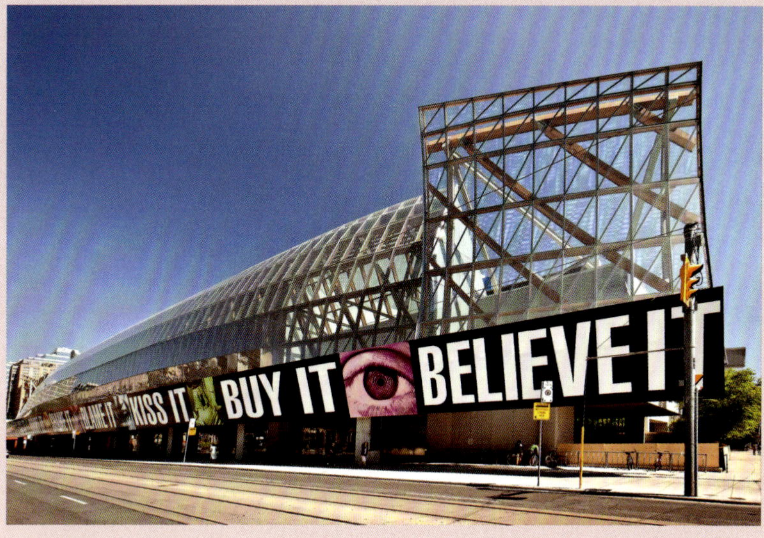

Barbara Kruger, *Untitled (It)*, Art Gallery of Ontario. Public installation in partnership with CONTACT Photography Festival, 2010. Courtesy of CONTACT.

The Scotiabank Photography Award is launched to recognize the outstanding contributions of Canadian artists. The inaugural winner in 2011 is **Lynne Cohen**.

2011

Hackett curates *Songs of Future: Canadian Industrial Photographs, 1858 to Today*. The show positions photographs of the built environment as Canada's other landscape tradition, and features works by artists as varied as **Alexander Henderson**, **George Hunter**, **Bill Vazan**, and **Isabelle Hayeur**.

Daniel Faria Gallery opens at 188 St. Helens Avenue, Toronto, showcasing work across all media by artists including **Steven Beckly**, **June Clark**, **Chris Curreri**, and **Mark Lewis**.

2012

Josef Sudek: The Legacy of a Deeper Vision presents 175 works by the Czech photographer, drawn entirely from the foundational 2000 gift, with an award-winning publication edited by Sutnik.

Max Dean presents *Album* during the CONTACT Photography Festival, touring Toronto in a custom Volkswagen "Foto Bug" and inviting the public to choose a photo album to take home. The AGO acquires over 200 albums as part of the initiative.

Berenice Abbott: Photographs opens at the AGO, curated by Dr. Gaëlle Morel, the first Exhibitions Curator at the Ryerson Image Centre (now The Image Centre at Toronto Metropolitan University).

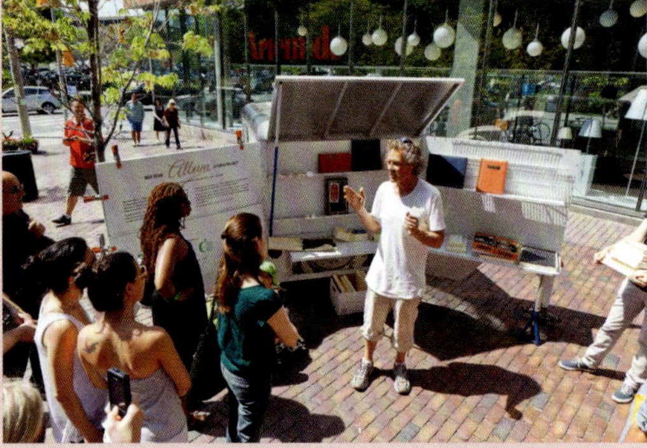

Max Dean, *Album: A Public Project*. The Distillery District, May 20, 2012. Courtesy of CONTACT.

The Ryerson Image Centre opens at Ryerson University. The inaugural exhibition, *Archival Dialogues: Reading the Black Star Collection*, showcases their foundational Black Star collection of press photography through newly commissioned work by contemporary Canadian artists.

The Image Centre hosts Toronto Convention. About Photographic Collections: Definitions, Descriptions, Access, the first symposium in a series, followed by The "Public Life" of Photographs (2013), Collecting and Curating Photographs: Between Private and Public Collections (2014), Photography Historians: A New Generation? (2015), Photography: The Black Box of History (2018), and Encoding the Image: How Does AI Affect the Future of Photo History? (2025).

2013

Light My Fire: Some Propositions about Portraits and Photography, curated by Hackett, is presented in two parts featuring over 200 works exploring portraiture's creative possibilities.

Paris Photo invites Sutnik and Hackett to curate a collection-based exhibition. They pair press photographs from the 1930s from the **Klinsky Press Agency** and Canadian artist **Arnaud Maggs**'s autobiographical series *After Nadar* (2012). Sutnik also serves as a juror for the Paris Photo–Aperture Foundation PhotoBook Awards.

Maia-Mari Sutnik and Penny Rubinoff *Performance Propositions, Paris Photo*, 2013.

2014

The Malcolmson Collection is acquired, enriching the AGO's holdings with modernist works by such pioneers as **Gustave Le Gray**, **Manuel Álvarez Bravo**, **Tina Modotti**, **Man Ray**, and **Bill Brandt**. A celebratory exhibition takes place later that year.

A comprehensive group of 442 works by American photographer **Garry Winogrand** becomes part of the collection.

Introducing Suzy Lake, a career-spanning exhibition co-curated by Georgiana Uhlyarik and Hackett, opens, highlighting Lake's pioneering work. The gallery hosts Radical Acts, an "unconference" bringing together feminist artists and scholars to discuss questions of feminism, performance, and self-representation. American dancer, choreographer, and filmmaker Yvonne Rainer delivers the keynote address.

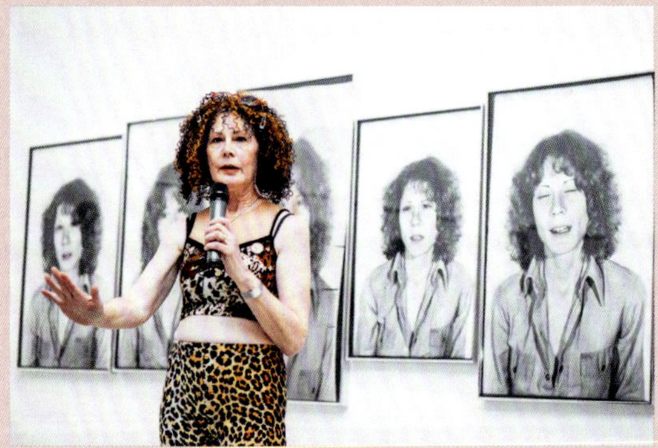

First Thursday: Suzy Lake in front of her work, November 6, 2014. *Suzy Lake (as Suzy Spice)*. Work shown: Suzy Lake, *Are You Talking to Me?*, 1979. AGO.

Toronto hosts WorldPride, marked by a pair of groundbreaking exhibitions curated by Hackett at the AGO and Ryerson Image Centre and the AGO: *Fan the Flames: Queer Positions in Photography* and *What It Means to Be Seen: Photography and Queer Visibility*, alongside Zanele Muholi's *Face and Phases*, curated by Dr. Gaëlle Morel. Together, the exhibitions examine how photographs have played a key role in the growing visibility of 2SLGBTQ+ communities and how queer artists have used the medium to express their experience and identity.

Curious Anarchy: The Photographic Collection of Maia-Mari Sutnik opens at The Image Centre, curated by FPPCM (Film + Photography Preservation and Collections Management) students.

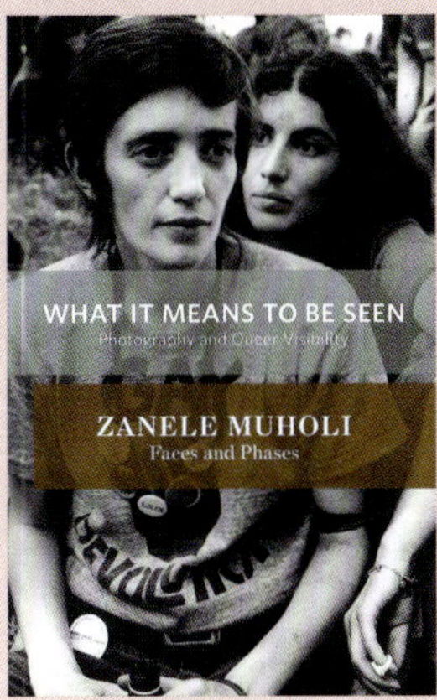

Publication for *What It Means to Be Seen: Photography and Queer Visibility* and *Zanele Muholi: Faces and Phases* (Ryerson Image Centre, Toronto: 2014).

The Kodak Lecture Series is revived in 2014 under a new name, the Howard and Carole Tanenbaum Lecture Series, and inaugurated in 2015 by renowned artist **Rebecca Belmore**.

2015

The Board of Trustees appoints Sutnik as Curator Emeritus, Photography. After a fifty-two-year career, Sutnik has grown the collection to over 55,000 photographs, curated more than seventy exhibitions, published over forty articles and books, established a dedicated curatorial department, and mentored a generation of professionals. In 2023, she receives the Order of Canada for her transformative contributions to the development and promotion of photography in Canada.

2016

Outsiders: American Photography and Film, 1950s–1980s, co-curated by Hackett and **Jim Shedden**, opens. The exhibition and book feature works by photographers and filmmakers like Kenneth Anger, Gordon Parks, **Diane Arbus**, Shirley Clarke, the cross-dressers of **Casa Susanna**, and **Nan Goldin**, who deployed their chosen media to reflect a complex and authentic view of the world they knew.

Hackett is promoted to Curator, Photography.

Scholars and curators gather in Toronto for the annual FOCUS conference, co-hosted by the AGO, The Image Centre, and the University of Toronto. Swiss curator Urs Stahel delivers the keynote address.

The AGO makes a landmark acquisition of 522 photographs by **Diane Arbus**, the largest collection of her work outside the United States.

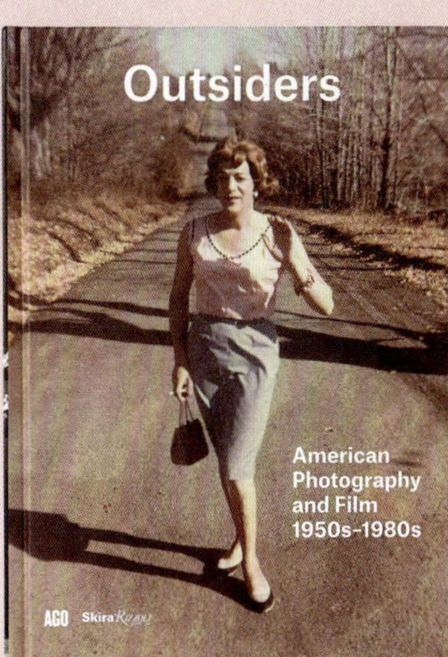

Outsiders: American Photography and Film, 1950s–1980s. Published by the Art Gallery of Ontario and Skira Rizzoli, 2016.

2017

Dr. Julie Crooks joins the Photography Department as Assistant Curator. Her first exhibition in the role, *Free Black North*, opens the same year, highlighting rare nineteenth-century tintype portraits of Black Ontarians.

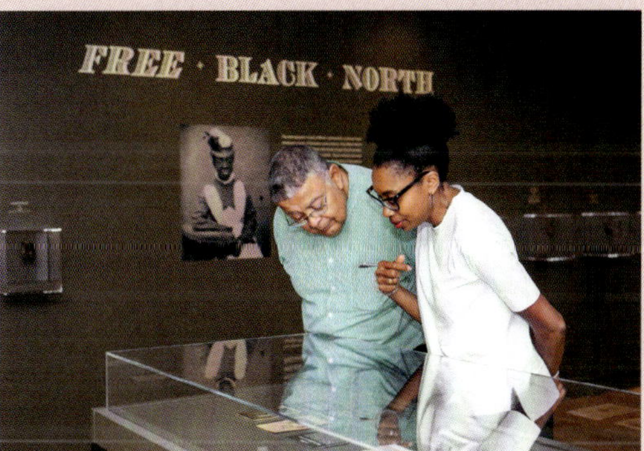

Dr. Julie Crooks points out to David Alexander a portrait of one of his relatives in *Free Black North*.

As part of *Look: Forward*, a major reinstallation of the AGO's permanent collection, new gallery spaces are dedicated to photography, inaugurated with the exhibition *Photography: 1840s–1880s* in the Odette Family and Robert & Cheryl McEwen galleries.

The Visibility symposium explores issues of representation, identity, and the power of photography in shaping cultural narratives. Presented in partnership with Aperture, the event brings together artists, scholars, and curators to examine the role of visual media in addressing contemporary social and political concerns. Featured artists include **Sunil Gupta**, **John Edmonds**, **Adrian Stimson**, and Liz Johnson Artur, with a keynote by Lyle Ashton Harris. This symposium also marks the final edition of the Aimia | AGO Photography Prize, with the last prize awarded to Hank Willis Thomas. To commemorate the prize's legacy, the book *Ten Years: Aimia | AGO Photography Prize, 2008–2017* is published, chronicling a decade of shortlisted artists.

The Reframing Family Photography conference, organized by The Family Camera Network, is hosted by the Royal Ontario Museum and the Munk School of Global Affairs as part of *The Family Camera* exhibition, exploring the significance of vernacular photography in shaping personal and collective histories.

2018

Anthropocene, co-organized with the National Gallery of Canada and the Fondazione MAST, Bologna, and co-curated by Hackett, Andrea Kunard, and Urs Stahel, opens. The exhibition explores the impact of human activity on the environment through powerful photographs, films, and augmented reality installations by **Edward Burtynsky**, Jennifer Baichwal, and Nicholas de Pencier. It becomes the most toured exhibition in the AGO's history.

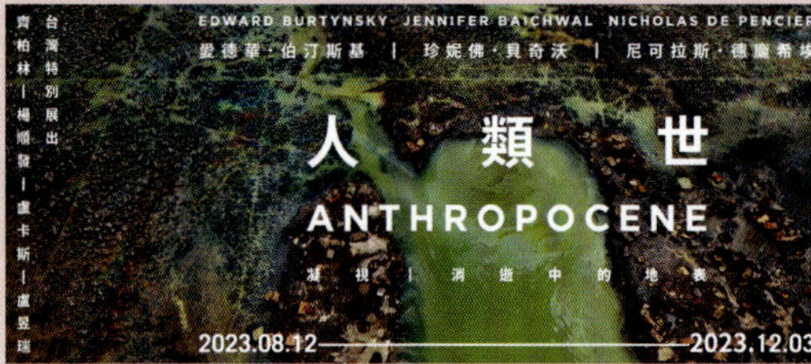

Anthropocene at the Kaohsiung Museum of Fine Arts, Taiwan, 2023.

Mickalene Thomas: Femmes Noires, curated by Crooks, the AGO's Assistant Curator, Photography, in collaboration with Andrea Andersson (Contemporary Arts Center, New Orleans), becomes the first major museum exhibition in Canada dedicated to a living African American artist.

The AGO acquires the Fade Resistance Collection, featuring over 4,000 instant photographs of Black family life. This leads to the 2022 exhibition *What Matters Most: Photographs of Black Life*, co-curated by Zun Lee and Hackett. The publication wins an AIGA 50 Books | 50 Covers award.

2019

With unprecedented support from members of Toronto's Black and Caribbean communities, the AGO acquires the Montgomery Collection of Caribbean Photographs, over 3,500 works from thirty-four countries, including Jamaica, Barbados, and Trinidad, spanning from 1840 to 1940. Many are later featured in the 2021 exhibition *Fragments of Epic Memory* curated by Crooks.

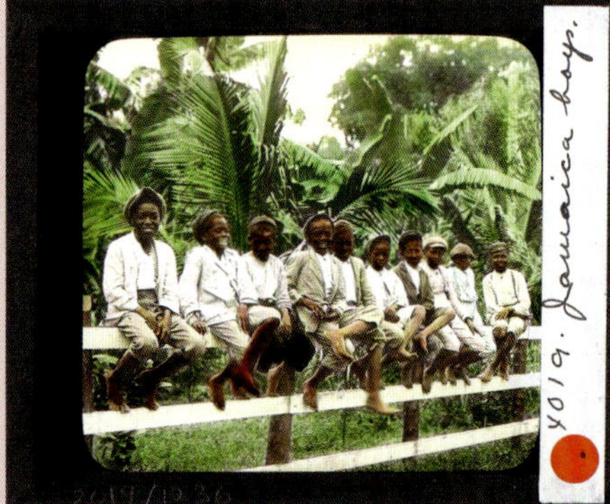

Brown & Dawson (Stamford, CT), *Jamaican Boys*, c. 1900. Glass slide. Montgomery Collection of Caribbean Photographs. Purchase, with funds from Dr. Liza & Dr. Frederick Murrell, Bruce Croxon & Debra Thier, Wes Hall & Kingsdale Advisors, Cindy & Shon Barnett, Donette Chin-Loy Chang, Kamala-Jean Gopie, Phil Lind & Ellen Roland, Martin Doc McKinney, Francilla Charles, Ray & Georgina Williams, Thaine & Bianca Carter, Charmaine Crooks, Nathaniel Crooks, Andrew Garrett & Dr. Belinda Longe, Neil L. Le Grand, Michael Lewis, Dr. Kenneth Montague & Sarah Aranha, Lenny & Julia Mortimore, and The Ferrotype Collective, 2019. 2019/1236

Nearly 5,000 photographs by Czech artists are acquired, including by **Petr Helbich**, **Josef Ehm**, **Tibor Honty**, and **Emila Medková**.

2010–2019

Newly dedicated photography spaces in the Odette Family and Robert & Cheryl McEwen galleries welcome a diverse range of exhibitions, including *Édouard Baldus: The Louvre Folios, 1855–1857* (2018), *Photography: First World War, 1914–1918* (2018–2019), and *Photography, 1920s–1940s: Women in Focus* (2019). Other notable exhibitions at the museum during this period include *"Where I Was Born...": A Photograph, a Clue, and the Discovery of Abel Boulineau* (2011–2012), *Scott McFarland: Snow, Shacks, Streets, Shrubs* (2014), and *Camera Atomica* (2015), guest-curated by scholar John O'Brian.

2020

The exhibition *Diane Arbus: Photographs, 1956–1971*, curated by Hackett and drawn entirely from the AGO's collection, closes three weeks into its run in March due to the COVID-19 pandemic. The show would continue its international tour as restrictions lift.

Dr. Julie Crooks becomes the founding Curator of the newly established Arts of Global Africa and the Diaspora Department.

Edward Burtynsky and Nicholas Metivier launch the Canada Now Photography Acquisition Initiative in response to the COVID-19 pandemic, supporting the AGO and the Image Centre to acquire work by twenty contemporary Canadian artists. The 2023 exhibition *We Are Story*, curated by Marina Dumont-Gauthier, presents ten of these artists.

2020–2022

With the gallery closed during the pandemic, the AGO programs *Art in the Spotlight*, a series of virtual conversations with artists, curators, and scholars, many engaged with photography, including Laura Jones, Deepali Dewan, Neil Selkirk, **Martha Rosler**, Hank Willis Thomas, and Michèle Pearson Clarke.

2021

The AGO acquires 945 photographs by **Harold Edgerton**, known for his pioneering high-speed photography.

Guest-curated by Emilie Croning, *Jorian Charlton: Out of Many* is presented at the AGO in partnership with Gallery TPW and Wedge Curatorial Projects.

2022

Felix Gonzalez-Torres: "Untitled" (Strange Bird), co-presented with Museum of Contemporary Art, Toronto, is presented at the AGO and on billboards throughout the city.

2023

Casa Susanna, curated by Hackett and Isabelle Bonnet, opens at Les Rencontres d'Arles. The exhibition later travels to the AGO and the Met in New York. The publication is shortlisted for the Paris Photo–Aperture Foundation Photobook Awards.

The exhibition *Building Icons: Arnold Newman's Magazine World, 1938–2000*, curated by Tal-Or Ben-Choreen and Hackett, opens. Drawn from the AGO's major holdings of 4,826 photographs by Newman, the exhibition travels to the Museum Hanmi in Seoul, South Korea in 2024.

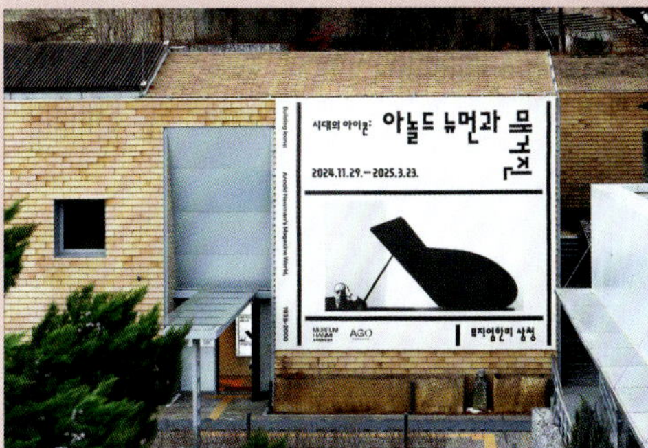

Building Icons: Arnold Newman's Magazine World, 1938–2000 at the Museum Hanmi, Seoul, South Korea, 2025.

2024

The symposium *Camera/Women: Rewriting the History of Photography*, organized by the Art History Department and Associate Professor Jordan Bear, in honour of Jane Corkin, recipient of an Honorary Doctor of Laws degree from the University of Toronto for her contributions as a visionary gallerist.

2025

A significant year for acquisitions: ninety-five photographs from **Tseng Kwong Chi**'s *East Meets West* series (1979–1989) enter the collection, alongside 1,220 photographs by **Lee Friedlander** and 210 lifetime prints by **Peter Hujar** spanning the full breadth and richness of their respective careers.

Recuerdo: Latin American Photography at the AGO opens, curated by Dumont-Gauthier. Over 150 works—among them key photographs by Mexican photographer **Graciela Iturbide**—offer an in-depth look at the museum's Latin American holdings.

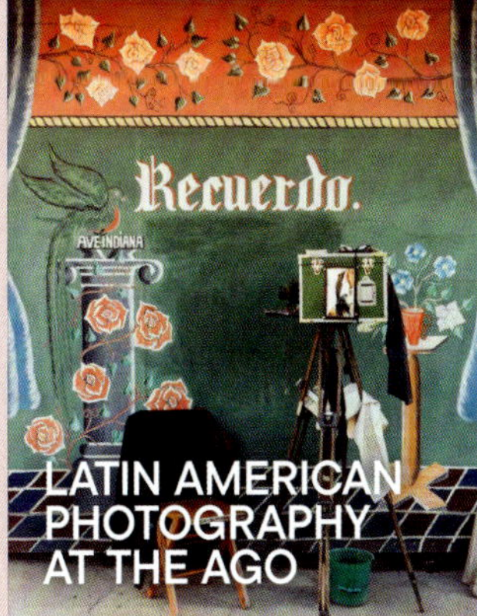

Recuerdo: Latin American Photography at the AGO. Published by the Art Gallery of Ontario, 2025.

The Photography Department celebrates its twenty-fifth anniversary with a special publication, the exhibition *Collective Visions: Celebrating Twenty-Five Years of Photography*, and a symposium.

Artist Index

André Kertész (born Budapest, Austria-Hungary [now Hungary], 1894 – died New York, New York, United States, 1985)

Ihei Kimura (born Shitaya-ku [now Taitō-ku], Tokyo, Japan, 1901 – died Nippori, Tokyo, Japan, 1974)

Susie King (born Toronto, Ontario, Canada, 1953)

Roy Kenzie Kiyooka (born Moose Jaw, Saskatchewan, Canada, 1926 – died Vancouver, British Columbia, Canada, 1994)

Klinsky Press Agency; Associated Press of Berlin, Associated Press, French, Associated Press, German, Eric Borchert, Alfred Eisenstaedt, Ihei Kimura, Willi Ruge

Paul Kodjo (born and died Abidjan, Ivory Coast, 1939–2021)

Luther Konadu (born North York, Ontario, Canada, 1991)

Rudolf Koppitz (born Schreiberseifen, Austrian Silesia, Austria-Hungary [now Skrbovice, Czechia], 1884 – died Perchtoldsdorf, Austria, 1936)

Barbara Kruger (born Newark, New Jersey, United States, 1945)

L

Suzy Lake (born Detroit, Michigan, United States, 1947)

Michel Lambeth (born and died Toronto, Ontario, Canada, 1923–1977)

Zun Lee (born Frankfurt am Main, Germany, 1969)

George Legrady (born Budapest, Hungary, 1950)

Gustave Le Gray (born Villiers-le-Bel, France, 1820 – died Cairo, Egypt, 1884)

Emmanuelle Léonard (born Montreal, Quebec, Canada, July 1971)

Christina Leslie (born Toronto, Ontario, Canada, 1983)

Nina Levitt (born Toronto, Ontario, Canada, 1955)

Elaine Ling (born Hong Kong [now Hong Kong, China], 1946 – died Toronto, Ontario, Canada, 2016)

Ken Lum (born Vancouver, British Columbia, Canada, 1956)

Lux Clock Manufacturing Co. (Waterbury, Connecticut, active 1914–) and G.F. Eschwei

George Platt Lynes (born East Orange, New Jersey, United States, 1907 – died New York, New York, United States, 1955)

Danny Lyon (born Brooklyn, New York, United States, 1942)

M

Peter MacCallum (born Toronto, Ontario, Canada, 1947)

Annie MacDonell (born Windsor, Ontario, Canada, 1976)

Arnaud Maggs (born Montreal, Quebec, Canada, 1926 – died Toronto, Ontario, Canada, 2012)

Man Ray (born Philadelphia, Pennsylvania, United States, 1890 – died Paris, France, 1976)

Robert Mapplethorpe (born Floral Park, New York, United States, 1946 – died Boston, Massachusetts, United States, 1989)

Étienne-Jules Marey (born Beaune, France, 1830 – died Paris, France, 1904)

Scott McFarland (born Hamilton, Ontario, Canada, 1975)

Meryl McMaster (born Ottawa, Ontario, Canada, 1988)

Emila Medková (born Ústí nad Orlicí, Czechoslovakia [now Czechia], 1928 – died Prague, Czechoslovakia [now Czechia], 1985)

Duane Michals (born McKeesport, Pennsylvania, United States, 1932)

Wardell Milan (born Knoxville, Tennessee, United States, 1978)

Michael Mitchell (born and died Hamilton, Ontario, Canada, 1943–2020)

Tina Modotti (born Udine, Italy, 1896 – died Mexico City, Mexico, 1942)

László Moholy-Nagy (born Bácsborsód, Austria-Hungary [now Hungary], 1895 – died Chicago, Illinois, United States, 1946)

Montgomery Collection of Caribbean Photographs; J. Murray Jordan, Publishers Photo Service

Abelardo Morell (born Havana, Cuba, 1948)

Jalani Morgan (born Toronto, Ontario, Canada, 1981)

Yasumasa Morimura (born Osaka, Japan, 1951)

Katharine Mulherin (born Grand Falls, New Brunswick, Canada, 1964 – died Toronto, Ontario, Canada, 2019)

N

N.E. Thing Co. [Iain and Ingrid Baxter] (Canadian, active 1967–1978)

Grazia Neri (born Milan, Italy, 1935)

Arnold Newman (born and died New York, New York, United States, 1918–2006)

Shelley Niro (born Niagara Falls, New York, United States, 1954)

William McFarlane Notman (born and died Montreal, Quebec, Canada, 1857–1913)

Alfred Noyer (French, active 1900s–1930s)

O

Isabel Okoro (born Lagos, Nigeria, 2001)

Bidemi Oloyede (born Port Harcourt, Nigeria, 1996)

Hugh Owen (born Market Drayton, England, 1808 – died Bristol, England, 1897)

P

Eli J. Palmer (Canadian, 1821–1894)

Louie Palu (born Toronto, Ontario, Canada, 1968)

Federico Patellani (born Monza, Italy, 1911 – died Milan, Italy 1977)

Mariette Pathy Allen (born Alexandria, Egypt, 1940)

Maurice Perron (born Montreal, Quebec, Canada, 1924 – died Sainte-Agathe-des-Monts, Quebec, Canada, 1999)

Jake Peters (born Haifa, Israel, 1952)

Dawit L. Petros (born Asmara, Eritrea, 1972)

Jacques-Philippe Potteau (born Menin, Belgium, 1807 – died Paris, France, 1876)

Photography Department 2000–2025

Staff

Sophie Hackett, Curator (2016–); Associate Curator (2014–2016); Assistant Curator (2006–2014); Intern (2002)

Tal-Or Ben-Choreen, Curatorial Coordinator (2023–); Research Assistant (2022–2023)

Marina Dumont-Gauthier, Curatorial Assistant (2023–2025); Curatorial fellow (2022–2023)

Emily Miller, Research & Collections Coordinator, Marvin Gelber Print & Drawing Study Centre (2023–); Research & Collections Assistant, Marvin Gelber Print and Drawing Study Centre (2021–2023); Research Assistant (2018–2020); Intern (2018)

Maia-Mari Sutnik, Curator, Emeritus (2015–); Curator, Special Projects (2009–2015); Curator (2000–2009)

Julie Crooks, Associate Curator (2019–2020); Assistant Curator (2017–2019)

Curatorial Administrative Assistant / Curatorial Coordinator

Jessie Snow (2011–2023)

Samantha Benjamin (2019)

Jill Offenbeck (2017–2018)

sol Legault (2016)

Jennifer Ward Bhogal (2007–2008; 2009–2011)

York Lethbridge (2008–2009)

Parin Dahya (2000–2006)

Wendy Hebditch (2000–2006)

Research Assistants

Sara Fruchtman (2014–2016)

Tracy Mallon-Jensen (2014–2015)

sol Legault (2013–2014)

Cataloguing Assistants

Malene Hjorngaard (2003–2004)

Brenda Renwick (2002–2008)

Manager, Curatorial Administration

Mara Meikle (2005–2011)

Interns

Samantha Ackerley (2013–2014); Kate Addleman-Frankel (2012–2013); Alex Arslanyan (2021); Olivia Babler (2016); Ariel Bader-Shamai (2017); Natalie Banaszak (2015); Andrea Beiko (2012–2013); Ekaterina Belilovsky (2013–2014); Sam Bernier-Cormier (2018); Lindsay Bolanos (2009–2010); Jesse Broissoit (2016); Connor Buck (2023); Zulay Jau Ting Chang (2009–2010); Joanne So Jeong Chung (2021); Anne Cibola (2013–2014; 2015); Sean Corscadden (2012–2013); Emilie Croning (2019); Samantha Diaram (2014–2015); Serra Erdem (2008–2009); Kaitlyn Fitzgerald (2021); Vanessa Fleet (2010–2011); Kate Fogle (2019); Laura Gentili (2014–2015); Liisa Graham (2014–2015); Jennifer Gray (2016); Shanice Frances Harriman (2022); Laura Hayward (2011–2012); Melodie Hueber (2011–2012); Christophe Jivraj (2013–2014); Elaine Jones (2025); Blanche Joslin (2017); Molly Kalkstein (2012–2013); Anne Kavanagh (2013–2014); Sarah Keane (2010–2011); Melika Khosravi (2024); Steven Kramer (2012–2013); Catherine Lachowskyj (2016); Katherine Lannin (2011–2012); sol Legault (2011–2012); Zoë Lepiano (2016); Emma Leverty (2010–2011); Jenny Li (2008–2009); Cassandra Lomore (2011–2012); Gabriela Macias (2023); Michelle Macleod (2011–2012); Rebecca Madamba (2013–2014); Tracy Mallon-Jensen (2010–2011); Julia Marcello (2021); Victoria Masters (2018); Danielle McAllister (2009–2010); Mélissa Mourez (2023); Sarah Munro (2010–2011); Jessica Murphy (2011–2012); Analiese Oetting (2018); Jill Offenbeck (2010–2011); Julienne Pascoe (2008–2009); Mary Patterson

(2017); Brian Piitz (2012–2013); Laura Ramsey (2013–2014); Heather Canlas Rigg (2011–2012); Juli Sheptytsky-Zall (2008–2009); Katherine Shoemaker (2009–2010); Luz Sierra Maldonado (2022); Valencia Sipes (2025); Cassie Spires (2021); Avery Steel (2019); Locrin Stewart (2016); Carla-Jean Stokes (2014–2015); Rebecca Streiman (2008–2009); Mallory Taylor (2009–2010); Harmony Trowbridge (2025); Rachel Verbin (2009–2010); Alexandra Wells (2024); Lisa Yarnell (2014–2015); Jennifer Yeates (2009–2010); Guanchen Yu (2017); Robyn Zolnai (2011–2012); Olga Zotova (2010–2011)

Photography Curatorial Committee members, 2002–2025

Julie Albert; Robin Anthony; Carol Appel; Cameron Bailey; Richard Balfour; David Banks; Claudia Beck; Diana Billes; David W. Binet (Chair, 2025–); Dr. Marta Braun; Dr. Stephen Brown; Robert Burley; Edward Burtynsky; Henry M. Campbell; Beverly Creed; Stephen Delaney; Janet Dewan; Susan Dime; Sarah Dinnick; Pamela Dinsmore; Rupert J. Duchesne (Chair, 2008–2011); Nicky Eaton; Andrew Federer; David Feldman; Mimi Fullerton; Leslie Gales; Lorne Gertner; Jennifer Grant; Hugh Hall; Jane Halverson; Robert Harding; Michael Infuso; Avrom Isaacs; Victoria Jackman; Dr. Parambir Singh Keila; Gale M. Kelly; James Lahey; Suzy Lake; Steven Latner; Jack Lazare; Zun Lee; Phil Lind; Ann Malcolmson; Harry Malcolmson; Dr. Paul Marks; Robyn McCallum; Cheryl McEwen; Patti Menkes; Aaron Milrad; Michael Mitchell; Dr. Kenneth Montague; Scott Mullin; Jeff Nolte; Deborah Palter; Dr. Sarah Parsons; Anjli Patel; Carol Rapp (Chair, 2002–2008); Tamara Rebanks; Edward Redelmeier; Dr. Penny Rubinoff; Judy Schulich (Chair, 2019–2025); Sandy Simpson; Dr. Jay Smith (Chair, 2011–2019); Bernice Smythe; Michael Stewart; Howard Tanenbaum; Jennifer Tanenbaum; Debra Thier

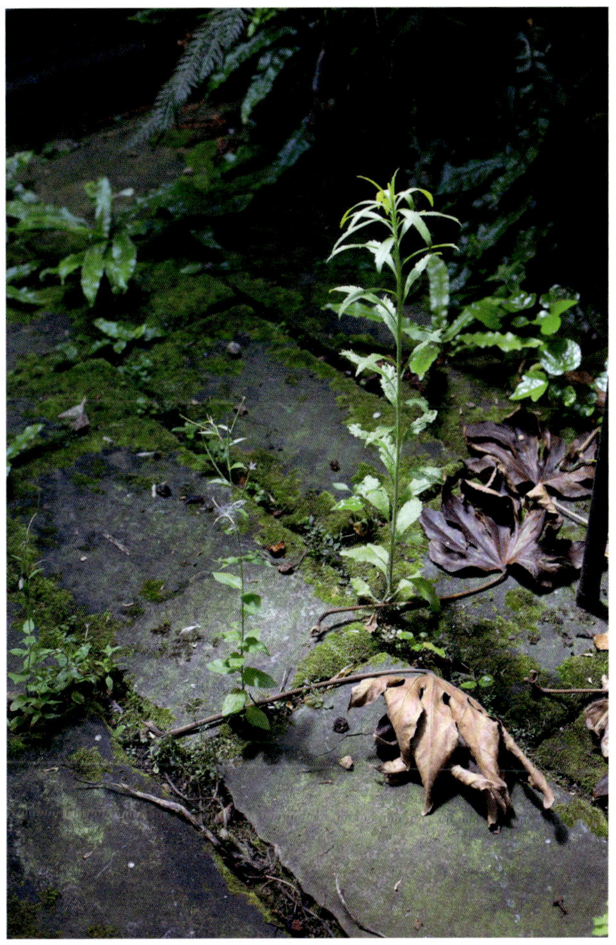

Wolfgang Tillmans
Weed
2014
Inkjet print, clips
410.8 × 274.6 cm
Gift of Glenn Pushelberg and George Yabu, 2022
2022/37

Thank you

Generous Support
David W. Binet
Gale M. Kelly
Penny Rubinoff
The Schulich Foundation
Jack Weinbaum Family Foundation
George Yabu & Glenn Pushelberg
Anonymous

Additional Assistance
Martha LA McCain

The Art Gallery of Ontario is partially funded by the Ontario Ministry of Culture. Additional operating support is received from the City of Toronto, the Department of Canadian Heritage, and the Canada Council for the Arts.

Contemporary programming at the Art Gallery of Ontario is supported by

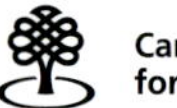

Canada Council for the Arts   Conseil des Arts du Canada

Goose Lane Editions acknowledges the generous support of the Government of Canada, the Canada Council for the Arts, and the Government of New Brunswick.

Goose Lane Editions is located on the unceded territory of the Wəlastəkwiyik whose ancestors along with the Mi'kmaq and Peskotomuhkati Nations signed Peace and Friendship Treaties with the British Crown in the 1700s.

Photo Credits

Society (ARS) New York/CARCC Ottawa 2025; p. 85 (top): © Nan Goldin; p. 85 (bottom): © Estate of Don Vincent; p. 85 (right): © Paul Graham; p. 87: © Estate of Robert Cohen/AGIP/Bridgeman Images; p. 88: © General Idea; p. 89 (left): © 2025 The Andy Warhol Foundation for the Visual Arts, Inc./Licensed by Artists Rights Society (ARS), NY/ CARCC Ottawa; p. 89 (right): © Suzy Lake; p. 90 (left): © Estate of Katharine Mulherin; p. 90 (right): © Cindy Sherman; p. 91: © Jin-me Yoon; p. 92 (top): © Estate of David Goldblatt; p. 92 (bottom): © George Legrady; p. 93: © Shelley Niro; p. 94 (top left): © Janieta Eyre; p. 94 (top right): © Mariette Pathy Allen; p. 94 (bottom): © Jake Peters; p. 95: © Barbara Astman; p. 96 (left): © Rebecca Belmore; p. 97 (left): © Estate of John Reeves; p. 97 (right): © Geoffrey James; p. 97 (bottom): © Estate of Tess Boudreau Taconis; p. 98: © Estate of George Platt Lynes; p. 99 (left): © Succession Man Ray/ADAGP Paris/CARCC Ottawa 2025; p. 103: © Raymond Boisjoly, Courtesy Catriona Jeffries; p. 106: © Jessica Eaton, Image courtesy of the artist and Bradley Ertaskiran; p. 107: © Edward Burtynsky; p. 108: Courtesy the City of Mississauga; p. 109 (left): © Estate of Ralph Greenhill; p. 109 (bottom right): © Robert Bourdeau, Courtesy of Stephen Bulger Gallery; p. 110 (left): © Edward Burtynsky; p. 111 (left): © Estate of Berenice Abbott/ Getty Images; p. 115: © Kelani Abass; pp. 118–19: © Lotus L. Kang, Courtesy of Franz Kaka; p. 120 (left): © Estate of Hannah Höch/VG Bildkunst Bonn/CARCC Ottawa 2025; p. 120 (right): © Chris Curreri; p. 121 (top): © Estate of Roy Kenzie Kiyooka; p. 121 (bottom): © Max Dean; p. 125: © 2010 MIT, Courtesy of MIT Museum; p. 126 (top left): © The National Archives and Records Administration; p. 126 (bottom left): © Estate of Jaroslav Rössler; p. 126 (right): © Arnold Newman Properties/Getty Images (2025); p. 127 (top): © Raymond Boisjoly; p. 127 (bottom): © Geoffrey Farmer; p. 128: © Dawoud Bey; p. 131: © Sunil Gupta, Courtesy of Stephen Bulger Gallery; p. 132 (left): © Sandra Brewster; p. 132 (top right): © Angela Grauerholz, Courtesy Olga Korper Gallery; p. 132 (bottom right): © Dawoud Bey; p. 133: © Estate of Reva Brooks, Courtesy of Stephen Bulger Gallery; p. 136: © Robert Kautuk; p. 138 (bottom): © Dawit L. Petros, Courtesy Bradley Ertaskirin; p. 139: © Estate of Robert Frank; p. 140 (top): © Max Dean, Photo: Isaac Applebaum; pp. 140 (bottom) and 142: © Estate of Tseng Kwong Chi, Muna Tseng Dance Projects; p. 143 (top): © Greg Girard; p. 144: © Sunil Gupta, Courtesy of Stephen Bulger Gallery; p. 145 (bottom): © Bhupendra Karia Estate, Courtesy sepiaEYE; p. 146: © Lola Álvarez Bravo/Artists Rights Society (ARS) New York/CARCC Ottawa 2025; p. 147: © Moyra Davey; p. 148 (right): © Estate of Roman Vishniac, Courtesy Magnes Collection; p. 150 (left): © Bill Brandt Archive; p. 150 (right): © Walker Evans Archive, The Metropolitan Museum of Art; p. 151 (left): © Estate of André Kertész, Courtesy of Stephen Bulger Gallery; p. 152: © Abelardo Morell; p. 153: © Gabrielle L'Hirondelle Hill, Courtesy Unit 17; p. 154 (top): © Estate of Lynne Cohen; p. 154 (bottom): © Lee Friedlander, courtesy Fraenkel Gallery, San Francisco and Luhring Augustine, New York; p. 155: © Cheryl Sourkes; p. 156: © Emmanuelle Léonard; p. 157: © Jalani Morgan; p. 159 (left): © Jeff Thomas; p. 159 (right): © The Estate of Garry Winogrand, courtesy Fraenkel Gallery, San Francisco; p. 160: © June Clark; p. 161 (top): © Estate of Michel Lambeth; p. 161 (bottom): © Thaddeus Holownia; p. 162: © Peter MacCallum; p. 163: © Steven Evans; p. 164: © Morris Lum; p. 165 (top left): © Jeff Thomas; p. 165 (bottom left): © Jorian Charlton; p. 165 (right): © Bidemi Oloyede; p. 166: © Cassils, Photo: Nir Arieli; p. 167: © Françoise Sullivan/CARCC Ottawa 2025; p. 170: © Wardell Milan; p. 171: © Ming Smith; p. 172 (right): © Estate of Emila Medková, Eva Kosáková; p. 173: © I & G Fárová Heirs; p. 174: © Graciela Iturbide; p. 175: © Lorna Simpson. Courtesy the artist and Hauser & Wirth; p. 176: © John Edmonds; p. 177: © Nina Levitt; p. 178: © Rodney Werden; p. 179 (top): © Gilbert and George; p. 179 (bottom): © Estate of Shelagh Alexander; pp. 180–81: © Luther Konadu; p. 182: © David Hlynsky and Elizabeth Chitty; p. 183: © Anne Collier, Courtesy Anton Kern Gallery; p. 184: © Estate of Herbert Bayer/VG Bildkunst Bonn/CARCC Ottawa 2025; p. 185: © Isabel Okoro; p. 188 (top): © Scott McFarland; p. 188 (bottom): © Gauri Gill; p. 189: © Cassils , Photo: Thomas McCarty; p. 190: © Sorel Cohen/CARCC Ottawa 2025; p. 191: © Alec Soth, image courtesy of the artist; p. 192 (left): © Duane Michals, Courtesy of DC Moore Gallery, New York; p. 192 (top right): © Spring Hurlbut; p. 193 (left): © Colette Urbajtel/ Archive Manuel Álvarez Bravo, S.C; p. 193 (right): © Lotte Jacobi Collection, University of New Hampshire; p. 194: © Estate of Diane Arbus; p. 195: © Meryl McMaster/Courtesy of the artist and Stephen Bulger Gallery and Pierre-François Ouellette art contemporain; p. 196: © Robert Burley; p. 202 (bottom right): © General Idea; p. 203 (right): Photo by Ron Bull/Toronto Star via Getty Images; p. 206 (right): © David Zapparoli/CARCC Ottawa 2025; p. 207: Photo: Dr. Dermon McCarthy, Courtesy of Stephen Bulger Gallery; p. 210 (top right): © Edward Burtynsky/Art Gallery of Ontario; p. 211: © Barbara Kruger; p. 212: Photo: Steven Evans; opposite p. 224: © Alan Belcher; back endsheet: © Robert Kautuk; back cover: © Paul Graham

This book was published to mark the 25th anniversary of the Photography Department at the Art Gallery of Ontario, alongside the exhibition *Collective Visions: Celebrating 25 Years of Photography*, on view November 8, 2025–May 10, 2026.

Published in 2025 by Art Gallery of Ontario and Goose Lane Editions.

Printed and bound in Belgium

ISBN: 9781773104799

10 9 8 7 6 5 4 3 2 1

Art Gallery of Ontario
317 Dundas Street West
Toronto, Ontario
M5T 1G4
Canada
ago.ca

Goose Lane Editions
500 Beaverbrook Court,
Suite 330
Fredericton, New Brunswick
E3B 5X4
Canada
gooselane.com

Editor: Sophie Hackett
Managing Editor: Jim Shedden
Publishing Coordinator: Robyn Lew
Production and Content Editor: Kieran Grant
Editorial Consultant: Sara Knelman
Designer: Polymode: Raleigh / Los Angeles, Brian Johnson, Randa Hadi, Silas Munro
Proofreaders: Judy Phillips, David Marsh
AGO Photographer: Craig Boyko
Pre-Press: Paul Jerinkitsch
Printing: Type A Print Inc.

Front cover:
Shelley Niro
Untitled (detail)
1991
(p. 93)

Front endsheet:
Max Dean
Snap (after Robert Frank) (detail)
2004
(p. 140)

Back cover:
Paul Graham
Untitled #55
1996-1997
(p. 85)

Back endsheet:
Robert Kautuk
Walrus Hunt (detail)
2016
(p. 136)

Library and Archives Canada Cataloguing in Publication

Title: *Collective States: Worlds of Photography at the AGO* / edited by Sophie Hackett.
Names: Art Gallery of Ontario, publisher, host institution. | Hackett, Sophie, 1971- , editor, organizer
Description: Accompanies an exhibition at the AGO marking 25 years of the photography department, held November 8, 2025–May 10, 2026. | Includes bibliographical references.
Identifiers: Canadiana 20250183498 | ISBN 9781773104799 (hardcover)
Subjects: LCSH: Art Gallery of Ontario—Photograph collections—Exhibitions. | LCSH: Photography—History—20th century—Exhibitions. | LCSH: Photograph collections—Ontario—Toronto—Exhibitions. | LCSH: Photography, Artistic—History—20th century—Exhibitions. | LCGFT: Exhibition catalogs.
Classification: LCC TR646.C32 T67 2025 | DDC 779/.074713541—dc23

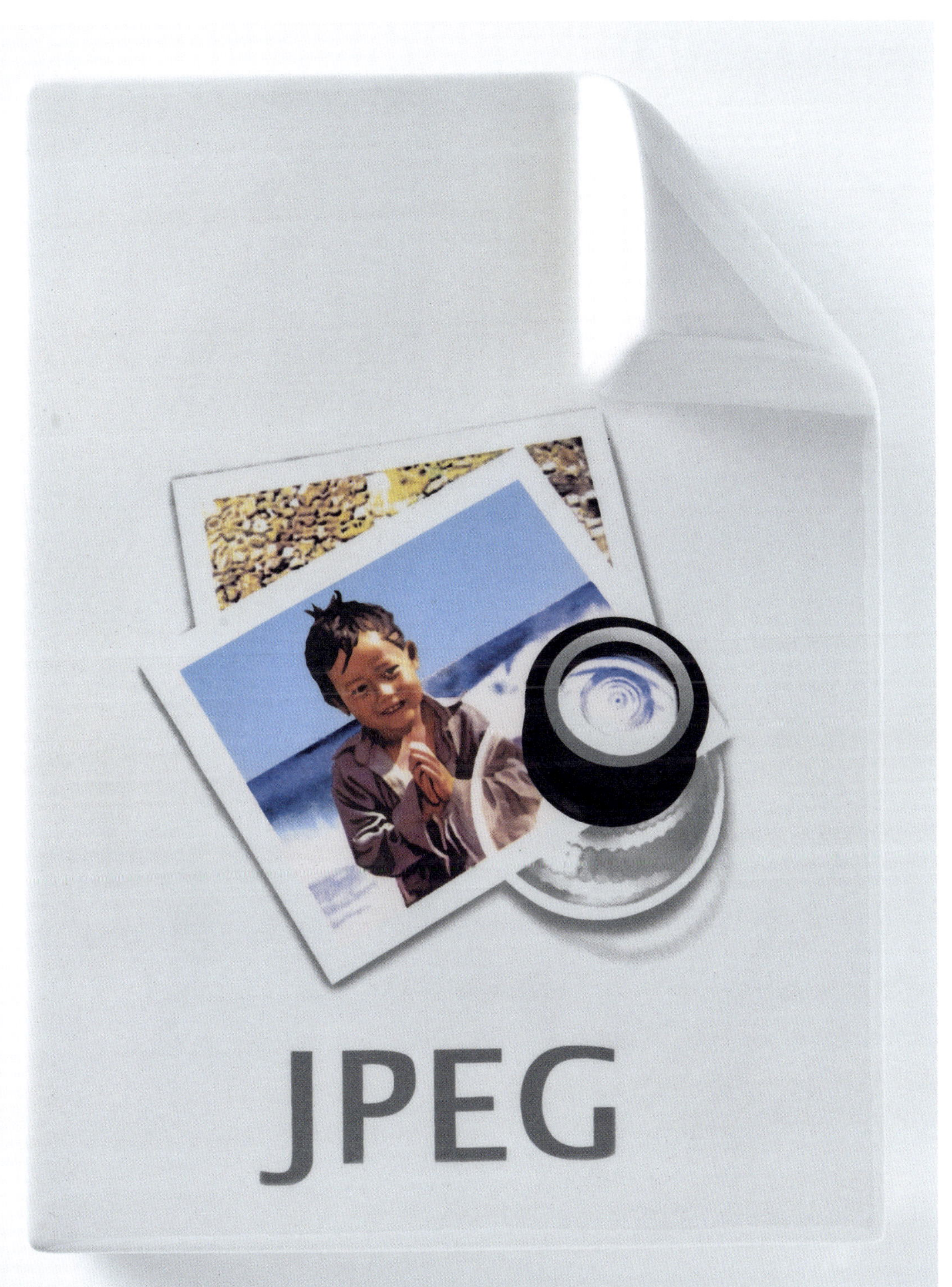

Alan Belcher
Stony milo.jpg
2012
Glazed ceramic multiple
25.4 × 19.1 × 7 cm
Purchase, with funds from the Photography Curatorial Committee, 2022
2022/13.1

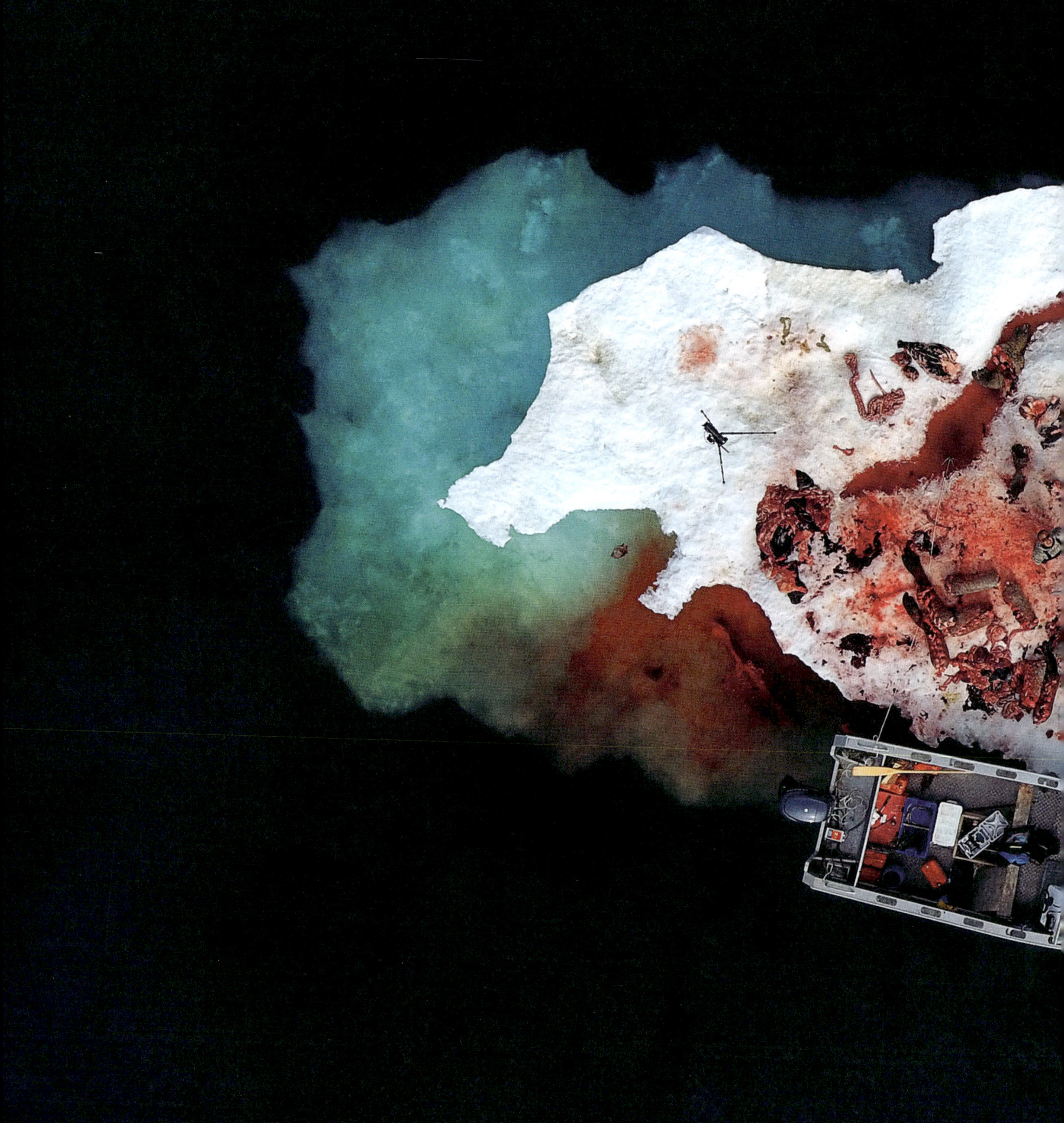